THE BASQUE SERIES

BOOKS IN THE BASQUE SERIES

A Book of the Basques
by Rodney Gallop

In A Hundred Graves: A Basque Portrait
by Robert Laxalt

Basque Nationalism
by Stanley G. Payne

Amerikanuak: Basques in the New World
by William A. Douglass and Jon Bilbao

Beltran: Basque Sheepman of the American West
by Beltran Paris, as told to William Douglass

The Basques: The Franco Years and Beyond
by Robert P. Clark

The Witches' Advocate: Basque Witchcraft
and the Spanish Inquisition (1609-1614)
by Gustav Henningsen

THE WITCHES' ADVOCATE

THE WITCHES' ADVOCATE

BASQUE WITCHCRAFT AND THE SPANISH INQUISITION (1609-1614)

by Gustav Henningsen

UNIVERSITY OF NEVADA PRESS
RENO, NEVADA
1980

Sources for illustrations: 1, 12-15: engravings by Adrian Schoonebech in Philip van Limborch, Historia Inquisitionis, *Amsterdam, 1692. 2: Biblioteca Nacional, Madrid. 3-10: sections of etching by Jan Ziarnko in* Pierre de Lancre, Tableau de l'inconstance, *Paris, 1613. 11, 16-21: Archivo Histórico Nacional, Madrid. 22: Royal Library of Copenhagen.*

Basque Series Editor: William A. Douglass
University of Nevada Press, Reno, Nevada 89557 USA
© *Gustav Henningsen 1980. All rights reserved.*
Printed in the United States of America
Designed by Dave Comstock

Library of Congress Cataloging in Publication Data

Henningsen, Gustav.
    The witches' advocate.

    (Basque series)
    Bibliography: p.
    Includes index.
    1. Inquisition. Basque Provinces. 2. Witchcraft
—Basque Provinces. I. Title.
BX1735.H44   272'.2'09466   79-20340
ISBN 0-87417-056-7

To Marisa, Jacob, Ulrik,
Gustav, and Maria

There were neither witches nor bewitched until they were talked and written about.

Inquisitor Alonso de Salazar Frías, 1612

We are still completely convinced that when the Council reads our report with the thoroughness and consideration which are customary, it will be bound to realize as a clear and obvious fact supported by unassailable arguments that this sect is a reality.

Inquisitors Alonso Becerra Holguín
and Juan de Valle Alvarado, 1613

When a detailed and systematic study of the witchcraft proceedings stored in the Inquisition archives has been completed, new facts will emerge which were unsuspected even by those who until now have devoted the greatest care to their examination.

Julio Caro Baroja, *Vidas mágicas e Inquisición*, 1967

CONTENTS

ILLUSTRATIONS, TABLES, DIAGRAMS, AND MAPS

ILLUSTRATIONS

TABLES

DIAGRAMS

MAPS

ABBREVIATIONS AND CONVENTIONS

A B B R E V I A T E D   T I T L E S *

ARGÜELLO *Instrucciones* — Gaspar Isidro de ARGÜELLO, (ed.) *Instrvciones del Santo Oficio* ... (1576), Madrid 1630.

CARO BAROJA *De nuevo* — Julio CARO BAROJA, "De nuevo sobre la historia de la brujería (1609-1619)" *Príncipe de Viana* 30 (1969) 265-328.

DE LANCRE *Tableau* — Pierre DE LANCRE, *Tableau de l'inconstance des mauvais anges* ... (1612), Paris 1613.

GARCÍA *Orden de procesar* — Pablo GARCÍA, *Orden qve comvnmente se guarda en el Santo Oficio de la Inquisicion, acerca del procesar en las causas* ... (1568), Madrid 1607.

HENNINGSEN *Papers of Salazar* — Gustav HENNINGSEN, "The Papers of Alonso de Salazar Frias. A Spanish Witchcraft Polemic 1610-14" *Temenos* 5 (1969) 85-106.

IDOATE *Documento* — Florencio IDOATE, (ed.) *Un documento de la Inquisición sobre la brujería en Navarra* Pamplona 1972.

LEA *Inquisition of Spain* — Henry Charles LEA, *A History of the Inquisition of Spain* 4 vols. New York 1906-07.

MONGASTÓN *Relación* — Juan de MONGASTÓN, (ed.) *Relacion de las personas que salieron al avto de la fee* ... *de Logroño* ... *1610* ... Logroño [1611].

MURRAY *Witch-Cult* — Margaret Alice MURRAY, *The Witch-Cult in Western Europe* (1921), Oxford 1962.

---

*For abbreviated titles of manuscript sources see Part 1 of Bibliography, "Alphabetic list of the sixty key documents."

OTHER ABBREVIATIONS AND CONVENTIONS

AGN	Archivo General de Navarra, Pamplona.
AHN	Archivo Histórico Nacional, Madrid.
Al	Province of Alava.
Auto de fe no.	Reference number in the *Second Report of the Auto de fe*, cf. tables 1, 4, 5, and see corresponding case nos. 1-31 of the Witch List.
BN	Biblioteca Nacional, Madrid.
Bu	Province of Burgos.
C.	The Council of the Inquisition, *"la Suprema,"* at Madrid.
Gui	Province of Guipúzcoa.
La	Pays de Labourd.
Leg	*Legajo* or manuscript file in the Section on the Inquisition at the Archivo Histórico Nacional, Madrid.
Leg.	*Legajo* found outside the AHN.
Lib	*Libro* or manuscript volume in the Section on the Inquisition at the Archivo Histórico Nacional, Madrid.
Lib.	*Libro* found outside the AHN.
Lo	Province of Logroño.
Na	Province of Navarra.
Olim	Latin "formerly," used before outdated archive signatures.
Rdo	*Reconciliado* or reconciled. Refers to number in *Relación de causas 1610/11*, see the corresponding case nos. 32-96 of the Witch List.
Rte	*Revocante* or "recanter." Refers to number in *Volume "F" of Salazar's Visitation Book*, see case nos. 441-521 of Witch List.
SD	*The Salazar Documents*. Author's forthcoming edition of Salazar's reports and other key documents, see end of Preface.
T.	The Tribunal of the Inquisition at Logroño.
Viz	Province of Vizcaya.

A number of other abbreviations are introduced and explained in the course of the text. Printed sources are rendered with the original spelling, while quotes from manuscript sources have been normalized. Square brackets are used for interpolations and conjectures. After a free or uncertain translation the original Spanish text is added in italics; the same practice is used after translations of Spanish terms. Serial numbers or other signatures used in the original sources are rendered in double quote marks; thus for example "Rte 60" is an original serial number of *Volume "F" of Salazar's Visitation*

Book and corresponds to *Rte* 61 or case no. 501 of the Witch List. "§" is used before clause numbers in the original documents.

The following principles will help the reader make full use of the notes. Full description is given when a source is mentioned for the first time. Cited books and articles are listed again in part 4 of the Bibliography, and so are major manuscript units such as *libros* and *legajos,* idem parts 2 and 3. All other source materials are described when they appear for the first time, and whenever they are mentioned again reference is made back to the first place of mention. An exception to this rule is made for the sixty key documents. Their short titles are found in an alphabetized list as part 1 of the Bibliography; here also are given references to the place where each source is first mentioned and fully described.

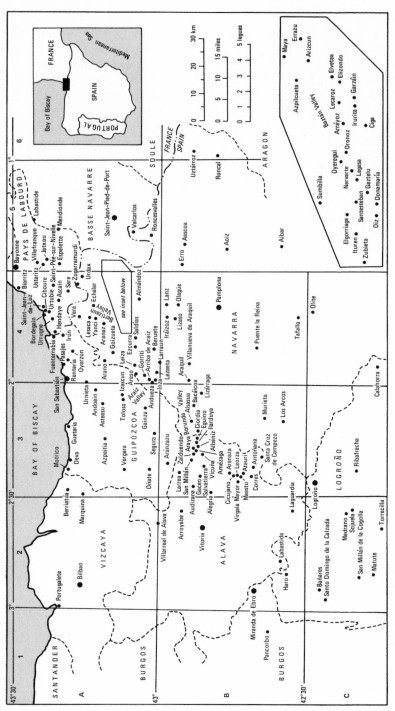

Map 1. Places mentioned in the text.

PLACE NAMES

List of place names mentioned in the text, followed by the name of the province (abbreviated), and location finders for use with map 1. Italics refer to inset map.

Aescoa, Na, B5
Aibar, Na, B5
Albéniz, Al, B3
Alegría, Al, B3
Almándoz, Na, A4
Alsasua, Na, B3
Alzate, *barrio* of Vera
Amaya. See Maya
Amézaga, Al, B3
Andoain, Gui, A3
Andueza, Na, A4
Antoñana, Al, B3
Aoiz, Na, B5
Araiz Valley, Na, A4
Aranaz, Na, A4
Arano, Na, A4
Aránzazu, Gui, B3
Araquil, Na, B4
Araya, Al, B3
Arce, *barrio* of Donamaría
Arenaza, Al, B3
Areso, Na, A4
Arizcun, Na, *A5*
Arráyoz, Na, *A4*
Arriba de Araiz, Na, A4
Arroyabe, Al, B2
Ascain, La, A4
Asteasu, Gui, A3
Atauri, Al, B3
Audizana, Al, B3

Aurtiz, *barrio* of Ituren
Ayabar. *See* Aibar
Azcárraga, *barrio* of Donamaría
Azpeitia, Gui, A3
Azpilcueta, Na, *A4*

Bacáicoa, Na, B3
Bañares, Lo, C2
Bayonne, La, A5
Baztán Valley, Na, *A4*
Berriatúa, Viz, A3
Bertizaun Valley, Na, A4
Beruete, Na, A4
Biarritz, La, A4
Bordegain, La, A4
Borunda Valley, Na, B3
Brujero. Not located

Calahorra, Lo, C4
Campezo. *See* Santa Cruz de Campezo
Ciboure, La, A4
Cicujano, Al, B3
Ciga, Na, *A4*
Ciordia, Na, B3
Corres, Al, B3

Deva, Gui, A3
Donamaría, Na, *A4*

Echalar, Na, A4
Eguino, Al, B3
Elgorriaga, Na, *A4*
Elizondo, Na, *A4*
Elvetea, Na, *A4*
Errazu, Na, *A5*
Erro, Na, B5
Espelette, La, A5
Ezcurra, Na, A4

Fuenterrabía, Gui, A4

Gaceo, Al, B3
Gainza, Gui, A3
Garzáin, Na, *A4*
Gaztelu, Na, *A4*
Goizueta, Na, A4
Gorriti, Na, A4
Guetaria, Gui, A3

Haro, Lo, B2
Hendaye, La, A4

Igunín, *barrio* of Donamaría
Ilarduya, Al, B3
Inza, Na, A4
Iráizoz, Na, B4
Irún, Gui, A4
Irurita, Na, *A4*
Ituren, Na, *A4*
Izascun, Gui, A3

Jatxou, La, A5

Labastida, Al, B2
Labastide, La, A5
La Calzada. *See* Santo Domingo
  de la Calzada
Laguardia, Al, B2
Lanz, Na, B4
Larraun, Na, A4
Larrea, Al, B3
Lecaroz, Na, *A4*
Legasa, Na, *A4*
Leiza, Na, A4
Leorza, Al, B3

Lesaca, Na, A4
Lezaeta, Na, A4
Lizárraga, Na, B3
Lizaso, Na, B4
Logroño, Lo, C3
Los Arcos, Na, B3

Maestu, Al, B3
Marquina, Viz, A3
Matute, Lo, C2
Maya, Na, *A5*
Medrano, Lo, C2
Mendionde, La, A5
Miranda de Ebro, Bu, B2
Motrico, Gui, A3
Murieta, Na, B3

Narvarte, Na, *A4*

Oiz, Na, *A4*
Olagüe, Na, B4
Olite, Na, C4
Oñate, Gui, A3
Oronoz, Na, *A4*
Oyarzun, Gui, A4
Oyeregui, Na, *A4*

Pamplona, Na, B4
Pancorbo, Bu, B1
Pasajes, Gui, A4
Portugalete, Viz, A2
Puente la Reina, Na, B4

Rentería, Gui, A4
Ribafrecha, Lo, C3
Roncal, Na, B6
Roncesvalles, Na, A5

Saint-Jean-de-Luz, La, A4
Saint-Pée-sur-Nivelle, La, A4
Saldías, Na, A4
Salvatierra, Al, B3
San Millán, Al, B3
San Millán de la Cogolla, Lo, C2
San Sebastián, Gui, A4
Santa Cruz de Campezo, Al, B3

Santesteban (de Lerín), Na, *A4*
Santo Domingo de la Calzada,
   Lo, C2
Sare, La, A4
Segura, Gui, A3
Sojuela, Lo, C2
Sumbilla, Na, *A4*

Tafalla, Na, B4
Tolosa, Gui, A3
Torrecilla, Lo, C2
Trapaza. Not located

Urdax, Na, A4
Urnieta, Gui, A4
Urrugne, La, A4
Urtubie, La, A4
Ustaritz, La, A5
Uztárroz, Na, B6

Valcarlos, Na, A5
Val de Roncal. *See* Roncal
Valderro. *See* Erro
Vera, Na, A4
Vergara, Gui, A3
Vicuña, Al, B3
Villa de los Arcos. *See* Los Arcos
Villanueva de Araquil, Na, B4
Villarreal de Alava, Al, B2
Villefranque, La, A5
Virgala Mayor, Al, B3
Vitoria, Al, B2

Yanci, Na, A4

Zalduendo, Al, B3
Zubieta, Na, *A4*
Zugarramurdi, Na, A4
Zuraurre, *barrio* of Ciga

PREFACE

HE BELIEF IN WITCHCRAFT BECLOUDING the minds of sixteenth- and seventeenth-century Europe makes it almost impossible to distinguish fact from fiction. How did the great witch-hunts originate, and how indeed were they brought to a stop? Did those who confessed believe themselves to be witches, and if they did not, how did they then fabricate their confessions? Could it really be possible that the witches indulged in some form of secret ritual?

When dealing with the formal records of firmly believing judges we can only conjecture about these questions. But south of the Pyrenees one meets with the expression of a skeptical temperament which enables us to discern the social and psychological realities lying behind the phenomenon. Spain is of special interest because belief in witchcraft, though never doctrinally substantiated, was a subject of constant discussion there, and thus many details that are not found in the source material from the rest of Europe are set forth clearly in the Spanish sources.

This is particularly true for the great Basque witch trial of 1609-1614 which is the subject of the present study. On account of the quite exceptional nature of the source material it is possible to trace this witchcraft epidemic from the moment of its inception in a remote valley of the Pyrenees on the border between Spain and France, until the spring of 1611, when it had spread into large areas of northern Spain, and on up to 1614, when the whole extensive region had returned to normal. It can be demonstrated how in village after village the persecution arose from particular causes which have little in common with the many general theories on witchcraft which are under consideration at the present time. Our investigation takes the form of a reconstruction and a critical appreciation of what really did happen, and aims above all to illustrate the psychological and social reality witchcraft held for those persons and communities which in one way or another came to be involved.

The phenomenon of witchcraft was in fact not at all the constant factor we normally regard it to have been, but was a dynamic and flickering element, now present, now absent, as in the case of modern collective delusions. The content of collective delusions may vary from one period to another, but the underlying human feelings seem to be quite constant. One could also reverse the situation and say that unless we understand in advance that human nature is unvarying and that only conditions change, historical research would be meaningless; for if we do not consider historical man as one of us, as an equal, how can we then ever hope to understand him or put ourselves in his place? The most precious tool of research is ourselves, and like the anthropologist we must persevere until we have searched so deep in our understanding that we can identify with the people we are studying, speak their language, and experience the world in their way. With this attitude history becomes something other than a mere study of past events; it turns into a journey of exploration backwards in time to a series of historical societies which tell us something new (and old) of man and his possibilities, under changing conditions.

The Basque witch-hunt which developed simultaneously both north and south of the French-Spanish border can be viewed today as a most sophisticated and cruel social experiment because of the very different measures used by the authorities in their respective countries. Traditional methods were utilized among the Basques north of the Pyrenees, in France. A large number of people were burned, and the witch judge, Pierre de Lancre, a parliamentary councillor from Bordeaux, returned to his home with the conviction that the entire Basque population formed one vast sect of witches. South of the Pyrenees, among the Basques in Spain, the all-powerful Inquisition instituted an equally comprehensive persecution, but after having burned a few people, they put entirely different methods into operation. This was chiefly at the instigation of the most junior of the inquisitors at the district tribunal at Logroño, Alonso de Salazar Frías. As a functionary working on official business he carried out an investigation of the witchcraft epidemic. But he did it in such a rationalistic way and with such purely empirical methods that it can be considered as the first systematic study in the history of witchcraft belief, revealing its social and psychological foundations and, needless to say, demonstrating the non-existence of witches.

Salazar's investigations might have changed the history of the European witch persecution had they been published. They were undertaken at the very time that witch burnings were flaring up as never before and were unopposed by anyone except for a few "reactionary" lawyers and priests. But the Spanish Inquisition kept Salazar's papers secret and the only consequence of their revolutionary conclusions was that they no longer allowed any more witch burnings within their vast territory of jurisdiction from Sicily in the east to Peru in the west.

Three hundred years later a few of Salazar's manuscripts were discovered by the American financier and self-taught historian Henry Charles Lea, who used them in his monumental history of the Spanish Inquisition (1906-07) for what he termed the turning point in the history of Spanish witchcraft. It seems odd, therefore, that to date Salazar has been the subject of superficial studies only. The reason for this deficiency is that the archives of the Spanish Inquisition were moved from Simancas shortly after the appearance of Lea's work. And although this may have been justifiable, it was the cause of Salazar's papers being completely lost to international scholarship. Certainly, until very recently, all succeeding scholars have relied entirely upon Lea, with the exception of the Spanish historian of witchcraft Julio Caro Baroja, who in 1933 published a single Salazar manuscript preserved in the Biblioteca Nacional in Madrid (where it still remains!).

During a fieldwork project (1965-67) on present-day witch belief among the Galicians in northwestern Spain I became interested in the witch trials of the Spanish Inquisition and it occurred to me to wonder whether Salazar's papers from the greatest trial of all could be rediscovered in either Simancas or Madrid. I consulted my distinguished friend Caro Baroja who presumed that they were still in Simancas, but after various abortive attempts I succeeded in December 1967 in locating the missing papers in Madrid, in the Archivo Histórico Na-

cional where they were catalogued in a form so misleading
that no one had realized what they were. Naturally I told
Caro Baroja of my discovery.

I abandoned my Galician project and began to delve sys-
tematically into the extensive archives of the Council of the
Inquisition (over five thousand files), and this investigation,
hand in hand with analysis and preparation, continued until
1972. The result showed that an exceptionally large amount of
source material was available, despite the fact that all the
original trial records had perished in the destruction (1808) of
the archives of the Tribunal at Logroño during the Napoleonic
war. A shorter article on my discovery was published in English in *Temenos* (1969). With the present monograph all available materials have for the first time been submitted to a
thorough study. One of my aims has been to demonstrate to
what extent Salazar's professional journey to the Basque
provinces and his reports to the grand inquisitor are comparable to modern anthropological fieldwork and to the modern
scientific study of collected data. Since this is, in other words, a
study of an old investigation, I have found it suitable to choose
a mostly descriptive approach for my presentation and to limit
my analyses to the most concrete form.

I have also been so fascinated by the exciting course of
events that I have often preferred to use straightforward nar-
rative and have banished all discussion and source criticism
to the notes (which originally were planned, however, to be
placed at the foot of the page). The non-specialist may well
wonder why I have presented such full accounts of archival
material. I hoped in this way to demonstrate a method which,
in my view, could be used to study the 342-year history of the
Spanish Inquisition throughout the whole Empire, for as far
as I know this is the first time that a monograph has been
based on a complete exploration of the immense archives of
the Council of the Inquisition.

This book was submitted in manuscript form to the University of Copenhagen on 10 January 1973 in satisfaction of
requirements for the Danish Doctor of Philosophy degree,
and on 22 August 1974 it was "approved for public defense"
by Professors Franz From, Arild Hvidtfeldt, and Niels
Skyum-Nielsen. During the long drawn-out process of
translating and editing, which has delayed the publication of
the book, it has been impossible for me to refer to most of the

recent research on early modern witchcraft. This, however, does not affect the main thrust of the book, which is concerned with the demonological and heretical aspects of witchcraft, about which nothing of importance has appeared (with the notable exception of Norman Cohn's splendid 1975 study, *Europe's Inner Demons*). Since the Spanish Inquisition was concerned with heresy — and *maleficium* only insofar as it bore upon heresy — the maleficent aspects of witchcraft (the object of many recent studies) are not essential to the subject of the present book. To avoid an expensive two-volume edition my editors have decided to leave out the lengthy Salazar Documents, wherein the whole story is told by the protagonists themselves through eighteen selected source manuscripts. They are now being prepared for publication elsewhere.

The Danish Folklore Archives
Copenhagen, Spring 1979   Gustav Henningsen

ACKNOWLEDGMENTS

URING THE COURSE OF MY RESEARCH I have met with kindness and received help and support from a great many people and institutions. I wish to take this opportunity to express my gratitude to them all and regret that I can mention only a few of them by name.

The Archivo Histórico Nacional offered me the greatest understanding and courtesy throughout my investigations, the archivists by allowing me unrestricted access to catalogues and registers, the staff by bringing hundreds of files up from the stacks. Copenhagen University granted me my traveling expenses and salary during my two periods of residence in Spain, 1965-68 and 1969-71. The Danish Council of Research in the Humanities provided for my subsistence during the first seven months of 1972 and also generously supported my research from the beginning with money to cover the cost of indexing of archives, study tours to visit archives in northern Spain and southern France, and duplicating. It has been of inestimable advantage to this book to have been able to work on the entire body of source material in copy form and also partially in bound volumes; this collection of copies of more than five thousand manuscript pages has now been deposited at the Danish Folklore Archives in Copenhagen. The Danish Folklore Archives granted me leave for almost seven years and kindly permitted me to devote a considerable amount of my working hours after my return from Spain to preparing the present book for publication. The Rask-Örsted Foundation paid for the translation of the manuscript from Danish to English. I am grateful to English-born Danish Magister Ann Born of Oxford for the enthusiasm and skill she brought to the work of translation. Particular thanks are due to my friends, the historians, and Hispanists Albert Lovett and William Callahan, for their help in translating the Spanish citations into English, and to my brother-in-law, the jurist Carlos Rey, for his invaluable aid with the systematic search for materials in the Archivo Histórico Nacional. Last, and far from least, I thank my wife, Marisa Rey-Henningsen, my permanent Spanish teacher, assistant, and critic, and my faithful "substitute" with our children every time I was gone with the witches.

There is no conclusive refutation of the belief in witch-craft, since whatever explanation one can give in scientific terms of impersonal causes, the question always remains "Why me? Why just then?" . . . In Europe we answer these questions by talking about chance, or, if we are more superstitious, luck.

–Lucy Mair

CHAPTER ONE
Introduction: Theories of Witchcraft

1. DID A EUROPEAN WITCH CULT EXIST?

N 1921 THE EGYPTOLOGIST MARGARET Murray published her classic study, *The Witch-Cult in Western Europe.*[1] Her work was to reopen an old question which two centuries of sophisticated Europeans had considered as settled, namely: were witches innocent victims of persecution? Since the Age of Enlightenment scholars had agreed that the persecutions had been a terrible mistake, and that the thousands of women and men who were burnt at the stake as witches had been the victims of a distorted theology, a corrupt judicial system, black superstition, or pure self-deception.[2] These explanations were repeated by the culturally optimistic historians of the era prior to World War I, and they were the basic concept on which the German Joseph Hansen[3] and the American Henry Charles Lea[4] based their superbly learned and unmatched works on the history of the Inquisition and the witch persecutions. All agreed that the witch phenomenon had been sheer illusion.

Now here was Margaret Murray asserting that the persecutions had not been mistaken in the least. For the witches, she

---

A preliminary version of this chapter was published by the Danish Folklore Archives as *The European Witch-Persecution* Copenhagen 1973 (DFS-Translations No. 1). The last section, however, on witch-hunts as related to changes in European class structure, was not included in the present chapter.

explained, belonged to a heathen fertility cult which had survived from pre-Christian times in certain remote Western
European regions. This phenomenon had formerly been
overlooked owing to the fact that the confessions of the
witches had never been subjected to scientific investigation.
They had always been either blindly accepted or completely
rejected:

> On the one hand are the writers who, having heard the
> evidence at first hand, believe implicitly in the facts and
> place upon them the unwarranted construction that those
> facts were due to supernatural power; on the other hand are
> the writers who, taking the evidence on hearsay and disbe-
> lieving the conclusions drawn by their opponents, deny the
> facts *in toto*.[5]

However, continued Murray, it had not been possible for
anyone to provide a satisfactory explanation as to why the
witches in their confessions should so strikingly corroborate
one another whenever they touched upon their rites and beliefs. "It is only by a careful comparison with the evidence of
anthropology that the facts fall into their proper places and an
organized religion stands revealed,"[6] she asserted. Thereupon
she went on to remove layer after layer of theology to expose
the rites of the witch cult. She tried to demonstrate that the
Devil was the horned god of the witches; she claimed that
many of their weirder exploits were none other than familiar
fertility rites; and she showed by means of lengthy lists that the
number of confederates in a witch trial supposedly turned out
to be thirteen (they were organized into covens or assemblies
of thirteen witches, one of whom stood proxy for the Devil, or,
more correctly, the god).[7]

It was five years later that the Roman Catholic priest and
Restoration scholar Montague Summers published *The History
of Witchcraft and Demonology*.[8] This book had no less impact
than Murray's. Father Summers showed himself to be not only
extremely well read in the demonology literature of authors
who had lain in oblivion for centuries, but also revealed himself to be their heir — if the book were to be taken seriously that
is, for several critics were in doubt on this point. However, the
book certainly *was* meant to be taken seriously, and Summers
set out to prove that the witch was indeed worthy of persecution as the vilest of creatures,

an evil liver; a social pest and parasite; the devotee of a loathly and obscene creed; an adept at poisoning, blackmail, and other creeping crimes; a member of a powerful secret organization inimical to Church and State; a blasphemer in word and deed; swaying the villagers by terror and superstition.[9]

He agreed entirely with Murray that the witches' confessions were genuine, but placed no credence whatsoever in her attempts to interpret them:

Her careful reading of the writers upon Witchcraft has justly convinced her that their statements must be accepted. Keen intelligences and shrewd investigators such as Gregory XV, Bodin, Guazzo, De Lancre, D'Espagnet, [and others] were neither deceivers nor deceived. The evidence must stand, but as Miss Murray finds herself unable to admit the logical consequence of this, she hurriedly starts away with an arbitrary, "the statements do not bear the construction put upon them," and . . . proceeds to develop a most ingenious, but . . . wholly untenable hypothesis.[10]

However, Summers fully agreed with Murray that the witches' meetings actually did take place. Thus the argument of an eighteenth-century writer[11] who explained away the sabbaths as dreams and fantasies is refuted by Summers in these words:

Happy sceptic! But unfortunately the Sabbat did — and does — take place; formerly in deserted wastes, on the hill-side, in secluded spots, now, as often as not, in the privacy of vaults and cellars, and in those lone empty houses innocently placarded "To be Sold."[12]

It is slightly disconcerting to be told that the modern witches' sabbath is none other than the spiritualist meeting of the twenties (to which Summers devotes a long chapter and which he condemns as purely diabolical). His attempts to demonstrate that the witches practiced a Satanic cult with origins in gnosticism and other ancient heretical movements are not very convincing. The chief weakness of the book is the author's complete ignorance of the criteria of folklore. Invokers of demons, practitioners of the black arts, fortune-tellers, spiritualists, devil-worshippers, and those possessed by demons are all accomplices of the Devil and, according to Summers, therefore witches. His book therefore made a dubious contribution to the history of European Satanism, which has yet to be subjected to a thoroughgoing and sober investigation, but the few examples of black masses that I have come across have convinced me that Satanism was — and is — something quite different from the chimerical world of the witches.[13]

Neither Margaret Murray's nor Montague Summers's hypotheses have proved themselves valid, but she has acquired a following,[14] while he has not. Her startling arguments, whatever their real merit, have fascinated her readers down to this day. The most effective criticism has been presented on anthropological grounds,[15] most recently by Lucy Mair, who remarks very aptly that

> the real weakness of Margaret Murray's theory is that if witches were merely the adherents of a religion as this is ordinarily understood *there would be no witches.* In the rest of the world witches are by definition those who reject the moral order, and the sign of their rejection is such an action as the murder of children to feast on.[16]

Mair draws the conclusion that Murray "in fact . . . invented a religion for the purposes of her argument."[17]

It would be interesting to discover whether there is any connection between Murray's book and the present-day witch cult. English and American witch societies have sprung up during the last few decades and as far as I know cannot be traced further back. It is true that the members themselves claim to continue to practice the ancient and primitive "witch religion," but as their rituals are carried out in secret we must be content for the time being with what Gerald B. Gardner, chief witch of the English witch societies, allowed to leak out in his dilettantish contribution to the history of witchcraft.[18] Judging from his books, the English covens would appear to hold their sabbaths in exact accordance with the religion discovered by Murray.[19]

Several modern scholars have put forward the hypothesis that the witches' confessions can be explained as visions produced by hallucinogenic substances. Some of them have even experimented with ancient prescriptions for witch ointment which are thought to be authentic. But as these researchers have a purely intellectual approach to witch belief, their laboratory experiments have not yielded the experiences they were seeking, apart from headache and certain sensations of flying.[20]

One exception, however, is the attempt made by Carlos Castaneda, an American anthropologist. By apprenticing himself to don Juan, an Indian shaman (in Arizona), he exposed himself to harsh training and possible danger to body and soul. Castaneda broke off the training after suffering a psychic breakdown which convinced him that he did not possess the courage necessary to continue. In *The Teachings of Don Juan* (1968)[21] he describes his initiation into the use of a number of narcotics and the Indian mysteries connected with them. Among other things, he describes some experiments with a flying ointment concocted from the root of the datura plant. Following his teacher's instructions he applied the ointment to his genitals, his calves, and the soles of his feet. Castaneda relates that the ointment smelled so strong that it practically suffocated him, and continues by describing its effects:

> Don Juan kept staring at me. I took a step toward him. My legs were rubbery and long, extremely long. . . . I moved forward. The motion of my body was slow and shaky; it was more like a tremor forward and up. I looked down and saw don Juan sitting below me, way below me. The momentum carried me forward one more step, which was even more elastic and longer than the preceding one. And from there I soared. . . . I saw the dark sky above me, and the clouds going by me. I jerked my body so I could look down. I saw the dark mass of the mountains. My speed was extraordinary.[22]

When Castaneda returned to normal he reported his experience to his teacher. But when he had finished, don Juan said:

> The unguent by itself is not enough. . . . As you learn more, and take it often in order to fly, you will begin to see everything with great clarity. You can soar through the air for hundreds of miles to see what is happening at any place you want, or to deliver a fatal blow to your enemies far away.[23]

The experience had been so convincing that Castaneda felt obliged to ask his teacher if he really had been flying. Don Juan affirmed that it had been so, but admitted that he had not flown like a bird, but like a man who had taken "the devil's weed" (i.e. the datura plant). Castaneda tried in vain to make his teacher define what he meant, and when he finally asked what would happen if he chained himself to a rock, don Juan looked at his unbelieving pupil and said: "If you tie yourself to a rock I'm afraid you will have to fly holding the rock with its heavy chain."[24]

Castaneda describes other experiments in which he met a deity in his hallucinogenic visions in the same manner as the European witches used to meet the Devil.[25] But it is still an open question whether a similar drug cult existed in Europe; and even if this could be proved I am convinced that it would account for only an extremely limited number of the witch trials. The same may be said of the attempts that have been made to prove that the witches were suffering from hysteric neuroses and other forms of insanity.[26] Such explanations are most relevant when it comes to shedding light on the psychological mechanism underlying so-called demonic possession,[27] but only occasionally can they be applied to explain the witch trials.[28] For by far the greater number of the victims of witch persecution probably enjoyed average mental and physical health.[29]

2. THE HYPOTHESES OF PEDRO DE VALENCIA

The above-mentioned hypotheses of twentieth-century witchcraft research were in fact anticipated by the Spanish humanist Pedro de Valencia. At the beginning of the seventeenth century he gave his views on the phenomenon during one of the greatest witch persecutions ever seen in Europe. The inquisitors at Logroño, in Spain, had instituted a thoroughgoing witch-hunt among the Basques in the Pyrenean mountain regions and had already held their first auto de fe in the autumn of 1610, at which some of the witches had been burnt while others had received prison sentences. Early in 1611, the Spanish inquisitor general wrote to a number of prominent people requesting them to give their opinion on "the witch sect."[30] One of those asked for comments was Valencia, who had himself previously approached the inquisitor general for permission to criticize a printed report of the auto de fe at Logroño.[31]

On 20 April 1611 Valencia sent his reply in the form of a long discourse, "Concerning the Witches' Stories."[32] It began by deprecating the fact that the sentences had been read out in full at the auto de fe and had subsequently been printed and published; the witches had confessed to such monstrous and abominable things as to defy imagination, and now that they had been made public everyone would be inclined to think that his own sins were peccadilloes compared with those committed by the witches; and there would undoubtedly be some weak spirits who would succumb to the temptation to imitate them.[33] Moreover, the disclosure was a disgrace to the whole populace in that area of Spain, a region which, according to Valencia, had always been considered one of the most Christian and unheretical in the realm. Lastly, for its own sake the Inquisition ought not to have entered into such a detailed proclamation of the prologues to the judgments, since the reputation of the Inquisition as a whole might suffer:

> Although on the whole it must be assumed that the witches have confessed to the truth, some of the things they have admitted are so improbable that many people will refuse to believe them and instead would consider the whole story to be something the witches have dreamed up. For such things have never been heard of before except in poems and fairy tales [*libros fabulosos*] which are written to entertain and terrify children and simple folk.[34]

Valencia proceeded to analyze the printed report of the auto de fe (which seems to have been the pamphlet published in January 1611 by the Burgos printer Juan Baptista Varesio).[35] In his survey of the witches' confessions the learned humanist constantly drew parallels with the religions of antiquity. On the other hand he gave very little consideration to the opinions of the theological authorities regarding the witches. He wisely confined himself to supplying explanations for what the witches had confessed to during this particular trial. Without indicating which was to be preferred, he propounded the following three hypotheses: (1) the witches' meetings were real, and took place without the cooperation of the Devil; (2) the witches' meetings were dream-visions produced by the witch unguent; or (3) the witches' meetings were sometimes real and sometimes only dreams, but in any case involved the cooperation of the Devil.

The first hypothesis postulated that the witches' gatherings were composed of people who met to indulge in the most depraved and licentious activities. The journey to these orgies was made on foot. The Devil was merely one of the participants, who appeared at the meeting wearing horns and a gruesome mask, and in this guise he had intercourse with the women, either in normal fashion or with the use of an artificial phallus.[36]

The second hypothesis postulated that the witches instructed each other in the concoction and use of a certain kind of poisonous ointment. After having committed themselves to the power of the Devil they anointed themselves with the unguent in order to fly to the witches' sabbath. But they did not really go anywhere. Instead they fell into a deep sleep during which the Devil fulfilled his part of the covenant and allowed them to experience the delights of the sabbath in dreams. He saw to it that the individual dreams were in agreement, and when the witches awoke they were completely convinced that what they had experienced actually happened. It was even possible, added Valencia, that the dream experiences were caused entirely by the ointment, which affected everyone in the same way, so that cooperation with the Devil was not necessary in order to explain why the dreams were in agreement.[37]

The third hypothesis postulated that sometimes the Devil transported people to a witches' sabbath so that they were in fact present in person, and at other times he deceived them and caused them to dream the whole experience. This, said Valencia, was the general view among the common people, and it was apparently supported by the witches' own confessions. But the theory was both fantastic and dangerous, he emphasized, for it was said that the Devil was able both to provide a counterfeit figure in the bed (so that the absence of the actual witch passed unnoticed) and to conjure up the figure of anyone he pleased at his witches' sabbath (thereby involving truly innocent people). In other words, the argument continued, this was a phenomenon which could be neither proved nor disproved. An accusation could never be substantiated, for though fifty witnesses might have seen a certain person at their witches' sabbath, the accused could always exonerate himself on the grounds that what the witnesses had observed was only an impersonation which the Devil, "who is man's declared mortal enemy," conjured up for them. By the same token an innocent defendant was prevented from proving his alibi, for it could always be objected that the witnesses who claimed to have seen and spoken to him at home were in fact deluded by a demon appearing in his place, and that the accused had really been with the witches.[38]

The long discourse to the inquisitor general ended with the recommendation that, whatever the outcome, the witches deserved to be severely punished if it could be proved that they had intended to make a pact with the Devil. However, the inquisitors were to ensure that the accused were not suffering from "melancholy," madness, or "possession," for in these cases flogging was a more effective remedy than the usual punishments enforced by the Holy Office. Finally, Valencia earnestly advised that in every concrete witch case one was always to search for a palpable corpus delicti in order to ensure that no person was sentenced for actions or injuries which had never been committed or which could be explained as natural occurrences or accidental misfortunes.[39]

Apart from the sociological explanations, no particularly new points of view have emerged in the witchcraft studies of the twentieth century. Today, indeed, the problem has become less complicated, since we feel we can leave the Devil out of account; but this is irrelevant for an evaluation of the efforts of Valencia. His treatise has not had any influence on present-day discussion;[40] it merely shows us how intelligent persons of the past were able to analyze witchcraft with no less penetration than modern commentators.

Yet, no matter from how many angles we view the problem, we are always left with a large number of witches, the majority, in fact, whose existence we cannot explain away with any of the above theories. Only when we turn to the study of witchcraft in its social setting do we begin to understand why so many people were suspected of being witches.

3. WITCH BELIEF IN ITS SOCIAL SETTING

Before there can be any satisfactory exposition, the complicated phenomenon of witchcraft must be clearly differentiated from sorcery. In a 1935 article on African witchcraft which paved the way for a fruitful study of the subject in primitive societies, the social anthropologist E. E. Evans-Pritchard wrote:

> There is much loose discussion about witchcraft. We must distinguish between bad magic (or sorcery) and witchcraft. Many African peoples distinguish clearly between the two and for ethnological purposes we must do the same. Witchcraft is an imaginary offence because it is impossible. A witch cannot do what he is supposed to do, and has in fact no real existence. A sorcerer, on the other hand, may make magic to kill his neighbours. The magic will not kill them,

but he can, and no doubt often does, make it with that intention.[41]

The distinction of Evans-Pritchard applies equally well in the study of European conditions. As a rule the Inquisition and the secular witch-judges in Europe distinguished quite successfully between witchcraft and sorcery (in Spain between *brujería* and *hechicería*). Thus, it was only seldom that wizards and sorcerers were accused of taking part in a witches' sabbath. They were tried for completely different crimes: whether they had made use of heathen spells or "superstitious" conjurations; whether they had made a compact with the Evil One or whether by the use of secret arts they could be considered to be in the Devil's clutches (that is, parties to an explicit or implicit pact); whether they had used their arts to do good or evil; from whom they had learned them; and finally, who had been their clients.

The trials of wizards and sorcerers reveal that one of their most important functions was to counteract the evil doings of the witches. The "wise" man or woman was in fact a kind of witch doctor in the European folk-communities. Like their African colleagues they had oracles and methods of divination which enabled them to discover who had bewitched a man or his possessions; they had magical remedies for enchantment which consisted chiefly of antiwitchcraft rites directed against the culprit; and they had powerful spells and charms which could protect their clients from new bewitchings.[42]

The witches were held responsible for all manner of critical situations in everyday life. People were quick to attribute the cause of any unusual misfortune or strange coincidence to witchcraft, and in a number of situations for whose relief there existed insufficient expert knowledge or defective skills it was traditional to put the blame on the witches. This was the case, for instance, when people wasted away with tuberculosis; when the milk in the churn failed to produce butter; when the brewer's mash was unsuccessful (bad yeast); or when the corn produced no grain and the ears were filled with a black powder (blight).

Outwardly, people thought to be witches were perfectly normal human beings. In the same way as other people they possessed only scraps of knowledge of the sorcerers' art. But witches were thought to have special powers or to be in league with supernatural powers. This enabled them to do things denied to ordinary mortals, such as flying through the air, transforming themselves into animals, and injuring their fellows merely by touching them or uttering a curse. There was no need to take any notice of what was said when ordinary people quarreled and hurled imprecations at each other, for that was perfectly commonplace. But sooner or later the curse of a witch was bound to come true; it might not happen for a long time, and it was only when a misfortune had finally occurred that one realized he had been cursed. (The argument was sometimes enforced from the opposite angle: after the damage was done people began to speculate about whom they had been on bad terms with; and when a witch was brought to court all her neighbors racked their brains to remember "mysterious incidents.") The witches carried out their evil deeds with such secrecy that a man could be married for many years before he realized that his wife was one of them, if, that is, he believed the charge made against her; for there are a number of examples of a husband taking his wife's part and accusing the person who had brought the charge of slander and defamation of character.

In some regions of Europe the witches invariably operated single-handedly ("the solitary pattern of witchcraft," as Macfarlane calls it[43]), and in other places in organized groups. It is not yet possible to say which was more common. In Denmark and Spain, where I have made a special study of the phenomenon, both types of witchcraft were to be found and in fact seem to have existed simultaneously. In both countries the concept of a witch organization was real, though vague, within the popular tradition. The local witches were thought to be in contact with each other and to assemble at night for secret meetings. Up to a point it might be said that the witches were thought of as a fifth column. As a rule their gatherings took place near a village. The meeting place (in both Denmark and northern Spain) was frequently near a spring. From here they set out on their nightly expeditions for the purpose of destroying their neighbors' crops, killing their children, and afflicting their cattle with sickness. But whether the witches operated in groups or singly, it is a characteristic feature of popular (in contrast to theological) opinion that as a rule the witches accomplished their evil work quite effectively without the assistance of the Devil.

People could only point the finger of suspicion at possible

witches, but from the records of the trials it is obvious that the first to come under suspicion were members of two social groups within the community (this is clearly shown when we consider who was accused of witchcraft and who the witches named as their accomplices). One group consisted of the weaker members of the community: beggars, cripples, widows, the very old, and orphans; in short, all those who could be accused without risk. The other group consisted of those who had rejected the moral order of society: fawning, envious, thieving, aggressive, spiteful, promiscuous, and odd people; in fact, all who were in any way unattractive.[44]

Thus we see that witchcraft in European village society during the sixteenth and seventeenth centuries had a great deal in common with the witch belief which social anthropologists have studied in primitive societies, particularly in Africa. Since Evans-Pritchard set the pattern for study in this field with his book *Witchcraft, Oracles and Magic among the Azande* (1937),[45] there has been much valuable research.[46] A survey of this is to be found in Lucy Mair's lucid and exceptionally fluent popular exposition, *Witchcraft* (1970), which dissociates itself from other easily approachable books on witches by taking the subject seriously: "This book," she says, "starts from the premise that in a world where there are few assured techniques for dealing with everyday crises, notably sickness, a belief in witches, or the equivalent of one, is not only not foolish, it is indispensable."[47]

This kind of research has not yet been undertaken in Europe. When social anthropologists compare witchcraft in Africa and Europe, it is significant that they invariably liken the results from recent African fieldwork to those from European studies covering the period of the witch trials.[48] The majority of social anthropologists appear to be unaware that there are local communities believing in witchcraft in many parts of Europe to this very day. Such communities are to be found even in a highly developed society like that of Denmark, where it is certainly no longer justifiable to speak of there being "few assured techniques for dealing with everyday crises." During 1960-62 I carried out an investigation into the patterns of ideas and behavior of a small group of convinced believers in witches which I happened to discover in a small Danish town.[49] During 1965-68 I undertook a similar piece of folkloristic fieldwork among the peasant and fishing communities in

Galicia in northwest Spain.[50] Here Lucy Mair's reasoning is more applicable. In both places I obtained results which agree to an astonishing extent with those reached by Evans-Pritchard and his successors in African communities. Both in Denmark and in Spain it is absolutely correct to say that witchcraft, to use Fortes's words, is "related to the notion of causation, the rules of moral conduct, the practice of divination and the art of healing to form with them a coherent ideology for daily living."[51] But it must be added that this social philosophy is constantly affected by and mixed up with the techniques and ideologies of the modern world. In Galicia the lifting of a spell may be achieved by any one of a series of experts — doctors and wise women, priests and fortune-tellers, psychiatrists and exorcists. And in Denmark several of my informants defined their belief in witchcraft in psychological terminology which they had acquired from reading weekly magazines.[52] Since education does not appear to play a decisive part in the matter, I find it difficult to elucidate why it is that so-called modern people do *not* believe in witches.

4. THE EUROPEAN WITCH CRAZE

There is not only a formal and structural resemblance between European and African witch belief, there are also such striking parallels in the substance of the ideas that there can hardly be any other explanation than that which presupposes that the witch mythology of the two continents rests on a very ancient common basis of tradition. The problem awaits closer investigation,[53] but it provides food for thought when in the fragmentary sources from the early Middle Ages we come across legal sanctions against witchcraft from which it appears that European witches as well as those in Africa were believed to eat human flesh at their nightly gatherings, and that the results could be seen by people being "consumed from within." In *Lex Salica*, dated ca. A.D. 500, it is stated that if a witch (*strix*) is convicted of devouring a human being the penance of blood money is to be imposed on her.[54] The comparatively light penalties which reappear in several laws reflect a skeptical attitude on the part of the authorities — skepticism not of the existence of the crimes, but of the difficulty of proving them.[55]

Advancing a little in time we see that both church and state condemn witch belief as heathen practice. According to Charlemagne's law for the newly christened Saxons (ca. 787), it was strictly forbidden to execute men and women who were, according to pagan views, man-eating witches (*striges*). In future any person who burned a witch according to ancient custom would himself be liable to the death penalty, as would any person who, by another ancient custom, slaughtered the witch and either ate the flesh himself or distributed it to others.[56]

The church continued to condemn witch belief as heathen superstition until well into the Middle Ages, and in *Canon episcopi*, an episcopal law of the tenth century which was incorporated into church law by none other than the twelfth-century canonist Gratian, priests were enjoined to preach against those who were foolish enough to believe the claims of women who alleged that they had ridden through the air at night on wild beasts in Diana's train, when it was obvious that Satan had inspired them with visions and illusions.[57]

The gradual change of attitude which finally resulted in the church becoming the enthusiastic advocate of witch persecution forms a long and complex saga. However, as recently demonstrated independently by two scholars, real witch trials did not occur until the beginning of the fifteenth century, when Spanish and French inquisitors began to persecute witches in the regions bordering on the Pyrenees, and witch-hunts were organized in the Alps as well.[58] Inquisitors and theologians wrote one learned treatise after another in which the witches' confessions were analyzed and theological significance was read into them. Eventually they hammered together popular ideas and learned treatises into a hard and fast theological system which certainly seems to have had very little in common with the witch belief of the common people. It therefore grew more and more difficult for the witches to answer the inquisitors' questions. The Holy Office had long since managed to circumvent Gratian's clause by declaring the witches to be a new sect which had nothing to do with those who had ridden in Diana's train. How the church managed to construe the witches of popular belief as a secret underground movement organized by the Devil is still puzzling. But it is not so strange that it happened in the Alps and Pyrenees; these regions had long been the haunt of heretical movements, and the Inquisition had tracked down and annihilated one sect after another.[59]

A milestone on the road was a handbook on witch persecution written by two German inquisitors, Jacob Sprenger and

Heinrich Institoris. *Malleus maleficarum* ("Hammer of Witches") was the title of their weighty work, which was published in 1487.[60] Two years previously they had secured a bull from Pope Innocent VIII, authorizing them to continue the witch-hunt in the Alps that they had already instituted despite resistance from both ecclesiastical and secular authorities. In the second edition of the "Hammer of Witches" the two inquisitors reprinted the bull of 5 December 1484 to make it appear that the whole work enjoyed papal sanction.[61] The "Hammer of Witches" became the standard manual for the persecutors of the next two hundred years, not only in Catholic but in Protestant countries as well.

For the remainder of the medieval period, however, witch-hunting was limited to the traditional areas of heresy in southern Germany, the Alps and northern Italy, and in southern France including the Pyrenees. In the rest of Europe, isolated trials for witchcraft and sorcery were held from time to time, but mass persecutions were unknown.[62]

Not until the sixteenth century did witch-hunting expand geographically, and then only to the north and west; Greek Orthodox eastern Europe apparently escaped.[63] The main cause of this development must surely be attributed to the increasing intolerance of Reformation and Counter-Reformation Europe where each camp zealously strove to maintain the purity of the faith. Any person who was associated with secret arts was suspect, irrespective of whether these were used for good or ill. Witches and wizards were persecuted relentlessly in both Catholic and Protestant countries, but as a rule the wizards were let off with lighter punishment on a first offense. Those who sought the advice of wizards were punished as well, as a rule with fines and penances, but in this respect legislation differed greatly from country to country and from period to period.

It is significant that witch-hunting did not really acquire momentum until after the Council of Trent in 1563 had initiated the Catholic Counter-Reformation. In the same year in England a statute enacted by Elizabeth created the legislation necessary to allow witch persecution. In Germany witch trials were not general until after 1570. Over the greater part of western Europe the persecutions culminated in the period between 1575 and 1650, at the time when denominational strife was at its most acute. It is therefore extremely misleading to describe the witch persecutions as a medieval phenomenon which survived into later times. Apart from the fact that in most parts of Europe the persecutions were practically unknown for the whole of the Middle Ages, we must remember that such a vital element as the witches' sabbath was only present in a rudimentary form in the witch mythology of the medieval theologians and lawyers and was not completely elaborated until about 1600.

In an important essay, "The European Witch-craze of the Sixteenth and Seventeenth Centuries," Professor Hugh Trevor-Roper has drawn attention to the fact that as early as the Renaissance intellectuals considered witch belief to be a thing of the past. "Erasmian Basel listened to the witch-stories of the surrounding mountains with polite amusement," writes Trevor-Roper. "But if the sceptics thought that they were prevailing, they were soon to know better."[64]

When Trevor-Roper says that the witch persecutions of the sixteenth and seventeenth centuries are "a standing warning to those who would simplify the stages of human progress,"[65] I support him warmly. However, it is questionable to what extent the witch persecutions can be explained as camouflaged heretic hunts. Trevor-Roper believes that when the Protestant and Catholic missionaries met with resistance which was too primitive to deserve doctrinal refutation, they resorted to the cliché coined by medieval preachers in the Alps and Pyrenees, that "the dissidents were witches." In this they were always able to count on the requisite support of the people, who wished for nothing more than to get rid of their witches.[66]

This seems a plausible argument, but if Trevor-Roper were correct we would find that the witch persecutions had been directed against dissidents of high estate. This, however, was not the case. The majority of witch trials were initiated against persons of lower social status who had been suspected of witchcraft for a considerable time. The witch-hunt might enter a second phase if all those people named by the first witches in their confessions were rounded up (the list of accomplices was frequently obtained when the accused was interrogated under torture). These were condemned without regard for whether they had done any harm; their having been seen at the witches' sabbath was more than sufficient to send them to the stake. There are plenty of examples to show that this provided an excellent opportunity to get rid of personal enemies as well as religious and political opponents. But the development from a small number of witchcraft trials to a full-fledged witch-hunt was in itself a natural consequence of the Christian zeal for the purity of the faith which was demonstrated by church and state in both Catholic and Protestant countries.

As a rule the ordinary citizen was only interested in whether a witch had caused harm or not, and if a witch could make good any damage he had done, he was seldom taken to court. For the leaders of society apostasy was the deciding factor, and they looked upon it as a sacred duty to clear the Devil's weeds from the garden of Christendom. However, it is worth noting that the authorities in several countries were aware of the vicious circle that the witch trials begot. In Denmark two legal provisions were made in 1547 to put a stop to mass persecutions. One laid down the ruling that torture was not to be resorted to until a death sentence had been pronounced; the other that no case could be brought against any person merely because a witch had named him as an accomplice.[67]

Even in areas where it might seem obvious to interpret the witch persecutions as camouflaged heretic hunts, such an explanation sometimes turns out to be completely untenable. Trevor-Roper saw a connection between the witch trials in Essex and the fact that "Catholicism was strong and the Puritan evangelists particularly energetic;"[68] but Macfarlane, who has studied the trials held over a period of more than two hundred years, reached the conclusion that there was absolutely no possibility of religious persecution. His reasoning is that

> when the Essex trials are seen in perspective, as moments of crisis in small communities, generated by quarrels between neighbours that come from the incidents of every day, the idea that they were nothing but a monstrous dramatic form of religious persecution becomes untenable.[69]

A study of the Danish and Spanish witch trials yields similar conclusions. By far the greater number of cases were brought on the initiative of ordinary citizens and were concerned with concrete witchcraft crimes such as killing children or slaying animals. It was, however, not at all unusual for the "witch" to be acquitted, either in the secular courts in Denmark or the tribunals of the Inquisition in Spain.[70]

Occasionally we can see that the persecutions were imposed

from above. Thus in 1626 the Danish king wrote to his chancellor and commanded him to deal severely with some witches in Copenhagen and Elsinore, regardless of whether their relatives were trying to shield them. "We have unfortunately far too many of these creatures, and it is desirable that they be thoroughly swept away once and for all, so that the house is free of this filth," wrote Christian IV.[71] But generally the witch persecutions were initiated locally. On several occasions in the sixteenth century we find the Basque peasants in the Pyrenees taking up a collection in the parish in order to raise the necessary sum to call in the commissioners from the High Court at Navarra to extirpate local witches.[72]

Thus the witch-hunting of the western European villages throughout the sixteenth and seventeenth centuries had very little to do with religious persecution. It was in fact entirely related to the function of witch belief in the social life of the time. That popular and traditional witch-hunting was encouraged by legislation and incited by sermons preached against "limbs of Satan" is quite another matter.

Significantly, when witch trials were abolished about 1700 and it was forbidden to lodge accusations, the mass of the people failed to comprehend and in several cases considered it necessary to take the law into their own hands and lynch witches.[73] Such murders are known to have taken place not only in the eighteenth and nineteenth centuries; they have occurred right down to the present. In 1976 at Hesloup, a village near Alençon in northern France, a fifty-year-old man was shot by two young men. During the trial it was revealed that the motive for the murder was that the two young men held him responsible for a series of misfortunes which had happened on their farm because, as they said, he had cast a spell on their family.[74]

If one disregards the popular environment of witch-hunting, as Rossell Hope Robbins did in his *Encyclopedia of Witchcraft and Demonology* (1959), and defines the subject as nothing more than "a Christian heresy" which thus "lies in the province of the theology,"[75] one has in advance ruled out any possibility of a deeper comprehension of the European witch craze. One must then, like Robbins, be content with simply condemning it as "the shocking nightmare, the foulest crime and deepest shame of western civilization, the blackout of everything that *homo sapiens,* the reasoning man, has ever upheld."[76]

Trevor-Roper demonstrates convincingly that the European witch craze was not a product of reason but a reflection of the whole ideology of the sixteenth and seventeenth centuries. Although the skeptics voiced their doubts throughout the period, Trevor-Roper maintains that rational witch belief remained unchallenged throughout the seventeenth century. "All that successive sceptics had done was to cast doubt on its practical interpretation: to question the value of confessions, the efficacy of torture, the identification of particular witches. The myth itself remained untouched, at least in appearance."[77] Trevor-Roper finds that at the end of the seventeenth century, when the critics had at last made themselves heard and the Dutchman Bekker[78] had given the coup de grace to the whole idea of Satan's kingdom, the witch trials had already ceased or were on the wane in most of western Europe. Trevor-Roper wisely refrains from pinning down the reason for this reversal:

> Why the witch-belief decayed — why the critical arguments which were regarded as unplausible in 1563 [Johan Weyer[79]] and in 1584 [Reginald Scott[80]] and in 1631 [Friedrich von Spee[81]] were found plausible in 1700 — is mysterious still.
>
> The nineteenth-century liberal historians did indeed offer an answer. They saw the controversy as a straight contest between superstition and reason, between theology and science, between the Church and 'rationalism'. The Englishman Lecky, the Americans White, Lea and Burr, the German Hansen, write as if the irrationality of the witch-beliefs had always been apparent to the natural reason of man . . .
>
> Today such a distinction between 'reason' and 'superstition' is difficult to maintain. We have seen the darkest forms of superstitious belief and superstitious cruelty springing again not out of half-purged religious systems, but out of new, purely secular roots [cf. for instance the persecution of Jews] . . . We recognize that even rationalism is relative: that it operates within a general philosophic context, and that it cannot properly be detached from this context.[82]

It requires specialized research to discover what social factors combined to bring about the cessation of witch persecution. Here we must be content with the generalization that with the philosophical and scientific revolution of the middle of the seventeenth century, witch belief and the demonological view of nature became obsolete. Witchcraft went out of fashion, but it was never disproved. The nature of the phenomenon made this impossible.

Trevor-Roper's long essay is the first attempt to place the witch persecutions of the sixteenth and seventeenth centuries in a broad historical context. His treatise is impeccably written and crackling with ideas, but on pondering over it one comes to realize how little in fact is basically known about the witch craze in the so-called enlightened centuries (this "perplexing phenomenon," as Trevor-Roper himself calls it).[83]

5. THE FALSE CONFESSIONS

Let us restrict ourselves to one main problem and ask with Pedro de Valencia: How are we to explain the witches' confessions? Trevor-Roper noted that many of them were made voluntarily and could not be ascribed to torture and leading questions. To explain these confessions, Trevor-Roper musters the usual battery of psychiatric terms, relying on the assumption, obviously correct, that "today, every psychopath has his or her private obsessions [while] in the past the neurotics and hysterics of Christendom centralized their illusions around the figure of the Devil."[84] But when we have exhausted psychiatric explanations we are still left with the problem that the bulk of the witches must be considered "normal," and if their confessions were always the result of torture and of leading questions we are forced to doubt the honesty of the examining judges. However, Trevor-Roper himself clearly demonstrates that the judges acted in good faith, and as they could even be "lenient" when people confessed, there still remains a possibility that a great number of confessions were in fact "voluntary."[85]

Intellectuals are often liable to forget that extremely gifted individuals are to be found among the rank and file of the population. Those familiar with the archives of the Inquisition are brought up short in amazement time and again when faced with the aptitude some heretics showed in outwitting their examiners. In normal life basically all of us show the same tendency. We learn from childhood to identify ourselves with the personality pattern that society expects of us, and we learn through our upbringing to conceal the characteristics and camouflage actions that are likely to be condemned. In every society the witch stands as the symbol of all that the moral order anathematizes as perversity and brands as of negative value. In short, the role of the witch is the complete inversion of the accepted personality pattern.

I therefore suspect that during a witch trial the accused person often suffered a complete reversal of identity. When he realized that the battle was hopeless, he felt he might just as well accept the negative personality pattern. Combining the most perverse side of his imagination with what he already knew about witches, he would fabricate the confession expected of him. For why should he give himself over to torture when he knew that no matter what he said, death at the stake probably awaited him? Then, too, there was always the outside chance that a voluntary confession might evoke judicial leniency.[86]

A few stoic characters chose the hard way. In 1628 the burgomaster of Bamberg, Johannes Junius, endured torture for so long that at last even the jailer grew sorry for him and begged him for God's sake to confess something. Burgomaster Junius managed to get a letter smuggled out of prison a few days before going to the stake, in which he took leave of his daughter in these words:

> Many hundred thousand good-nights, dearly beloved daughter Veronica. Innocent have I come into prison, innocent have I been tortured, innocent must I die. For whoever comes into the witch prison must become a witch or be tortured until he invents something out of his head and — God pity him — bethinks him of something.[87]

If we read the interviews held by the psychiatrist Robert Jay Lifton in 1954 with a number of people who were permitted to leave China after having been subjected to Chinese Communist "thought reform," we cannot help wondering whether similar methods were not used in the witch prisons.

> They will have their false confession. But I don't want to make a false confession. Maybe there is a way to say something that is not totally untrue to satisfy them — but what? . . . I've said the truth. They don't want the truth. I've only one way to escape: to guess what they really want.[88]

These were the thoughts of Francis Lucas, a Catholic priest, while he was sitting in a Chinese prison accused of anti-Communist activities.

Time and again, in the records of both the European witch persecution of the sixteenth and seventeenth centuries and the outbreak of African witch-hunting which took place in the forties and fifties of the present century, we note how accused persons have been able to fabricate witch confessions so convincingly that we constantly find ourselves on the point of believing in them and are thus tempted to adopt the fantasies of Margaret Murray.[89]

If a human being is isolated for a considerable time from all the stimuli which confirm his identity, and if, by both violent means and sympathetic persuasion, he is constantly induced to confess all his crimes, it is not only probable that the false confession will be obtained, but the accused is likely to identify so much with his false confession that he betrays his own personality and begins to doubt who he really is. Lifton believes that this sort of personality mutation occurred in some of those who underwent the Chinese brainwashing.[90]

6. WITCH PERSECUTION IN SPAIN IN THE SIXTEENTH CENTURY

Some western European countries escaped infection from the prevalent witch craze; others did not keep pace with the general development. Catholic Ireland was practically untouched. Protestant Holland had very few trials and after 1610 no witch was burned. In Sweden persecution did not get under way until the middle of the seventeenth century, but then continued until well into the eighteenth. In Italy and Spain, the motherlands of the Inquisition, the peak of the persecutions was reached as early as the beginning of the sixteenth century, but subsequently the Inquisition displayed remarkable restraint.

In Spain there were hectic witch persecutions in the Pyrenees and the Basque provinces in 1507, 1517, and the 1520s,[91] but thereafter witch burning ceased for the rest of the century. While more and more witches were burned at the stake in France and Germany, the witches in Spain were sentenced to light punishments or freely acquitted. And there are even records of cases in which the Inquisition attempted to rehabilitate the witches by forcing them to move to villages where their unsavory reputation was unknown.[92]

In spite of the fact that some of the earliest treatises on witchcraft were written by Spanish theologians,[93] witch mythology never seemed to take firm root amongst the learned in Spain. In 1526 the inquisitor general summoned a number of the most learned lawyers and theologians to a meeting in Granada in order to discuss the witch question and to define an attitude toward some witch confessions that had been sent by the inquisitors at Navarra. They reached the conclusion that the existence of a sect of witches was still to be regarded as a dubious matter about which the judges could easily be deceived. New instructions were drawn up for witch trials which necessitated concrete proof of guilt before a person could be condemned for witchcraft.[94] The Council of the Inquisition kept witch persecution under control for the rest of the sixteenth century. In southern Spain this was not difficult, for the notion of the witches' sabbath never really penetrated that area. Cataluña and the Basque provinces including Navarra, however, were the first to be infected by the witch scares which flared up periodically in the wake of persecutions in France and set secular authorities in motion. As a rule, action ended with the intervention of the Holy Office.[95]

The auto de fe at Logroño in 1610 used procedures different from those which had been used by the Inquisition at witch trials for more than eighty years. It led to a witch persecution of hitherto unmatched proportions. Witches confessed by the hundreds and in the course of two years the number of suspects rose to several thousand.

7. PIERRE DE LANCRE'S WITCH-HUNT

The auto de fe at Logroño and the investigation of Basque witch belief which followed it are of special interest because they occur almost simultaneously with the witch-hunt of the French judge Pierre de Lancre which took place north of the Pyrenees in the Basque-speaking Pays de Labourd (map 1). De Lancre's investigation led to a mass burning of witches and to the suspicion that the entire population, numbering about thirty thousand, was infected by the witch sect. In 1612 he published a book about his witch-hunt in the Pays de Labourd: *Tableau de l'inconstance des mauvais anges et demons* ("Description of the inconstancy of evil angels and demons").[96] It was larded with quotations from demonological and other learned works, but today the greatest value of the book lies in the long extracts and reports reproduced from the witch confessions in the Pays de Labourd. When de Lancre was writing his book he had access to the original records,[97] and after these were lost in a fire in Bordeaux in 1710,[98] his book acquired considerable importance as a primary source.

Until recently, practically the only available information about the Basque witch trials was that contained in de Lancre's book.[99] He even devoted a chapter to the auto de fe at Logroño.[100] Many of the examples quoted in support of the fantastic theories of Murray and Summers, and before them by Jules Michelet, are taken from de Lancre's book, and if the references are examined closely some of them can even be traced back to the auto de fe at Logroño.[101] Although dealing only with the Spanish source materials the present study has thrown new light on de Lancre's witch persecution, revealing some of its underlying mechanisms. A detailed study of de Lancre, however, falls outside the scope of this book. I restrict myself to a short account in order to provide a background for the exposition that follows.

In 1608 a complaint was sent from the Pays de Labourd to Henry IV to the effect that the number of sorcerers had increased so alarmingly during the previous four years that no corner of the region was free of them.[102] Two noblemen were responsible for the denunciation, Jean d'Amou, the lower court judge (*bailli*) whose chateau was situated in Saint-Pée-sur-Nivelle,[103] and the Lord of Urtubie, Tristan de Gamboa d'Alsatte, commandant of the troops at Labourd and *bailli d'espée*.[104] On 10 December 1608, by a Royal Decree to the parliament at Bordeaux, the fifty-six-year-old lawyer and parliamentary councillor Pierre de Lancre was appointed to investigate the matter. He was to be sent to Labourd with authority to interrogate under torture and pronounce summary death sentences. "For certain good reasons," which the Bordeaux parliament must have stated in high quarters, the commission was extended to include the parliamentary president, Jean d'Espaignet (decree of 17 January 1609).[105] On 1 July the two commissioners embarked on their punitive expedition.[106] They were vested with extraordinary authority and in fact constituted a traveling high court for sorcery cases. The commission was valid until 5 December 1609,[107] but as d'Espaignet was obliged to be at Nerac by Martinmas to open *la Chambre de l'Edict en Guyenne*, the two witch judges ended their campaign as early as 1 November.[108] It is not known how many witches were burned in the course of that summer. The figure six hundred, so often repeated by historians writing on de Lancre, cannot possibly be correct and probably derives from a misinterpretation of some figures given in the preface to his book.[109] In the *Tableau* de Lancre refers to only forty-six actual witches (among them twelve priests) and thirty-five witch witnesses (children and young people, who more or less unwillingly had been to the witches' sabbath).[110] It is stated definitely that three priests and eight other witches were burned;[111] but as the prisoners were later transferred to the prisons at Bordeaux, where the trials were continued for several years,[112] it is hardly possible to ascertain the total number of those who died at the stake. Salazar, who was well-informed regarding the witch persecutions in the Pays de Labourd, states, in 1612, that the French judges managed to burn over eighty persons as witches during the course of the commission,[113] and this is undoubtedly as near to the truth as we shall ever get.

When d'Espaignet and de Lancre reached the Pays de Labourd in the month of July 1609 the witch-hunt was already in full swing and the local authorities had imprisoned many witches.[114] The Spanish Inquisition had begun its investigations on the other side of the frontier considerably earlier, and all was now in readiness for a wholesale persecution of the abominable sect.

CHAPTER TWO
The Witches of Zugarramurdi

HE WITCHES WHO APPEARED AT THE FA-
mous auto de fe at Logroño in 1610 came almost
without exception from Zugarramurdi and
Urdax, two Spanish villages on the north side of
the Pyrenees mountains near the Pays de Labourd. Zugarramurdi was a daughter-parish of Urdax and its church was
served by a monk from the Premonstratensian monastery at
Urdax.[1] The combined population of the two villages hardly
exceeded three hundred.[2] The abbot at Urdax had jurisdiction
over both the secular and spiritual affairs of the people — those
of Zugarramurdi were peasants and shepherds, while those of
Urdax were simple farm laborers who worked at the monastery estates.[3] Twenty-five of the thirty-one witches at the auto
de fe came from these two villages;[4] they were men and
women ranging in age from twenty to eighty and appear to
have made up about a quarter of the adult population of the
two remote mountain communities.

The aim of this chapter is to determinate the local reputation
of these unfortunate people *before* the Inquisition transformed
them into monsters. We shall leave the supposed secret rites
out of account and restrict ourselves to what ordinary persons
might have known or witnessed. I believe this to be the only
way to reconstruct the witchcraft notions of daily life in this
region of the Pyrenees at the turn of the century.

The most common indictment in the roster of crimes for
which the witches were tried was infanticide by vampirism.

An extended Spanish version of this chapter was published in
Saioak. Revista de Estudios Vascos 2 (1978) 182-195.

The sixty-six-year-old shepherd Miguel de Goiburu confessed to the Inquisition that "thirty years ago" he took part in the murder of his sister's little daughter. He explained how the witches broke into her house during the night, bit the child, and sucked blood from the wounds. Only the witches knew about this, but every person in the village was able to confirm that the child was found next morning, her body covered with black marks, and that she died a few days later (the villagers had all been to see the injured child). Miguel's sister had complained to him that the witches had sucked her child's blood; but he replied that he knew nothing about it.[5]

Ten years later, Goiburu admitted, he had joined in sucking the blood of a widow's child. Afterwards the witches took the child out and played ball with it in the square, then left it on the ground outside the widow's house. A chance passer-by heard it crying, woke the family, and delivered the child to its mother. The next morning the town was in an uproar over what had happened.[6]

It seems that in these two cases no one person in particular was under suspicion; it was enough to determine that "the witches" were to blame for the misfortune. Generally, however, people were not content with this vague collective term, but seem to have demanded the concrete identities of the evil-doers.

Evans-Pritchard found that in Azande society "sufferers from misfortune seek for witches among their enemies."[7] In Zugarramurdi it was a common assumption that the witches revenged themselves on their enemies' *children*, and by far the greater number of child murders confessed to by the witches follow this pattern. Miguel de Goiburu related that he killed an eight-year-old child in Urdax because its father had been an unsatisfactory middleman in a cattle deal.[8] Likewise, eighty-year-old Graciana de Barrenechea confessed to having killed a four-year-old girl in revenge for a thrashing the child's father had given the old woman (she and another witch were gathering firewood in the forest and the man had caught them helping themselves to a pile he had just chopped).[9] In another murder case the parents of Graciana's child victim had accused the old woman of stealing a hen, and later when the hen reappeared with chicks they had forgotten to apologize to her.[10] Likewise in a third case of child murder the victim's parents had let their herd of pigs stray into Graciana's garden, where they ruined a large pile of apples she had collected for making cider.[11]

On rare occasions it was the child itself who had offended the witch. Thirty-six-year-old Estevanía de Yriarte confessed to bewitching a child for this reason. Estevanía had been given permission to use her neighbor's oven for her baking, but then the neighbor's children ate one of her loaves. In her anger Estevanía revenged herself on the eldest child, a boy, so that he developed a throat inflammation which lasted twenty days. This took place about 1604.[12]

The witches also revenged themselves directly upon adults. For example, forty-year-old María de Yriarte, the sister of Estevanía, made the following confession: Three years ago (in 1606) she and other witches broke into the house of a neighbor who had threatened her with a knife because she had stolen apples from him. She poured witch powder down his throat while he was asleep. The man survived, however, because he vomited immediately, but the next morning his wife told the neighbors that her husband had vomited so violently that it had nearly killed him.[13] María de Yriarte also confessed that she and her sister, together with their mother, Graciana de Barrenechea, had murdered three men and a woman who had once caused them trouble.[14]

If we sum up the crimes for which these four witches were held responsible, it appears that they were accused of committing about eighteen infanticides, eleven adult murders, a smaller number of bewitchings with nonfatal results, and various instances of injury done to their neighbors' domestic animals.[15] Added to this was the damage that they and other witches had done to the crops.

The harsh climate made farming, the chief means of livelihood in Zugarramurdi, difficult. Hail storms and night frost prevailed far into the spring.[16] And even if the crops had escaped damage from cold and were ready for harvest, new dangers threatened. If the south wind "that in Castilla they call *bochorno*"[17] began to blow, it meant that the witches were abroad with their destructive powders. No one could see how it was done, but the results were obvious to everyone: if the wheat had been bewitched, hardly any grain was formed and the diseased ears were filled with a blackish-yellow powder, sticky and evil-smelling (i.e. blight). If the apple trees had been attacked the flowers withered without forming fruit. If the chestnut trees had been stricken there were no nuts in the shells, or only a single chestnut instead of the usual three.[18]

The texts do not reveal whether the witches had been under suspicion before they were exposed, although in the case of Graciana and her two daughters it is highly probable, even though they may not have been openly accused. It is clear from their confessions that they were constantly quarreling with their neighbors, that they stole when they could get away with it, and were beaten when they were caught red-handed. Of course this does not prove anything more than that they were unpopular and regarded as bad neighbors. But in peasant villages where belief in witchcraft is strong, a "bad neighbor" is almost synonymous with a witch.

For the inhabitants of Zugarramurdi it was not a meaningless coincidence when a small child who had previously been healthy suddenly fell ill and died, nor an inexplicable misfortune when a pig began to sicken. All this was thought to be the work of "evil folk." Here, as in other societies which believe in witchcraft, the price of this "ideology for daily living"[19] was an atmosphere charged with age-old and unresolved suspicions which lingered on. To spark an explosion in such a community it was necessary only for someone to succeed in convincing the people that he possessed proofs. This is what happened at Zugarramurdi.

At the begining of December 1608, one of the young girls of the village returned home after having lived for three or four years in the Pays de Labourd. Her name was María de Ximildegui, and she was twenty years old. Her parents were French and apparently had lived in Zugarramurdi, but when María was about sixteen they had moved to Ciboure, a town on the coast three leagues away. Her father was called Adame de Ximildegui, her mother's name is unknown.[20] The parents stayed on in France, but María returned to Zugarramurdi alone to take employment as a servant.[21] No doubt the first few days after her return were spent in exchanging news, for María had experienced some very remarkable things during her stay in France. She had been a member of a witches' coven. A girl in Ciboure had persuaded her to become a witch and had taken her to their gathering. Before being admitted into the secret society of the witches she had to renounce her Christian faith, and although she never completely denied it she had in fact been an active member of the coven for eighteen months. An experience during Lent in 1608 reconverted her to Christianity, but she was too frightened of the witches to break away from them. After a serious crisis and seven weeks of illness, which almost proved fatal, she finally resolved to seek the help of a learned priest at Hendaye. He heard her confession and gave her some powerful spiritual remedies with which to resist the Devil until he could obtain permission from his bishop to give her absolution. The permission arrived at the end of July and the priest was able to give her communion.[22]

María de Ximildegui was able to reveal much more about the witches in France than simply her own experiences. It happened that she was there at the time of the witch-hunt which preceded that of Pierre de Lancre and which particularly affected Ciboure and the neighboring town of Saint-Jean-de-Luz.[23] Before she left for Zugarramurdi the new persecution was in preparation, and most probably vigils were already being kept in the church at Ciboure to prevent children and young girls from being taken off to sabbaths by the witches.[24]

However, what was most interesting about María de Ximildegui was that during her time as a witch she had attended sabbaths at Zugarramurdi as well, and accordingly knew who the other witches were. When the French girl proceeded to mention individuals by name, protests were soon heard. The first to remonstrate was the farmer Esteve de Navarcorena. He and his relatives presented themselves in a body and called her to account for having brought his wife, twenty-two-year-old María de Jureteguía, into disrepute and causing her suffering by circulating false rumors.[25]

María de Ximildegui replied that if she might speak to Esteve's wife she would certainly get her to go to confession. Esteve and his kinsmen took her back with them to María de Jureteguía. The two young women were confronted with each other, and a lengthy exchange took place. María de Ximildegui described everything she had seen at the witches' sabbath at Zugarramurdi, and the other denied the accusations as soon as they were uttered and swore they were all lies. But the French girl recounted the details so vividly and spoke so eloquently that the listeners gradually became convinced, and at last the family began to put pressure on María de Jureteguía to make her confess. When the young wife realised she had no way of escape she fainted. Shortly afterwards, when she had recovered, she went to confession and admitted that everything the

French girl had stated was true. She confessed to having been a witch since she was a small child. She named fifty-two-year-old María Chipía de Barrenechea, her maternal aunt, as her instructor in the evil arts.[26]

María de Ximildegui was victorious; public opinion in Zugarramurdi had accepted her "evidence." The next step was to bring María de Jureteguía before the priest, Fray Felipe de Zabaleta, who resided at the monastery at Urdax. Here she repeated what she had previously admitted and confessed to being a witch. The priest urged her to make a public confession in the Zugarramurdi church and beg forgiveness from the congregation for all the damage she had caused. During the next few days various other people denounced by the French girl followed María de Jureteguía's example and made public confessions.[27]

Meanwhile María de Jureteguía began to feel she was being pursued by the witches. Shortly before Christmas she and her husband heard that the witches were about, so the following night they collected a crowd of neighbors to stay with them at the home of Esteve's father, Petri de Navarcorena. They stoked up a huge fire in the big kitchen and also kept three wax candles burning. They made a circle around María de Jureteguía and settled down to await events.[28]

That night the Devil and his witches came to reclaim her. People could see them out in the garden in the shape of dogs, cats, and pigs. Some of the older witches broke into the house with the Devil and climbed onto a bench to see where she was. María could see them peering at her and pointed at them, but the others could not see them. From the flue of the open chimney her "instructor" and another maternal aunt made signs for her to follow them and threatened her by putting their fingers to their foreheads. But María grasped the cross on her rosary and lifted it up in the air, at the same time shouting up the chimney that she had finished with serving the Devil.[29]

Thereupon the witches disappeared. But the next morning it was discovered that in their rage the witches had revenged themselves on María's father-in-law by tearing up fruit trees and vegetables in the garden and destroying his water-mill by splitting the wheel and leaving the millstone lying up on the roof.[30]

The situation rapidly grew more and more alarming. Shortly before New Year's a dozen or so people took the law into their own hands and broke into the houses of those neighbors who were under suspicion in order to look for the "toads" believed to accompany all witches (i.e. their imps). They went to Miguel de Goiburu, to Estevanía de Yriarte, and to old Graciana de Barrenechea.

Next day Estevanía's husband, the shepherd Juanes de Goiburu, went to the priest at the monastery and complained about what had happened. Fray Felipe told him to fetch his wife. When he returned with her the priest declared that she had already been exposed as a witch. But Estevanía denied the

Table 1. The Ten Inhabitants of Zugarramurdi Who Confessed to Witchcraft Between December 1608 and January 1609[32]

Name, age, spouse, occupation	Relationship to other witches	Auto de fe no.
Estevanía de Navarcorena, "over 80," widow of Petri de Telechea, farmer	Mother of no. 10[33]	5
Graciana de Barrenechea, 80, married to Juanes de Yriarte, shepherd	Mother of nos. 3 & 4; aunt of no. 9?	1
María Pérez de Barrenechea, 70 (or 46),[34] married to Juanes de Burua (Burga), carpenter		6
María de Yriarte, 40, unmarried, daughter of Juanes de Yriarte, shepherd	Daughter of no. 1; sister of no. 3	4
Juana de Telechea, 38, married to Juanes de Lecumberri, miller	Daughter of no. 5	10
Estevanía de Yriarte, 36, married to Juanes de Goiburu, shepherd	Daughter of no. 1; sister of no. 4; wife of no. 11	3
María de Jureteguía, 22, married to Esteve de Navarcorena, farmer	Niece of no. 1?	9
Miguel de Goiburu, 66, married (wife's name unknown), shepherd	Father of no. 11; maternal uncle of no. 12[35]	2
Juanes de Goiburu, 37, married to Estevanía de Yriarte, shepherd	Son of no. 2; husband of no. 3; cousin of no. 12	11
Juanes de Sansín, "over 20," unmarried, son of Sansín; servant of his uncle the shepherd Miguel de Goiburu and also sieve-maker	Nephew of no. 2; cousin of no. 11	12

charge. Then the priest laid his stole and some relics on her head, all the while exhorting her to tell the truth. Eventually, after having been threatened by him and by others who were present, Estevanía went to confession and admitted that she was a witch. Some other people under suspicion were dragged to the priest by force and threatened with torture if they too did not confess.[31]

By January 1609 a considerable number of people had made such confessions and publicly asked pardon in the church at Zugarramurdi. We do not know the names of all who proclaimed themselves witches on this occasion, but ten men and women were definitely included (see table 1).

The ability to practice witchcraft was not considered hereditary, as it is in many African tribes. Zugarramurdi followed the general European pattern of witch belief; witchcraft was an art that had to be learned. However, what we know about the mutual family relationships of those making confessions to the Inquisition suggests that the occupation of witchcraft was thought to be handed down within certain families.[36] Six out of the ten on the list were related to each other either by blood or by marriage, and if we assume that eighty-year-old Graciana de Barrenechea and fifty-two-year-old María Chipía de Barrenechea (María de Jureteguía's maternal aunt) were sisters, the witch-family of Zugarramurdi numbers eight members in all. Diagram 1 shows the mutual kinship and teacher-pupil relationships between living as well as deceased witches.

Graciana de Barrenechea confessed to the inquisitors that she had learned the art from her mother, María de Telechea.[37] She herself had initiated two of her daughters, María and Estevanía,[38] whilst a third daughter, who was also called María and who was married to Juanes de Marigorre, was not a witch.[39] Estevanía de Yriarte confessed to having made two of her small children witches (probably the two oldest, for according to her husband they had five small children).[40] Miguel de Goiburu declared that his maternal aunt, Mari Juan de Otazarra,[41] had initiated him into the art and that he himself had made witches of his son and of his nephew, Juanes de Sansín.[42]

I admit that it is only guesswork when I assume that Graciana and María Chipía de Barrenechea were sisters, but it is clear from the confessions that María de Jureteguía had two

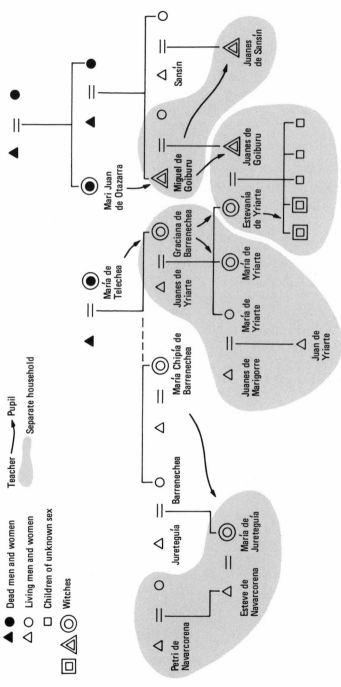

Diagram 1.   The large "witch family" at Zugarramurdi, 1609.

maternal aunts who were witches,[43] and there can be little doubt that she herself was thought to be a witch because she belonged to the Barrenechea family.[44] It is stated in the sentence passed upon Miguel de Goiburu, Graciana de Barrenechea, and two of her daughters that these four witches with five other relatives worked together at producing poison. They usually gathered at the house of Estevanía de Yriarte, where the husband and children were witches, and where they therefore felt secure. It is also stated that they sometimes went to Graciana de Barrenechea's house; but this was possible only when her husband and her son-in-law (Juanes de Marigorre) were out, as they were not witches.[45] It is at this point that the most remarkable fact about diagram 1 emerges, namely, that the dividing line between witches and non-witches cuts right through marriage and sibling ties. Faced with this fact it is interesting to note that the inhabitants of Zugarramurdi solved the problem by a compromise — reconciliation with the witches after they had confessed and asked pardon.[46] If the Inquisition had not been alerted, Zugarramurdi would undoubtedly have found the way out of the difficulty by dealing with its witches in this admirable manner. But unfortunately the Inquisition *was* informed.

CHAPTER THREE
The Inquisition

1. THE INQUISITION IN THE SIXTEENTH AND SEVENTEENTH CENTURIES

ROM THE VANTAGE POINT OF THE TWEN-
tieth century it seems incomprehensible that
people could have become so fanatical about religion as to burn their fellow men for holding
beliefs different from their own. However, in the sixteenth and
seventeenth centuries religion was as vitally important as, for
instance, political ideology today; or, more correctly, religion
and politics were two aspects of the same question, for in
Catholic as well as Protestant countries the structure of society
was based entirely on religious foundations. The purity of the
faith was guarded on both sides of an "iron curtain" which at
that time divided Europe into a north and a south; but only in
the southern states was there an institution especially devoted
to this task: the Inquisition. In Italy it was active well into the
eighteenth century, and in Spain and Portugal right up to
1820. However, the last remainder of the Inquisition was formally in existence until 1965, when the Congregation of the
Holy Office at Rome (founded in 1542) was dissolved as a
consequence of the Second Vatican Council's declaration of
religious liberty (7 December 1965).[1]

2. THE SPANISH INQUISITION CIRCA 1600

The Inquisition in Spain had been reorganized in 1478 and
introduced into Castilla, which in contrast to Aragón had not
been subject to the papal Inquisition of the Middle Ages. In

this respect the Spanish Inquisition had acquired a particular status; unlike the situation in other countries, it did not come under the direct jurisdiction of Rome, but had its own inquisitor general appointed by the Spanish king subject to papal confirmation. The inquisitor general appointed his inquisitors himself, and by virtue of his position had such extensive authority that the Spanish Inquisition was practically autonomous in carrying out its task, which consisted of guarding the purity of the Catholic faith in the whole of the Spanish Empire from Sicily in the east to Peru in the west.

The Inquisition had its own ministry, *el Consejo de la Suprema y General Inquisición*, or simply *la Suprema*. It had its own courts, the tribunals of the Inquisition. It had its own prisons and houses of correction. In the prisons (*las cárceles secretas*, literally, secret prison cells), the prisoners were completely isolated from the world and cut off from one another except for their cell-mates; in the houses of correction (*las casas de penitencia*), the prisoners had exit permits during the day so that they could work to earn their subsistence.[2]

The Inquisition had its own secret intelligence service, whose chief agents, the district commissioners, were for the most part parish priests. Each commissioner was assisted by an Inquisition notary and by lay agents (*familiares*). He received information, interrogated witnesses, and made arrests, and in addition carried out a number of regular inspections. The agents of the Inquisition fulfilled the functions of customs officers in the harbors and border towns, where they were especially on the lookout for a particular type of contraband: forbidden books — for instance vernacular Spanish translations of the Bible![3] Before a man was accepted for employment by the Inquisition, it was necessary to provide documentary proof that his own family and his wife's family had no heretical antecedents. A certificate of family purity (*limpieza de sangre*) was liable to be particularly expensive, as all checking of records and questioning of witnesses was undertaken at the applicant's own expense. The work of the agents of the Inquisition was unpaid, but the posts were much sought after because of the prestige and the privileges they provided. The most important of these rendered the officeholder immune from secular authority. Thus whether a case involving a member of the Inquisition was civil or criminal, it came under the jurisdiction of the Holy Office.[4]

Finally, the Inquisition had its own fraternity, La Hermandad de San Pedro Martir, the functions of which were mainly of a ceremonial nature. Every employee of the Holy Office, paid or unpaid, could become a member, but membership was not obligatory.

Thus, as far as the whole of its administrative organization was concerned, the Inquisition was self-supporting. And yet even this was not its greatest source of strength. The key to the power of the Inquisition lay in the principle of secrecy which permeated every branch of its activity. The Holy Office was not responsible to any temporal authority for what it undertook in matters of faith. No person, not even the king, could demand to know any more than the Inquisition chose to divulge.[5] All its employees, paid or unpaid, were sworn to secrecy, and witnesses and accused were likewise enjoined to remain silent. Information and reports were received with the promise not to reveal the name of the informer, and entered in *los libros de testificados,* the secret files of the Inquisition which were kept in each court. The records of heretics in *el secreto,* the secret archives and offices of the tribunal, were accessible only to the inquisitors and their closest collaborators. As far as the accused person himself was concerned, he disappeared completely from the face of the earth for the year or two which the trial might last. Before the case was closed and sentence passed at an auto de fe, the Inquisition was not even bound to reveal that it was holding a suspect in its secret prisons, let alone whether he was alive or dead. The only thing the Inquisition was answerable for was its own finances, since the king could claim his share of the property confiscated from heretics.

There was one redeeming feature of this state within a state: its tremendous self-control. *La Suprema* was vigilant in ascertaining that its laws and regulations were strictly adhered to, and this was primarily ensured by the inspections which each provincial court was subjected to from time to time and which could last for years. The inquisitor general was always ready to listen to complaints of abuse, and it was possible for these complaints to be anonymous. Thus in order to control the tribunals *la Suprema* applied the very same methods towards its own officials as ordinarily applied to heretics.

The aim of the Holy Office was not to eradicate the heretics but to convert them into good Catholics. Only those who refused to cooperate in this "thought reform"[6] — "the stubborn and impenitent deniers" (*protervos e inpenitentes negativos*), as they were termed in the somewhat biased terminology of the Inquisition — went to the stake. A trial was chiefly aimed at arousing the heretic's sense of guilt, which would provide the motivation for him to amend his erring ways. He was not informed of the charge until the trial was well advanced, and after the preliminary inquiries had taken place. Normally there were three preliminary hearings, and according to the regulations they were to be effected within ten days of the arrest.[7] During the first hearing at the inquisitor's table (figure 1) the prisoner was asked whether he knew why he had been arrested. If the answer was no, the inquisitor proceeded to acquaint him with the set formula in the regulations for interrogation:

> In this Holy Office it is not customary to arrest anyone unless sufficient evidence is available to confirm that he has said or done, or seen others do, something... which... appears contrary to our Holy Catholic Faith.[8]

During this interrogation and the two which followed, the prisoner was repeatedly urged to confess and divulge everything that was on his mind; then his case could be wound up quickly and the Inquisition could mete out to him the mercy that was generally shown to those who made a complete confession before the indictment was revealed to him. But when the *fiscal*, the "public" prosecutor of the tribunal, was called in to inform him of the nature of the charge, it was too late; then the law was bound to take its course.[9]

However, the preliminary inquiries could be broken off if no confession was forthcoming, and the prisoner could be detained for an indefinite period with instructions to speak out when he had more to add to his confession. On occasion the inquisitors found it convenient to wait for months for a prisoner to request to be interrogated.[10]

If the accused person acknowledged his guilt, he was classified as *confitente* (from Latin *confitens*) or *diminuto confitente* (having made an incomplete confession) according to whether he had admitted to the whole charge or only to part of it. During the remainder of the trial the *confitente* was obliged to signify clearly that he sincerely repented of his crimes and was willing to cooperate with the inquisitors in every respect. He was to provide them with information which might assist them

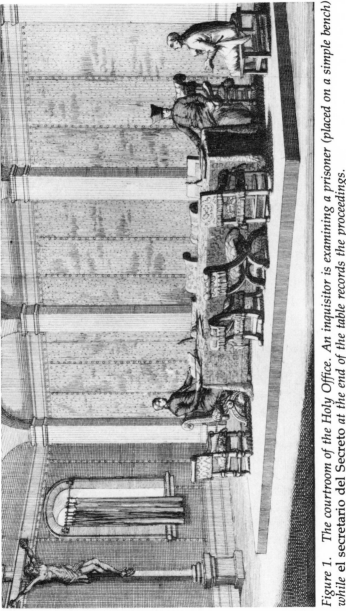

Figure 1. The courtroom of the Holy Office. An inquisitor is examining a prisoner (placed on a simple bench) while el secretario del Secreto at the end of the table records the proceedings.

in discovering other heretics, and he was expected to expose all his accomplices and not to shield anyone.

The *fiscal* drew up the indictment, which was a concise document based on the statements of witnesses and the facts that had emerged from the preliminary inquiries. This indictment was restricted to the definition of the type of heresy the prisoner was accused of and to the recapitulation of his crimes under particular counts. After reading out the indictment the *fiscal* invariably demanded that the accused should in due course be interrogated under torture if there were any doubt regarding his sincerity.[11] Immediately following the indictment the prisoner had to answer to the charge point by point. No time was permitted for reflection and normally he was not given a written copy of the indictment. After this he was assigned a defending lawyer, who was summoned to the courtroom and informed orally of the prisoner's confession and of the charge and what the prisoner had answered to it. The accused was not permitted to call his own counsel and the lawyer allotted to him by the tribunal was in fact prevented in advance from providing a defense. As a Christian he was naturally bound to exhort the prisoner to confess the truth, and his only defending function was to advise his "client" to beg for mercy and penance for the section of the charge which he acknowledged,[12] and to instruct him in any other possible ways of defending himself. All communication between the defending lawyer and his client had to take place in the presence of the inquisitor.

Thereupon the case proceeded to trial (*a prueba*). All the witnesses were now reexamined so that their previous statements could be confirmed and any necessary corrections and amendments made. This "ratification" was simply a condition for establishing the validity of the witnesses' statements, and during this fresh examination each witness was expressly told that the Inquisition intended to make use of his statement against the person concerned. Much time could pass in getting all the witnesses ratified,[13] and in the meantime the inquisitors were obliged to give the prisoner a hearing whenever he requested it. This was emphasized in the regulations of the Inquisition for two reasons: "partly because it is a comfort to the prisoners to be heard, partly because it happens often that a prisoner may one day make up his mind to confess or to recount something which may prove important for the resolution of his case; but the next day may change his mind."[14]

When the ratification had been completed the contents of the witnesses' statements were revealed to the prisoner according to the following formula: In this month of this year *a certain person* stated that at such and such a place and such a time he saw the accused doing such and such (or heard the accused say this or that).[15] The accused answered to the witnesses' charges point by point, after which his defending counsel was summoned and made acquainted with the witnesses' statements and the accused's answers. Then the prisoner and his counsel, in the presence of the inquisitor, discussed the possibilities of defense. The policy of the defense might consist of seeking to prove that the defendant was a good Catholic, and it might consist as well in trying to prove that the anonymous witnesses — whom the accused would have to try to identify from their statements — were hostile towards him, or were his declared mortal enemies. Whether the defendant sought to substantiate his Christian virtues or to disqualify the witnesses, he was obliged to give the inquisitors a list containing the names of persons who could be interrogated by the tribunal in order to confirm these points. The regulations of the Inquisition required the tribunal not to avoid inconvenience but to interrogate every witness who might speak for the benefit of the accused — as far as this could improve his case.[16] But as in practice it was a matter of opinion whether it might benefit the accused to have the witnesses interrogated, it was in fact for the inquisitors to decide how much consideration they would give to the defense.

Before the case was ready for sentence the prisoner and his defending counsel were to be informed that the investigations they had requested had been undertaken "to the extent that it might benefit the case." But the result of this questioning of witnesses (if in fact the tribunal had taken the trouble to interrogate anyone at all) was not to be revealed, as this would conflict with the principle of secrecy.[17] Finally the accused and his defending counsel were asked if they had anything to add, as the case would otherwise be considered closed.

The cases were decided by a jury consisting of the inquisitors, the bishop's representative (*el ordinario*), and the theological and legal advisers to the tribunal (*los consultores*). The material for the consideration was a résumé of the trial which was to be drafted by the senior inquisitor, who was not to reveal his own opinion (however this may have been possible). The report was read out by a clerk of the Inquisition (*secretario del secreto*), and each person present gave his opinion, which was immediately noted in the record. The advisers were the first to give their verdict, followed by the bishop's representative, and finally the inquisitors, beginning with the most junior.[18] If there was much circumstantial evidence, but lack of proof, in some cases the jury sentenced the accused to interrogation under torture.[19] If a person withstood the torture without confessing, the charge was considered insufficiently proved and he escaped with renunciation of heresy and a light punishment.[20] A prisoner could also be sentenced to interrogation under torture if there were evidence to show that he was seeking to shield his accomplices, but even if he bore this *tormento in caput alienum* without revealing any information, it had no influence on his own case.[21] The Inquisition was skeptical of torture as a means of proof and therefore used it to a relatively limited extent. No prisoner was brought to torture until the case was ready for judgment, and all the inquisitors of the tribunal together with the bishop's representative were obliged to be present while the prisoner was being tortured.[22]

The accused was not informed of the outcome of his case until the auto de fe. The *confitente* was ceremonially readmitted to the Church (*reconciliado*) if he had been found guilty of apostasy. One who denied his guilt (a *negativo*) was sent to the stake (*relajado*) or charged to renounce his heresy, according to whether the tribunal considered his guilt to be proven or not. However, in cases involving the less serious forms of heresy, *negativos* almost always escaped with light punishment simply by renouncing their heresy. The Inquisition was not empowered to execute a burning; it could only deliver a delinquent over to secular authorities for the execution of justice. The same applied in the case of persons condemned to flogging. They too were handed over to the secular authorities, who carried out the penalty.

The Inquisition did not *punish*, it merely imposed penance. As a rule the penance consisted of several years in the penitentiary. But able-bodied men were generally sentenced to do penance "unpaid at the oar" in the galleys of the Spanish fleet. Those reconciled were also required to wear a penitential garment, a *sambenito* (from *saco bendito*, blessed sack), for a considerable time. Banishment to another district was a less severe punishment. This was often meted out in two periods. The first was obligatory and came into force immediately; the second was a deferred period of banishment which would be imposed only if the delinquent violated the first period. In this category were also the so-called pecuniary penitential acts, which consisted of making over one's property, or a part of it, to the Holy Office, or of larger or smaller fines.

Apart from re-admitting the heretics into the Church, the Inquisition did nothing to rehabilitate them. On the contrary, those who had been penalized by the Inquisition were excluded for life from all posts of importance and in no circumstances whatever were they permitted to make use of status symbols such as arms, silks, gold, silver, and pearls; and they were not even allowed to travel on horseback.[23] If the heretic had been burned, the infamy (*infamia*) affected his children and grandchildren. In short, the victims of the Inquisition were excluded from so much that it would not be an exaggeration to say that they became the pariahs of Spanish society.[24]

When the sentence had been served the penitential garment was hung up in the delinquent's parish church bearing a label stating his name, his crime, and the year in which he had been sentenced. The *sambenitos* of the heretics who had been burned were also hung up. These sackcloths remained on display indefinitely, a constant reminder of heretical infamy.

The procedures of the Inquisition are open to very stringent criticism when judged by modern ideas of justice. Above all, we would consider it legally indefensible to make the outcome of the case stand or fall on the principle that the accused person had to prove his own innocence.[25] And yet it is undeniable that within the framework of their legal system the inquisitors endeavored to act justly. When false witnesses were exposed they were severely punished, and although it was a rare occurrence, a wrongly accused person could appear at the auto de fe carrying a palm branch in token of absolute acquittal.[26] The lengthy duration of the trials is one of the clearest marks of this desire for justice. This was the cause of the very limited capacity of the inquisitorial courts; fifty cases of heresy a year was a good average for a tribunal.[27] The reason for the Inquisition's frequent delay in pouncing on suspected persons was not only the wish to avoid errors, but also simply the impossibility of dealing with more cases.

The Catholic population did not in fact hate and fear the Inquisition as much as so many of its historians would have us believe. The great majority would undoubtedly have regarded the Inquisition as a necessary bulwark against the heresy which threatened society from within and without. The inquisitors were neither monsters nor torturers but sober theologians and lawyers, greatly respected and esteemed. Most of them were ordained priests. Many had started out as monks or priests and had a long theological career behind them when they entered the service of the Inquisition. Some, chiefly noblemen, later left the Holy Office to become bishops.[28] Occasionally a bishop or archbishop reached the zenith of his career by becoming inquisitor general. This happened to the bishop of Valladolid, Juan Bautista de Acevedo, in 1603. After his death, Bernardo de Sandoval y Rojas (figure 2)[29] was appointed, on 12 September 1608. By then he had already become cardinal of Rome and archbishop of Toledo and he retained these titles after becoming inquisitor general. His term of office, which lasted for ten years, was marked by two important events: the expulsion of the Moors in 1609 and the witch craze in the Basque provinces from 1609 to 1614.

3. THE TRIBUNAL AT LOGROÑO[30]

In 1608 great changes took place in the Tribunal at Logroño, one of the nineteen regional Inquisition courts spread throughout the vast Spanish empire (see below, chapter 13.2). The senior inquisitor, Juan Ramírez, had been appointed *fiscal* (prosecutor) to the Council of the Inquisition;[31] the next in seniority, Doctor Alonso Becerra Holguín, had been advanced to senior inquisitor and president of the Tribunal; and the most junior had died.[32] The details of the hierarchical order were, however, of minor importance since all the inquisitors enjoyed the same status and acted in concert. Any disagreements they might have were settled by *la Suprema*. When the inquisitors were in unanimous agreement they conducted the Tribunal almost independently of *la Suprema*, but if they differed amongst themselves the Tribunal was in constant correspondence with the Council of the Inquisition.

Becerra, aged forty-eight, was a monk of the Order of Alcántara. He had been received into a monastery of this order in his birthplace, Cáceres, when young, but had lived mostly in Salamanca and Alcántara. He entered the service of the In-

Figure 2. Bernardo de Sandoval y Rojas, inquisitor general from 1608 to 1618. Protector and benefactor of Cervantes.

quisition when he was forty and took up the post of third inquisitor at Logroño on 26 March 1601.[33]

The first assistant sent to help Becerra was the *licenciado* Juan de Valle Alvarado, and these two were soon on good terms. Valle received the post of second inquisitor as Becerra had two years' seniority.[34] Valle was a priest of fifty-five. He came from the province of Santander in northern Spain, where he had held a living and served as an inquisitorial commissioner. After this he had been secretary to the archbishop of Burgos for many years and then to the bishop of Valladolid, Juan Bautista de Acevedo.[35] When the latter became inquisitor general in 1603 Valle accompanied him into the Council of the Inquisition, where he became the bishop's confidential secretary (*secretario de cámara*).[36] Before Acevedo died on 9 August 1608,[37] Valle presumably obtained the promise of an inquisitorship, but it was not until later that autumn that he acquired the vacant post at Logroño.[38]

The *fiscal* of the Tribunal, Juan Laso de Vega, had also been transferred.[39] He was succeeded by twenty-nine-year-old Doctor Isidoro de San Vicente, who arrived in September 1608.[40] The two inquisitors found him easy to get on with, although this was of little consequence since he was their subordinate.

Lastly, one of the clerks to the secret archives of the Tribunal was also a new arrival. He was the twenty-nine-year-old *secretario del secreto*, Luis de Huerta y Rojas.[41] The post of third inquisitor remained empty until 20 June 1609, when it was filled by the forty-four-year-old *licenciado* Alonso de Salazar Frías.[42] Becerra and Valle did not get on well with him, but this was not to affect the trial of the first Zugarramurdi witches.

Salazar was born about 1564 in Burgos, where his family were officials and wealthy merchants.[43] He matriculated at the age of fifteen and entered the University of Salamanca, where he obtained a bachelor's degree in canon law after five years. Following this he retired to his birthplace in order to prepare for his licentiate, which he took at the University of Sigüenza in 1588. In the same year he was ordained a priest and took service with the bishop of Jaén as a legal adviser. On 18 September 1590 the bishop appointed young Salazar canon with an annuity of 1,500 *ducados,* and not long afterwards he made him his visitor general. During the years that followed, Salazar made visits over the whole diocese of Jaén until, as he writes in his autobiography, there was no church or font that he had not seen. After this he was appointed vicar general, and he was named executor when the bishop died in 1594. In the same year the cathedral chapter sent Salazar to Madrid to defend the interests of the diocese in a law suit with the archbishop of Granada. Salazar won the case in two and a half years, during which time he also represented Jaén at a synod in Madrid. During the period from 1600 to 1608 he was diplomatic agent in Rome for the Castilian bishops (*agente y procurador general de la Corona de Castilla y León*). But he must have spent a good deal of time in Spain as well, for he took part in synods in 1602 and 1608, and the archbishop of Toledo, Bernardo de Sandoval y Rojas,[44] made him his representative in Madrid. In his autobiography Salazar recounts that he was on such intimate terms with the archbishop that the latter entrusted him with some of his private "very important and confidential business." While Salazar was in Rome the pope sent several written recommendations requesting that the Spanish inquisitor general Acevedo bestow an office upon him, but not until the archbishop of Toledo became inquisitor general did Salazar reach the goal which he appears to have desired for so many years. He was the first inquisitor to be appointed by Sandoval y Rojas and was assigned to the vacant post at Logroño on 23 March 1609.[45]

4. WHO TOLD THE INQUISITION?

The Logroño Tribunal covered a large area. It included the whole of Navarra, the Basque provinces of Guipúzcoa, Vizcaya, and Alava, the diocese of Calahorra and Santo Domingo de la Calzada, and a portion of the archbishopric of Burgos.[46] From the whole of this area highly effective agents fed back a constant stream of confidential information to the Tribunal.[47] However, in the case of Zugarramurdi and the Baztán Valley of Navarra there was a hole in the Inquisition's intelligence network. Thus, in September 1609 when the abbot of Urdax, Fray León de Araníbar, applied for a post with the Inquisition, he drew attention to this situation. He stated that the mule caravans from Saint-Jean-de-Luz and Bayonne passed close by the monastery walls and had safe conduct right down to Pamplona — for on the whole of this road there was not one agent of the Inquisition to examine their loads for heretical books.[48]

The Tribunal had been aware of the problem but, as the

inquisitors explained in a letter to *la Suprema,* had been unable to find suitable candidates: "Since this . . . area comes within the jurisdiction of the bishop of Bayonne, and the people pay tithes to him, the majority of the priests are French; and we cannot entrust the affairs of the Holy Office to them." The inquisitors added that the same conditions applied to the other approach route via Vera de Bidasoa and the Bertizaun Valley.[49] However, the area was not completely without agents of the Holy Office. At Arráyoz in the Baztán Valley there was a *familiar,* the notary of the royal justice (*escribano real*) Miguel de Narvarte;[50] and at Lesaca in the Bertizaun Valley there was an Inquisition commissioner, the elderly parish priest Domingo de San Paul.[51] But as the mule caravans did not pass through any of these towns the abbot of Urdax was correct in stating that the Inquisition had no control over what was brought in by these little used but unguarded frontier crossings.

Both Arráyoz and Lesaca were a considerable distance from Zugarramurdi, and it is unlikely that the agents we have mentioned would have been aware of what was going on there in December 1608. The nearest official who could report the matter was the abbot of Urdax. Zugarramurdi and Urdax came under the jurisdiction of the monastery, and Fray León possessed the title of *abad mitrado* (priestly feudal lord) and a seat in the parliament of Navarra (*las Cortes de Navarra*). He likely knew that witchcraft was dealt with by the Inquisition and was too grave a matter to be disposed of — as Fray Felipe had done — by means of public confession and private reconciliation. It was therefore most probably Fray León who informed the Tribunal at Logroño and requested its intervention.

CHAPTER FOUR
The Trial (First Part)

T THE BEGINNING OF JANUARY 1609 A commissioner of the Inquisition and his notary made their appearance in Zugarramurdi in order to prepare a report. These two agents interrogated eight adult men, who made statements under oath about the people who had confessed to being witches and repeated what they had heard the witches admit.[1] The identities of the commissioner and his notary are not known; we know only that a notary from the Baztán Valley helped to prepare the first report. Presumably he was the *familiar* from Arráyoz.[2] Neither is it known who the eight witnesses were,[3] although they would not have included the witches. The two agents disappeared as quietly as they had arrived, without further activity.

The report was received at Logroño on 12 January. Initially the inquisitors Becerra and Valle seem to have been somewhat at a loss; one almost gets the impression that they thought they were confronted with a hitherto unknown sect based on "apostasy from Our Holy Faith and worship of the Devil."[4] (The Tribunal had had no cases of witchcraft since 1596,[5] which would have been before both Becerra's and Valle's time.) But when the two inquisitors began to search through the archives of the Tribunal they soon discovered a large number of records of witch trials. They also found letters from *la Suprema* showing what had been prescribed for dealing with the witch sect on previous occasions. Their investigations went back almost a century: "Thus we looked up what had been dictated in the letters of 14 December 1526, 2 October and 12 September 1555, and in the instructions therewith," Becerra and Valle wrote in their letter to the inquisitor general and the Council of the Inquisition in Madrid (dated 13 February 1609). "These instructions," they continued, "were sent by *la Suprema* in order to obtain proof of the existence of the sect, since this was doubted at the time and thought to be something which people might have experienced while dreaming."[6]

Once the two colleagues had firm ground under them they began to consider what was to be done with the large number of persons who, according to the report, were guilty or under suspicion. So as not to arouse too much attention they picked out four people from among those who had confessed of their own accord, and made a point of selecting those who, according to the report, were the most notorious.

By summoning these four to the Tribunal, the inquisitors went on to explain in their letter to *la Suprema*, they would also have the opportunity to interrogate them in accordance with the old questionnaires used in witch cases, and to investigate whether the affair at Zugarramurdi rested on firm foundations or was caused by dreams and illusions. "For," the two inquisitors assured the Council, "none of the commissioners would have been able to manage this [investigation] satisfactorily."[7]

2. THE FIRST GROUP OF PRISONERS

We do not know who took the first four witches to Logroño, but it was possibly Juan de Monterola, inquisitorial commissioner at Arano. In any case, he was "detained for many days at the Tribunal" to serve as Basque interpreter during the questioning of the first witches.[8] As was customary, the arrest warrant included sequestration of property, but on account of the uncertainty prevailing in witch cases, the warrant carried the injunction that the sequestration should not be enforced until further notice.[9] The four prisoners were: eighty-year-old Estevanía de Navarcorena, seventy-year-old María Pérez de Barrenechea, thirty-six-year-old Juana de Telechea, and twenty-two-year-old María de Jureteguía.[10] On 27 January they were jailed in the Tribunal's secret prison.

The four women confessed during the very first hearings and reaffirmed all that they had stated in their extrajudicial confessions at Zugarramurdi.[12]

María de Jureteguía confessed to having been a witch since she was a child. When she reached the age of discretion she had renounced her Christian faith and had been received into the witch sect, but her status had never reached that of senior witch.[13] As a child she had been set to guard a flock of toads at the sabbath. It was impressed upon her that the toads were to be treated with great respect. One night after María drove a toad back to the flock by pushing it with her foot instead of with the little shepherd's crook she had been given for the purpose, she was cruelly punished by the witches so that she was covered with bruises for several days. Her tutor witch was identified as her aunt María Chipía. It was she who had rubbed her with ointment when she was going to the sabbath. Once when they where about to go out through a little hole in the wall María de Jureteguía noticed that she had become quite tiny, and she asked her aunt why she had made her so small; but her aunt replied that she was not to worry, that afterwards she would make her big again.[14] According to a statement from the inquisitors it was largely the confessions of María de Jureteguía which led to the discoveries at Zugarramurdi; but unfortunately these few fragments are all that remain today.[15]

Juana de Telechea admitted to having been a witch for eighteen years and to making four of her children witches. Nothing more is known about her confession.[16]

María Pérez de Barrenechea confessed that she was the third highest in rank amongst the witches at Zugarramurdi, and that she had initiated three of her children. Of the remainder of her confession we know only that she admitted taking part in the murder of several people.[17]

Old Estevanía de Navarcorena confessed to having been a witch since she was a child and admitted to many murders and acts of revenge. She stated that she was the second highest in rank in the Zugarramurdi coven[18] and confessed among other things to having poisoned her own grandchild with witch powder which she put into the child's food. This was in revenge for the child having soiled her new apron while sitting on her lap. She had also killed a bigger boy in Zugarramurdi because once he had shouted at her: "Go break your neck, you old whore [*Ah puta vieja, el pescuezo se te tuerza*]."[19]

Not until they had completed the preliminary inquiries and obtained confessions from all four witches did the inquisitors inform the inquisitor general and his Council in Madrid of the witchcraft affair at Zugarramurdi. On forwarding the records and the report with the witnesses' statements for inspection the two inquisitors admitted in their letter (the one quoted above, of 13 February 1609) that the interrogations were long and drawn out and the confessions rambling. But it could not have been otherwise, as the witches were only partially *confitentes* and were trying to extricate themselves and back out the whole time. The length of the proceedings was also due to the fact that the witches had been questioned in the old manner to ascertain whether they really had committed the crimes they confessed to. If Becerra and Valle had entertained any doubts to begin with, these had certainly vanished when they reported to the Council, for in their letter they constantly assumed the existence of the witch sect as a fact.[20]

It is not possible to state with certainty what made the four women repeat their confessions of witchcraft at the Tribunal. They were most probably tempted with promises of mild sentences, promises which the Inquisition did in fact keep at the auto de fe. We only know that the confessions were voluntary in the sense that the women were not subjected to torture.

However at a much later stage of the trial a piece of information came to light which revealed that one of the four witches had made a false confession because she thought this was her only chance of escape. The information derived from a conversation held one night between María de Jureteguía and her maternal aunt, María Chipía, who had been imprisoned in the meantime. The jailer had waited outside their cell and listened to their conversation, and he repeated it next day at the Tribunal. María Chipía had said to María de Jureteguía that she could not bring herself to confess the things the inquisitors asked her about in the courtroom for she was not a witch and she did not believe any of the others were. To this María de Jureteguía replied that if she hoped to get out of prison at all she would have to make a confession even if it was false from start to finish; and she confided to her aunt that this was what she herself had done.[21]

3. THE SECOND GROUP OF PRISONERS

When the other suspects at Zugarramurdi saw the first four witches taken away by the Inquisition they grew extremely anxious about what might happen to them. Six of those who had made public confessions were advised by their families to go to Logroño and tell the Inquisition the real facts of the case. They hired a man to show them the way, and about 6 February they reached Logroño, where they requested an interview at the Tribunal.[22]

The six persons were: Graciana de Barrenechea and her two daughters María and Estevanía de Yriarte, Estevanía's husband Juanes de Goiburu, and finally Miguel de Goiburu and Juanes de Sansín.[23] That they hardly succeeded in changing the inquisitors' minds is clearly seen from the Tribunal's letter of 13 February which tells how they were examined individually and how they all gave the same explanation, word for word, to the effect that they had been compelled to make false confessions because they had been accused and threatened with violence if they did not confess; that their local magistrates had instituted proceedings against them and demanded severe sentences; and that now they had come to the Tribunal in order to tell the truth, as in fact not one of them was a witch. When the inquisitors had heard all six, they summoned the guide and asked him who had brought them to court. The man replied that no one had been brought to court at Zugarramurdi.

The inquisitors saw fit to employ delaying tactics in order to complete the questioning of the first four witches. So the newcomers were told to wait in the town for some days. But their fate had already been decided; the inquisitors had drawn their conclusions from the guide's statement: "We gather," they wrote in the letter of 13 February, "that either it must be on advice from the Devil — with whom the Graciana in question is on intimate terms — or at the request of their relatives that they have presented themselves to the Tribunal in order to explain away the confessions they made to the parish priest in the presence of other people."

The commissioner's report containing the declaration of the eight adult witnesses at Urdax and Zugarramurdi confirmed that all six according to their own confessions had separated themselves from the Holy Catholic Faith, and the questioning of the four witches at the Tribunal provided further details. All six turned out to belong to the inner circle of the Zugarramurdi witches, and as far as Graciana de Barrenechea and Miguel de Goiburu were concerned, it was discovered that they were indeed no less than the leaders; the inquisitors were in other words honored by a most important visit.[24]

The *fiscal* to the Tribunal set to work to formulate a provisional charge (*clamosa*),[25] while the inquisitors had transcripts made of everything that, according to the commissioner's report, the six had confessed at Zugarramurdi. This information was sent to the theological experts of the Tribunal (*los calificadores*) with a request for their opinion on what type of heresy these witches were guilty of.

Having read the theologians' reply the inquisitors issued the six warrants of arrest, but added the same proviso as with the first four, to the effect that the confiscation of property should be postponed. In fact this was of relative unimportance, for whereas the first prisoners had some few possessions the second group had virtually nothing that the Tribunal could dispose of.

All this took place during the week before 13 February when Becerra and Valle sent their letter to *la Suprema*. The letter closed with a request for further instructions. They were particularly anxious to know what was to be done with all the other suspects. The two inquisitors had already formulated a plan of campaign themselves: "We are of the opinion," they wrote, "that we could avoid arousing attention and save expense if we have the commissioners summon the persons to be arrested to the Tribunal; and then after we have got them here we can make the arrests."[26]

Shortly afterwards — presumably as early as 14 February[27] — the six waiting witches were fetched from their lodgings by the Tribunal's constable (*el alguacil*) and taken to the secret prison. Here they were apparently parted from each other and confined in separate prison cells so that they had no opportunity to converse.[28]

During the days that followed they were taken to the preliminary inquiries one at a time. In the course of the first hearing they took the usual oath to reveal all they knew to the Holy Office, not to shield any other person, and not to bear false witness against themselves or others. Next followed the usual questions: Were there any heretics in their families? Had they been baptized and confirmed? Did they go to church? Did they make their confession and take communion at the times stipulated by the Church? Then they were examined in their Paternoster, Ave Maria, and Creed and questioned on the course of their lives. All six apparently confirmed that they were good Catholics and had no heretical forbears, but what details they related about their lives is unfortunately unknown to us, as the original records have not been preserved.[29]

To the question whether they had any idea about why they had been arrested, they answered that it was presumably due to certain persons at Zugarramurdi, whom they mentioned by name. (Unfortunately the names are not stated in the source materials preserved today.) These people had victimized them and accused them of being witches, declared the six in their respective interrogations, and they went on to repeat the explanation of how they had been forced to make false confessions.[30]

Despite the inquisitors' earnest injunctions to them to confess the truth, all six stoutly maintained their innocence during both the first and second preliminary interrogations. Becerra and Valle realized that the six had conspired together to say nothing and therefore decided to break off the hearings for the time being to see whether a spell of imprisonment would make the witches change their minds.[31]

4. THE FOURTEEN QUESTIONS FROM *LA SUPREMA*

The letter from Becerra and Valle, the report of the commissioner, and the trial records of the four witches were received in Madrid on 2 March 1609.[32] The Council of the Inquisition did not show a great deal of enthusiasm for the activities of the two inquisitors at Logroño. Its first reaction consisted of a brief letter ordering the inquisitor whose turn it was to make a visitation to hold himself in readiness to go to Zugarramurdi. But he was to await further instructions.[33] Four days later, on 11 March, *la Suprema* returned the four records with a questionnaire which was intended for the imprisoned witches as well as for those witches still at liberty in Zugarramurdi and for certain outside witnesses — that is, persons who were not themselves witches.[34] It was the intention of *la Suprema* to have these three groups interrogated simultaneously (thus providing a means of continual cross-checking), and it was therefore vitally important not to delay the journey of visitation to Zugarramurdi.

Several of the questions were aimed at establishing whether the experiences of the witches were dreams or reality. If the latter, the Tribunal was ordered to obtain concrete proof. For instance:

Question 1. Did the witches during the sabbath, or on the way to and from it, hear clocks, bells, dogs, or cocks from nearby villages and farms?

Question 3. Was their absence noticed by those who slept in the same room with them, and if not how did they succeed in concealing their absence?

Question 6. How long did it take them to get from their homes to these gatherings, and what was the distance? Did they meet anyone on the way to and from them, and did they, while at the sabbath, see any travelers, shepherds, or other persons pass by?

Question 9. Was it necessary to anoint themselves with flying ointment to go to the sabbath?

Question 10. Did they speak together after a sabbath and discuss what had happened there?

Question 12. Were they convinced that they had participated corporally in the sabbath, or did the ointment make them fall asleep, so that these things were merely imprinted in their imagination or fantasy?

The questionnaire also contained instructions for the undertaking of certain investigations. Question 8 on the list, which inquired into the preparation and use of witch salve, required the inquisitors to procure the salve if the witches confessed to possessing it, and to obtain the opinion of doctors and apothecaries as to its composition and the natural effects that it might produce.

The two final items on the lists were merely instructions for procedures. Question 13 concerned the interrogation of outside witnesses to the witches' crimes: if the witches confessed to having murdered children or adults and taken their hearts out, witnesses should be sought to confirm that these crimes really had been committed. Question 14 gave directions for the cross-examination of the witches: when a witch is interrogated, it stated, the accomplices must be questioned afterwards; each in turn must be asked the same questions with regard to what they do at the witches' sabbath, what crimes they have committed, and who the members of their coven are.[35]

The fourteen questions did not merely bear witness to the skeptical attitude of *la Suprema*, they also showed how the Council had searched through its archives for precedents. Many of the items on the questionnaire were in fact literal transcripts of older instructions dating from the sixteenth century.[36]

Finally in the letter of 11 March *la Suprema* ordered the inquisitors to search the archives of the Tribunal and send copies of all letters and ordinances they found there concerning the witch sect.[37]

5. PREPARATIONS FOR THE VISITATION

Becerra had been on a journey of visitation in 1607, and therefore it was now Valle's turn.[38] But he did not set out. The two inquisitors continued to interrogate the witches at the Tribunal for more than two months after they had heard from *la Suprema*. They did not reply to the letters nor did they inform the Council of the state of affairs.

On 22 May 1609, at long last, the inquisitors wrote to *la Suprema* explaining what had been happening in the meantime: Valle had been unable to begin his journey of visitation because the ten witches had provided so much work for the inquisitors that it had even been necessary to work on Sundays and holidays to finish it all. Also *la Suprema*'s inquiries had occasioned them extra work in the archives, where the inquisitors and their secretaries were in the process of going through the old registers of correspondence to find the details the Council had requested. As for the trials of the witches, the first four prisoners were continually making additions to their confessions, and the women members among the six people of the second group had now confessed, though the men were still refusing to admit anything. The latter had nevertheless supplied some valuable information about witches' sabbaths which were held in other parts of Navarra. The Tribunal had been kept busy writing down everything that came to light about the witches' accomplices at Zugarramurdi and Urdax — anything they considered would be of use to Valle on his journey of visitation. However, the inquisitors continued, there was little hope that the witches would come forward voluntarily when Valle arrived there. The interrogation of the women in the second group of prisoners had shown all too clearly that the Devil meanwhile had terrorized his followers into revealing nothing. Before Valle left, it was also necessary for him to have more specific instructions on how to deal with the varying age groups among the witches, juveniles (girls under twelve and boys under fourteen), minors (under twenty-five), and adults. The Inquisition would have to be prepared for the fact that even among the juveniles there might be some who had renounced their faith.[39]

One month later, on 20 June, the vacant inquisitorial post was filled by Salazar Frías, who joined the Tribunal as its third and most junior member.[40] This invalidated Valle's chief excuse for postponing his journey, for — as a new order from *la Suprema* stated — there were now two inquisitors to attend to the affairs of the Tribunal while the third was in the field.[41]

But Valle still did not leave. Obviously he himself wished to take part in winding up the preliminary hearings. On 11 July the records of the interrogation of the last six witches were sent off to the Council for their inspection. Also *la Suprema*'s inquiries of 11 March were answered on this occasion by a file from Logroño containing copies of the old archival letters and ordinances regarding witches.[42] On 24 July the Council returned the records with a letter declaring satisfaction with the Tribunal's proceedings and enclosing new instructions for witchcraft cases. I have been unable to trace the latter, which has presumably been lost. It would appear, however, that in spite of its apparent approval the Council remained doubtful, since it still did not permit the inquisitors to confiscate the witches' property, a custom which otherwise prevailed in all cases of heresy. In the letter of 24 July *la Suprema* gave the Tribunal permission to confiscate only what would produce the necessary amount to provide subsistence for the prisoners.[43] (The Inquisition invariably claimed the cost of board from its prisoners, but this was a general practice of all prison administrations in the sixteenth and seventeenth centuries.)

Time had been on the side of the inquisitors. When they sent the trial records to *la Suprema* for inspection on 11 July they had obtained confessions from all ten witches. It was true that one of the men had subsequently revoked his confession, but a month later he gave in and confessed all (see chap. 4.6, below). On 4 September the Tribunal was able to report that the preliminary inquiries had been brought to an end — they had lasted for more than six months! — and that they were about to make the indictment known to the witches.[44] Meanwhile, in a new letter dated 26 September the inquisitors wrote that they had made no more progress with the cases as all the witches had fallen ill (see chaps. 8.2 and 8.5, below). Valle's signature is missing from the last two letters. He had at long last set out on his visitation to Zugarramurdi.

The list of questions from *la Suprema* had not shaken the convictions of the two inquisitors, and the third member of the Tribunal was as yet too new to the task to have formulated a personal opinion on the matter. We cannot ascertain how Becerra and Valle applied the questionnaire in the interrogations as the original records are not preserved. *La Suprema* had compiled the list to take account of every conceivable possibility and, as an extra precaution, the Tribunal had been instructed to interrogate the witches who were still at large and to put questions to outside witnesses regarding the damages to which the witches confessed. It was true that the inquisitors had only applied the questionnaire to the closed circle of prisoners, but there they had managed to make the pieces fit together. From the answers given it was apparent to the inquisitors that the witches' sabbaths were not based on dreams or imagination, but were as real as the daily services in Zugarramurdi's church. Unless we accept this and proceed in the belief that a witch cult really did exist at Zugarramurdi, we shall be obliged to explain why *la Suprema*'s questionnaire failed so completely to disprove the cult's existence.

The correspondence with *la Suprema* is important because it informs us of *when* the witches confessed and who was first to do so. As for the first witches, we have already referred to the little that is known about their confessions. For the second group of prisoners we have considerably more detail. In the next chapter I shall discuss how far these last confessions in themselves made the existence of a witch sect at Zugarramurdi seem probable; but first it will be necessary to consider some of the sources of error inherent in the inquisitors' method of interrogation and to consider some of the information that reveals how the six *negativos* were induced to confess.

6. WERE THE WITCHES BRAINWASHED?

It is undeniable that the Inquisition's practice of keeping a charge secret was an extremely effective means of getting at the truth in the great majority of cases. As long as a person under interrogation is ignorant of the charge against him he is unable to protect himself. But it is a dangerous method, for even if the accused person is innocent he can easily involve himself in erroneous answers and suspicious explanations; very few people can account for their actions as accurately as the method presupposes.[45]

With the Inquisition's method, in which an accusation could be kept secret for months and a prisoner could communicate only with the examining judge, who continually exhorted him to confess the *truth*, the system had every possibility of serving as a form of brainwashing, in Lifton's sense of the word.[46] This type of brainwashing must, however, have been a psychological process in which the examining judge and the accused person involuntarily misled each other, for the inquisitors were not the sort of cynical examining judges who would drag a confession out of their victims at any price.[47] I believe there is much evidence pointing to this having been the case with the six *negativos*.

On 10 July 1610 the Tribunal requested permission from *la Suprema* to allow the witches to confront one another in court (according to the regulations of the Inquisition this was forbidden, for any confrontation of the accused with the witnesses or accomplices was contrary to the principle of secrecy).[48] In this connection the Tribunal admitted to a similar practice with the six *negativos* the previous year. The first to confess, stated the inquisitors, was Estevanía de Yriarte, and they continued: After she had confessed "we gave orders" that "chance" meetings should be arranged when the prisoners went to the storeroom to fetch their rations. Two Basque interpreters were ordered to be present and to listen to what was said. Estevanía had been told that when she saw her relatives she was to say only "that now she had told the truth" and to call upon the others to do the same. "These few words were enough to make the others give up and confess," states the inquisitors' letter.[49] If we combine this statement with the reports of the six *negativos'* confessions we are given a further insight into the way in which the inquisitors dealt with the witches' "conspiracy."

The inquisitors obtained Estevanía de Yriarte's confession during an interrogation in Holy Week[50] (that is to say, from 12 to 19 April 1609),[51] which she had herself requested. She began by saying that for a long time the Devil had prevented her from confessing anything, but that now God had given her the courage to tell the truth, and that she was prepared to save her soul even if it cost her her honor and she lost her possessions.

Next she began to relate how her mother had made her a witch when she was fourteen years old, and she proceeded to give many more details to which we shall return in the following chapter.[52]

The next to confess was Estevanía's sister, María de Yriarte. Her first attempt at confession took on an element of drama and gives us an instructive glimpse into the interrogation technique of Becerra and Valle. Like her sister, María commenced by saying that she had wanted to confess for a long time, but that "the evil Lord" had constantly forced her to keep silent. The truth was that two years earlier she had become a witch. At this point she began to be indisposed. According to the report of the interrogation:

> she was coughing and trying to speak, but was unable to do so. When we encouraged her to tell the truth, she kept swallowing and groaning loudly, and several times she moaned and said, "Ah, Joan Gaicoa, Joan Gaicoa!" and explained that the evil Lord would not let her speak [see chap. 5.2]. After we had said a great many things to her to encourage her to continue, we asked who made her a witch. She answered that it was her mother, Graciana de Barrenechea, and said that her mother had told her that to become a witch she would have to hold "the filthy thing" in her hand. But she had answered, "No, Mother, you will never make me touch that!" And then she again became silent and troubled and could say no more. We began to tell her many things so that she should understand how important it was for her to save her soul, and finally we exhorted her to tell us what it was she had to hold in her hands. She answered that it was some toads.

The report goes on, stating that thereupon she began to tell the inquisitors about her first sabbath and to describe how she had kissed the Devil and renounced her faith, but in the middle of her explanation she stopped and again began to groan and wail. Becerra and Valle realized that her difficulties were the Devil's work and agreed to break off the interrogation:

> In consideration of the fact that the matter was so grave and was a question of her stating what she had believed as a renegade, and of her begging sincerely for mercy, we agreed that it was best to give her more time and more admonishments in order that she might reach a complete realization of

her sin and in addition come to a better understanding of the
salutary effects of reconciliation, so that she herself would
beg to be reconciled. She was therefore sent back to her cell
with an earnest exhortation.[53]

When María de Yriarte next asked for an audience she was
more composed and made a coherent statement about how
she had been received into the witch sect.[54] But she created
more dramatic scenes in the court of inquiry on later occasions.
Once, for instance, when she was asked how many children
she had put to death, she first denied having murdered any.
But after a while she began to cry and admitted she had killed
five. The inquisitors encouraged her to give more details but
she began to cry again and implore them "by God's wounds"
(*por las llagas de Dios*) not to tell anyone, for if it ever came out
she would be damned. After this she confessed to no less than
nine child murders. Later she declared, without having been
asked, that her mother and sister had taken no part in these
murders. When the inquisitors queried this she corrected her
explanation and said that she could not remember them taking
part; but if they themselves had admitted it she was willing to
confirm it.[55]

It must not be forgotten that the above is taken from a
summary of María de Yriarte's confession. There is no means
of telling how many self-contradictions and how many "en-
couragements" her original trial-record contained (not to mention all that was not written down during the interrogations).[56]

Concerning old Graciana de Barrenechea, we know only
that she confessed during a hearing which she herself had
asked for "after having refused to confess for many days." But
it must have occurred before 22 May when the inquisitors
informed *la Suprema* that they had obtained confessions from
all the women.[57]

We do not know which of the men was the first to confess.
Juanes de Sansín confessed on 19 June at an interrogation he
himself had requested,[58] but perhaps old Miguel de Goiburu
had already confessed by then.[59] The one who held out longest
was Estevanía's husband, Juanes de Goiburu. According to
the summary of his trial he did not confess until 3 July, but as it
was growing late the inquisitors decided to continue the interrogation next day.[60] The following day the thirty-seven-year-
old shepherd came before the inquisitors again and went on

with his confession, but then suddenly fell silent. And when they exhorted him to confess the truth he hesitated a little, but

> then rose up, in fierce anger and disrespect, and struck the inquisitors' table, saying his father had betrayed him, for when they met in the storeroom his father had told him to confess the truth and own up to being a witch as he himself had just done and to reveal every detail. This was what had made him give way. But now they could do what they liked with him, he had nothing more to confess, and what he had already said was a pack of lies. And even though he was exhorted to go on with his confession, he continued to deny his guilt. He was therefore returned to his cell and orders were given for him to be treated more severely.[61]

We do not know what was done to Juanes de Goiburu, but twenty-five days was sufficient to break him down. On 29 July he again asked for an audience. He excused himself by saying that the Devil had made him think of certain dangerous consequences that his confession might have. It was this that had caused him to retract it, he explained to the inquisitors. The report ends by stating that he then again admitted everything that he had confessed during the examination of 3 July and that he "went on to tell the court many interesting details about the witch sect which agreed with what the others had [confessed and] witnessed against him."[62]

7. LOS ACTOS POSITIVOS

Heresy was a moral crime which consisted not only of words and actions but also of thoughts and feelings, and the latter were the more weighty. If a woman was accused of crypto-Judaism (i.e. of practicing Judaism in secret) and there was evidence that she changed her bed linen on Saturdays, this was circumstantial evidence of her guilt. But if it could be proved that she changed her linen on other days of the week as well and in addition was known to be a good Catholic, the evidence was set aside. The fact that she changed the sheets on Saturday could not be used as an *acto positivo*, a positive proof, as long as it was not definitely proved that she did it to observe the Sabbath.[63] When the inquisitors sentenced a prisoner to interrogation under torture it was often to find out what had been the intention of the words or actions that the accused could be proved to have said or done.

The evidence in witch trials was especially perplexing in that it was practically impossible to pin down palpable actions. The inquisitors were faced with the identical problem that confronted the anthropologist Friedrich Nadel in the case of African witch belief and which he formulated so lucidly. "Witchcraft," says Nadel, "creates an imaginary world of cause and effect to which the criteria of our own reality are almost inapplicable. Witchcraft constitutes, in one word, a belief which protects itself from being 'found out.' "[64]

One of the main intentions of *la Suprema*'s fourteen questions was to isolate details from the mass of the witches' fantastic confessions, details which it was possible to verify by statements from witnesses who were not witches. That the list had been made use of is clear from the summaries of the trial records included in the joint sentence of Graciana de Barrenechea, her two daughters, and Miguel de Goiburu. For instance, they were asked if they had been missed while they were at the *aquelarre* (see chap. 4.4, above, question 3). Without specifying who the spokesman was, it is stated that the four witches revealed that the Devil would cause the non-witch members of the household to fall into a deep sleep from which they would not awaken; and also he would replace each of the witches with a demon in the witches' own likeness, to serve as their substitutes in bed while they were at the witches' sabbath.[65] Old Graciana, however, added that once her husband had noticed she was missing from the bed, and when he asked where she had been she merely said she had been spinning at a neighbor's house.[66] The answer of the four to question 9 on the list, about the necessity of witch salve, was that the senior witches had the ability to travel to the sabbath without anointing themselves.[67]

On three occasions the witches had met with people on their nocturnal expeditions (see question 6). Once, in the company of other witches, they were going along the road in the shape of dogs and cats, and they terrified the miller Martín de Amayur. He defended himself with a stick and landed a hearty blow on one of them, seventy-year-old María Presona, so that she had to keep to her bed for three or four days afterwards. On another occasion they terrified three men, who backed away from them with drawn swords and ended up by falling into a pond. A third time they lay in wait for two brothers who were coming home from seeing to the cows in the field. When they came up the witches fell upon them, but as the brothers cried "Jesus, Jesus!" the witches could not harm them. The two brothers, however, had been so badly frightened and reached home in such a state of terror that they died shortly afterwards.[68]

We do not know what the witches' answers were to the other questions from *la Suprema*,[69] but these examples give us reason to assume that the suspects had enough basic intelligence to grasp the intention of this part of the questioning, and that they very soon discovered what kind of *truth* Becerra and Valle wanted to hear.

CHAPTER FIVE
The Witch Cult

1. THE SOURCES

NLY A FEW FRAGMENTS REMAIN TO US of the first four witches' confessions referred to in the last chapter. There is much more at our disposal regarding the second group. The trials of Juanes de Goiburu and his cousin Juanes de Sansín are summed up in their *méritos,* and we can read the other four confessions in the long joint sentence.[1] We can be almost certain that the confessions of these six witches were made before 4 September 1609, when the Tribunal reported that the preliminary investigations were completed. As far as Graciana de Barrenechea, Estevanía de Yriarte, and Miguel de Goiburu were concerned, a natural limit was set on their presentation of any new facts or modifications — all three of them died during the course of the autumn. María de Yriarte died too, but not until August of the following year.[2] It is therefore of little consequence that the joint sentence of the four witches was not drafted until shortly before the auto de fe. Apart from what María de Yriarte may have added, it shows us the content of the witches' confessions in the summer of 1609, that is, before the Tribunal proceeded to compare the results of its interrogations with new investigations in the field.

Taken together the confessions of the six prisoners provide a description of the rites and social organization of the witch sect in a wealth of detail that would be hard to equal in any other witch trial. Becerra and Valle became convinced that the sect did in fact exist, mainly because the witches' own descriptions of their assemblies and rites were in such close agreement. The inquisitors returned constantly to this argument in their letters to *la Suprema*: the same argument was used repeatedly by many of the witch judges of the sixteenth and seventeenth centuries, and it is precisely the same as that used by Margaret Murray and Montague Summers. All of them accept the witches' confessions on the ground that they are in agreement. The conclusion drawn by the witch judges and Summers, that they were devil worshippers, does not need further refutation. But Murray's thesis that they were continuing an old pagan religion is still most popular in spite of what serious scholars have written against it. Although I don't at all share her views I shall for the moment convert myself into a Murrayist and, utilizing all possible evidence from my examination of the witches' confessions, attempt to support her theories. One thing is certain: Murray and her followers never saw such abundant descriptions of the witches' rituals as in the present case, so if her theory has any solid foundations it is bound to be vindicated here.

2. T H E G O D[3]

Throughout the confessions of the six witches their God was referred to as "the Devil" and the witches addressed him as "Lord."[4] He apparently had no name. When María de Yriarte twice called upon "Joan Gaicoa" during an interrogation, she was in fact calling upon the Christian God (*Jaun Goicoa* in Basque).[5] Miguel de Goiburu described him as a dark-skinned man with wide, glaring, horrible eyes. He was thought to speak in a low voice that sounded like the bray of a mule. He wore a good quality black suit, but his body was deformed and he had an ass's tail. He had three horns on his head. His hands were like a cock's feet, with bony fingers and nails like hawks' claws. He had the feet of a gander. Sometimes his body was in human form and at other times like a he-goat, and sometimes he appeared in the shape of a man without horns.[6]

Graciana de Barrenechea said that the Devil had a vile smell.[7] According to the description of her daughter, María de Yriarte, he had two long horns and a number of small ones like a crown.[8] Her sister Estevanía maintained that the Devil had only two horns, one on his forehead and the other on the nape of his neck.[9] Several of the six witches said that he generally sat on a chair, and María de Yriarte described the chair as being black with twisted arms.[10]

All things considered, the six witches' descriptions of the Devil may be said to complement each other. The only noticeable discrepancies are to be found in their mention of the Devil's horns.

3. THE ASSEMBLIES

Among the witches the assemblies were known as *aquelarres* (*aquelarre*, the Castilian spelling of the Basque word *akellarre* from *akerr* 'he-goat' and *larre* 'meadow').[11] They were held in the neighborhood of Zugarramurdi in the meadow called Berroscoberro[12] or in the meadows called Sagardi and Sagastizarra, which Estevanía mentioned.[13] The assemblies took place Monday, Wednesday, and Friday nights each week.[14] The witches also gathered on the eves of the festivals of the Christian year: Christmas, Easter, Whitsunday, Ascension Day, Corpus Christi, St. John's Day, All Saints' Day, and all the feast days of the Virgin Mary.[15] The assemblies began "when the evening is well advanced"[16] and went on "until the cock begins to crow."[17]

According to the confessions, before the witches set off they anointed themselves with a very evil-smelling fluid of a greenish-black color. They rubbed it on their hands, temples, face, breast, genitals, and the soles of their feet, saying these words:

> I am a devil.
> From now on I shall be one with the Devil.
> I shall be a devil,
> and I shall have nothing to do with God.

Then they committed themselves to the Devil and set off. Sometimes they got out through cracks in the doors, windows, or chimneys and flew through the air to the assembly. At other times they walked out of the door and made their way on foot through the village until they reached the meeting-place.[18] (The meadow of Berroscoberro lies only a few hundred meters from Zugarramurdi near a grotto which even today is said to be the witches' gathering place.)[19]

When they arrived they would fall to their knees before the Devil, whom they worshipped by "kissing him on the left hand, on the breast just above the heart, on the privy parts,

Figure 3.   Witches en route to the aquelarre.

and beneath the tail." Two of the witches, María and Miguel, added that it was the Devil's habit to break wind into their faces (*los ventoseaba por los hocicos*) when they reached the last part of the worship ritual. Then the witches would begin to dance and cavort to the music of the band of the *aquelarre,* which consisted of flute, bass drum, and side drum, and sometimes a violin as well.[20]

While at the sabbath they were strictly forbidden to cross themselves or to speak the names of Jesus, Mary, or the saints. (These names were used only during the denial of faith, to be discussed below.) If anyone broke these taboos the assembly dispersed with a tremendous din and disturbance and all fled away in terror. But afterwards the witches would return and punish the causers of the disturbance with the greatest brutality.[21]

4. ADMISSION CEREMONIES

The witches were formally admitted to the sect when they reached the age of discretion (*edad de discreción,* which it would appear from the confessions was at about the age of nine years).[22] Two of the witches, Miguel de Goiburu and Juanes de Sansín, declared that they became child witches at an even earlier age, Miguel when he was four, and Juanes at the age of seven;[23] they were merely presented to the Devil, who marked them by making some scratches on their foreheads.[24] The other four were older and all declared that they were admitted at their first *aquelarre.*[25] But whether the aspirant took part in the assembly as a child witch or not, he was to have the denial of faith explained to him in advance by his tutor witch, so that he would be fully aware of what he was doing.

Estevanía admitted that her mother took her aside "one Friday noon after the meal, and confided to her that she would make her a witch. But to enable her to do this it would be necessary for her to deny God and Mary and all the saints." She would also have to be prepared to forswear her baptism and confirmation — as well as the sacramental oils which she had received on these occasions — and she was to deny her godparents, her parents, and all other Christian people; for she would have to accept the Devil as her Lord and Master.

After Estevanía had assented, her mother took her to the *aquelarre* that same evening and presented her to the Devil with the words, "I bring thee this maiden [*ésta*], Lord." The Devil

Figure 4.   Girls and old women dancing naked to the witches'
orchestra.

replied, "I accept her," and bade her kneel so that she could undertake the denial of faith. Then he began to speak the same words that she had heard from her mother and she repeated them after him. When she had forsworn her Christianity the Devil said that from then on she was to honor and worship him only. As a sign that she had received the Devil as her Lord and Master Estevanía kissed him on the genitals and under the tail. Thereupon the Devil stuck a nail into her left shoulder and drew blood. As a reward for supplying him with a new subject he gave her mother some money and a toad. The toad, which was intended for Estevanía, was dressed in clothes of green material.

Estevanía related that she had suffered violent pain from the witch-mark for more than a month after her initiation, and the inquisitors noted in parentheses that they could certainly see a scar from the mark in the place she had indicated.[26]

To judge from the reports of the six witches' confessions there was not a great deal of discrepancy in their descriptions of the admission ceremony. Old Graciana declared that she had been made a witch at the age of fifteen (that is to say about 1545) by her mother. The Devil marked her by tearing a lump of flesh out of her nose. He also stamped the pupils of both her eyes. The Devil made these marks with a gold instrument and she felt no pain. Her toad had been dressed in three colors, dark violet, red, and black.[27]

Her daughter María first said that she was thirty-eight when her mother initiated her, and in a later interrogation that she was sixteen. She was marked in the eye and over the left ear. Her toad was "dressed in various colors and the clothes fitted tightly to its body." Her description of the admission ceremony included one particular point which was not present in the others', for she declared that the Devil had intercourse with her and deflowered her, and that she returned from her first *aquelarre* with her chemise covered with blood. She complained about it to her mother, but her mother took no notice.[28]

Miguel de Goiburu confessed that his aunt had taken him to the assemblies from the time he was four (about 1545). He forswore the Christian faith when he was nine years old. But there was one item in his account of the admission ceremonies not mentioned by the other witches. The first thing the Devil did was to give him his "blessing." But since the Devil cannot make the sign of the Cross, the blessing was made in the following manner: "He lifted his left hand in the air with the palm upwards and the fingers wide-spread; then he suddenly lowered his hand and made some fumbling gestures above the ground. He repeated this four or five times," concluded Miguel, who then went on to describe the admission ceremonies in the same manner as the other witches. He was marked in his left eye and under one ear. The Devil pressed some blood out of the wound under the ear, which he preserved in a jar. Afterwards he gave Miguel an herb with which to cure the wound. (The Basque name for the plant is *belarberza*.) It is stated of his toad only that it was dressed in various colors.

Both witch-marks were carefully inspected by the inquisitors. On Miguel's cheek they found a patch without any beard, while the rest of his face was "thickly covered," and they could see that there was a very fine scratch in the pupil of his eye.[29]

Juanes de Goiburu declared that his father had made him a witch. The Devil marked him on his left shoulder. His dressed toad was the size of a chicken and its face resembled that of the Devil.[30]

Juanes de Sansín confessed that it had been his uncle, Miguel de Goiburu, who had initiated him. He was marked by the Devil on the left side of his head, and his toad was the size of a dove and dressed in various colors. He continued his confession by going on to tell how he fed it every day, and how he also fed the toads belonging to his uncle and his cousin. According to Juanes de Sansín, Miguel de Goiburu's toad was dressed in red and Juanes de Goiburu's had black clothes;[31] but unfortunately the trial résumés do not tell us what colors the uncle and cousin themselves said that their toads were dressed in (however, see note for additional information).[32]

The summaries of the six witches' confessions are, however, composed in such a way that they allow little chance for discrepancies to appear; the only place we find any is where the time of admission to the sect is referred to. Both tutors and pupils were questioned as to this. Graciana de Barrenechea declared that her daughters were "ten or twelve years old" when she made them witches.[33] But María states that she was sixteen,[34] and Estevanía that she was twenty-two or younger.[35] Miguel de Goiburu said that his son and nephew were "two or three years old" when he presented them to the

Figure 5. A child witch being presented to the Devil.

Devil and that they were admitted to the sect as ten-year-olds.[36] But Juanes de Goiburu says nothing about being a child witch; nor does his declaration that he was admitted "twenty-four years ago," that is, at the age of twelve, agree with his father's statement.[37] Juanes de Sansín says that he began to take part in the assemblies when he was seven and that he was admitted to the sect three years later.[38] The last but not the first statement agrees with his uncle's declaration. However, these discrepancies are not particularly alarming especially as the mistakes of the eighty-year-old Graciana can easily be explained as errors of memory natural to a person of her age.

The inquisitors' assertion that the witches' statements agreed on all important points is fully confirmed by the reports of the cases, and moreover these seem to have been composed so accurately that we cannot lightly accuse the inquisitors of omitting everything the original records may have contained in the way of contradictions.[39]

5. WITCH POWERS AND FAMILIAR SPIRITS [40]

Besides the ability to transform themselves into animals, (cats, dogs, pigs, horses, and "various other animals"),[41] the witches claimed no personal powers of magic. Everything they undertook was done with the help of the Devil or of demons. But one thing differentiated them from ordinary people: When the priest in church elevated the Host for the congregation to worship, the witches — who went to church to avoid arousing suspicion — could not see it; instead they perceived a black object in the priest's hands. But as soon as they broke with the witch sect, confessed their errors, and went to Communion, they were again able to see the Blessed Host.[42]

The witches' familiar spirits or imps were dressed toads, which were handed to the tutor at the admission ceremonies. Each toad was intended for the novice but was nevertheless for the time being placed in the care of the tutor. Not until the novice was initiated into the senior grade of witches was the toad at his disposal. The toad was the witch's "guardian angel" and adviser. It lived in the witch's house, where it had a special hiding-place so that it could not be seen by intruders. The witch fed it every day on maize, bread, and wine, and the toad ate with its forelegs and guzzled like a pig. If it did not get enough to eat, it complained and threatened to tell the Devil. If the witch were asleep when it was time to leave for a sabbath, the toad announced that it was time to get up. But the toad was more than an alarm clock, for it was the toad that made the journey to the *aquelarre* possible. Every day when the toad had finished eating, the witch would begin to whip it with a small switch. The toad would swell up, take on a poisonous color, and finally say "that will do." Next the witch would tread on it with the left foot so that excrement burst out of it at both ends. The substance was a greenish-black fluid. The witch would collect it carefully and put it into a little bowl; this was the salve that was used as the means of traveling to the sabbath. Whether the journey was undertaken on foot or through the air, the witches were always accompanied by their toads, which could either hop along or else fly at the witch's left side.[43]

6. THE RITES AT THE THRICE-WEEKLY MEETINGS

We have already mentioned the Devil-worship which was a standing ritual at the ordinary weekly meetings on Monday, Wednesday, and Friday. The same applies to the music, which Murray considers is also of a ritual nature.[44] At the *aquelarre* there was moreover a fire which did not burn human flesh. The Devil explained to his witches that it was the fire of Hell, and when they danced around it he called upon them to leap in and out of the fire so that they might accustom themselves to entering Hell without fear.[45] Another feature of the *aquelarre* was the herd of toads. According to the confessions of some witches these were the toads that the witches had collected from the fields to be made into poison.[46] Others, however, maintained that the herd was made up of the dressed toads which were stabled there while the witches disported themselves at the sabbath. The latter theory would explain why the children, according to María de Jureteguía, were enjoined to treat the toads with respect.[47]

7. "FERTILITY RITES"

In addition to the dance, sexual intercourse with the Devil was an integral part of all the assemblies. Copulation with the Devil took place with the use of both vagina and anus. The male or female witches whom the Devil had selected for himself were brought to him in triumphal procession by "the queen of the *aquelarre*" (Graciana de Barrenechea), who was accompanied

Figure 6.   Child witches guarding the herd of toads.

by the witch band. As Juanes de Goiburu was "drummer to the *aquelarre*" it fell to his lot to join the procession when his mother-in-law led his wife, Estevanía, to the Devil, and to be present with the orchestra and play while the Devil enjoyed her. The witches also indulged in mutual intercourse without the slightest regard to sex or blood relationship.[48]

It seems the Devil also found it necessary to practice these "fertility rites," as Murray would call them,[49] at other times, for he constantly sought out witches both in their homes and in the fields in broad daylight.[50] María de Yriarte even confessed to having had a visit from the Devil in Logroño before she was imprisoned. He came to her at the lodging house where she and her companions lived during the week when they were awaiting an answer from the Tribunal.[51]

8. THE FEAST

Black Mass was celebrated on festival nights throughout the year. The witches would come to an assembly with money, consecrated bread and wine, and other things that they were in the habit of offering their Lord on these occasions. "The Devil's minions" — subordinate devils — would erect an altar and cover it with a black cloth. The altar-piece was adorned with portraits of the Devil, and over the altar they would have a worn and tattered black canopy.

Before the "service" the Devil would hear the confessions of all the witches. Their sins were all the Christian actions they had been unfortunate enough to carry out, and all the harm they had neglected to cause when they had had the opportunity. When the Devil had heard all the confessions he would robe himself in a kind of vestment consisting of "long, black and filthy garments," and the mass would begin. The choir, which was made up of the Devil's minions, would sing in "hoarse, gruff, and tuneless voices." In his sermon the Devil would generally tell the witches to hold firmly to their belief in him and not in their vanity to seek other gods, for even though in this life they must endure poverty and adversity, they must constantly bear in mind that perpetual rest awaited them in the after life. After the sermon came the offering. The Devil would seat himself facing the congregation, and the "queen of the *aquelarre*" would take her place on a chair beside him. She wore a gold chain around her neck. In one hand she held a medal bearing a picture of the Devil, in the other she had an alms box.

Figure 7.   Witches dancing with demons.

The witches would file past them; one after another they would kiss the medal and place their offering in the box, "some a *sos* [*sou* in French], which is equal to half a *tarja* [*targe* in French], others offer a whole *tarja,* and the richest and most prosperous give a frank, which corresponds to three Spanish *reales."* And to each the Devil would say: *"Pax tecum* [Peace be with you]. This you give for the glorification of the world and in honor of the Feast." Before returning to their places they would fall to their knees and kiss the Devil in the usual manner.

Finally the communion would take place. The Host resembled the black sole of a shoe and bore the Devil's portrait. The blessing was made as the Devil held the Host while intoning the words: "This is my body." And the kneeling witches would answer in chorus: "Aquerragoiti, aquerrabeiti!" which, according to the translation of the inquisitors, meant: "Up with the goat, down with the goat!" Meanwhile they would beat their breasts and gaze at the Host in adoration. Likewise the Devil would bless the chalice, which was a wretched black wooden cup. Then the witches would come forward to communion. The wafer handed them by the Devil was tough and almost impossible to swallow. The liquid in the cup, from which they all took a sip, was acrid and left them with a freezing sensation around the heart.[52]

After the mass the witches would devote themselves to the customary carnal pleasures. However, on Midsummer Night there was an additional ritual. The witches would make their way to "the church" (presumably that of Zugarramurdi) and break into it while the Devil waited outside. They would tear down all the statues of the saints and throw the great cross to the floor with the reliquaries downwards.[53] (It must be assumed that it was a part of the witches' ritual to put the church in order again after the desecration, for at no time did any outside witnesses come forward to confirm that the church had ever been ransacked.)

9. VIOLATION OF TOMBS

After a witch's death and burial the senior witches accompanied by the Devil and his minions would go to the churchyard carrying spades and axes. The Devil and his minions would then dig up the coffin, and the next of kin would take out the corpse and quarter it with axes on the spot so that the blood and intestines fell into the grave. The entrails and winding sheet were replaced in the coffin and the grave was covered over again with such skill that it appeared completely undisturbed. The quartered corpse would be carried off by the nearest relatives and taken to the witches' meeting-place. Likewise they also dug up the corpses of the children and adults they had murdered on their nocturnal expeditions.[54]

10. THE BANQUET

The corpse would be served at the *aquelarre* roast, boiled, or raw, and the witches declared that it tasted better than partridge or capon. The heart was considered to be the greatest delicacy and was always reserved for the Devil. Some of the meat was thrown to the dressed toads, who hurled themselves upon it with grunts; the Devil's minions also had a share. All the witches without exception joined in the banquets, for even if the meal consisted of one's own father or mother, husband or wife, or even his own child, no witch would ever dream of missing it.[55]

The witches were allowed to take what was left over from the banquet home with them. They kept the human flesh in their breadbins and ate it gradually.[56] The bones and brains of the corpses which had been devoured were however buried at the witches' meeting-place, for the witches used them later in the manufacture of poison.[57]

11. POISONS, POWDERS, AND OINTMENTS

At the next meeting the bones and brains would be dug up again and put in a pot to boil with an herb which made the bones as soft as cabbage (and which the documents say is called *belargusia* in Basque).[58] The witches produced a poisonous salve out of the boiled bones[59] and moreover obtained a deadly poison which was called "yellow water."[60]

The witches also made a powder which was considerably more complicated to produce; they therefore usually met in one of their homes to make it, although it was sometimes also prepared at the *aquelarre*. It was concocted from toads, snakes, lizards, salamanders, slugs, snails, and puffballs (Latin *lycoperdon*), which were collected in great quantities in the fields and on the mountain slopes.[61]

When the witches were setting out to collect the ingredients,

Figure 8.   Witches and demons feasting on a child.

the Devil divided them into groups, appointed group leaders, and allotted an area for each to cover. Before they started work he would give them his "blessing" and then they would go off on foot or through the air. The Devil and his minions overturned boulders and pulled the snakes out of their holes with sticks. But the witches had to pick up the creatures with their own hands and throw them into heaps.[62]

When they had found enough, they carried what they had collected to the meeting-place or to the home of the member whose house was at their disposal. The Devil again gave them his "blessing" saying: "Powders, powders, powders, and poisons!" Then under the direction of the "queen of the *aquelarre*" they would begin to skin the toads. They flayed them by biting a hole in the skin of the toad's head and pulling the head free. Then, closing their teeth on the skin, they would get hold of the head with their fingers and with a sharp tug they stripped the skin off the toad, which was still alive and kicking them in the face. The Devil put the skins on one side, while the bodies were given to the "king of the *aquelarre*" (Miguel de Goiburu), who would chop them all into small pieces on a little board and throw them into some old pots. When the bones and brains of the corpses had been added the mixture was put on to boil and stirred the whole time until the Devil said it had cooked long enough. Then it was poured onto boards and tiles and left to dry in the sun or in a chimney.

When this substance had dried out for two or three days the witches would gather again. The Devil would give his "blessing" and they would grind the dried matter to powder in mortars. The powder was green, yellow, and black, and was shared out among the senior witches, who took it home in their jars.[63]

12. DAMAGE TO HUMAN BEINGS

When the witches wished to revenge themselves on someone, they would present their complaint to the Devil and beg either for sickness or death to fall on the person concerned. The Devil was glad to grant the revenge, but the injured witch had to be the one to carry it out. In the night he or she went together with the Devil and the other witches to the house where the revenge was to be accomplished. The Devil opened the doors and lighted their way, either with smoke that issued from his horn

Figure 9. Two witches flaying a toad.

or with a torch of pitch and resin which he held in his left hand. When they got to the beds where the sleepers were lying the Devil gave a "blessing" to all the inmates of the house and cast upon them a sleep from which they could not awaken. Then they would approach their victim. The witch who was to be revenged mixed some powder in a toad skin, the Devil opened the sleeper's mouth, and the witch poured the powder down his or her throat.[64]

The effects were nausea and violent vomiting. The vomit was often seen to be of a black or green color and was very evil smelling. Those who did not vomit anything either died quickly in fearful agony or wasted away slowly. Sometimes a witch would request a lesser revenge, for instance that his victim suffer stomachache or fever or be paralysed and become a cripple. When the witches wished to be quite certain of their victim's death they would administer some "yellow water," for no human remedy was effective against this poison. The witches killed young children by sucking blood from the fontanelle or the genitals while they pressed down on their backs and on other parts of the body. At other times they pierced their temples or heads with nails.[65]

13. DAMAGE TO CROPS AND DOMESTIC ANIMALS

Poisonous powders were also used for destroying corn and other crops. When the fields were ready for harvest the Devil flew or walked out to those that were to be damaged and the witches followed him in the shape of dogs, cats, and pigs. It was the duty of the "king of the *aquelarre*" to carry "the Devil's kettle" containing the powder and distribute it to the witches. First the Devil would throw some powder backwards with his left hand, saying "Powders, powders, let it all be ruined!" (or "Let half be ruined," according to how much revenge was asked for). When the witches threw their portions they repeated these words and added: "But let mine be spared." However this did not help them much, for their fields were ruined along with their neighbors'.[66]

Rituals for causing damage to animals[67] and calling up storms[68] were also included in the repertoire of the Zugarramurdi witches, but these show us nothing especially new. We will therefore leave the rites and turn to the social organization of the witches.

14. THE COVEN

There are two separate meanings of the word *aquelarre;* it can signify either the meeting or the group which meets together. The first meaning corresponds to *witches' sabbath,* the second, to what Margaret Murray calls the *coven.* One of her stronger arguments points out that the number of members in these covens is always thirteen. If we take all the witches at the auto de fe of 1610 at Logroño and exclude those who did not come from Zugarramurdi and Urdax we find twenty-seven. This is one too many for two covens. But as one of them was the priest from Fuenterrabía, who presumably belonged to the coven of that town, he may be excluded on this count and the sum is then correct.[69] Murray's list of English witch-covens in the appendix to her book is impressive on first sight;[70] but here as elsewhere the sources are open to so many interpretations that it would most probably be feasible to "prove" that the covens consisted of twelve members, or fourteen. Moreover, where Zugarramurdi and Urdax are concerned there is nothing to warrant an assumption that there were *two* covens instead of one.

15. DEGREES

We have touched several times on the different grades among the witches. There seem to have been only three stages:[71] (1) child witches and the uninitiated; (2) novice witches; and (3) senior witches.

The child witches participated in the sabbath without having renounced their faith. The Devil marked them with a scratch and their task was to guard the toads.[72] They could not get to the *aquelarre* by themselves but had to be fetched and taken by a tutor witch or other senior witches.[73] The witches could take very small children to the sabbath whether they were willing to go or not, provided that the parents had not hung a holy medal on them or blessed them and made the sign of the cross over them before they fell asleep.[74] The older children had to give their consent, but to obtain this the witch needed only to ask if they wanted to go somewhere where they would have a good time.[75]

The novice witches had renounced their faith and been received into the sect, but they were permitted to join only partially in the witches' rituals. Thus, twenty-year-old Juanes de Sansín was too young to have been initiated into all the

Figure 10.   A tutor witch taking small children to the aquelarre.

secrets of poison-making, and was therefore limited to collecting ingredients and skinning toads. On the other hand, he was not excluded from violating graves and devouring corpses.[76] The novice remained under the tutelage of his instructor, who took charge of his toad and anointed him with flying ointment when they were going to the *aquelarre* (see chapter 5.5, above).

The senior witches were initiated into the mysteries of poison-making. They had control of their own toads and traveled to the *aquelarre* independently. Besides enjoying greater responsibility and higher degrees of dignity the senior witches had the task of enlisting new members and serving as their teachers.[77]

16. OFFICERS

There was a clearly defined system of rank within the senior grade. Graciana de Barrenechea confessed to being the most distinguished witch. In the provisional charge of the *fiscal* based on the statements of the witnesses and the first prisoners, she was described as "queen, head, and chief of the *aquelarre*."[78] It was she who directed the assemblies. She instructed the other witches as to when poison was to be made, and during the Black Mass she sat in the most honored place beside the Devil.[79] The next highest in rank among the witches was old Estevanía de Navarcorena,[80] and the third in importance was María Pérez de Barrenechea[81] (see table 1).

Miguel de Goiburu held the title of "king of the *aquelarre*." He was the chief among the male witches, who respected him as their head, but there is no doubt that he was subordinate to the queen. In recognition of many years of faithful service the Devil had allotted him the honorable task of carrying the kettle on the expeditions of destruction.[82]

Estevanía de Yriarte is referred to as being on intimate terms with the Devil and both she and her sister were most distinguished among the senior witches.[83] Juanes de Goiburu was "bass drummer to the *aquelarre*,"[84] and his cousin Juanes de Sansín, despite his youth and novice status, had been appointed "side drummer."[85]

17. DISCIPLINE

It was compulsory for the witches to attend the assemblies. If a member failed to appear, the other witches went to his or her

house and cruelly beat and ill-treated the truant.[86] The witches
were also bound to silence and were strictly forbidden to
discuss with each other outside the assemblies what they had
been doing at the *aquelarre*.[87]

18. THE ZUGARRAMURDI COVEN AND OTHER *AQUELARRES*

The witches were in contact with other covens. They sometimes paid each other visits. The group at Zugarramurdi were
in contact with the witches at Ciboure, Trapaza (*sic*, uniden-
tified locality), Ascain, and other villages over the border in the
Pays de Labourd.[88] Normally the witches undertook the visit
in a body with the Devil at their head. According to the confessions it turns out that each *aquelarre* had its own Lord or Devil
and these devils respected each other's territories. Thus, in
order to get to the coast to destroy some ships the Devil of
Zugarramurdi was obliged to obtain permission from the Devil
at Ascain to pass through his area.[89]

19. THE WITCHES' GENERAL MEETING

The witches of Zugarramurdi belonged to an organization of
Spanish witches which held a general meeting every few
years. In the long joint sentence of the four witches there is a
description of such an assembly which was held in Pamplona
"twenty years ago" (that is, about 1590). The Lord of Zugarramurdi made his appearance with his witches and met with
twelve other devils. The protocol and rituals of the local
aquelarre were repeated, only more elaborately. The Lord of
Pamplona was respected by all the others as their head "because he was the most distinguished and handsome; and even
though the other devils were not so handsome," the record
goes on, "yet they were all white and of a handsome appearance. Only the Lord of Zugarramurdi was black, ugly, and
horrible." But he was nevertheless the next highest in rank and
sat on the left of the Lord of Pamplona the whole time. He was
also the first to appear with his witches to greet the Lord of
Pamplona and kiss him under the tail.[90]

We do not know which of the four witches it was who gave
this extremely interesting description (they were, it will be
recalled, Graciana, María, Estevanía, and Miguel), but it was
probably Miguel de Goiburu. We know from the correspondence with *la Suprema* that the male witches had given valuable

information about *aquelarres* in other parts of Navarra[91] and we possess various examples of the sixty-six-year-old shepherd's inventiveness during the interrogations.[92] Certainly it is also to him we owe the following description of the general assembly at Pamplona where one of the zeniths of the witches' art in story-telling is reached:

> Since the Lords of all the *aquelarres* were summoned to the meeting, there was a great throng of witches, and it could be seen from their costumes that they came from different regions. There was also a deafening din as each devil was accompanied by his official drummers and musicians. All of them amused themselves and copulated in the most outrageous and indecent manner. Afterwards the Lords feasted their witches at separate tables. When the festivities were at an end they approached the Lord of Pamplona with great deference and with many reverences took their leave of him with affection and gratitude, which he accepted with the solemnity and calm befitting his exalted rank. Three hours later when the cock was beginning to crow, they were back at Zugarramurdi.[93]

20. WAS THERE A WITCH CULT AT ZUGARRAMURDI?

Reassuming my own identity I do not doubt that the Murrayists will point to the indisputable fact that thirteen devils were present at the witches' general assembly and begin to calculate whether it might be possible to cover the fifty miles from Pamplona to Zugarramurdi on horseback in three hours. But the rest of us, who do not share Murray's views, what are we to make of the above?

We have long since confirmed that the confessions were not extorted under torture; and we have not been able to disprove the inquisitors' assertion that the witches' statements were identical. However, there is hardly any doubt that the joint sentence is the sum of the four witches' confessions. The inquisitors obviously had no hesitation in combining Graciana's, María's, Estevanía's, and Miguel's confessions, and were quick to generalize even when a rite or a detail was supported by only a single witness. If, however, one reads the summaries of the trials of Juanes de Goiburu and Juanes de Sansín, one has a strong suspicion that the amount of detail and particulars was not nearly as impressive when the confessions were dealt with separately.[94]

Moreover, if we consider the description of the witch cult as a whole, the first question to raise itself is the problem of who would have wished to be a witch under these wretched conditions. The Murrayists will presumably account for it by explaining that many of the negative and excessively perverse elements are due to exaggeration on the part of the inquisitors who could not conceive of any happiness outside Christianity and who therefore begrudged the witches their pleasures. But even if we chose to discount the theological bias of the Inquisition it would be impossible from the remaining evidence to recreate anything bearing resemblance to any known religion. On the contrary, if we accept the description of Basque witchcraft as it stands with all its motifs of horror and obscenity it can be argued that these are in fact striking confirmation of the principle of inversion; a universal feature of witchcraft notions (see above, chapter 1.5).

It might be tempting when interpreting the confessions to make use of the assumption that the Zugarramurdi witches were adherents of some drug cult. It could be pointed out, for instance, that it is well known that the toad is imbued with hallucinogenic substances. The American ethnopharmacologist Michael Harner, with whom I have corresponded regarding the phenomenon, is convinced that the excrement of toads could be used as an effective flying ointment.[95] Many details in the witches' confessions could be explained in the terms of the sensations and visions produced by this type of narcotic. This, however, can never be more than indirect evidence, and in view of the fact that the inquisitors themselves thought of the possibility of a drug cult, we shall leave the question open and return to it later when discussing the investigations that the Tribunal undertook in this connection.

Whatever the witches' source of inspiration and although their confessions were probably lies from beginning to end, the structure built upon them by the Inquisition was indeed impressive. The inquisitors had succeeded in revealing a witch cult at Zugarramurdi in all its frightful detail. All that was needed was for Valle to confirm the results of the court hearings by personal investigations at the scene of the crime.

CHAPTER SIX
The Visitations and the Edict of Faith

ALLE'S JOURNEY IN 1609 TO ZUGAR-ramurdi and other towns in northern Navarra and Guipúzcoa took the form of a normal visitation, as did Salazar's journey two years later. The particular commission entrusted to each inquisitor in connection with the witch sect was executed within the framework of the procedure usually employed for any inquisitorial visitation.[1]

Much information was filtered into the tribunals of the Inquisition by their secret intelligence service. Sometimes interrogation of prisoners resulted in the exposure of accomplices, which in turn could lead to the discovery of heretic cells in a variety of places, whereby the inquisitors would be able to unravel a whole heretical movement. This process was helped by the fact that the tribunals were constantly exchanging information with each other via *la Suprema*. But without any doubt the tribunals obtained their most vital information on the district visitations, during which the inquisitors themselves traveled around taking statements.

It was incumbent on each tribunal to undertake one journey of visitation per year through a part of its area.[2] The routes were planned to ensure that the whole area was visited region by region over the years, and when this had been done the process was started again.[3] The duration of the visitation was a stipulated four months[4] and the inquisitor whose turn it was to undertake the journey was required to start out on the first Sunday in Lent.[5] (The date could not have been better chosen, for Lent was the time when those who were not in fact regular churchgoers made a point of going to confession in order to comply with the *precepto pascual*, the Church's command that every person go to communion at least once during the period between Lent and Whitsunday. Confessors were strictly ordered not to give absolution for any form of heresy. They could not break the seal of confession, but they had instructions to defer absolution and to direct the penitent to the nearest tribunal so he could present himself voluntarily and clear himself with the Inquisition.)[6]

The most important function of the journey of visitation was the publication of the Edict of Faith (*el edicto de fe*). The Edict of Faith was the Inquisition's questionnaire, which enumerated on eight printed folio pages every imaginable form of heresy.[7] When an inquisitor arrived at the town where a visitation was to be held he sent around copies of the edict to be read out in all the churches and convents of the surrounding district.[8]

According to the accompanying printed instructions the publication had to be made the following Sunday. On Saturday night the town crier was ordered to make his rounds and proclaim that all the inhabitants were to attend church next day with their children and everyone else in the household (except for boys under 14 and girls under 12); they were told to hear High Mass with a sermon and the proclamation of the Edict of Faith if they wished to spare themselves excommunication from the Church and legal proceedings from the Inquisition.[9]

The next day at High Mass after the reading of the Gospel the whole congregation with one accord took the solemn oath of loyalty to the Inquisition. They declared themselves one and all to be on the side of the Holy Catholic Faith; they swore to assist the Holy Office to expose heretics and promised to report any who either shielded heretics or helped them in any way.[10] Next followed the reading of the long Edict of Faith, which must have taken more than half an hour.

The introduction varied at different tribunals. The edict of the Logroño Inquisition opened with a lengthy preamble (see figure 11):

> We, the apostolic inquisitors sent to combat heretical depravity and apostasy throughout the whole kingdom of Navarra, the diocese of Calahorra y la Calzada, the county of Vizcaya with the province of Guipúzcoa, and the entire

OS LOS IN-
QVSIDORES APOS-
tolicos, contra la eretica pravedad, y Apoftafia,
en todo el Reyno de Navarra, Obifpado de Calahorra, y la Calçada, Códado y Señorío de Vizcaya,
con la provincia de Guipuzcoa, con toda la tierra, y juridicion que cae
en el Arçopifpado de Burgos, de los montes de Oca a efta parte, y
fu diftrito, por autoridad Apoftolica &c. A todos los vezinos, y moradores, eftantes, y refidentes, en todas las ciudades, villas, y lugares defte
nueftro diftrito, de qualquier eftado, y condicion, preeminencia, o
dignidad que fean , efentos, o no efentos, y cada vno, y qualquier
de vos , a cuya noticia llegare lo contenido en efta nueftra carta en
qualquier manera; Salud en nueftro Señor IESVCHRISTO , que es
verdadera falud, ya los nueftros mandamientos, que mas verdaderamen
te fon dichos Apoftolicos, firmemente obedezer , guardar , y cumplir.
Hazemos faver, que ante nos parecio el promotor Fifcal del Santo Offi
cio, i nos hizo relacion diziendo; Que bien faviamos, y nos era notorio
que de algunos dias, y tiempo a efta parte, por nos en muchas ciudades,
villas, i lugares defte diftrito, no fe avia hecho Inquificion, ni vifita Gene
ral, por loqual no avian venido a nueftra noticia muchos delitos que fe
avian cometido, i perpetrado, contra nueftra Santa Fè Catolica, i fe efta-

A   van

*Figure 11.   First page of the Edict of Faith from the Logroño Tri-
bunal.*

region within the archbishopric of Burgos as far as the Oca
Mountains . . . [11]

After this enumeration of the localities of the district, the text
of the Edict of Faith was the same for all tribunals. It began with
a Christian greeting and went on to state that the *fiscal* of the
tribunal had made his appearance before the inquisitors and
reported that many parts of the district had not been visited for
a considerable time, and it was therefore very likely that in
these places offenses might have been committed against the
Holy Catholic Faith without the knowledge of the tribunal.
(This of course was a purely legal formality, for as will be
recalled the *fiscal* was the inquisitors' subordinate, and they
could consequently order him to make such an appearance.)
For this reason, the edict continued, the inquisitors had promised their *fiscal* to go on a journey of visitation, and they now
charged every citizen to come and report if he knew or had
heard it said of any person — alive or dead, present or absent
— that that person had said, thought, or done anything that
conflicted with the tenets of the Catholic Faith. [12]

Following this came the enumeration of the many different
forms of heresy. Firstly there was a detailed account of Jewish
customs and the concepts of Judaism. Then followed similar
descriptions of Mohammedanism, Protestantism, and the
mystical movement of *"los alumbrados."* These religious
minority groups together made up the chief object of the
Inquisition's concern. [13]

The edict continued with a section containing miscellaneous
information, including a description of blasphemous speech
such as "I renounce my God [if what I am saying is not true]"
and heretical opinions such as "there is no such thing as
Paradise for the good or Hell for the wicked, but only birth and
death." After this followed the passage which is of particular
interest to our study, because it asked whether those who were
being warned had knowledge of any people who practiced
supernatural arts or were "in possession of familiar spirits
[*familiares*]"; or who invoked demons, or drew magic circles on
the ground and put questions to demons; and finally, whether
they knew or had heard of any who were "warlocks or witches
[*brujos o brujas*]" or who had made a pact with the Devil. [14]

The edict continued with a section dealing with forbidden
books and finally turned to inquiries regarding offenses

against the Holy Office: whether any person was known to have neglected to report his knowledge of heretical activity to the Inquisition; whether any person was known to have borne false witness to the Inquisition or bribed others to do so; whether any person was known, after having been punished, to have stated that what he had confessed to the Holy Office was not true but had been said out of fear or for other reasons; whether any person was known to have broken his oath of silence as given to the Holy Office; and, finally if any person had been heard to say of persons who had been burned by the Inquisition that they had been innocent and had died martyrs.[15]

Under threat of excommunication, any person who had knowledge of any of these points was charged to present himself and make a secret declaration to the Inquisition without mentioning the matter to anyone. The time allowed in which to fulfill this obligation was six days. Confessors were reminded of the prohibition against giving absolution to any persons who were guilty of heresy or who were aware of heretical activities which they had omitted to report to the Inquisition.[16]

As a rule, after the edict was read a sermon was preached on the subject. According to the printed instructions, the priest was to exhort every citizen to fulfill his Christian duty and reveal everything he knew, and when addressing the heretics he was to make a point of mentioning the lenience shown by the Inquisition toward those who presented themselves voluntarily and confessed their errors.[17]

The following Sunday, when the time limit had run out, the Anathema was proclaimed. As with the Edict of Faith, the town crier went around the preceding evening announcing that the people were to present themselves in church next day.[18] The Anathema was an excommunication, it was read from the pulpit after the Gospel in the same way as the Edict of Faith, but was briefer and from the start sounded a harsher note.[19]

It first stated that the populace had now had six days in which to make their declarations. However — and here followed the usual story — the *fiscal* of the tribunal had again presented himself to the inquisitors, this time for the purpose of accusing those who in their inveterate disobedience had been unwilling to fulfill their obligations to Holy Mother

Church. The inquisitors thus declared that these reprobate persons were to be expelled from Christian society.[20]

The Anathema continued by giving punctilious directions on how this excommunication should be enforced:

> On the day when the congregation is assembled at High Mass and our letter is read out, you are to declare them publicly expelled. You are to excommunicate them while sprinkling holy water to ensure that the demons who have them in their toils and snares may flee away. [Here we may visualize the reading accompanied by a symbolic sprinkling of holy water in the direction of the whole congregation, as of course it would not have been revealed who the guilty members were.] At the same time you are to pray and beseech our Lord Jesus Christ that He may be pleased to convert these people and bring them back into the bosom of the Holy Catholic Church so that they may not end their days in such obstinacy and wickedness.

Every Christian was given three days' notice in which to sever all connections with those who had been excommunicated if he did not wish to be struck by the same Anathema.[21]

At this point the priest in the pulpit bade all the ecclesiastics present to step forward "in dignified apparel" to perform the ceremony of excommunication. During the reading of the Anathema the priests and monks had been holding themselves in readiness in the sacristy clothed in their albs and with lighted candles in their hands. The words "in dignified apparel" were the signal for them to enter the church. At the head of the procession was carried a cross swathed in black. Then followed the monks and priests bearing candles and singing *"Deus laudem meam, ne tacueris."* When they had sung this to the end, they would strike up the antiphon, *"Media vita in morte sumus,"* followed by the response, *"Revelabunt coeli iniquitatem judae."* When the procession reached the altar they would come to a halt and continue to sing softly, thus providing a background of music for the last and most terrible part of the Anathema.[22]

Now the priest in the pulpit would begin to utter the excommunication whose phraseology was similar to the one applied by black magicians in their conjurations: "May the wrath and damnation of God Almighty come upon them," began the Anathema. It then went on implacably to invoke curses from "the Blessed Virgin Mary . . . from the holy apos-

tles Saint Peter and Saint Paul, and all the saints in Heaven."
Those excommunicated were to be afflicted by all the plagues
of Egypt, and the miseries of Sodom and Gomorrah were to
come upon them. "Their food and drink, their waking and
sleeping, shall be damned . . . The Devil will always be at their
right hand. They will lose their court cases and their days shall
be numbered and evil. They shall forfeit their goods and property to others. Their children shall be orphans and always in
want. Fire shall reduce them to penury and wheresoever they
shall turn their steps they will be met with abhorrence and
shown no pity." The Anathema concluded by invoking "all
the curses of the Old and New Testament" upon the expelled
individuals and delivering them over to "Lucifer and Judas
and all the devils in Hell," who were to be "their Lords and
companions."[23]

When the reader came to the words "Lords and companions" the monks and priests stopped their muted singing and
responded in chorus with a resounding "Amen." A symbolic
ritual succeeded the excommunication. One by one the
ecclesiastics thrust their burning candles into a vessel of holy
water, at the same time pronouncing the words: "As these
candles die in this water, so shall the souls of these rebellious
and obstinate people die and be buried in Hell." After this
ceremony was concluded there would be ringing of the small
bells and tolling of the large bells for some time, as at funerals.
The excommunication remained in force until those expelled
returned to obedience and showed themselves worthy of the
Church's forgiveness.[24]

Before 1632, when the Edict of Faith was revised, the texts
varied considerably from tribunal to tribunal.[25] In a printed
Anathema from Logroño (undated but presumably from the
beginning of the seventeenth century) those excommunicated
were allowed a further period of time in which to report. For
the inquisitors had their suspicions, as stated in this text, that
many had refrained from reporting their friends and relatives
and allowed regard for them (or other motives) to stand in the
way of their Christian duty.[26] But even though the Anathema
may have varied, the ceremony of excommunication seems to
have been much the same in the various tribunals at the beginning of the seventeenth century.

It would be interesting to make a detailed study of the effects
of the exhortations of the Edict of Faith and the curses of the

Anathema. There is a good deal to indicate that people gradually became inured. Naturally enough the documents of the Inquisition give only an occasional suggestion of this. Thus during a visitation in Galicia in 1581 it appeared that a man at Racamonde had urged all the inhabitants of the parish to keep silent when "an excommunication" was read in their church "next Sunday," for if one spoke up, others would follow suit and then they would all be lost. He told them not to worry about the excommunication, which was nothing more than an order issued by a secular court of law, and said God would not allow them all to be anathematized for saying nothing. The man was summoned and the case was settled with a reprimand and a fine.[27]

In 1611, when Salazar was on his journey of visitation in Vitoria, a respected woman resident reported two people for committing adultery. She told Salazar that she had been in doubt whether to bring the matter before the Inquisition and explained further that the reason for her not coming earlier was that many people had assured her that it was a trivial matter and that she was not obliged to report it.[28] On the same journey, Salazar discovered that the commissioner to the Inquisition at Irún, an eighty-year-old priest, had the reputation of being something of a womanizer and was particularly dangerous in the confessional. For safety's sake the old man had left out the section relating to unchaste confessors when he read out the Edict of Faith in his church. On his return home Salazar read through the registers of the Tribunal and discovered that his case was by no means unique.[29]

The witnesses were questioned by the inquisitor, and his secretary entered their statements in the so-called *libro de visita,* or visitation book. According to some instructions dating from the beginning of the seventeenth century, an inquisitor was to ensure that each witness was asked if other witnesses (*contestes,* literally co-witnesses) could corroborate his evidence. The names of these people were to be carefully noted down so that the inquisitor could summon them for interrogation in due course. The instructions advised the traveling inquisitor to embark on these interrogations immediately, "for if he postpones them until later he will make a lot of trouble for himself [*porque si dejase los contestes para la postre le será muy molesto*]."[30]

The traveling inquisitor had other duties besides publishing the Edict of Faith and receiving denunciations. Wherever he visited he had to ensure that the *sambenitos* of those whom the Inquisition had burned or reconciled were hanging (complete with labels) in the churches, and that those which were very old and dilapidated were renewed. The inquisitors were furnished with lists so that they could see whether any of the *sambenitos* were missing.[31] From the list for Salazar's visitations it may be seen that some of the penitential garments had been hanging up for over a hundred years, the oldest being for the year 1500.[32] The *sambenitos* hung in all the churches of Spain, a constant reminder of the crimes of the heretics against the Holy Faith and a permanent disgrace to the heretics' descendants.

The traveling inquisitor also took with him from the secret files of the tribunal particulars of suspected persons, so that he could collect new information about them. Finally, during his journey he was obliged to make inquiries regarding the local representatives of the Inquisition to ascertain whether they were leading exemplary lives and attending to their duties without taking advantage of their position.[33]

The autos de fe in the town where a tribunal was based, the journeys of visitation which reached a region from time to time, and the *sambenitos* hanging in the church were what the Inquisition signified to the ordinary citizen; the remainder of its activities were concealed in darkest secrecy.

The Inquisition was as jealous of its prestige on the journeys of visitation as at the autos de fe. When a traveling inquisitor was approaching the place where a visitation session was to be held, he sent word on ahead so that representatives of the ecclesiastical and secular authorities might come out to greet him and accompany him to his quarters. The Inquisition secretary who went along on the journey had orders to note down the details of these receptions and state whether they had been sufficiently ceremonial and whether they had been warm or cool.[34] Besides finding quarters for the inquisitor and his entourage, the townspeople would have to provide premises where a temporary courtroom could be set up. Here a table was placed at which the inquisitor presided beneath a canopy which he brought with him. Along one of the walls was placed the tribunal's traveling altar, where the inquisitor and his company said Mass before settling down to the business of the day.[35]

At the beginning of the seventeenth century the journey of

visitation still retained something of the character of a traveling inquisitorial court, but this was only an outward appearance, for the tribunals had long since been stationary. The traveling inquisitor's duty was purely and simply to obtain evidence, although he could settle trivial matters on the spot with warnings or fines. However, if there was any danger of the suspected person taking flight, the inquisitor had authority to make arrests. All other matters were to be discussed at the tribunal after the journey of visitation.[36]

Upon his return to the tribunal the inquisitor drafted a report covering the cases resulting from the visitation, with an account of how many *contestes* had been interrogated in each case. This *relación de visita* was forwarded to the Council of the Inquisition, and months, perhaps years, later, the arrests were made.[37]

Since the visiting inquisitor charged each witness with the customary pledge of silence, the Inquisition might appear and disappear without any person realizing what it had discovered during its stay.[38] Something was sure to leak out, for even if the inquisitor did his best the principle of secrecy could not always be upheld on these journeys. People's tongues wagged both before and after they had been interrogated, and even if the witnesses held their tongues, the promise of complete anonymity could not always help them. In village society, where everyone knew everyone, it was bound to be noticed when someone suddenly started out on a journey the week after the reading of the edict; and generally it was possible to guess what one or another had to tell the Inquisition.

The fact that the informers might be exposed to threats and bodily attacks is illustrated by a number of trial records of persons accused of "having hindered the Inquisition in the execution of its duty." The examples I know are in fact remarkable for the relatively mild sentences that were meted out to the accused.[39]

The regulations of the Inquisition stipulated that visitations be carried out annually, but the lengthy and troublesome journeys could never be other than an unpleasant duty for the inquisitors. The correspondence between *la Suprema* and the tribunals is, as Lea aptly remarks, punctuated with orders to the touring inquisitor to set off, and with apologies from the tribunals for postponing the journey.[40] The inquisitor who was to start off on the first Sunday in Lent "without delay"[41] seldom left before the summer. It almost seems probable that the reason for the inquisitors' setting off on the journeys at all was due to a regulation introduced in 1578 according to which the annual bonus was not to be paid to any inquisitor who had neglected to make his visitation.[42] The bonus (*la ayuda de costa*) formed one-sixth of the inquisitor's annual salary. However, it would seem that in practice *la Suprema* always ended by accepting the excuses of the tribunals. If for instance we take the period from 1600 to 1620 in the Lorgroño Inquisition, we see that journeys of visitation were made only in 1607, 1609, 1611, 1616, and 1617,[43] but the annual bonus was paid out every year to all the inquisitors.

CHAPTER SEVEN
Valle's Visitation

 A *SUPREMA* HAD TO REPEAT ITS TRAVEL orders to Valle as late as 21 July 1609.[1] But the Council could not have disapproved of the constant postponement of the journey to Zugarramurdi too much, for three days later a new letter was sent with final instructions for Valle. In it he was ordered above all to visit the home villages of the imprisoned witches — that is to say, Urdax and Zugarramurdi. There he was to take statements and confessions in connection with the sect, which, as the Council wrote, "is causing us so much anxiety," and he was to keep up a frequent correspondence with the Tribunal about the progress of his investigations. When examining members of the sect and also those outside it, the chief object was to verify the things the imprisoned witches had confessed to, "such as keeping toads, producing ointments and powders, killing children, and exhuming and devouring the corpses of witches and unbaptized children." The damages, which according to their confessions the witches had caused, were to be more closely investigated by Valle, by means of questioning the injured persons or others who might have any knowledge of the events, in order to establish whether the damages were actual or imagined. Valle was to search for the ointments, powders, toads, and other things which the witches used in their evil arts in the places where the witches declared they were hidden. When these articles were found he was to have them examined by doctors and apothecaries and obtain their opinions as to what they were composed of and what effects they might have. The letter concluded with a request to Valle and his colleagues at the Tribunal to carry out these investigations with the greatest care, "as the matter stands or falls on whether it can be demonstrated that these evil deeds actually took place and that the tangible objects [witches' ointments, powders, toads, etc.] actually exist."[2]

This instruction[3] was a supplement to the first set of instructions (which accompanied the fourteen questions discussed in chapter 4.4, above). It reveals that the Council of the Inquisition was far from convinced by its reading of the records of the trials of the first ten witches but still maintained that the examinations at the Tribunal should be followed up by investigations at the scene of the crime.

2. THE VISITATION AT ZUGARRAMURDI

The letters were received at Logroño on 7 August, and on Sunday 16 August Valle set off at last.[4] He was accompanied by Francisco Pardo de la Fuente,[5] an Inquisition secretary who took with him in his document chest the fruits of the efforts of the spring. There were copies of everything the witches had confessed to at the Tribunal; there was material for indictment against the witches' accomplices who were still at large in Zugarramurdi; and there was information which the Tribunal hoped would lead to the discovery of witches in other places in Navarra (see chapter 4.5, above).[6]

Valle and his company reached the monastery at Urdax at 6 o'clock on Wednesday evening, wearied after the day's journey over steep and stony roads across the Velate Pass and up through the Baztán Valley. There was a peal of church bells as they arrived. Fray León and his monks bade Valle a warm welcome and the reception would have done justice to a bishop. The following day, 20 August, Valle reported all this with satisfaction in his letter to the Tribunal. He interpreted such striking marks of respect as the expression of a positive attitude towards the Inquisition.

However, Valle's letter went on to say that the place was not really suitable for a visitation as it lay so close to the French border. He had therefore decided that the Edict of Faith was to be published only in the Baztán Valley, but even so some people would have to travel more than five *leguas* (about 15 miles) over mountains and valleys to reach him. Valle had been informed at the monastery that the commissioner to the Inquisition at Lesaca, who had been selected by the Tribunal as official Basque interpreter, was too old and not sufficiently alert, though he was otherwise an honest man and a zealous worker. He had therefore decided to send for the commissioner at Arano, the priest Juan de Monterola, to come and serve as interpreter. The letter concluded with Valle's first impression of the witch problem, which he must have formed from what the abbot, Fray León, had told him after his arrival:

> The whole district, both here in Navarra and on the French side of the border, is extremely alarmed about the witches. [On the way here] we could hear people shouting on the paths between their fields, and hear that they were shouting "Jorguinas, jorguinas! [Basque *sorgiñak*, witches]." In many places on the other side of the border witches have been discovered, and the authorities are prosecuting them very severely. They are burning one after the other and concluding the cases very quickly. But I am assured [by Fray León] that the judge, who is a president of the Parliament at Bordeaux [Jean d'Espaignet], is conducting the cases efficiently. The villages in which this wicked sect is to be found have themselves requested the investigation. The judge's commission runs for four months, as the whole area is infested with witches, especially the countryside from here to Bayonne, which is five leagues distant. But I believe the situation to be equally serious here in the mountains of Navarra, and I shall keep Your Grace [Inquisitor Becerra] informed on what develops.[7]

The Edict of Faith was read from the pulpits of the Baztán Valley on Sunday 23 August, and a week later the Anathema was pronounced upon those who had concealed what they knew.[8] Only five witches presented themselves, and three of those did not come forward until after the time limit for reporting had run out. The meager result confirmed only too well the inquisitors' supposition that the Devil had terrorized his underlings so much that they dared not speak.

The five who defied the Devil's prohibition were all from Zugarramurdi. There is no exact record of the five witches, but from contemporary lists and references we can infer the names of those in question (see table 2).[9] In addition Valle also examined María de Ximildegui, the French girl who had denounced the first witches at Zugarramurdi.[15]

Table 2. The Five Zugarramurdi Witches Who Reported Themselves
During Valle's Visitation of 1609

Name, age, status	Date of confession[11]	Relationship to other witches	Rdo
María de Lecumberri, 20, (alias María Chipía?), unmarried daughter of Juanes de Lecumberri, miller	25 Aug.	Daughter of Juana de Telechea[12] (auto de fe no. 10)	15
Juana de Telechea Garagarre, 17, unmarried	27 Aug.		16
María de Burga, 15, unmarried daughter of Juanes de Burga, carpenter (?)	31 Aug.	Daughter of María Pérez de Barrenechea (auto de fe no. 6)?[13]	17
María de Lecumberri, 12, unmarried daughter of Juanes de Lecumberri, miller (?)	5 Sept.	Daughter of Juana de Telechea (auto de fe no. 10)	18
María Pérez de Burga, 12, unmarried daughter of Juanes de Burga, carpenter(?)	9 Sept.	Daughter of María Pérez de Barrenechea (auto de fe no. 6)?[14]	19

We have only secondhand knowledge of what the five
witches confessed.[16] On 15 September 1609 Becerra and
Salazar wrote to *la Suprema* and forwarded two letters which
they had just received from their colleague. In addition to
Valle's letters (which unfortunately have not been preserved),
they had received a copy of the confessions of the five witches.
The two inquisitors observed that the statements of the new
witches agreed on almost every count with the confessions of
the imprisoned witches, but contained fewer details. An echo
of Valle's letter can be heard in the statement that in particular
the confessions of the four minors bore witness to the tight
hold the Devil was keeping over his young witches for fear
they would betray him. But the Devil had also discovered a
new stratagem: He took the young witches to the sabbath after
they had fallen asleep, so that afterwards they could "support
the theory that has arisen that the whole thing is something
that the witches are dreaming."

Nevertheless, a few new facts had emerged. It seems that on

every Midsummer Night the witches ransacked the church at Zugarramurdi and tore down the crosses and stamped on them, while the Devil waited outside. It also came to light that on the nights of festivals the Devil donned clerical vestments and celebrated communion at the witches' sabbath. When he raised the chalice all the witches uttered "certain meaningless words," which the five witches declared signified "Down with the goat, and up with the goat." The witches also said this when they were in church and the priest elevated the bread and wine for the congregation to worship.

The letter went on to relate how Valle, while examining these five witches, had succeeded in confirming some of the particular events described by the prisoners at the Tribunal. Twenty-year-old María Chipía (presumably identical with María de Lecumberri, senior) described in detail how the Devil and his witches attempted to carry off María de Jureteguía, and how they damaged the garden and ruined the water-mill when the abduction attempt failed. Her statement agreed with what María de Jureteguía herself confessed to the Tribunal, and all five recounted how the other witches, who did not go into the house, waited outside in the garden in the shape of pigs and mares. Valle was able to substantiate this last occurrence by an outside witness who declared that he saw the witches in the garden. This witness, the letter went on to say, was one of the eight men who made a declaration in connection with the inquisitorial report in January 1609. Valle also questioned the miller Martín de Amayur, who corroborated the assertion that the witches had accosted him in the road one night and played some of their tricks on him (see chapter 4.7, above).

Enclosed with the letter were copies of the outside witnesses' statements; Valle's two colleagues at the Tribunal considered these of such importance (unlike the witches' confessions) that they sent them on with the other material to *la Suprema*. In their letter Becerra and Salazar pointed out that the miller's account and that of the eyewitness who had seen the witches in the garden corresponded exactly with what the imprisoned witches had confessed.

By contrast, the two inquisitors went on, certain evidence that Valle had received concerning the monk Fray Pedro de Arburu at the Urdax monastery was not at all so clear-cut. Several of the other monks testified to Fray Pedro's presence at the monastery at times when the witches declared they had seen him at their sabbath. The inquisitors admitted in their letter to *la Suprema* that this was causing them some doubt; but as the result of the inquiries on all other points had been confirmed so explicitly, they were inclined to disbelieve the monk and account for his presence in the monastery with the explanation that "the Devil sometimes places a counterfeit body in the bed," or that now and again the monk had simply decided not to go to the witches sabbath. "If he remained in his bed every night," the argument of the inquisitors continued, "there would be far less agreement in the witches' evidence. However, all the *confitente* witches declare they have seen him in person in his monk's habit taking part in the *aquelarre*, and they also maintain they have seen him taking part in their other activities." The two inquisitors were hoping to obtain more detailed information regarding the counterfeit-body phenomenon, as this was one of the new manifestations which had emerged during this visitation. One of the witches at Zugarramurdi (presumably María de Lecumberri, senior) declared to Valle that "when she was about to go to the *aquelarre* she saw a ghostly body having her appearance place itself [in the bed] and remain there as long as she was away."[17]

After having received a new letter from Valle the inquisitors again wrote to *la Suprema* about the monk's alibi. Valle had requested that they interrogate all the witches at the Tribunal on whether they had seen such bodies acting as their substitutes. If the existence of counterfeit bodies could be established as a fact it would settle the questions still in doubt. (This seems to have been important not only in the case of the monk, but in the case of two other people referred to in Valle's letter as well; unfortunately we do not know the result of this questioning.) However, one more fact had emerged: it was not possible to rouse the monk when he was asleep, and this had strengthened the inquisitors in their suspicions that it was *not* his own body in the bed.

The second letter from the Tribunal to *la Suprema* went on to relate how Valle had also carried out investigations into the deaths and damages confessed to by the witches imprisoned at Logroño. He had questioned the people involved, and these witnesses confirmed that the deaths and injuries had in fact occurred because the witches had been at work with their poisons and had sucked blood (*chupado y ponzoñado*) from their victims. But the explanations as to exactly how the crimes were committed varied significantly, for they had always taken place while the witnesses were asleep.[18]

To judge from the Tribunal's letters, the investigations at Zugarramurdi had led to the results expected: the new witches described the rites of the sect exactly as the imprisoned witches had confessed them; the injured persons confirmed that the bewitchings had taken place, and other outside witnesses acknowledged having seen or met the witches on the occasions referred to by the witches themselves. On the other hand, Valle had found neither dressed toads, witch ointment, nor any of the other material evidence that *la Suprema* had so expressly enjoined him to search for. And it seems very likely that there had been few other outside witnesses besides the miller and the man who saw the witches in the garden (see chapter 4.7, above).

The considerable difficulty of the monk's alibi, which had caused the inquisitors almost insuperable difficulty at the outset, was overcome by the counterfeit-body theory, an interpretation which was subsequently validated by the evidence of some of the imprisoned witches.[19] It is also clear from other sources of reference that while Valle was away the interrogations continued at the Tribunal, and the witches were questioned about the new details that had been added. If we go so far as to assume that the Devil's Mass and the desecration of the church on Midsummer Night were first confessed to during the visitation, this means that these important details cropped up at a late stage of the imprisoned witches' confessions.[20]

It could be argued that since Valle interrogated the witches at both Logroño and Zugarramurdi this worked as a unifying factor. However, we must not jump to the conclusion that the confessions were merely a product of leading questions. These may well have been used with effect, but we cannot be certain to what extent, as the original records from the trial and from the visitation have not been preserved. However, in the six files which have come down to us from the last part of Valle's visitation at Zugarramurdi it appears, firstly, that Valle examined the witches in a reasonably objective fashion and on the whole accepted their answers; and secondly, that the witches possessed an amazing knowledge of witchcraft practices.[21]

I am inclined to believe that the agreement between the testimony given by the witnesses during the Zugarramurdi visitation and the evidence presented by the witches at the Tribunal can be explained in the following way: Similarities in the descriptions of the witches' rituals must derive from a background of witch-tales and notions about witchcraft which were common knowledge in the village long before the arrests. The same applies to the agreement between the eye-witnesses' accounts; this may also have resulted from the witnesses having talked to one another, before their arrest, about their nightly encounters with the witches. Finally, regarding the crimes, the witches at the Tribunal probably restricted themselves to the misfortunes which village rumors had ascribed to witchcraft. Those malefic acts which had not been accounted for in the witches' confessions during the preliminary inquiries may very well have been included by the inquisitors in their charges, which (as mentioned in chapter 4) were not published until long after Valle's visit to Zugarramurdi.

Indeed, the information that Valle managed to collect during his month-long stay at the monastery of Urdax did not amount to very much. From some page references to his missing visitation book it appears that the witches' confessions and all the other witnesses' statements together took up no more than 184 pages, for at the next session the record began at folio 93 in the visitation book.[22] Perhaps the positive attitude towards the Inquisition which Valle was rejoicing over did not extend very far outside the walls of the monastery. Only the five girls from Zugarramurdi had made confessions of witchcraft; the rest of the witnesses, whom Valle presumably summoned himself and interrogated as *contestes*, seem to have restricted themselves to confirming facts that the Inquisition was already familiar with.

The last thing Valle did before he left Urdax and Zugarramurdi was to make the arrests. Becerra and Salazar had sent him a list of twenty-two persons whom they had selected as suitable candidates. They charged him to arrest up to fourteen of these, ensuring that the monk Pedro de Arburu and the priest Juan de la Borda y Arburu were among them. These two, who were cousins, had been included in the list not only because there were many witnesses against them but also because the Tribunal was in great need of them. "Since they are priests," wrote the inquisitors in a letter to *la Suprema*, "it must be assumed that they can speak Castilian or at least Latin."

In order not to arouse attention the Tribunal instructed Valle to arrest the monk a few days in advance. As an added security — presumably so that his cousin, who was assistant priest at Fuenterrabía, should not be alerted — the arrest was to be camouflaged in the following way: Valle was to arrange with the abbot to have Fray Pedro sent off on some fictitious errand or other. He was to be accompanied by a friar and a boy, who would have instructions to lead him to Logroño. Once en route Fray Pedro would soon enough find out where they were going.[23]

On 26 September Becerra and Salazar wrote to the Council of the Inquisition with the information that they had now received the monk, the priest, and thirteen other prisoners from their colleague.[24] This was one more than the Tribunal had requested.

3. THE REST OF THE JOURNEY

The next session was held at Lesaca, where Valle stayed during the period 23 September to 14 October.[25] He then moved on to San Sebastián,[26] where he remained until 20 November. Finally he went to Tolosa to hold the last session of the visitation,[27] and here we find him still on 14 December 1609.[28] After Urdax and Zugarramurdi, where the mystery of the witch sect had been partially unraveled beforehand, the assignment had grown considerably more difficult. From the references to Valle's missing visitation book the yield may be seen to have been particularly meager at Lesaca, at least as regards volume, for only seventy-six pages were written (folios 93-131) during the twenty-two days of the stay.[29] In San Sebastián there was a considerable improvement and here almost three hundred pages were written (up to folio 278 in the visitation book).[30] In Tolosa some two hundred pages were added.[31] However, the greater part of the details that Valle recorded in San Sebastián and Tolosa were confessions made by witches from Lesaca, Vera, Yanci, and Echalar. It seemed that after the Inquisition had left their district the witches changed their minds and now started to follow Valle and seek him out at the succeeding sessions of the visitation. This, for instance, was the case with the six persons whose confessions are preserved in the transcripts from Valle's visitation book.[32]

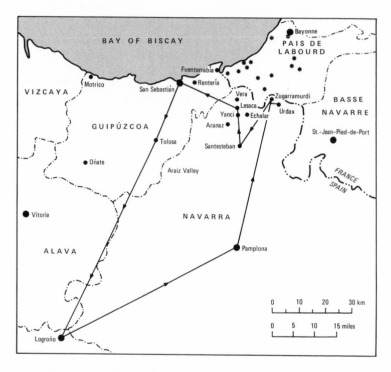

Map 2.   *The route taken by Valle during his journey of visitation in 1609 and the thirteen sites of* aquelarres *in Labourd discovered by de Lancre in the same year (see chapter 1 n. 110, below).*

In two long letters which Valle wrote home to the Tribunal from San Sebastián he described how he had fared since leaving Urdax and Zugarramurdi. In the first letter,[33] dated 13 November, Valle wrote that in all there were now fifteen child witches (including the four minors from Zugarramurdi) who had confessed and admitted to renouncing their Christian faith. He asked permission to reconcile these during the visitation as their parents were poor and could not afford to travel with their children to Logroño. Valle went on to say that he had exposed a confederacy of witches at Lesaca. Seven of the members, children whose ages ranged from twelve to fifteen, had come to him and made their confessions.

In the second letter,[34] written one week later (20 November), Valle stated that three more members of the *aquelarre* at Lesaca had reported themselves to him. Two were women aged respectively fifty-five and thirty-three. Since María Chipía at Zugarramurdi these were possibly the first adults to make confessions. Certainly the great majority were minors, and if we compare the list with the page references to Valle's visitation book our assumption that his witch-hunt had yielded comparatively little is confirmed.

However, Valle's two letters give the impression that he was quite satisfied and several times in them he gives spontaneous expression to his feelings. At one point he tells triumphantly how he himself has had the opportunity to examine some Devil's marks:

> It is a fact that the Devil sets his mark on them, for I have seen it with my own eyes on the Lesaca witches. The mark is a small one. On some it can barely be seen. When it is pricked with a needle they feel nothing even if pressure is exerted; and even if the needle pierces the skin and is pressed right in they feel nothing. The witch marks that I have seen are the size of a pinhead and form a small depression in the skin. It has really amazed me![35]

We hear no more about the concrete evidence which was to have been obtained. From Valle's letters we gather that things had taken a completely new turn which made it doubtful whether he would be able to allot much time to this task. Now it was vital not to waste time, as the Devil for his part was not wasting any. At Lesaca alone, said Valle, in the month that had passed since the Inquisition left the town, the Devil had gained no less than twelve children for his sect. Valle assured the

Tribunal that "for God's sake" they would have to arrest two
or three women in the village, "the greatest scoundrels under
the sun, limbs and accomplices of Satan. These women,"
continued Valle, "are constantly wheedling the children and
luring them with a particular type of apple which they give
them. And as soon as they have enticed the children to the
sabbath they get them to renounce their faith, even if they are
only nine or ten years old."[36] He said he had given orders that
the witches at Lesaca should be gently persuaded to report
themselves, and in addition to those who had already come to
him at San Sebastián he had been informed that several more
were to come to him during the visitation at Tolosa. "And I am
very happy about this," remarked Valle, "for the apostasy in
this place is very serious, and almost seventy persons are
suspected of being witches."[37]

Neither did the Devil seem to have been wasting his time at
Rentería, a town midway between San Sebastián and France.
Since Martinmas (12 November) "eight days ago," said Valle
in his letter of 20 November, one woman alone had enlisted
more than fifteen new witches. One was a twenty-year-old
French girl, the rest children aged from five to thirteen. They
had all since been to see Valle. The parents were distressed and
the town was in a turmoil. To save the woman from being
lynched the authorities at Rentería had put her in prison.
Afterwards they approached Valle in order to hand the prisoner over to him, and Valle gave them an evasive answer to
gain time to ask the Tribunal for advice. "But I rejoice that she
has been detained," he confided to his colleagues, "for otherwise she would certainly have fled to France, if for no other
reason than fear that they might kill her."[38] The woman was
eighty-year-old María de Zozaya.[39] According to a report dating from 1618, she was the witch discovered by a notary at
Rentería, Miguel de Michelena, who exposed her with the help
of evidence from the children and other information that had
come to light during a secular trial against Crazy Jane (*Juana la
Loca*), a witch from the neighboring town of Pasajes, who had
been arrested at San Sebastián but was later released by the
authorities.[40] In December 1609 María de Zozaya was transferred to Logroño with another witch from Rentería, twenty-six-
year-old Juanes de Lambert.[41]

However, the visitation had not been entirely without difficulty. Valle described in detail how he discovered in the

middle of it that the High Court of Navarra (*Consejo Real de Navarra*) was undermining his work. A notary from the Baztán Valley sent him a confidential report about this, the same notary who had assisted the Tribunal over the first examination of witnesses at Zugarramurdi (see chapter 4.1, above).

The case concerned "three or four" persons who had the reputation of being witches, as well as some others appearing on behalf of deceased relatives. These had all applied to the High Court at Pamplona where they had charged two girls with libel and slander. These two "decent girls," as Valle called them, had come to him at Lesaca and alleged that according to local opinion the persons mentioned were witches. The High Court had taken the case up for investigation and had sent a commissioner to examine witnesses and make arrests. "This caused much indignation and fear all over the district, especially among those who had been to me and given their evidence," wrote Valle and he went on to say that his first step was to protest to Dr. Ximenes de Oco, one of the High Court judges. In his letter Valle had sharply criticized them for opening a trial on the basis of what in his eyes was a completely unmotivated complaint. He had pointed out further that the Holy Office was thereby hindered in discharging its duty, since, as he wrote: "None will dare to come to the Inquisition in order to relieve his conscience and make statements if he is punished for it afterwards."[42]

When Valle wrote to his colleagues on 20 November he was able to enclose a friendly letter which he had just received from Dr. Oco,[43] who wrote that the High Court had decided to recall its commissioner and not to arrest or summon anyone; as long as the Inquisition was dealing with those cases the High Court would not accept any new complaints of defamation or of slander.[44] So the matter had turned out favorably for the Inquisition; and Valle held yet another trump card: "And the best thing is," he burst out just afterwards, "that I have discovered an *aquelarre* in these villages, which are in the neighborhood of Santesteban. It has been exposed by two witnesses aged fifteen and nineteen respectively, who are themselves members, and those they name as their accomplices have already been reported."[45] Whether these two witnesses were identical with the two "decent girls" we are unfortunately unable to determine from the records.[46]

The letters from San Sebastián not only gave a copious

report on the course of the journey to date, but also elaborated Valle's plans for the last part of the visitation, the session at Tolosa. Thus, from the letter of 13 November it appears that the Tribunal had sent him a copy of a witch trial from 1595, an action which had been taken by the Lord of Andueza against four witches in the Araiz Valley. In this connection Valle was able to tell his colleagues that on his way through Pamplona he chanced to hear that "thirteen or fourteen years ago" the High Court had arrested many people in this valley for witchcraft and that some had died in prison, while others were released. With the help of the information the Tribunal had sent him he hoped to succeed in exposing something in the Araiz Valley, which was only two *leguas* (ca. 6 miles) from Tolosa. In any case he would have the Edict of Faith published there, "and if it proves necessary," added the zealous Valle, "I will go to the valley myself and remain there as long as may be needed regardless of whether the time for the visitation is at an end."[47]

On 17 December, having been away for the obligatory four months plus one day,[48] Valle returned to the Tribunal at Logroño.[49] He did not after all seem to have felt any urge to visit the Araiz Valley and spend Christmas there.

4. THE FRENCH CONNECTION

During the course of 1609 Valle had established himself as the Tribunal's witch expert. The chief basis of this expertise had been the study of old witch trials, the interrogation of the prisoners at the Tribunal, and his experiences on the journey of visitation. In addition to these sources of knowledge he established a valuable contact with the French witch judges while he was at Urdax, and this gave him fresh insight into the hidden world of the witches.

Even before Valle had set out on his journey of visitation the Tribunal had begun to take notice of the French witch-hunt. On 19 July the commissioner in the coastal town of Motrico reported that the previous day two French agents had presented themselves with an indictment against a certain Catalina de Lesalde, who during the last six months had been living in this town. The two Frenchmen had requested the authorities to arrest her and hand her over to them so that they could take her back to "Semper," where she had been accused of witchcraft.[50] ("Semper" is unknown as a placename in Labourd. It is obviously a Spanish distortion of Saint Pée, where lay the castle of the Lower Court judge Jean d'Amou (see chapter 1.4), and where d'Espaignet and de Lancre had their headquarters for a considerable time.)

It seems extremely probable that the two French agents went on to San Sebastián, for five days later the Inquisition's commissioner there reported a similar case. His letter contained a remarkably well-informed introduction to the conditions prevailing in France, so even though it is not mentioned directly it is obvious that there had been an occurrence similar to that at Motrico:

> For many days there has been talk here of nothing else but the rumors reaching us from the Labourd Valley, which borders on this province. The rumors have it that great numbers of witches are being arrested and that so many have been discovered that the King of France has entrusted the prosecution of the witches to a president [d'Espaignet], and a judge [de Lancre], both from the Parliament at Bordeaux. These have already arrived [see chapter 1.4] and taken up residence in the valley where they have arrested a large number of witches and some French priests who also are accused of this crime.
>
> A widow from "Semper" in France was held in custody for examination regarding this witch affair. But it is said that, being a wealthy woman, she bribed the jailer and fled across the border to Spain. As far as we know, they need her in order to help with their inquiries, as they are certain that she was one of the ringleaders. She has moved about from place to place here in Spain before taking up residence in a small house which comes under the jurisdiction of this town, but which is in an isolated position completely by itself...[51]

(Here as in other instances the Spanish sources provide some interesting information about the events which preceded de Lancre's witch-hunt.)

The authorities in San Sebastián and Motrico had already arrested and examined the escaped French witches, but as doubts were raised as to whether the cases came under secular jurisdiction, the trial records were handed over to the above-mentioned commissioners of the Inquisition, who in turn forwarded the records together with the other documents for the Tribunal's consideration.[52] It appears from a letter to *la Suprema* from the inquisitors, dated 22 August, that the Tribunal returned the cases to the district commissioners with the comment that the Inquisition had not been informed that the women in question were witches, let alone that they had committed any crimes on Spanish territory. Therefore they would leave it to the secular authorities to decide what they would do with their prisoners. However, while reporting on these facts the inquisitors at the same time proposed to *la Suprema* that on principle the Inquisition should adopt a favorable attitude towards the extradition of French refugees, since the time might soon come when they would need the help of the French authorities in tracking down and returning Spanish witches who might be fleeing in the opposite direction.[53]

On 24 August another letter was delivered to the Tribunal, this time from a judge at Oñate. He had imprisoned and initiated proceedings against a certain Mariana de Yriart and one or two other French citizens who had fled from Ustaritz right down to the southwest corner of Guipúzcoa, and whom he had suspected of being witches. At the request of the Inquisition's commissioner in the town the judge had sent in the cases for the Tribunal's inspection.[54]

The next day, 25 August, Becerra and Salazar, now gravely worried over the situation, again wrote to *la Suprema*. It can be seen from these reports, says the letter, "that these witches, who have fled from France and invaded our realm, are numerous. We fear that wherever they may settle they will do great harm." Therefore the inquisitors were inclined to believe that the mass flight of the witches to Spain was a new technique invented by the Devil with the object of "infecting and corrupting this realm" with the witch sect. As a counter measure the two inquisitors had written to Valle at the monastery at Urdax urging him to make contact with the French witch judges and to obtain a list of all escaped witches, so that the Inquisition could track down those who had crossed the frontier. But, continued the letter to *la Suprema*, the district commissioners could not handle this task alone. In order to clear the area in an effective manner the Tribunal needed the support of the secular authorities. Therefore the inquisitors requested *la Suprema* to arrange for a royal ordinance to be issued to all municipal authorities warning them to be on the watch for any French subjects who might appear or who might already have settled in their town without a specific reason which would put them above suspicion.[55] We do not know whether such a royal ordinance was in fact issued. But in Pierre de Lancre's book about the witch-hunt in the Pays de Labourd there are more details of the mass flight of the witches to Spain and about the letter from the Spanish inquisitors:

> On our arrival they were fleeing in great numbers both by land and sea . . . and the crowd at the Spanish frontier grew larger by the hour. They professed to be traveling pilgrims on the way to Santiago [de Compostela] and Montserrat . . . But they put Navarra and Spain into such a state of alarm that the Spanish inquisitors, who had journeyed to the frontier, wrote asking us to send them the names, ages, and descriptions of the escaped witches, so that they could return them to us, which, they wrote, it would give them great pleasure to do. But we replied that it would be better for them to watch them carefully and prevent them from returning home, for they ought to take pity on us and save us from getting them back. They are an unnecessary commodity which does not need to be inventoried.[56]

Instead of the list of escaped witches, the French witch judges seem to have sent Valle a copy of the records of some of the witch trials that they had held. This is made apparent in a letter from the Tribunal to *la Suprema* dated 26 September 1609 which states that Valle had received two letters, one from d'Espaignet and the other from the Lord of Urtubie, along with "seven small trial records containing evidence of the things confessed to by the witches." The letters are stated to contain the judges' comments on the seven trials.[57] Unfortunately these interesting documents have not been kept. After having been examined by the Council of the Inquisition they were returned to the Tribunal on 10 October 1609 with an encouraging letter telling the inquisitors that it had now been decided that they were to be given a free hand to go ahead with all the witch cases that might occur, stipulating only that they should consult with *la Suprema* in the last instance.[58]

The witch-hunt in France must undoubtedly have enhanced the prestige of the Logroño Tribunal in Madrid. For theoretically speaking, it could be maintained that the French judges were in no doubt at all as to the existence of the witch sect; and practically speaking, it could be pointed out that there was imminent danger of the French witches fleeing to Spain in great numbers.

5. THE POSTPONEMENT OF
THE EDICT OF GRACE

A few days after Valle's return the Tribunal received a letter
from *La Suprema* which caused the inquisitors some surprise.
The inquisitor general had decided to publish an Edict of
Grace. This was the traditional answer of the Inquisition to
mass apostasy, but on account of the ancient doubt in cases of
witchcraft the inquisitor general had gone further than usual in
this case. In the Edict of Grace which the Tribunal was to issue
to the witch sect, all those who reported themselves within the
time limit set by the edict would be expressly promised exemption from confiscation of property and other penalties. Valle
was to be instructed to continue his visitation and await further
orders. The two inquisitors at the Tribunal and their colleague
on visitation were to cooperate in ensuring that the edict was
published in every region where they felt it to be necessary. *La
Suprema* wished to be informed of the effect the edict had had
after the time of grace had expired and of how many witches
had taken advantage of it.[59]

In their first reply to the Council, dated 2 January 1610, the
Tribunal confined itself to reporting that Valle had been unable
to comply with the order as he had already returned. The letter
bore the signatures of Becerra and Salazar only. The two inquisitors explained that their colleague had been relieved of
normal duties since he was working on the report of his visitation. However, from what he had told them they gathered that
he had had an extremely arduous journey through some of the
bleakest and most desolate areas of the Pyrenees. Also it had
been an expensive undertaking for the Tribunal. Owing to the
poverty of the people, Valle had been obliged to bear the cost
of subsistence for those who came long distances to testify. He
had even been forced to take some of the child witches along
with him on the journey, for after having made their confessions they were frightened that the adult witches would take
their revenge on them. (The rest of this letter is concerned with
some newly-arrived witches who had just been brought to the
Tribunal from Rentería, with an accompanying letter in which
the town begged for permission to be allowed to burn these
witches at Rentería, partly to set an example and partly to
compensate the parents of the bewitched children for the grief
they had been caused.[60])

It must have been a bitter blow to Valle to learn that the

inquisitor general — after all that had emerged during the visitation — was still in doubt and that he was even prepared to give free legal aid to all the Devil's assistants if they would only report themselves. That had certainly not been Valle's intention in November when he requested permission to reconcile the child witches on his visitation.[61] Thus it was doubtless on Valle's initiative that a new letter was sent off by the inquisitors on 9 January, requesting permission to hold up the publication of the Edict of Grace until after they had held the auto de fe and captured the leaders of the witches.[62]

La Suprema sent a reply on 25 January 1610 in which it was stated that the inquisitor general had accepted the suggestion of the Tribunal and at the same time was issuing the order for the visitation for the current year to be postponed until after the auto de fe.[63] The letter was received on 5 February and delighted the Tribunal: "We are absolutely convinced that everything contained in the letter has been guided and dictated by the Holy Ghost," wrote the inquisitors to the inquisitor general a few days later, when thanking him for his indulgence.[64]

6. THE WITCH-HUNT IN LAS CINCO VILLAS

Las Cinco Villas ("The Five Towns") was the common designation for the towns of Vera, Lesaca, Echalar, Yanci, and Aranaz in the Bertizaun Valley. Together they made up the northernmost jurisdiction of Navarra.[65] The witch-hunt which took place there in the autumn of 1609 was a direct result of Valle's stay at Lesaca. By the time he moved on to Guipúzcoa in the middle of October, he had, as we have learned, instructed the preachers to continue to preach against the witches in order to get them to report themselves, and we know that during the last part of the visitation, at the sessions at San Sebastián and Tolosa, Valle himself managed to reap the first fruits of his propaganda campaign.

We should not censure Valle too much for believing that the witch phenomenon was a reality. The six confessions which have been preserved in transcript from Valle's visitation book all give the impression of having been made without any sort of compulsion. These six witches (see table 3) came from Lesaca and Echalar and confessed to Valle at the sessions at San Sebastián and Tolosa. Their accounts of the rituals agree to an extraordinary extent, and apart from a few additional de-

Table 3. The Six Witches Who Confessed During Valle's Visitation
and Then Revoked Their Confessions Two Years Later

Rte	Name, age, status; domicile	Place and date of confession; folio reference to Valle's lost visitation book; folio no. of the transcript in Salazar's visitation book	Place and date of revocation; folio no. in Salazar's visitation book
17	María Martín de Legarra, 31, unmarried, servant to parish priest of Lesaca; Lesaca (born at Echalar)	San Sebastián, 17 Nov. 1609; fol. 220; ff. 108^r-117^v	Lesaca, 11 Aug. 1611; ff. 118^r-119^r
12	María de Gardel, 72, widow of charcoal burner; Lesaca	Tolosa, 11 Dec. 1609; fol. 332; ff. 70^r-72^v	Lesaca, 8 Aug. 1611; ff. 73^{r-v}
22	María de Dindur, 40, unmarried; Lesaca	Tolosa, 12 Dec. 1609; fol. 337; ff. 144^r-150^v	Lesaca, 13 Aug. 1611; ff. 151^r-152^v
23	Juanes de Picabea, 11, son of charcoal burner; Lesaca	Tolosa, 13 Dec. 1609; fol. 372; ff. 156^r-158^r	Lesaca, 14 Aug. 1611; ff. 159^r-160^r
24	Gracia de Lizárraga, 17, unmarried, daughter of charcoal burner; Lesaca	Tolosa, 13 Dec. 1609; fol. 375; ff. 164^r-165^v	Lesaca, 17 Aug. 1611; ff. 166^{r-v}
25	María de Yturría, 9, daughter of charcoal burner; Echalar	Tolosa, 14 Dec. 1609; fol. ?; ff. 170^r-172^v	Vera, 19 Aug. 1611; f. 173^r

NOTE: The dates are taken from *Volume "F"* of *Salazar's Visitation Book* (see case nos. 457, 452, 462-465 of the Witch List). The ages are as stated in 1609. The revocations were all made before Salazar, with the exception of *revocante* 24, whose statement was taken down by commissioner of the Inquisition Domingo de San Paul.

tails their descriptions correspond in the main to the Zugarramurdi confessions. On the other hand, none of them had
been guilty of bewitching human beings, animals, or crops.
The witch-hunt in Las Cinco Villas distinguished itself from
that at Zugarramurdi in that it was purely a heretic hunt. The

principal counts on which people were indicted were participation in witch assemblies, abjuration of the Christian faith, and attempts to acquire new members for the sect. On the other hand Valle could certainly be reproached for having forgotten his chief task en route — the procuring of tangible evidence — by turning his journey of visitation into a veritable campaign against the witch sect. But what Valle neglected to undertake, a scientific investigation of the grounds underlying the whole witch phenomenon, was soon launched from a very different quarter. Indeed, even before he returned to Logroño this appears to have been under way.

Las Cinco Villas fell within the jurisdiction of the bishop of Pamplona, the influential Antonio Venegas de Figueroa.[66] When he heard of the uproar over the witches he decided to take the matter into his own hands and make a personal visitation in order to discover what was afoot.[67] But he did not make directly for the areas infested by the witches. It was possibly in order to give the impression of a routine visitation that he began his journey by traveling around the eastern area of Guipúzcoa, which came within his diocese. From a letter sent later from the inquisitors to *la Suprema* it is clear that the bishop's action took the Tribunal entirely by surprise. When Valle left Lesaca and went on to San Sebastián and Tolosa, he discovered that the bishop of Pamplona and his train were also on a journey of visitation, runs the letter, and the surprise was not diminished when the bishop later continued his journey of visitation to Lesaca, Vera, and the other places so recently visited by Valle.[68]

Another bishop would certainly not have dared to poach on the preserves of the Inquisition so tactlessly, but Venegas seems to have had little to fear from the Tribunal. He had been an inquisitor himself, in Granada, and later a member of the Council of the Inquisition.[69] The bishop was still on visitation at Lesaca at the beginning of March 1610,[70] but he must have moved on shortly after that, for about 10 March he was holding a visitation in the Baztán Valley.[71]

On this journey Venegas was collecting an important part of the material which was to form the basis of his letters and report to the inquisitor general the following year (SD Texts 5, 7, and 8). The bishop's investigations led him to the conclusion that the witch craze was almost entirely based on deceit and self-delusion, and he gave expression to this view in a letter to the Tribunal, which he wrote as early as his stay at Lesaca.[72] The fact that his investigations of the infested area were carried out a few months after the outbreak of the persecutions provides us with a unique opportunity for observing how a witch-hunt was initiated.

Thus one of the chief aims of the bishop's investigations was to ascertain when talk of witches had first started in Las Cinco Villas. After interrogating various people the bishop was able to establish that there had been no mention of witches before the persecutions had commenced on the other side of the border. Many inhabitants of Las Cinco Villas had been over to France to witness the witch burnings and they had heard the sentences read out. On the basis of this knowledge and the many rumors which reached Las Cinco Villas from the Basques on the other side of the border, it was not long before the witch sect was a common topic of conversation. Thus ran Venegas's letter to the inquisitor general dated 4 March 1611 (SD Text 5).[73] In the report of 1 April the same year (SD Text 8) we find even stronger expression of his amazing assertion that the inhabitants did not know anything about the witch craze in advance:

> Although the same *licenciado* [Valle] Alvarado visited Las Cinco Villas and other places in person, it did not appear that he found therein a single person contaminated by this evil sect. Notwithstanding the large number of old people in these places not one knew what it was to be a witch nor anything which savored of this evil art, nor what an *aquelarre* signified.[74]

(*Excursus:* From the registers of the Inquisition we know that in 1524 or 1525 legal action was taken against a large number of witches from Vera and its neighborhood.[75] Was it really possible that all recollection of the witch sect had vanished in less than a century? Perhaps the explanation is that witchcraft had reverted to its traditional popular form. If popular witch beliefs in Las Cinco Villas had followed the general European pattern (see above, chapter 1.2), presumably people would have believed in witches as individual miscreants who operated by their own ability without the assistance of the Devil. There was such a world of difference between this and the Devil-worship that the Inquisition claimed to have exposed in 1609 that Venegas was within his rights in asserting that the witch sect had not previously been known in this area.)

Venegas's contention that nothing was revealed during

Valle's stay must surely reflect the general opinion prevailing in the place. However, the statement is not entirely correct, for during his visitation at Lesaca, Valle had already obtained the first witch confession from this area. It was made on 10 October 1609 by a fourteen-year-old boy, Diego de Marticorena, from Echalar.[76] As was customary, this confession took place in strictest secrecy, and it is therefore not so strange that the bishop had no knowledge of it.

There is no complete list in existence of those who reported themselves during Valle's visitation at Lesaca, so we are unable to determine whether the case of Diego de Marticorena was unique. But we know that all the other witches from Las Cinco Villas whose names are available to us made their confessions during the visitation sessions at San Sebastián or Tolosa. It was here that the witches' sabbath at Echalar was confirmed by yet another witness, the nine-year-old child witch María de Yturría, who exposed eleven accomplices;[77] and it was here that the existence of the witch coven at Lesaca, mentioned before, was corroborated by the admissions of thirteen witches, five adults, and eight children.[78] (Five of the confessions from Lesaca have been preserved and together they bear witness against ninety-four persons or one in every thirteen of the population of the town!)[79] Two very young child witches, who made their confessions during the visitation at Tolosa, asserted that a coven existed in Vera as well (see p. 137, below). A similar group at Yanci was exposed by an eight-year-old girl named Mari Juri who also confessed at Tolosa.[80] In the fifth town, Aranaz, strangely enough no witches were discovered until a year after Valle's visit (see below, chapter 10.3).

One of the Lesaca witches, the thirty-three-year-old María Martín de Legarra, gives us a glimpse in her confession of the propaganda campaign that Valle set in motion during his stay in the town. When the Inquisition was at Lesaca, she recounts, both in and outside the church there was already a great deal of preaching against this evil sect, and it was said that "the witches were going to Hell."[81]

Venegas's report gives us a clearer idea of how the priests at Lesaca and Vera complied with Valle's orders to continue his work of "gently" persuading the witches to report themselves. The bishop tells how after Valle had left, the priests began to thunder from their pulpits in earnest. If the people had not

known previously what an *aquelarre* was, they soon got to
know about it now, when the priests:

> gave sermons on the theme of the innumerable persons
> belonging to this evil sect in both towns. They claimed that
> they knew who they were and that they had lists of the
> names. They consequently urged these people to come
> forth since, however anxious they were to escape detection,
> their identities were already known. In their sermons they
> maintained that out of the entire population of the two
> villages more than three quarters were witches. This, they
> declared, was a fact and they would repeat it a thousand
> times. According to the same priests, many of those who
> had that very day confessed to them and received Holy
> Communion from their hands, belonged to the hateful sect.
> They added that they knew of the *aquelarres* in the said
> villages . . . and . . . preached from their pulpits exactly what
> the child witches of France had said both in regard to the
> witches' catechism and everything else related to the sect
> and its doctrine.[82]

The ringleader in this propaganda campaign was the rector
at Vera, the young *licenciado* Lorenzo de Hualde. He was a
Frenchman and originated from the Pays de Labourd, where
his parents were still living (see p. 137, below). He was a great
friend of the Lord of Urtubie, who was also the Lord of Alzate
and as such held the patronage of the living of Vera. He had
installed Hualde as parish priest some years previously in spite
of the protests of the town at being given a French priest.
"Because of this," the report of Venegas states, "the said rector
and the lord of Urtubie have always been and are bitter
enemies of most of the residents of the town of Vera." But the
extremely well-informed bishop was also able to reveal
Hualde's close involvement in the French witch-hunt and to
expose its most embarrassing origin, which has remained unknown to all historians up to the present:

> The Lord of Urtubie, A French nobleman whose manors lie
> in the kingdom of France two leagues from Las Cinco Villas,
> seized certain old women on his own authority and, holding
> them prisoners, extracted from one of them an account of all
> the witches in the village of Urrugne, where the said Lord of
> Urtubie resides. On the said account being submitted to the
> Parliament of Paris this body sent a judge to the village of
> Urrugne and the Pays de Labourd to investigate and to
> sentence those found belonging to the witches' sect. And

because those mentioned in the account — both religious and lay — were enemies and opponents of the Lord of Urtubie... and it seemed that the judge who was holding the said witch trials was condemning them without due process of law, the affair came to the notice of the Parliament which suspended the commission of the judge, giving orders that he was to return home and that the matter was to be left as it stood.

It happened that the first old woman from whom the account was taken and the others who later confirmed the same were condemned to death. In their last confession they declared the statements they had made to be false, explaining that they had made them at the promptings of the Lord of Urtubie. They added that they had implored the said judge and the Lord of Urtubie to tear up their statements and to consider their contents as false and invalid; for unless this was done their souls were damned on account of the false witness they had borne against the previously mentioned persons.

And as assistant and adviser to the Lord of Urtubie there happened to be involved in all these matters the *licenciado* Hualde, the rector of Vera... And at that time the said rector always accompanied the said judge and the Lord of Urtubie to all the above mentioned places.[83]

Thus we see how Hualde in 1609 had become a witch expert, like Valle; and from other sources we can infer that he served as a Basque interpreter as well, when he accompanied the Lord of Urtubie and the judge, Pierre de Lancre, throughout the summer campaign in the Pays de Labourd.[84] While Valle was staying in Las Cinco Villas Hualde assured him that the witch sect was active in this region as well, and promised to do his best to assist the Inquisition to expose it.[85] In return Valle had given Hualde hopes of getting him an inquisitorial commissionership, despite the fact that Hualde was French and that there was already a district commissioner at Lesaca.[86]

At Lesaca the preachers were the eighty-year-old priest and Inquisition commissioner Domingo de San Paul and his assistant priest Juan Martínez de San Paul. The latter had just been appointed by Valle as notary to the Inquisition, so he had a particular reason for exhibiting Christian zeal.[87] At Yanci the preacher was presumably the learned parish priest, Martín de Yrisarri, who to begin with gave the witch-hunt his whole hearted support.[88] Later he was to become one of its bitterest opponents. It is doubtful whether any preaching against the witches was carried on at all at Echalar, since both the parish priest (the *licenciado* Labayen) and two other priests in the town (the doctor Miguel de Oragaray and Tomás de Urrutía) were skeptical and soon began to undertake their own experiments, which will be discussed later. The attitude of the priests in the fifth town, Aranaz, is unknown, but, as we have already mentioned, this town was for the time being spared witch persecution.

Other methods were being used in addition to the exhortations from the pulpit. According to the bishop's report the priests at Lesaca were putting severe pressure on the child witches who would not confess. The children were confined night and day in certain rooms where they were attended by two women who subjected them to threats and promises.[89] I have not been able to confirm this information from other sources, but that Domingo de San Paul exerted pressure on people in order to get them to confess was revealed by his own maid servant, the María Martín de Legarra mentioned above. This happened two years later when she recanted the long confession she had made at San Sebastián on 17 November 1609 (in which she had not mentioned the fact that she was in the priest's employ). The recantation took place during the visitation of 1611. In her statement to Salazar the elderly servant explained how she, who had never been a witch, had come to make a false confession under pressure from her master, the old priest and inquisition commissioner:

> At that time [when the Inquisition was at Lesaca] there was a great deal of talk about the witchcraft which was thought to be rampant in the town and about the punishment that awaited the witches. The whole town was talking about the things that went on in this sect, and some adults as well as many of the children stated openly who the witches were and named names. It was thus that María Martín acquired her first knowledge of the witch organization. One day her master asked her if she were one of them and she ended up by confessing that she was. Thus, on the basis of what she had learned from street gossip she made a confession to the priest, and when he pressed her further she agreed to repeat her confession before the Holy Office. [This she did] to the *licenciado* Juan de Valle Alvarado when he was holding the visitation at San Sebastián.[90]

The confession at San Sebastián did not rely only on street

gossip. The priest had been preparing her for a considerable time and "was constantly instructing her" in what she was to say to the inquisitor.[91]

When reading María Martín's confession to Valle one cannot help wondering which is the false statement: the confession in 1609 or the recantation in 1611. Her description of the rites of the witch sect is not only astonishingly full in detail but is also so realistic that the whole story bears the stamp of something that had really been experienced. On the other hand her list of accomplices is far less convincing, embracing as it did no less than sixty-one persons (seventeen men, thirty-seven women and seven children). All were from Lesaca except one. This was a twenty-five-year-old widow, the beautiful and wealthy María de Endara, who owned an ironworks in the town of Echalar and was a local aristocrat. She was, however, a native of Lesaca.[92]

Bishop Venegas tells how at Vera Hualde summoned a large number of children and adults from all quarters of the town. He worked on them for more than forty days to make them confess and for the whole of this time he allowed no one to leave the rectory, apart from some very old people who were permitted to go home.[93] The result of this method was that Hualde was able to write to Valle on 11 January 1610 that at long last he had succeeded in exposing the witch sect at Vera.

> It caused me great pain and sorrow that matters did not progress in the way that I had hoped with regard to the assignment with which Your Eminence had charged me. ["Your Eminence" refers to Valle, who should in fact have been addressed as "Your Grace."] My addresses from the pulpit bore not fruit. Perhaps this is the reason for Our Lord having now graciously revealed the evil and heretical witch society [la maldad y heregía de la brujería] in this town, whose existence I have suspected the whole time, as I told Your Highness when we were speaking together. I have been exerting every effort to clarify the matter. You will see from the enclosed evidence how hard I have been working, and how much light has been shed on things by children of six, seven, eight, nine, ten, eleven, and twelve years old — and the Frenchwoman in particular.[94]

In his letter Hualde urgently requested the Tribunal to arrest a number of women his investigations had shown to be the ones who took the children to the nightly sabbaths. The women were Mari Juan de Aguirre (alias Mari Juanto, no. 7 at the auto de fe), "the French woman" Beltrana de la Fargua (no. 16 at the auto de fe), and three other women. These witches were to be removed from the town with all speed as the people were threatening to lynch them and "four days ago" would have cut their throats if Hualde had not intervened.[95]

Hualde recounted that his rectory was filled with children sent to him by their parents in the hope that he could provide a remedy. From the context, it appears clearly that these were the very same children whom the witches took to the sabbath and forced to swear allegiance to the Devil. Hualde had not ventured to absolve these child witches on his own responsibility, but he was doing what he could to prevent the witches from taking them to the sabbath at night. His "remedy" was a Christian invocation in Latin:

> Jesus † Nazarenus † Rex † Judeorum †
> Verbum caro factum est.
> Jesus, Maria, Joseph.

This invocation (which was presumably written on a piece of paper) was placed in the children's bedroom with some blessed bread, blessed herbs, candles, a bottle of holy water, and a crucifix or a picture of Our Lady. Besides this Hualde impressed on the children that they must bless themselves when they went to bed and upon arising. The blessing consisted of their crossing themselves three times over the heart while repeating the words: "Jesus propitius esto mihi peccatori." "When the children have made their confessions and started using these remedies they say that they are not taken to the *aquelarre* any more," stated Hualde, at the same time requesting the Tribunal to approve his remedies. He asked permission to send the children home to their parents for he could not go on having thirty or forty children filling his rectory.[96]

This last remark in no way signified that Hualde was growing tired of his witch-hunt. On the contrary! It was merely that he needed the Tribunal's sanction before taking further steps — and we can read between the lines that Hualde was extremely anxious to proceed, even though he was obviously restraining himself in order not to seem too eager. Thus Hualde mentioned that if he were to receive orders from the Tribunal to undertake more radical investigations and to imprison the French woman, he would then confront her and the children with some of the suspected adult witches who were in doubt whether to go to confession. But until he received such orders he dared not continue.[97] He immediately concluded that the problem could not possibly be solved by the two agents of the Inquisition already assigned to the region:

> Although the good old priest at Lesaca is doing his best to tackle the task, he is in fact past it; and this is no work for the old and weary. His notary, Fray Juan [Martínez de San Paul] has his hands full at Lesaca, and they have therefore asked for the witches from Vera to come to them. But the children would rather confess to me, for I fetch them from school and take them home with me, where I can ask them my questions when I have them to myself. If they were to go to Lesaca they would be more afraid of the authorities. But for my part I always preach to them that if they confess what they have done I will help them to obtain forgiveness from the Holy Office.[98]

Once we have obtained a clear picture of Hualde's interrogation technique it is very easy to understand his hesitation over sending the witches to Lesaca. For Hualde stated that he himself wrote down the confessions of these child witches while he was examining the children in the privacy of his rectory. When he had finished examining a child he called in witnesses, read out the confession in their presence and the child's, and afterwards had the witnesses put their signatures to the document to attest that the child declared it to be the whole truth.[99]

Hualde's long letter closed with an extraordinarily vivid description of the situation at Vera on 12 January 1610:

> I wrote all the above last night after having put the children to bed and taking the usual precautions. Now this morning when I questioned them, they tell me that the witches have taken them to the sabbath again, and all the children have confirmed this. From eleven o'clock last night onwards the witches have been at work in this house and the neighboring one. It sounded almost as if they were taking tiles off the roof. One moment they uttered their fearful howls, the next they burst into roars of ribald laughter. The whole neighborhood was stricken with terror, but I myself heard nothing; so I think that they [the witches] must have given me some herb or other [*me echaron alguna hierba*] to ensure that I did not wake.

When the children told how they had been taken [to the sabbath] and been whipped because they had betrayed the witches, the town was in turmoil. And if it had not been for those who dissuaded them they would undoubtedly have murdered the old women who take the children [to the sabbath]. I therefore once again would beg Your Highness and the Holy Office to intervene without delay and take action before it is too late to prevent further attacks [on the suspected women].

The men and women under suspicion [of being witches] are possessed with the greatest impudence and audacity. They are not ashamed to let either ecclesiastical or secular [persons in authority] hear their villainous talk. They declare without flinching that there are no witches, but that I fabricate them in my house; that everything I say in church is a lie and a fable and that I am not to be believed; that I get people to affirm things that do not exist at all by means of promises and threats; and they go on with a thousand shameless imputations . . . But I have resolved to say nothing . . . before the Tribunal gives me authority and further orders. The residents grow more furious daily, nay hourly.

For my part I can only offer to do everything in my power to help [the Inquisition] as I have done hitherto, with the greatest diligence and care. And Your Eminence must not think that I am doing it in order to become an Inquisition commissioner. Even if I should never attain to this eminence I shall devote myself to this work with the greatest happiness, simply to serve God and the Holy Office . . .[100]

On the same day the matter was taken up by the town council of Vera for the first time. For a long time the council had expressed doubts over Hualde's witch-hunt, but after hearing about the children's confessions they seem at last to have given him their support. At all events, during this meeting the town council wrote a letter to the Tribunal, in which it was suggested that authority should be given to Hualde and other "ecclesiastical and secular persons" in the town to enable them to arrest the guilty persons. The council declared that to date over twenty children together with a number of adults had publicly confessed to being witches. "To avoid too many signatures," the letter concluded, "the letter bears only the town seal and signatures of two members who sign on behalf of the remainder."[101] Perhaps the truth was rather that no other members of the Vera town council wished to put their names to this application.

The letters were received at Logroño on 16 January and were sent on to Madrid the same day with a covering letter from the inquisitors, in which they wrote:

> We are firmly resolved to put a stop to the Devil's audacious designs with all our might, but we are greatly hampered by the fact that our actions can necessarily only be carried out under the regulations of the Inquisition. Since the Devil knows the rules he is doing everything he can to hinder us; first and foremost by ensuring that the witnesses' statements [which come into the hands of the Tribunal] are so incomplete that they do not meet with the requirements of the Inquisition.[102]

The existence of the *aquelarre* at Vera had already been supported by two witnesses from Valle's visitation, the inquisitors continued, but they admitted that the statements of these witnesses suffered from the same defects as those received from Hualde's child witches, for in both cases these had been very young children. The letter concluded with a request to *la Suprema* to waive the regulation that no person of foreign origin was eligible to hold office. Hualde's parents were foreigners, but they had both been born in the Pays de Labourd, where the people were also good Catholics. Moreover, the Tribunal was greatly in need of an Inquisition commissioner at Vera, and Hualde was "better fitted than any other man on account of his uprightness and learning."[103]

We have no further particulars of how the witch-hunt began in the third town, Echalar, but from what we know about the two child witches from this town (see above, in this section) we may allow ourselves to infer that as early as Valle's stay at Lesaca, Echalar had been infected by the dream epidemic. Fourteen-year-old Diego de Marticorena, who confessed on 10 October 1609 at Lesaca, reported himself two weeks after the publication of the Edict of Faith in this region.[104] His trial record has not been kept, but that of nine-year-old María de Yturría has. She made her confession on 14 December at Tolosa and from it we get the first impression of what the children had been experiencing in their dreams. María de Yturría was a charcoal-burner's daughter from Echalar. She told Valle that her father had wished to present her during the visitation at Lesaca (that is, earlier than 14 October, when Valle recommenced his journey); but the night before she was to have made her statement, the Devil frightened her, and they had to return home with their mission unaccomplished.[105]

The nine-year-old girl began her confession by recounting how she had been made a witch by Catalina de Topalda, a girl who was a *serora* (a kind of church servant or female "sacristan") at Echalar. One day early in September, "about the time of Lady Day," María met Catalina de Topalda, who told her she would take her somewhere where she would enjoy herself very much. That same night the "sacristan" came to her bed, which she shared with her grandmother. In spite of the fact that she was asleep, she was aware that Catalina de Topalda lifted her from her bed and took her out of the window, and then carried her at great speed through the air to a field that she did not know. She awoke as they arrived and noticed Catalina de Topalda standing beside her fully dressed. The confession went on to describe the Devil as a black he-goat with the face of a man. He was sitting on a gilt chair with the witches dancing around him. The "sacristan" led her to the place where the child witches were and handed her a small stick so that she could help to look after "the clothed toads." After amusing themselves for some time the witches disappeared with the he-goat. The "sacristan" again bore María with great speed through the air and took her home to her grandmother. She fell asleep the moment she got into bed and slept until broad daylight. When next day she told her father what had happened he was astonished and could scarcely believe her. But the "sacristan" went on taking María to the *aquelarre*. In all she took her there nine times. On the sixth night the "sacristan" forced María to renounce her faith and worship the Devil. Afterwards the Devil marked her left shoulder with his claw. When María told this to her father next morning "he grew anxious about her" and took her to church so that the priest could read some words of exorcism over her (*para que le dijesen los evangelios*). But the "sacristan" went on coming for her at night and the child went on complaining. Finally the father decided to take her to the inquisitor who was on visitation at Lesaca. They went over there "on a Wednesday afternoon" and spent the night with a relative. But that night the "sacristan" again took María to the *aquelarre*. (Here as well the times of meeting were Monday, Wednesday, and Friday.) She was brought before the Devil, who gave her strict orders to keep silent, and to make her realize he was in earnest he threatened to drown her in a huge and terrible ocean which he showed to her.[106]

It is hard to decide whether the little girl really believed all this had actually happened or was merely terrified by her strange dreams. Be that as it may, two years later, on Salazar's visitation, she recanted her confession and declared that her father and other persons had forced her to say she was a witch.[107] But if one believes, as Valle did, that the Devil took the young witches to the sabbath while they were asleep, so that they could later on support the "dream theory," it was of little importance what the child witches themselves believed. The judgment of the social environment was the deciding factor. In 1609 there was alarm in Spain over the French witches and an urgent need was felt to forestall the Devil on the Spanish side of the frontier. So it was not possible for people to accept the children's accounts (which for us are symptomatic of the extent of this mass-psychosis)[108] merely as dream-experiences. When Salazar came to Las Cinco Villas on his journey of visitation two years later the witch craze had passed its peak and the chief cause for anxiety was now the vast number of people (about a thousand from Las Cinco Villas alone) who had meantime been stigmatized by the hundred or so witches who had by now made their confessions to the Inquisition. Therefore many people were now eager for the witches to recant their confessions and clear their neighbors of suspicion.[109]

During the bishop's stay at Las Cinco Villas there had already been murmurs of skepticism. At Echalar there were several open discussions during which the priests Labayen and Oragaray, supported by the visitor, Dr. Zalba, and others of the bishop's company, claimed that it was completely ridiculous to believe in all this witch nonsense (*era cosa de risa la materia de brujos*). The inquisitors later narrated these episodes to *la Suprema* with deep regret:

> They started to stir up discussion and put forward foolish contentions that witches could not possibly exist and that the whole thing was nothing but fabrication and calumny. They even carried on some of these discussions when the bishop was present and for all to hear, without having the slightest regard to the harmful effect it might have. The commissioners told us that this had had a serious effect in slowing people from coming forward with the confessions

and statements of evidence they were collecting, and they said that the priests in question had even grown so bold as to openly declare the whole thing to be lies, and to begin to threaten the witnesses [i.e. the witch *confitentes*]. We therefore gave orders [to the commissioners] to make a report on this [i.e. to collect evidence against Labayen and Oragaray].[110]

In the same letter the inquisitors recounted with great disgust how the three priests at Echalar had repeatedly brought two "attractive young witches" to their rectory in order to watch over them. After spending the whole night talking to the women, next day the priests questioned the child witches closely on whether they had seen them at the *aquelarre*, and the children said that they had.[111] The two young witches were the serora or "sacristan" Catalina de Topalda and the rich widow María de Endara, who had both come under suspicion during Valle's visitation, and who were both arrested at the beginning of March 1610.[112] Later in the summer María de Endara was discovered to be pregnant, and when she declared Labayen to be the father, the inquisitors were not slow to put the priests' "experiment" down as nothing more than a pretext for playing fast and loose with the charming young witches.[113]

We cannot say exactly when the children in the fourth town, Yanci, were infected by the dream epidemic. The confession of the eight-year-old Mari Juri at Tolosa, in the autumn of 1609, is the earliest indication of witchcraft in Yanci, but unfortunately her confession is known only through a brief reference (see note 80 to this chapter). However, the witch-hunt does not seem to have been in full swing before the beginning of 1610. But here less severe action was taken than in the other towns. After a whole year of persecution, only ten witch confessions had been obtained.[114] (When Salazar was on visitation at Las Cinco Villas in 1611 three of the Yanci witches revoked the confessions they had made to the elderly Inquisition commissioner at Lesaca on 3, 20, and 23 February 1610. The three witches were girls aged twelve, thirteen, and fifteen. Their records have been preserved and show most clearly that the witch persecution in Las Cinco Villas was purely and simply a heretic hunt. The list of accomplices takes up almost twice as much space as the other details they confess.[115] These young witches had respectively accused 40, 52, and 29 persons, of whom the great majority were children. However before

Salazar the three girls declared that the motive for their false confessions had been fear caused by threats from their parents and relatives, who had insisted that they confess, since the other child witches in the town claimed to have seen them at the *aquelarre*. For example, thirteen-year-old Juana Fernández de Arbiza told Salazar how her father came home drunk several times and dragged her out to a field, where he beat her and told her the Inquisition would burn her alive if she did not confess.)[116]

At the beginning of February 1610 the local authorities of Vera, Lesaca, Echalar, and Yanci (but significantly not of the fifth town, Aranaz) resolved to make application to the Inquisition to take action against the witch plague. On 5 February a messenger conveyed the letters from the four town councils to the Tribunal at Logroño. A few days previously the Tribunal had received a similar application from Rentería.[117]

In a letter dated 13 February the inquisitors informed *la Suprema* of the situation and reported that they had decided to arrest sixteen of the most notorious witches. The Tribunal hoped by doing this to stem the Devil's advance and at the same time satisfy the towns so that they could more patiently await the solution to the witch problem that the Tribunal was formulating.[118] On 3 March the sixteen prisoners were received at Logroño. Six of them came from Vera and the others were taken from Lesaca, Echalar, Yanci, and Rentería.[119]

Later in the summer Valle forwarded a report of his journey of visitation to the Council of the Inquisition. Unfortunately I have been unable to trace this report, but an accompanying letter from the inquisitors reveals that it contained evidence against 280 witches and in addition a large number of children, not included by Valle in the calculations since they had taken part in the witches' sabbaths without forswearing their faith. The inquisitors admitted that there was only slender proof against many of the suspects, though in many cases it was being strengthened by evidence from the fresh witch confessions which were constantly coming in from the commissioners in the area.[120]

On his journey of visitation Valle had designated a considerable number of new agents to fill the gaps in the Tribunal's intelligence system. For instance, besides the priests at Vera and Lesaca, he had appointed the abbot of Urdax, Fray León de Araníbar, to the post of Inquisition commissioner for the

Baztán Valley. He was to play a prominent part in the fierce witch persecution which broke out in the autumn of 1610, when the pattern of "the little witch-hunt" in Las Cinco Villas was repeated on a grimmer and larger scale. But for the time being the witch-hunt had quieted down. The imprisonment of the sixteen witches had had its effect; the Tribunal was fully occupied with all the cases to be completed for the auto de fe; and perhaps the fact that Hualde had finally been appointed an Inquisition commissioner[121] also had something to do with it.

CHAPTER EIGHT
The Trial (Second Part)

1. THE NEW PRISONERS

HE ONLY INFORMATION WE POSSESS about the fifteen witches whom Valle sent to the Tribunal in September 1609 (see chapter 7.2, above), is that there were six men and nine women, and that the monk Fray Pedro de Arburu and the priest Juan de la Borda y Arburu were included in this group.[1] Apart from the priest, who was from Fuenterrabía, all the prisoners came from Urdax and Zugarramurdi. However, if we combine these facts with the report of the auto de fe (SD Text 2) and the food accounts of the prisoners (in which the food seems to have been calculated at one *real* per day, although sometimes other expenses were added), it is possible to reconstruct the list of fifteen prisoners (see table 4, third group).

In November the Tribunal received one more witch from Zugarramurdi, an old charcoal-burner who had fled to Guipúzcoa, where Valle had captured him (see table 4, fourth group).[2] In December María de Zozaya and Juanes de Lambert, who had been imprisoned by the authorities at Rentería, were transferred to Logroño (table 4, fifth group).[3] The secret prison had been full for some time and new prison cells were being installed in the "house of penance."[4]

The sixteen witches who had been arrested in Las Cinco Villas and Rentería were imprisoned by the Tribunal about 3 March.[5] As will be recalled they were arrested to satisfy the local authorities and they were the last to be detained before the auto de fe. The twelve women were put in the "house of penance," but the monks at the Dominican monastery were requested to take charge of the four men.[6] Two of the women, Mari Juanto (alias de Aguirre) and Beltrana de la Fargua from Vera, and one of the men, a forty-year-old smith from Echalar, were at the auto de fe (table 4, sixth group). The others had to wait for almost nine months for their cases to be dealt with.[7] Counting the ten trials from the previous year (table 4, first and second groups), the Tribunal now had thirty-one witch cases to complete. In addition there were twenty-three other heresy cases to prepare for the auto de fe.[8] It was simply not feasible for the inquisitors to contend with any more.[9]

We are told that seventeen of the new prisoners (auto de fe nos. 7, 8, 13-15, and 20-31) were arrested on the basis of the commissioners' report of January 1609.[10] If this information is reliable it implies that they were already under suspicion at that time (see table 1) and that perhaps some of them had even made a public confession in the Zugarramurdi church. In chapter 2 we pointed out that María Chipía de Barrenechea was a member of the large "witch-family" at Zugarramurdi (see diagram 1); this was probably also the case with María de Echalecu[11] and with Juanes de Odia.[12] None of the other new prisoners would seem to have belonged to the Barrenechea family, but several of them were mutually related. If we combine the facts contained in the sources it is possible to tabulate three more "witch families" at Zugarramurdi.

It is obvious that the priest at Fuenterrabía was implicated because he belonged to the Arburu family. He was the son of María Bastán de la Borda and first cousin of the monk at Urdax on his father's side.[13] It is therefore possible that his father was also regarded as a witch and that the suspicion had spread to include his mother as well (see diagram 2). The widow of Martín de Borda, Graciana Xarra,[14] may possibly have belonged to this family as well; but we can only speculate on these relationships, for in fact the sources throw no light on them.

The sole basis of our reconstruction of the Arburu family is the statements of the other witches, since throughout the trial the priest, the monk and their mothers — the two sisters-in-law — all maintained stoutly that they were *not* witches.

In the case of the other two witch-families we possess the members' own admissions of witchcraft. Juanes de Echegui, who died during the course of the trial, certainly denied being

Table 4. The Thirty-One Witches Whose Trials Ended Before the Auto de Fe

Group	Name, age, home; spouse, occupation	Auto de fe no.	Attitude during trial	Food charges (reales)	Imprisonment	Death in prison
1.	Estevania de Navarcorena, "over 80," Zugarramurdi; widow of Petri de Telechea, farmer	5	Con	180	27 Jan. 1609	Aug. 1609
1.	María Pérez de Barrenechea, 70 (or 46), Zugarramurdi; married to Juanes de Burga, carpenter	6	Con	445	''	Autumn 1609
1.	Juana de Telechea, 38, Zugarramurdi; married to Juanes de Lecumberri, miller	10	Con	826	''	
1.	María de Jureteguía, 22, Zugarramurdi; married to Esteve de Navarcorena, farmer	9	Con	900	''	
2.	Graciana de Barrenechea, 80 (or 90), Zugarramurdi; married to Juanes de Yriarte, shepherd	1	Con	224	14 Feb. 1609	Sept. 1609
2.	María de Yriarte, 40, Zugarramurdi; unmarried	4	Con	526	''	Aug. 1610
2.	Estevanía de Yriarte, 36, Zugarramurdi; married to Juanes de Goiburu (auto de fe no. 11)	3	Con	326	''	Sept. 1609
2.	Miguel de Goiburu, 66, Zugarramurdi; shepherd, married	2	Con	294	''	Autumn 1609

Table 4, continued

Group	Name, age, home; spouse, occupation	Auto de fe no.	Attitude during trial	Food charges (reales)	Imprisonment	Death in prison
2.	Juanes de Goiburu, 37, Zugarramurdi; shepherd, married to Estevania de Yriarte	11	Con	1,083	14 Feb. 1609	
2.	Juanes de Sansín, 20, Zugarramurdi; sieve-maker, unmarried	12	Con	1,098	,,	
3.	Maria Presona, "over 70," Zugarramurdi; unmarried	13	Con	453	Sept. 1609	
3.	Maria de Arburu, 70, Zugarramurdi; widow of Juanes de Martinena, miller	24	Neg	457	,,	
3.	Maria Bastán de la Borda, 68, Zugarramurdi; widow of Martín de Arburu	25	Neg	550	,,	
3.	Graciana Xarra, 66, hospitalera at the inn at Urdax; widow of Martín de Borda, shepherd	27	Neg	461	,,	
3.	Maria de Echachute, 54, Zugarramurdi; married to Juanes Francés of Saint-Jean-de-Luz	26	Neg	434	,,	

3.	María Chipía de Barrenechea, 52, Zugarramurdi; married to Sabat de Celayeta, carpenter	14	Con	472	,,	Aug. 1610
3.	María de Echegui, 40, Zugarramurdi; married to Martín de Machingorena, farmer	15	Con	448	,,	Aug. 1610
3.	María de Echalecu, 40, Zugarramurdi; widow of Pedro Sáenz, carpenter	21	Neg	363	,,	Aug. 1610
3.	Estevanía de Petrisancena, 37, Urdax; married to Juanes de Azpilcueta, farmer	23	Neg	448	Sept. 1609	Autumn 1609
3.	Martín Vizcar, "over 80," Zugarramurdi; farmer, married	8	Con	408	,,	
3.	Juanes de Echegui, 68, Zugarramurdi; farmer and shepherd, father of María de Echegui (auto de fe no. 15)	20	Neg	120	,,	
3.	Domingo de Subildegui, 50, Zugarramurdi; charcoal burner, born in Pays de Labourd	29	Neg	582	,,	
3.	Fray Pedro de Arburu, 43, Urdax; Premonstratensian monk	30	Neg	537	,,	
3.	Petri de Juangorena, 36, Zugarramurdi; farmer	28	Neg	560	,,	
3.	Don Juan de la Borda y Arburu, 34, Fuenterrabía; assistant priest, born at Zugarramurdi	31	Neg	662	,,	

Table 4, continued

Group	Name, age, home; spouse, occupation	Auto de fe no.	Attitude during trial	Food charges (reales)	Imprisonment	Death in prison
4.	Juanes de Odia y Berechea, 60, Zugarramurdi; charcoal burner and sieve maker	22	Neg	308	Nov. 1609	Aug. 1610
5.	María de Zozaya y Arramendi, 80, Rentería; servant (?), born at Oyeregui	19	Con	279	Dec. 1609	Aug. 1610
5.	Juanes de Lambert, 27, Rentería; born in Pays de Labourd, where father was burnt as a witch	17	Con	334	Dec. 1609	
6.	Mari Juanto (alias de Aguirre), 60, Vera; born at Zugarramurdi, widow of Juanes de Zapaguindegui, day-laborer	7	Con	197	3 Mar. 1610	Aug. 1610
6.	Beltrana de la Fargua, 40, Vera; born at "Ayamau" in France, married to Martín de Huarteburu, beggar	16	Con	263	''	
6.	Juanes de Yribarren (alias de Echalar), 40, Echalar; smith	18	Con	257	''	

NOTE: *Neg = negativo(a); Con = confitente.* For death in prison, see chapter 8.2 with nn. 22, 23, 24, and 28.

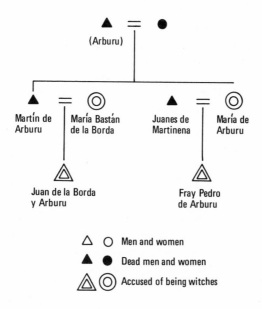

Diagram 2. *The Arburu family in 1609.*

a witch to the last.[15] But his daughter, María de Echegui, went to confession and gave evidence against her father. She herself declared she had initiated her own daughter.[16]

María Presona of Zugarramurdi[17] and Mari Juanto of Vera[18] were sisters. They both confessed to being witches and gave evidence against each other (see below, chapter 8.3). We do not know whom they exposed as their tutors, but María Presona admitted to having made her illegitimate daughter and two grandchildren witches.[19]

These "witch dynasties" had no more real existence than did that of the Barrenechea family. However, the information contained in the second part of the trial serves to confirm our impression that people *believed* that witchcraft was handed down within certain families.[20]

2. THE TWO PRISON EPIDEMICS

When the date of the auto de fe came round in the autumn of 1610, two epidemics had drastically thinned out the witches in the overcrowded prisons. The first epidemic began during the hot August of 1609 and by the time Christmas was drawing near six of the twenty-six witches, who up to then had been imprisoned, had died. The second epidemic began in August 1610. It carried off another seven witches.

The six who died in 1609 were all members of the first and second groups of prisoners, with the exception of Juanes de Echegui, who had arrived in September. Old Estevanía de Navarcorena was the first victim of the epidemic. Becerra and Salazar reported her death to *la Suprema* on 22 August. In their letter the inquisitors explained that the "ninety-year-old" woman was so stone-deaf that they had been unable to reconcile her, let alone "ratify" her evidence.[21] In order that the old woman might die a Christian the two inquisitors had released her from her state of excommunication (which she had incurred automatically on being charged with heresy), and they saw to it that she made her confession and received Holy Communion. The letter stated further that the other nine witches were all ill. As these were the chief witnesses against the remaining witches at Zugarramurdi, the two inquisitors had begun the work of "ratifying" their evidence *ad perpetuam* to ensure that it could be used for accusations even if the witnesses were to die in the meantime.[22]

A month later the two inquisitors wrote that the "queen of

the witches," old Graciana de Barrenechea, and one of her daughters, Estevanía de Yriarte, had now died as well. Becerra had been able to release the latter from excommunication and reconcile her, but when he came to ratify her evidence she suddenly became delirious. The two inquisitors were of the opinion that there was something suspicious about the whole affair, for when Becerra arrived at "the house of penance" he found her fever had almost abated, although she was very weak. While he was releasing her from excommunication and reconciling her she was completely lucid, the letter relates, but afterwards, when she was asked "whether she recalled giving evidence against anyone to the Holy Office," she made an effort to rise from her chair. "When she was asked why she rose, she replied that she wanted to go to the window and show the inquisitor some beautiful groves."

The following day Becerra went to the "house of penance" to go through the same process with the sister, María de Yriarte. When he began she looked well enough and was able to hold herself erect, but during the proceedings she grew weaker and weaker and when he arrived at the point where she was to confirm what she had stated in her evidence "she became very sorrowful and would say no more. She would not even answer questions. But at last she acknowledged what she had said previously."

In their letter Becerra and Salazar wrote that they were not disinclined to believe that the Devil was behind the strange illness among the witches, which suddenly brought them to the point of death when they seemed to have survived the illness and the doctors had declared them almost recovered and given them permission to get up. This suspicion was strengthened by certain reports that the Devil appeared to the witches in the "house of penance" and had sexual intercourse with them. The doctors themselves considered that something was amiss, continued the two inquisitors, "and since yesterday they have been of the opinion that we should have new clothes and bed [linen] made for the witches, and that the old [clothes and bedding] should be thrown away." If their suspicions should be confirmed on closer investigation, the inquisitors planned to install a temporary infirmary in the secret prison and requisition the jailer's accommodation for this purpose. The rooms were small and not particularly suitable, but they would have served to secure the witches against the

Devil, as it had been found that he never dared to show himself in the secret prison where all the other witches were confined.[23]

On 28 November, Becerra and Salazar wrote that they had now lost a total of six witches. Since their last communication the "king of the witches" (i.e. Miguel de Goiburu), María Pérez de Barrenechea, and "one of the *negativos*" had died.[24] It is possible to identify the last-named as Juanes de Echegui (see table 4, third group). The inquisitors had gone to great pains to persuade him to confess but he persisted in denying his guilt to the last,[25] and they had therefore had to let him die without receiving the sacraments.[26]

On 21 August 1610 the Tribunal informed *la Suprema* of a new epidemic in the prison, and on 30 August the inquisitors reported that it had carried off six witches.[27] These were María de Echalecu, Estevanía de Petrisancena, and Martín Vizcar (from the September group), Juanes de Odia and María de Zozaya (who had arrived in November and December 1609 respectively), and Mari Juanto (one of the sixteen who were imprisoned in March 1610).[28] Yet one more witch was to die in this outbreak, namely María de Yriarte. She had been arrested in February 1609, and judging from the food accounts, she was in prison for eighteen months.[29] Her case had been completed and in the judgment it is stated that since her confession she had behaved like a good Catholic and shown every sign of being sincerely penitent, and that on her deathbed she "wept, and begged for God's forgiveness."[30]

In their letter of 30 August the inquisitors went on to tell the Council that they had several conversations with the doctors about the cause of the witches' illness. On the one hand the doctors felt that the illness might be due to natural causes: "Since they are healthy mountain-dwellers who are accustomed to hard work and whose diet consists of milk and varied nourishment, the illness may well be caused by their having been brought here and all their habits changed." On the other hand the doctors did not exclude the possibility that the illness and deaths might also have a supernatural origin for which the Devil was responsible. The inquisitors were in no doubt about this last explanation being the correct one. "We are convinced that this must be the case," runs their letter, "for those who are dying off are the very persons we most need in order to pursue our investigations and reveal the witches' confederacies."[31]

Of the thirty-one people whose cases were included in the auto de fe only eighteen, therefore, survived to hear the result of their trials. The others who died in prison during the course of the trial, which lasted nearly two years, were to be presented in effigy. Five of them would have been burned alive, so for them the epidemic undeniably meant an easier death. Their bodies were carefully preserved, however, so that their earthly remains might be presented at the auto de fe, where they were to be burned together with their effigies. The other eight had all confessed and obtained the forgiveness their penitence entitled them to. They received Christian burial, for it was sufficient that their effigies were present at the auto de fe.[32]

Death did not bring the work of the Inquisition to an end. In contrast to other earthly courts the Holy Office sought to extend its jurisdiction beyond the grave. In various ways the autos de fe called to mind the Day of Judgment, and this resemblance was deliberately cultivated by the Inquisition. But even if the Inquisition regarded its judgments on the quick and the dead in this perspective it did not consider them as being definitive, since none could predict the final sentence of the Last Day.

3. THE WITCHES' CONFESSIONS

Only nine of the twenty-one witches whose cases were prepared for the auto de fe confessed. Four came from Zugarramurdi, and five came variously from the towns of Vera, Echalar, and Rentería. We have only a fragmentary knowledge of these witches' confessions,[33] with the exception of María de Zozaya, whose case will be discussed separately.

Of the four from Zugarramurdi, fifty-two-year-old María Chipía de Barrenechea admitted to having made her niece, María de Jureteguía, a witch (see chapters 2 and 4.2). She also confessed to having initiated a niece of her husband. This is all we know of her confession.[34] It has already been stated of forty-year-old María de Echegui that she gave evidence against her father and admitted having made one of her daughters a witch. Beyond this we know only that she confessed to having been a witch for thirteen years.

It is stated of eighty-year-old Martín de Vizcar that he confessed to "serious crimes, murders, and acts of revenge," and that he admitted to being the superintendent (*alcalde*) of the children at the *aquelarre*. At the ceremonial black masses he and Miguel de Goiburu performed as the Devil's train-bearers (*caudatarios*) and it was their task to lift up the Devil's robes when the witches approached in order to "worship" him.[35] Martín Vizcar furthermore confessed to having been a witch since childhood, but said that the Devil did not have intercourse with him until he was an adult. The first time it had caused him severe hemorrhage. He was by then a married man, and on his return home his wife had asked him why he was bleeding. But he had made the excuse that he had grazed his leg on a branch.[36]

The two sisters, María Presona, who was seventy, and Mari Juanto, sixty, confessed to having been witches all their lives and that they were both members of the *aquelarres* at Zugarramurdi and at Vera.[37] Mari Juanto had moved to Vera, where she had a son, and no doubt her sister visited her there.[38] In any case they both confessed to having been present when some child witches were cruelly punished during the *aquelarre* at Vera because they had betrayed the witches by telling their parents who took them to the sabbath.[39] The two sisters also confessed to having killed each other's children on a certain occasion after the Devil had said at the *aquelarre* that they had not perpetrated any wickedness for a long time. To satisfy him the two arranged that one should poison her sister's son and the other her sister's daughter.[40]

Mari Juanto also confessed that when she was at the *aquelarre* a demon appeared as her substitute. One night some neighbors came around to buy eggs, but the demon had called from within the house saying that she had none. When Mari Juanto returned from the witches' meeting, the demon told her what had happened. But when she heard that the neighbors had come in vain she told him that he could very well have given them some of the eggs on the shelf in the kitchen.[41]

The forty-year-old beggar-woman Beltrana de la Fargua — alias "the French woman" who had made a provisional confession to the parish priest Hualde at the beginning of 1610 (see above, p. 134) — came from Vera. She confessed at the Tribunal to having taken part in "various *aquelarres*" in Navarra and to having been present at all the scandalous ceremonies of the witches. She also confessed to making witches of three small children and admitted that two of these were her own daughters. Furthermore, she owned to having a "dressed toad" which she breast-fed. Sometimes when she was suckling her own child, she said in her confession, the toad began to stretch and crane upwards from the floor until it caught hold of her nipple. At other times it changed itself into a child so that she should pick it up in her arms and suckle it.[42]

It is stated of Juanes de Yribarren, the forty-year-old smith from Echalar, that

> He was accused by four boys aged from eleven to fourteen years, who declared that he was one of the witches at the *aquelarre* at Echalar, at which he held the post of jailer and had to whip the children on the Devil's orders. He was taken to the Tribunal in error and was detained on account of the witnesses' statements mentioned above, so that he could be interrogated. During the first interrogation he admitted to being a witch and to having been one "with conviction and apostasy" since he was quite small.[43]

During subsequent interrogations he said that "some years ago he had stopped being a witch and stayed away from the meetings";[44] but he must later have relapsed, since he acknowledged having acted as jailer at the Echalar *aquelarre.* He also admitted that he had whipped the children when they talked too openly and let slip the identities of the witches. The whip was made of hawthorn twigs and the thorns became embedded in the children's flesh. The Devil usually healed them afterwards with special ointment, but sometimes the thorns were stuck fast and on several occasions Juanes de Yribarren had noticed next day that people in Echalar were sitting and pulling thorns out of the children he had whipped the previous night.[45] He also declared that he had a devil-mark on his stomach. The inquisitors examined him carefully, and when they pricked him with a needle he felt nothing even though they pressed it right into his flesh.[46]

Two more fragments of Juanes de Yribarren's confession are available to us in Mongastón's pamphlet. The first of these contains a detail not found in the other witches' confessions. He describes a torch made out of the left arm of an unbaptized child, which the witches used on their nocturnal forays when the Devil did not accompany them to provide a light.[47] The second reports something that Juanes de Yribarren claimed to have experienced himself. The first time he went out with the other witches on a crop-destroying expedition he forgot the ban against uttering the name of God. He tells how when the witches were traveling through the air they made as much noise as forty galloping horses. He was so astonished that he cried out "Jesus," and at that moment they all vanished. He fell to the ground and remained lying lifeless in a field in the dark. Soon afterwards he heard the church clock. He realized that he was not far from the village and crawled towards the sound as best he could. When he reached home he fainted, and remained ill for some days on account of the shock he had suffered. The next time he went to the sabbath the witches punished him with a beating for mentioning the name of Jesus.[48] Basically this could very well be interpreted as an authentic record of the hallucinations induced by drugs, for the forty-year-old smith's description of his awakening is extraordinarily realistic. But here once again the sources offer us no definite proof.

Twenty-seven-year-old Juanes de Lambert of Rentería was also a smith. He came from Labastide in French Navarre on the border of the Pays de Labourd, where his father, Martin de Lambert, had been burned as a witch. Juanes himself had been initiated by his father when still a small child, but a priest had helped him to stop practicing as a witch and for many years he had not taken part in the gatherings. "Fourteen months ago" runs the résumé of his confession, "he settled down at Rentería. Here María de Zozaya [again] initiated him and took him with her to the *aquelarre* at that town. . . . [He also confessed] to having helped [her] to take a boy to the *aquelarre* in order that the child might become a witch."[49] For her part María de Zozaya, the last of the nine *confitente* witches, does not seem to have witnessed against Juanes de Lambert; he is certainly not mentioned in the very detailed report of her trial that was preserved (see the following section).

We know very little about the trials of the twelve *negativos*. But as they all, except for the priest Juan de la Borda, came from Urdax and Zugarramurdi, and as they all denied being witches, it is hardly likely that they would have provided any details about the "witch cult" which we are not already familiar with. The only one who seems to have confessed anything during the questioning was forty-year-old María de Echalecu from Zugarramurdi. According to Mongastón's pamphlet she told how one day about noon Graciana de Barrenechea carried her through the air to a field "where there is a cave." A little while later she saw Graciana coming out of the grotto with Estevanía de Telechea (*sic*, alias de Navarcorena) and the Devil, the latter walking between the two women, who had their arms around him. As they came toward her she screamed and cried "Jesus," whereupon they immediately vanished. She realized that she was in the Berroscoberro meadow, so she returned on foot to the village, which was only a short distance away.[50]

The contents of the trial record of Juan de la Borda, the thirty-four-year-old assistant priest from Fuenterrabía, are reported in his so-called *méritos*. It appears from this report that, according to the usual procedure of the Inquisition, he was asked at the first hearing whether he knew why he had been arrested. When he replied that he did not, he was given the standing formula that the Inquisition arrested nobody without cause. The only possible offense he could recall was having learned some charms for curing toothache, stomach pains, and worms. He admitted having made use of these spells a few times, recited the charms to the Tribunal, and came out with a few other things as well. But the inquisitors attached little importance to all this. However, after further consideration he said that he suspected that the witches who had been taken to Logroño by the Inquisition had borne false witness against him, as well as against his mother, his aunt, and his cousin, the latter being a monk. Perhaps they had brought these false charges, the priest went on, in the hope that by so doing they might save themselves; but this must have been an impulse instilled into them by the Devil.[51]

All we know of Juan de la Borda's aunt, the miller's widow, seventy-year-old María de Arburu, is that she was accused of being successor to Graciana de Barrenechea in the office of "queen of the *aquelarre*," but, as we know, she denied being a witch to the last.[52] Of the other *negativos* we know only that for the entire duration of the trial they remained "stubborn and impenitent" to use the terms of the Holy Office (see chapter 3.2, above).

4. MARÍA DE ZOZAYA'S CONFESSIONS

We know more concerning María de Zozaya than about any of the other accused witches. We have already described her unmasking at Rentería (chapter 7.3) and heard how she had recruited fifteen new witches in the course of eight days (from

12-20 November 1609) and that these later testified to Valle in San Sebastián. After the Tribunal (that is to say, Becerra and Salazar) had seen the statement of the proceedings that the secular authorities at Rentería had instituted against her, they felt that there was no cause to demand that she be handed over to the Inquisition. They therefore returned the documents and instructed the secular authorities to continue the proceedings themselves. But "if it should emerge from her later confessions that she has committed any offense against our Holy Catholic Faith," they would wish to inspect her case-record again.[53]

The upshot of this correspondence ended with María de Zozaya being delivered over to the Inquisition. A few days after Valle's return in December she was transferred to Logroño (see chapter 8.1, above). At first she was ill and there are indications that her interrogation (to be discussed shortly) was not begun until some time in March. It is not possible to say whether María de Zozaya's confession to the secular authorities at Rentería was the product of torture, but at the interrogations at the Tribunal no form of *physical* violence was used against her. María de Zozaya's confession is reported in great detail in the forty-page-long sentence which was read out at the auto de fe. It is this text which forms the basis of the following analysis:[54]

María de Zozaya y Arramendi was born circa 1530 at Oyeregui, a village in the neighborhood of Santesteban in Navarra. When she was fourteen she moved with her parents to Elizondo in the Baztán Valley. At the age of twenty she went to Rentería where she held various posts as a servant-girl for eight to ten years. When she was thirty years old she inherited a small house from one of her mistresses, in which she was still living in 1609 when she was arrested.[55] We have no knowledge of her means of livelihood during the last fifty years of her life.

To gain an idea of popular witch belief in Rentería we will for the moment ignore the secret rites of the witches (as we did when analyzing the Zugarramurdi witches' confessions) and concentrate on the facts that those who were not witches would know about. If we take this part of her confession it will be seen that María de Zozaya's social situation differed somewhat from that of the Zugarramurdi witches. She had a private motive for revenge in only two out of the eight bewitchings to which she confessed. In one case she accused a neighbor of having stolen a hen from her. When the woman denied having taken the hen, María grew so furious that she killed her with a poisoned apple. On the second occasion, which occurred about 1605, she had ordered a petticoat from a neighbor who was a dressmaker, and had told her to make the garment full. The dressmaker made it tight-fitting and when María protested she offered to buy some more material herself and make another petticoat. But the witch could not control her rage. She gave the dressmaker a poisoned pear, the effects of which caused her death — but remarkably enough not until six months later!

María de Zozaya's other bewitchings took the form of ill-treating and killing several of her neighbors' children by vampirism, and terrifying and maltreating a ship's captain so much that he was paralyzed; but in none of these cases does there seem to have been any previous personal conflict. [56]

It is my impression that for a long time María de Zozaya had been in the second phase of the witch role and had become the public scapegoat of the entire neighborhood. There are several instances of her having been accused of entering houses in broad daylight and molesting children whose parents had left them alone in their cradles while they were at work; and when the young priest of the town came home without a single hare after having been out hunting all day even he blamed María de Zozaya. In this case, however, she got no more than she deserved, for when the priest passed her house she would say: "See that you catch plenty of hares, Father, so the neighbors can have jugged hare." The priest no doubt swore at her, for it is a well-known fact that no hunter takes kindly to being wished good luck with his hunting. María de Zozaya confessed to the inquisitors that as soon as the priest had passed by she turned herself into a hare and ran ahead of him and his hounds the whole day long so that they returned home exhausted. This, she added, had occurred eight times during 1609. [57]

María de Zozaya confessed that she had recruited a total of twenty witches. She had initiated five of these long ago, one of them "five years ago" (i.e. in the year 1605). As for the other fifteen (an eighteen-year-old French girl and fourteen children aged between three and fourteen), she declared having taken them to the *aquelarre* "three or four months ago." If we assume that the inquiry did not take place until February or March, these statements are in agreement with those of Valle in the letter of 20 November 1609 (see chapter 7.3, above).[58] All in all it would seem reasonable to conclude that María de Zozaya had been suspected of witchcraft several years before the commencement of the persecutions. However, there can be little doubt that her notoriety was rapidly increasing in 1609, when fear of witches entered a new and heightened phase. Apart from a couple of occurrences which it is not possible to date, all the tangible crimes for which María de Zozaya was indicted seem to have been committed after 1605.

On the other hand her secret life as a witch went right back to the Oyeregui period. When she was ten years old (that is, about 1540) a neighbor made her a witch, María de Zozaya relates in her confession. The woman visited her several times and told her about some marvelously fair gods that she knew and would like to show her. At first María would not listen, but one day she allowed herself to be persuaded and promised the neighbor to go with her to see what these gods were like. That same night, about ten o'clock, as she was undressing by the light of a tallow candle, having quite forgotten her conversation with the neighbor, the woman suddenly entered the room accompanied by the Devil, who had the appearance of a big, ugly, and sinister man. They asked what she was doing. María answered that she was sprinkling holy water so that no evil could come to her. The Devil and the woman told her to throw that away for they had something far better. As María hesitated they told her firmly: "Come along then! We are going tonight." "For Jesus' sake, this very night?" exclaimed the girl, and as soon as the Devil heard the name Jesus he vanished with a muffled clatter. The neighbor remained and explained to the girl that in future she must not utter the name of Jesus, for she would teach her something better. In a little while the Devil returned and took out a small bottle. The neighbor pulled off María's shift, and taking a little salve out of the bottle she began to rub it on the girl's face, on her breasts and shoulders, her knees, the soles of her feet, and the palms of her hands. She then replaced her shift and put an old petticoat (*faldellín*) on over it. All this was done with the utmost haste, for the next moment the woman and the Devil took her out through the window and then to a meadow "which lies half a *legua* from Rentería [*sic*, but this must be an *erratum* for Oyeregui]. This meadow," continues the statement, "is known as Macharena's Meadow [*Prado de Macharena*], but the witches call it *Acheguin Soro* in Basque, and this means The Meadow of Pleasure [*Prado de Placer*]."[59]

María de Zozaya saw two figures in the meadow, sitting in an extremely dignified manner on black chairs. One of the figures was a large, ugly, grim man with horns on his forehead and claws on his hands and feet. A beautiful woman was sitting on his left in the other chair. She was somewhat taller than most and was elegantly dressed in black. Her face was hidden by her shawl. In front of these two figures a great crowd of men and women was dancing to the noise of drums and flutes. A huge bonfire was blazing in the center of the meadow. The witches were dancing in a number of small circles, but sometimes they joined together in a large group of over two hundred which encircled the bonfire. When they were dancing round the fire the Devil urged them to leap into the flames. It was the fire of Hell, he said, and they would see that it neither scorched nor burned them. Besides the light of the fire there was a strange glare over the meadow. It issued from the horn that was in the center of the Devil's forehead. It was brighter than moonlight and shone so clearly that it was possible to recognize who was present and see everything that was going on in the meadow.[60]

María de Zozaya's confession continues by describing her admission to the witch sect. She tells of her participation in the witches' sabbaths at Oyeregui, Elizondo, and Rentería. She was initiated into the senior witch grade at Rentería; some time after she had moved into her little house, her erstwhile neighbor and the Devil came all the way from Oyeregui and presented her with a "dressed toad" in order that she might travel to the *aquelarre* by herself. María de Zozaya's descriptions of the witches' black masses, sexual orgies, violations of graves, devouring of corpses, preparation of poisons, powders, and ointments, destruction of crops, and injuries to human beings agree to an astonishing extent with the repertoire of the Zugarramurdi witches.[61] In fact, only two new elements are evident. One is the woman in black seated beside the Devil, whom María de Zozaya declared she had seen only at the Oyeregui *aquelarre*;[62] the other is the light shining out of the Devil's horn (a detail recounted by several of the witches from Las Cinco Villas).[63] The remainder of María de Zozaya's divergences are of less moment; for instance, her statement that the "dressed toads" were equipped with a collar hung with bells when stabled with the toad flock at the *aquelarre*. (This feature is also common to several witches' confessions from Las Cinco Villas.)[64]

In other words, we are brought back to the chief argument of the inquisitors: the general agreement between the witches' descriptions of their rituals; and this time the argument is all the more convincing when the witch concerned comes from a region far from Zugarramurdi. I am not sure how we are to explain this agreement. (It would be necessary, in order to get to the heart of the problem, to undertake a historical/ geographical analysis of the traditions inherent in the material relating to the witch belief as it existed in both Spanish and French Basque regions, and to compare this with the scholastic tradition in the demonological works of the period.) I shall therefore limit myself to indicating a few possibilities that should be noted in the particular case of María de Zozaya.

Her description of the elaborate methods of producing the powder is in an obvious state of confusion (compare the straightforward account of the Zugarramurdi witches, chapter 5.11, above). The toads, snakes, lizards, and so on, are first of all chopped, then grated, and then crushed in a mortar. This substance is then mixed with liquid obtained from toads and cooked in pots, after which it is dried and crushed once more in a mortar.[65] It might seem natural to conclude that María de Zozaya's testimony had been shaped by leading questions posed by the inquisitors. But it is also a possibility that she had been in the same prison cell as one of the Zugarramurdi witches, who could have instructed her in what she should say at the inquiries.

Salazar drew *la Suprema*'s attention to the fact that this possibility should be taken into account when the witches' confessions were being judged. However, this was not until 2 March 1611, when he reported this and certain irregularities of the Tribunal. Lack of space in the prison led to contact between the witches, which in turn posed a particular problem; as Salazar noted, a good *confitente* could instruct a bad *confitente* if they were sharing the same cell.[66]

There is an indication that this was precisely what happened in the case of María de Zozaya. In her confession she declared that nobody ever missed her when she was at the *aquelarre*, for while she was away a counterfeit figure took her place: The moment she rose and got out of bed this figure lay down in her place, she explained, and went on to say that it must have been a demon. Once "three or four years ago" she had just come back from a sabbath and was undressing beside her bed. Suddenly the phantom began to speak to her and tell her that while she had been away a woman had come and knocked at the door. The demon had answered from the bed and asked her what she wanted. The woman outside had replied that she had come for some eggs, but the demon said there were no eggs in the house, and the woman had gone away again. When María heard this she told the demon that another time he should give the woman the eggs, as there were always some in the house.[67]

This story is repeated almost word for word in a fragment of Mari Juanto's confession (see near beginning of chapter 8.3, above), so it could be assumed that these two witches shared a cell. Unfortunately very little else of Mari Juanto's confession is extant and it is therefore impossible to check this hypothesis by a closer comparison of these two witches' confessions.[68]

On the other hand María de Zozaya was also committed to the confession she had made at Rentería and which was known to the Tribunal, which had already inspected it. But even at this stage of her trial there would seem to be a possibility of agreement with the Zugarramurdi repertoire. We have seen that Valle was involved in María de Zozaya's trial at an early stage; for one thing, he personally interrogated all fifteen of the witnesses who maintained that she had taken them to the sabbath and made them witches. It is therefore most probable that Valle supplied the secular authorities with points for indictment, or at least with a questionnaire regarding the witches' rites, which by then he had such detailed knowledge of. These reflections may serve as an indication of the difficulties to be encountered when analyzing witch confessions by a folkloristic approach.[69]

The list of fourteen questions from *la Suprema* (see chapter 4.4, above) may be seen to have been applied in María de Zozaya's trial, though to little effect. She answered to Question 1 that she had heard bells and clocks both when she was at the sabbath and when she was on her way to and from it. She even claimed to have counted the strokes of the hours. While at the sabbath she had heard cocks crowing on the farms, at both ten and eleven o'clock, but never after midnight, for the witches were always back in their beds by twelve o'clock.[70] To

Question 6 she answered that at the assemblies in broad daylight she had heard the sound of bells, dogs, and pigs, and had
seen people working in the fields. But people were unable to
see the witches, she explained, for the Devil had enveloped
them in a cloud.[71] The witches were similarly invisible when
they flew over the rooftops of Rentería in broad daylight, though she herself could see people down in the streets
quite well.[72] When the witches broke into houses at night in
order to fetch the children and take them to the *aquelarre*, or to
do them some harm, they sprinkled some powder over the
parents which prevented them from awakening.[73] In answer
to Question 10 she said that the witches never discussed the
assemblies when they met during the daytime, for the Devil
had strictly prohibited them from talking about these things
outside the *aquelarre*.[74] To Question 12 María answered that
she was absolutely convinced that she actually participated in
the witches' sabbaths and did not merely dream about them.[75]

María de Zozaya's confessions are of particular interest
where sexual intercourse with the Devil is concerned. When
she was going to attend the sabbath on Mondays, Wednes-
days, and Fridays she got out her toad and whipped it. On
some occasions this happened in the middle of the day, at
others in the evening. When she was whipping the toad during the day the Devil was in the habit of appearing in the shape
of a goat or a man in order to look on. After the toad had
expelled its fluid and been put back into its box, continues the
description, the Devil always had

> intercourse with her, by means of the usual parts and the
> rear ones [*por las partes ordinarias y por las traseras*]. When it
> took place in the normal way she had the same satisfaction
> as if it had been with a man, although it was somewhat
> painful, for the Devil's member was big and hard. But when
> he used the anus it gave her more pain than pleasure. When
> the Devil was about to have intercourse with her he always
> threw her down onto the floor. [She confessed further] that
> many times he came in the night and got into her bed and
> lay beside her like a real human being. . . . While they were
> lying together his skin and limbs felt just like a man's. He
> embraced her and she kissed him; and they had intercourse
> and talked together as intimately as if they had been man
> and wife. But his skin was always colder than a man's and
> never grew really warm. Even when they were embracing,

his skin remained quite cold. He usually stayed with her for two or three hours and left her shortly before dawn.[76]

The description is so realistic that one gets the impression that it is based on personal experience. In the case of María de Zozaya it would seem to be quite justifiable, for once, to talk of a sexual neurosis. This explanation also helps to throw some light on another passage in her confessions. "Twenty years ago," it runs, "she confessed to a priest at Rentería that she was a witch. The priest gave her some good advice and hung some *nominas* (i.e. printed or written exorcisms) on her. But twenty days after the priest had gotten her to stop practicing witchcraft (*dejar aquel mal oficio de bruja*), and despite her good resolutions, she suffered a relapse and continued again in the old manner. She had been to confession and communion many times, both before and after, but that was the only time she had confessed that she was a witch.[77]

If we could with certainty believe the story of the "dressed toad" we would be able to provide an explanation not only for María de Zozaya's erotic experiences but also for many more of the things she described about her secret life as a witch. For it could all be something that she experienced as a result of anointing herself with the fluid she extracted from the toad. We have previously discussed the fact that toad vomit contains hallucinogenic substances (see chapter 5.20, above), but in María de Zozaya's case, as well, there is no definite proof to warrant such an interpretation. According to her own confession the following witch requisites were in fact hidden in her house at the time of her arrest: (1) María de Zozaya's own "dressed toad," which lived in a wooden box which was hidden in a pot with a wooden lid; (2) five "dressed toads" which she was keeping for her pupils and had hidden between the chest and the wall; (3) a pot of toad vomit, which it was María's duty to take to the *aquelarre*; (4) a pot of poisonous ointment; (5) a pot of poisonous powder; (6) a small glass bottle of "yellow water"; and (7) powder made from ground toadskin wrapped in a piece of paper.

After she was imprisoned the authorities searched the house but found nothing. María de Zozaya explained to the inquisitors that the Devil must have removed all the things she had listed in order that they should not be found.[78] To Becerra and Valle this must undoubtedly have seemed to be yet another example of how the Devil was doing all in his power to prevent them from obtaining evidence against his sect. But it was becoming increasingly difficult for Salazar to accept the explanation that the witch sect, thanks to the Devil's wiles, was consistently able to avoid confrontation with empirical reality. The negative result of the search of María de Zozaya's house was one of the arguments Salazar produced in his first criticism of the evidence used at this trial (see near end of chapter 8.7, below).

5. THE TRIAL

As early as 26 September 1609, when Becerra and Salazar wrote to *la Suprema* reporting the arrival of the fifteen prisoners sent by Valle to the Tribunal, the inquisitors had stressed that they could not then undertake any more witch trials. "We have decided not to imprison any more for the time being," declared the two inquisitors. "We shall have more than enough to do with those we already have, and when we consider the complexities involved in this type of case and the length of the witnesses' statements it is questionable whether we shall have the strength for the task that lies ahead of us." The letter continued with a report of the trial of the first witches which had had to be broken off on account of the epidemic at the prison, and of the preliminary inquiries to be held with the newly arrived witches:

> We had been intending to spend these days in informing those who were already here of the charges against them; but as they have now all fallen ill and are very weak, this is not possible. We shall therefore commence to examine the new prisoners, all of whom seem firmly resolved to deny their guilt.[79]

Not until six months later, on 13 February 1610, was *la Suprema* informed of the progress of the trial. Fourteen out of the twenty-eight witches now at the Tribunal had confessed, and their cases (apart from two, which remained incomplete) were all ready for sentence. The other fourteen denied their guilt; all of these had been informed of the charge, and their trials had progressed to the point where they were to be acquainted with the statements of the witnesses (cf. page 43, above). On account of the large number of witnesses the inquisitors had decided to inform them of only six witnesses' statements *in extenso* and merely to give them a summary of the other evidence. If, in the light of the immense amount of evidence against the witches, the defending lawyer abstained from presenting witnesses on behalf of the fourteen *negativos*, the inquisitors thought that they would be able to conclude the cases and have them ready for an auto de fe in the near future. The letter ended with a plea for financial assistance, as all the witches were poor and had to be supported at the Tribunal's expense. (The fact that no less than half the number of people accused insisted that they were innocent must in itself have given food for thought; but when we look more closely at the Tribunal's statement the situation appears more serious still: only four of the eighteen new prisoners had confessed, for the other ten admissions had been made by the first group of prisoners, who had all pleaded guilty.)[80]

On 10 July the Tribunal sent the records of the by then thirty-one witch trials to *la Suprema*.[81] In the meantime the cases had been completed and the verdicts had been decided at a number of *consultas de fe*. One *consulta de fe* was held on 8 June 1610, and the others had presumably taken place previously. The situation regarding the *confitentes* and *negativos* was now as follows: nine of the most recently arrived prisoners had produced witchcraft confessions, and there were now nineteen *confitentes* in all. The inquisitors had recommended all of these for reconciliation and "penance," with the exception of María de Zozaya. The latter they condemned to the stake because she had been a proselytizer (*dogmatizante*) for the witch sect and had been to blame for sending many people to perdition. While the judgments of the nineteen *confitentes* seem to have been agreed unanimously, the Tribunal was not in agreement regarding the fate of the twelve *negativos*. Not being convinced of their guilt, Salazar voted they should be interrogated under torture; but Becerra, Valle, and all the other judges considered it to be a foregone conclusion that they should be sent to the stake, and sentenced them accordingly (see below, chapter 8.7).

It was presumably on this occasion that the *fiscal* to the Tribunal, Dr. San Vicente, sent in his twelve-point consideration to *la Suprema*. This report is extant, but is merely headed "1610."[82] In it San Vicente argued that the witches were being tried with far too much clemency and demanded that all be sentenced to the stake and to forfeiture of property. As a precedent for the death sentence he recalled that the archives of the Tribunal contained the files of a large number of witches burned in 1508 and 1509 "with far less evidence than we have now." Others received less severe sentences, he admitted, and were reconciled and condemned to life imprisonment and confiscation of property. As a precedent for the confiscation of property he recalled that in the years 1528 through 1531 many witches were reconciled with confiscation of all their property. It was true that during the period 1532-1536 on orders from the inquisitor general only half the property was confiscated, but San Vicente was able to explain this fact away as follows: the scholars at that time were in a state of uncertainty, as the witch sect was little known and the evidence that the Tribunal now possessed was not then available. Finally San Vicente revealed that in 1576 proceedings were instituted against some witches from the Carranza Valley, and on advice from *la Suprema* all their goods were sequestered on their imprisonment.[83]

It would take too long to reproduce more of the *fiscal's* tortuous arguments based on precedents which provided a line of reasoning that was far from clear (and in which he omitted a large number of precedents, to be found in the archives, for more lenient treatment of the witches).[84] The last point in the *fiscal's* consideration is however, of interest, as it touched on the "foreign policy" element in this witch trial. San Vicente drew attention to the fact that that year in France a large number of witches had been burned, among them two priests. In France, they were watching eagerly to see what the Spaniards would do with their witches. Too much leniency, warned the *fiscal*, would not only result in a loss of respect for Spain, but would cause all the French witches who felt their lives in danger to flee over the border into Spain, where they could be more secure.[85]

Finally the inquisitors sent with the thirty-one trial records the long letter of 10 July reporting on the witch situation in general (quoted above, pp. 62 and 141). In this the three inquisitors wrote:

> Even though these are but few witch trials compared with the great number that are awaiting us, and although they have given us a great deal of work, we are in good heart; for we are aware that this is a new type of case of which we had no previous experience. Therefore we have been obliged to proceed slowly . . . and to pose many questions in order to

reach an understanding of the content and principles of this form of heresy. In future we shall be able to get along faster and to follow a routine.[86]

This was the letter in which, as was mentioned previously, the Tribunal asked for permission to confront the witches with one another in court; the inquisitors were certain that this would save much time. In addition to the experiment with María de Yriarte and her relatives (see chapter 4.6, above), they had gained some experience with the new group of prisoners that Valle had sent down from Zugarramurdi. Several of them were apparently completely convinced that the first witches fetched from Zugarramurdi by the Inquisition had been burned "because they had confessed the truth." Martín de Vizcar and María Presona among others firmly believed this, relate the three inquisitors, and they continue: "Merely bringing one of them [the first prisoners] into the court [so the newcomers could see that he or she was alive] was enough to break their [the newcomers] resistance and make them tell us what the Devil had got them to believe in order that they should not confess."[87] The sources do not inform us whether *la Suprema* gave this permission. In all the letters to the Tribunal at this period the inquisitors' proposal is ignored.

La Suprema returned the thirty-one trial records on 9 September, having noted on each record a recommendation for what steps were to be taken. We have mentioned that the records were lost, so that we are precluded from knowing whether *la Suprema* changed the judgments of the Tribunal. However, apart from the cases of the monk and the priest, which will be discussed below, *la Suprema* would seem to have abided by the decisions of the Tribunal. This anyway is the impression given in three accompanying letters dated 9 September 1610, which are available to us from *la Suprema*'s letter book.[88]

In the longest of these letters, the inquisitors, the *fiscal*, and all the other employees of the Tribunal were warmly praised for the industry and speed they had manifested in this matter. The inquisitor general was grateful to them for this and would bear it in mind. The letter continued by enjoining the Tribunal to ensure that the witches who had been transferred from the secular authorities were not exposed to legal prosecution from those authorities after having served the sentences imposed on them by the Inquisition (see the request from Rentería, chapter 7.5, above). Since the cases were not wound up, concludes the letter, the inquisitors might hold the auto de fe whenever they wished, providing they notified *la Suprema* in advance. The Tribunal was to see that the date of the auto de fe was announced in Logroño and its neighborhood as well as in the more distant towns where it could be expected to be of interest. They should also make sure that the announcement was made in good time, as it was anticipated that many would wish to come to Logroño to witness the witches' punishment.[89]

A fourth letter, also dated 9 September 1610, was concerned with the trials of Juan de la Borda and Pedro de Arburu.[90] While *la Suprema* recognized that the ten other *negativos* were condemned to the stake by an overwhelming majority, they made an exception of the priest and the monk. In their cases the Council was in accord with Salazar and ordered the Tribunal to interrogate the two accused clerics under torture.[91]

On 12 October the Tribunal reported that the orders of *la Suprema* had now been effected and that both the monk and the priest had undergone the torture without confessing. The torture device had consisted of eight *garrotes*.[92] (Eight ropes (*cordeles*) binding eight separate parts of the body were tightened by turning transverse rods, or *garrotes*, so that they cut into the flesh.) According to the rules of the Inquisition all three inquisitors and the bishop's representative, *el ordinario*, were to be present during the torture. As will be recalled from chapter 3 the Inquisition was extremely reluctant to impose torture. Thus none of the other twenty-nine witches were exposed to this treatment.

Torture was a means of proof resorted to by the Inquisition only if, when the case was complete, doubt still prevailed as to the guilt of the accused person. The accused was to be naked during the torture, and when it was finished the executioner was obliged to treat the injuries he had inflicted on the prisoner. In his imposing work on the Spanish Inquisition Henry Charles Lea is completely justified in writing that

> the popular impression that the inquisitorial torture-chamber was the scene of exceptional refinement in cruelty, of specially ingenious modes of inflicting agony, and of peculiar persistence in extorting confessions, is an error due to sensational writers who have exploited credulity. The system was evil in conception and in execution, but the

Spanish Inquisition, at least, was not responsible for its introduction and, as a rule, was less cruel than the secular courts in its application, and confined itself more strictly to a few well-known methods.[93]

The inquisitors write that an unfortunate occurrence took place during Pedro de Arburu's torture. After the executioner had given the monk "the first turn" on all eight *garrotes,* and was about to give him "the second turn" on the first *garrote,* the rope broke before he had finished turning the rod. The rope was applied again and the jailer again gave him "the first turn." When the inquisitors commanded the executioner to give "the second turn" to the rope around the monk's right upper arm, he began to scream and cried: "Let me go! I will tell you the truth. I am a witch. Let me go, then I will tell the truth." But when the inquisitors had the torture stopped he denied the charge more vehemently than ever. Thereupon they ordered the executioner to continue and to give the monk the "second turn" of the rope around his left forearm. However, when the rod had been turned half way they saw that the monk, who was beside himself with rage, was apparently feeling nothing, and they therefore resolved to discontinue the torture.

Describing Juan de la Borda's torture the inquisitors related that he was given the "first turn" of all eight ropes, but when he suddenly collapsed they found it inadvisable to continue.

The letter continued with the information that the sentences of the monk and the priest were voted for at a new *consulta de fe.* The inquisitors had decided to impose a sentence on them comparable to the death sentence in view of the substantial number of witnesses and in view of the fact that the mothers of the monk and the priest were to be sent to the stake. These women had refused to confess, but according to the witches' evidence, they had themselves initiated their sons, the monk and the priest, into the witch sect. The inquisitors, together with the other judges (the *consultores*), recommended, this time unanimously, that the two priests be sentenced in the following manner: they were to be presented at the auto de fe in penitential garb with a half St. Andrew's Cross (*hábitos de media aspa*). Here they were to hear their sentences read out, renounce their heresy *de vehemente,* and be deprived of all priestly orders. Finally they were to be banished for five years to the king's galleys "unpaid at the oar," after which (if they survived!) they were to be confined in an enclosed monastery for life (see chapters 9.5 and 9.6, below).

The remainder of the letter was concerned with the eleven *negativos* who were to be burned. Only six of these were now alive, for since July the prison had been ravaged by the second epidemic (see chapter 8.2, above). Among those still alive were María de Arburu and María Bastán de la Borda, the mothers of the monk and the priest.

The inquisitors were in doubt about what they should do with the *negativos* if they decided to confess when they heard that they were going to die. (It was the custom to break this news to the prisoners the night before the auto de fe.) They also wished to know what course they should take if the prisoners confessed during the auto de fe, or after they were handed over to the secular authorities and were on their way to the stake. The inquisitors still considered it possible that the *negativos* would confess at the last moment; but the regulations of the Inquisition did not offer any clear direction on what to do in any of these events.[94]

In another letter, also written on 12 October 1610, the inquisitors reported that the auto de fe was appointed for Sunday 7 November. "At that time," they wrote, "the people are finished with the wine-harvest and the feast of All Saints is over." For the sake of speed these letters were not sent by post, but by courier. The Tribunal needed a reply from *la Suprema* as soon as possible, as they would have to announce the auto de fe "in a week's time."[95]

On Wednesday 20 October the Council sent a reply stating that it needed to see the trial records of the monk and the priest again in order to come to a decision regarding their sentences; they also wished to have another look at "the file containing the evidence against them." The letter was delivered by a courier named Pedro Ibañez. He received two-hundred *reales* for the journey and was instructed to bring back an answer.[96]

The letter was received by the inquisitors at Logroño on Saturday evening between ten and eleven o'clock, and on Sunday morning at eight o'clock the courier was sent off on his way back to Madrid with the trial records, the statements of evidence, and a letter to *la Suprema*. The inquisitors wrote that besides the documents that had been requested they were also sending a copy of the verdicts in the cases of María de Arburu and the other *negativos* (cf. chapter 8.7, below) as these verdicts contained some reasons and arguments to which the inquisitors had referred in their new judgments regarding the monk and the priest.

The letter concluded with news of the announcement of the auto de fe. This was the first the general public had heard about the great witch trial on which the Tribunal had been working for so long, the inquisitors assured the Council, there had been a positive reaction:

> The auto de fe was announced on the nineteenth [of October] and was received enthusiastically throughout the district, and we assume that the announcement has also been made in the other districts of the region. With a multitude of people converging from all sides it promises to be a very great auto de fe. All over the region people are bent on coming, in particular the population in the districts that have been afflicted by this odious sect [*afligidos con tan gran miseria*].[97]

6. THE REPORT TO THE KING

During September and October of 1610 Philip III was staying with the duke of Lerma, Francisco de Sandoval y Rojas (a cousin of the inquisitor general).[98] Thus it was from Lerma that the king sent his letter to the bishops and the provincials of the religious orders commanding them to send preachers into the mountains to instruct the people and halt the advance of the witch sect (see below, chapter 10.2). The Inquisition at Logroño received an inquiry regarding the date of the auto de fe, and as the king was staying no more than a day's journey distant, this was taken to be an indication that he was going to grace the Tribunal with his presence. The inquisitors later heard that His Majesty had been prevented from making his appearance. And they resolved in their disappointment to compose a report of the auto de fe, so that the king could at least read about it.[99] The inquisitors decided to make copies of two of the sentences to be read out at the auto de fe. On the title page they explained that the sentences had been selected from two different *aquelarres* so that it could be seen how on all vital points the witches concurred in their descriptions of the rites and ceremonies of the sect. Finally the inquisitors drew attention to the fact that the first sentence was composed of the sentences of four witches which had been combined for the purpose of saving time at the auto de fe.[100] This was the joint sentence of Miguel de Goiburu, Graciana de Barrenechea, and her two daughters (see chapter 5, above). The other sentence was that of María de Zozaya which we have discussed above.

Luis de Huerta y Rojas, secretary to the Inquisition, was detailed to write out the sentences in his elegant hand. In their letter to *la Suprema* of 24 October the inquisitors stated that, having put the bulk of their preparations behind them, they were now preparing a report for the king, which they intended should be presented to him on the day the auto de fe was held at Logroño.[101] When Luis de Huerta had finished his work, and the inquisitors saw that the sentences took up sixty-eight closely-written folio pages, they must have realized that it was too much to inconvenience the king with, so they began to edit a shorter report, which reduced the number of pages to twenty-two. This report (SD Text 2) consists mainly of the lengthy joint sentence of the four witches, which is frequently quoted word for word, though material from other judgments is also included.[102]

This short report was addressed to the king with a letter dated Logroño, 31 October 1610 (SD Text 1).[103] The inquisitors had the idea of sending the sixty-eight-page report to the duke, in order that he could inform the king of its contents and give it to His Majesty to read if the king felt so inclined. The inquisitors explained all this to the duke in another letter which they had deliberately dated 1 November, that is, a day later than the king's letter.[104]

Though the letters were signed by all three inquisitors they had been composed on the initiative of Becerra and Valle only. Salazar had done what he could to prevent their being sent, as he himself stated in a later document. This was partly because he could find no precedent for the inquisitors addressing themselves directly to the king without first going through the usual channels of *la Suprema* and partly because he felt that all this editing and calligraphy was a waste of the Tribunal's time, especially in view of the fact that there were people languishing in prison whose cases had not yet been attended to.[105]

Salazar's objections resulted in the plans being changed so that the letters were not sent directly to the king and the duke. Becerra and Valle yielded to their colleague's objections on this point. On 1 November all the documents were sent to *la Suprema* with a covering letter from the inquisitors begging the inquisitor general — provided he approved their plan — to see that His Majesty received the reports on the day of the auto de fe. They had left a space after the account of the trials of the monk and the priest which they asked *la Suprema* to fill in when the final decision regarding their sentences had been taken. (In their previous letter of 24 October the inquisitors had been far-sighted enough to request *la Suprema* to make copies of the definitive sentences.)[106]

On 6 November *la Suprema* replied with a reprimand. The inquisitors could have spared themselves the trouble, as it was quite unheard of to compose auto-de-fe reports in advance. It was always necessary to be prepared for last-minute alterations in the sentences. When the auto de fe was over the Tribunal could send its report to *la Suprema* as usual, and if then the inquisitor general so pleased he might forward it to His Majesty.[107] The letters and the manuscripts for the king and the duke came to rest in the Council's archives, and the fact that they are still to be found there among the other correspondence from Logroño is the surest proof that they went no further.

7. SALAZAR'S VOTE

The various indications of disagreement between Salazar and his two senior colleagues which I have referred to from time to time (chapters 8.4 to 8.6, above) are all to be found in rather later sources. The letters of 1609 and 1610 depict a Tribunal that conscientiously and harmoniously sought to mete out punishment as justly as possible to each of the witches. They depict a Tribunal that had long since ceased to doubt the existence of the witch sect. The inquisitors had patiently gathered instance after instance and set proof upon proof far in excess of what had been necessary for conviction in any other case of heresy, and in the process every detail of the rituals and beliefs of this new sect had been charted. The results of all these investigations were embodied in the long and detailed prologues to the sentences which were to be read out at the auto de fe, when the general public was to learn for the first time about this secret trial which had lasted almost two years.

Had it not been for Salazar's verdict in the case of María de Arburu we might well believe that the inquisitors prepared the auto de fe in harmony. But Salazar's vote tells a different story. It was owing to something of a coincidence that it was preserved at all. For it is available to us only through a copy of the minute book of verdicts (*Libro de votos*), the original having been lost with the rest of the Tribunal's archives at Logroño. The document is written in Salazar's hand and at a later date he has added the heading "Relating to the sentence of María de Arburu and the other persons presented at the auto de fe."[108]

The verdicts were given at a *consulta de fe* held in the courtroom of the Tribunal on 8 June 1610. The jury consisted of the following eight persons:[109] (1) *el doctor* Alonso Becerra Holguín, senior inquisitor; (2) *el licenciado* Juan de Valle Alvarado, second inquisitor; (3) *el licenciado* Alonso de Salazar Frías, third inquisitor; (4) *el licenciado* Lazaro de Badarán, canon of the cathedral chapter at Logroño, representative of the bishop of Pamplona (*el ordinario*); (5) *el licenciado* Martín Pérez de Amasa, judge of confiscations; (6) *el doctor* Juan González, dean of La Calzada; (7) Fray Pedro Venero, prior of the Dominican convent at Logroño, Nuestra Señora de Valcuerno de Extramuros; and (8) Fray Antonio de Villacre, Franciscan provincial for the province of Burgos.

The three last members of the jury are described as *consultores* and *calificadores* (advisers to the Tribunal and theological experts). According to the rules for delivering judgment, first the *consultores*, next the bishop's representative, and last the inquisitors, beginning with the most junior inquisitor, were to deliver their verdict. Each verdict was to be noted down immediately, before proceeding to the next, and it was the duty of the senior inquisitor to see that each member had the opportunity to state his opinion freely.[110] The five who delivered their judgment before Salazar voted that all be burned at the stake, as did Valle and Becerra. The sole person who was not convinced of the prisoner's guilt was Salazar.[111] His vote went against all the others', but even so Salazar later on reproached himself for not having interfered more directly with his colleagues then. (In a communication to *la Suprema* a couple of years later Salazar stated that he had been aware that on various essential points his colleagues' arguments were at variance with the actual facts and the contents of the trial records, but he had kept silent. For one thing he was uncertain whether the regulations for judging permitted him to make amendments after he had delivered his verdict, and for another he hoped that the Council would take steps when it saw the contradictions between the verdicts and the original trial records.)[112]

The first part of Salazar's verdict was given in an extremely compact style and presupposed that the case was already familiar to those present. Reproducing it in paraphrase will help to make it understandable: Salazar commenced his consideration by saying that he was not convinced that there was sufficient evidence to condemn María de Arburu to the stake. On the one hand it was probable that an ignorant peasant such as she did not dare go to confession for fear of being condemned to death — as was the case, according to the opinion of some of the accused, with some of the first persons to be arrested by the Inquisition (see p. 169). On the other hand the statements of the witnesses (i.e. the other witches) suffered from a number of serious defects: instead of being in complete agreement on the most decisive points, the statements were made in general, vague, and ambiguous terms. For instance the witnesses were unable to state on exactly which night they saw the accused received into the sect; and some of these even contradicted themselves on this point (see chapter 5.4, above). Neither did the witnesses give reliable information as to their accomplices, for in this respect they added or subtracted names that they or others had already, during many interrogations, certified as being involved. Salazar pointed out that:

> On the contrary some of the witches have to date failed to mention the priest, Juan de la Borda, and the monk, Pedro de Arburu. This is true of María de Xumeldegui [i.e. Ximeldegui], María de Lecumberri, Juana de Garagarra, María de Burga, and María Pérez de Burga — the five unmarried women who confessed spontaneously to the inquisitor Juan de Valle Alvarado at Zugarramurdi.[113]

This, continued Salazar, was all the more remarkable since the other witch-witnesses maintained that these two were so distinguished that the Devil honored them particularly by keeping them always beside him and allowing them to assist him at the Black Mass. Therefore it seemed incredible that any of the witches could have avoided noticing them.[114]

He continued by saying that María de Jureteguía, Graciana de Barrenechea, Estevanía de Navarcorena, and Estevanía de Yriarte, as well as others in the first group of prisoners, made no mention at all of the witches' confessions to the Devil, of the Black Mass, or of the Devil's sermons, in spite of the fact that they had all been good *confitentes* and these were matters that all the witches must have known about.

Neither did anyone testify to having seen María de Arburu forswear her faith; nor were there witnesses to any of the other renunciations of faith (apart from the tutor witch who accompanied the novice). It was true that Miguel de Goiburu had begun to assert that he had been present at several persons' renunciations, but he expressed himself in very general terms only. All the rest merely said that they assumed that so and so forswore his faith as they saw him taking part in the sabbath, the dance, and the Devil-worship, and because they witnessed him or her going out on the witches' expeditions of destruction; and since none might do this who were not members of the sect, they assumed that the person concerned had renounced his faith. In other words, contended Salazar, the conclusion that they were guilty of apostasy had been drawn from the evidence of these persons having taken part in the witches' sabbaths and the assumption that they consquently must have renounced their faith. But as the apostasy was *the* crucial question, the evidence should not be regarded as fulfilling the demands of the law as long as it rested only on assumption and suspicion. Besides, it should also have been recalled that the accused people might have been present at the witches' sabbath without having renounced their faith,

> as is the case with the small children and some of the adults who after having come to the sabbath refused to renounce their faith. This, for instance, is apparent from the statements of witnesses against María de Zozaya, and from what María Xumeldegui [i.e. Ximeldegui], the French girl, declared regarding herself, for even though she took part in the *aquelarres* she never renounced her faith, although she was ordered to do so.[115]

The style of the latter part of Salazar's verdict is more explicit,[116] and therefore lends itself more readily than the above to direct quotation:

> Item, according to what scholars say of these phenomena, it is demonstrable that the witches go to the sabbaths many times in dreams [*spiritual y mentalmente;* literally, spiritually and mentally], even though perhaps at other times they participate bodily [*corporalmente*]. This phenomenon is also described in the trial record of Fray Pedro de Arburu by the witnesses' statements concerning his alibi and his [deep] sleep. In spite of the great divergence in the methods of participating in the assemblies, to date none of the accused

[i.e. the witches] have been able to distinguish between these two methods; on the contrary they maintain that they always participate personally and bodily.

But when they err on such a material point it is extremely probable that they are also in error with regard to those they name as their accomplices. It is all the more probable since the scholars say also that at the sabbaths the Devil can with the greatest ease conjure up figures [of innocent people] whom the witches believe are the authentic persons. The same phenomenon may also be seen to appear outside the witches' sabbaths. Thus some of the accused declare that an apparition replaces them in their beds when they are going to the sabbath; in particular María de Zozaya, Miguel de Goiburu, Mari Juanto, María de Echegui, Beltrana de la Fargua, and those to whom María de Echegui refers. This objection could very well be made to many of the most compromising witnesses' statements against the accused, for if, for instance, we take the evidence of witnesses against Juan de la Bastida [alias Lambert], there are some who maintain they have seen him at the *aquelarre* on the selfsame days and times when he was under lock and key in the Tribunal's secret prison.

Similarly [all] the witnesses are [also] mistaken in claiming that the miller Martín de Amayur gave María Presona a blow with a stick. In fact she denies this in all her interrogations during which she otherwise makes such frank confessions both with regard to herself and to the other witches.

Neither have definite proofs been produced by the things that outside witnesses have been brought to confirm, concerning the witches' assemblies, the ointments, the sexual intercourse with the Devil, and the other tangible witch phenomena. In part these investigations suffer from the same uncertainty as those discussed above; and also in the trial of María de Zozaya, the very opposite was proved [i.e., that the witches' requisites were not to be found (see end of chapter 8.4, above)].[117]

Salazar ended his consideration with the conclusion that the Tribunal had considered the evidence to be sufficient in the cases against the witches who had themselves confessed and thereby substantiated the charge. With regard to María de Arburu and the other *negativos*, however, he considered the evidence to be inconclusive, especially on the important counts of the renunciation of faith and subsequent apostasy. Salazar, therefore, suggested that María de Arburu be interrogated under torture in order to ascertain her intentions with regard to the actions of which, according to witnesses, she had been guilty. He thought that similar measures should be taken with the other accused persons who had been with her at the assemblies.[118] What Salazar proposed be done with the other *negativos* does not clearly appear from his verdict, but he probably proposed that they should all be interrogated under torture, this being their only hope of survival.

By voicing these suggestions Salazar had acquired a mortal enemy in the second inquisitor, Juan de Valle Alvarado. Not long afterwards Salazar was assured by Valle that he would never have a moment's peace if he did not adhere to the latter's opinion. "And another time," Salazar related, "when we were sitting in the Tribunal, he rose from his chair screaming and cursing, and shouted that if I ever contradicted him he would never leave me in peace. And this he said so beside himself with rage that he completely neglected to conduct himself with the decency and decorum befitting the grave nature of the matters we were in process of resolving."[119]

Thus, even before the sinister discoveries in Zugarramurdi were revealed to the public in all their horror, Salazar had expressed his doubts as to whether the conclusions of the Inquisition rested on solid foundations. It is hard to define exactly how skeptical Salazar had become. We have seen that his judgment in the cases against the *confitente* witches which was made at another *consulta de fe* (see p. 167) was in agreement with his two colleagues; and when the monk and the priest had been subjected to torture and their cases had been judged at a fresh *consulta de fe* the inquisitors' verdict was unanimous here too. It is obvious that Salazar had become skeptical about the premises on which his colleagues had based their conduct of the trial, but he probably realized with resignation that he could not prevent them from holding their auto de fe. The affair had reached the point of no return.

CHAPTER NINE
The Auto de Fe

1. THE FINAL PREPARATIONS

HE INQUISITORS HAD PREPARED TWENTY-five miscellaneous heresy cases, in addition to the witch cases, in readiness for the auto de fe.[1] Six persons were to be condemned for Judaism,[2] one for Mohammedanism, one for Lutheranism, one for bigamy,[3] twelve for blasphemous and heretical utterances,[4] and two for masquerading as agents of the Inquisition.[5] Normally these, and not witches, were the types of delinquents to be seen at the autos de fe; the auto de fe at Logroño in 1610 was significant enough that many years afterwards it was remembered in Inquisition circles as "the one with the witches" (él de las brujas).[6]

A Spanish auto de fe (literally: act of faith) was an extremely ceremonious occasion, something in the nature of a dramatic representation of the Day of Judgment, though at the same time it was a public entertainment.[7] The autos de fe were events which drew an audience from many miles around, just as throughout Europe people eagerly traveled for miles to witness an execution. In both cases the punishment had the effect of being both a terrifying example and an official confirmation of basic social values, whether it was concerned with the protection of the rights of property or the purity of the Christian Faith.

A general auto de fe had not been held at Logroño for many years. There had been small autos de fe (autillos) in the cathedral church, Nuestra Señora de la Redonda, in 1600, 1601,

1602, and 1603,[8] but a "general public auto de fe" (*auto publico general*) in the town square had not taken place since 1593.[9] Toward the close of the sixteenth century the burning of heretics was perceptibly on the decline and this coincided with a decrease in the number of autos de fe, but when these ceremonial demonstrations of the power and might of the Holy Office did take place they were held with the greatest pomp and magnificence.[10]

While the inquisitors were spending the last days before the auto de fe of 1610 working on the report for the king, the town bustled with activity as everything was prepared for the event. In the square the carpenters erected the stage and stands for the spectators. This edifice consisted of a square wooden structure eighty-four feet long on each side.[11] On the side which adjoined the town hall (*las casas del consistorio*), the carpenters built a terraced stand with eleven levels which provided seating for a thousand spectators. In the center of the top level they constructed a box for the inquisitors, which was accessible from the top floor of the town hall. This last had been the inquisitors' invention, so that, as they wrote in one of their letters to *la Suprema*, they could mount by the staircase *inside* the building and make their appearance before the crowd with all the greater solemnity![12] On the opposite side of the stage a similar stepped platform was erected with seats for the delinquents.[13] It is not clear from the description whether the stage was enclosed in any way on the other two sides, but presumably the floor of the stage would have been raised above ground level so that all the spectators who had to make do with standing room out in the square could see what was going on.[14] A square platform was placed in the center of the stage on which the delinquent was to sit while his sentence was announced. Two pulpits, from which the declamations were to be made, were placed at other points on the stage,[15] and the remaining space was taken up with portable benches.[16] On payment of forty *reales* to the owners of the surrounding buildings the Tribunal obtained the right to use, as box seats, all the windows facing the square.[17] The stage and the seating accommodation cost the Tribunal fifteen hundred *reales*.[18] (In order to establish monetary value: the annual wage of the Tribunal porter was fifteen hundred *reales*, and the prisoners' food was calculated at one *real* per day.)[19]

In various workshops scattered about the town other work-

Figure 12.   The setting for a Spanish auto de fe. In the middle of the scene a bishop is removing all the ecclesiastical signs of dignity from a priest who is going to be sentenced by the Inquisition.

ers busied themselves preparing the garments to be worn by
the delinquents at the auto de fe and also the effigies of the
dead witches who were to be sentenced in absentia. The effigies (las mascaras y estatuas) were made by a certain Cosme de
Arellano, who received 142 reales for the work. Afterwards
they were painted and decorated with the customary symbols
of the Inquisition by the artist Mateo Ruiz for 130 reales. Finally
the placards for the sambenitos were produced by the printer
Juan de Mongastón for 31 reales.[20] One item in the account, for
397 reales, which was paid out in thirteen portions, apparently
was for thirteen loads of wood for the thirteen negativos who
had originally been condemned to the stake.[21] After the addition of other items the total expenses of the auto de fe
amounted to 2,541 reales, which was not excessive in comparison to what other tribunals spent on their autos de fe.[22]

2. SATURDAY

On Saturday 6 November, the day preceding the auto de fe,
people poured into Logroño from far and wide. The scene was
described by a member of the Inquisition in a long letter to the
inquisitorial commissioner at Vitoria, the treasurer Pedro
Gámiz:[23]

> I was in no doubt, up to the night before the auto de fe, that
> Your Grace would be coming, particularly since you could
> be certain of accommodations with any of us. I kept my
> [guest room] available up to that day in case Your Grace
> should need it; and this caused me no little difficulty, for I
> can assure Your Grace that never before have so many
> people been gathered together in this town. It is estimated
> that over thirty thousand souls have assembled here from
> France, Aragón, Navarra, Vizcaya, and various parts of
> Castilla. The reason for such enthusiasm was the publica-
> tion of the announcement that the vile sect of the witches
> was to be revealed at this auto de fe.[24]

We shall return later to the letter from this anonymous
member of the Inquisition (or ministro to the Holy Office at
Logroño, as he calls himself) to his colleague at Vitoria. We
must accept his figure of thirty thousand spectators with certain reservations, but there is no doubt that the response to the
announcement was overwhelming. Thus the inquisitors could
write in a letter to la Suprema dated 13 November that so many
had arrived "from all parts of the kingdom and from abroad

that there were simply not enough accommodations for them in the town. Many found lodgings in the neighboring villages but [even so] the streets of the town were completely blocked by the crowds."[25] (Presumably a great proportion of the visitors were camping out in the streets of Logroño.)

The auto de fe commenced at two o'clock on Saturday afternoon with "the procession of the Green Cross." Leading the procession were a thousand or so *familiares,* commissioners, and notaries with their staves and golden emblems and with the standard of the Inquisition fraternity at their head. Next came all the religious orders of the town, Dominicans, Franciscans, Mercedarians, Trinitarians, and Jesuits, followed by all the parish priests and monks from the surrounding districts. Finally, in the last section of the procession came "the Green Cross," the emblem of the Inquisition. It was borne by the prior (*guardián*) of the Franciscan monastery, who was also *calificador* to the Tribunal. Before him walked a large group of church choristers and musicians, followed by two distinguished ecclesiastics of the cathedral chapter, then came the inquisitors and other employees of the Tribunal, and at the very end the constable (*alguacil*) to the Inquisition with his scepter.

The procession wound its way through the crowded streets and came to a halt in the square. Here the Green Cross was solemnly borne up the steps of the spectators' stand and set down at the highest point. When darkness fell lanterns were lit which brightly illuminated the stage and the Brothers of the Inquisition mounted a vigil around the Green Cross throughout the night.[26]

Nothing further took place in the town that day. But behind the walls of the Tribunal the six who were to be burned alive were acquainted with their fate, and so that they should not spend their last night on earth alone, monks were sent to sit up with them in their cells. The inquisitors hoped that the announcement of the death sentences would have the effect of making the six *negativos* confess, so that they would not then need to send them to the stake.[27] But the *negativos* stood firm. María de Arburu (the mother of the monk), María Bastán de la Borda (the mother of the priest), sixty-six-year-old Graciana Xarra, fifty-four-year-old María de Echatute, fifty-year-old Domingo de Subildegui, and thirty-six-year-old Petri de Juangorena all went through the night without succumbing to the temptation to save their lives by making a false confession. The other delinquents were kept in ignorance of the result of their cases, which would not be made known to them until the auto de fe next day.[28]

3. SUNDAY

Before sunrise on Sunday morning all the prisoners were awakened and taken up to the courtroom of the Tribunal. Here they were dressed and given cakes to eat in company with the Brothers of the Inquisition who were to accompany them to the auto de fe and the monks who had watched throughout the night with those under sentence of death.[29]

Between six and seven o'clock the procession began to emerge from the Tribunal's building. All the delinquents went barefoot and each one walked between two Brothers of the Inquisition. First came a group of twenty-one men and women; from their garments and from the symbols painted on them the spectators could see that they were to do penance for less serious offenses such as heretical utterances, blasphemy, and bigamy. Six had scourges around their necks to indicate that they were to be punished by whipping.

After them followed another twenty-one delinquents wearing *sambenitos* and *corozas* (a kind of tall bishop's mitre). The painted symbols on their garments and caps showed that they were to be reconciled. There were in reality only fourteen persons in this group, for the others were present only in effigy: these were the seven witches who had died during the trial as "good *confitentes*."

Finally there were eleven delinquents whose *sambenitos* and caps were covered with figures of devils and flames. These were the eleven witches condemned to the stake. Only six of them were alive; the other five were in effigy. The effigies were carried on long poles, and behind each followed a man bearing a small coffin on his head. The coffins contained the remains of the deceased, which had been carefully preserved for the occasion.

The fifty-three delinquents were followed by the four secretaries of the Inquisition, who rode on horseback. In their midst was a mule carrying on its back a velvet-covered document chest, containing the sentences to be read out at the auto de fe. The *fiscal* to the Tribunal, Dr. San Vicente, rode behind them carrying the standard of the Inquisition. Lastly came the

Figure 13. Procession, including delinquents, going to an auto de fe. Each delinquent is accompanied by a familiar of the Inquisition.

three inquisitors, together with a number of local dignitaries, all on horseback.

When the procession reached the square all the delinquents were led to their seats on one side of the stage. The eleven who were to be burned were placed highest up in the back row; the twenty-one who were to be reconciled had seats in the middle rows; and the other twenty-one who were to receive milder penalties were placed in the front rows. There they sat facing the spectators in the large stand on the opposite side of the stage adjoining the town hall. Meanwhile the inquisitors mounted the staircase in the building and appeared solemnly before the crowd. They took their seats in their box, which was adorned with the canopy of the Tribunal. On the highest row to their right were the ecclesiastical dignitaries, and to their left the representatives of the secular authorities. Lower down in the stand sat the rest of the employees of the Tribunal together with the *consultores, calificadores,* and a great number of specially invited ecclesiastical guests. The remainder of the spectators' stand and the portable benches on the stage were occupied by noble lords and distinguished persons invited from far and wide.

The auto de fe commenced with a sermon preached by the Dominican prior Fray Pedro de Venero, who, it will be recalled, had himself been a member of the jury which had judged the accused. Immediately following the sermon the oath of loyalty to the Holy Office was read out and responded to with a resounding *amen* from the thousands of spectators out in the square.

Next began the pronouncement of the sentences. One by one each accused was taken down onto the stage and made to take his place on the platform where he was to sit facing the inquisitors while listening to the outcome of his case. Two inquisitorial secretaries took turns reading the sentences from the two pulpits. However, on the first day the only sentences read were those of the eleven witches who were to be burned. The prologues to the judgments were immensely long and detailed (for instance, it must have taken at least two hours to read out María de Zozaya's sentence alone, since it filled forty folio pages). When all the ghastly deeds of the condemned prisoners had finally been revealed to the gaping multitude, there remained only one hour until sunset.

The day ended with the transfer of the six *negativos,* together with the five effigies and coffins, into the hands of the secular authorities so that the punishment might be carried out. Accompanied by soldiers they were then led out to the place where the faggots and the stakes stood ready. Beside each of the six walked a monk who prepared the person for death with consolation and admonition. The inquisitors seem to have continued to the last to hope that the "stubborn *negativos*" would confess. But the six men and women remained resolute to the end; as the inquisitors wrote to *la Suprema* on 13 November, "nothing occurred to warrant any alteration in the sentences."[30]

4. MONDAY

When the sun rose on Monday morning the forty-two remaining delinquents were already in their places. As the Tribunal building was situated outside the town they had been confined for the night in some rooms provided by the town hall. The auto de fe opened with a sermon preached by the Franciscan provincial Fray Antonio de Villacre. Like the preacher on the preceding day he had been a member of the sentencing jury.[31]

Next the reading of the sentences began. According to Mongastón's pamphlet, which is an eyewitness account, the eighteen witches were not dealt with immediately. The sentences of the twenty-four delinquents who were guilty of other forms of heresy were read out first.[32] (Twenty-one were to receive milder penalties, three were to be reconciled, as were also the remaining witches.) We shall take a closer look at four of these cases, as they are of some interest for our study.

A twenty-five-year-old student, Francisco Ruiz, from Portugalete in Vizcaya, was sentenced to a six-year exile from the district of the Tribunal. His crime consisted of having "personified" the Holy Office. He had posed as a secretary to the Inquisition and played the part of a self-appointed witch-finder.[33]

A merchant from Vitoria, Pedro González de Trocanis, had also passed himself off as a secretary of the Inquisition; he, however, was sentenced to two hundred strokes of the lash, five years in the galleys, and exile for life from the district of the Tribunal. The résumé of his case merely states that he went about Navarra with forged credentials giving him power to question witnesses and make arrests. When he had collected

Figure 14.   The condemned prisoners are taken to the stake by soldiers while friars are making a last effort to make them confess their heresy so that at least their souls may escape perdition.

sufficient evidence for indictment he would confront the persons involved with the materials he had gathered and extort
money from them for destroying it.[34] Unfortunately the
sources give no indication of what sort of evidence he collected
or tell us whether he was interested in witch-hunting at all.

Two thirty-year-old parish clerks were sentenced for heretical utterances and sorcery. They were both made to renounce
their heresy *de levi* and were exiled for four and six months
respectively. One of them, *el bachiller* Dionisio de Lerma, confessed that he made a living by curing people with spells and
writing prescriptions for medicine, and he admitted having
made use of vestments and baptismal oil for some of his
"frauds and sorceries" (*embustes y hechicerías*).[35] The other,
Pedro Manrique, was parish clerk at Laguardia. He had also
cured people with magic spells, and he confessed that one of
his spells contained the words of transubstantiation in the
communion service.[36]

Presumably it took the greater part of the morning to acquaint the first twenty-four delinquents with their sentences.
Next began the reading out of the horrific deeds of the eighteen
witches who remained from the preceding day. Probably the
first to be dealt with were the sentences of Miguel de Goiburu,
Graciana de Barrenechea, and her two daughters (see chapter
5). As we have mentioned previously, the inquisitors had
prepared a combined sentence for these four cases; but even so
it must have taken at least two and a half hours to read out the
thirty closely written folio pages.[37] The other witches' sentences were also fairly verbose, and as the afternoon wore on
they were still far from finished. The inquisitors therefore gave
orders for the remaining sentences to be read in a shortened
form.[38]

With the advent of evening the reading came to an end and
the seven effigies, the eleven live witches, and three other
heretics were led before the inquisitors' box, where the ceremony of reconciliation was to take place. They were all made to
kneel down, and while the many thousands of spectators out
in the square observed the deepest silence, the solemn ceremony commenced.[39] One by one the witches repeated a formula whereby they dissociated themselves from all their errors
and embraced the teaching of the Catholic Church, which they
swore to follow for the rest of their lives. Thereupon the senior
inquisitor, Alonso Becerra, released them from excommunica-

Figure 15.   The preparation of the stake.

tion and received them again into the Holy Catholic Church.[40]
The reconciliation ceremony ended half an hour after sunset.[41]
Afterwards the senior inquisitor approached María de
Jureteguía and took off her penitential garment. While he was
removing the *sambenito* he cried out that the Inquisition was
being thus merciful to her because she had been a truly re-
morseful *confitente* and also so that she could stand as an
example for all other heretics. This act, according to Mongastón's account, made a deep impression on all those present,
who offered up prolonged praise to God and the Holy Office.[42]

The auto de fe ended with the returning of the Green Cross
to the Tribunal. Immediately behind it followed the church
musicians and choir intoning the Te Deum. The rear of the
procession was made up of the penitent delinquents who were
to be taken back to the Tribunal.[43] Slowly the square began to
empty. The mood of the people returning to their homes was
recorded for us in the last lines of Mongastón's pamphlet:
"Having listened to so many ghastly monstrosities for the
space of two whole days ... we all returned to our several
homes, crossing ourselves the while."[44]

5. OFFICIAL AND UNOFFICIAL REPORTS OF THE AUTO DE FE

While the sentences were being read out several spectators sat
taking notes, and these notes were later expanded into coherent accounts of the auto de fe. An example is the thirteen-
page report sent by the anonymous member of the Inquisition
staff to the commissioner at Vitoria. By way of introduction he
assured his colleague that it was the most reliable and the
longest account of those circulating in the town. He continued
with the following most interesting information regarding the
effect of the auto de fe:

> As Your Grace is aware, doubt prevailed previously as to
> whether the sect actually existed or not, and whether they
> participated in the Devil's assemblies with soul and body or
> it was merely something they experienced in dreams. Now,
> however, all these questions have been clarified, as Your
> Grace will see from this report ... The witches themselves
> have described most fully how they subject themselves to
> the Devil and revealed what rewards and advantages the
> Devil grants them in recompense.[45]

The anonymous writer dated this report 14 November, only a

few days after the auto de fe. Like the author of Mongastón's pamphlet, he had been deeply affected by what he had heard; he ended with the heartfelt words: "May God in His mercy assist us to stamp out this devilish and pernicious sect which is so alarmingly widespread."[46]

The Tribunal sent off an account of the auto de fe to *la Suprema* as early as 13 November: "The people observed the deepest silence during the entire ceremony and paid the greatest attention, and no untoward incidents of any kind occurred," ran the inquisitors' letter, and it went on to assert that the auto de fe "has been to the great edification of the people. For all agree that never before have they experienced anything more solemn, more strange, and more authoritative."[47]

The inquisitors continued by stating that on that very day they had pronounced sentence on the monk and the priest behind the locked doors of the Tribunal courtroom. Here they had had them renounce *de levi* (i.e. dissociate themselves positively from the heresy that, according to the final result of the trial, they were only suspected of to a lesser degree; see chapters 3.2 and 8.5). Fray Pedro de Arburu had been sent to the Premonstratensian monastery at Buxeda by Miranda de Ebro, and Juan de la Borda to the Benedictine monastery at San Millán, seven *leguas* (27 miles) north of Logroño.[48] (After having examined the trial records of the monk and the priest for the second time, *la Suprema* had returned them with considerable mitigation of the sentences. The inquisitor general had first and foremost released them from hard labor in the galleys and from the deep disgrace of being put on view to all and sundry at the auto de fe.[49] In the report to Philip III a space had been left open for a short comment on the final sentences of the two ecclesiastics. The inquisitors certainly had not foreseen that they would not appear at the auto de fe at all.)[50]

The letter of 13 November also contained a report on several French persons of rank who came to the auto de fe. It mentioned the witch-judge Armand (?) de Gourgues's participation: Among others, runs the letter, was one "Monsieur *de Gorgos* [*sic*]," a rich nobleman and councillor of the Parliament of Bordeaux, to whom the Queen has entrusted the prosecution of Portuguese Jews and Moors in the Basses-Pyrénées. On the Queen's orders he came in disguise to the auto de fe in order to observe how the witches were punished. He was accompanied by the commissioner of Vera (i.e. the parish priest Hualde; p. 130 ff.), and afterwards expressed his admiration for the clemency which was shown by the Tribunal. He asked the inquisitors for copies of the sentences, but they were not able to grant him this. Nevertheless, it had been noticed that his servants stood all the while at the auto de fe and noted down the sentences as they were read out.[51] On 25 November *la Suprema* sent a reply instructing the inquisitors to send M. de Gourgues a short report of the auto de fe. "Since he is a judge of witches in that country," it is stated in *la Suprema*'s letter, "we may perhaps in this way serve God's case."[52]

Some time later the Tribunal forwarded the customary report on the auto de fe to *la Suprema*.[53] This report, which is the official account of the auto de fe, was based largely on the one that had been intended for the king. Long passages of the text are repeated almost word for word, but the delinquents' names are in a different order and the résumés of their cases are slightly more detailed than in the first version.[54]

Outside the walls of the Tribunal the printers were making the most of the auto de fe. At the beginning of 1611, at Logroño, Juan de Mongastón published the pamphlet of which we have made such frequent use in the preceding sections. On the title page Mongastón revealed that his work was based on a handwritten report of the auto de fe that had come into his possession. The pamphlet fills twenty-eight quarto pages. The first section (folios 2^r-3^v) depicts the course of the auto de fe and describes the processions and the rest of the ceremonial. As mentioned earlier this part is an eyewitness account and therefore of primary historical source value. The second section (folios 3^v-14^v) gives a long and extremely detailed report of the witches' confessions. Portions of it had obviously been noted down during the auto de fe while the sentences were being read out. But long passages of the text bear a highly suspicious resemblance to the reports that the Tribunal had compiled (see diagram 3); as these were not read at the auto de fe, the only reasonable explanation would seem to be that the anonymous author of Mongastón's pamphlet in some way or other had access to the reports of the Tribunal. Although it contains some references from the individual sentences which have not been preserved in other sources, on the whole this section is of only secondary source value. It is worth bearing this in mind when reading what has previously been written

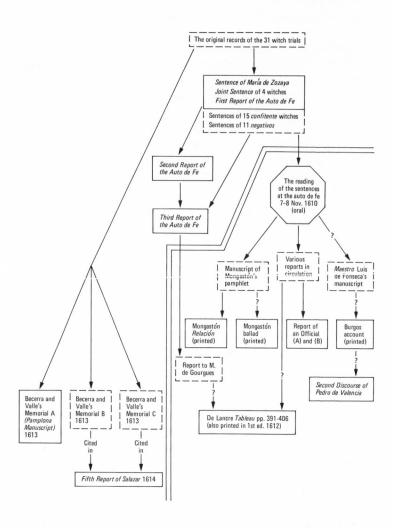

Diagram 3.   Stemma showing how the information about the witch trials was spread. Information below the double line was available to the public; the rest was secret, known to the Tribunal and **la Suprema,** *only.* **Note:** *Regarding Becerra and Valle's Memorials A, B, and C, and the* **Fifth Report of Salazar,** *see below, chapters. 12.5, 12.6, and 12.7 (near end).*

about the renowned auto de fe at Logroño, for those accounts are based almost entirely on Mongastón's pamphlet. The fact that all the handwritten accounts mentioned above are also in existence seems to have escaped the attention of most investigators.[55]

In addition to the lengthy auto de fe report, Mongastón also published a broadsheet ballad with a rhyming account of the witches' confessions.[56] The only surviving example of this is in the Biblioteca Nacional in Madrid. Agustín González de Amezúa, the Cervantes scholar, made use of it at the beginning of the century and even states its accession number in the library's pamphlet section. But no one has since been able to trace this intriguing document.[57]

A printer at Burgos, Juan Baptista Varesio, published an account of the auto de fe at Logroño which filled forty-eight folios in octavo. The author was one Master (*maestro*) Luis de Fonseca. The imprimatur bears the date 8 January 1611, while Mongastón's imprimatur is dated 7 January, so that it is difficult to determine which was the first on the market. At present the Burgos account is known only through Amezúa, who describes a copy which was in the possession of the bibliophile Fray Justo Cuervo at the beginning of the century.[58]

6. THE SENTENCES

After the auto de fe only twelve of the original thirty-one witches were alive. Thirteen had died in prison and six died at the stake (see table 5). The death sentences did not mean that the judgment of the Inquisition had been unusually severe on this occasion. It was the fate which awaited every *negativo* convicted of the graver forms of heresy; and it was also the custom of the Inquisition to sentence "agitators" to be burned at the stake, even when, like María de Zozaya, they were penitent and had made confession. Compared with the penalties that were generally meted out, several of these sentences may be said to have been exceptionally light. María de Jureteguía, who had been the inquisitors' chief witness in exposing the other witches, was sentenced to reconciliation, confiscation of property, *sambenito*, and a six-months' exile. But she had already been relieved of the *sambenito* at the auto de fe, and the place of exile was Urdax, where her husband would have been able to visit her every day. It was not possible to exempt her from the confiscation, but as she had no per-

Table 5. The Sentences of the Thirty-One Witches

Auto de fe no.	Name, age, domicile	Attitude during trial	Position in aquelarre	Food costs (in reales): Charge/Payment		Sentence	No. in Third Report
1	Graciana de Barrenechea, 80, Zugarramurdi	Con	Queen	224	0	Reconciliation in effigy	32
2	Miguel de Goiburu, 66, Zugarramurdi	Con	King, Devil's train-bearer	294	0	"	33
3	Estevanía de Yriarte, 36, Zugarramurdi	Con		326	0	"	34
4	María de Yriarte, 40, Zugarramurdi	Con		526	0	"	35
5	Estevanía de Navarcorena, 80, Zugarramurdi	Con	Second most senior witch	180	116	"	36
6	María Pérez de Barrenechea, 46, Zugarramurdi	Con	Third most senior witch	445	118	"	37
7	Mari Juanto (de Aguirre), 60, Vera, (born at Zugarramurdi)	Con	Superintendent of children	197	0	"	38
8	Martín Vizcar, 80, Zugarramurdi	Con	Devil's train-bearer	408	11	"	39
9	María de Jureteguía, 22, Zugarramurdi	Con		900	0	Reconciliation and 6 mos. exile	25
10	Juana de Telechea, 38, Zugarramurdi	Con		826	60	Reconciliation and 1 yr. imprisonment	26
11	Juanes de Goiburu, 37, Zugarramurdi	Con	Bass drummer	1,083	0	Reconciliation and life imprisonment	27
12	Juanes de Sansín, 20, Zugarramurdi	Con	Side drummer	1,098	0	"	28

	Name		Role			Sentence	
13	María Presona, 70, Zugarramurdi	Con		453	0	′ ′	29
14	María Chipía de Barrenechea, 52, Zugarramurdi	Con		472	0	′ ′	30
15	María de Echegui, 40, Zugarramurdi	Con		448	0	′ ′	31
16	Beltrana de la Fargua, 40, Vera	Con		263	0	Reconciliation and 6 mos. imprisonment	40
17	Juanes de Lambert, 27, Rentería	Con		334	0	Reconciliation and exile for life	41
18	Juanes de Yribarren, 40, Echalar	Con	Jailer	257	0	Reconciliation, 1 yr. imprisonment and exile for life	42
19	María de Zozaya y Arramendi, 80, Rentería	Con	Agitator	279	32	Burning in effigy	43
20	Juanes de Echegui, 68, Zugarramurdi	Neg		120	0	′ ′	44
21	María de Echalecu, 40, Zugarramurdi	Neg		363	0	′ ′	45
22	Juanes de Odia, 60, Zugarramurdi	Neg		308	0	′ ′	46
23	Estevanía de Petrisancena, 37, Urdax	Neg		448	105	′ ′	47
24	María de Arburu, 70, Zugarramurdi	Neg	Queen	457	0	Burning alive	48
25	María Bastán de la Borda, 68, Zugarramurdi	Neg		550	0	′ ′	49
26	María de Echatute, 54, Zugarramurdi	Neg		434	0	′ ′	50
27	Graciana Xarra, 66, Urdax	Neg		461	0	′ ′	51
28	Petri de Juangorena, 36, Zugarramurdi	Neg		560	0	′ ′	52
29	Domingo de Subildegui, 50, Zugarramurdi	Neg		582	0	′ ′	53

Table 5, *continued*

Auto de fe no.	Name, age, domicile	Attitude during trial	Position in aquelarre	Food costs (in reales): Charge/Payment		Sentence	No. in Third Report
30	Fray Pedro de Arburu, 43, Fuenterrabía (born at Zugarramurdi)	Neg		537	0	Renouncement *de levi* and 10 yrs. exile	54
31	Don Juan de la Borda, 34, Urdax	Neg		662	290	Renouncement *de levi* and 3 yrs. exile	55

NOTE: *Con* = *Confitente*; *Neg* = *Negativo(a)*. The last column indicates the numbers assigned to the witches in the *Third Report of the Auto de fe*. The property of all these people was confiscated, and all of them had to wear *sambenitos*. Nos. 16 through 19 were not members of the Zugarramurdi *aquelarre*. Nos. 30 and 31 were presented in the courtroom of the Tribunal. For further details of the penalties and inquisitorial terminology see chapter 3, above.

sonal property, this part of the sentence had no practical significance.[59] Thirty-eight-year-old Juana de Telechea, who was imprisoned together with María de Jureteguía, escaped with a year in the house of penance because she confessed straight away at the first hearing.[60] Juanes de Yribarren, the smith from Echalar, also confessed during the first interrogation, and he too was only imprisoned for one year, but in addition he was sentenced to six years' banishment from Navarra and Guipúzcoa, presumably because he had been jailer at the Echalar *aquelarre*.[61] Beltrana de la Fargua, the French beggar-woman who had made her confession to Hualde at Vera, was let off with six months in prison, though it is true that following that she was to be exiled from Navarra and Guipúzcoa for life.[62] The twenty-seven-year-old smith from Rentería, Juanes de Lambert, was exiled immediately from Navarra and Guipúzcoa; but as he came from Pays de Labourd, this presumably meant merely that he went home to his birthplace. This particularly light sentence no doubt was connected with the fact that he, like so many others, had been a victim of María de Zozaya's recruiting campaign at Rentería.[63] None of the five who were condemned to "life imprisonment" had made early confessions.[64] "Life imprisonment" in fact seldom meant more than three or four years in the house of penance, providing that the delinquent comported himself as a good and repentant *confitente*. Despite their partial acquittal it was, paradoxically enough, the monk Pedro de Arburu and the priest Juan de la Borda who received the hardest sentences: ten and three years' confinement respectively in a monastery outside the borders of Navarra, and exile for life from the dioceses of Calahorra and Pamplona.[65] This was far more than was normally imposed on those who endured the torture without admitting anything.

During the period of the trial, almost two years, the Tribunal had spent 14,495 *reales* on the prisoners' subsistence. They had recovered only 732 *reales* of this, almost half of it paid by the priest Juan de la Borda. He owed 662 *reales* and paid 290. Only six of the other prisoners were in a position to pay anything toward their food (see table 5 "food costs"). When the account was made up the Tribunal had a deficit of 13,763 *reales*, which was five times as much as the auto de fe had cost.

To all outward appearances the auto de fe had been a triumph for the inquisitors. The witch sect was now an established fact, for who would dare to doubt the existence of the witches after they had been judged at such a great ceremony as the auto de fe at Logroño? The ratio of *confitentes* to *negativos* at the auto de fe had been nineteen to ten (the two ecclesiastics who denied had not been present). This considerable predominance of penitent confessions had been sufficient to produce the conviction that the trial was well founded.[66] Salazar's criticism of the premises of judgment and his efforts to give the accused a fair trial never became known outside the Inquisition. On the contrary, as an irony of fate, it was put about in ecclesiastical circles in Pamplona that it was *Salazar* who had been the "cruel and despotic" judge during the trial, and that he was to blame for several witches having gone to the stake.[67]

But it was not long before Becerra's and Valle's sinister achievements began to be undermined by persons outside the Tribunal. These were nearly all working for the bishop of Pamplona, the influential and politically experienced Antonio Venegas de Figueroa. He had adopted a critical attitude toward this witch trial at an earlier stage, and when the Tribunal held the auto de fe he dissociated himself from it by absenting himself despite repeated invitations from the inquisitors.[68]

CHAPTER TEN
The Great Persecution

HE WITCH-HUNT THAT FOLLOWED IN THE wake of Valle's visitation was, as we have seen, limited to a very few towns. In the province of Guipúzcoa, Rentería was the only victim, with the mass hysteria centering round the bewitched children. In Navarra the epidemic was confined to Vera, Lesaca, Yanci, and Echalar, while Aranaz, the fifth town of Las Cinco Villas, was not affected.[2] Judging from the sources there was no outbreak of the witch epidemic in other places, although there were some isolated instances of confessions and accusations.[3]

At Zugarramurdi, where the epidemic had reached its crisis around Christmas 1608, it seems already to have been on the decline when Valle arrived there the next summer. And after the Tribunal had arrested the sixteen witches, on 3 March 1610 (see chapter 8.1), the other towns too became quieter. Indeed, it would seem that in the mountains of Navarra and on the seaboard at Rentería all was quiet during the entire spring and summer of 1610. No mention is made of fresh persecutions, and from the end of March until well on into August not even a single witch confession is known.[4]

During the autumn the trouble began to flare up again throughout the whole mountain region of northern Navarra. The first report came from the abbot of Urdax, Fray León de Araníbar, who had become an inquisitorial commissioner in the meantime. On 4 October he wrote to the Tribunal that the situation in the area was worsening day by day. He therefore felt obliged to remind the inquisitors that they had promised to provide a solution to the witch problem. Fray León described the gravity of the situation with simplicity and urgency:

> The evil has now gone so far that we are no longer concerned that there are witches, although they are being exposed by the dozen, if only they refrain from bewitching or infecting others. I am thinking particularly about the children, for it makes me weep blood when I see the parents crying to Heaven for aid.

The abbot went on to describe the desperation of the people, who could do nothing to combat the witches. And if it had not been for his admonitions they would have murdered some of the witches by now, Fray León maintained, for he knew of an instance in which the inhabitants of a village in France had lynched an old woman "a few days" earlier. The village was only two *leguas* (7.6 miles) from the monastery. The old woman had made a confession of all her witchcraft, but nonetheless she kept on taking children to the witches' sabbath. After repeated warnings she admitted that she had been unable to stop herself from fetching the children, and so they burned her.[5]

Fray León took this opportunity to enclose confessions of witchcraft made by five girls who lived near the monastery. He stated in his letter that they were the same five who had denounced themselves on Valle's journey of visitation (see table 2). They had all relapsed in the meantime, and even after having made their fresh confessions to Fray León and an inquisitorial notary, they had all again been to an *aquelarre* which took place on the very night after they had been interrogated, and as meanwhile the notary had returned home, Fray León had been obliged to write the last statements himself with two monks as witnesses.[6] Matters had now gone so far, Fray León wrote further, that even quite small girls had begun taking children to the witches' sabbath; for instance, in her most recent confession, thirteen-year-old María de Burga admitted having taken two children to the sabbath.[7] After these last experiences Fray León did not hold out much hope of the witches mending their ways. Therefore he suggested to the Inquisition that they should no longer be given any protection. It would be preferable for the people to stab to death those who took the children to the sabbath, for otherwise the whole region would go to ruin.[8]

Fray León concluded his letter by informing the Tribunal of two new *aquelarres* that were in course of being exposed. He himself had discovered one of them at Elgorriaga. He told the Tribunal that there was "a fearful amount of wickedness" in the village, which lay next to Santesteban, but that he was not yet finished collecting information.[9] The second *aquelarre* was exposed by the prior Fray Josef de Elizondo, who was second head at the monastery and who received his information from a thirteen-year-old niece at Elizondo. "This has cost him a great deal of trouble," related Fray León, "for the girl had scruples and at first would not reveal the names of her accomplices. The zeal with which he is applying himself to the case, both in his preaching and as confessor, makes him deserve every possible reward with which Your Eminence [i.e. Valle] can recompense him." This nicely set the scene for the prior's first request to the Tribunal, which asked that he might have dispensation to give his niece absolution.[10] Fray Josef must without any doubt have promised the girl "legal aid" in return for her divulging the names of the other witches.[11]

When the inquisitors submitted the report of Valle's visitation on 10 July 1610 they stated that at the time of writing twenty *aquelarres* had been discovered.[12] In the letter to the Duke of Lerma of 1 November (see chapter 8.6) the figure had increased to twenty-two.[13] Presumably the two sabbaths mentioned above had been added to the Tribunal's original total.

On 14 December the inquisitors wrote anxiously to *la Suprema* that during the last two months (that is, since the middle of October) they had received a large number of new witch confessions from various places. However, in order not to trouble the inquisitor general with such a quantity of documents so near Christmas, they thought it sufficient to include only the confessions collected by Fray León at Elgorriaga and Santesteban, two towns where the witches held their sabbath in common.[14]

Three days previously, on 11 December, the dean of Santesteban, *el licenciado* Miguel de Yrisarri, presented himself before the Tribunal. He had come on behalf of his town to inform the inquisitors of the terrible plague of witches which had afflicted Santesteban and Elgorriaga. Soon after Fray León had questioned a large number of "bewitched" children, no fewer than nine had been taken to the sabbath. This had happened the night before the dean's departure, and in order to calm the agitated parents the town had felt compelled to imprison two of the most notorious witches. At the same time, he was delivering a letter to the Tribunal from the authorities at Santesteban beseeching immediate assistance. The dean seems to have had with him fifteen-year-old Juanes de Narvarte, who was the son of one of the imprisoned witches.[15] That very day this boy made a copious confession to the Tribunal in which he gave evidence against, among others, his own mother.[16] We cannot tell whether the Tribunal had received reports of witch disturbances from other places, but shortly after New Year's the persecutions began to increase greatly in violence and then spread to the whole of northern Navarra.

It is beyond doubt that the auto de fe had served to stimulate this development, but, as we have seen, the hunt was already on several weeks previously. The auto de fe could not therefore have been the sole reason for the fresh outbreak of the witch craze. At Urdax and Zugarramurdi we can put the blame on the persecutions in France. But why had the preaching friars at Urdax suddenly taken to operating so far away from their base? Why had Fray León been on a witch-hunt in distant Santesteban? Why was Fray Josef working at Elizondo? And why had Dean Yrisarri, who had previously been of a peaceful disposition, suddenly turned into a zealous witch persecutor?

2. THE PREACHING CRUSADE

It is absolutely certain that the recrudescence of the witch craze arose out of the preaching crusade launched in the autumn of 1610. The inquisitors had suggested, in the long letter of 10 July 1610 to *la Suprema*, that preachers should be sent up into the mountains to give Christian instruction to the people. The registers of the Tribunal showed that this had been done in a similar situation in 1527. To institute the action the Inquisition required a letter from the king to be sent to the bishops in the Logroño district and to the heads of the various preaching orders requesting them to send preachers to the infested area.[17] On 3 August the Council of the Inquisition forwarded the proposal to the king, with a report describing how the witch sect was gaining ground in Navarra on account of the ignorance and simplicity of the people.[18] On 5 September Philip III wrote his letter. It was sent to the bishops of Pamplona, Calahorra, Burgos, and Tarazona; to the heads of the

Franciscans in the provinces of Burgos and Vizcaya, to the provincials of the Dominicans and the Jesuits in Castilla, and to the heads of other orders. All received instructions to dispatch preachers as soon as possible in order to convert all those who might be influenced by the evil sect.[19]

In the meantime, the Tribunal at Logroño was possibly experiencing some misgivings, for when later on in the autumn it received applications from several monasteries in the town stating that they were prepared to send off preachers, the Tribunal replied that they would be informed when the time was ripe.[20] Many months later the inquisitors learned that preachers had in fact been up to the witch-plagued regions of Navarra under instructions from the bishop of Pamplona but without the sanction of the Tribunal.[21]

About 21 November a group of Jesuits arrived in Lesaca.[22] One of them was Hernando de Solarte. He was accompanied by two or three other Jesuits. They all came from a college in Vizcaya and were therefore proficient in the Basque language.[23] They limited themselves to visiting Las Cinco Villas: Lesaca, Vera, Echalar, Aranaz, and Yanci. Their stay was relatively brief, for by the New Year they had returned home via Santesteban.[24]

At the same time as the Jesuits — or perhaps slightly earlier — a group of Basque-speaking Franciscan monks arrived and these too came from Vizcaya.[25] Like Solarte and his companions they stayed for a while in Las Cinco Villas, but they also visited a number of other places and presumably penetrated as far as Zugarramurdi; in any case they did not get home before some time in March of 1611. They went first to Pamplona to make their report to Bishop Venegas de Figueroa, and from there they continued to Logroño to inform the inquisitors of their activities.[26] One of the Franciscan preaching friars was Fray Domingo de Sardo. Some months later he was to accompany Salazar as interpreter on his journey of visitation.[27]

Extremely detailed reports of the Jesuits' journeys were preserved in the letters written by Solarte to his provincial at Valladolid and to the bishop of Pamplona (SD Texts 3, 4, 9, and 10). The Franciscans also composed a report on their journey, but this unfortunately has not been kept. We know only that the bishop of Pamplona made use of it when preparing his report of 1 April 1611 to the inquisitor general (SD Text 8). It is most likely that he would have quoted the most notable results of the Franciscans' journey. The bishop's report claims to relate to the period June-December 1610 only, but it nevertheless mentions events occurring both earlier and later.[28]

Various references suggest that the Franciscans preached against the witches with great zeal. They were successful in the confessional in persuading many suspects to turn themselves in and confess to the Inquisition.[29] On the contrary Solarte and his companions became increasingly skeptical during their journey. In their confessionals they heard how several so-called witches had made false and fictitious confessions. When the inquisitors realized the true nature of the Jesuits' mission they were no doubt extremely glad that no other preachers had been sent to the area.

3. THE TRIBUNAL'S WITCH-HUNT

By having launched the battle against the witches, the Inquisition had put itself in the position of guarantor of the reality of witchcraft. The evidence had been exhibited at the auto de fe and now the time was ripe to make a broad-fronted attack on the abominable sect. Now the towns plagued by the witches, after long and patient expectation, could recommence the hunt. Now the inquisitorial commissioners and other zealous souls could set about reexamining with a fine-tooth comb the villages where nothing previously had been discovered. Now the Tribunal could again send an inquisitor on visitation to the infested area to investigate matters on the spot. But as time passed and no action was taken by the Tribunal, the people began to grow impatient.

Shortly after New Year's Day the inquisitorial commissioner at Vera, Hualde, wrote that he had been forced to lock up the fathers of the "bewitched" children three times in order to prevent them from murdering the witches, and he continued in reproachful tones:

> I fear that they will carry out their threats in earnest at the first available opportunity. For the people are highly incensed and have utterly lost hope of the law ever being put into effect. The auto de fe is already so far in the past and they believed — as I had certainly promised them — that as soon as it was over Your Eminence [Valle] would set out [on visitation].[30]

In other places the people lost patience and took matters into their own hands. In the towns around Santesteban the local authorities took the lead by sanctioning acts of violence, imprisonment, and torture, which cost a number of lives. The charge that the Inquisition had prepared, and which preachers and other agitators had distributed so efficiently, produced explosions of such force that the Tribunal was well on the way to losing control of the situation. Three months after the auto de fe the whole of this area of the Pyrenees was ablaze. From Vera down to Santesteban and on up through the Baztán Valley to Zugarramurdi, there was hardly a town without "bewitched" children who were taken to the witches' sabbath at night and who named all those they had seen there.[31]

It is quite difficult for us to imagine the extreme which popular violence reached on this occasion, but the bishop's report, based as it is on primary sources, gives us an impression of the lynch-hysteria which dominated the area:

> The moment a person is accused [of witchcraft] on the basis of the statements of two, three, or more children, a large crowd of people rush to his house and in the name of justice they seize him, submitting him to monstrous and cruel tortures because of the hatred and bitterness felt towards anyone accused of this crime.
>
> The crowd tortured some by laying them on their backs along benches and binding them round with ropes from their feet up to their arms. Then using the garrotte or stick they twist the rope tighter and tighter. Under this form of torture a woman in Sumbilla died. Others they torture by tying them from their feet up to their arms to the trunk of an apple tree; and turning the garrotte, they tighten the ropes so that they suffer hideous pain. Some even die, as did a pregnant woman in Aurtiz, a *barrio* of Ituren.
>
> They torture others with a long ladder; that is, they place some four or five of the said persons [between the rungs] at one end of the ladder and then force them to walk dragging the ladder. Now and again someone lifts the end which is trailing along the ground and, giving the ladder a good push, throws them all to the ground so that they fall flat on their faces. Then they pull up the end of the ladder and force them with great violence to get up; but before they have found their balance they hurl them backwards, this time, so that their bodies receive severe bruises.
>
> In this fashion they bring them to the bridges found in the said villages. On arrival, having stripped and bound the accused, they lower them until they touch the water. They keep them here some time, slackening the rope sufficiently

so that they sink right to the bottom of the river, and they duck them in the water several times until certain that they are thoroughly exhausted. Thereupon they haul them up and — having ducked them one after the other — place them anew in the ladder and make them wander through the streets of the town, throwing them to the ground as mentioned above. This goes on all night to the accompaniment of shouts and cries and lights in the streets while a thousand insults are hurled at the victims.

They torture others by placing them in stocks with their feet and calves set in tubs of water; and as soon as the weather becomes cold enough the water freezes and they suffer agony. In the village of Legasa they tortured five persons thus, and these, while under such pain, confessed to being witches although later on they again retracted their confessions. (*The Bishop's Report* fol. 8^{r-v}, SD Text 8)

There seem to have been two stages to the witch craze. The mass hysteria centered on the "bewitched" children spread like wildfire, but before the witches could be denounced there was a barrier to be overcome in every village. The parents of the "bewitched" children were often in doubt about what to believe; especially when, as a father at Elgorriaga did, they sat up with the child all night and saw that he did not go anywhere.[32] In the village of Aranaz, which had escaped the previous year's epidemic (see p. 129, above), the witch-hunt did not get under way until November of 1610. It happened after a father had wormed out of his son that it was the cowman Yricia who took him to the *aquelarre*. The father went straight to Yricia, and pointing a dagger at his chest, asked him why he had bewitched his son. After Yricia had confessed to witchcraft he was taken to the commissioner at Lesaca, who received his confession and sent him on to Logroño as a prisoner. During the days following, thirty other child witches at Aranaz confessed that the cowman Yricia had taken them to the *aquelarre* also. After Yricia was removed, the children soon agreed amongst themselves that they were then taken by Juana de Argarate, a sixty-year-old widow. And when she too was arrested the children accused another woman, whose name is unknown.[33]

Now it was no longer necessary for the inquisitorial commissioners to put pressure on the witches in order to make them confess, for this was seen to by the local priests, town councillors, and village elders (*jurados*), assisted by the parents and relatives of the accused persons. The commissioners' chief task was now to interrogate the witches and write down their confessions so that they fulfilled the demands of the Inquisition. For most of the witches, like the cowman Yricia, had already made a confession before being brought before the commissioner.

The abbot of Urdax was the most active of all the commissioners in the district. At the end of January he wrote a long letter to the Tribunal about his work in the towns around Santesteban and in the Baztán Valley, at the same time forwarding the confessions he had received up till then. Lately he had exposed witch confederacies at Donamaría and Gaztelu south of Santesteban and at Arráyoz, Oronoz, and Elizondo in the Baztán Valley (see map 3). In addition he had begun making interrogations at Zubieta, where the parish priest had discovered a witch coven. The energetic abbot had also commenced interrogations at Legasa, but here he complained of slow progress with the intelligence work.[34] Fray León remarked of the enclosed confessions that he had not noted down the names of all the child witches. There were so many of them, he explained, and still more were to come. But as everyone in each town knew who the child witches were, he could easily make lists of them if the Tribunal so wished.[35] The abbot made the following extremely interesting comment on the confessions of the adult witches:

> Some of the confessions are very brief despite the fact that they have been made by elderly persons who have been witches for many years. This is not because I have neglected to put questions to them, for you may be sure that I have grilled them regarding all the things that we already know the witches do at their *aquelarres*, but they answer that they know nothing. However, the truth is that they do not come [to me] out of penitence or remorse, but because they are sent by the civil authorities, or are frightened of them. Others again present themselves because they have been publicly denounced by witches. For these reasons, only very few of them mend their ways [after having made a confession] and abandon their evil arts. No, the witches do not tell me the half of what they know![36]

The messenger who carried Fray León's papers also brought two prisoners with him from Santesteban, two witches whom *la Suprema* had given the Tribunal permission to arrest. In his letter Fray León stated that there was much dissatisfaction in the district because the Inquisition had taken away only these two witches and left all the others "who were much worse."[37] The local authorities themselves had now begun to imprison the witches who were at large. Fray León had attempted to protest against this and warn the towns that they were exceeding their authority, but had then met with strong opposition:

> Some have actually turned on me and asked what I mean by saying that they and their authorities cannot arrest these witches [*brujos y brujas*] who take the children of the village to meetings where they make them renounce their faith, and whip and maltreat them.[38]

Fray León fully realized that he had taken on a task that was utterly insuperable. "There is a fearful amount to be done in every place," he exclaimed in his long letter, "so there is work and to spare here for a thousand years."[39]

On 9 March the Tribunal sent the inquisitor general a preliminary report on the situation. The witch plague, it stated, was particularly bad in a belt of about ten or eleven *leguas* (some 40 miles) broad, stretching from the Baztán Valley to two *leguas* (7.6 miles) west of San Sebastián. In this area alone the Tribunal had exposed witches in twenty-seven towns, and the inquisitors were convinced that there was an *aquelarre* in almost every town and village. From here the sect was spreading eastward toward Aragón, southward to the lowlands of Navarra, and westward along the coast to the provinces of Vizcaya and Santander. They were in the process of exposing *aquelarres* even in the towns in the neighborhood of Logroño and if the towns where *aquelarres* were suspected but not confirmed were included the total would amount to over fifty infested towns.[40] The letter was accompanied by statistics (see table 6) of witchcraft confessions and suspected persons grouped into *aquelarres*.[41] Some of the towns in the list are grouped together as they have *aquelarres* in common (e.g. Zugarramurdi and Urdax, Aranaz and Sumbilla). There are therefore only forty-two *aquelarres* on the list of the inquisitors.

We could spend much time in pondering over this highly unusual statistical document. These figures reveal to us more clearly than any other source of information how the witch persecution in northern Navarra was reaching the proportion of a social disaster. Thus in Urdax and Zugarramurdi, out of

Table 6. Statistics on Witches as Issued by
the Tribunal on 9 March 1611

Towns holding aquelarres	No. of inhabitants	Confitente witches	Persons under suspicion	Total no. of witches
1. Zugarramurdi and Urdax	390	34	124	158
2. Vera	595	32	187	219
3. Echalar	425	19	82	101
4. Lesaca	1,190	23	230	253
5. Yanci	255	10	84	94
6. Aranaz and Sumbilla	650	19	110	129
7. Elgorriaga and Santesteban	440	50	119	169
8. Zubieta and Ituren	515	23	72	95
9. Donamaría	215	20	109	129
10. Gaztelu	70	4	9	13
11. Legasa	165	15	32	47
12. Oronoz, Narvarte, and Oyeregui	570	17	73	90
13. Arráyoz and Ciga	370	20	40	60
14. Garzáin	270	1	0	1
Total for northern Navarra	6,120	287	1,271	1,558
15. Arriba de Araiz		2	9	11
16. Lezaeta		2	18	20
17. Tafalla		1	0	1
Total for the whole of Navarra		292	1,298	1,590
18. Fuenterrabía		4	162	166
19. Rentería		27	84	111
20. San Sebastian and Asteasu		7	41	48
21. Urnieta		2	9	11
22. Andoain		1	3	4
Total for Guipúzcoa		41	299	340

Table 6, continued

Towns holding aquelarres	No. of inhabitants	Confitente witches	Persons under suspicion	Total no. of witches
23. Eguino		3	6	9
24. Alegría		1	?	1
25. Labastida		1	1	2
26. Miranda de Ebro		1	3	4
Total for Alava and other towns in the neighborhood of Logroño		6	10	16
Total results as of 9 March 1611		339	1,607	1,946

Aquelarres in process of exposure

27. Villa de los Arcos (Na)	32. Murieta (Na)	37. Bañares (Lo)
28. Espelette (La)	33. Pamplona (Na)	38. Sojuela y Medrano (Lo)
29. Gorriti (Na)	34. Puente la Reina (Na)	39. Haro (Lo)
30. Aoiz (Na)	35. Ribafrecha (Lo)	40. Matute (Lo)
31. Oyarzun (Gui)	36. Ajamil (Lo)	41. Brujero (not located)
		42. Santander

the 390 or so inhabitants, no fewer than 158 had been branded as witches (34 had made confessions, 124 were under suspicion). At Vera the witches numbered 219, or 36.8 percent of the inhabitants. Nos. 1-14 on the list show clearly that the persecutions were still limited to northern Navarra and Rentería.[42] It is, moreover, worth noting that the figures from some of the first *aquelarres* exposed show signs of stagnation. Twenty-two of the thirty-four confessions which were made at Zugarramurdi and Urdax dated from the auto de fe and Valle's visitation; and of the twenty-three *confitente* witches at Lesaca, thirteen at any rate had made their confessions during Valle's journey (see p. 129 above).[43] Map 3 shows the geographical distribution of exposed witches' sabbaths in northern Navarra and Guipúzcoa. The Tribunal had obtained a total of 339 witch

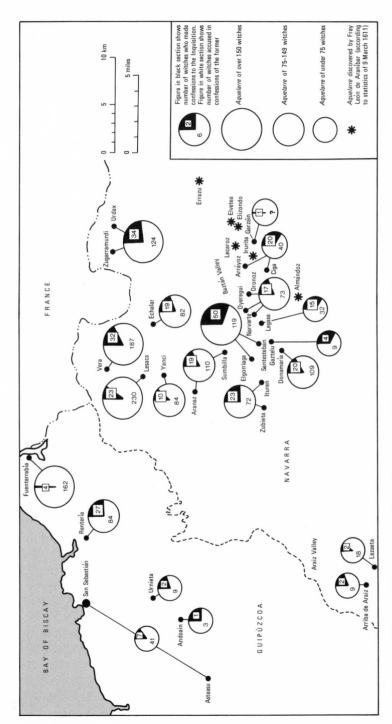

Map 3. *The witch-hunt in northern Navarra and Guipúzcoa, Spring 1611.*

confessions from the whole of this area, and in addition 1,607 persons were under suspicion.

With the advent of May the *fiscal* to the Tribunal estimated that a round figure of 500 witches had been to confession and that over and above these, 2,000 persons were under suspicion.[44] The majority of the 150 or so confessions that had been added were presumably obtained by Fray León who, according to a statement made by Salazar, collected more than all the other commissioners put together.[45] And a letter from the Tribunal to *la Suprema* of 9 April stated that Fray León had sent in more than eighty confessions and that they had almost all been made by adults.[46]

Thirty of the witch confessions that Fray León heard are extant and he himself wrote down most of them. They show the abbot as a tireless man, constantly journeying from one part of the region to another.[47] Eleven of the confessions were made after the Tribunal had completed its witch statistics. These show that Fray León had continued to expose *aquelarres* in the districts south of Santesteban, in Almándoz, and eastwards up through the Baztán Valley, at Irurita, Lecaroz, Elvetea,[48] Elizondo, and Errazu.[49] We can thus add six more *aquelarres* to the fourteen which had already been discovered.

In addition to the preachers, the inquisitorial commissioners, and the local secular and ecclesiastical authorities, there was also a witch-finder at work in the area. This was a fourteen-year-old boy from France, whom the Jesuit Solarte came across on his journey to Las Cinco Villas. The boy claimed to be able to recognize witches by looking them straight in the eye. He asserted that a mark which he had on his body was a sign of his supernatural powers. But under questioning in private the boy admitted to Father Solarte that he had been lying because some woman had persuaded him with blandishments and given him nice things to eat. In his report to the bishop of Pamplona, Solarte told how this witch-finder had been active in Aranaz and Sumbilla and had caused great harm in both places.[50]

4. THE BISHOP OF PAMPLONA
AND OTHER WITCH DEFENDERS

As the witch craze continued to increase, the skeptics began to rouse themselves. They had made themselves heard even during the outbreak of the previous winter (1609-10) (see p. 139 ff.), but now a political battle broke out between those who believed in witches and those who were skeptical. On one side were the Tribunal, the agents of the Inquisition, and the majority of the local ecclesiastic and secular leaders. On the other side were the bishop of Pamplona, the priests at Echalar, the Jesuit Solarte, and an unknown number of parish priests and local officials. In December 1610 the skeptics gained an important ally in the *licenciado* Martín de Yrisarri, the parish priest at Yanci, who crossed over from the enemy camp. Hitherto he had supported the Inquisition's witch-hunt, and this support was all the more important for the Tribunal since he was esteemed all over the area for his great learning.[51]

When Father Solarte arrived at Yanci some time in December, Yrisarri at once began to put him in the picture. He told the Jesuit of all the experiments that had been made with the witches and of all the evidence that had been obtained relating to the existence of the sect. After listening to the licentiate for a considerable time, Solarte inquired one day when they were alone whether the witch phenomenon could not be explained in a different manner; in order to safeguard himself he added that he was only putting forward his explanations as theoretical possibilities. But Yrisarri listened with the greatest interest and admitted afterwards that these possibilities had never occurred to him. He promised to respect Solarte's confidence,[52] whereupon the Jesuit presumably went on to tell him what he had uncovered in the other towns, where in the confessional and in the course of confidential conversations with several of the so-called witches he had discovered that their confessions had been false and that they had been forced to make them under torture or by threats and bribes. One of Solarte's informants, a sixteen-year-old boy at Vera, had produced some quite compromising statements about the inquisitorial commissioner and parish priest Hualde. The boy, who was Hualde's own nephew, confided to Solarte that his uncle had tied him naked to a bed and thrashed him cruelly because he would not admit to being a witch after the other children had denounced him. Others had told Solarte how their own parents ill-treated them and threatened to kill them if they did not confess. Some of those concerned had even gone so far as to encourage their suspected relatives to make a false confession, as this, they explained, was their only means of escaping the stake and confiscation of property and saving their families from infamy.[53]

At any rate, whatever it was that Solarte told Yrisarri, he succeeded in shaking Yrisarri's convictions so much that next day the priest summoned a nineteen-year-old witch from Lesaca, who was known to have denounced many others. When he began to question her as to whether she had borne false witness against anyone the girl burst into tears and said that two women had threatened to kill her if she did not denounce the persons they then named. A certain Fray Juan López who was present at this interrogation afterwards told Solarte that Yrisarri turned as white as a sheet when he heard the girl utter these words.[54]

From that day onward, Yrisarri's eyes were opened to what was really going on in the witch-plagued villages, and he became one of the "witches'" most energetic and courageous defenders. In fact, shortly after the meeting with Solarte he wrote to a friend in Rome asking him to obtain a letter of indulgence (jubileo) from the pope for all members of the witch sect.[55] This would enable the priests to hear their confessions and give them absolution without the interference of the Inquisition. Yrisarri must also certainly have made contact without delay with the skeptical priests at Echalar, whom we have already discussed in a previous chapter (see page 139 ff.).

Hualde at Vera was the first to feel the opposition of the skeptics. In his letter of 10 January to the Tribunal he complained that he had been threatened that if he did not keep quiet about the witches he would certainly pay for it with his life. Others had threatened that he would soon be put in prison.[56] Two days later Hualde and the inquisitorial notary Sebastián de Huarte went to Echalar to question four persons there who confessed to having attended the witches' general meeting at Pamplona on Christmas Night (cf. chapter 5.19, above). The "witches" were unable to give other than vague statements; but during the visit to Echalar, Hualde had a confrontation with the parish priest Labayen, who declared that he could not believe there was so much wickedness in his town. He went on to say that the Inquisition would not get away with what they had started and that they would be called to account for what they had done. That same evening, in a letter dated 12 January, Hualde informed the Tribunal of the episode at Echalar.[57]

It is obvious from Hualde's letter that despite the efforts of the skeptics, the town of Echalar was completely dominated by the witch craze. People sat up with their "bewitched" children every night in order to prevent them from sleeping, but this apparently only resulted in the witches taking them to the sabbath by day. For every time an exhausted child dozed off for a moment he would wake up immediately claiming that the witches had been to fetch him.[58]

Hualde had another piece of disturbing news for the Tribunal. The Jesuits had visited Vera during his absence at Christmastime, and had then refused to give absolution to a woman who confessed to having persuaded her niece, María de Peña (age twenty-one), to make a witch confession. To give her courage before being examined the aunt had given her niece a glass of wine, which the girl had requested herself. The Jesuits enjoined the woman to go to Hualde as soon as he had returned and tell him that her niece had made a false confession. Hualde's letter continues:

This has made me realize how little they have helped us; and perhaps this is why people have grown so silent at Yanci, and Lesaca. It is true that the witches say nothing unless they are forced to; and even with persuasion and all the other methods it is with the greatest difficulty that we expose them.[59]

Some time in March Bishop Venegas convened a meeting at Pamplona to which he summoned the persons who had undertaken investigations at his request in the witch-plagued areas. We do not know whether the Jesuits attended, but the Franciscans were present to submit their report.[60] They had with them the first material proofs of the existence of the witch sect. During their wanderings in the Pyrenean mountain regions they had ferreted out four jars containing witch salve and, what was even more exciting, a "dressed toad" (about which, unfortunately, nothing further is heard).[61] On the other hand, one of the Franciscan friars was able to state that he had come across no fewer than eighty persons who admitted to having made false witch confessions.[62] So that after all there was some doubt about how much the Franciscans had in fact "helped" the Inquisition.

The Franciscans delivered the "dressed toad" and the four jars of ointment to the Tribunal when they arrived at Logroño. The inquisitors had the jars examined by doctors and apothecaries, together with five other jars of witch ointment and powders that had been sent down by the dean of San-testeban and the abbot of Urdax. First, however, the nine jars were shown to some of the imprisoned witches, who declared that some of the jars contained the unguent they anointed themselves with in order to fly to the sabbath, and that others contained the deadly poison that they used in their criminal dealings. The jars were then sent to the doctors and apothecaries for their opinion. They declared unanimously that the contents:

> were unknown to medical science and pharmacology and they were therefore unable to analyse the ingredients of the salve. If it had been ointment for curing harness sores on oxen they would have been bound to recognize it, for that is to be obtained from any apothecary.

This quotation is taken from a letter to *la Suprema,* dated 15 June, in which the inquisitors write that they are enclosing a report of all the tests that had been made with the witch salve; but unfortunately this report was not preserved. The last sentence was aimed at the parish priest Martín de Yrisarri, who had assured the bishop that three of the Franciscans' jars came from some carters who used the ointment for healing the sores of their draught beasts.[63]

We thus have indirect evidence that the learned parish priest from Yanci attended the meeting. But Yrisarri went to Pamplona several times to discuss the situation with the bishop. On one of these occasions he brought with him several people, one of whom was a postmaster from Irún. All of these made statements regarding maltreatment and torture that they had been subjected to by the local authorities. On the basis of these statements the bishop arranged for the High Court of Navarra to institute proceedings against a number of local magistrates and others who were responsible for the ill-treatment.[64]

One of the first trials to be opened was the case against two village elders (*jurados*) from Elgorriaga and their accomplices, who were accused of defamation and maltreatment directed at several of the so-called witches of the village. From 30 April

1611 until the middle of the June following, the High Court commissioners were examining witnesses at Elgorriaga. The defense witnesses were almost without exception persons who had been exposed to witch persecution. The record of this trial, which is extant and which takes up several hundred pages, therefore gives an invaluable impression of the witch craze in one village alone, from the first hint of its inception right up to its culmination — seen invariably, of course, from the "witches' " standpoint. The trial was concluded in December 1611. One of the elders was exiled for two years, the other and his three accomplices were each exiled for one year.[65]

On 15 May 1611 the dean of Santesteban appeared at the Tribunal to present a report on the case conducted by the High Court at Elgorriaga.[66] The inquisitors wrote several letters of protest to the viceroy of Navarra,[67] but this time they were unable to induce the High Court to recall their commissioners. The viceroy replied by sending the Tribunal a long report of the injustices and ill-treatment to which the victims of the witch persecution had been exposed.[68]

On 17 June we find the Tribunal complaining to *la Suprema*, in a long letter which ended by requesting that a royal command be issued to the High Court of Navarra to suspend proceedings until the investigations of the Inquisition were at an end. The letter, which is written by Becerra and Valle only, states among other things that:

> It pains us greatly to see how the promises that the Devil made to his witches have been fulfilled. According to the statements of evidence from many *confitente* witches to the Holy Office, they consulted with the Devil and begged him to help them endure all the arrests which were made in the villages. The Devil told them to be of good courage, for he would see that the lawsuit for their defense made good progress, and they would go free while the Christians would be convicted and punished.... Since we now see this carried out and enforced with such severity by the judges [of the High Court] we cannot do other than deeply regret the protection afforded to the witches and the punishment that is falling to the lot of Christians in these mountains. These good Catholics have pursued the witches with holy zeal, even though it must be admitted that in their revulsion for the members of the sect they have overstepped their authority. They have helped to expose the witches'

confederacies with great success, and experience has shown
that the only true remedy against this pernicious league is
the rigor of the law. If it pleases Your Eminence [the inquisitor general] to peruse the confessions of nigh on thirty
witches who have been reconciled [by the Tribunal] in the
course of the last few days, you will find abundant proof of
this truth. It will also be apparent that everything which
occurs in the witch sect is an undeniable reality and not a
figment of dreams.[69]

On 28 June the Council of the Inquisition replied with a letter
that was in many ways epoch-making. The Tribunal received
express orders not to interfere with the cases of the High
Court, but to allow it to make its investigations without hin-
drance.[70]

As spring wore on the skeptics were on the point of acquiring a new ally in Inquisitor Salazar, who was growing more
and more critical of his two colleagues. Thus on 2 March he
reported a long series of abuses to *la Suprema*. He accused
Becerra of despotism, and of wanting to make decisions without asking the advice of his colleagues. For instance when the
Tribunal was writing to the Council Becerra insisted on dictat-
ing his own opinion and would not listen to Valle's and
Salazar's views. He had also tried to prevent them carrying out
research in the Tribunal archives when he himself was not
present. Recently Becerra had sent a threatening letter to the
parish priest Labayen at Echalar and this happened just at the
time when the Tribunal was considering whether to arrest him
for "hindering the Inquisition in the execution of its duty."
Salazar complained that the Tribunal was wasting too much
time on the witch trials. He went on to inform the Council how
the Tribunal had neglected to record when the prisoners for
one reason or another had been able to talk to each other,
either because they shared a cell or because the inquisitors had
given them an opportunity to meet. This, Salazar explained,
was a particularly crucial factor in cases of witchcraft, since a
good *confitente* could instruct a *negativo* or a bad *confitente* in
what he was to confess. Salazar had drawn the attention of his
colleagues to the fact that the regulations for interrogation
were not being followed in this respect but he had only succeeded to a limited extent in getting these details inserted in
the records. It was also in this document that Salazar reported
Valle's unseemly conduct toward him on account of his iso-

lated vote in the judgment of María de Arburu and the other *negativos* (see end of chapter 8.7).[71]

The day after Salazar had written his report, 3 March, the inquisitors met to decide whether the Tribunal should receive some witches as prisoners. Those in question were one man and three women, who had been brought to Logroño by the authorities of the village of Zubieta on their own initiative. Salazar, as the junior inquisitor, had the first vote. He fastened upon the fact that the accused had been exposed to ill-treatment. They had been thrown into water, and they had been kept tied to some fruit trees for several nights running. Salazar considered that there was no cause to imprison them before these things had been looked into and the case laid before the Council of the Inquisition.

The two senior inquisitors then voted. Both of them emphasized quite different points. Seven *confitente* witches had witnessed against the accused, and they themselves had made voluntary confessions to the inquisitorial commissioner Fray León de Araníbar. Valle and Becerra therefore voted for imprisonment. The ill-treatment received by the accused could be completely left out of account: it was excusable because of the indignation the residents of Zubieta must feel toward these people, who had carried off their children and enrolled them in the witch sect.[72]

Here we have yet another example of how the belief in witches did not stand or fall by a more or less logical argument, but rested on a fundamental concept: that witchcraft was an undisputable reality. In fact the argument of Becerra and Valle was in no way less "reasonable" than that of Salazar, it just developed from a completely different point of departure.

The Council of the Inquisition occupied a position of relatively neutral authority over the opposing parties. As the witch persecutions in Navarra gradually developed into an embarrassing situation, so the letters from the Tribunal at Logroño grew longer and longer. The first long report from the inquisitors, dated 14 February, was concerned with the letters of Solarte, which had been delivered to Becerra a few days previously by the rector of the Jesuit college at Logroño. Presumably when he received Solarte's reports on the journey to Las Cinco Villas, the Jesuit provincial at Valladolid, Fray Gaspar de Vegas, dared not withhold them from the Inquisition. He therefore chose to betray Solarte. The Tribunal's report began by detailing all the prehistory of the "witches' party," as the inquisitors called their opponents. They could not touch the bishop of Pamplona, but he was represented as having been deceived by his subordinates, first and foremost by his visitor, Dr. Zalba, who, the inquisitors had discovered, was related to María de Endara, the rich widow from Echalar. The experiments of the priests at Echalar could be ignored completely after it had emerged that the parish priest Labayen had fathered the child to which María de Endara had given birth while in prison. This had certainly revealed the real intention of the priests' night watches at Echalar (see page 140). As regards Solarte himself, the inquisitors went on, he was young, and besides he had no experience with the witch problem. Neither could his investigations be taken too objectively, for it was obvious that they had aimed at satisfying the hopes that had been placed in his mission beforehand from a higher quarter.[73] The Tribunal could not as yet lay any blame on the learned parish priest at Yanci, *el licenciado* Yrisarri, but Valle, who knew him, was able to state that in fact he was only a *bachiller* and therefore presumably by no means so learned after all.[74]

Two months later the inquisitors were in a position to disqualify their last opponent, Yrisarri, for they had intercepted the letter he had written to his friend in Rome. In the letter Yrisarri revealed that his own mother at Yanci had been denounced as a witch. The Tribunal registers showed that other relatives of Yrisarri were also under suspicion. Thus his motives in attempting to obtain a letter of indulgence from the pope were perfectly clear.[75]

The inquisitors informed *la Suprema* of their new findings in a letter dated 9 April and appended several points to Yrisarri's list of sins. The Franciscans had just visited the Tribunal and delivered their report — which was about their journey and what had transpired at the meeting in Pamplona. One of the Franciscans, Fray Domingo de Sardo, had related that in "a certain town" he had found sixteen witches who were firmly resolved to make their confessions to the Inquisition. However, next day, when they were interrogated, they all denied that they were witches. This volte-face had been brought about by the persuasions of "a certain person." The Franciscans refused to divulge the name of this individual because he had been their host during their stay in the town. But later on,

when their statements had been written down, the Franciscans revealed orally to the inquisitors that these things had
taken place at Yanci and that it had been the parish priest
Yrisarri who had persuaded the witches not to confess. The
Franciscans also stated that Yrisarri had among other things
suggested to the bishop that instruction should be issued
ordering the inquisitors at Logroño to cease working on these
cases. Yrisarri had furthermore proposed that an inquisitor
from a different Tribunal should be sent on visitation to the
witch-plagued area.[76]

Later in the spring Becerra and Valle attempted to have
Yrisarri arrested and charged with opposing the Inquisition.
But Salazar refused to go along with this, and the divided vote
was forwarded to *la Suprema* where the matter was allowed to
rest.[77] Becerra was no more successful in his attempts to have
Labayen, the parish priest at Echalar, arrested.[78] There was a
reprimand for the inquisitors in this connection in the epoch-
making letter from *la Suprema* of 28 June (see earlier in this
section).

> If there be in this affair any zealous and pious Christian
> persons who may wish to elucidate something to you which
> might be at variance with the opinion you yourselves have
> formed, you are not to be angered. On the contrary, you
> should hear what they have to say with mildness and
> gratitude. For it is vital for everyone to realize that you are
> constantly seeking to expose the truth, and ready to accept
> the facts as you find them.[79]

This letter marks the definitive turning-point in the battle
between the Tribunal and the "witches' party." From then on
the Tribunal was to take up a defensive position, and it was to
become first and foremost a matter of prestige for the inquisitors to prove the existence of the witch sect.

It is, however, an open question as to whether Salazar could
any longer be considered a member of the Tribunal's party. He
had already been away for a month on visitation at Santesteban and had realized that the doubt he had expressed at the
Tribunal on various occasions had most certainly not been
without foundation.

CHAPTER ELEVEN
Salazar's Visitation

A. THE FIRST PART OF THE JOURNEY
1. THE TASK

ARLY IN 1611 THE TRIBUNAL HAD AL-
ready suffered its first defeat at the hands of the
"witches' party." The cause of this defeat was
the inquisitor general's instructions for Salazar's
journey of visitation with the Edict of Grace to the witches (SD
Text 6). The instructions are dated Madrid, 26 March, and they
were received at Logroño on 31 March 1611.[1]

The inquisitor general had sent a letter in advance of these
instructions, on 25 February, requesting the Tribunal to send
him a detailed report on the situation and to make suggestions
as to how best to combat the witch sect. The inquisitor general
wished steps to be taken as soon as possible. He had himself
considered moving the Tribunal temporarily to Pamplona (so
that it would be closer to the infested area). The Tribunal was
also asked for an opinion as to whether it would be necessary
to summon inquisitors and staff from other inquisitions, or
whether they felt able to deal with the task themselves. The
inquisitor general appears to have been alarmed by the latest
reports from the Tribunal at Logroño, for the letter spoke not
only of the Edict of Grace, but also of dealing severely with the
witch sect.[2]

In reply, on 9 March, the Tribunal sent the report and statistics of the witches' sabbaths that had been discovered and
which we discussed in the preceding chapter (p. 212 ff.). But
the letter was much longer. After the harrowing report of the

proliferation of the sect the inquisitors launched a grandiose plan for a solution to the problem. Their suggestions may be summarized as follows:

1. In the witch-plagued towns, priests and other persons were to be prohibited from holding public or private discussions as to whether witches existed.

2. Prohibitions were also to be issued against threatening or influencing the witches to make confessions.

3. Orders were to be issued from the king to the frontier guards to assist the Inquisition by intercepting possible refugees.

4. Orders from the king were also to be issued to the towns in the area to assist the Inquisition by supplying board and lodging to all who presented themselves in order to make confessions during the visitation.

5. As the Tribunal had been informed that people who went to the Inquisition were exposed to threats and ill-treatment, measures were to be taken to prevent a recurrence of this, so that anyone might feel free to report and avail himself of the Edict of Grace. It should also be ensured that those witches who had been reconciled were not subsequently subjected to any persecution.

6. Since legal proceedings could not be instituted against the witches during the period of the Edict of Grace, there would be no necessity to move the Tribunal to Pamplona.

7. The Edict of Grace was to be valid for four months.

8. Two inquisitors were to go on visitation following different routes. One was to travel to the infested area with the Edict of Grace to the witches. The other was to travel through the rest of Navarra with the Edict of Faith, as on a normal visitation, but was in addition to publish the Edict of Grace so that all existing *aquelarres* might be discovered.

9. The inquisitor who went to the witch-plagued area was to be accompanied by two secretaries (*secretarios del secreto*).

10. The Edict of Grace was also to be published in Logroño, so that the third inquisitor, who was to stay behind at the Tribunal, could deal with the witches who might present themselves there.

11. It was to be anticipated that it would be impossible for the inquisitor in the infested area to interrogate all the witches. He should therefore stay for only four to eight days in each

place in order to publish the Edict of Grace. Before leaving he was to charge a local ecclesiastic with the task of "redeeming the witches from their errors by urging them to go to confession and beg for mercy." The inquisitor was also to arrange to leave a commissioner and a notary in each place so that they could hear confessions. He could if necessary nominate new commissioners and notaries to carry out this work. When the inquisitor had published the Edict of Grace in five or six different places, he was to retrace his steps in order to examine all the witch confessions that had emerged meantime. He was to make lists of all the accused and to reconcile the witches who had made satisfactory confessions.

12. The other inquisitor was to travel in a similar series of loop movements, but when the period of grace had expired he was to make his appearance in the area visited by the first inquisitor. Here he was to institute proceedings against all those witches who had made insufficient confessions and against all those who might have failed to avail themselves of the Edict of Grace.

13. Since it was anticipated that this whole operation would be a costly procedure, the bishops in the area and the authorities in the witch-plagued towns were to be urged to contribute adequate financial support.

14. The local bishops and the provincials of the various religious orders were to be requested to obtain the necessary Basque-speaking interpreters and preachers, and to direct them to go to the monasteries in the area in order to be available when the Inquisition sent for them. (The inquisitors, after their experience with Solarte, wanted to make sure that preachers were not allowed free access to the area again!)

15. When the period of grace had ended, severe measures were to be taken, and then would be the time to transfer the Tribunal temporarily out into the area, as the inquisitor general had suggested.

16. When all guilty persons in Navarra and Guipúzcoa had been punished, a general visitation was to be made through the remaining parts of the district of the Tribunal (the provinces of Alava and Vizcaya etc.) so that any further manifestations of the witch sect might be eradicated.

17. Finally, one of the inquisitors was to return to Navarra on visitation in order to punish all those witches who might have relapsed.[3]

There might have been disastrous consequences for the Basque population if the Tribunal's plan had been carried out. But fortunately the inquisitor general had felt it necessary to ask the opinion of *others*. He not only wrote to the inquisitors at Logroño on 25 February; similar inquiries were sent to the bishops of Calahorra and Pamplona, to the humanist Pedro de Valencia, and probably to other prominent people as well.[4] All were asked what should be done about the witch sect.

The bishop of Calahorra replied on 6 March that there were, thank God, no witches in his area, and since the inquisitor general constantly addressed himself to the bishop of Pamplona, he assumed that it had been sent him in error. As far as Calahorra was concerned he could state that nobody from his diocese had been at the auto de fe, and that in fact there were no records to show there had been any witches there. The letter was received in Madrid on 14 March.[5]

On 14 March the inquisitor general also received an answer from Antonio Venegas de Figueroa, the bishop of Pamplona. The letter was written on 4 March and was a provisional reply (SD Text 5). In it the bishop announced that he had just called a meeting at Pamplona. As soon as he had spoken to the preachers he had sent up to the infested area and to the other persons who were to make reports, he would send the inquisitor general a detailed account. At present he would merely assure the inquisitor general that there was a great deal of deception and swindling going on in this affair, "especially in all that related to the children." He had had a personal opportunity to convince himself of this when (in the winter of 1609-10) he had been on a journey of visitation to the witch-plagued towns. Most of it consisted of rumors started by children and simple folk, who had heard about the witches in France. The inquisitorial commissioners were the ones chiefly responsible for persecutions being instituted on the Spanish side of the frontier. They had employed quite unheard-of methods in order to get people to confess. Some of them were prompted by Christian zeal, but others had made use of the witch-hunt to gain their own ends. The conviction that the bishop had reached on his journey of visitation had later been further strengthened by the reports from the parish priests which he received subsequently, and from the preachers whom he himself had sent up to the area; for these had told him that they were sought out by unhappy people who were suffering pangs of conscience because they had made false confessions to being witches and denounced blameless neighbors as their accomplices.[6]

The reply from Pedro de Valencia, which we discussed in the first chapter, arrived too late to exert any influence on the decisions of the inquisitor general relating to his instructions of 26 March for Salazar's visitation.[7] The same may be said of the second letter from the bishop of Pamplona (SD Text 7), written on 1 April, which contained the report and two enclosures from Solarte the Jesuit[8] (SD Texts 8, 9, and 10). But the first letter from Antonio Venegas was sufficient to open the eyes of the inquisitor general.

The instructions endorsed the view of the skeptics on nearly every count. The Edict of Grace was to run for six months and not four as suggested by the Tribunal. It was to include all witches, even those confined in the Tribunal's secret prison. Only relapsed witches (*relapsos*) were to be excluded from the Edict of Grace for the time being; the inquisitor general asked to have these cases submitted to him so that he could consider them in due course. Only the most essential points of the witches' confessions were to be written down, and they were not to be questioned about their accomplices at all, since this was merely "wasting time." Preachers were to be sent up to the area, however, without restriction to the monasteries (see item 14 in the Tribunal's plan above). No person was to be allowed to put pressure on others for the purpose of forcing witch confessions out of them, and none who made confessions were to be subjected to reprisals. (But discussion on whether witchcraft actually existed was not to be forbidden.) The priests were to be requested not to deny the Sacraments to the witches who had made confessions; and the Tribunal was not on any account to forbid the priests to hear the witches' confessions. The inquisitors were to accord the secular and ecclesiastical authorities liberty to institute witch trials, as it was to be assumed that they would transfer the cases to the Tribunal if it was revealed that the accused were guilty of apostasy (i.e. having forsworn their Christian faith). Finally, the inquisitors were once again enjoined to take particular care to interrogate the witches who attended the same *aquelarre* in order to see if their statements tallied.[9] This last point was a repetition of the instructions of 11 March 1609, "The Fourteen Questions from *la Suprema*" (chapter 4.4). But it had since come to take the form of a rigidly scientific experiment, which will be described in detail below (chapter 11.C.6).

The Tribunal had by now become accustomed to *la Suprema*'s skeptical instructions. The two senior inquisitors had tailored these commands to suit themselves. Their conviction of the reality of the witch phenomenon had never wavered since they began the proceedings in 1609. As for the junior inquisitor, Salazar, he had been obliged to show Becerra and Valle the trust he owed them as a colleague, though during the voting of the sentences when he could give expression to his personal opinion of the case, he had not sought to conceal his doubts. What was most decisive about the new instructions was therefore the ruling that "the inquisitor whose turn it was" — i.e. Salazar — was to go on visitation, and that he was to undertake the journey *alone*.[10] In this way it was more likely that the instructions of *la Suprema* would be closely adhered to and the investigations carried out with greater frankness and from a more critical standpoint than had previously been the case.

If the inquisitor general had complied with the Tribunal's request, reasonable enough in itself, to send off two inquisitors, it is true that it would have been Valle's turn (or Becerra's) to make a visitation to the witch-plagued area, while Salazar would probably have been delegated to tour the rest of Navarra. We know from a later report made by Salazar that both Becerra and Valle were eager to administer the Edict of Grace, and he describes how hard they found it to hide their jealousy when the lot fell to their junior colleague.[11]

Now the two senior inquisitors had to resign themselves to sitting at home in Logroño while Salazar traveled around taking the Edict of Grace to the witch sect. In their eyes Salazar was certainly far too inexperienced for the assignment, especially since the edict had been granted under such favorable conditions that catastrophic consequences might ensue if the most vigilant watch was not kept to prevent any new attacks being launched by the Devil.

2. THE FINAL PREPARATIONS

On 9 April the Tribunal wrote that the instructions of the inquisitor general had been received and that Salazar was making ready to set out on visitation. Everyone at the Tribunal was busy with the final preparations in order that he could leave at the end of the month. Regarding the wording of the edict, they had thought to employ the same formula as that used for previous Edicts of Grace:

> We, the Apostolic Inquisitors to the Kingdom of Navarra, etc., hereby make known that our Lord the King has commanded his ordinance to be issued, and the Most Venerable Cardinal and Inquisitor General [has resolved to issue] his Edict of Grace...

The inquisitors' intention was to follow this by quoting the ordinance of the king and the inquisitor general's edict *in extenso*, concluding with a statement that the Tribunal would keep all promises that had been made to the witches. They had decided to have the edict translated into the Basque language so that all the people should understand it. The inquisitors had agreed that Salazar was to go first to Las Cinco Villas and to Santesteban, the two places which most needed his presence. Finally, they had decided that the Tribunal was to have the Edict of Grace published at Logroño, Pamplona, and other places considered necessary, on the same day that Salazar published it on his journey of visitation.[12] This was all entirely in accordance with what had been prescribed in the instructions of 26 March. But we shall soon see how, with the help of district commissioners and special delegations, Becerra and Valle used this opportunity for stealing a march on Salazar in connection with the publication of the Edict of Grace.

Meanwhile the Tribunal was proceeding with the preparation of the documents Salazar was to take with him on his journey. With the exception of the records of the imprisoned witches and the records of those who had been reconciled at Logroño during the spring, all the witch confessions obtained since 1609 were handed over to Salazar in their original form or in transcript. Then during his visitation it was intended that he should call in the persons concerned so that they might be reconciled by virtue of the Edict of Grace. (Salazar was entrusted with a total of 338 witchcraft confessions, presumably the *confitente* witches who had turned up by 9 March 1611; see the statistics in table 6, where the total number of witch confessions is 339, and cf. below, chapter 11.A.7, near beginning.)[13]

Presumably Salazar was also supplied with a list for each region of the many hundreds of persons who were suspected of being witches.[14] The Tribunal further supplied Salazar with questionnaires for use in interrogating the witches. The records show that during the visitation he made use of the original list of fourteen questions from *la Suprema*,[15] and also a shorter list containing eight questions extracted from the instructions of 26 March (see below, chapter 11.C.6). Where child witches under six were concerned, Salazar was merely to read some exorcisms over them, and the texts for these were carefully selected by the three inquisitors together.[16]

In order to facilitate the quick dispatch of the cases, *la Suprema* had given permission for printed forms to be used at the reconciliation ceremonies.[17] The Tribunal was to have these forms printed (leaving blank spaces for the insertion of details) before Salazar's departure.[18] Presumably they also had copies of the Edict of Grace printed,[19] and of another edict which ordered that the witch problem be treated calmly. This last edict warned all — and particularly parents — against threatening, persuading, or ill-treating anyone in order to force him to make an admission, or to call someone to account for a confession which might already have been made to the Holy Office.[20]

Finally, there were the papers that always accompanied the inquisitors on their journeys: information regarding all persons suspected of heresy, lists of inquisitorial agents, lists of *sambenitos,* and lastly, printed copies of the Edict of Faith and the accompanying instructions for its publication (see chapter 6, above). While the papers for Valle's visitation could no doubt have been contained in a single document chest, several chests would have been needed to hold the archive Salazar was to take with him.

On 7 May the inquisitors reported that Salazar had now "put all his papers in order." Meanwhile, he had not been able to leave, as the royal ordinance granting dispensation from confiscation of property had not yet been received.[21] It had, however, already been issued (Aranjuez, 25 April 1611)[22] and was on its way accompanied by a letter from *la Suprema.* The letter, dated 29 April, was a reply to that of the inquisitors, dated 9 April, and informed them that it would be sufficient to mention in the edict that the king had promised exemption from confiscation of property to all witches who confessed before the time-limit expired.[23]

This mention of the Edict of Grace in the correspondence is of the greatest importance, since not one copy has been preserved, despite the fact that it had presumably been printed.

Nor have I been able to trace anything about the edict in the registers of *la Suprema*. We know only that it was issued as early as the end of 1609 (see chapter 7.5) and that it established the period of grace at four months. This was now to be altered to six months (according to the new instructions mentioned above).[24]

The letter of 7 May from the Tribunal to *la Suprema* also contained a plea for financial assistance. The inquisitors requested urgently that other Tribunals might be enjoined to help the impoverished Inquisition at Logroño. The Tribunal was now so short of money that it was in arrears with the salaries of its staff. The inquisitors had even been forced to borrow the money to pay Salazar's salary before he set out on his journey of visitation. The letter went on to state that if the economic position was not improved the Tribunal would not "dare to open the doors to the many people who are anxious to come to Logroño in order to beg for the means of their souls' salvation."[25] This was obviously a reference to the witches who, the inquisitors expected, would present themselves at Logroño after the publication of the Edict of Grace. The Tribunal knew by experience that the witches were poor and therefore calculated that it would have to be responsible for their meals while they were being interrogated and reconciled.

3. THE VISITATION TO THE INFESTED AREA

On Whitsunday, 22 May, Salazar finally set out on his journey,[26] which was to last for almost eight months (see chapter 12.1, below). He was accompanied by two inquisitorial secretaries, the *licenciados* Francisco Ladrón de Peralta and Luis de Huerta y Rojas,[27] and by two Basque interpreters, designated by the Tribunal, who were also to preach on the publication of the Edict of Grace and to act as witnesses during the reconciliation ceremonies. Both were especially well qualified for this mission. One was Fray Domingo de Sardo, the Franciscan monk who had been traveling around all winter preaching against the witch sect. The other was Fray Josef de Elizondo, who had been Fray León's right-hand man in the witch-hunt that had been directed from the monastery at Urdax.[28] By appointing them to these honorable posts the Tribunal was recognizing their contribution, and they later received a handsome monetary reward for their efforts.[29]

The first destination of the visitation was Pamplona. Salazar had come to an agreement with his colleagues that he should visit the local bishop, Venegas de Figueroa. Salazar handed him a letter from the Tribunal requesting him to instruct his parish priests to assist Salazar in every way possible.[30] Venegas was expecting the visitation, for his representative at the Tribunal (*el ordinario*) had already given formal authority to the Inquisition to hold a visitation in his diocese. But Salazar had instructions to furnish the bishop with more detailed information regarding the witch sect.[31] On his part, Venegas presumably told Salazar of the investigations he himself was undertaking and of the letters and reports that he had sent to the inquisitor general. It is most probable that Salazar knew nothing of these matters, for according to the normal inquisitorial practice *la Suprema* had completely omitted to inform the Tribunal of the information that had reached it from other sources. We have no other details of this meeting, but the atmosphere must surely have been a cordial one; for the bishop lent Salazar his own damask canopy, which Salazar adorned with the coat of arms of the Inquisition and under which he presided throughout his visitation.[32] Salazar seems to have spoken of the bishop with so much enthusiasm after his homecoming that his colleagues began to suspect that they had held secret meetings. But in fact the meeting at Pamplona was the first and only time the two witch-defenders met each other.[33]

Also at Pamplona Salazar met the viceroy of Navarra. Becerra and Valle had instructed him to persuade the viceroy to suspend the proceedings instituted by the High Court at Elgorriaga. The viceroy apparently complied with the request to some extent but shortly afterwards Becerra and Valle wrote to *la Suprema* that he had not kept his promise.[34] It was undoubtedly at Pamplona that Salazar first became acquainted with the rumor that he was to blame for the witches having been burnt at the auto de fe the previous autumn (cf. p. 202, above).

For the first four months, Salazar traveled about northern Navarra and ended up at Fuenterrabía in Guipúzcoa. For the second four months he visited the rest of Guipúzcoa and continued on to the two other Basque provinces, Vizcaya and Alava. In a long letter to the inquisitor general dispatched from Fuenterrabía on 4 September, Salazar made a provisional report on his visitation of the infested area. This letter will be studied more closely below; for the present I shall merely cite what Salazar writes concerning his route during the first part of the visitation (see map 4):

> I have held a visitation at the following towns in the mountains of Navarra: Santesteban de Lerín, Zubieta, Ezcurra, Iráizoz, Lizaso, Olagüe, Elizondo, Urdax, Zugarramurdi, Valderro, Las Cinco Villas de Lesaca, and Vera.[35]

If we combine this list with the inquiry dates from the visitation cases that are extant for this part of the journey we can obtain a reasonably accurate chronological survey of Salazar's movements during the first four months. We can see that his stay at the first town, Santesteban, lasted right up until 5 July.[36] By 14 July, however, Salazar had already completed the session at Zubieta and had moved on to Ezcurra.[37] The next three sessions must have been still more brief, for as early as 23 July Salazar had reached Elizondo, where he stayed until the end of the month (inquiry dates were 23, 24, 29, and 30 July).[38] The next three sessions were held at Urdax, Zugarramurdi, and Valderro.[39] Despite the fact that the latter place involved a long detour, we see that Salazar had already reached Lesaca on 8 August (8, 11, 13, and 14 August).[40] From here he went on to Vera (16 and 19 August).[41] Presumably he also visited the towns of Echalar, Yanci, and Aranaz, and in any case he had got as far as Fuenterrabía on 22 August.[42] His stay here lasted until the beginning of September.

The Edict of Grace had long since been published in Fuenterrabía (5 June 1611),[43] so that when Salazar arrived there he published only the Edict of Faith. It was the first time this was done during the entire journey; in all the other places Salazar had published only the Edict of Grace to the witches.[44]

The sources do not clarify whether it was obligatory for all men and women (aged respectively from fourteen and twelve years of age upwards) to be present at the reading of the Edict of Grace, as was the custom with the Edict of Faith (see chapter 6, above). Neither can we tell whether copies of the Edict of Grace were circulated to the adjacent parishes for publication, or were read only in the towns where Salazar held visitations. But in any event an announcement would have been made in advance, similar to that used on the publication of the Edict of Faith. Salazar himself states merely that at each session he

summoned people from the surrounding villages and

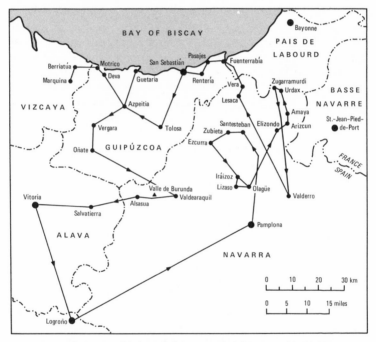

Map 4.   The route of Salazar's journey of visitation, during which he carried the Edict of Grace to the witches, 1611.

deaneries who usually attend on such occasions. Thus being informed in this way of the visitation and of the edicts, everyone was able to come and see me without difficulty.[45]

4. THE VISITATION AT SANTESTEBAN

We have seen that the Edict of Grace was first published at Santesteban, and we shall now attempt to give a clearer picture of Salazar's activities during the five weeks he stayed there. On Sunday 29 May he had the edict published.[46] It was read out during High Mass at Santesteban church by the dean, Miguel de Yrisarri, who had recently been promoted to inquisitorial commissioner by the Tribunal.[47] The town was soon full of witches who had come from far and wide and were awaiting examination so that they could avail themselves of the Edict of Grace.[48]

Thirteen original visitation files are extant from the session at Santesteban (see table 7).[49] They give us a basic idea of Salazar's working technique. The instructions permitted him to write the confessions down on loose sheets of paper and they authorized him to obtain assistance by letting others undertake the examinations. He had even obtained permission to send his assistants out to the surrounding villages to receive the witches' confessions.[50] We can see that Salazar made full use of these possibilities on his visitation, although to begin with he preferred to keep his assistants working under his supervision at Santesteban.

In a later connection Salazar revealed that he took over five or six rooms in the places that he visited on this journey.[51] The thirteen cases illustrate how he established his "office for witch-cases" and rapidly acquired a staff of assistants. Thus on the morning of 2 June Salazar examined the forty-year-old Juana de Labayen (the first witch of table 7), whose serial number shows her to have been the eighth witch on the visitation. The Franciscan monk Fray Domingo de Sardo and the dean Miguel de Yrisarri assisted as Basque interpreters, and the secretary Luis de Huerta y Rojas acted as clerk. While interrogating the ninth witch in the afternoon Salazar found it sufficient to have only Domingo de Sardo as interpreter. On the morning of 3 June Salazar examined his tenth witch, this time with the priests Miguel de Arramendía and Pedro de Aranguren as interpreters. But Miguel de Yrisarri had already been delegated to examine witches single-handed "on special

Table 7. The Thirteen Visitation Cases From the Session at Santesteban

Serial no.	Witch's name, age, marital status, domicile (date of previous confession, commissioner)	Inquiry date	Examiner	Inter-preter(s)	Notary	No. of MS pages	Recon-ciled	Rte
"8"	Juana de Labayen, 40, married, Zubieta (15 Apr. 1611, MY)	2 June A.M.	ASF	MY & DS	LHR	4	26 June	67
"9"	Mari Juan de Joanes Congoa, 50, widow, Zubieta (15 Apr. 1611, MY)	2 June P.M.	ASF	DS	LHR	4	26 June	71
"10"	Hernautón de Hualde, 60, widower, Zubieta (19 Feb. 1611, LA)	3 June A.M.	ASF	MA & PA	FLP	3	28 June	78
"12"	Juana de Hualde, 27, unmarried, Zubieta (daughter to no. 10) (20 Feb. 1611, LA)	3 June	MY		ME	2	28 June	69
"19"	Juana de Yrurita, 40, widow, Zubieta (18 Apr. 1611, MY)	4 June	MY		PA	3	28 June	75
"23"	Catalina de Yrurita, 16, unmarried, Zubieta (daughter of no. 19) (11 Feb. 1611, LA)	4 June A.M.	ASF	MA	LHR	3	28 June	77
"24"	Juanes de Arroqui, 40, married, Zubieta (married to no. 8) (16 Apr. 1611, MY)	4 June P.M.	FL		FLP	5	28 June	62
"26"	Hernautón de Arrosarena, 20, unmarried, Zubieta (son of *Rte* 55) (11 Feb. 1611, LA)	4 June	MY		TZ	2	28 June	66

"30" María de Mindeguía, 40, married, Zubieta (mother of no. 26, married to *Rte* 55) (16 Apr. 1611, MY)	6 June A.M.	FL		FLP	5	22 June	68
"32" María de Saldías, 19, unmarried, Zubieta (17 Feb. 1611, LA)	6 June	FL		FLP	5	28 June	64
"33" Gracia de Marquesarena, 16, unmarried, Zubieta (25 Feb. 1611, LA)	6 June	MA		TZ	3	28 June	65
"59" Mari Pérez de Larralde, 18, unmarried, Ciga (6 Feb. 1611, LA)	10 June	MA		TZ	3	26 June	63
"126" Tomás de Saldías, 14, unmarried, Zubieta (Spring 1611, LA)	4 July	MA		TZ	2	5 July	76

Abbreviations:

ASF	Alonso de Salazar Frías, inquisitor
DS	Fray Domingo de Sardo, Basque interpreter (appointed by the Tribunal)
FL	Fernando de Lizasu, priest at Santesteban, Basque interpreter (appointed by Salazar)
FLP	Francisco Ladrón de Peralta, inquisitorial secretary
LA	Fray León de Aranibar, abbot of Urdax, inquisitorial commissioner
LHR	Luis de Huerta y Rojas, inquisitorial secretary
MA	Miguel de Arramendia, priest at Alsasua, Basque interpreter (appointed by Salazar)
MY	Miguel de Yrisarri, dean of Santesteban, inquisitorial commissioner
PA	Pedro de Aranguren, priest, inquisitorial notary
ME	Martín de Elizondo, public notary (*escribano*) for the Baztán Valley, Elizondo
TZ	Tomás de Zozaya, citizen of Santesteban, inquisitorial notary (appointed by Salazar)

orders from Inquisitor Salazar Frias," as it is stated in Juana de Hualde's examination of that day.[52] It is obvious why Salazar changed the interpreters; he intended to get to know his assistants before he allowed them to undertake examinations. The number of assistants on the staff increased steadily during the next few days until there were at least four groups interrogating the witches (if we include Salazar's own group).

If Salazar had kept to the normal working hours of the Tribunal (three hours in the morning and three in the afternoon)[53] each group would not have dealt with more than two witches a day.[54] Even if the task was relatively easy for the Basque-speaking assistants it must be remembered that everything had to be recorded in Spanish. The tempo might possibly have been a little faster in the groups which had a Basque-speaking clerk, as in the case of Tomás de Zozaya, appointed by Salazar as inquisitorial notary. But he would still, of course, have to write the record of the interrogation in Spanish.

During the visit at Santesteban the number of witch cases is seen to increase pari passu with the number of assistants (see table 7 and compare serial numbers with inquiry dates). Thus on 2 June, four days after the publication of the edict, Salazar had completed the examination of only nine witches; on 3 June the 12th witch was dealt with, on 4 June the 26th, and on 10 June the 59th witch. Judging from the list, 126 witch cases had been recorded by 4 July, but this figure included the confessions that were sent to Salazar from other places. Thus nos. "68" through "70" were in fact confessions made at Fuenterrabía on 10 and 11 June.[55]

However, the serial numbers include only those witches in the category old enough to be reconciled. The minors, who were to be absolved *ad cautelam,* formed a separate series, and their cases presumably were expedited speedily since Salazar, unlike Valle, spent as little time as possible on the child witches. A third group was made up of witches over twelve (women) or fourteen (men) who stated that they had been to the *aquelarre* without having forsworn their Christian faith. These were not to be reconciled either, but were to renounce their errors *de levi.* Finally, a fourth and last group were those persons who were not themselves witches but who reported in order to testify regarding bewitchings and persons they had suspected of witchcraft.[56]

The thirteen witches mentioned above had all previously

made admissions to one of the inquisitorial commissioners (in this case either Fray León de Araníbar or Miguel de Yrisarri). They had all traveled to Santesteban from Zubieta (ca. 5 miles from Santesteban) with the exception of one who came from Ciga (about 9 miles away). They all declared that they had presented themselves voluntarily in order to take advantage of the Edict of Grace, but this was probably not so. The record of sixteen-year-old Gracia de Marquesarena (serial number "33") states that she had already been examined by Miguel de Yrisarri on 4 June, but had not then wished to say anything.[57] And we know that all thirteen later recanted their confessions. This is basically why we know about their confessions, for they were removed from the numerical order in the list of those reconciled and bound together in the extant volume "F" of Salazar's visitation book.[58]

If we compare the examinations of these thirteen witches we see that they all conform to an identical pattern. The previous confession was produced and after a short interrogation it was read aloud to the culprit so that he could confirm the contents. On the basis of the confession the person was questioned on his apostasy and his desire to return to the Catholic Faith. The last part of the interrogation concerned the so-called *actos positivos*, or material proofs. In the case of the first of the thirteen witches, Juana de Labayen (see table 7, no. "8"), her answers to Salazar's questions on this point are recorded in the following manner (see figure 16):

[Appended in margin:] *Actos positivos*	And she said likewise that throughout all the time she had been participating in the witches' meetings she does not recall having met anyone either on the outward or the homeward journey, neither the other members of her *aquelarre* nor persons who are not witches, in spite of the fact that she would have been able to recognize them if she had met anyone. Neither does she remember having heard the sounds of dogs, church-bells, or such things, during the outward journey, the assembly, or on the return journey, although she herself feels that these things should be clearly audible from the witches' meeting-place. The only thing she
got wet!	has noticed is that the witches get soaked when it rains or snows and this applies par-

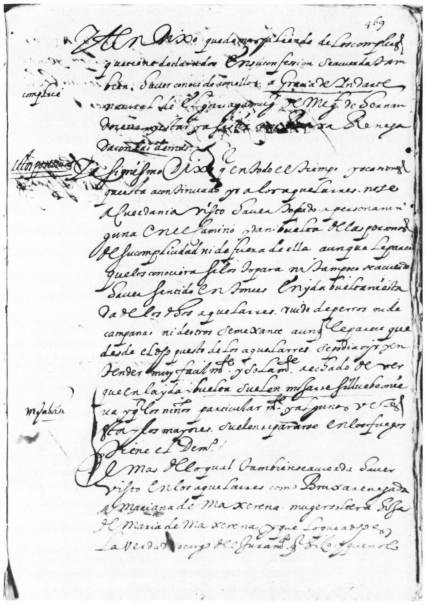

Figure 16.   Page from Volume "F" of Salazar's Visitation Book
with marginal notes: complice *(accomplice);* actos positiuos;
mojabase *(got wet).*

ticularly to the children. But she and the
other witches usually dry themselves at bon-
fires which the Devil has [lit for them].[59]

The examinations carried out by Salazar himself reflect steadily increasing skepticism. His questions are not included in the
report, but we can read between the lines that the witches were
grilled, not least with regard to what they had said about third
parties.

On 3 June Salazar examined Hernautón de Hualde from
Zubieta (table 7, no. "10"). When his previous confession was
read to him, the sixty-year-old farm laborer began to back
down: whereas he had formerly said that the Devil had intercourse with the men and the women, now it was strictly
speaking only with the women. Regarding the marriages he
had said that the Devil arranged between male and female
witches, he had in fact never actually seen that kind of union
entered upon at the *aquelarre*. On reaching the point at which
he had to confirm his evidence against eighteen persons whom
he had previously alleged were his accomplices, the record
runs as follows:

> He tried to enlarge on or detract from his statement in the
> same manner, and in such a confused and mulish way that
> the whole story seemed to the Lord Inquisitor so hard to
> credit . . . that this item was omitted and nothing relating to
> the accomplices was written down.

And in order that there should be no possible doubt about the
matter Salazar later added a note in the margin to the effect
that the statements against the accomplices had been revoked.[60]

On the following day, 4 June, when Salazar examined
Catalina de Yrurita (table 7, no. "23"), he had the clerk make
the following note in her record:

> She showed much uncertainty and inconsistency when
> reexamined about the accomplices she had named in her
> confession. We emphasize this so that it may be seen how
> little trust can be placed in her testimony on this issue.[61]

(In her previous confession to Fray León de Araníbar this
sixteen-year-old girl had accused no fewer than forty-six of her
neighbors at Zubieta of witchcraft, and she claimed to have
seen all of them worshipping the Devil at their *aquelarre*.)[62]

Salazar did not question these two witches on the subject of *"actos positivos"* at all, and we may certainly assume that the reason for this was that he felt it was not worth his trouble as he was so certain they were not witches. Perhaps he intentionally omitted to ask them questions that were too pertinent. Providing that they would only revoke their accusations against third parties, they could still benefit from the Edict of Grace; but a full recantation could involve them in grave trouble, since according to the general regulations of the Inquisition this almost invariably meant death at the stake.[63]

There are also several examples of how Salazar kept a check on his assistants when they were examining witches in the adjoining rooms. Here too his skeptical attitude is apparent. On 4 July a fourteen-year-old boy (table 7, no. "126") was examined by Miguel de Arramendía. The record notes at the very end that the boy wished to name some accomplices but that Salazar gave orders that he was not to be believed on account of his youth.[64]

When a convenient number of witches had been examined Salazar set aside several days for the reconciliations, which took place in the courtroom in the presence of all his staff and a number of other witnesses. It appears from the visitation records extant that Salazar kept to a strict routine in order to wind up the cases as speedily as possible. Thus on the morning of 28 June alone, Salazar reconciled eight witches, and on this occasion forty-eight pages were filed (see table 7, nos. "10" through "26," "32," and "33").[65] Each reconciliation invariably takes up six pages of the record. First, the previous statements were ratified and here there remained an opportunity to retract the names of accomplices.[66] Next followed the ceremony of reconciliation, in which the witches were released from excommunication and renounced all errors according to a formula printed in Spanish, which presumably would have been translated into Basque for them. The last two pages contained the sentence signed by Salazar. The identical trifling penance was imposed on all eight witches: for two months they were to say ten Paternosters and ten Aves daily, while at the same time begging God's pardon for their sins. In the course of these two months they were furthermore to make a confession to their parish priests, and to fast every Friday. Finally, the reconciled person was strictly admonished against relapsing and warned that if he did he could expect no mercy, for the law would take its course with regard to both persons and goods (i.e. by the stake and confiscation of property).

Only the renunciations of heresy were printed but it can be seen that the greater part of the remaining material was written beforehand. Even the sentences were prepared in advance but with blank spaces left for individual details. It is obvious that Salazar instructed his secretaries to prepare these handwritten forms with blank spaces for names, dates, and brief remarks.[67] Presumably this work was done in the free periods between the working hours of the visitation. Many years later one of the secretaries, Francisco Ladrón de Peralta, recalled the tempo of work on this journey of visitation. He tells how Salazar worked "more indefatigably than he had thought possible for any man, and by his example encouraged his secretaries to work without ceasing."[68]

Thanks to the thirteen case-records which were preserved from the visitation at Santesteban, it has been possible to get an idea of how Salazar organized the work. The sessions in the other towns were presumably carried out in the same manner, but they were all of considerably shorter duration. It is clear that Salazar gradually gave his assistants ever more rein. For instance, Fray Domingo de Sardo was sent ahead on several occasions to publish the Edict of Grace and to begin to hear the witch confessions. When Salazar caught up with him a few days later he could start straightaway on the reconciliation ceremony, which his instructions prohibited him from delegating to others.[69]

5. THE WITCHES' LIES

It is not easy to determine whether Salazar believed anything at all of what the witches told him. But in spite of his unmistakeable skepticism he went steadily on with the investigations he had been instructed to undertake. Throughout the whole journey he listened patiently to the things the witches confessed and simultaneously built up a body of evidence proving that the supposed sect was nothing but a chimera. If Valle had shown only half as much frankness on *his* journey of visitation he would undoubtedly have returned with a very different result.

But only an inordinately gullible person could have swallowed all the lies the witches hit upon. In Salazar's second report, which contains a detailed analysis of the witches' con-

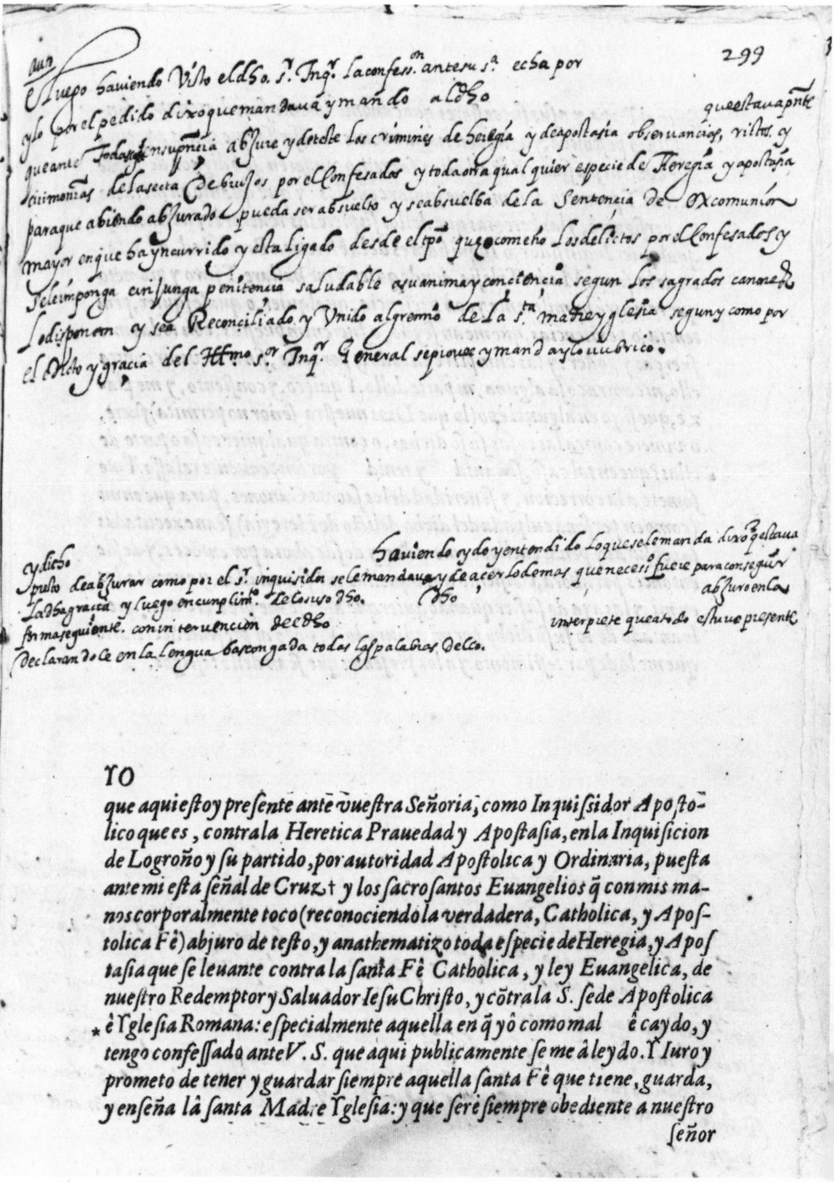

[Handwritten manuscript facsimile — folio 299]

To

que aqui estoy presente ante vuestra Señoria, como Inquisidor Apostolico que es, contra la Heretica Prauedad y Apostasia, en la Inquisicion de Logroño y su partido, por autoridad Apostolica y Ordinaria, puesta ante mi esta señal de Cruz,† y los sacrosantos Euangelios q̃ con mis manos corporalmente toco (reconociendo la verdadera, Catholica, y Apostolica Fè) abjuro de testo, y anathematizo toda especie de Heregia, y Apostasia que se leuante contra la santa Fè Catholica, y ley Euangelica, de nuestro Redemptor y Saluador Iesu Christo, y cõtra la S. sede Apostolica è Yglesia Romana: especialmente aquella en q̃ yõ como mal è caydo, y tengo confessado ante V. S. que aqui publicamente se me à leydo. Y Iuro y prometo de tener y guardar siempre aquella santa Fè que tiene, guarda, y enseña la santa Mádre Yglesia: y que seré siempre obediente a nuestro
señor

Figure 17. Manuscript form with blank spaces, from Volume "F" *of* Salazar's Visitation Book. *At the bottom is the beginning of a printed form, the renunciation of heresy: "I [blank space] who stand here before your Lordship..."*

fessions, there is one girl to whose case he returns time and again on account of her fantastic tales. It is that of seventeen-year-old Catalina de Sastrearena. Her file has not been kept, but if all the references to it are collated one is left with the impression that her case was somewhat unique.[70]

One must use caution when applying psychiatric explanations to the witch phenomenon. I have previously pointed out that the great majority of the victims of the witch persecutions were normal human beings whose behavior we can classify as natural in the particular circumstances. But we must surely be justified in describing Catalina de Sastrearena as a psychopathic personality. For her, the role of witch seems to have provided the ideal opportunity to display the mythomaniac tendencies she must undoubtedly have possessed previously.

When Catalina arrived at Elizondo in order to be reconciled by Salazar she declared that her fellow witches had accompanied her through the air the whole way. One of Catalina's accomplices had traveled to Elizondo with her and was questioned about it, but she declared Catalina's story to be nonsense, for she had not seen any witches.[71] Catalina also stated that she had been fetched and taken to the sabbath while she was waiting to be summoned for the reconciliation ceremony.[72] Salazar questioned some of those who had been waiting with Catalina, and they declared that they had talked to her and even eaten with her without noticing the slightest change at any time.[73]

Catalina had recounted being similarly taken to the witches' sabbath in broad daylight in her previous confessions. Thus, when everyone in her village had assembled in church to hear Fray Domingo de Sardo's sermon on the Edict of Grace to the witch sect, Catalina was suddenly translated to the *aquelarre*. The people who were standing beside her in church did not notice her absence, but Catalina herself asserted that she had missed the whole of the sermon.[74] (This also provides us with an impression of Fray Domingo's power of suggestion as a preacher; cf. the case of Olagüe near beginning of chapter 11.A.7.) On another occasion, when the whole of Catalina's village was taking part in a religious procession, she and some others fell out of the group in order to join a similar ceremony that the Devil had organized at his sabbath.[75] Like many others Catalina was unable to explain exactly how she was taken to the *aquelarre*;[76] but this inventive girl at least could explain that she flew there in the shape of a raven.[77]

Catalina also related that the witches were in the habit of revenging themselves on their persecutors by burning them at the *aquelarre*. She said they had inflicted this fate on the inquisitor (Salazar!), the parish priest at Arizcun, and "the preacher mentioned above" (i.e. Fray Domingo). And she even maintained that they sometimes went into the examination room in order to carry out their reprisals. But later, when she was questioned more closely, Catalina admitted that perhaps the witches only burned effigies at the *aquelarre*. However, she continued to insist that the reprisals in the examination room were directed at living persons.[78]

Arizcun is only three miles away from Elizondo, and the fact that the parish priest of this town was also on the witches' blacklist might serve to indicate that Catalina herself was from Arizcun.[79] On the other hand Salazar tells how Catalina and four of her fellow witches had already decided to get rid of him when he was at Santesteban. In his report of this particular case Salazar relates that Catalina and her confederates flew together with the Devil "one and a half *leguas*" (about 5 miles) from their *aquelarre* to Santesteban,[80] where:

> they entered the Chamber at midday and were present in person during the hearing. More than forty witches, men and women, came in there. On this point the witnesses were all in accord. Nonetheless, they became confused in the cross-examination since, as so often happens, the very effort to make such an extraordinary lie sound convincing confounds itself. For all of us happened to be present in the room, and this was so low, so small, and so narrow, that with the altar for the celebration of Mass and the table for the Tribunal there was scarcely space left for anybody, let alone so many persons, unless they were exercising the privilege claimed for them of being invisible so that their presence could not be felt.[81]

Catalina was cross-examined with four of her accomplices: a boy of thirteen, two girls of fourteen and nineteen, and a third girl whose age is not established.[82]

She and her friends also described another death sentence pronounced upon Salazar, which was fixed for St. James's Night (i.e., the night of 24 July). On this occasion they several times broke into the room where Salazar lay sleeping and poured their poisonous powders down his throat.[83] Pierre de Lancre, in his book on the witch-hunt in the Pays de Labourd, describes with a shudder how similar attempts were made on his life.[84] But while de Lancre took the witches' stories seriously, Salazar describes the attacks with amused forbearance. Thus he can write of the attempt to poison him on St. James's Night in these words:

> It would seem not entirely surprising, however, that I survived this attack without any difficulty, since I apparently suffered no ill effects from the other attempts to kill me, not even when, as I presided over the hearing in that room, the Devil and some witches bound me fast, and others set fire to my person and to the chair on which I was sitting.[85]

Catalina and her friends had ample time to fabricate new lies while they were waiting to be examined. Thus, three of her friends seem to have had a mutual agreement to make the same scene when they were called in to the examination room one after the other. They stopped short in the middle of their confessions and made gestures and signs indicating that they were unable to continue as their mistresses and the Devil were invisibly present and were cruelly maltreating them in order to prevent them from revealing anything further. The fact that this happened on the same day during three successive interrogations, and that all the witches concerned came from the same village, was sufficient to arouse Salazar's suspicions that it had been a put-up job.[86]

6. THE REVOCANTES

Shortly after Salazar had arrived at Santesteban, Dean Yrisarri — not to be confused with the priest Yrisarri at Echalar — told him that some of his flock had been suffering from pangs of conscience after making their confessions and being reconciled by the Tribunal at Logroño. Yrisarri knew that seven out of a total of ten witches wished to revoke their confessions.[87] Salazar immediately informed his colleagues of the problem in a letter in which he asked for permission to receive the recantations during this visitation.[88] But on 6 June Becerra and Valle replied that there could be no question of accepting recantations from persons who had been ceremonially reconciled by the Holy Office. If any should attempt it, Salazar was to send them as prisoners to Logroño, where they would receive the punishment they deserved. Salazar was forbidden by his colleagues even to grant interviews to persons who came to him with this intention.[89]

We do not know whether *la Suprema* was informed of the problem, but in one of Becerra's and Valle's long reports the question was touched upon, although in a completely different connection. It was in the letter of 17 June mentioned previously (see quotation in chapter 10.4, above) when the inquisitors complained that the High Court was continuing its investigations in spite of repeated appeals not to do so. In this connection Becerra and Valle complained that great numbers of witches were being encouraged to retract their confessions.[90]

However, the epoch-making letter of 28 June from *la Suprema* put an end to this question as well. The inquisitors were not only to leave the High Court in peace and to take a courteous interest in people holding different views of the witch problem, but there was yet another bitter pill for Becerra and Valle to swallow:

> You are to take note also that whenever the accused come to make confession or to recant, you are to receive their statements and enter them in the records, even though they may already have been reconciled or sentenced. You are to inform your colleague of this in order that he may act in conformity with these orders on the visitation. You are also to write to the commissioners ordering them to receive such statements without delay... as they can inform the Tribunal or your colleague of them later.[91]

Salazar received the first recantation on 14 July, when the visitation had reached Ezcurra.[92] As we mentioned above, a total of eighty *revocantes*[93] came forward during the journey. But Salazar was convinced that there would have been many more if he had not been forced to turn the firstcomers away with harsh words at Santesteban.[94]

The geographical distribution of the eighty *revocantes* was as follows: Navarra 55 (Almándoz 2, Aranaz 4, Arráyoz 4, Ciga 7, Ciordia 1, Echalar 1, Elvetea 2, Irurita 1, Lecaroz 5, Lesaca 5, Oronoz 3, Santesteban 1, Vera 2, Yanci 3, and Zubieta 14); Guipúzcoa 16 (Asteasu 1, Fuenterrabía 13, Oyarzun 1, and San Sebastián 1); and Alava 9 (Araya 1, Atauri 1, Cicujano 2, Corres 1, Ilarduya 1, Larrea 2, and Maestu 1). See map 5 and case nos. 441-520.

7. THE LETTER FROM FUENTERRABÍA

The letters Salazar wrote to the Tribunal during his journey

Map 5.   Distribution of the eighty revocations of witchcraft confessions received by Salazar during his journey of visitation.

through northern Navarra have not been preserved. In consequence the letter which he sent on 4 September from Fuenterrabía direct to the inquisitor general is of the highest importance. It fills five pages and reports on the first four months of the journey of visitation. After describing the route of his journey (see quotation in chapter 11.A.3, above), Salazar continued by saying that he had been received with gratitude all along the route and that people had accepted the Edict of Grace calmly. All who had presented themselves had derived benefit from the edict, and none had been left unreconciled or unabsolved. All the cases had been dealt with as quickly as possible, and thanks to the Inquisition's principle of secrecy it was possible to shield the people concerned from public scandal. News of the Edict of Grace had reached as far as France, and Salazar had been sought out by several distinguished persons from that country who had come in strictest secrecy to be reconciled. He had admitted them to reconciliation on an equal footing with the Spanish witches.[95] The figures Salazar was able to produce spoke of the success of the Edict of Grace:

When I left Logroño only 338 confessions had been made . . . But by now, with God's help, I have dealt with 1,546 cases on my journey. These may be divided up into the following groups: 1,199 children under twelve and fourteen have been absolved *ad cautelam;* 271 persons of twelve and fourteen and upwards have been reconciled (these were of varying ages; many of them were elderly, and some were even senile); 34 have renounced [their errors] *de levi;* finally, there are 42 *revocantes,* some of whom have recanted their confessions after having been reconciled by the Holy Office, and some of whom have made the recantations on their deathbeds. In addition there are a large number of children of five years old and under. After consultation with my colleagues I have read some exorcisms over them chosen by all three of us for this purpose. So that people of all ages have had a share in the comfort and consolation which has been anticipated by them, and by their children and relatives, and this has served to generally reassure the whole district.[96]

While Valle spread and increased the witch craze as he journeyed, Salazar's visitation seems to have had the opposite effect; there were of course some exceptions, for the Basque interpreters appointed by the Tribunal seem to have continued to follow Valle's lead at first. For instance, before Fray Domingo published the Edict of Grace at Olagüe this town had no witch problem. But in the course of a few days the Francis-can's suggestive sermons had children dreaming that they were taken to the *aquelarre,* and this village had still not recov-ered from the witch epidemic by the following year.[97]

Salazar for his part did what he could to establish peace wherever he went in an attempt to scotch any possible reason for talk in these isolated mountain communities. He fully realized how much damage had been caused:

> A great deal of terrible injustice had already been imposed in the name of Christian zeal on those who were suspected of belonging to this sect; and this was done even when the suspicion rested only on the allegations of children. Pro-hibiting the suspects from [taking] the sacraments of the church — which has been practiced quite openly and been very extensive — has also caused great harm.[98]

Salazar continued by describing what he had been doing to halt the witch craze. Wherever he had been he had published the edict, which commanded that the witch question should be dealt with calmly and sensibly, and this had obviously taken effect. But he had also taken the utmost care to ensure that the principle of secrecy of the Inquisition was adhered to, first and foremost by never permitting local agents of the Inquisition to learn what the witches from their own town had confessed during interrogation.[99]

Salazar sent this provisional report to the inquisitor general because certain problems had arisen during his journey. He had already mentioned them in his letter to the Tribunal, but as his colleagues' reply was slow in coming he had resolved to write directly to the inquisitor general.

The first problem concerned some witches who had re-lapsed after their reconciliation.[100] Salazar reports two very informative cases, which are especially interesting as they are taken from the lost volume "C" of his visitation documents:

> On 23 July a young girl came to me begging for aid. It was sixteen-year-old María de Tanborín Xarra, from the village of Irurita, whom I had reconciled on 23 June [at Santeste-ban]. She told me, weeping, how she had twice been taken to the witches' sabbath since her reconciliation. It had hap-pened while she was asleep, without her will or consent, and she had neither kissed the Devil nor participated in any of the other things to which she had been accustomed when she was a witch. She had been deeply miserable day and

night about these relapses. She begged me to help her and
give her fresh absolution. As a sign of her good intentions
and resolution she described certain concrete events which
her mother and others were able to confirm, as — according
to the girl — they had seen her returning from the assemblies. However, when these witnesses were interrogated they declared they had seen nothing.

Similarly Catalina de Echetoa came to me on 3 August. I
had reconciled this young girl of 14, from the village of
Urdax, on 28 July [at Elizondo]. With just as much anguish
as the other girl, she and her parents told me, weeping
ceaselessly, how she had been taken to the sabbath by the
same tutor witch who had taken her previously. It had
happened after the girl had gone to bed and fallen asleep;
and she was unable to say how or when it took place, nor
was she able to prevent it from happening.

I have for the time being reassured and comforted these
two while I await Your Highness's decision on these cases,
on which Your Highness has reserved the right of judgment
(see p. 231). This decision will serve as a guide in similar
cases. I expect a few more to come in, although so far only
these two have reported themselves, as well as two others,
who are under ten years old. But as the latter are so young I
shall refrain from commenting on their confessions at present.[101]

Salazar continued by saying that he had had similar problems with many of the other witches. While at the same time
copiously "making their confessions" they also declared that
they were still being taken to the *aquelarre* after they had fallen
asleep at night. It happened against their will and they were
unable to explain how it occurred. Some of those who came to
be reconciled confessed that they had been to the *aquelarre* the
very night before. On first consideration this seemed to be
incompatible with their reconciliation. But after Salazar had
discussed the matter with Fray Domingo de Sardo and Fray
Josef de Elizondo they agreed that the reconciliation ought not
to be postponed on this account. Salazar and the monks had
made their decision,

in consideration of the particular character of the confessions and the obvious results we have obtained through the
investigations we have carried out on Your Highness's instructions in order to ascertain whether the witch assemblies occur in dreams or in reality. These investigations
have amply provided us with clear answers to all the points

Your Highness wished to be informed of. This will be seen in detail from the reports of this visitation, which are extremely lengthy and are not yet complete. I should therefore prefer not to forward them until [after my return], when I shall submit an account [of the whole journey of visitation]. But if Your Highness wishes to have a sight of the reports before then, I will hasten their preparation.[102]

We know from later sources that the two Basque interpreters and preaching friars returned with a completely changed view of the witch phenomenon.[103] We also know that Salazar was already in process of drawing up his reports during the course of the journey of visitation.[104] The letter from Fuenterrabía demonstrates that Salazar had already then made a great deal of progress in his analysis of the witch confessions, and that Fray Domingo and Fray Josef had long since begun to lose their unquestioning belief in the existence of witchcraft.

The second problem concerned the *revocantes*. Despite the fact that *la Suprema* had already permitted witches to recant confessions (chapter 11.A.6, above) the problem was not yet solved. For the priests dared not give communion to the witches who had revoked their confessions. Several priests had been to Salazar to request special permission; but in accordance with the instructions of 26 March, Salazar had told the priests that they were to decide for themselves whether the persons concerned should be excluded from the sacraments or not. The priests had objected to this, saying that they must have express permission, since the Tribunal had previously forbidden them to give the church's sacraments to the witches, regardless of whether the witches had confessed or were merely under suspicion. Therefore Salazar considered that it would be desirable for *la Suprema* to issue a command to the priests not to exclude the "recanters" from the sacraments.[105]

The third problem was of a purely practical nature. Salazar requested permission for his assistants to carry out the reconciliation ceremonies. The work had been held up considerably by the ruling that all witches were to be reconciled by Salazar personally. He had for instance wasted a great deal of time by making a long detour to visit Valcarlos, where some elderly sick people had confessed to an inquisitorial commissioner that they were witches.[106]

The long letter from Fuenterrabía contained a few other points to which we shall return in the section dealing with the special investigations. Towards the conclusion Salazar described how the towns were appealing to him:

> There have been a great many cases to attend to here at Fuenterrabía in connection with the Edict of Grace. But now I must go on. I have received urgent requests from Rentería, Tolosa, Oyarzun, and San Sebastián asking me to come personally on visitation to their towns, which are all in this neighborhood. I shall go first to San Sebastián, which is the largest town, and which is the one, moreover, which appears to need me most.[107]

The letter was received in Madrid on 12 September. *La Suprema* replied that same day praising Salazar for his work and assuring him that the inquisitor general had complete trust in him. The case of Catalina de Echetoa had been discussed with His Excellency — who had in the meantime read both the report of Venegas and the discourse of Pedro de Valencia (see chapters 1.2 and 11.A.1, above) — and it was agreed that her experiences were nothing but dreams and imaginings (*ha parecido sueño y cosa de fantasía*). It was therefore perfectly in order for Salazar to absolve her *ad cautelam*. He was to treat María de Tanborín likewise, and any others who might report themselves. With regard to the priests, *la Suprema* merely referred Salazar to the instructions of 26 March and otherwise gave him a free hand. Finally, as regards the reconciliations, Salazar was given permission to have them carried out by his assistants, but he himself was to inspect the witches' confessions first in order to determine whether they should be reconciled.[108]

These remarks were written as notes in the margin of Salazar's letter, which was sent to the Tribunal at Logroño for its information, with instruction that it was to be forwarded to Salazar. In a second letter addressed to the Tribunal the two inquisitors were informed that the inquisitor general had resolved to extend the Edict of Grace for a further period of four months after the expiration of the six months already granted (it was thereby valid until 29 March 1612). The inquisitors were to see to the publication of the extension of the edict and also inform their colleague accordingly.[110]

The decision to extend the period of grace was only reasonable, considering that after the first four months Salazar still had to visit the whole of Guipúzcoa and the other districts where witches had been exposed. When we further consider that

1,546 cases had been dealt with in northern Navarra and Fuenterrabía alone, six months was certainly not over long. Even though Salazar did not directly request it there was much in his letter that indicated the necessity for an extension of the edict. It could be read between the lines as a fourth problem requiring a solution. It must hardly have come as a surprise to Salazar, but it did so to Becerra and Valle. The two inquisitors felt bitter because the inquisitor general had not thought to ask for their opinion at all. They did not trouble to hide this when on 5 October they wrote one of their lengthiest letters to *la Suprema* attempting to persuade the inquisitor general to alter his decision to extend the Edict of Grace.

But before I describe this attempt — and before we accompany Salazar further on his journey — we must return to Logroño in order to find out what his colleagues had been up to during Salazar's absence; for they had certainly not been idle.

B. THE LAST BASTIONS OF THE TRIBUNAL

1. THE REMAINING GROUP OF PRISONERS

Since Salazar's departure Becerra and Valle had changed their tactics. They now set about obtaining confessions from the remaining group of prisoners whom they had been holding captive ever since March 1610 (see table 8). Only the three who had been presented at the auto de fe had confessed; five had died in prison as *negativos*, and the other eight, whose trials had commenced immediately after the auto de fe, still firmly maintained their innocence.[111] Besides these eight there was one other witch in the secret prison of the Tribunal; this was forty-year-old Graciana de Amézaga from Oronoz, who had been arrested somewhat later than the others.[112] All nine witches were now informed of the Edict of Grace. This was done during the period from 26 May to 3 July 1611,[113] but at first the inquisitors secured only two confessions.[114] One was made by the Graciana de Amézaga mentioned above, and as early as 30 June she was reconciled and released.[115] The other came from María de Endara, the aristocratic young widow from Echalar, whose fortune had been estimated by the Inquisition at ten thousand gold ducats (*ducados*).[116] She was acquainted with the Edict of Grace on 1 July and she confessed

Table 8. The Sixteen Prisoners From 3 March 1610 and the Seventeenth From Autumn 1610 (an Attempted Reconstruction)

No.	Name, age, residence, occupation	Reference no. or source	Food charges in reales	Final attitude	Death in prison	Confession
1.	Juanes de Yribarren (alias de Echalar), 40, Echalar	Auto de fe 18	257	Con		Spring 1610
2.	Felipe de Vizcancho Casanova, 40, Lesaca, muleteer	Rdo 51	1,087	Con		30 July 1611
3.	Juanes de Aguirre Luberriseme, Vera	Hualde to Tribunal, 10 Jan. 1611	270	Neg	1610	
4.	[Pedro de Andrade, shepherd, (?)]	Food Accounts 53 (see chap. 11.B.7)	976	Neg	After 8 Oct. 1611	
5.	Mari Juanto (de Aguirre), 60, Vera, born at Zugarramurdi, widow of day laborer	Auto de fe 7	197	Con	Aug. 1610	Spring 1610
6.	Beltrana de la Fargua, 40, Vera, married to beggar	Auto de fe 16	263	Con		Spring 1610
7.	María de Erausate, 48, Vera, widow	Rdo 47		Con		8 July 1611
8.	María de Aranaz, 28, daughter of no. 7	Rdo 48	1,099	Con		15 July 1611
9.	Juana Legasa Cucurro, 72, Vera, widow	Rdo 49	564	Con		9 Aug. 1611

10.	Dominja de Casanova, 40, married, Lesaca, sister of no. 2	Rdo 50	617	Con	22 July 1611
11.	María de Endara, 25, Echalar, widow of owner of iron foundry	Rdo 52	2,554	Con	4 July 1611
12.	Magdalena de Agramonte, 36, Renteria, widow	Rdo 54	777	Con	24 July 1611
13.	[Catalina de Ydiarzabal, Renteria, mother of no. 12 (?)]	Food Accounts 45		Neg	1610
14.	Catalina de Topalda, unmarried girl, Echalar, "serora"	Food Accounts 53	324	Neg	1610
15.	[Margarita de Casanova (alias Vizcancho), widow, Lesaca, sister of no. 2]	Food Accounts 44	193	Neg	1610
16a.	[Catalina de Antoco, Lesaca, widow]	Food Accounts 37	294	Neg	1610
16b.	[Magdalena de Argareta, Yanci, widow]	Food Accounts 55	395	Neg	1610
17.	Graciana de Amézaga, 40, Oronoz	Rdo 57	464	Con	7 July 1611

NOTE: *Con = confitente; Neg = negativo(a).* The chief sources are *Second Report of the Auto de fe; Relación de causas 1610/11; Accounts of 27 Sept. 1614;* and *Leg* 1679 Exp. 2.1 No. 27 F. 1ᵛ (Hualde to Tribunal 10 Jan. 1611; chapter 8 n. 38, below). The arguments for our reconstruction are presented in chapter 11 n. 111, below.

during an interrogation on 4 July, which she had requested herself. Becerra undertook the examination and Martín de Aguirre, a familiar of the Inquisition, assisted as interpreter. It would therefore seem that María de Endara was able to speak only Basque, yet her noble birth shone out in other ways in her confession. She stated, for instance, that when she arrived at the *aquelarre* the Devil received her with the greatest courtesy, and when she had renounced her faith she was merely obliged to kiss his hand (in contrast to all the other witches who were made to kiss him beneath the tail and in other unmentionable places). On 15 July she was reconciled by virtue of the Edict of Grace, and released with her fortune intact.[117] But the young woman was not permitted to enjoy her freedom for long; by 5 November she had died. She was buried at Yanci by the parish priest Martín de Yrisarri with all the honors due a person of her standing.[118]

2. PUBLICATION OF THE EDICT

As well as conducting the cases of the imprisoned witches, Becerra and Valle were intent upon discovering more *aquelarres*. The northern areas of the district were left to Salazar, but in the region bordering on Logroño the two inquisitors made the most of the permission granted by the inquisitor general to the Tribunal to publish the Edict of Grace where it was felt to be necessary. In southern Navarra the edict was published in the towns of Olite and Tafalla. In Alava publication was made at Vitoria, San Millán, Santa Cruz de Campezo, and several other towns.[119] The edict was also sent to Salvatierra, but here the inquisitorial commissioner opposed the Tribunal and refused to publish it, saying there were no witches in his district.[120]

As will be recalled, the Edict of Grace had been postponed until after the auto de fe (see chapter 7.5, above), and even when the edict was put into force the inquisitors used it only for reconciliation of prisoners and of witches who for other reasons ended up at Logroño. Forty-five persons were reconciled in this way (*Rdo* 15-59, see case nos. 32-76). Thus as a direct result of Becerra and Valle's publication of the Edict of Grace it appears that only seventeen witches came forward (*Rdo* 60-76, see case nos. 77-93). The extremely low figure is the more remarkable in view of the fact that the two inquisitors ensured that sermons were preached repeatedly against the evil sect in the towns where the edict was published.[121]

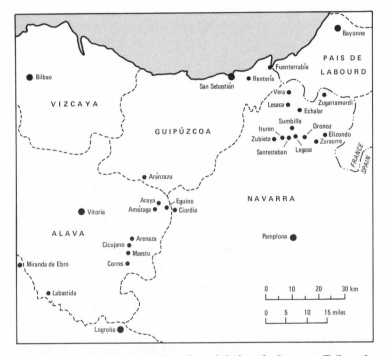

Map 6.   Confessions to witchcraft made before the Logroño Tribunal
in order to be reconciled by the Edict of Grace (December 1610-August
1611).

Map 6 shows the geographical distribution of all sixty-two witches reconciled in the courtroom of the Tribunal at Logroño by virtue of the Edict of Grace from December 1610 to August 1611. Forty-three came from Navarra: Ciordia (*Rdo* 67); Echalar (*Rdo* 52, 53); Elizondo (*Rdo* 36-40); Ituren (*Rdo* 46); Legasa (*Rdo* 44, 45); Lesaca (*Rdo* 50, 51); Oronoz (*Rdo* 57); Santesteban (*Rdo* 20-35); Sumbilla (*Rdo* 59); Vera (*Rdo* 47-49); Zubieta (*Rdo* 41-43); Zugarramurdi (*Rdo* 15-19); and Zuraurre (*Rdo* 58). Six came from Guipúzcoa: Aránzazu (*Rdo* 60-62); Fuenterrabía (*Rdo* 56); and Rentería (*Rdo* 54, 55). Eleven came from Alava: Amézaga (*Rdo* 66); Araya (*Rdo* 65); Arenaza (*Rdo* 68); Cicujano (*Rdo* 69); Corres (*Rdo* 70); Eguino (*Rdo* 72); Labastida (*Rdo* 74-76); Maestu (*Rdo* 71); and Miranda de Ebro, which strictly speaking belonged to the Burgos province (*Rdo* 73). And two came from the town of Logroño (*Rdo* 63, 64).

The only place where Becerra and Valle's summer campaign bore fruit was in eastern Alava, in the districts around San Millán and Santa Cruz de Campezo (see map 7, below), for here the witch-hunt of the Tribunal was followed up by special emissaries. But before subjecting the Alava campaign to closer analysis we will make a brief mention of the witch-hunt that the two colleagues themselves instituted at Logroño. For the Edict of Grace had been published here as well.

3. THE INVESTIGATIONS AT LOGROÑO

On 9 July the two inquisitors wrote to *la Suprema* regarding their investigations at Logroño; they made express mention of the skeptical attitude they had at first adopted:

> During the last two months many rumors have been circulating in this town to the effect that witches are abroad here, holding assemblies and *aquelarres* at night. Various happenings have taken place and finally we have been obliged to realize that the rumors are in fact true. First and foremost, a large number of people have seen mysterious fires in various parts of the town between 10 o'clock and midnight. On the night of Whitsunday [12 May], for instance, no fewer than seven witnesses, who were gathered in a [paper] mill, saw a bonfire around which some strange figures were dancing.[122]

The seven persons afterwards reported to the Tribunal in order to make a report on the strange sight, and when the inquisitors also received accounts of bewitchings which had taken place in the houses of certain citizens, they had, as they explained to *la Suprema*, felt obliged to look into the matter more closely. Becerra and Valle continued their letter by relating that they

Figure 18. Certificate of the witch Catalina de Echevarría (case nos. 73 and 493). Immediately after reconciliation the witches were furnished with a certificate stating that they had been tried by the Inquisition for "a certain case," and that they were no longer banished from Holy Communion or the other sacraments of the church.

had already made the first arrests, three Frenchmen from "Uztures" (i.e. Ustaritz in the Pays de Labourd). The chief witness against these persons was a nine-year-old boy, the son of a thatcher, who like so many other Frenchmen had made his home at Logroño. The thatcher had himself brought his son along to the Tribunal, where the boy described how the three had taken him at night to the *aquelarre*. One was actually the boy's uncle. The father and other witnesses told the Tribunal that all three of the accused were refugees from Ustaritz, where warrants for their arrest had been issued at the time when the authorities there were prosecuting the witches with great severity, and where many had been burned. However, the letter from the inquisitors states further that only one of the Frenchmen had confessed. He confessed among other things to having visited the *aquelarre* at Logroño three times and to having seen many people there, but he had been unable to recognize anyone apart from his two fellow prisoners.[123]

La Suprema sent a reply on 23 July upbraiding the Tribunal for having imprisoned people during the period of grace. They were to release the three Frenchmen immediately and acquaint them with the Edict of Grace so that they could avail themselves of it if they wished.[124] However, only one of the Frenchmen, the thirty-five-year-old Domingo de Orlaneche, took advantage of the edict. Presumably he was the one who had previously made a confession. He was reconciled by the Tribunal on 19 August.[125] The thatcher's nine-year-old son, Juanes de Sorraiz, also benefited from the Edict of Grace, for apparently as early as the month of June he was absolved *ad cautelam* on account of his extreme youth.[126]

4. THE MEMORANDUM OF THE FISCAL

On 9 July Becerra and Valle wrote two more letters to *la Suprema*. One of them gave an account of the trial of the nine witches (see table 8, nos. 2, 4, 7-12, and 17), which we have already mentioned; the other was a covering letter to a number of requests that had been submitted by the *fiscal*, San Vicente, in a memorandum, and which the Tribunal was now forwarding to *la Suprema*. His suggestions may be summarized as follows:

1. In order to effect some reparation the Tribunal was to proceed to sell the property of the Zugarramurdi witches in accordance with the sentences of confiscation pronounced at the auto de fe. It had now

been sequestered for more than two and a half years, while the cost of the witches' upkeep in prison had been met entirely by the Tribunal.

2. The *sambenitos* of those who were burned at the auto de fe were to be hung up in the churches with the *sambenitos* of those who died during the trial as *confitentes* and who were reconciled at the auto de fe in effigy. At the very least the garments were to be painted so that they were ready for display as soon as Salazar had completed his visitation to Zugarramurdi, from where the majority of the witches originated.

3. The trial of the witches imprisoned at the Tribunal was to continue regardless of whether the Edict of Grace was in force. Experience had shown that practically all of them went on denying their guilt even though they were informed of the benefits they could obtain from the edict. If their trials were not continued until after the period of grace there was a risk that they might all die in the meantime. "Out of sixteen persons who were imprisoned . . . ," wrote San Vicente, "eight died in the course of the sixteen months' imprisonment."[127] The *fiscal* went on to mention that the case of María de Endara gave an example of how hard it was for the witches to confess, for it was necessary to drag her confession out of her by means of a long series of questions (*preguntas y repreguntas*). However, San Vicente had no doubt that the truth was obtained: "Her confession agrees on practically every point with the witnesses' [i.e. the other witches'] statements, and the actions that the witnesses maintain she has participated in take place under conditions of such secrecy that it would be impossible for her to have knowledge of them unless she were a witch. For she has never spoken to the witnesses, either in the jail or before her imprisonment."

4. The Tribunal was to ensure that all the witchcraft confessions obtained to date were "ratified" in order that they could be used as evidence after the period of grace was over, and legal proceedings were to be instituted against all those who had not availed themselves of the edict. Since many of the *confitente* witches were between seventy and one hundred years old, and since almost all of them lived a great distance from the Tribunal, it was desirable for their evidence against third parties to be ratified *ad perpetuam;* and it would be quite convenient for Salazar to attend to this as he was on visitation in the area.[128]

In the interests of decorum, the two inquisitors were rather more reticent in their covering letter. Concerning points one and two, they considered that the witches might be deterred from confessing if these measures were adopted before the period of grace came to an end. They left the third point for *la Suprema* to decide. But the fourth point they strongly endorsed.[129] However, Becerra and Valle can certainly not have been enthusiastic about sending the concluding item of the *fiscal*'s letter on to the inquisitor general. For San Vicente wrote:

And since the Inquisitorial Secretary Francisco Pardo [de la Fuente] has seen fit to draw my attention to the fact that the instructions given us by Your Highness are not being followed in the examinations recorded by him, I pass this information on so that it shall not devolve upon me and so that he will not worry me further over this question. I must confess that hitherto I have not taken these details very seriously for I felt that in the witch trials it was correct to proceed in this manner especially considering the good results of this method in the case of María de Endara. The inquisitors themselves adopt this method partly because they observe how much doubt is expressed by so many people in various places [and they wished to allay this doubt]. And I myself hope that with God's help these people may be convinced by clear and obvious proof; on the other hand I admit the numerous deceits and deceptions practiced by the Devil [which must be taken into consideration when judging the evidence of the witches] against their accomplices.[130]

San Vicente concluded by asking the inquisitor general to pardon him if he had overstepped his authority in his closing remarks.

It cannot have been a coincidence that the inquisitors had mobilized the *fiscal* to the Tribunal to put forward his recommendations at precisely this moment. We can interpret all this correspondence of 9 July as a reply to the epoch-making letter of 28 June from *la Suprema* — although this is nowhere actually mentioned.[131] Becerra and Valle had swallowed their bitter pill, and now wished to find out where they stood with *la Suprema*. The request of the *fiscal* contrasted greatly with the mildly tolerant outlook of *la Suprema* as revealed in the instructions of 26 March, and it appeared at so inopportune a moment, that it could have had only one aim, namely, to force the inquisitor general to show his hand.

On 23 July, when *la Suprema* sent orders to the Tribunal to free the three Frenchmen, a reply was also given to the *fiscal*'s communication. His requests were all rejected,[132] except for the third, which asked for the trial of the imprisoned witches to continue. But this was to take a different form from that envisaged by the Tribunal. Thus, the Edict of Grace was to be read twice more to the accused, both when the trial was half completed and also when their cases were ready for sentence.[133] In reality this meant that the accused was given the choice of denying his guilt and being condemned to the stake with confiscation of property, or of confessing and being reconciled and released without any punishment whatsoever.

5. THE WITCH-HUNT AT ALAVA

Strangely enough the witch-hunt at Alava received no mention at all in the Tribunal's letter of 9 July to *la Suprema*. It was then in full swing, but possibly the inquisitors felt that the time was not yet ripe to report on it. The statistics of 9 March 1611 show that there had already been four confessions from the eastern part of Alava, which during the course of the summer was to become the scene of the Tribunal's most strenuous activities. We do not know the identities of the four witches; we know only that one of them came from Alegría and that the other three were from Eguino (see table 6, above). The inquisitorial commissioner of that place was the parish priest Pedro Ruiz of Eguino. On 25 March Pedro Ruiz obtained a long confession of witchcraft from an eighty-year-old man in the neighboring town of Araya. The name of the old man was Juan Díaz de Alda and on 21 April he was reconciled at Logroño after having repeated his confession to the inquisitors and denouncing a large number of persons from his district as witches.[134] Presumably he had been taken to the Tribunal by Pedro Ruiz, who despite being the incumbent at Eguino had a house in Logroño and resided there most of the time. This commissioner was particularly well-acquainted with the witch problem, for as a Basque interpreter he had taken part in the examination of almost all the imprisoned witches. When the Tribunal resolved to have the Edict of Grace published in eastern Alava by special emissaries, Pedro Ruiz was the obvious candidate for this confidential mission.[135]

During the course of the summer Pedro Ruiz made several journeys to his native district and each time returned to Logroño with witches who had come to make their confessions to the Tribunal and receive the benefits of the edict.[136] On 2 August he brought along a ninety-five-year-old priest, Diego de Basurto, who lived in the village of Ciordia in the Borunda Valley on the border of Alava,[137] but who was in the habit of coming to say Mass at the commissioner's church at Eguino. Basurto was subjected to a very searching interrogation at the Tribunal and after a time they succeeded in getting a coherent confession of witchcraft out of the old man, whose memory, as

Becerra and Valle wrote to *la Suprema*, was much impaired by his great age. On 12 August the two inquisitors sent Basurto's trial record to the Council for perusal, together with a letter containing a report of the campaign in Alava. They explained that the large numbers of witches there had made it necessary for the Edict of Grace to be published before Salazar reached this district. The Tribunal had more than a hundred people under suspicion and among these were no fewer than ten priests. The letter explained further that the priests were doing all in their power to obstruct the investigations of the Inquisition, and in several cases they had threatened *confitente* witches and told them not to confess anything. However, Diego de Basurto, who was already under suspicion before he made his confession, had given evidence against all of them and had in addition denounced two priests in the Borunda Valley as witches.[138] In their letter to *la Suprema* the inquisitors revealed that Basurto was an ignorant and disreputable old priest without learning, who was unpopular besides, and who had fathered several illegitimate children in his district. The Tribunal was therefore of the opinion that despite the rulings of the Edict of Grace, he should be instructed to refrain from exercising his priestly function in the future.[139]

On 23 August *la Suprema* returned Basurto's confession with orders for the old priest to be reconciled and to receive all the benefits of the Edict of Grace. The Tribunal obeyed the orders and reconciled Basurto on 3 September.[140]

Later in the summer another inquisitorial commissioner began activities similar to those of the commissioner at Eguino. This was the parish priest Felipe Díaz de Bujanda of Maestu.[141] He too specialized in bringing priests to book. Thus on 22 September Felipe Díaz examined fifty-year-old Magdalena de Elorza from the village of Atauri. The only people this woman could recall having seen at her witches' sabbath were six priests who (strangely enough) happened to be neighbors of the inquisitorial commissioner. She mentioned them all by name and one of them was no less than the dean Francisco Ochoa of Antoñana, who lived about four miles from Maestu.[142] The number of suspected priests in Alava was now twenty, to which can be added the two in the neighboring Borunda Valley (see below, table 9 and map 7).

The witch-hunt in Alava would be worth a closer study in itself. It is an example of a centrally conducted campaign which appears to have been only half-heartedly supported by the populace. Several hundred people came under suspicion, but the suspicion rested on the evidence of fewer than twenty *confitente* witches, and half of these revoked their confessions when Salazar arrived in the area.[143]

6. THE FISCAL IS SENT TO SAN SEBASTIÁN

In the middle of September the Tribunal sent the *fiscal* San Vicente to San Sebastián. He left Logroño on Sunday the 11th and returned in the evening of Wednesday the 21st.[144] He undertook this sudden journey in order to have a meeting with Salazar, who had just completed the visitation at Fuenterrabía and was about to commence a fresh session. Both the Edict of Grace and the Edict of Faith were published at San Sebastián, and on the latter occasion the sermon was preached by a Dominican monk from the monastery of San Telmo in that town, who was a firm believer in witchcraft.[145] It is unlikely that the *fiscal* would have arrived in time for the publication itself, but during his week's stay at San Sebastián he was present when fifty-two child witches, most of them under the age of seven, were absolved by virtue of the Edict of Grace. This was the only result of the Edict of Grace at San Sebastián; all the adult witches held back, apart from one woman who had previously been detained by the authorities and who regained her freedom by availing herself of the edict.[146] The object of the *fiscal*'s sudden dash to San Sebastián was clearly to obtain detailed information for the Tribunal of the results of Salazar's visitation. In his letters to the colleagues, Salazar had displayed extreme reticence and had consulted them only when obliged to do so.[147] The *fiscal* made use of the few days he spent at San Sebastián to undertake a hasty perusal of the visitation papers in order to get a general idea of what had emerged as a result of the Edict of Grace.

7. THE TRIBUNAL'S OBJECTIONS TO EXTENSION OF THE EDICT

By the time the *fiscal* had returned from San Sebastián the Tribunal had probably already received the orders from *la Suprema* regarding the extension of the Edict of Grace, and had read the copy of the report Salazar sent from Fuenterrabía to the inquisitor general (see chapter 11.A.7). The Tribunal spent the remainder of September in composing the longest report on the witch affair it had yet sent to *la Suprema*, four pages from the *fiscal* and seven very close-written pages from Becerra and Valle. As usual the *fiscal's* communication was addressed to the inquisitors. On 3 October San Vicente read it out himself to Valle in the courtroom of the Tribunal and requested that it be forwarded to *la Suprema*.

Becerra was absent on that occasion and on the whole it is hard to assess how much responsibility he had for the Tribunal's witch prosecutions during this period. In the middle of July he was stricken with quartan fever and since then had been bedridden most of the time.[148]

The contents of the *fiscal's* document, which concluded by recommending that the Edict of Grace ought not to be extended, may be summarized as follows:

1. In the areas around Logroño where the Tribunal had published the Edict of Grace, it had had little effect: only twelve out of three hundred suspects had turned themselves in and made confessions.

2. The effect of the Edict of Grace had been unsatisfactory on the journey of visitation as well. The yield might have been substantial, but the figure was to be seen in the light of the following considerations: (a) A large proportion of the (adult) witches who had presented themselves had already made a previous confession to the Inquisition, and many had recanted their confessions later on, while others had relapsed. These witches, following the advice of the Devil, had made false and incomplete confessions in order to benefit from all the provisions of the Edict of Grace; (b) Far the greater number of the latest witches to report were minors, and these could still be absolved regardless of whether the period of grace was extended. As far as the adult witches were concerned it was obvious that not even a tenth of the suspects had taken the outstretched hand of the Inquisition and availed themselves of the Edict of Grace.

3. The Edict of Grace had an effect completely opposite to that originally intended, and had encouraged the Devil's minions to greater insolence and aggressiveness: (a) Previously they held meetings three times a week, now they met every night; (b) Recently they had begun to take many more children to the sabbath, and while before they did not admit them to the witch sect until the girls were twelve years old and the boys fourteen, now they had no compunction in making them renounce their Christian faith at the age of eight or nine; (c) The witches previously had a certain amount of respect for the Inquisition, but now they even had the effrontery to attack the staff of the Tribunal and their families. (As an example of this San Vicente related how on the previous day Salazar's housekeeper had come weeping to him and had shown him how she was covered with bruises caused by the witches' ill-treatment.)[149]

If we set the demonological aspect of San Vicente's argument aside for a moment, there is little doubt that it was based on an accurate assessment of the effects of the edict. The small section of the records of Salazar's visitation which has survived confirms that it was predominantly the Inquisition's "old offenders" who appeared at the sessions to avail themselves of the edict. Since San Vicente had access to all the records his statements must therefore be regarded as an important source of information regarding the greater part of Salazar's visitation book which was later lost.

The conclusion of the *fiscal's* letter is worth quoting in full. It provides striking evidence of the mood prevailing at the Tribunal after Salazar's departure:

> It is not my intention to dwell upon the many other misfortunes and strange diseases that the staff of the Tribunal are being plagued with, and all the damage which has occurred to the crops in the surrounding areas, for I have only my suppositions [regarding the causes of these things] . . . Nor shall I enlarge upon the tricks that the Devil plays every day in front of our very noses. However, it is not without good reason that some of the commissioners have grown so frightened that they say they will resign their office and leave their homes if the period of grace is extended. This is particularly true of the commissioner at Maestu [Felipe Díaz]. He finds it unthinkable to extend the edict, when he sees that almost his entire village — including the other priests and his own household — are members of this accursed sect. [It is his experience that] the witches have become [more] vicious and [more] tenacious after observing the mercy that has been shown to their [*confitente*] neighbors. For the Edict of Grace has merely had the effect of making them threaten and maltreat those [who have confessed]. It is therefore hopeless to expect the witches to show any improvement.
>
> The only possible step to take now is to make them feel the strong arm of the law and send them to the stake — and to do this not here in the town [i.e. Logroño], but at home in their own villages outside the very doors of their houses. One should at least burn the tutor witches in this way, for then it is to be hoped that the apprentices will come forward and give themselves up. After they have witnessed the severity of the penalties they will surely stop listening to the persuasions of the Devil and the instructors in this diabolical sect [who tell them not to reveal anything], and tear them-

selves away from the delusions they have been under. And I
say this not so much from my position as *fiscal*, but in order
to relieve my own conscience and to pass the responsibility
on to Your Éminence [Inquisitor Valle]. However, should I
be so permitted, I should have the greatest pleasure in
presenting myself to His Eminence the Cardinal [i.e. the
inquisitor general] and the Lords of the Council in order to
set forth these proofs and to explain more fully the documents relating to the case (*para comprobar con papeles y razones
esta verdad*).[150]

It is somewhat difficult to determine exactly who shared the
views expressed at the end of the letter. As far as San Vicente
himself was concerned, he was so strictly circumscribed by
virtue of his office that despite his own assurances we cannot
take his words as a straightforward expression of his *personal*
view of the matter. The meeting at the Tribunal ended with
Valle promising that the inquisitors would write to *la Suprema*
and enclose the *fiscal's* memorandum.[151]

Two days later Becerra seems to have been at work, for we
find his signature at the foot of the seven-page letter to *la
Suprema*, dated 5 October, in which the two inquisitors elaborated on the arguments of the *fiscal*.[152] Concerning Salazar,
they complained that he had not complied with their request
that he should send them detailed reports of the results of the
visitation. However, the Tribunal had received letters from the
inquisitorial commissioners in the districts visited by Salazar
and they were all in the following vein:

Only very few of the adult [witches], who had not already
previously confessed, availed themselves of the Edict of
Grace. Therefore, say the commissioners, no progress has
been made in combating the plague of witches. It is true that
many juvenile witches have been helped by the Edict of
Grace, but the old witches and the tutors have grown excessively insolent during the six months' respite afforded them
by the edict. They believe the Inquisition will take no further
steps in this matter, and feel they are completely safe. This is
why they are now victimizing and maltreating the Christians with the utmost lack of restraint.[153]

Becerra and Valle were in full agreement that even though
the Edict of Grace had benefited the young witches, it had
served very little, if at all, to achieve the chief aim of the
Inquisition, which was to exterminate the witch sect (*extirpar*

esas maldades).[154] After having commented on Salazar's visitation, the two inquisitors proceeded to give a detailed report of the witch investigations they themselves had carried out during the course of the summer.

There was only one person, a shepherd, remaining to be tried at the Tribunal (see table 8 no. 4 and n. 111). He had several times begun to confess something but had not been able to bring himself to make a complete confession. The Tribunal was convinced of his guilt as there were many witnesses against him. This was also the case with a woman who had died in the prison without making a confession. The other witches had made confessions "amidst copious weeping which showed their sincere penitence," and had now all been reconciled and set free.[155]

The results of the witch-hunt in Alava were summed up by the two inquisitors as follows: twelve adult witches had confessed at the Tribunal, and had been reconciled through the Edict of Grace. In addition to this there were five who had made their confessions to the district commissioners, but who had still not been to Logroño to be reconciled by the Tribunal.[156] Seven of the witches belonged to a big *aquelarre* in Alava, which counted no fewer than twelve priests amongst its members. Almost all the other witches came from another *aquelarre* in the province of Alava "five *leguas*" (ca. 19 miles) from Logroño, where a further five priests were under suspicion.[157]

The letter went on to state that the Logroño witches were as active as ever. Every night they held an *aquelarre* in the square of San Francisco. The two inquisitors were able to mention several citizens who had been exposed to persecution and ill-treatment by the witches, and in a lengthy passage they described how the commissioner Pedro Ruiz had met with sudden death under extremely mysterious circumstances:

> Terrible things are happening in this town in front of our very eyes, and every citizen is now afraid to show that he is on the side of the Inquisition for fear of what the witches might do to him. We are deeply grieved because they have killed Pedro Ruiz de Eguino — of this we are quite certain... We entrusted him with the publication of the Edict of Grace in the Province of Alava because of his great talents and his knowledge of the locality, which was his birthplace. As a result of his energy and competence he uncovered the

large *aquelarre* mentioned above, to which the twelve priests are under suspicion of belonging. He spared no one and thus detected some more witches who were his own relatives. The wicked priests mentioned above did, and are still doing, everything in their power to prevent any further confessions being made, and several months ago they began a campaign of harassment against the commissioner at his home here in Logroño. Things became particularly bad after we had confined the witch priest, Diego de Basurto, to his house. Basurto described in his confessions how the Devil and many witches continued to come to fetch him and take him to the *aquelarre*. It ended with Basurto assenting, and on the night of Lady Day in August [the night before 25 August?], three of the twelve priests together with the Devil and a distinguished nobleman came and took him to the sabbath... The witches made such threats and created such disturbances in the house of the commissioner that he fell into a state of melancholia and declared he would have no more to do with the affair. We talked to him at the Tribunal and made him see reason, and he regained his strength and courage, and determined to continue both for God's sake and for the sake of his own honor, even if it should cost him his life. However, the news leaked out that Eguino had been entrusted with a new mission and was to go to the Borunda Valley and other places where there are many witches. Before he had left on his journey he awoke one morning and found a plaster (*un pegote*) on one of his legs. He tore the plaster off with great difficulty. He realized at once that this was the witches' work, as he had received a warning from them. He was afflicted with a fever that same day and next morning he was aware of a powder in his mouth and throat, which seemed to be composed of ground brick and which he declared tasted of cheese. This quite broke his spirit. He told the doctors what was wrong with him and afterwards begged for the last rites. Then he began to suffer the vomiting and diarrhea which is the usual effect of the powders, and four days later he died. Judging from the course the illness had run, the doctors declared that he must have died of poisoning.[158]

The two inquisitors also related how the witches had attempted to murder other members of the Tribunal staff with witch powders. This had all happened *after* the publication of the Edict of Grace, and the agents who had assisted the Tribunal with the publication were now making daily complaints to the inquisitors. All were looking forward to the end of the period of grace and for "severity and punishment" to be enforced. Thus Becerra and Valle were quite convinced that to extend the period of grace would bring about grave harm. "And," they added, "Your Highness would be equally convinced, were He as closely affected by the events as we are." The two inquisitors concluded with something of a concession when they requested the inquisitor general at least to confine the extension of the edict to the areas where it had not yet been published or had only been in operation for a short time. On the other hand, in the remainder of the district, where the witches had had the opportunity to present themselves voluntarily, it was high time to "step in firmly" with "the severity of the law."[159]

The following day, 6 October, the Tribunal received a letter from Salazar which will be discussed below. It concerned fourteen witches who had been imprisoned by the authorities at San Sebastián (see chapter 11.C.2, below). The inquisitors forwarded this letter to *la Suprema* with a covering note stating that this was the first time that Salazar had written to them about the witches.[160]

On 25 October *la Suprema* replied by ordering the extension of the Edict of Grace "despite the objections of the *fiscal*." The Tribunal was to undertake further investigations into the causes of the maltreatment of Salazar's housekeeper and the death of Eguino. Also fresh investigations were to be made concerning the witches' meeting places and new experiments undertaken with their ointments, poisons, and powders. Those who carried out the investigations were to feed the poisonous substances to animals and then observe the effects after a day had passed — all, as the letter states, "in order to establish what it is possible to establish in such a difficult type of case."[161]

The inquisitor general did not panic over the alarming reports from Logroño and the pessimistic evaluation of the effects of the Edict of Grace. With its usual circumspection *la Suprema* ordered its servants to prove their claim with empirical evidence.

On 15 November Becerra and Valle promised, in a letter to *la Suprema*, to comply with the request and forward a detailed report (but as scientific investigation was not their strong point the report seems never to have materialized). And then the letter was chiefly concerned with two new "political" leads on the part of the Tribunal. The first proposal related to the witches who had revoked their confessions and were now trying to get others to follow their example. This was particularly serious in Navarra, and Becerra and Valle therefore requested permission to take action against these agitators even though the Edict of Grace was still valid. The second proposal concerned two of the witches from the auto de fe in 1610, María Chipía de Barrenechea and María de Echegui. The Tribunal requested permission to release these two women. They were the only witches remaining at the House of Penance after the auto de fe, and they felt they were being treated unjustly when they saw the other witches — who had not been willing to confess until they heard of the Edict of Grace — had now been released.[162]

La Suprema replied on 29 November. In its usual manner the Council neutralized the proposal to take steps against the agitators. The inquisitors could recommend the arrest of four or five of the most notorious, and send their votes in to the Council without taking further steps in the matter. As for the second proposal, la Suprema for once reacted positively. The inquisitor general had decided to remit the remainder of the term of imprisonment of the two women at the House of Penance. The Tribunal was to release them and to allow them freedom to go wherever they wished.[163]

C. THE SECOND PART OF SALAZAR'S JOURNEY

1. RECONSTRUCTION OF THE ROUTE

It is not feasible to reconstruct the last part of Salazar's journey of visitation with the same degree of certainty as exists for the journey through northern Navarra. In the first report to the inquisitor general there is a list of all the places where Salazar stayed to publish the Edict of Grace, but it is obvious that the towns were not listed in the order in which they were visited. Thus, in the first section of the list we find the Borunda Valley and the Araquil Valley in western Navarra placed together with all the places in northern Navarra which were visited during the first part of the journey, but in fact Salazar did not reach these two valleys until the last part of the journey (see map 4). The list merely reels off towns where Salazar "held sessions and published the Edict of Grace":

In the Province of Guipúzcoa I visited Fuenterrabía, San Sebastián, Tolosa, Azpeitia, Rentería, Los Pasajes, Vergara, Deva, Guetaria, and Motrico; in Vizcaya I saw Berriatúa, Marquina, and Oñate; and in Alava, the town of Salvatierra and the city of Vitoria.[164]

The dates of the interrogations help us a little further, but documentation is extant only for the sessions at San Sebastián (12 September through 8 October),[165] Tolosa (13 October),[166] Alsasua in the Borunda Valley (18 November),[167] Salvatierra (26-27 November),[168] and Vitoria (29-30 November and 22-27 December).[169] We must use different methods to discover the dates of Salazar's visits to the other towns.

It is quite likely that he visited Los Pasajes and Rentería on the way to San Sebastián. There is a description by Salazar of how he sailed from Rentería and went ashore "at two o'clock in the morning" at a place outside San Sebastián, where the authorities of the town were waiting to receive him. We learn about this in connection with Salazar's mention of a new attack made against him by the witches; for — according to a confession — they too had come out to meet him (flying through the air in a troop).[170] Presumably Salazar had already reached San Sebastián to enable him to publish the Edict of Grace as early as Sunday, 11 September.[171] The sessions at Los Pasajes and Rentería must therefore have been held some time between 4 September (when Salazar wrote to the inquisitor general from Fuenterrabía) and 10 September.

Salazar must have visited the towns in western Guipúzcoa and Vizcaya during the thirty-five days from 14 October to 17 November — a period during which there is no record of his whereabouts.[172] Eight towns are listed: Azpeitia, Guetaria, Deva, Motrico, Berriatúa, Marquina, Vergara, and Oñate. At Azpeitia the Edict of Faith was published together with the edict to the witches. This would have required a stay of at least a week, for the Anathema would have been published only after seven days had elapsed. Possibly Salazar maintained his headquarters at Azpeitia for a longer period of time and from there made excursions to the towns in western Guipúzcoa and in Vizcaya.

2. THE VISITATION AT SAN SEBASTIÁN
AND EASTERN GUIPÚZCOA

The visitation at San Sebastián seems to have commenced with the publication of the Edict of Grace on Sunday, 11 September.[173] From the previously mentioned letter of Salazar to the Tribunal (dated San Sebastián, 28 September), it would appear that the Edict of Faith was published on Sunday the 18th, while the *fiscal* was at San Sebastián, and that the Anathema was read the following Sunday, after his departure for Logroño (see chapter 11.B.6, above). The preacher at the publication of the Anathema, wrote Salazar to his colleagues, was the provincial of the Franciscan Order, "and his authority and scholarship contributed much towards making this ceremony a very solemn occasion" (cf. chapter 6).[174]

The rest of Salazar's letter to his colleagues was concerned with fourteen women who before his arrival had been arrested for witchcraft by the authorities at San Sebastián. Only one of them had confessed, and she had been reconciled through the Edict of Grace. The others maintained stubbornly that they were innocent, and Salazar had therefore sent them back to their prison without concerning himself further with their cases. However, after he had inspected their trial records, Salazar seems to have taken the trouble to draw the attention of the authorities to the fact that there was no evidence against any of the accused. For the letter states that the magistrates were extremely downcast at having no evidence, and angry with Salazar for not having instituted proceedings against these thirteen witches. In defending these women Salazar had incurred the displeasure of the entire town:

> Whatever I say to make the authorities see reason and to calm the agitated people has no effect. They all shout with one voice that there can be no doubt that these women are the witches who take their children [to the *aquelarre*]. None can understand why they should not be punished, or why I will not hear of accepting them as prisoners of the Inquisition.[175]

Salazar had also had trouble over the fourteenth witch, whom he had reconciled. The authorities could not understand why she should benefit from all the provisions of the Edict of Grace and they had insisted that they should at least have permission to banish her from their town. On the one hand Salazar was prepared to help the woman; on the other hand he did not want to appear too unyielding to the townspeople, who might easily lose heart if they saw that the Inquisition was defending their "witch." Salazar ended by asking his colleagues' advice on how he should act in this case.[176] (The problem is one which constantly recurs in the history of Spanish witch persecution. The civil authorities were always prepared to acknowledge the jurisdiction of the Inquisition in these cases, but they could not tolerate the witches escaping unpunished.)

During his stay at San Sebastián, Salazar summoned two seventeen-year-old girls from Fuenterrabía[177] in order to question them regarding the following event: on Saturday, 10 September, four women ate their lunch together on the mountainside outside Fuenterrabía. All four were reputed to be witches, and all four had made confessions to Salazar. During their alfresco meal the women discussed their good fortune in getting through the examination so easily. For they had feared, while they were waiting to be interrogated, that Salazar would order them to show him how they had held their *aquelarre,* to discover if they were telling the truth. However, all had gone smoothly for them at the hearing, and afterwards they had merely been very curious as to how much of their tall stories the inquisitor really had believed. But now that it was over and done with the four women promised each other not to breathe a word of this conversation but to stand firm by what they had said in their confessions. As for those they had denounced as their accomplices, the women on the mountainside agreed that they had nothing to fear, for they were all such poor and simple folk that you could call them witches to their faces.[178]

The two girls were interrogated at San Sebastián on 16 and 20 September respectively. The story just described was repeated to both of them and both denied any knowledge of it. Salazar warned each of them against bearing false witness, since the Inquisition had been informed that they had been present on the occasion in question — one of them, the servant girl María de Azaldegui, was even supposed to have taken part in the conversation — but both maintained that they knew nothing of the matter.[179] Unfortunately this is as far as we can get with this extremely interesting evidence of the cynical manner in which some of the "witches" at Fuenterrabía had acted in order to save their own skins.[180]

From San Sebastián Salazar went on to Tolosa. Here a twelve-year-old girl from Asteasu revoked the witch-confession she had made the previous autumn to the district commissioner of the Inquisition.[181] We do not know where Salazar went after leaving Tolosa, for, as I mentioned, we almost lose sight of him for the next month. Perhaps there were no witch cases at all on this part of the journey. However, the witches turned up again as soon as Salazar entered the area where his colleagues had directed their campaign during the summer.

3. THE LAST THREE SESSIONS

The records are extant for a total of eleven visitation trials from the Borunda Valley and Alava. Ten of these concern men and women who recanted the witch-confessions they made during the summer and autumn;[182] the eleventh, a thirty-six-year-old woman, María de Ulibarri, stood firm by her confession and was reconciled, making her the 289th reconciled witch on the journey of visitation.[183] From a total of 290 cases of witchcraft we see that 271 witches had already been reconciled by the time Salazar left Fuenterrabía (see near beginning of chapter 11.A.7). This means that the last nineteen must have been distributed over the whole of the remainder of the journey.[184] We are therefore able to state with certainty that only very few availed themselves of the Edict of Grace during the last three visitation sessions, at Alsasua, Salvatierra, and Vitoria, and this despite the fact that the Tribunal had several hundred persons under suspicion. However, it did not take Salazar long to realize that the real problem in this area was not the witches, but the inquisitorial commissioners and the monks who had been sent up by the Tribunal to preach and instruct the populace.[185]

The visitation in the Borunda Valley commenced on 18 November. On this day, which was a Friday, the Edict of Grace was published in the principal town of Alsasua during a morning service at which the preacher was Fray Josef de Elizondo. After the ceremony, an elderly priest, who had hovered close to Salazar the whole time, approached Fray Josef and said that he would stay in the town for the rest of the day as there was something he wished to discuss with the inquisitor. Salazar sent for him in the afternoon. It turned out to be the ninety-five-year-old Diego de Basurto from Ciordia.

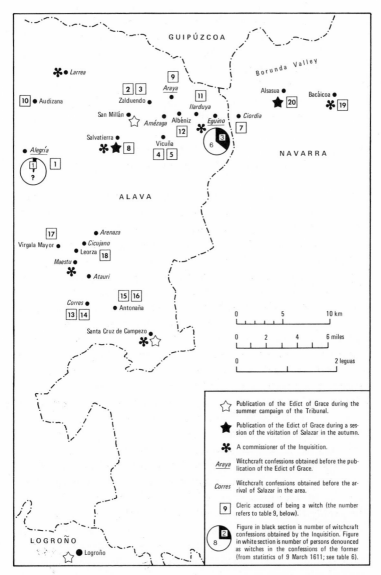

Map 7. *The witch persecution at Alava and the Borunda Valley, 1611.*

The old priest commenced by saying that he had already been reconciled at Logroño, but when Salazar asked what he had on his conscience the old man grew frightened and replied that he had nothing more to say. Salazar tried to loosen his tongue by asking where the witches held their meetings and how long it was since he had been to the *aquelarre*. But the old man replied: "The truth is, Sir, that I know nothing and have never known anything of these things, and therefore I cannot in truth answer such questions." He continued by describing how the commissioner Pedro Ruiz had tricked him into making a witch confession (cf. chapter 11.B.5, above). They had known each other from Eguino, where the commissioner was parish priest, and where Basurto was in the habit of going to say Mass. One day, when they had met, the conversation had turned to the witches, and Pedro Ruiz had said: "You must be a witch, then." It had been spoken in jest and Basurto had merely smiled and answered in the same vein. However, Ruiz went on with the joke and said that a scar Basurto had on his left temple was the sign that he was a witch. Here Basurto had broken off the conversation and said very definitely to Ruiz: "My good Sir, I am no more a witch than Your Grace."

However, each time they met, the commissioner had reopened the discussion. On one occasion Basurto replied that "he was no more a witch than St. Peter." On another occasion, when the commissioner had been particularly pressing, the old priest was rash enough to make the following remark: "I cannot imagine how I could have become a witch, as Your Grace thinks, unless perhaps old Agneda de Lezcano at Zubielgui [Zubildegui?] anointed me when I was small, for they used to say she was a witch."

However, the commissioner had continued to keep up the banter and one day he invited Basurto to be his guest on a journey. The shabby old priest was incautious enough to accept the invitation without asking the object of the journey. They ended up at Logroño, where the commissioner installed Basurto in his house and showed him every hospitality. But here Ruiz began to put pressure on the old man to make him confess that he was a witch. Basurto, however, had continued to deny it most strongly. Finally the commissioner's patience snapped and he threatened to deliver Basurto over to the Inquisition, where he could rot away in the prison if he did not go to confession. This had frightened the old man, and he had agreed to make a voluntary confession to the Inquisition.

A few days later Ruiz had taken him along to the Tribunal. They had entered a chamber where Basurto was left alone with an inquisitor (probably Valle), who immediately began to interrogate him concerning all the witches' activities and how they made their unguents. As the old priest was unable to give any real answers to the questions the inquisitor grew angry and in a rage sent for Ruiz. When the latter came into the room he at once let it be understood that Basurto had already confessed all these things to him. Ruiz then went on to fire questions at him so that, as he said, Basurto might "repeat" his confession in the presence of the inquisitor. It was only at this point that the written record began, and they continued to hear his confession during several examinations in the days that followed. Everything that Basurto confessed at the Tribunal, however, had been put into his mouth by Ruiz, including the names of the persons he denounced as accomplices. Basurto told Salazar that he was under the impression they were all people with whom Pedro Ruiz was on bad terms. Among other things, Ruiz had made him say that the dean of Alegría was a witch, and this in spite of the fact that Basurto had never even seen the dean.

When Basurto had finished his account he burst into tears and begged Salazar's forgiveness for having borne false witness. Salazar asked him if he had discussed this matter with anyone else or if he had any other reasons, apart from those he had already given, for making this recantation. But the old man replied: "No, Sir, only God and the Holy Spirit have moved me to make this declaration."[186]

The next session was held at Salvatierra, the principal town in eastern Alava, and here more facts came to light about the activities of Pedro Ruiz. Two old women, who had been among his first victims, and who had made their confessions in the month of June, were called in so that Salazar could reconcile them on the visitation. Salazar had had their earlier confessions sent up from the Tribunal. The two old women came before him on 26 and 27 November respectively, and here they revoked all that they had declared against themselves and those whom they had denounced as accomplices.

One of the old women was called Catalina Fernández de

Lecea. She was an eighty-year-old spinster from Araya, a village some few miles from Eguino. The confession she had made earlier to the commissioner at Eguino was read out to her, but after hearing all the perverse things she was supposed to have taken part in at the witches' sabbath, the old woman declared point-blank that "he who wrote that" must have invented those things, for she had certainly never confessed to them. She admitted, rightly enough, that she had made a confession of witchcraft but said she had been forced to do so by the commissioner. He told her that she had a witch-mark in her left eye, and that besides he had already heard from others that she was a witch. Thus she, a harmless old woman, had been tricked into bearing false witness against herself and many other innocent persons.[187]

The other old woman was called Ana Sáenz. She was a seventy-year-old widow from Ilarduya, a mile or so from the commissioner's village. She told Salazar that the commissioner had threatened to take her to Logroño if she did not confess.[188]

The records of these two old women are extant and they show that Pedro Ruiz made his two victims accuse over fifty persons of witchcraft. In their lists of accomplices we find old Basurto and also the names of eleven other priests (see table 9).[189]

The last session was held at Vitoria and went on for over a month. The Edict of Grace must have been published on 28 November,[190] for on the morning of 29 November Salazar was interrogating María de Ulibarri (whose trial is discussed in a separate section below). On 30 November Salazar examined three women whom he had summoned in order to ratify their witch-confessions and to reconcile them by virtue of the Edict of Grace. However, at the examination the three women declared that they were not witches at all and thereupon revoked everything that they had said in their earlier confessions. Two of them were young girls, aged thirteen and fourteen respectively. They told Salazar how the priest at Larrea, Martín López de Lazárraga, had summoned them to the rectory and bound them by the hands and neck while threatening to take them to Logroño if they did not confess. He had thereby intimidated them into making confessions and also witnessing against their own mothers. They denounced, however, no priests.[191] These were presumably some of the first witch confessions acquired by this priest for the Tribunal, for he had just been appointed inquisitorial commissioner to succeed Pedro Ruiz de Eguino, after the latter had allegedly been killed by the witches. The third *revocante* was a fifty-year-old widow, Magdalena de Elorza, from Atauri. She retracted the confession she had made to the priest at Maestu, Felipe Díaz, on 20 September.[192] This priest, as has been mentioned, was also a commissioner and was responsible for the discovery of the other large *aquelarre* in Alava, where six priests were under suspicion (see the case of Magdalena de Elorza, chapter 11.B.5 and table 9 nos. 13-18).

The young girls and the widow also spoke of a third person who had aided in the extraction of their false confessions. This was the Franciscan monk Fray Juan de Ladrón. He took part in the witch-hunt in Alava in the capacity of one of the Tribunal's special emissaries, and as such he had helped the commissioner at Larrea to tie up the two young girls, and the commissioner at Maestu to put the idea of the six priest witches into the widow's head.[193]

Towards Christmas Fray Ladrón himself went to see Salazar at Vitoria. His purpose was to report five witches in the Maestu district. These had all been to Logroño during the course of the summer and had shared in the Edict of Grace after making their confessions, but they were now going about the district saying they were not witches. Salazar had them all summoned to Vitoria, where they were examined between 22 and 27 December. One of them held to what she had said at Logroño. The other four admitted that they were not witches and described how they had been threatened and cajoled into making false confessions.[194]

Thus Gracia González, a young farmer's wife from Cicujano, told how she and some others had been taken to Logroño one day in July. When they reached Logroño they were told that if they confessed, their cases would be dealt with quickly and they would go unpunished, while if they refused to confess they would be detained. The young wife was awaiting her husband's return from a journey and therefore decided to confess. Most of what she confessed at the hearings, Salazar learned, she had picked up from some fellow villagers who had been to the auto de fe the previous year. Other details she had acquired from a neighbor who had been taken to Logroño with her. The rest she had assimilated from

Table 9. The Twenty Priest Witches From Alava and the Borunda Valley

Name, ecclesiastical rank, domicile	Eguino			Maestu	
Domicile of Inquisition commissioner:					
Date of confession: / Signature of record:	26 June Rte 46	28 June Rte 47	2 Aug. Rte 58	20 Sept. Rte 48	No date Rdo 76b
1. Juan Martínez de Alegría, dean of Alegría	•		•		
2. Sancho Abad, priest at Zalduengo	•		?		
3. Graviel López de Lazárraga, parish priest of Zalduengo	•		?		
4. Pedro López de Aldoín, assistant priest at Vicuña	•		?		
5. Juan Ruiz, assistant priest at Vicuña	•		?		
6. Bernardo de Guridi, priest at Segura, previously priest at Eguino	•	•	?		
7. Diego de Basurto, parish priest at Ciordia, also affiliated to Eguino	•	•	•		
8. Juanes de Hualde, assistant priest at Church of Santa María at Salvatierra, born at Ciordia	•		?		
9. Juan Abad de Lecea, assistant priest at Araya	•	•	?		
10. Martín Abad de Audizana, parish priest at Audizana	•		?		
11. Juan Ruiz de Arriola, parish priest at Ilarduya		•	?		
12. Martín Sáenz de Ilarduya, priest at Albéniz		•	?		
13. Francisco Abad, priest at Corres				•	•

14. Fausto Abad, priest at Corres
15. Francisco Ochoa de Abiria, dean of Antoñana
16. Juan de Alda, parish priest of Antoñana
17. Juan Abad Ochoa, parish priest of Virgala Mayor
18. Martín Abad de Suso, priest at Leorza
19. Juan Martínez de Larraiza, 76, inquisitorial commissioner for the Borunda Valley, parish priest at Bacáicoa
20. Miguel de Arramendia, parish priest of Alsasua, inquisitorial notary for the Borunda Valley and interpreter on Salazar's journey of visitation, 1611

NOTE: *Rte* 46 is Catalina Fernández de Lecea, age 80, from Araya (see chapter 11.C.3); *Rte* 47 is Ana Sáenz, 70, Ilarduya (see chapter 11.C.3); *Rte* 58 is Diego de Basurto, 95, parish priest from Ciordia (see chapter 11.B.5 and 11.C.3); *Rte* 48 is Magdalena de Elorza, 50, Atauri (see chapter 11.B.5 and 11.C.3); *Rdo* 76b is Mariquita de Atauri, 65, Atauri (see chapter 11.C.4).

the inquisitors themselves, for, as she explained to Salazar: "when they asked her whether she had seen this or that she learned from these very questions what it was they wished her to say."[195]

Ana de Corres, a fifty-four-year-old widow from Maestu, told Salazar how she and her sister Inés had been detained at Logroño for almost a month before they were reconciled and allowed to go home. Before they left Logroño they went to confession at the Franciscan monastery. The confessor was a young monk whom they recognized from the hearings at the Tribunal; despite this the two sisters confessed that they had made false statements as they were in fact not witches at all. The monk tried to calm their consciences by telling them that even if they were not witches the reconciliation had been in order, since there were many witnesses against them. However, Inés was in such despair over having made a false confession that she fell ill and died soon after her return from Logroño. Therefore Ana de Corres recanted not only her own but her sister's confession as well.[196]

Salazar also had the Edict of Faith published at Vitoria. Originally this was to have taken place on 3 December, which was a Sunday, but the proclamation was postponed owing to a dispute with the cathedral chapter. On Saturday, after the ceremony was announced by the town crier, Salazar went to the church in order to see where he was to sit and to give orders for the erection of his canopy. At this the priests began to protest, saying that he, as an inquisitor, was not entitled to sit under a canopy; but Salazar defended his right to this mark of dignity and had it set up. Next time he entered the church he found that the priests had dismantled his canopy and placed it in the sacristy. Salazar thereupon postponed the publication of the Edict of Faith and reported the episode to *la Suprema*.[197]

On 13 December *la Suprema* made its reply and solemnly reprimanded Salazar. He was instructed to publish the Edict of Faith in another church where he was to sit without a canopy and without a high-backed chair and to use only a rug, a stool, and a cushion; and in addition he was to endeavor to ensure that the Inquisition should not be exposed to further criticism.[198] This episode reveals some of the limitations experienced by the Inquisition as soon as it ventured outside its sphere of influence.

If this clash with the priests had not occurred, Salazar would certainly have been able to reach home by mid-December. No other places required the Edict of Grace, and publication of the Edict of Faith normally took a week. But now Salazar was obliged to remain in Vitoria throughout Christmas while *la Suprema* corresponded with the Tribunal and the authorities in Vitoria (these latter had also reported the episode and had complained in addition that Salazar insisted on being addressed as Your Eminence although he should only have been called Your Grace).[199] Salazar probably used most of this delay to arrange the enormous accumulation of documents resulting from his journey and to work on his reports for the inquisitor general.

4. MARIQUITA FROM ATAURI

Shortly before Salazar reached Alava an old woman committed suicide. Her thirty-six-year-old daughter, María de Ulibarri, gave the news to Salazar when she was reconciled in Vitoria on 29 November,[200] and we know that it made a deep impression on him.[201]

María de Ulibarri was married to a peasant at Corres. She had made her confession, on 9 September, to the inquisitorial commissioner, *el bachiller* Martín Pérez de Carrasco, who was the priest at Santa Cruz de Campezo,[202] one of the places at which the Edict of Grace had been published (see chapter 11.B.2 and map 7). We shall never know why María held to her confession of witchcraft. But the fact is that she retracted her accusations against the mayor's wife at Corres and four other persons, for after Salazar had interrogated her she was no longer certain that she had seen them at the witches' sabbath.[203] On the other hand she retracted the names of a large number of persons her mother had accused of witchcraft when she was examined at Logroño in order to be reconciled. María could remember the names of up to thirty-three persons against whom her mother had regretted bearing false witness.[204] However, before María reached this point in the hearing she unburdened her soul to Salazar and related how her mother had committed suicide "twenty days ago."

The mother's name was María Pérez, but she was called Mariquita de Atauri and she lived on a farm at Atauri a few miles from Corres. She had returned heart-broken from the Tribunal at Logroño. María had tried to cheer her up and told her she should be glad that it was all over and done with. But her mother had answered very sorrowfully that there could be no salvation for her, her soul was damned because of all the innocent people she had denounced at Logroño, and all because two persons had subjected her to so much pressure that she had given in to them.

The mother had not named the two in question, but to judge from her description María believed that one of them must have been the Franciscan monk Fray Ladrón, for he had also tried to make her accuse some priests.

As the mother had continued to grieve, María had finally advised her to speak to a member of the Inquisition. So Mariquita went to Maestu and sought out the commissioner, Felipe Díaz, but he was furious and drove her away. He called her both a liar and a hussy because she now wished to recant what she had truly confessed to the Holy Office. And he shouted after her that if she began to cross names off the list by herself she could count on being burned.

Thus, the mother had returned unsuccessful in her attempt to unburden her conscience. María had advised her to try to speak to the priest at Corres, but she had come home instead. María visited her one Sunday at Atauri. And then shortly afterwards she received the news that her mother had drowned herself.

One Friday morning a few hours before sunrise the herdsman had gone out to see to the cattle. Mariquita had told him to leave the gate open so that the animals could go out later. The next morning they found her body in the river at a place where there was a small dam. The old woman was floating in the water. She was bare-headed and her face was upturned to the sky.[205]

5. THE COMMISSIONERS OF THE INQUISITION

An earlier chapter mentioned that it was customary for a traveling inquisitor to acquire information regarding the local employees of the Tribunal wherever he went (see chapter 6, above). Salazar did not neglect this side of his work on his journey of visitation, showing a particular interest in discovering how the commissioners reacted during the witch scare. Only a small proportion of them had been involved, but they were each given attention in Salazar's first report to the inquisitor general (summarized here):

The commissioner at Santesteban, Dean Miguel de Yrisarri, had been very reluctant and unwilling to receive revocations of witchcraft confessions after the new orders from *la Suprema* took effect. Apparently he had completely forgotten the anxiety he had expressed to Salazar when the latter had just arrived at Santesteban; therefore several *revocantes* from his area had preferred to go to the commissioners at Arano and Urdax and some had even undertaken the long journey to San Sebastián in order to seek out Salazar. Salazar had privately appointed the commissioner at Urdax to investigate the matter, but it was not possible to discover why Yrisarri was so unwilling to admit the witches' recantations.[206]

The commissioner at Urdax, Fray León de Aranibar, had collected more witch confessions than all the other commissioners together. Salazar found that he was "a mature and intelligent man" and had acted in a thoroughly correct manner in the witch cases that he had handled.[207]

Regarding the commissioner at Lesaca, Domingo de San Paul, Salazar had heard nothing apart from what had emerged in some of the witches' recantations [see p. 130 ff., above]. On the whole however, Salazar had the impression that the old man had treated these cases calmly and not allowed himself to become as emotionally involved as the rest of his town.[208]

The commissioner at Vera, the priest Lorenzo de Hualde, received an extremely bad testimonial: "The whole time — and even before the visitation — I had the suspicion that he showed far too much emotion in all his actions relating to the witch sect. In this way he has exceeded his authority time and again, either by wanting to imprison people according to his whim in order to send them to the Tribunal without delay, or by actually imprisoning them and keeping them confined without the Tribunal's authorization, all under the pretext that it was the townspeople who complained that they were witches and forced him to make the arrests." When Salazar arrived at Vera, Hualde confided to him that he felt his life was in danger because he had been dealing with the witch affair. In order to mediate between Hualde and his enemies Salazar resolved to hold a session at Vera, and as far as he was able to determine, he had succeeded in restoring peace. For Hualde had promised Salazar not to meddle in any future witch cases, but to leave them to a commissioner from elsewhere. To help Hualde keep his promise Salazar gave him several missions, once sending him as far away as Roncesvalles. Hualde did not keep his word however, but continued his activities at Vera as before. This convinced Salazar that it was personal desire for revenge and not Christian zeal that motivated the commissioner's witch persecution. The Lord of Urtubie and Alzate had presented Hualde with the living only a few years previously and these two had not forgotten how Vera had protested at being given Hualde as their priest, since he was both French and very young.[209]

The commissioners in the rest of northern Navarra were given good references. Both Juan de Monterola at Arano and Juan de Arangoa at

Arriba (in the Arraiz Valley) were mentioned as intelligent and dutiful persons.[210] (It is significant that these two priests were already concerned in the Tribunal's witch investigations from as far back as 1609, but that, as Salazar emphasizes, very few witches appeared in their respective districts.)

At Fuenterrabía the commissioner Miguel de Berrotarán, assisted by two "brothers" of the Inquisition (the *familiares* Pedro de Zuloaga and Martín de Berrotarán), had collected more witch confessions than in any other town. However, it did not appear to Salazar that they had been in any way biased or had overstepped their authority, even when out of "Christian zeal and in order to pacify the town" they had allowed the populace, helped by the municipal authorities in certain cases, to deal roughly with people who were suspected of being witches.[211]

Not until Salazar mentions the commissioners in the Borunda Valley and Alava do we again hear about witchcraft cases.[212] In fact the witch craze seems to have been limited to eastern Alava, for neither the commissioner at Salvatierra or the commissioner at Vitoria had to deal with any of these cases.[213] Again, summarizing Salazar:

In the Borunda Valley Salazar found that the accusations of witchcraft had proliferated so much that hardly anyone escaped them. Even the seventy-six-year-old inquisitorial commissioner at Bacáicoa, the priest Juan Martínez de Larraiza, had fallen under suspicion, as had the priest at Alsasua, Miguel de Arramendía, who accompanied Salazar for the entire journey of visitation (cf. p. 239 ff.).[214]

Salazar states of the commissioner of Larrea, Martín López de Lazárraga, that he had previously served as notary to Pedro Ruiz de Eguino and helped the latter with the publication of the Edict of Grace. However, both had allowed their feelings to affect the investigations, and both had gone so far as to claim that their own households and relatives had bewitched them. Thus, Salazar reports: "He told me that the witches NN and NN, his neighbors, had cast a spell on him." Furthermore, this commissioner went around openly accusing the persons concerned of being witches, and he threatened to take revenge on them by means of the investigations the Tribunal had ordered him to undertake (in which he was still engaged when Salazar reached his town). Salazar had therefore given him strict instructions to refrain from handling future witch cases.[215]

Three monks who had participated in the witch-hunt in Alava as special emissaries of the Tribunal were also given poor testimonials in Salazar's report. The Dominican Fray Francisco de Zarate and the Franciscan Fray Tomás de Galarza had both been far too eager to get the accused to witness against others, but their behavior was excusable as they had been motivated by Christian zeal and were without any personal desire for revenge. This excuse however could not be extended to the third monk, the Franciscan Fray Juan de Ladrón, for he, said Salazar, had taken a part in both imprisoning and ill-treating the suspected witches.[216]

6. *AQUELARRES*, OINTMENTS, AND OUTSIDE WITNESSES

Time after time, ever since the first witches from Zugarramurdi had been exposed, *la Suprema* had asked the Tribunal to produce material proofs of the existence of the witch sect. The Council had evolved one experiment after another, but the Tribunal had either cut short the investigations or ignored them completely. On Salazar's journey of visitation these investigations were at long last undertaken thoroughly and scientifically. A hundred and eight witches over the ages of twelve and fourteen and of adequate intelligence were examined regarding *"actos positivos"* according to *la Suprema's* list of fourteen questions (cf. pp. 57 ff., 233 f., and 243 f.).[217] However, in addition to this, three more comprehensive investigations were undertaken. The first concerned the witches' meeting places, and this Salazar completed during his stay in Navarra. The second, involving the witches' ointments and powders, and the third, concerning outside witnesses to the witches' exploits, were kept under way throughout the entire journey.

We mentioned earlier that detailed directions concerning verification of the witches' meeting places were given in the instructions of 26 March 1611 (SD Text 6 § 13). However, there is extant in Salazar's hand a copy of the questionnaire which was used on his visitation. It is a transcript of the instructions, but for the sake of clarity Salazar made certain changes in the text. The questionnaire is reproduced here in full as it is our most valuable source of knowledge regarding this experiment, which is unique in the history of witchcraft.

> The following experiment is to be undertaken with the witches from one and the same *aquelarre* and coven at the place where they hold their meetings or in the immediate neighborhood. The subjects for the experiment must be chosen from among the most intelligent.
>
> On different days and at different times the persons concerned are to be taken to the meeting place one by one. They are not to be told where they are going and care must be taken that no one sees them and that the other persons to be subjected to the experiment do not learn anything about the

experiment [beforehand]. Each person is to be questioned, by a competent commissioner and notary, on the following matters:

1. They are to indicate the exact place at which the witches gather and state the distance of this place from their homes.

2. They are to show the place where the Devil sits, where they make sacrifice to him, and where they eat, dance, and take part in the other activities.

[They are also to be questioned on the following details:]

3. Whether doors and windows are locked when they leave for the *aquelarre*; how they get out of the house; whether they are taken off by the Devil; whether they are carried through the air or how the Devil takes them to the sabbath; and how long it takes for them to get there.

4. Whether a number of witches make the journey to the *aquelarre* together and whether they are able to recognize each other there clearly, or if they travel to the *aquelarre* separately.

5. Whether they meet anyone on either the outward or homeward journey and whether they speak to them or avoid them.

6. How they re-enter their houses; and at what time they usually go to the sabbath, and when they return.

7. Whether there are clocks or bells [in the neighborhood of the meeting place], where these are, and whether they hear them.

8. And [they are to be questioned further] on any other circumstances which might serve to clarify the problem and provide us with sure proofs of these things.[218]

The experiment was carried out on a total of thirty-six subjects taken from nine different witch covens in the following towns: Santesteban, Iráizoz, Zubieta, Sumbilla, Donamaría, Arráyoz, Ciga, Vera, and Alzate[219] (all in northern Navarra, see map 3, above). In each place four witches from among those who had previously made their confessions were chosen.[220] When all four had been separately taken out to the witches' meeting place and the interrogation had been completed, their answers to the questions were compared. At Vera and Ciga the witches' answers were in agreement, but in all the other towns the subjects of the experiment contradicted each other. Some had also contradicted what they themselves had declared in their earlier confessions at the Tribunal, and some had stated roundly that they knew nothing at all of these things.[221] The witches at Zubieta declared that when they were at the *aquelarre* they could see neither the trees nor the houses near their meeting place; on the contrary it appeared to them that the mountains were flattened out and the place became a level plain.[222]

One of the subjects of the experiment at Zubieta was the forty-year-old farmer Juanes de Arroqui, who had been reconciled at Santesteban (see table 7, no. "24"). On 6 July he was fetched from his field, where he was reaping. He was immediately taken to the witches' meeting place, where the inquisitorial secretary, Peralta, was standing waiting for him. But when the secretary began to question him, Juanes de Arroqui replied: "Sir, I am not a witch, and it has been to no avail to bring me here. Even if they kill me, this is the honest truth. I confessed to being a witch because of the ill-treatment I was subjected to by the magistrates (*los jurados*) and the authorities." Peralta reported this answer the same day to Salazar during the visitation at Santesteban. A week later, when Salazar had reached Ezcurra, he had this farmer summoned, and here Juanes de Arroqui recanted the whole of his witch confession and related how he had been subjected to torture. Among other things they had tied a rope round him and dipped him into the river from a bridge.[223] Juanes de Arroqui was the first *revocante* on Salazar's visitation (see chapter 11.A.4, above).

Apart from Juanes de Arroqui's statement none of the original documents relating to this investigation are preserved. Our knowledge of the results relies entirely on the brief mention found in Salazar's report to the inquisitor general. We are therefore precluded from adopting a critical attitude with respect to the positive results of the experiment at Ciga and Vera and must restrict ourselves to noting that Salazar did not attach any great importance to them.

The investigation into the witches' ointments and powders produced a negative result as well. Salazar made great efforts to trace the unguents with which the witches anointed themselves in order to get to the *aquelarre,* and the powders they used to spread death and destruction. But the twenty-two jars of ointment and powder which came to light proved to contain nothing but fake materials. The witches admitted to having cooked up some of the substances themselves with various worthless ingredients in order to satisfy their persecutors. Some of the other jars were handed to doctors and apothecaries who made experiments with the contents and tried them out on a large number of animals to discover whether they were poisonous. But all the jars turned out to contain perfectly harmless substances. On one occasion the powders were in fact eaten in the presence of a great many people by a woman reputed to be a witch, but she too emerged from the experiment unscathed.[224] Most of the jars came to light during the first part of the visitation, and the letter of 4 September from Fuenterrabía shows clearly that even at this early stage Salazar was losing hope of ever finding authentic witch ointments: "Not a single one out of the sixteen jars I have discovered to date seems traceable to the witches' *aquelarre*," Salazar writes to the inquisitor general, and continues: "On the contrary I have acquired a grave suspicion that the jars which were shown to us in the Tribunal at Logroño were not authentic either."[225]

On the last part of his journey Salazar obtained clear proofs that the Inquisition had been tricked in the matter of the jars sent down to the Tribunal during the spring. In October he appointed Juan de Monterola, the commissioner at Arano, to investigate the origin of three witch-jars that had been discovered by the parish priest at Zubieta, *el licenciado* Yrigoyen. The commissioner questioned the witches who had presented the jars, and all admitted that the witch ointment was faked and that they had made it themselves to escape the persecution of the priest and the village authorities.

María de Mindeguia, a farmer's wife, and Juana de Hualde, a miller's wife, described how they had together made their unguent. The parish priest and a certain Franciscan monk had threatened that they would be burned in the marketplace next day if they did not produce their jars. They melted down some pork fat and added a little water; into this they stirred some soot from the chimney, and then put the mixture into a jar, which they gave to the priest.[226]

Mari Juan de Juanesgoncoa, a widow, told how she had taken some asphodels and wild plums (*gamones o prunes silvestres*), that they usually fed to the pigs. She first boiled them, then put them into a cloth and pressed out the liquid, and subsequently packed the substance into a jar, which she delivered to the priest.[227]

The forty-year-old widow Juana de Yrurita and her daughter Catalina both described how they had attempted to concoct a real witch unguent. They had boiled buttercups and mint "which had been blessed on Midsummer Day [St. John's Day]" in some holy water that had been kept from Easter Eve. To give the ointment green coloring they had added an extract from a plant known in Basque as *Zaradona*. Finally they drained off the liquid and put the pulp into a jar, which Catalina took to the priest. (This recipe has an almost authentic ring about it, but if we study the facts more closely it is obvious that mother and daughter chose magical ingredients for the sole purpose of giving the concoction a more genuine character. That same day Catalina had been interrogated by the priest Yrigoyen. By using the threat of sending her to Logroño, he had made the girl confess she was a witch. She had also told the priest that she and her mother had a small quantity of the unguent with which they anointed themselves. When Catalina went home and related what she had confessed, her mother scolded her, saying she had made a terrible mistake in confessing, since she was certainly not a witch. But as there could now be no going back, mother and daughter had set to work to concoct the witch ointment.)[228]

Shortly before Salazar returned to Logroño he received proofs that the Tribunal had also been duped over the ointments and powders that had been sent down by the commissioner at Maestu, Felipe Díaz. This was revealed during the hearing of two of the four women who retracted their witchcraft confession in Vitoria at the end of December (see chapter 11.C.3, above). One of them was Gracia González, the young farmer's wife who confessed at Logroño in order to be able to get home quickly to her husband. The other was Magdalena de Arza, who was single, but the mother of Gracia. These two now told Salazar how they had come to say, when they were at Logroño, that they possessed the unguent. It was true that they had also said that they had thrown their jars into a river before going to Logroño. But when they returned the commissioner began to press them and demanded that they should find the jars and deliver them to him. As a means of getting peace from their tormentor the mother and daughter finally decided to make the ointment. They made it from muck and kitchen waste and put it into two jars. Graciana put the jars under her apron and, taking care to be seen by no one, she went down to the river and placed them in the water among some stones. Afterwards they told the inquisitorial commissioner where they had hidden their witch ointment, and he went down there himself and retrieved the jars.[229]

Unfortunately, only the documents relating to the false unguents were preserved. The results of the other investigations are known to us only through Salazar's reports to the inquisitor general. Salazar came to the conclusion that the unguents were neither "harmful or poisonous." However, he did not say whether the witch ointments were also tested for what in his parlance would have been called "soporific" effects. It is therefore an open question as to whether any of the twenty-two jars might have contained toad vomit or other hallucinogenic substances. Here once again the sources let us down.

The third investigation — that relating to outside witnesses to the witches' activities — also produced a negative result. In his second report to the inquisitor general, Salazar examines no fewer than twenty-seven cases where attempts to verify concrete acts of witchcraft by means of evidence from persons who were not themselves witches had led to negative results.[230] I shall restrict myself here to scrutinizing three of these "negative *actos positivos*."

During the visitation at Santesteban a large number of children declared that they had been to the *aquelarre* on Midsummer Night. However, Salazar's two secretaries, the licentiates Huerta and Peralta, had been out to the witches' meeting place that night and testified that apart from themselves, not a single person had been there. Presumably Salazar had sent them out on watch to see whether the witches actually did forgather.[231]

At Vera several young girls confessed to having had intercourse with the Devil, but when they were examined by midwives they were all found to be virgins. Salazar had not authorized this investigation, but since it had been carried out he saw fit to include it in his report to the inquisitor general.[232]

At the town of Leiza on the border of Guipúzcoa Salazar ordered an inquiry into the deaths of two infants. The circumstances of their deaths and certain marks which had been found on the children's bodies had convinced the whole town that they had been murdered by the witches. However, the inquisitorial commissioner who investigated the matter found no grounds for such a suspicion.[233]

7. THE RESULTS OF THE JOURNEY

One month after his return home Salazar completed his reports to the inquisitor general. Salazar commenced the second report (SD Text 12) with a survey of the witch cases that had been dealt with on the journey of visitation:

> In a letter which I addressed to Your Highness from Fuenterrabía, on 4 September, I reported how, as a sequel to the Edict of Grace . . . 1,546 persons of all ranks and ages came forward to avail themselves of it . . . I now report that — during the period from 22 May 1611, when I set forth on the visitation, to 10 January this year, when I concluded it — a total of 1,802 cases has been dispatched . . . The figure can be broken down into the following groups: 1,384 children, of twelve or fourteen years of age and under, were absolved *ad cautelam*. Of those older than twelve or fourteen, 290 were reconciled; 41 absolved *ad cautelam* with abjuration *de levi*; 81 retracted the confessions which they had made to the Holy Office . . . ; and finally 6 confessed to having relapsed by returning to the *aquelarres*. Among the 290 whom I reconciled there were a hundred persons over twenty . . . many of them being sixty, seventy, eighty, or even ninety years old.[234]

If we compare this survey with that from Fuenterrabía (see chapter 11.A.6, above), we can clearly see a startling reduction in the number of witch cases during the last part of the journey (table 10). Out of a total number of 256 cases, we find that three-quarters were child witches (185 cases of girls under twelve and boys under fourteen), while the remaining 71 were divided into 19 *reconciliados*, 7 absolved *de levi*, 39 *revocantes*, and 6 *relapsos*. We know that 52 of the child witches came forward at San Sebastián (see chapter 11.B.6, above) and the remaining 133 can doubtless be assigned to Rentería and other towns in northern Guipúzcoa, where the dream epidemic had proliferated; on the other hand I have discovered no indications that children were involved in the Borunda Valley and Alava.

Salazar himself in his first report to the inquisitor general commented on the discrepancy between the numbers of cases on the first and second parts of the journey:

Table 10. Distribution of Cases Dispatched During the First and
Second Parts of Salazar's Visitation, 1611

Data from:	Reconci-liados	Absolved de levi	Revo-cantes	Relap-sos	Absolved children	Total
Fuenterrabía as of 4 Sept.	271	34	42	0	1,199	1,546
Second part of visitation	19	7	39	6	185	256
Entire journey	290	41	81	6	1,384	1,802

NOTE: Salazar is here reckoning *cases* and not *persons*. The 19 who recanted after having been reconciled (see chapter 11 n. 49, above) are counted among both the 290 *reconciliados* and the 81 *revocantes*. In the same manner the 6 who had relapsed seem to have been listed in two places. Thus only 1,777 persons were involved in the 1,802 witchcraft cases. When Salazar quotes the total results of the first part of the journey at 1,546 cases, it is presumably due to the fact that he is overlooking the 4 *relapsos* whose cases are mentioned in *Letter from Fuenterrabía* (see quotation in chapter 11.A.7, above). Thus on the last part of the journey there were in fact only 2 *relapsos*.

This disparity shows that in all the latter regions [Guipúz-coa, Vizcaya, and Alava] the trouble [from witchcraft] was not so severe as in the mountains of Navarra. I should like to call attention to the care with which I endeavored to dis-cover the evil by tarrying longer over the sessions of the last part of the visitation. This was especially true of the prov-ince of Alava and the Borunda Valley, which lie near to the city of Vitoria. Here we expected to discover great evil in view of all the information and evidence presented in the Tribunal. However, very few witches came forward; and from people who were not members of the sect we received only the few testimonies which have been set down in the [general] records of the visitation. From the latter and from the statements of those who revoked their confessions it can clearly be seen that this province is in fact not as infested with witchcraft as the Tribunal had concluded from the confessions of the first witches. . . . This can also be said about all the other places I visited after the mountains of Navarra, except for Fuenterrabía which is nearby, and for San Sebastián which, although unaffected by witchcraft [*sin fundamento*], had been thrown into panic by the news of what was happening in the vicinity.[235]

In many ways the journey of visitation with the Edict of Grace served as a witch-craze barometer. As soon as Salazar left northern Navarra and Guipúzcoa the manifestations ceased completely, but when he went down into the Borunda Valley and Alava they reappeared. It was in precisely these two areas that the propaganda of the Tribunal had touched off the charge, and where the witch persecutions had been set in motion. In the rest of the area normal conditions seem to have prevailed. No doubt witches of the traditional popular type existed there, but there was no fear of a witch conspiracy. Any witches who might have been found were here as in other parts of Europe held in check by counter-magic.

Salazar relates that in almost all the larger towns, but in particular at San Sebastián, Azpeitia, and Vitoria, there were more or less professional practitioners of magic who devoted themselves to the superstitious arts of sorcery and divination. These "white witches" were generally well-regarded, and the local authorities, both ecclesiastical and civil, left them alone, as this type of case, according to a Bull promulgated by Pope Sixtus V (Rome, 9 January 1585) fell within the jurisdiction of the Inquisition. Some of them called themselves *santiguadores* or *ensalmadores* (persons who healed by means of magic formulas), and among them were a number of priests, writes Salazar. One of their specialities was in fact to cure the effects of witchcraft. They claimed to have special powers in this sphere and were able to say who was to blame for a bewitching.[236] According to Salazar, the clientele of these "white witches" were predominantly country folk: "The villagers have come to believe in them and they supply as many remedies as requested in return for payments and benefits which they shamelessly extort," he wrote. Unfortunately it was not in Salazar's terms of reference to make a thoroughgoing investigation of the activities of the "wise folk." He had to be content with summoning some of them and cautioning them, but did not institute proceedings against them or keep any record. "It would quite simply have been impossible," says Salazar, "for there were so many of them."[237]

Besides the 1,802 cases in connection with the Edict of Grace there were 17 cases of bewitching which Salazar included in a special report concerning general cases from the visitation.[238] Unfortunately this report was lost, but a couple of the witchcraft cases are described in Salazar's second report to the inquisitor general and they provide us with an instructive glimpse of what may certainly be assumed to have been a facet of popular superstition. Thus the following incident, which was reported during the visitation at San Sebastián, reveals the existence of a legend common to both European and African witchcraft.

An old woman named Simona de Gabiria presented herself during the visitation and related that one night when she was lying in bed she had seen a misshapen dog in her bedchamber. She realized at once that it was a witch who had assumed this shape, and she rose to throw the dog out. At that moment a man appeared on the scene and managed to wound the dog with his dagger before it disappeared. Next day a woman who lived nearby complained of pain from a wound, and since she already had the reputation of being a witch her neighbors soon came to the conclusion that it was she who had been transformed into the dog. Simona de Gabiria stated the names of both the witch and the man with the dagger, but Salazar was unable to trace either, or find anyone else who could verify her story.[239]

Becerra and Valle had already suffered a decisive defeat by the epoch-making letter from *la Suprema* of 28 June 1611. Salazar's provisional report from Fuenterrabía, which had won him the approval of the inquisitor general, had further nourished the suspicions of the Council that the witch-hunt of the Logroño Tribunal was a mistake. With the extension of the Edict of Grace Becerra and Valle suffered a further severe defeat, and when Salazar went down into Alava and uncovered the methods used by the agents of the Tribunal during the summer campaign his colleagues were forced to acknowledge, whether they liked it or not, that they had lost the battle in the field. Apart from the village of Olagüe (see chapter 11.A.7 and n. 97) and the Roncal Valley in the depths of the Pyrenees,[240] peace now reigned in the area.

In his second report to the inquisitor general, Salazar summarized the results of the journey. His conclusion was in complete contrast to the interpretation of his colleagues. Salazar wrote:

> I have not found a single proof nor even the slightest indication from which to infer that one act of witchcraft has actually taken place ... Rather I have found what I had already begun to suspect in these cases before my experiences during the visitation; that the testimony of accomplices alone — even if they had not been submitted to violence and compulsion — without further support from external facts sub-

stantiated by persons who are not witches is insufficient to warrant even an arrest.[241]

But if Salazar thought that he had won the battle over the witches by submitting all the proofs he had acquired through his investigations, he was soon obliged to think again; the hardest struggle was yet to come, and it was to be fought out within the four walls of the Tribunal.

CHAPTER TWELVE
The Battle Over the Witches

ALAZAR ARRIVED HOME FROM HIS JOUR-
ney on Tuesday, 10 January 1612.[1] He had been
away from Logroño for almost eight months.
Instead of depositing the visitation papers in the
archive according to custom he had all his documents taken to
the "second courtroom" of the Tribunal; and instead of delivering the customary report on the journey to his colleagues he
shut himself up with the two secretaries, Peralta and Huerta,
and set to work on the reports for the inquisitor general.[2]
Salazar did not show the papers to anyone on the pretext that
he was afraid of disturbing "the order that they were in," since
the visitation book still consisted of loose sheets and had to be
bound first.[3] Though hardly a complete explanation this was at
least plausible, for more than 5,600 folios (or 11,200 pages of
manuscript) had accumulated during the eight months of the
visitation. Thus Salazar's visitation book was sixteen times as
large as Valle's.[4]

During the first weeks after his homecoming Salazar and
Valle were alone at the Tribunal. Becerra was still confined to
his bed with quartan fever, from which he had been suffering
ever since July when the Tribunal received the severe reprimand from *la Suprema* (see near the end of chapter 10.4,
above). However, Salazar's presence in Logroño seems to
have caused the fifty-year-old Becerra some anxiety, for on 17
January he wrote to a certain eminent member of *la Suprema*
requesting a transfer to an inquisitorial post at Valladolid

which was then vacant. The name of the eminent personage is nowhere stated but it was presumably Juan Ramírez, formerly an inquisitor at Logroño, who had now become the *fiscal* to *la Suprema* (see near beginning of chapter 3.3, above). Becerra gave as his reason for making this application the bad effect on his health of the bad climate at Logroño. However, it is hard to say how seriously Becerra intended this application for a transfer to be taken. For immediately after making it he went on to stipulate that it should only be granted on condition that "Your Highness does not consider that my presence may be of some use in solving the problem of the great number of people in this area who are infected by the witch sect." If necessary, continued Becerra, he was willing to remain at his post in Logroño and devote himself utterly to this matter. He ended the letter with the assurance that he was now recovering and said that the doctors had promised him that as soon as the weather grew milder he would get well.[5]

On 28 January Becerra was up and about and in the afternoon was feeling so well that he ventured to go to the Tribunal to call upon his colleagues. By the time he arrived it was four o'clock, but he found them all so busily engaged that he decided to return home again. Before he left, Valle approached him with a letter from *la Suprema*, which Becerra took home with him. It contained a severe reprimand to the Tribunal, saying that the inquisitorial secretaries were neglecting their work by constantly going out to question witnesses regarding *limpieza de sangre*.[6] (In this way the secretaries were supplying themselves with valuable perquisites, see chapter 3.2, above.)

On 3 February Becerra wrote personally to assure the Council of the Inquisition that the trouble over the secretaries was less serious than *la Suprema* believed. That the secretaries had been guilty of certain irregularities was not to be denied, but the person who had reported the affair had exaggerated its importance not a little.[7] At the end of his letter Becerra put the blame on the Devil for the adversity the Tribunal had been suffering during the past year:

> I am quite convinced that this affair [of the secretaries], as well as the entirely unprovoked interference from the judges of the High Court of Navarra, and many other problems, are one and all due to the work of the Devil. He it is who causes all these troubles to distract our attention and prevent us from dealing effectively with this accursed witch

sect, which indeed may well reduce this part of the country to chaos. Having to watch all this, and the understandable pain I have felt at seeing God's name blasphemed by acts of such abomination, has kept me bedridden for seven months. May God send a solution to it all, and may he also remedy the differences of opinion which have recently arisen in this Tribunal. Although for my part I have no intention of avoiding my responsibilities I must admit that this latest trouble has greatly motivated my desire for another post with more peaceful conditions of work.[8]

Becerra's illness continued and he does not seem to have resumed his work before the end of February or possibly the beginning of March. The last words of his letter therefore probably refer to the conflict between Valle and Salazar, for the latter had already resumed his daily work in the service of the Tribunal at some date around 24 January.[9]

On 8 February Salazar presented a report on the general visitation cases resulting from the journey.[10] The report covered a total of 110 persons, 17 of whom were suspected of witchcraft. After Valle and Becerra had examined the report the three inquisitors voted on how each of the suspects should be dealt with. The report, as I have mentioned (see near end of chapter 11.C.7, above) was not preserved, but as far as the 17 cases of witchcraft were concerned it appears from other sources that Salazar considered the evidence to be so insubstantial that he felt there was no cause to institute proceedings against any of the accused.[11]

A few days later Salazar produced a further "eight or nine reports" at the Tribunal[12] and at the same time requested his colleagues to inspect the original visitation documents which had been bound in the meantime and which comprised eight volumes (Volumes "A"-"H").[13] These nine reports all dealt with the witches; they will be discussed in a separate section below.

On 17 March Becerra again wrote to *la Suprema* regarding the inquisitorial secretaries. The letter is addressed to Miguel García Molina, secretary to the Council of the Inquisition, and its closing lines clearly reflect the turmoil that Salazar's reports had caused at the Tribunal:

> I cannot understand what has caused so much trouble to arise in this Inquisition, where previously there had always been understanding between us. But I assume that the Devil

is plotting to prevent us from carrying out our sacred duty and taking firm action to combat all the evil that is rife. Your Grace will soon receive an opinion on the matter in the form of some more lengthy considerations. May God provide a remedy to it and open the eyes of all concerned so that they may realize how serious the situation really is [*para que claramente se vean y conoscan tan grandes engaños*].[14]

Becerra and Valle had been informed beforehand that Salazar had been drawing his own conclusions in the eight months that he had been away; but even so they had probably not expected him to come back as obviously skeptical as his reports indicated. They came to the immediate conclusion that their colleague had used the entire journey of visitation to accumulate material that would justify his opposing vote on the sentences passed on the witches who were burned at the auto de fe.[15]

It was Salazar's intention that the Tribunal should vote on the next steps to be taken in the witch affair on the basis of the reports (which together constituted his opinion); but Becerra and Valle were quite unable to agree to this. They objected that the reports did not accord with the usual practice of the Inquisition, for Salazar had neglected to "compose the most important report of all, which would give an account of how many witches had been recorded [of those who had made confessions in connection with the Edict of Grace], the nature of the crime for which each was under suspicion, and how many witnesses had testified against them on the journey of visitation as well as in the registers of this Holy Office." Therefore his colleagues requested that Salazar begin work on this report while they themselves prepared their opinion. But Salazar refused. He had already made an attempt and found the task both impossible and valueless.[16]

Salazar's colleagues then tried to persuade him not to send off his reports until they had completed their own considerations, so that they could all be dispatched at the same time. However, Salazar would not agree to this; he was willing to put his rough drafts at his colleagues' disposal, but he wished to send off the fair copies immediately. In the end Becerra and Valle suggested that the question should be submitted to *la Suprema* for decision, but Salazar was so insistent on getting his reports sent off that they conceded the point.[17]

On 24 March the three inquisitors jointly dispatched the

report covering the 110 general visitation cases, with their votes.[18] Salazar sent his nine reports on the witches,[19] and his colleagues wrote a long letter in which they requested permission to defer their considerations. Becerra and Valle excused their delay by stating that Salazar had been working on his reports throughout his journey of visitation and had accumulated such a quantity of material that they required further time in which to examine the papers before they could be in a position to make any rejoinders to his arguments. The letter reflects the first reaction of Salazar's colleagues to his reports and shows clearly that they had not allowed themselves to be budged one iota from their previous stand:

> After having read them [i.e. the reports], we are astonished to the highest degree that he should have produced such unheard-of arguments to defend the isolated vote that he cast against the other eight of us when we were voting upon the sentences of the witches who were presented at the auto de fe. For all of it conflicts with the vast amount of evidence and confessions which we have at this Tribunal. And when he maintains that it can all be reduced to dreams and illusions suggested to the witches by the Devil, it is completely incomprehensible to us. . . . We are convinced that we can refute his interpretation — and that held by the bishop of Sigüenza, previously bishop of Pamplona, with whom our colleague is on particularly intimate terms — merely by what is contained in his own papers. In the long run the attempts of all who seek to spread doubt over the existence of the sect . . . and who try to prevent us taking steps against the witches with all the resources of the law, will meet with failure. However, strong measures are necessary if we are to have any hope of stopping this fearful scourge, which is making its way into every part of our district.[20]

On 31 March Salazar's reports reached Madrid, but once there they remained unread for the time being. The reason for this was that Becerra and Valle had requested in their letter that the Council refrain from reading the reports until it had received their considerations — a wish respected by *la Suprema*.[21] However, the colleagues' vote was a long time in coming, and Salazar had to wait around in Logroño for a year and a half for a reply to his reports. From his time as a secretary of the previous inquisitor general, Valle was familiar with the machinery of the Council. The two colleagues, therefore, wittingly allowed Salazar to send in his reports, since they were aware that they still had the possibility of stopping Salazar and forcing him to await their opinion.

In many respects the waiting time in Logroño became a test, not only for Salazar, but for his two colleagues as well. The disagreement spread quickly from the witch question to almost all the other fields of the Tribunal's activity. Becerra and Valle were so embittered over Salazar's reports and visitation papers that they repeatedly told him that the whole lot deserved to be burned.[22] For his part, Salazar returned from the visitation with more self-confidence than he had when he set out, and there was now hardly a case at the Tribunal in which his opinion did not differ from that of his colleagues.[23] The *fiscal*, San Vicente, who was transferred at his own request in September 1612,[24] wrote a desperate letter to *la Suprema* on 13 July. He related that the inquisitors had declared open war on each other and this was affecting the work of the Tribunal so seriously that he personally would consider it a lesser evil if they were all living in sin or taking bribes.[25] When the three inquisitors were sitting in the courtroom at the Tribunal voting on current cases they often fell to disputing loudly; and on several occasions San Vicente, who worked in the adjoining archive, was obliged to enter the courtroom and reprimand the inquisitors, remarking that their voices could be heard out in the street.[26]

This information originates from an examination of San Vicente made in 1620 in connection with *la Suprema*'s inspection of the Logroño Tribunal. San Vicente was now an inquisitor at Zaragoza, but he had warm memories of Salazar. According to the one-time *fiscal* at Logroño, Salazar was invariably courteous and mild in manner towards his colleagues even when this required much self-control. However, there were times when Becerra and Valle provoked him excessively, and then Salazar too lost patience and became really angry. He also recalled Salazar as a man who never neglected his duties or his work. And when the Tribunal was closed, continues San Vicente's statement,

> he would spend his time in his library among his books. Even when going for a country walk it was his custom to take a book with him and walk alone without any desire for company. And when the witness [i.e. San Vicente] once asked him why he [always] walked alone, Salazar had replied that he found refreshment in reading.[27]

In San Vicente's view the inquisitorial secretaries Juan de Agüero and Juan de Zorilla were responsible for a great deal of the dissension at the Tribunal. They were both faithful followers of Valle and they neglected no opportunity of sowing discord between him and Salazar.[28]

According to Gregorio de Leguizamo, who succeeded San Vicente as *fiscal* in Logroño, on a certain occasion Juan de Agüero exclaimed that the Devil had sent Salazar to Logroño.[29] Perhaps this was the thought that lay behind Becerra's repeated complaints to *la Suprema* that the Devil had forced his way into the Tribunal.

2. SALAZAR'S PAPERS (EXCURSUS)

Salazar's first report (SD Text 11) bears the title "A General Account of the Results of the Visitation and the Edict of Grace. First Report."[30] It consists of twenty-three manuscript pages and is dated Logroño, 24 March 1612. The report is divided into fifty-five clauses, but only the first eight deal directly with the witches; clauses 9-15 give an account of other types of heresy; 16-44 form a report on the agents of the Inquisition; and 45-55 are concerned with the *sambenitos* in the churches. We have already made reference to a substantial part of the contents of this report (see chapters 6, 11.C.5, and 11.C.7, above), which relate to our topic. I shall therefore restrict myself to a few items which have not previously been mentioned. In clauses 5 and 6 Salazar described the progress of two projects which, according to the instructions of 26 March, he was to carry out during the journey of visitation.

The first project was to exhort the people to build chapels and erect crosses in the places where the witches held their gatherings; but the request was to be made courteously and without any form of coercion.[31] Salazar was now able to report that the mountain people had taken up the idea with great enthusiasm: "particularly in Santesteban, where a very beautiful chapel was completed by Michaelmas (29 September)" and consecrated at a great festival. In the village of Errazu in the Baztán Valley the people had begun building a similar chapel which was already well advanced when Salazar left their district, and he hoped that other villages as well had complied with the request.[32]

The second project prescribed the founding of new monasteries in the witch-infested areas.[33] Salazar stated in his report that he had not found this to be feasible. Even the monastery at Urdax had difficulty in maintaining itself although it was well-endowed. However, he had reached the opinion that the founding of further monasteries was not essential: "for although the people are rough and uncultivated they are kindly, intelligent, and devout, and above all well-disposed towards the Church, faithful in attendance, and respectful to the clergy." Salazar therefore felt that occasional missions sent out from the monasteries of Pamplona should suffice; but care should be taken to ensure that the monks did in fact carry them out, since experience had shown that they were often discouraged by the rough terrain and the poverty of the area.[34]

Salazar's second report (SD Text 12) bears the title "An Account of the whole Visitation and Publication of the Edict relating to the Witch Sect. Second Report."[35] It is dated Logroño, 24 March 1612, and consists of forty-five manuscript pages, including the notes or glosses. This is by far the most important of all the Salazar reports, and even though we have already given an account of much of the contents (see above, chapters 11.A.5, 11.C.6, and 11.C.7), there is still far more detail remaining than can be summarized here. For the report in itself is a highly condensed analysis of the witchcraft confessions from the eight-volume visitation book, which is constantly referred to. I shall therefore limit myself to an analysis of the composition and the technique of presentation employed by Salazar.

The report is made up of seventy-seven clauses arranged in four chapters, each of which forms a main item of discussion. Attached are a large number of notes (or "glosses" as they are called) which amplify and document the report. Salazar himself provided the following headings:

[Introduction].

I. Of the manner in which the witches set out to, are present at, and return from their *aquelarres* [clauses 1-9].

II. Of the activities they undertake and experience as witches [clauses 10-24].

III. Of the *actos positivos* or external proofs, which we have endeavored to substantiate [clauses 25-51].

IV. Of the evidence which might result from the above and serve to convict the guilty [clauses 52-77].

[V.] Witches: The glosses of the preceding report [glosses 1-90].[36]

In the first nine clauses which made up chapter 1 of the report, Salazar analyzed the results of the interrogation regarding the nightly gatherings of the witches. The great majority, runs the report, answered that they always set out for the *aquelarre* after they had gone to bed and fallen asleep. In gloss 1 Salazar refers to no less than 102 witches who stated this in their confessions. It was true, the report continues, that there were others who maintained they were taken to the *aquelarre* while awake and before they had gone to bed, but there were very few of these; in gloss 2 Salazar refers to seven files:

> [Gloss] 2. The persons who say that they always, or at least on some occasions, went and came back awake are the following: E 303, C 393, B 335, E 361, E 473, C 477, D 522. [For the identities of these witches, see respectively case numbers 326, 225, 171, 332, 342, 231, and 284 of our Witch List, part 3, being simultaneously a reconstruction of volumes A through H of Salazar's visitation book.][37]

Referring constantly to original records, Salazar went on to relate that almost all the witches declared that they flew to the sabbath, although there were also a few who maintained that they went on foot or were carried on the shoulders of their tutor witches. The greater majority maintained that they left their houses through chinks and holes in the wall, or through the windows or the chimney; but there were also a few who declared that they left by the doors and went down the stairs of their houses. They also maintained firmly that they met no one en route, never heard any sounds of people, animals, or church bells, nor did they get wet even if it was snowing or raining; gloss 8 refers to 108 files. However, twenty witches maintained the opposite and asserted that they had met with people, heard noises, and had gotten soaked; gloss 10 refers to twenty files, and an additional eight files from people who answered that this had happened to them at least occasionally.[38]

Salazar then proceeded to give his opinion on this evidence. Firstly, he found it extraordinary that when, as reported, so many witches were abroad, they had never been seen by anyone. Secondly, it was remarkable that certain witches who claimed to have been to the sabbath in broad daylight did not ever seem to have been missed by those with whom they were eating, speaking, or in company. Thirdly, it was also remarkable that a large group of more than fifty witches declared that they were quite unable to give any explanation whatsoever of how they were taken to the sabbath. "It is therefore not surprising," remarked Salazar, "that we are unable to discover anything when even the witches themselves fail to understand what goes on."[39] After giving some examples he concluded the first chapter thus:

> Let us suppose that one was willing to give credence to all this, and to believe that the Devil is able to make persons present when they are not, and make others invisible when they pass before people who would certainly recognize them, with the result that nobody can be sure that he or she who is present is any more real than he or she who is with the witches; then surely, one could conceive another explanation far more readily: The Devil only deludes those "invisible" ones, or those who think that they have been absent, without this ever happening, in order that the deceived person should speak in good faith and find acceptance for these and similar lies, and consequently also be believed when he says that he has seen other people at his *aquelarre* whom he subsequently denounces. Thus immediately and without any effort the Devil leaves the village in an uproar [and] those unjustly incriminated exposed to condemnation.[40]

With these words Salazar put the basic problem of the Basque witch craze in a nutshell. In the remainder of the report he merely elaborated different facets of this compact formulation.

In the second chapter Salazar, not without humor, discussed the extraordinary things that were experienced by the witches, and which they had related to him. A lengthy series of points which were discussed in our section on the witches' lies (see chapter 11.A.5, above) are derived from this chapter and serve as examples of its contents.[41]

The third chapter dealt with external proofs. Salazar examined twenty-seven *actos positivos* which he had subjected to close investigation and which all produced negative results.[42] We have already referred to three examples from this list (see chapter 11.C.6, near end). I shall therefore limit myself to mentioning that as the twenty-fifth *acto positivo*, Salazar analyzed the experiment with the witches' meeting-places, and as the twenty-sixth he summarized the investigations into the witches' ointments and powders. It will be recalled that both investigations had produced negative results (see chapter 11.C.6, above).[43]

In the fourth and final chapter Salazar reasoned, with dazzling virtuosity, that no legal validity whatsoever should be ascribed to the witches' evidence against third parties. Apart from the fact that the existence of the witch sect had not been proven, said Salazar, it was not enough for the witches to declare they had seen a certain person at their sabbath; for that person may have been present without committing any criminal offense. However, against this must be weighed all the factors which were demonstrably valid and which must be taken into consideration when judging the witches' evidence. Time after time the *confitente* witches had denounced their neighbors as accomplices out of personal enmity. Others had gone so far as to accept bribes for stating the names of innocent persons in their confessions. Salazar went on to say that the relatively small number of *revocantes*, eighty-one in all, who came forward during the journey of visitation must be considered in the light of the strict prohibition of revocation which was still in effect at the commencement of the visitation. Thus, it was Salazar's opinion that at least three-quarters of the witches had made false confessions and that therefore a large number of revocations was to be expected in the future.[44]

After stating the radical conclusion that he had found no proofs of the existence of a witch sect (see quotation at end of chapter 11.C.7, above), Salazar ended by assuring the inquisitor general that a further prolongation of the Edict of Grace was unnecessary. And here Salazar drew attention to the fact that the witches in France had disappeared of their own accord after the bishop of Bayonne (the learned Bertrand d'Echaux) had prohibited further reference to them in speech or writing.[45]

The lost reports. In contrast to the first and the second, the other reports of Salazar seem to have been mere collections of material consisting of extracts from the records in the eight-volume visitation book. In the introduction to the second report Salazar himself makes explicit reference to the existence of these materials. For, after having recorded the various groups of children and adults who have benefited from the Edict of Grace (see table 10, above), he says that summaries of the cases in each of the groups are made in separate surveys.[46] The information about the lost reports is scanty[47] but sufficient to enable us to attempt to compile a list:

a. Survey of the cases against the 1,384 children who were absolved *ad cautelam*.

b. Survey of the cases against the 290 adults (i.e. women over twelve, men over fourteen), who were reconciled.

c. Survey of the cases against the 41 adults who were absolved *ad cautelam* with renouncement of heresy *de levi*.

d. Survey of the cases against the 81 adults and children who revoked their confessions.

e. Survey of the cases against the 6 adults and children who relapsed.

f. Survey of the hearings in connection with the experiment with the witches' meeting-places.

g. Survey of the investigations which were made into the witches' ointments and powders.

Salazar's Visitation Book contained the 5,600 folios of original records bound into eight volumes designated "A"-"H." We have already mentioned that the greater part of this extremely valuable source material was lost. This happened at the beginning of the nineteenth century during the Napoleonic wars, when the archive of the Tribunal at Logroño was destroyed.[48] However, one of the volumes was lodged in the archive of *la Suprema* and thereby did not suffer the same fate as the other seven. This is the previously-mentioned volume "F" with the files of the eighty *revocantes*. For each of these eighty persons (of both sexes and all ages from nine to ninety-five) we have the original confession of witchcraft, as made to an official of the Inquisition, and also the recantation made later, with an account of the motives and circumstances which led to the false admission. In nineteen instances the "witch" had actually been reconciled before he or she recanted the confession. The original foliation of the volume runs from 1 to 627. Some of the witchcraft confessions originate from Valle's journey of visitation in 1609.[49]

A single fragment is extant from volume "E," which formed the final volume of reconciled persons. This is the file of María de Ulibarri (see chapter 11.C.3, above). The serial number 289 indicates that she was the penultimate of the total number of 290 witches who were reconciled during Salazar's journey of visitation. The original foliation from 671 to 684 shows that the leaves must have been torn out of a volume of size similar to that of volume "F."[50]

Salazar's second report refers to the visitation book over four hundred times. Forty-five of his references are to volume "F" and the isolated file from volume "E," and we are thus able to verify these.[51] But moreover these two sections of Salazar's visitation book are so abounding in fascinating source-material that what I have described of it in this study has far from exhausted it.

In the introduction to his second report Salazar points out that he employs a special method of reference. Instead of making reference to the specific page in the visitation book where the item is to be found he invariably refers to the first page of the file of the person concerned. For, as Salazar explains, the records are so brief that it is possible to leaf through them rapidly, and furthermore there is always a note in the margin opposite the point in the record which is cited.[52] If, for instance, we look at note 12, which gives examples of witches who set off for the sabbath from one and the same bed without noticing each other, we find the following reference: "E 671,"[53] meaning volume "E" of the visitation book, folio 671. This is the first page of María de Ulibarri's record, and if we leaf through it we find that on the verso of folio 681, the record deals with the forementioned item — this being announced by a marginal note in Salazar's own hand: "Mother and daughter, witches, neither met nor saw one another."[54] (As a further example see the extract with marginal notes, chapter 11.A.4, above.)

Thanks to Salazar's note system, where the first page of a file always stands for the whole file, it has been possible to reconstruct the contents of the lost parts of his eight-volume visitation book and find out with reasonable accuracy how many files and what sort of materials each volume was made up of. The following is only a short outline of my findings (the reconstruction is reproduced entirely as section C of the Witch List, below).

We can see that *Volume "A"* was compiled as a general visitation book. It contained all the cases of heresy which emerged in connection with the Edict of Grace, plus the evidence of outside witnesses of witchcraft[55] and, finally, some documents in connection with the various investigations which were made during this journey. Thus folios 453-475

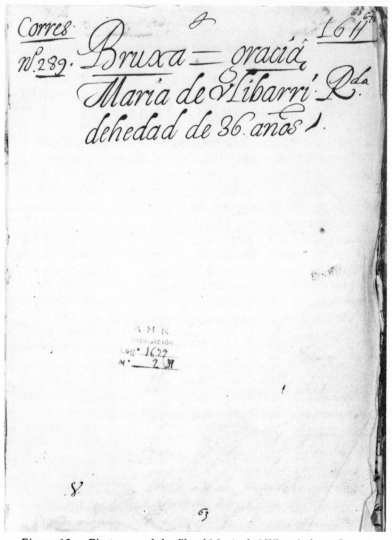

Figure 19.   First page of the file of María de Ulibarri, from Corres.
"671" indicates that the file began at folio 671 and was torn from
Volume "E" of Salazar's visitation book (no longer extant); "n° 289"
means that she was the 289th witch (Bruxa) reconciled (R[econ-
cilia]da) by the Edict of Grace (Gracia). The significance of the figure
"63" at the bottom of the page is unclear, although it may mean that
the present file was no. 63 among those contained in Volume "E" (cf.
case nos. 291-355 in the Witch List, below).

contained all the records made during the experiment concerning the witches' meeting-places. When we consider that
the experiment included thirty-six persons and that the notes
occupied fewer than fifty manuscript pages, we realize that the
hearings must have been extremely summary.[56] Immediately
before this, on folio 410 ff., were to be found all the investigations and experiments which were made with the witches'
ointments and powders.[57]

Volumes "B"-"E" contained the trial records of the 290 persons who were reconciled on the journey of visitation.[58] Actually these four volumes can only have comprised 271 records,
for as previously mentioned (see above, chapter 11 n. 49)
nineteen of the reconciled witches later retracted their confessions and their files were removed from the series of the
reconciled and placed in volume "F."[59]

The extant *Volume "F"* contains, as we have said, eighty
records. The fact that the eighty-first *revocante* is not among
them may be because Salazar did not receive her recantation
until after the other records had been bound.[60]

Volume "G" contained the records of the forty-one persons
who renounced their witchcraft *de levi.*[61]

Volume "H" contained the records of the 1,384 children. The
volume does not seem to have been over five hundred folios in
length, so on the whole the children's trials must have been
extremely summary.[62]

The six *relapsos* did not form a separate section in the original
visitation papers. It can be seen that their trial records were
bound in with the consecutively numbered *reconciliados.*[63]

If we examine the distribution of the references in Salazar's
second report it is obvious that he almost entirely ignored the
1,384 child witches and confined himself to the confessions of
the "adults." There are in all only sixteen references to volume
"H"; the rest refer to the "adult" witches (women over twelve
and men over fourteen) in volumes "B"-"G" of the visitation
book, together with a number of outside witnesses in volume
"A."[64] This is consistent with what Salazar himself states in a
report submitted in 1614 (SD Text 16), where he says that apart
from a few minor details he left the records of the 1,384 children entirely out of account; and he emphasizes that the
analysis of the witches' confessions was only made in regard to
"the 420 adult" persons.[65] Salazar arrives at the figure of 420 by
subtracting 1,384 from 1,802 — which strictly speaking equals

418 — but here our inquisitor overlooks the fact that he is counting *cases* in place of *persons*. The number of adult persons does not seem to have exceeded 393.

3. THE LONG WAIT

After having waited for two months Salazar wrote to the inquisitor general on 20 May 1612 requesting that the Council at least read his first and second reports, which he had deliberately forwarded under separate cover. He explained that the reason for his request was the fact that the Tribunal could not proceed with the hearings of a number of general visitation cases (see pp. 303 and 309, above), since the inquisitors had agreed to consult *la Suprema* before taking steps against the persons concerned. The letter was received in Madrid on 29 May and a note was appended to it ordering that the two reports be produced for inspection.[66]

It is open to question, however, if even then they were read, for on 28 May Becerra and Valle wrote another letter in which they earnestly repeated their request that the Council refrain from the reading until it had received their verdict. They were now in the process of perusing Salazar's papers and, as the letter states, "preparing a report on the real facts of the case which are apparent from his own visitation papers and which prove the indisputable reality of the witch sect." The two inquisitors maintained that they were in a position to prove this truth beyond a doubt; the visitation papers entirely confirmed the experiences from the auto de fe and from the witches who had been reconciled at the Tribunal; and when the inquisitor general had read their report he would undoubtedly be convinced of the gravity of the situation in this region and resolve to combat the witch plague with effective measures.[67] Becerra and Valle ended with a request for continued postponement

> partly owing to the fact that the accumulation of papers [*la maquina de papeles*] of our colleague is so vast, partly because he has amassed so many things in his reports. . . . We are thus not in a position to forward our opinion on this matter to Your Eminence as speedily as we would have wished. We must have more time than we first believed necessary. Not least with regard to the immense body of undisputed facts which are being recorded and which are gradually being confirmed as proof.[68] We are therefore obliged to entreat

Your Eminence to agree to our continuing our investigation as carefully and thoroughly as is demanded in so important a case. . . . We promise to complete [our work] as rapidly as possible, despite the fact that the current business of the Tribunal prevents us from dealing with this matter for most of our working hours.[69]

Later in the summer Salazar had another opportunity to draw the attention of *la Suprema* to his journey of visitation. It occurred on 22 September, when the Tribunal was recommending an application from the inquisitorial secretary Luis de Huerta y Rojas, who had accompanied him on the journey. Salazar inserted half a page into the letter on which he listed the numbers of witchcraft cases in connection with the Edict of Grace, mentioned the eight-volume visitation book "of over five thousand folios," and concluded with a strong recommendation in favor of Huerta, which cited his untiring work at all hours of the day and night in dealing with the total number of 1,802 witches.[70]

On 2 October *la Suprema* wrote a very sharp letter to the Tribunal at Logroño. It began amicably enough by stating that the inquisitor general had decided to release the inquisitors from a fine of two hundred *reales* each, which had been imposed on them for having permitted the secretaries to spend so much time away from the Tribunal (see near beginning of chapter 12.1, above). But then the blow fell. Salazar received the worst of it. He was reprimanded very sharply for refusing to sign a letter from the Tribunal to *la Suprema* because he claimed the letter had been altered during the fair-copying. A discussion of the matter with the inquisitor general had resulted in the opinion that Salazar had willfully wished to demonstrate his unreasonable reluctance to agree. He was therefore charged to exercise self-control and conquer his personal feelings in order not to damage the routine at the Tribunal. If his conduct failed to show considerable improvement, the letter went on, it would be necessary to take steps without further warning, and this would be chiefly to Salazar's detriment. *La Suprema* then proceeded to call all three inquisitors to order over complaints that had been made of their not having attended to applications for posts in the Inquisition. They were also reprimanded for not answering letters from *la Suprema*. It concluded by saying that if these delays continued, the Council would have no alternative but to send up persons who could dispatch the cases (i.e. exchange the inquisitors).[71]

On 13 October *la Suprema* returned the report relating to the general visitation cases (see beginning of this section) at the same time also returning the report on Valle's journey of visitation of 1609 (see p. 141, above).[72] Unfortunately these two reports are not extant, but in the margins of both *la Suprema* had noted what should be done with each one of the suspects. However, the brief covering letter from *la Suprema* dated 13 October does not mention whether the Council had found it necessary to read Salazar's first and second reports to assist them when it decided on the general visitation cases.

In December *la Suprema* sent another letter sharply reprimanding the inquisitors at Logroño. But this time Becerra and Valle were the chief targets of their wrath. Most of the complaints were directed at conditions reported by Salazar in his letter of 2 March the previous year[73] (see chapter 10.4, above). These reprimands from *la Suprema* furnish us with instructive examples of the discipline imposed within the Inquisition itself. The inquisitors may have had a free rein, but this did not exclude the intervention of *la Suprema* when a Tribunal went astray.

For almost a year Salazar had no further opportunity to jog the memory of the Council about the reports. But he did so when on 5 March 1613, the Tribunal formulated its judgment on two petitions from Juanes de Sansín and Juanes de Goiburu. These two witches had been in the House of Penance ever since the auto de fe in 1610. They both petitioned for release and for exemption from wearing *sambenitos*. Sansín pleaded that he was ill and had been afflicted with quartan fever the whole time he had been in the House of Penance. Goiburu stated that he had an elderly mother at Zugarramurdi who was unable to fend for herself, and that he had five motherless children of whom the eldest was only nine years old. He also stated that the monks at the Dominican monastery where he worked could vouch for his good Christian behavior during the past few years, for he had not only attended Mass and been to confession at the prescribed time, but also on many other occasions, solely out of piety.[74]

The inquisitors were agreed in their verdict to the extent that in view of the Edict of Grace the two prisoners could be released and exempted from wearing *sambenitos*. But there the agreement stopped. Salazar was of the opinion that they should be freely permitted to go home to Zugarramurdi.[75] For any objection to such permission was invalid on the basis of the investigations carried out, the reports of which now reposed in the archive of the Tribunal, and which had also been referred to *la Suprema*. Besides, only in the last few days the Tribunal had received another proof of the validity of the results reached by Salazar on his journey of visitation, through examining Catalina de Echevarría, who had been sent for from Fuenterrabía at the request of *la Suprema*. Becerra and Valle, however, would not permit the two men to return to their home district "or to any other place where we have information that witch conspiracies exist [*que hay aquelarres de brujos*]." Their arguments may be summarized as follows:

1. Many persons at Zugarramurdi against whom there were large numbers of witnesses had neglected completely to avail themselves of the Edict of Grace.

2. The *confitente* witches at Zugarramurdi and other places were being encouraged to retract their confessions. Among the women who had been released and permitted to return to Zugarramurdi, María de Echegui — against whom no fewer than twenty-four witnesses testified — had retracted her confession, and "the four others" (among them María de Jureteguía and María Chipía de Barrenechea, see chapter 4.2, above) had been strongly encouraged to do likewise.

3. It was the practice of the Devil to persuade the *confitente* witches to revoke their confessions and return to his sect. "Similarly," the two inquisitors continued, "he makes us fall back time and again into the same sins from which we have been cleansed by the sacrament of confession. And when we who are protected by the immovable steadfastness of the Holy Catholic Faith and strengthened through frequent use of the sacraments nevertheless succumb to the temptations of the Devil and fall prey to his wiles, there must be every reason to fear that these poor wretches [Sansín and Goiburu] will give in to the blandishments to which they will be subjected constantly by the Devil and the witches in their region."

4. "These two young men," it is further stated, "have neither land, parents nor wives in their home district. It will therefore be much easier for them to earn a living in this prosperous area [around Logroño] or some other place, for wherever they choose to go they will never find any place quite as poor as their own district." [It was true that more than a year had passed between the presenting of Goiburu's petition and the determination of the case, but unless Goiburu's old mother and five children had died in the meantime the last argument was not true.]

Becerra and Valle concluded their opinion by referring to their report on the witch sect and Salazar's journey of visita-

tion. From it and from the opinion they had delivered in the
case against Catalina de Echevarría the inquisitor general
would soon "learn the indisputable truth concerning this matter and realize that strong measures were essential" if this
fearful scourge was to be combated. The two inquisitors regretted that their report was still unfinished. This, they
explained, was partly because they had both been dogged by
ill-health and partly because they had been occupied in bringing all the business of the Tribunal up to date in accordance
with the inquisitor general's orders (see immediately above).
Finally, they had also been obliged to deal with the Tribunal's
current cases of heresy. Becerra and Valle ended their letter
with a petition for permission to withdraw from normal service
as soon as they had dispatched all delayed business except for
three or four cases. Salazar was capable of handling the current
business of the Tribunal during the time they needed to write
their report.[76]

Together with their opinion, the inquisitors also dispatched,
on 5 March, a report that they had just received from the
commissioner at Oyarzun in Guipúzcoa. It concerned a
sixteen-year-old *saludador* or witch finder, Pedro de los Reyes,
and another person, Juanes de Goizueta, who had confessed
to being a witch. The boy had been going about the Oyarzun
Valley maintaining that he had special powers to recognize
witches, and also that he had been authorized by the Holy
Office to carry out his activities. The second suspect had made
a confession of witchcraft to the authorities at Oyarzun, but
only after Pedro de los Reyes had exposed him. However,
there seems to have been collusion between the witch and the
witch finder, and as the inquisitors could not agree on what the
Tribunal should do, they were laying the case before the
Council.[77]

La Suprema replied to the inquisitors' letter without delay, on
14 March. They rejected the request of Becerra and Valle for
exemption from normal service as quite unheard of. They
would make a pronouncement on the applications from Juanes
de Sansín and Juanes de Goiburu in the near future (they were
in fact released shortly afterwards).[78] As far as the witch and
the witch finder were concerned, the Tribunal was given detailed instructions on how it was to proceed. A *new* inquisitorial commissioner was to be instructed to make a fresh investigation of the matter, and if the two persons were still pre-

sumed guilty they were to be taken to Logroño. Juanes de Goizueta (who seems to have already been in the custody of the local authorities) was to be transferred to the prison of the Inquisition. Pedro de los Reyes was to be arrested and taken to Logroño, there to be confined in the town prison. In order to ascertain whether he really had the ability to recognize witches he was to be confronted with Fray Pedro de Arburu and made to carry out the same witch test on the monk that he had done with Juanes de Goizueta.[79] (Fray Pedro de Arburu was still immured in a monastery, as was his cousin, the priest Juan de la Borda. It was an irony of fate that these two, whom the Tribunal had been obliged to partially acquit, were still serving their sentences more than a year after the other survivors of the auto de fe had been released.)

La Suprema was emphatically not prepared to declare the Tribunal at Logroño in a state of emergency so that the inquisitors could put the finishing touches to their report on the witches. On the contrary, the Council wrote on 24 March that if the inquisitor whose turn it was to go on visitation had not yet set forth he was to leave immediately. This was followed by a reminder that the journeys of visitation were "extremely necessary on account of the many benefits" they usually produced.[80]

The letter was received in Logroño on 5 May. Salazar was in complete agreement with the Council that a visitation should be made, but as Becerra and Valle disagreed, he composed a written opinion that same day and read it out to his colleagues. Salazar declared in this verdict that the journey should be made in that part of the area that had been longest without a visit. The witch plague in northern Navarra and Guipúzcoa no longer presented a problem, for it had come to an end after he had dealt with the 1,800 cases in connection with the Edict of Grace. Salazar terminated his opinion with the complaint that it was now more than a year since he had submitted his reports on the journey of visitation. He therefore begged the inquisitor general to order the Council to read his first two reports without further delay, since they contained the most urgent facts of the case.[81]

Becerra was the inquisitor whose turn it was to go on visitation. He did not reply to *la Suprema*'s letter until 31 May, explaining that he had not yet set out because of the pressure of work at the Tribunal, of which the Council was well aware.

Becerra was now in good health, so he could not make his quartan fever the excuse for omitting the visitation for this year, but he had another excuse ready:

> It is now late in the year, the season is fruitful, and the crops are ripening. It is therefore to be expected that people will be busy seeing to their fields and getting the harvest home. The visitation will thus inconvenience them greatly and it is to be feared that they will not be as guided by the exhortations of the Holy Office as they ought to be. On the contrary it is certain that many will avoid coming to us [at the visitation sessions] to unburden their consciences so as not to neglect their fields and holdings [*por no desamparar sus campos y haciendas*].

Becerra assured the Council that apart from the witches there was no urgent need for a visitation, and that before the inquisitor general had come to a decision in the matter of the witches it would be inadvisable for the Tribunal to undertake new assignments. Becerra promised that his and Valle's report would be sent shortly, and he concluded the letter with a request to the inquisitor general to cancel the journey of visitation for the current year.[82]

On 12 June *la Suprema* replied excusing Becerra from the journey of visitation on the grounds that Salazar's reports from the previous journey had still not been voted upon. But the Tribunal was expressly instructed to see that next year the visitation should start on the first Sunday in Lent, as was stipulated in the general decrees (*por carta acordada*).[83]

On 15 June Salazar presented a memorandum at the Tribunal. It was an enumeration of a total of thirteen items that, despite the efforts of the inquisitors to bring everything up to date, were still outstanding. At the end Salazar promised his colleagues that for his part he would do everything possible to assist them in resolving the cases. After being read at the Tribunal, Salazar's memorandum was sent on to *la Suprema*, where it was received on 1 July.[84] The intention of Salazar was obviously to provoke a decision on the witch affair. More than half the cases mentioned in his memorandum had some connection with this matter and depended directly on a solution being found to the witch problem as a whole.[85]

This time, however, our inquisitor could have spared himself the trouble, for *la Suprema* had already lost patience. On 20 June, long before Salazar's memorandum reached Madrid, the

Council wrote to the Tribunal informing it that the inquisitor general had agreed that the inquisitors should spend the whole month of July completing their opinion in connection with Salazar's journey of visitation, but if there was any further delay the matter could not be postponed.[86] The letter reached Logroño on 3 July and on the 6th the inquisitors sent a reply promising to do their utmost to comply with the inquisitor general's orders.[87]

Becerra and Valle now employed the same tactics as Salazar. Without a word to their colleague they shut themselves up with all the papers from the journey of visitation and the other witch trials and worked on their report.[88] Towards the end of the month Valle wrote a long letter to the archbishop of Burgos, Fernando de Acevedo, who had been *fiscal* to the Council of the Inquisition during Valle's time there, and who had just been appointed archbishop.[89] The object of this letter was obviously to acquire an influential ally in the battle over the witches. The letter opens with a summary of the conclusions reached by Becerra and Valle, and this summary is all the more important since the whole of this part of their verdict was lost. Valle commenced by saying that he had heard from Burgos that the archbishop was in good health, and he promised to pay him a visit in the near future. After these initial courtesies Valle continued:

> I have felt it right to inform Your Eminence of the matter of the witches on which we are at present working, for it looks as if the Devil is endeavoring to cloak the truth in every possible way. He is naturally very eager to bring souls to perdition, and unfortunately there is no shortage of people to help him realize his intentions.
>
> The Council has commanded Dr. Alonso Becerra and me to send our opinion on the papers concerning *el licenciado* Alonso de Salazar's journey of visitation in the course of this month. But even though we are working every day of the week and on Sundays as well it will not be possible within such a short time to pronounce an opinion on such a momentous matter (from which [i.e. the visitation] he returned completely duped). It is true that we have completed the most important part of our report, which will be sent off in a week's time. We shall take the opportunity then of requesting more time in which to formulate the remainder. We are still completely convinced that when the Council reads our report with the thoroughness and consideration

which are customary, it will be bound to realize as a clear and obvious fact supported by unassailable arguments that this sect is a reality. And this is in spite of all the delusions and deceits employed by the Devil, and which all purport to show that the witches do not exist. It will also be evident that the witches really do go to the sabbath and participate corporally in the meetings, and that they believe absolutely that their devil is God — as they state it in their confessions.

We have also collected a great many material proofs [*actos positivos*] which are completely unassailable, and I should be very glad to send a copy of this information to Your Eminence. For this subject has never been investigated and explored so thoroughly before, and moreover it will have to be acknowledged that the confessions of the accused agree on all points with what earlier authors have written regarding these matters.

I cannot understand how any sensible and intelligent person can bring himself to doubt this truth [i.e. the existence of the witches]. People have known about the sect for centuries in all neighbor countries and in all adjacent provinces, and its members have been punished with the greatest severity. In this very district the Inquisition has been aware of the existence of the sect for over a century, and *la Suprema* has held several meetings in order to subject the problem here to thorough investigation and consideration. It is therefore impossible to comprehend how anyone can dare to challenge these facts and misrepresent the truth that has been absolutely proved and acknowledged by all the scholars in Christendom, and how anyone dares to assert that it is the scholars and the Council of the Inquisition who have been in error and who have committed injustice for all this time — all this with no other basis than his [Salazar's] own whim, because from the very beginning (without knowing what he was doing) he clung to an erroneous interpretation. But now he is defending it tooth and nail. He is seeking to ally himself with persons who have no experience in these matters, and in particular he is leaning on that friend who used to live in this neighborhood [Venegas de Figueroa], who had espoused his case quite openly, and has done much to influence in his favor those superiors [in *la Suprema*] on whom he is continually exerting pressure.

All this grieves us [i.e. Becerra and Valle] deeply, and the only thing that relieves our pain is the knowledge that Your Eminence is on our side and is ready to defend this case of God. For Your Eminence has, like ourselves, understood the gravity of the matter and has realized what vile actions are rife in blaspheming God's Divine Majesty and sending so many souls to perdition. The very thought of it arouses horror and makes the heart bleed.

The long interruption in the legal proceedings as a result of the publication of the Edict of Grace has made the Devil and his witches bolder. The sect is spreading in all the districts where the Edict was read and is constantly acquiring more members, and those who are not witches [must look on helplessly while they] see their children taken to the *aquelarre*. So now they can only hope that the necessary steps will be taken [*todos están esperando el remedio*]. But when the case is brought up in the Council I am certain that the Noble Lords — may God guide them — will make the decision that is needed, so that this fearful scourge may be eradicated.

Until that time I trust that Your Eminence will, with your indomitable courage, lend your aid and cast light on this matter, for if we are to serve God and defend His honor we must realize that this is the most momentous and grave case which has ever come up before the Inquisition....[90] [We can disregard the second part of the letter. It is a long attack on Salazar, who is depicted as a quarrelsome intriguer and indescribably arrogant.][91]

At the beginning of August, Becerra and Valle sent off the portion of their verdict that they had managed to complete. It was made up of two parts (see below, chapter 12.4) and accompanied by a letter signed by the three inquisitors, in which they promised to forward the missing part of Becerra and Valle's opinion in ten or twelve days' time. (The dating of the letter, 3 July 1613, is obviously a mistake. Presumably the writer had forgotten to change the month, so that we should read 3 August; however that may have been, the letter with the two parts of the verdict was not received in Madrid before 21 August.)[92]

In the middle of August Becerra was notified that he had been appointed *fiscal* to the Council of the Inquisition. In a letter dated 17 August Valle and Salazar expressed gratitude on behalf of the Tribunal for the honor shown to their colleague.[93] However, Becerra did not relinquish his post at Logroño until some time around the middle of October.[94]

On 1 September Salazar read a fresh memorandum to his colleagues at the Tribunal. He commenced by drawing attention to the fact that there had still been no progress in several of the cases mentioned in his previous memorandum (of 15 June 1613). No less unfortunate was the fact that the Tribunal had kept Juanes de Goizueta and Pedro de los Reyes (the witch and the witch finder who had been imprisoned in the meantime) in detention for over two months without deciding their cases, although both were perfectly straightforward. These delays resulted directly from the fact that his colleagues had still not completed their report despite having been excused from normal service for almost two months. Salazar also complained of the jealous manner in which his colleagues concealed their work. They had read out their findings to him only moments before the letter was sealed (according to Salazar the letter was dated 23 July), so he had been prevented from acquiring a thorough understanding of the contents or replying to their criticism. The reading had taken place just as the Tribunal was writing to *la Suprema* promising that the rest of Becerra and Valle's report was to follow in "ten or twelve days' time." But Salazar had been informed neither as to whether the letter and the two parts of the verdict (see chapter 12.4, below) had been dispatched, nor whether his colleagues had completed their opinion and sent it off. Salazar concluded with an earnest request to his colleagues to allow him to examine their verdict. After his memorandum had been read to the Tribunal Salazar sent it off to *la Suprema* for its information.[95]

On 24 September Salazar wrote personally to the inquisitor general asking him again to come to a decision on this matter, "the most regrettable affair in the history of the Inquisition," as he calls it in his letter. Salazar drew the attention of the inquisitor general to the many thousands of people involved who now for the second year in succession were uncertain as to their fate. He continued by complaining that his colleagues were not only prolonging the case but that they also refused to discuss their views with him, let alone allow him to see their considerations. Salazar also felt bitterness over what he thought to be the real reason for his colleagues' dilatoriness. He was convinced that Becerra had merely been waiting for his appointment as *fiscal* to *la Suprema* to be confirmed. For this would put him in a position to follow up the matter at the Council in person and argue his own opinions there, while Salazar sat in Logroño with no possibility of reply. Salazar concluded by mentioning the tense atmosphere that prevailed at the Tribunal on account of the witch affair. Therefore, to avoid further trouble he requested that this letter should not be mentioned to his colleagues before the case came up for consideration at the Council.[96]

The letter to the inquisitor general was accompanied by some notes emphasizing the detrimental effect of a prolonged postponement of a decision on the matter.[97] These notes have not been kept but they were presumably identical with an undated three-page document in Salazar's hand which I have called his "Third Report" (SD Text 13), although this is not strictly speaking a report but a memorandum and moreover Salazar numbered only his first and second report. The document carries the heading "So that the Council without further delay may reach a decision on this matter." It addresses a certain "Your Grace," Alonso Becerra's proper title, so presumably the memorandum was read out at the Tribunal before Salazar sent it on to the inquisitor general.[98]

In the document Salazar suggested that normal procedure, whereby first the Tribunal and then *la Suprema* voted on the cases, should be waived. Since all three inquisitors had now sent in their opinions for the Council to examine, the Tribunal ought to refrain from further discussion and allow *la Suprema* to reach a decision on the matter. In order to get his colleagues to agree to his suggestion Salazar showed himself most willing to cooperate wherever possible. He thus reassured them that a decision on the case would by no means exempt the guilty from punishment. But five thousand persons had been branded as witches, and all these — together with their relatives — were awaiting the Inquisition's next step. In Salazar's opinion, it would be the most inhuman cruelty to keep all these people in suspense merely because "fourteen to twenty of them" might in the end turn out to be guilty.[99]

On 3 October Becerra and Valle read out the remainder of their verdict in the Tribunal to Salazar, but as with their previous reports Salazar was not permitted to examine it. This portion of his colleagues' opinion contained among other things a criticism of Salazar's second report and a sharp attack on Salazar for his behavior throughout the whole affair. His colleagues hereby expressed the greatest astonishment that Salazar had recently been attempting to get *la Suprema* to make a decision by going over the heads of the inquisitors of the Tribunal.[100] But Salazar had already prepared his next contribution to the controversy, a document of nineteen closely written pages (SD Text 14). We shall examine this part of his opinion below under the heading *Salazar's Fourth Report*. It would appear that Salazar said nothing to his colleagues about the new report but followed their practice of simply reading it at the Tribunal before sending it on to *la Suprema*.[101]

At the end of October Valle wrote to one of the members of the Council, probably Juan Ramírez (see chapter 12.1, above), complaining that he and Becerra had heard nothing concerning the two parts of the verdict that they had "sent in at the beginning of August." He went on to say that the remaining sections (i.e. the rest of their opinion) were now complete and that after fair-copying would be ready for dispatch. Valle assured his correspondent that the new considerations "will undoubtedly smooth out any difficulties that may have arisen in the meantime" (i.e. with Salazar's fourth report?). In the rest of his letter Valle was concerned with recounting the story of a violent argument he and Becerra had had with Salazar on "Thursday the 17th [of October]." The matter concerned an application for the post of inquisitorial commissioner and the quarrel ended with Salazar going home and staying away from the Tribunal until the following Monday.[102] Valle assured the Council that he for his part was doing everything he could to placate Salazar and keep the peace at the Tribunal:

> And even though this [i.e. Salazar's behavior at the Tribunal] provides every reason for me to give vent to my annoyance I shall not do so. On the contrary I answer him . . . by avowing how much I care for him, value him, and hope that he will curb his unruly nature, which is the most contentious and quarrelsome I have ever come across. For my part I have never given him cause for grief; on the contrary, as a long-standing friend I have, ever since his arrival at this Inquisition, attempted to help him to improve himself. I have striven to avoid everything that might cause painful conflict by yielding and letting him have his own way except when my conscience or the duties of my office forced me to oppose his wishes. By this means I hoped he would improve himself.[103]

Valle continued to recount how these tactics had only resulted in Salazar taking advantage of his compliance by actually attempting to treat him as his subordinate. Since Becerra left for Madrid Salazar had badly tried Valle's patience: "But," concluded Valle, "I am prepared to ignore it provided he mends his ways and leaves us in peace."[104]

Valle's letter must have crossed in transit one that *la Suprema* had sent to Salazar on 24 October, in which the Council at long last confirmed that it had received both his reports and the considerations of his colleagues concerning the matter of the witches; but as his colleagues had not conferred with him when composing their verdict, the Council suggested that Salazar should be handed the draft of the verdict and should read it through "very slowly," and thereafter send any further comment he might wish to make on his colleagues' opinions.[105]

Salazar complied with these instructions and composed an official rejoinder to his colleagues' opinion of 3 October. The document is divided into twenty-one paragraphs. It was read out at the Tribunal on 13 November. Those present were Valle and the new *fiscal* Leguizamo and two of the inquisitorial secretaries.[106] Becerra had long since left, and Salazar was soon to follow him, for he had asked the inquisitor general for three months' leave in order to go to Jaén to carry out some business in connection with the office of canon which he held there (see chapter 3.3, above).[107]

On 19 November *la Suprema* granted Salazar his leave on the condition that he would await the arrival of the new inquisitor, Juan Laso de Vega, before departing.[108] The latter had in fact arrived at Logroño on 12 November, but owing to illness was unable to take up his position before the 14th.[109] However, Salazar stayed on in Logroño to the end of the month. Shortly before his departure he assisted in judging the cases of Gracia Luxea and two other child witches from the Roncal Valley[110] and a sixteen-year-old boy from Larraun. The boy's name was Cristóbal de Mayza and he had been reconciled on Salazar's journey of visitation. He had now turned himself in to the Tribunal to tell how he had suffered a relapse, and had again been taking part in the witches' assemblies.[111] Once again Valle's and Salazar's opinions conflicted and therefore the cases were sent on to the Council for decision.[112]

Salazar did not leave for Jaén before about 1 December.[113] Here at last he had an opportunity to relax after the two years of stress caused chiefly by the controversy with his colleagues at the Tribunal. But he could not unwind completely, for he carried with him the draft of his document of 13 November. After expanding it with a few extra paragraphs he forwarded it to the inquisitor general in a letter dated Jaén, 7 January 1614 (SD Text 15, *Salazar's Fifth Report*).[114] Now Salazar began his wait; the next move had to come from the Council.

4. THE VERDICT OF BECERRA AND VALLE

The two parts of the verdict sent in by Becerra and Valle to *la Suprema* in August 1613 are no longer extant. However, the letter of 3 August to the Council (see preceding section) gives us some idea of their contents. One of the documents, to which we shall refer below as "Memorial A," is said to contain "the evidence and the facts that have emerged from the confessions of these witches"; the other document, which we shall designate "Memorial B," is stated to contain "the facts that have been proved."[115] At the beginning of the second document (or possibly in both?) was a list of the facts that had been proved, and then followed copies of all the statements of evidence. Thus ran the letter to *la Suprema*, and Becerra and Valle went on to mention that their report remained unfinished:

> These two documents contain in principle all the material which provides incontrovertible proof that the witch sect is a reality and that all the monstrous things that the witches confess actually do take place. However, in order to gain a greater understanding of it all we consider it expedient for us to demonstrate how the arguments that our colleague propounds to the contrary carry but slight — if *any* — weight. We shall have completed this part of our verdict in ten or twelve days' time, when it will be immediately forwarded to Your Highness [i.e. the inquisitor general].[116]

We can have no idea of how many more installments were needed for the remainder of Becerra and Valle's verdict, but I shall include them below under the designation "Memorial C." There are some inferences of what they contained in Salazar's Fourth and Fifth Reports, which we shall discuss in a separate section below.

5. THE PAMPLONA MANUSCRIPT (MEMORIAL A)

In 1971 I learned that a sizeable manuscript relating to the dispute over the witches had come to light in Pamplona in the Archivo General de Navarra. The news of this exciting discovery was given me by Julio Caro Baroja, who had just returned from Navarra. Two months later, thanks to the exceptional kindness of the director of the Archive, Florencio Idoate, who was to publish the manuscript himself, I succeeded in acquiring a photostatic copy.[117]

It has not been possible to ascertain how this manuscript ended up in Pamplona.[118] However, there is absolutely no doubt that we have here a transcript of our lost Memorial A together with a section of Memorial B. As early as July 1613, in his letter to the archbishop of Burgos, Valle expressed the idea of sending him a copy of his and Becerra's verdict (see chapter 12.3, above). The Pamplona Manuscript would seem to confirm that the two colleagues did in fact carry out their plan to circulate copies to their allies. It is not known to whom the Pamplona Manuscript was sent. It may possibly have been forwarded to the High Court of Navarra, which was in Pamplona (the archive of which is today included in the Archivo General de Navarra); but if this was the case the Tribunal must have broken the Inquisition's principle of secrecy. Perhaps the two inquisitors wished to exonerate themselves from the criticism of the High Court, and had therefore found it necessary to disclose the matter.[119]

The first part of the manuscript is in the hand of the inquisitorial secretary Juan de Agüero.[120] It ends on the reverse side of folio 53, which bears the original signatures of Becerra and Valle.[121] This portion of the transcript must therefore have been completed *before* the middle of October 1613 when Becerra left for Madrid. The remainder of the manuscript is written in Valle's hand and therefore may well come from a slightly later date. The whole manuscript takes up 134 closely-written folio pages — and is thus the longest extant statement relating to the witch polemic.[122]

Apart from the final section, which is stated to be an extract from Memorial B,[123] the Pamplona Manuscript seems to be an authentic copy of the lost Memorial A.[124] This part of the colleagues' verdict is first and foremost a collection of evidence, or *actos positivos* as the inquisitors preferred to call it. Becerra and Valle restrict their arguments greatly. They merely state a proposition and then proceed to present the documentation. The manuscript is made up of thirty-two chapters each dedicated to a specific *acto positivo* and all written in the same monotonous way. If for example we look at chapter 3, or *"Acto*

3" as it is called, we see that it is introduced by the following proposition: "The witches go to the *aquelarre* on foot many times and some of them even without anointing themselves." This is followed by extracts from the trial records of twenty-five witches and further documentation is referred to in the cases of thirty-one other witches who also declared that they went to the *aquelarre* on foot. Of the twenty-five witch trials quoted from in extracts, three originate from the auto de fe, twelve from persons reconciled at Logroño, one from Valle's thirty-one references, four refer to witches reconciled at Logroño, and twenty-seven to witches reconciled on Salazar's journey of visitation.[125]

The chief value of the Pamplona Manuscript is its abundance of quotes from the original trials, which were later lost in the destruction of the Logroño archives. If this source material had come to light only a year earlier it would have facilitated the writing of the present book. Now, on the other hand, it has offered an unexpected opportunity for checking the exposition of the preceding chapters and for supporting the weak points in my reconstruction of events with fresh evidence. This material has mainly been incorporated in the notes. The Pamplona Manuscript has also confirmed our assumption of an increase in the motifs of witchcraft beliefs. An examination of all references to the confessions of the nineteen witch *confitentes* at the auto de fe demonstrates clearly that new elements emerged in the confessions of the subsequent groups of prisoners (see table 11). Of course we cannot be sure that Becerra and Valle have exhausted the material, but they show a clear predilection for the confessions obtained during this first part of the trial.

The thirty-two *actos positivos,* which the two colleagues established during the hearings of the witches in the course of the whole trial, can be summarized as follows: (1) The tutor witch obtains the consent of the novice before initiation. (2) Adult witches are awake when they anoint themselves and while traveling to the sabbath. (3) The journey may sometimes be undertaken on foot, and (4) if it rains the witches get wet. (5) On the journey they are able to hear the sounds made by shepherds, cattle, pigs, and dogs. (6) They meet with other persons on their way, who may be their comrades but also may be people who are not witches. (7) When the witches happen to meet each other during the day they discuss what has

Table 11. Contents of the Confessions of the Nineteen Witch *Confitentes* at the Auto de Fe (1610), According to the *Pamplona Manuscript* (1613)

Acto no.	Acto positivo	5	6	10	9	1	4	3	2	11	12	13	14	15	8	19	17	7	16	18
Initials:		EN	MPB	IT	MJ	GB	MY	EY	MG	JG	JS	MP	MCB	ME	MV	MZA	IL	MJ	BF	IY
Age:		80	70	38	22	80	40	36	66	37	20	70	52	40	80	80	27	60	40	40
Imprisonment:		27 Jan. 1609				14 Feb. 1609						Sept. 1609				Dec. 1609		30 Mar. 1610		
1.	Consent of the novice	Q	Q	R		Q	Q	Q	R	Q	Q	Q			Q	Q		Q		
2.	Anointed and awake	Q	Q	R			R	Q	Q	Q	Q			R	Q	Q		Q		
3.	On foot to the sabbath											Q								
4.	Getting wet in rain																			
5.	Hearing noises	R	R				R	R	Q		Q		R		R	R			R	
6.	Meeting people					Q			Q				R			Q		Q	R	
7.	Discussing the meetings									R	R									
8.	Witness to a sabbath	Q	R	R	R	Q		Q												
9.	Naming Jesus								Q											Q
10.	Obligation to appear	S	Q	Q	S	S	S	S	S	S	Q	S	S	S	S	S	S	S	S	Q
11.	Belief in Devil day and night	S	S	S	S	S	S	S	S	Q	S	S	S	S	S	Q	S	S	S	
12.	Unable to see the Host		S	S		R	Q	Q	Q	R	S	R	R			R	R	R		Q
13.	Devil's mark			R		R	R	R	Q	Q	Q	Q	Q		Q	Q		R	Q	R
14.	The dressed toad					Q			Q		R	R								
15.	Money to the mistress									R	Q	R	R	R	Q	Q				Q
16.	Senior degree and poisoning	Q	Q			Q	R		R	Q	R	R			Q	Q		R		Q
17.	Poison-making at home	Q				Q	Q		Q			Q	R	R	R	R		R		
18.	Harm to crops		Q	Q		R	R		Q	R	R			R		Q		Q		
19.	Harm to people	Q		Q		Q														R

Table 11, *continued*

Acto no.	Acto positivo	5 EN 80	6 MPB 70	10 JT 38	9 MJ 22	1 GB 80	4 MY 40	3 EY 36	2 MG 66	11 JG 37	12 JS 20	13 MP 70	14 MCB 52	15 ME 40	8 MV 80	19 MZA 80	17 JL 27	7 MJ 60	16 BF 40	18 IY 40
	Imprisonment	27 Jan. 1609		1609		14 Feb. 1609						Sept. 1609				Dec. 1609		30 Mar. 1610		
20.	Eating corpses at the sabbath										Q					Q				
21.	Eating corpses at home					Q	Q			Q	Q				Q	Q				
22.	Violation of tombs	R				R	R	Q	Q	Q	Q					R				
23.	First copulation with Devil							Q	Q	Q					Q	Q				
24.	Copulation outside the sabbath					Q	Q								Q					
25.	Giving birth to toads																			
26.	Meetings by day	Q				Q	Q	Q	R	Q		Q				Q				
27.	Persuaded not to confess					Q	Q	Q	Q	Q	Q	Q				Q				
28.	Demon as substitute					Q							Q		Q	Q		Q		
29.	Witch's absence noted	Q				Q						R			Q					
30.	Offerings on solemn sabbaths						Q	Q	Q	Q	Q									
31.	Devil's advice for false evidence			R	R	R	R	R	R	R	R									
32.	Punished for revealing the sect		Q	Q	Q				Q		Q									
	Total number of actos	12	10	11	5	16	16	12	19	15	20	13	8	5	14	19	3	11	5	9

NOTE: Q = Quotation from the record; R = Reference to the record; S = Reference in general to several records.

The initials of the witches are given in the order in which they confessed; thus the first prisoner from January 1609 appears on the left. Reading towards the right of the table it will be seen that the witches' repertoire increases considerably, although none of the nineteen witches claims examples of *acto* 25, "giving birth to toads." This *acto positivo* does not occur until after the *auto de fe*.

occurred at the assemblies. (8) The sabbaths have been seen by persons outside the witch circle. (9) If the name of Jesus is uttered during the assembly, all the witches flee in horror. (10) The witches are punished for not attending meetings. (11) When the witches have forsworn their Christian faith, they remain faithful to their belief in the Devil night and day, and (12) if they go to church they are unable to see the Host. (13) On admission the Devil marks the witch, and the mark remains for life; (14) the witch is given a dressed toad to serve as his familiar and "guardian angel," and (15) the tutor receives money in payment for the new recruit. (16) When the novice has attained a ten-year seniority he is eligible for promotion to the senior grade and is instructed in the art of poison-making. This generally takes place at the sabbath, but (17) sometimes the witches meet in their own homes to make poison. (18) The powders are used to destroy crops, and (19) other poisons are used to harm persons the witches wish to revenge themselves on. (20) Eating of corpses is practiced at the sabbath, and the proof that it is real flesh is the fact that the witches' stomachs are affected by it and that they vomit it next day in their homes. (21) The flesh of corpses left over from the banquet is allotted to the senior witches, who take it home and keep it in their food chests to eat by degrees. (22) When the witches go out to rob graves they take with them spades, butcher's knives, and spits. (23) Loss of blood is suffered by virgins, both women and men, on the first occasion they copulate with the Devil, and they return home with their clothes bloodstained. (24) The witches also copulate with the Devil in broad daylight as well as at the sabbath, and (25) they may sometimes conceive and give birth to toads. (26) Assemblies are also held in the day-time. (27) Occasionally the Devil seeks out individual witches during the day and persuades them not to confess. (28) When a witch is at the sabbath a demon substitute appears in his place at home, but there may however be instances when (29) a witch's absence is noticed by the other members of the household. (30) When the witches go to the sabbath on festival nights they take sacrificial gifts with them, which are kept by the Devil. (31) The Devil advises witches not to confess, not even when they feel a desire to do so, and tells those who have already confessed to recant their confessions and return to his sect. (32) Those witches who break the oath of silence and go to confession are punished cruelly by the Devil and the other witches. Many witnesses have seen the marks of such punishment on those who have suffered it.

Roughly two-thirds of the documentation originates from the eighty-four witch trials which Becerra and Valle had themselves dealt with at the Tribunal. The other third is taken from the eight-volume visitation book and this provides completely new possibilities of checking Salazar's references in the reports to the inquisitor general, above all the second report (see chapter 12.2, above). However, a critical comparison of the references made by the two parts to Salazar's visitation book would require a special investigation. I shall therefore content myself with giving a short demonstration to show how the new source material can be utilized. For my example I again select *Acto 3*, relating to the means employed by the witches to get to the sabbath.[126] I have mentioned that nine of the examples are from Salazar's visitation book. Four of these instances are also referred to by Salazar in gloss 10 to his second report (visitation files "C 1," "C 381," "C 615," and "D 164"), but, it must be noted, as examples of a minority who gave affirmative answers to Salazar's question as to whether they had met with people, etc. (see my comment on Salazar's gloss 10, p. 315, above). Two others of the colleagues' examples ("D 420" and "D 502") are referred to by Salazar in his gloss 1 and gloss 8. Salazar quotes them as instances of persons giving negative answers to his questions. Thus in the latter case we find an obvious disagreement between Salazar and his two colleagues, though the explanation of it may possibly be that the colleagues are citing an earlier confession made to one of the inquisitorial commissioners, while Salazar is referring to the visitation hearing. As for the seventh of the colleagues' instances, we can ignore it as it is merely a duplication of the above-mentioned case "D 164." On the other hand, with regard to the last two instances, they are not included at all in Salazar's memorials.

In their letter to *la Suprema* of 24 March 1612, Becerra and Valle had committed themselves to proving the existence of the witch sect solely by what was contained in Salazar's own papers. A closer study of the Pamplona Manuscript reveals how the two inquisitors went about fulfilling their promise. Thus one can observe three marked tendencies in their use of Salazar's visitation book: (1) Becerra and Valle made use only of examples which confirmed their suppositions and they failed entirely to mention when these were exceptions to the general rule. (2) They made extensive use of cases not quoted by Salazar in his reports. (3) They frequently quoted from earlier confessions made by the witches before the journey of visitation without any regard as to whether these same persons later altered their statements at new hearings or perhaps entirely revoked the confessions.

The two inquisitors obviously left no stone unturned in order to prove their assertions. And the product is certainly impressive. In "*Acto 1*," 99 examples were cited to prove that the witch mistresses had to obtain the consent of the novices before turning them into witches.[127] That all *adult* witches went to the *aquelarre* anointed and while awake ("*Acto 2*") was proved by 124 instances, and 74 of these were taken from Salazar's visitation book.[128] The arguments continued in this manner up to "*Acto 32*," relating to the prohibition against revealing the secrets of the sect; this was proved by 18 instances.[129] The lengthy memorial contains a total number of over two thousand references to the original records.

At times the examples cited by Becerra and Valle are so fantastic that their allies in the witch polemic must have had some difficulty in accepting them. The following example, from "*Acto 28*," on demons acting as substitutes for persons, must have contributed more than anything else to raise doubt as to whether the two inquisitors were sufficiently critical to make judgments in such difficult cases:

> Graciana de Amézaga, 40, no. 65 [on the list of 84 witches; case no. 74 of our Witch List] folio 22, declares that when she went to the *aquelarre* a demon stayed in her house as her substitute, taking her shape and form. And when asked [by the inquisitors] why it stayed there, she replied that it was so no one should notice her absence. If anyone should come to ask for her, the demon at once rushed to the sabbath to warn her and fetch her home. And this all happened so quickly that she was in time to answer the people who were calling on her. . . . Thus one night when she was at the *aquelarre,* Juana de Arquinarena came to borrow a pair of scissors. The demon hastened at once to the sabbath to tell her she had a visitor, and took her home in time for her to answer the neighbor and give her the scissors. After we had asked her how the demon could take her home so quickly from such a distance she answered that the Devil was able to do such things. And [she continued by saying that] when

she got home she saw that the Juana in question was sitting on the doorstep. So she entered by the back door and after having answered [from inside the house] she threw the scissors out of the window.[130]

Graciana de Amézaga was the witch who, while in the Tribunal prison, confessed right after she heard about the Edict of Grace (see chapter 11.B.1, above).

However, the substantial memorial contained some items that could not be disregarded lightly. In the case, for instance, of "*Acto 8*" — *aquelarre* observed by outside witnesses — Becerra and Valle quoted from a total of thirteen instances and several of these seemed to support their assumption that the witches belonged to a secret organization worshipping a horned god.[131] One of the quotations is taken from the trial record of Catalina de Echetoa of Zugarramurdi, whom we have mentioned previously (see chapter 11.A.7, above). She was not a completely uncompromised witness; but presumably the two inquisitors used the example on the supposition that the statements referred to the time before Catalina became a witch:

Catalina de Echetoa, 14, visitation book [vol.] C folio 644, no. 23 [in the list of 174 witches; case no. 241 of our Witch List] states that about three months ago she went out at midday to weed a field of maize. When she came to the field she saw a great gathering of people dancing before a tall black man with three horns who was sitting on a chair. She did not see them until she came quite close. When she caught sight of them she was afraid and tried to run away; but at that moment her aunt came up to her. The aunt had a field close by and had gone out earlier to weed. Two girls who were taking part in the dance... also approached her. All three of them told her not to be frightened. Then they grasped her by the hands and said that she could choose: she could either do as the others and join their assembly, or she could die on the spot. For fear that they should kill her Catalina decided to stay. She now saw that many people from Zugarramurdi and the farms of Urdax were there — women, girls, and children... And she grew very frightened and wept to see all the terrible things [that were going on] for it was all so new to her [*viendo aquellas cosas tan nuevas y espantosas*]... When the assembly dispersed, some [of the witches] assumed the form of pigs and other animals, but some of the women kept their own shapes and went off with the children . . . in order to take them home. When her aunt saw that Catalina was terrified she told her that the witches would not harm her [as long as she revealed nothing]; but if she gave them away they would kill her. The two girls also told her this. Then she began to weed the field in question and her aunt worked in another field nearby.[132]

6. THE LOST MEMORIALS

From some references in the Pamplona Manuscript it is possible to obtain a fair idea of the contents of the lost Memorial B. In some ways it seems to have been even more interesting than Memorial A, for it contained, inter alia, extracts from the statements of the outside witnesses questioned by Valle when he was on visitation at Zugarramurdi in the summer of 1609. Here was the account of the miller, Martín de Amayur, about the witches who went out into the road and played tricks on him (cf. p. 111 , above);[133] and here was the statement of the witness who had seen the witches in the garden on the night when they attempted to carry off María de Jureteguía. As was previously mentioned (p. 111, above) this witness was one of the eight men who gave evidence to the inquisitorial commissioners who made a report in January 1609, but the fact that the witness was Petri de Navarcorena, María de Jureteguía's own father-in-law, emerges only in the Pamplona Manuscript.[134] Memorial B seems also to have contained an account of the experiments with the witch ointments and powders which had been taken to the Logroño Tribunal.[135] There may also have been more details about the "dressed toad" that was brought back by the Franciscan monks from their preaching crusade and which only receives a passing mention from the other sources (see page 220, above).[136] While Memorial A relied on the witches' own confessions, the documentation in Memorial B consisted chiefly of evidence from outside witnesses.[137] This distinction is noted on the title page of the Pamplona Manuscript (see chapter 12, n. 122, below):

The other volume, which is bound in parchment, also contains proven acts [of witchcraft], but in that one the concrete actions confessed to by the individual witches are proved by means of outside witnesses. In the present volume the common acts admitted by the witches are proved by their individual confessions, which are in agreement with one another.[138]

The Pamplona Manuscript is bound in contemporary half binding. It is to be hoped that the parchment volume with the intriguing Memorial B will also reappear one day, for it must undoubtedly contain the answers to many questions about which the other sources are silent.

We have scant knowledge of the remainder of Becerra and Valle's verdict, those parts which I have put together under the common designation Memorial C.[139] Our only sources are the quotations, extracts, and references which are to be found in Salazar's rejoinder to his colleagues' verdict.[140] But from these we can conclude that the Memorial in any case contained the following:

1. A criticism of Salazar's second report in which his arguments are attacked paragraph by paragraph.[141]

2. A complete account of the development of the witch affair from the first disclosures at Zugarramurdi at the end of 1608 up to the auto de fe in 1610 (in other words, a contemporary description of what I have attempted in chapters 2-8 to reconstruct on the basis of the existing sources).[142]

3. An attack on Salazar himself and a sharp criticism of his treatment of the cases at the Tribunal and on the journey of visitation.[143]

7. SALAZAR'S REJOINDER

Salazar's Fourth Report (SD Text 14) is dated Logroño, 3 October 1613 (the same day that his colleagues' Memorial C, or anyway a part of it, was read out at the Tribunal). The extant manuscript is written in Salazar's hand, and the fact that it contains some corrections indicates that it is the original draft.[144] The report is set out in forty-five clauses. It is divided into four chapters and an epilogue, for which Salazar has supplied the following headings:

[Introduction (clause 1)].

I. Concerning the documentation in the archives of this Tribunal that has not been brought to the attention of the Council [clauses 2-12].

II. Of the errors that have been incurred during the course of this affair — both inside and outside the Tribunal — with the harmful effects that have resulted [clauses 13-26].

III. Of the significance of the *actos positivos* which both parties have brought forward [clauses 27-32].

IV. Of the objections raised against my person and against my handling of this matter [clauses 33-45].
[V.] The epilogue to the whole controversy [see table 12, below].[145]

In the introduction Salazar said that at the time he sent in his opinion on the matter of the witches he pointed out that he was keeping back certain facts for another occasion. He did so in order not to offend his colleagues, but he had now decided to disclose everything. Whereupon Salazar proceeded to recount all the omissions he had witnessed during his three years as a member of the Tribunal.[146]

In the first chapter Salazar pointed out that when on 9 July 1609 the inquisitors replied to *la Suprema*'s inquiry about previous instructions in witchcraft cases, they forwarded only the details that supported their own interpretation of the whole affair. As a result, Salazar now forwarded to *la Suprema* an account of everything that had been held back by his colleagues on that occasion. He cited old letters and instructions received by the Tribunal from *la Suprema* in connection with nine extensive witch cases in the sixteenth century, from 1526 to 1596.[147] During the whole of that period, Salazar demonstrated the Tribunal had not burned a single witch and never once had it been permitted to make imprisonments in these cases before asking the advice of *la Suprema*. The instructions that Salazar quoted reveal an astonishing degree of skepticism on the part of the Council of the Inquisition. For instance, a letter dated 27 November 1538 advised the inquisitors not to believe everything they read in *Malleus maleficarum* (see chapter 1.4, above), even if "he [i.e. the authors Sprenger and Institoris] writes about it as something he himself has seen and investigated, for the cases are of such a nature that he may have been mistaken, as others have been."[148]

Salazar continued with his revelations in the second chapter. He started off with a crushing indictment of the procedure followed by the Tribunal during the present witchcraft outbreak, and here he did not attempt to disclaim his own responsibility as third inquisitor:

As for the proceedings, we failed to write down all the important things which related to the defendants both within and outside the Tribunal, for we omitted to record the disputes and rejoinders, writing only the final resolu-

tion of each point. We thus suppressed the inconsistencies
and irrelevancies which could have further weakened the
defendants' creditworthiness. When, for example, a certain
Juan de Espinar, from Santesteban , . . . stated that he had
seen the three inquisitors at his gatherings entwined with
three women, this was abridged to [his having seen] the
figures of three inquisitors, and nothing more. Nor was
mention made of the continued promises and guarantees
with which we assured those who denied everything that if
they confessed they would be set at liberty.

Nor was mention made of the communications and con-
frontations among the prisoners which the Tribunal had
permitted or arranged in order to make people confess or
supply certain missing information about their offences or
accomplices. On some occasions specific retractions of what
had already been confessed were omitted from the records
in the hope that the renunciations would be withdrawn
through the use of the aforesaid procedures, which were
not mentioned either.[149]

It went so far, continued Salazar, that nothing whatsoever was
written down of what the jailer, Martín de Igoarzabal, declared
he had heard two women confide to each other one night while
he was standing listening outside their cells. Salazar next
reported the nocturnal conversation between María de
Jureteguía and her aunt (mentioned near the end of chapter
4.2, above). But la Suprema was only now being informed of
this fact — three years after the two women had been reconciled at the auto de fe and María de Jureteguía had been held
up as an example of a particularly good confitente. But most of
the criticism that followed in the report fell on Salazar's colleagues. They had tacitly accepted the violence to which the
witches had been subjected by local authorities, while Salazar
had protested strongly when the vote was proposed on
whether the Tribunal was to accept the maltreated prisoners
who had been brought from Zubieta by the authorities in the
spring of 1611 (see page 223 f., above).[150] The Tribunal had
concealed the new orders from la Suprema (issued 28 June 1611)
so that in fact the district commissioners had not been informed that the witches were now permitted to retract their
confessions.[151] (But in this too Salazar was blameless, since it
happened while he was away on visitation.) Finally, Salazar
stated that Becerra and Valle did everything in their power to
sabotage the journey of visitation; they had slandered him to

the district commissioners and given them secret orders to offer him as little assistance as possible.[152]

Concerning the procedure in dealing with witch cases, Salazar admitted that there had recently been some slight improvement, for the witches' confessions were now being written down: "with all the imperfection and confusion of the replies" — as his colleagues had commented. And this had resulted in such confused confessions that it was now impossible to either reconcile or absolve the accused.[153]

As proof of how utterly mistaken the Tribunal's method of dealing with the witches had been, Salazar referred to the "universal peace and quiet" that he had already predicted when he sent in the report of his journey of visitation.[154] The permanence of this state of affairs was illustrated by a letter from the commissioner at Lesaca, dated 2 June 1613, which Salazar enclosed with the new report. It will be recalled that Lesaca had been one of the places hardest hit by the witch craze. But now, four years after the outbreak, old Domingo de San Paul was able to write:

> ... Otherwise there is nothing new to report from this district. The child witches are sleeping peacefully through the night and they say that now the witches no longer take them to the *aquelarre*, either by night or day.[155]

In the third chapter Salazar discussed what he and his colleagues understood by proofs. He began with a sharp criticism of Becerra and Valle's use of the term *actos positivos*:

> Until it has been clearly and distinctly ascertained that certain events resulted from *maleficia* and came about by such means, they cannot call them *actos positivos*. For the fact that people "saw her [i.e. the witch] pass by" here or there, or that someone was killed, crippled, or injured does not imply anything and no conclusion can be reached unless this is proved to be the work of witches through statements from people who are not witches which leave no room for doubt. We have no more ground for believing the accomplices about this than for believing the other details about the gatherings, dances, and *aquelarres* (where we pass beyond the limits of credulity) if these are not corroborated by outside witnesses or by circumstances and arguments which would back up the claims of the accomplices. However, up to the time of writing we have had no proof of this kind.[156]

Salazar went on to criticize the demonological aspect of his

colleagues' argument and in doing so formulated some exceptionally rational principles regarding evidence at witch trials:

> My colleagues are wasting their time in maintaining that the
> more theoretical and complex aspects of this can be properly
> understood only by the witches, since in the event witch-
> craft has to be dealt with by judges who are not members of
> the sect. . . it is not very helpful to keep asserting that the
> Devil is capable of doing this or that, simply repeating over
> and over again . . . the theory of his angelic nature; nor is it
> useful to keep saying that the learned doctors state that the
> existence of witchcraft is certain. This is only a needless
> annoyance, since nobody doubts this. . . . The real question
> is: are we to believe that witchcraft occurred in a given
> situation simply because of what the witches claim? It is
> clear that the witches are not to be believed, and that the
> judges should not pass sentence on anyone, unless the case
> can be proven by external and objective evidence sufficient
> to convince everyone who hears it. However, who can
> accept the following: that a person can frequently fly
> through the air and travel a hundred leagues in an hour; that
> a woman can get out through a space not big enough for a
> fly; that a person can make himself invisible; that he can be
> in a river or in the sea and not get wet, or that he can be in
> bed and at the *aquelarre* at the same time . . . and that a witch
> can turn herself into any shape she fancies, be it housefly or
> raven? Indeed, these claims go beyond all human reason
> and many even pass the limits permitted the Devil.[157]

In the fourth chapter Salazar defended himself against the
criticism his colleagues had directed against him personally.
He rejected among other things the charges that he had carried
on a secret correspondence with the inquisitor general and
with Antonio Venegas, previously bishop of Pamplona, who
in the meantime had been promoted to the wealthy see of
Sigüenza.[158] Salazar also pointed out that in their "dark
brooding" over his reports his colleagues had time and again
quoted things he had never said.[159] Toward the end Salazar
reached the conclusion that all his colleagues' attacks were
being made with the sole aim of provoking him into making
another extensive contribution to the controversy, "which
would take as long to draw up as theirs, thus postponing the
examination of the papers in the Council as they have succeeded in doing until now by procrastination and presentation of interminable papers."[160]

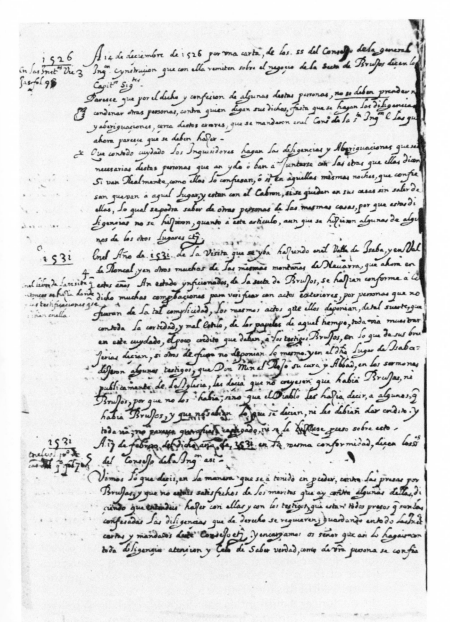

Figure 20. Manuscript page from Salazar's fourth report, in his own hand.

In the epilogue Salazar first demonstrated that the controversy between him and his colleagues seemed destined in advance to preclude any compromise, and he therefore restricted himself to giving a brief outline of the main points in the interpretations of the opposing sides. Table 12 is a summary of the twelve main points posited by Salazar.[161]

Salazar's Fifth Report (SD Text 15) is dated Jaén, 7 January 1614 (see end of chap. 12.3, above). It covers nine pages and is divided into twenty-four clauses.[162] The report does not contain any appreciably new arguments on the part of Salazar, so we may concentrate on the criticism he levels at his colleagues' memorials, and chiefly to that which was read aloud at the Tribunal on 3 October 1613. It is presumably this last that Salazar was quoting at the start of his report when he said that Becerra and Valle felt they were justifying their basic conception when they reasoned thus:

> "We marvel that he [Salazar] tries to insinuate that the majority of the witches' confessions and everything else that emerges from the visitation are dreams and fantasies; for it is clear that the tricks, intrigues, and contrivances of the Devil have been powerful and strong enough to blind the understanding of many people. All of this, naturally, has allowed the Devil to better protect his witches."[163]

In another place, continued Salazar, they go so far as to say that "blinded by the Devil I defend my witches."[164] After refuting this charge, he proceeded to develop a critical analysis of the three fundamental opinions on which his colleagues in principle based their argument:

> Firstly, they accept at face value the rules observed by the Devil and his witches; that in order to go to the *aquelarre*, to be anointed, or to hold a toad, people sometimes must give their consent, while at other times these things happen without their permission; that some witches have permission to do what is forbidden to other witches; that sometimes the person seen at the *aquelarre* is only a counterfeit figure of the real person and at other times is the person himself. All of this they reduce to accepted conclusions, as if the doctors and authorities had enjoyed revelations or had succeeded in limiting the Devil to a uniform pattern of activity without variations in time, place, or occasion; with the result that a gathering of witches in Zugarramurdi should be exactly the same as one in Fuenterrabía or in France. . . .

Table 12. The Twelve Main Points in the Witch Polemic of the Tribunal

Becerra and Valle	Salazar
1. All the *confitentes* have done the things they confess to and have personally seen the things they testify to about their accomplices.	Even though this may well be possible, not a single one of the existing statements of evidence is convincing in this respect.
2. The evidence regarding these things is absolutely and unmistakably true.	Even the strongest evidence contains the element of uncertainty that has always been present in cases of this nature.
3. We are dealing with an ancient and well-known sect which has always been severely punished ever since it was discovered.	Nevertheless, *la Suprema* has time and again found it necessary to subject the sect to investigation and has gradually mitigated its original severity.
4. Proceedings should be instituted against all who are under suspicion.	It is inadvisable to institute proceedings against anyone unless the testimony is supported by other sources of evidence.
5. In view of the secret nature of witchcraft, less definite evidence should suffice to indict the offenders.	Even if this were conceded, the existing evidence would be suspect, for that part of it which is claimed to be well-known is not in fact known to anyone insofar as I have been able to ascertain.
6. We must take precautions to ensure that one of the gravest forms of apostasy that has ever been experienced within Christianity does not go unpunished.	We can ignore this entirely as long as proof is lacking against those suspected and as long as there is no certainty in any one case that the offenses have been committed.
7. We should at least seek to make reparation to God for the offense to which these miserable wretches have subjected His honor.	For the sake of the honor of God it would befit us to make reparation for all the violence and coercion that has been employed completely illegally, and which has ruined the good name and reputation of so many.
8. All the accused should suffer the same punishment as other heretics, and the procedures of the Inquisition should not be altered in cases of witchcraft by allowing witnesses to retract their statements and the witches to revoke their confessions.	The law ought not to be applied to witches with the same rigor as it is applied to other heretics.
9. When composing the trial records we should write down only the final, well-reasoned confessions that agree with what is already known about witchcraft.	We must write down the confessions in full with all their contradictions and absurdities.

Table 12, *continued*

Becerra and Valle	Salazar
10. *Our* verdict is based on the experience gained when we instituted proceedings against this sect and from the evidence that emerged in the course of trying the eighty-four cases concluded at the Tribunal in Logroño.	*I* too have acquired a good deal of experience with the eighteen hundred witches whose cases I dealt with single-handedly on the journey of visitation, in addition to my share in trying the eighty-four cases at the Tribunal.
11. Since we enjoy seniority of office and instituted this case, and since the members of the jury who judged the cases at the auto de fe all endorsed our opinion, we should be given preference over our colleague, who stood alone.	The voting of the sentences at the auto de fe should play a subordinate part in this discussion when the truth is at issue.
12. All the papers from our colleague's visitation are directed solely towards reinforcing his negative vote at the Tribunal.	This is in conflict with the fact that my colleagues have bolstered their own arguments with so many citations from my visitation papers.

Their second assumption has the same end. In order to resolve the contradictions which emerge from the confessions, my colleagues divide the defendants into three categories: good, bad, and indifferent [*diminutos*] *confitentes*. However, we have no method or rule which allows us to evaluate each confession other than the arbitrary one that they have used and refer to in the same paper. Thus the name of bad *confitente* is given to someone whom another [judge] might call good, and vice versa. . . .

Thirdly, they assume that the Devil exercises great astuteness and constant vigilance in concealing his sect and in avoiding the danger that he fears will result if it should become known, lest his detestable designs for corrupting the Christian religion should fail. All this flies in the face of the copious testimony from over two thousand suspects which led to the discovery of the sect. Similarly it does not seem that the Devil's machinations, the product of an angelic sagacity and a nature far superior to the human, could be exposed so easily by children of such tender years — eight and under. (More than fifteen hundred of the witnesses have not reached twelve!)[165]

Salazar devoted the remainder of the report to the detailed

items in his second paper that his colleagues had criticized. Thus when the colleagues in their memorial had tried, by an inspired metaphor, to evade the issue in his clause 8 — regarding the fifty-odd witnesses who attended the *aquelarre* but were unable to explain how they got there (see page 316, above) — Salazar demonstrated how their comparison is completely misguided:

> My colleagues make a forced comparison with seafarers who, without knowing how to use the compass or pilot chart, nevertheless find their way to the Indies or to the ports they are seeking. I see no basis for a comparison here, since these two cases are completely unrelated to one another. In the former case, the seafarers whilst on the high seas are prepared for any eventuality by day or by night; but in the latter case, when the witches are traveling to the *aquelarre*, it is only the witch, or at most the novice and the mistress, who see the way. Furthermore, no one can be found to confirm this, nor can anyone outside the sect tell anything about it. [166]

Salazar concluded by saying that in spite of all the conflicting opinions in the controversy, he and his colleagues were agreed on one point: that it was absolutely necessary to come to a decision in the case. Therefore Salazar once more begged the inquisitor general to put an end to the matter with all possible speed. [167]

CHAPTER THIRTEEN
The Resolution of the Witch Problem

1. SALAZAR IS SUMMONED TO THE COUNCIL

T WAS NOT UNTIL MARCH 1614 — TWO years after Salazar had presented his reports — that *la Suprema* began to deal with the great witch affair. Salazar should have returned to Logroño by this time, but he was in fact still at Jaén, for on 4 February the inquisitor general had extended his leave for another two months.[1]

On 7 March one of the inquisitorial councillors, Juan Zapata Osorio, wrote to Salazar assuring him that all the members of the Council would welcome his presence during the examination of the papers,[2] and he went on to say that if they had not realized that his way home to Logroño from Jaén would take him through Madrid, the inquisitor general would undoubtedly have sent for him. The Council, wrote Zapata, was now about to commence deliberating the matter, but they would not finish examining all the papers until after the Easter vacation. Nevertheless he urged Salazar to come to Madrid as quickly as possible:

> Although we gather that Your Grace will arrive before a decision is reached in the case, and their Lordships are all anxious to hear your opinion on these matters — and I not least — I would wish Your Grace's arrival might be in time for the examination [of the papers], or at least some of them. For my opinion on these matters coincides with that of Your Grace, and I feel that it is necessary to proceed with great caution, in the way that our predecessors have always done.[3]

Four days later the Secretary to *la Suprema,* Hernando de Villegas, wrote to Salazar in the name of the Council requesting his presence in Madrid during the week following *cuasimodo* Sunday. The letter stated that the examination of the papers relating to the witch affair was about to be undertaken, and Salazar's presence was required in order that he could furnish detailed explanations.[4]

Cuasimodo Sunday is the first Sunday after Easter and in 1614 it fell on 6 April. Salazar was to begin his service at the Council of the Inquisition the following week. However, he may have arrived in Madrid earlier, for on the same day the secretary sent his letter, Juan Zapata wrote again to Salazar urging him not to delay, but to leave for Madrid at once. Since he last wrote, the Council had begun to work on the case and Juan Zapata had become convinced that Salazar's presence would be "of great gain to God's case."[5] (Table 13 shows the personnel of *la Suprema* in 1614. It can be seen from the dates of appointment that only Juan Zapata and a few other members of the Council had followed the Logroño case from its commencement.)

On 15 March the Council wrote to the Tribunal at Logroño requesting that all the papers relating to the witch case be sent to Madrid immediately. The visitation books of both Valle and Salazar were required along with the records of the eighty-four trials that had been concluded at the Tribunal. In addition the Council asked that two witches be sent down, with the greatest secrecy: Juanes de Yribarren (auto de fe no. 18) and Juanes de Goizueta (see above, chapter 12.3). The Tribunal was to assure the two witches that they had nothing to fear; they were to go to Madrid not as prisoners but as normal travelers, and the agent who accompanied them was not to carry a staff of office. On arrival they were to report to Secretary Villegas, who would tell them why they had been sent for.[7]

On the same day that the Council wrote to Logroño, a letter was dispatched to the inquisitor general, who had gone to Toledo. The letter stated: "As His Eminence ordered before His departure, we have now begun to examine the witch question in the afternoons." It went on to inform the inquisitor general of what had been written to the Tribunal. The trial documents, explained the Council, had been requested "in order to facilitate the resolution of the problems presented by the case," and the two witches were to be brought to Madrid

Table 13. Members of the Council of Inquisition, 1614[6]

Title	Name, position	Date of appointment (Date of swearing-in)
Inquisitor general	Bernardo de Sandoval y Rojas, cardinal & archbishop of Toledo	12 Sept. 1608
1st councillor	Pedro de Tapia, *licenciado*, member of the Council of Castilla	26 June 1603 (27 June 1603)
2nd councillor	Juan de Llano y Valdés, *licenciado*	17 Mar. 1608 (24 Mar. 1608)
3rd councillor	Juan Zapata Osorio	17 Mar. 1608 (24 Mar. 1608)
4th councillor	Rodrigo de Castro y Bobadilla, *doctor*	(3 Dec. 1608)
5th councillor	Gabriel de Trejo Paniagua, *licenciado*, member of the Council of Castilla	(3 June 1610)
6th councillor	Enrique Pimentel, *licenciado*, former member of the Council of Orders (*Consejo de Ordenes*)	4 Sept. 1613 (5 Sept. 1613)
7th councillor	Juan Ramírez, *doctor*, former *fiscal* to *la Suprema*, and one time inquisitor at Logroño	3 Sept. [Aug.?] 1613 (9 Aug. 1613)
8th councillor	Francisco de Mendoza, *licenciado*, one time inquisitor at Toledo	3 Sept. 1613 (28 Sept. 1613)
Fiscal to *la Suprema*	Alonso Becerra Holguín, *doctor*, monk of the Alcántara order, former inquisitor at Logroño	2 Sept. 1613 (19 Oct. 1613)

"so that here in the presence of Your Eminence and the Council we may attempt to determine the truth and really get to the bottom of the matter."[8] The original of the letter to Toledo is extant and here for the first time we have direct evidence of how the grand inquisitor regarded the problem. In the left-hand margin of the letter we find the following note written by the inquisitor general himself:

I am well pleased with what Your Graces have here written to me and would merely reiterate that I am interested in the speedy conclusion of this case. May God preserve Your Lordships for many happy years. Toledo, 17 March 1614.

B[ernardo de Sandoval y Rojas][9]

2. LA SUPREMA

The Council of the Spanish Inquisition had its seat in the old royal castle of Madrid (*el Alcazar del Rey*) along with the other government bodies.[10] The administration was divided into two secretariats (see map 8), one for the inquisitorial tribunals of Castilla (Toledo, Valladolid, Sevilla, Granada, Córdoba, Murcia, Llerena, Cuenca, Santiago, and the Canary Islands) and the other for the tribunals of Aragón (Zaragoza, Barcelona, Valencia, Mallorca, Sardinia, and Sicily), Navarra (Logroño), and America (Mexico, Peru, and Cartagena de Indias, the latter established in 1610). Each of the two offices was staffed by a secretary (*secretario*) and a reporter (*relator*).[11] The reporter's work included filing the incoming correspondence and making summaries of the appeal cases which came in from the tribunals.[12] These four officials took part regularly in the meetings of the Council. But the other employees were permitted to enter the Council chamber only when they were summoned.[13] This subordinate staff consisted of the following employees: one chief constable (*alguacil mayor*), one messenger (*nuncio*), three porters (*porteros*), one assessor (*tasador de procesos*), two doctors (who attended the employees when they fell ill), and a cashier (*receptor general*).[14] Each successive inquisitor general usually had a private secretary (*secretario de cámara*), although this does not seem to have been a permanent post.

The Council of the Inquisition began each day with Mass in a private chapel, attended by the whole staff.[15] Strict etiquette, too complicated to describe in detail here, marked Council meetings. These meetings occupied three hours every morning and two hours every Tuesday, Thursday, and Saturday afternoon.[16] The inquisitor general presided over the Council. He was seated on a dais under a crimson canopy. The two most senior inquisitorial councillors were also seated under the canopy. They sat one on each side of the inquisitor general, and chaired the meetings in his absence.[17] The inquisitor general normally took part in the meetings for only two hours every morning,[18] and the two councillors, who were at the same time members of the Castilian Council (see table 13), were generally present only at the afternoon sessions.[19] In front of the inquisitor general and the two senior councillors stood a small table on which were writing materials and a bell, which was rung to summon the porters from the entrance hall. A long

Map 8. The tribunals of the Spanish Inquisition, the year of their founding, and their dependence on the Council of the Inquisition.

table was placed below the dais. Here sat the other councillors in order of seniority, and the *fiscal* had a seat at the bottom of the table. Before him on the other side of the table stood a chair for the king's secretary, but as a rule this was unoccupied. In fact the king's secretary could enter the chamber only when summoned by the inquisitor general, and his presence was necessary only when the Council was considering cases which were to be put before the king. A bench at the far end of the long table allowed the two secretaries and the two reporters to sit facing the inquisitor general.[20]

This then was the Council which dealt with cases coming in from all over the Spanish Empire. First the letters were opened and read out in this assembly. In order to facilitate the resolution of the cases the inquisitorial councillors seem to have divided up the twenty provincial tribunals amongst themselves, and so as to ensure that there was always a member present to sign the letters that were dispatched to the tribunals, the councillors took turns serving as *"semanero"* (i.e. being on duty for the week).[21] However, the senior inquisitor and the *fiscal* were exempted from this duty. A great deal of the Council's time must have been taken up with the reading of the incoming mail. As a rule the inquisitor general — or the senior councillor in his absence — dictated the reply on the spot, but if there were any doubts regarding the decision, the matter was put to a vote. As at the *consultas de fe* at the tribunals, the voting at *la Suprema* was carried out according to seniority, beginning with the most junior councillor. During the voting it was the duty of the inquisitor general to supervise and see that no councillor's vote was interrupted and that none of the others attempted to influence him by gestures or facial expressions. However, the decisions that were reached had to bear the signatures of all the councillors present without regard to whether they had voted for or against them. If the vote was tied the inquisitor general could submit the question to a fresh jury.[22]

3. THE COUNCIL'S TREATMENT OF THE AFFAIR

On 15 April — one month after the Council had written to the Tribunal at Logroño — a courier arrived with the two visitation books and the eighty-four trial records that had been requested. He also brought with him the witch Juanes de Goizueta, a letter from Valle, and the new inquisitor, Laso de

Vega. In the letter, dated Logroño, 9 April, the two inquisitors wrote that Juanes de Goizueta had set off very willingly after being told that this journey would expedite the conclusion of his case. They also explained that the second witch, Juanes de Yribarren, had not been sent (the inquisitors had learned that he was wandering about as a beggar and was sometimes to be found at Urdax or Zugarramurdi, although most of the time he was in France; therefore they had written to the abbot of Urdax asking him to get hold of Yribarren). A note attached to the letter from the inquisitors at Logroño contains orders for the Council's porter to arrange lodgings for Juanes de Goizueta (four *reales* a day for board and lodging).[23] It thus appears that the young Basque was permitted to move about freely while he was in Madrid.

In a letter dated 17 April the Council informed the Tribunal at Logroño that they had received the papers and also the witch Juanes de Goizueta, whom they were retaining for the time being. "All the papers," concluded the letter, "are now being examined, and you will be informed of our decision."[24]

On 19 April the Council again wrote to Logroño requesting that the Tribunal forward a folder containing the letters that had been exchanged between Salazar and his two colleagues during Salazar's journey of visitation, and also the trial record of Juanes de Goizueta, which had not been received with the other records.[25]

By the beginning of May *la Suprema* was in receipt of the long awaited papers which arrived with a letter from the Tribunal dated Logroño, 23 April.[26] The inquisitors had also included in the package the reply they had received in the meantime from the abbot of Urdax regarding the other witch. Fray León (writing from Elizondo on 14 April) stated that after Juanes de Yribarren had returned from Logroño he had begun to steal and to attack travelers. As a result the High Court of Navarra had condemned him to ten years in the galleys, and he had now served eighteen months of this sentence. It was obvious that the inquisitors forwarded the original of the abbot's letter so that *la Suprema* could read what this commissioner had written about the witches in his region. The letter continued as follows:

> If anything of further interest to the Holy Office should occur, Your Eminence [i.e. Valle] has in me a servant who is perpetually on guard, particularly regarding everything

concerning this devilish riff-raff. For they [the witches] rest in the belief that all is past and forgotten, and this has made them so presumptuous that they are utterly intolerable.[27]

A few days later, on 7 May, Valle wrote to *la Suprema* with the news that his colleague, the inquisitor Juan Laso de Vega, had died that morning after a long illness.[28]

Now Valle was the sole inquisitor at the Logroño Tribunal, while his former colleagues Becerra and Salazar were in Madrid participating in the deliberations on the witch affair. In the middle of July the witch Juanes de Goizueta returned from Madrid. *La Suprema* had concluded the hearings and the Tribunal was instructed in a letter to terminate his case as speedily as possible. (The precise directions were entered in the trial record, which is no longer extant, but apparently he was released *ad cautelam*.)[29] During the month of July Valle received the information that Salazar was trying to institute disciplinary proceedings against him. This information reached Valle through "certain persons" (presumably employees of the Tribunal), who had returned from a journey to Madrid. They told him that Salazar had tried to persuade them to give evidence against Valle at the Council of the Inquisition, and when they had replied that they knew nothing about the matter, Salazar had said that they need not present themselves at the Council after all. When Valle heard this he jumped at the conclusion that Salazar intended to have him and the secretaries Agüero and Zorilla dismissed from the Inquisition at Logroño (see chapter 12.1, above).[30] However, as far as can be ascertained from the sources, Salazar did not succeed in getting this case instituted at the Council. On 14 August the annual report of the cases (*relación de causas*) concluded by the Tribunal was submitted by Valle alone. It contained twenty-seven trial records terminated during the period 20 July 1613 to 20 July 1614.[31] Among other things, the report described the result of the cases against the three child witches from the Roncal Valley and that of the sixteen-year-old boy from Larraun, that we mentioned previously (see chapter 12.3, above). A fifth witch case concerned an old beggar-woman, Isabel Folca, who had been exposed by a witch-finder at Alava. All these witches had been released *ad cautelam*. This was in fact the first time since 1611 that this type of case had figured in the Tribunal's *relaciones de causas*. This is all that we know about Valle's activities at Logroño during this period. We can now, therefore, return to Madrid, where the deliberation on the great witch affair was in full swing.

Doubtless one of the first tasks undertaken by Salazar after he had commenced his spell of service at the Council of the Inquisition was the preparation of his sixth report to the inquisitor general (SD Text 16). It bears the title "The Account and Summary of the Findings of the Visitation carried out by the Holy Office in the Mountains of the Kingdom of Navarra and other areas, and of the Outcome of the Edict of Grace granted to the Witches' Sect, according to the Reports and Papers Remitted to the Council." The report covers eight pages and is undated.[32] We need not dwell on the contents; they are merely a résumé of Salazar's second, fourth, and fifth reports, which contained all his main viewpoints. The last section bears the title "Summary of the whole discussion," and it is a slightly abbreviated version of the epilogue to the Fourth Report, in which Salazar made a comparison between the opinions held by the two opposing sides (see chapter 12.7, above, and table 12).[33]

Salazar's sixth report was adopted almost word for word in a seven-page letter written by the inquisitor general. The letter was to have been sent to a number of bishops who had previously been members of *la Suprema*. The inquisitor general had intended that they should help the Council come to a decision in the case, but he later changed his mind and the circular letter — as a note in Salazar's hand states — was not in fact sent to anyone.[34] However, the very fact that the letter was written at all is indirect testimony to the esteem in which Salazar was held by his old patron. The inquisitor general now stood by Salazar whole-heartedly and supported him on behalf of the "witches" (insofar as his office allowed).

Presumably Salazar took part in the meetings only when the witch affair was on the agenda. Here it became his task to conduct the witches' defense at the highest level, and here he was face to face with his erstwhile colleague Becerra, who in his capacity of *fiscal* to the Council undoubtedly spared no effort to ensure that the witches would not escape so easily, and that the fiendish sect would eventually be dealt with severely. Unfortunately we are unable to discover who took Becerra's side since no records of the Council meetings were preserved.

Halfway through the summer the Council seems to have

completed its perusal of all the material that had been sent down from Logroño. On 11 August a letter was dispatched to the Tribunal informing it that Salazar had finished his term of service at the Council and was now returning to his post at Logroño.[35] His signature begins to appear with that of Valle on the Tribunal's letters as of 23 August.[36] However, twelve days later, on 2 September, Valle made an application for twenty days' leave. He stated that he was requesting this because he had been suffering for some time from gallstones and that the doctors had advised him to visit a health spa in France, as he was too old for an operation. He went on to explain, in order to reassure the inquisitor general, that the spa was only three miles from the Spanish frontier in a region where the people were all good Catholics.[37] Instead of the twenty days he had asked for, Valle was granted two months leave and it would seem that he managed to get away from the presence of his old opponent quite soon, for as early as 15 September his signature is missing from the Tribunal's correspondence.[38]

4. SALAZAR'S DRAFT FOR THE NEW INSTRUCTIONS

On his departure from the Council of the Inquisition Salazar left behind a very detailed draft for *la Suprema*'s new instructions for witchcraft cases. Two copies of this "bill" are extant; they were undoubtedly compiled at the request of the inquisitor general. On one of them Salazar made a note that this was the last document he presented to the Council. The manuscript, Salazar's *Seventh Report* to the inquisitor general, covers four pages and bears the title, "Measures suitable for the Resolution of the Affair of the Witches."[39] In the introduction Salazar emphasized, as so often before, the necessity of a speedy decision by the Council:

> This matter disclosed by the Inquisition at Logroño has now reached a point where an immediate solution is demanded. To meet the urgent need, to safeguard the future and also to remedy the past abuses, I, Inquisitor Alonso de Salazar Frías, recommend the following articles and clauses:[40]

The proposals were set out in twenty clauses. The first part (clauses 1-9) was a criticism of the past errors that had been made, and the second part (clauses 10-20) was an attempt, bordering on pedantry, to exclude any possibility of similar errors in the future. For the sake of clarity Salazar's clauses are here reproduced in paraphrase:

1. The Holy Office is to make known its deep regret for the ill-treatment suffered by the accused at the hands of the district commissioners, their own relatives, or the local authorities. It is also to be announced that for the present the Inquisition is referring the punishment of the guilty to the High Court of Navarra, but that in the future, any persons who are guilty of inflicting such injustice will incur the severest penalities imposed by the Inquisition.

2. The Tribunal is to open proceedings against the commissioners who have been party to the abuses, and in addition to the penalty to which each of them is condemned the Tribunal must ensure that these people never again take any part in witchcraft cases. As obvious subjects for such "disciplinary enquiries" Salazar mentions specifically the commissioners at Vera, Maestu, and Larrea (see above, pp. 133 ff., 270, and 286).

3. Permission to revoke confessions of witchcraft is to be given out so effectively that all those who have hitherto held back may come forward without fear.

4. The parish priests are to be expressly ordered not to deny the sacraments to any of the accused, unless their guilt has been determined by the Tribunal.

5. All confessions and testimonies in the present witchcraft case are to be declared invalid, so that it will not be possible to institute proceedings against any person on the basis of these statements (unless new charges are preferred), and no suspect or his relatives will be debarred from the right to occupy honorable posts.

6. On account of the deficiencies of the trials, the *sambenitos* of the persons sentenced at the auto de fe of 1610 are not on any account to be displayed in the churches.

7. For the same reason the property that was sequestered is not to be confiscated.

8. The Tribunal is to discontinue the proceedings against those prisoners who died in prison before their trials were concluded. And their children and dependents are to be summoned in order that they may be informed that these proceedings have not debarred them from honorable posts. These details are to be entered in their files.

9. The proceedings against Fray Pedro de Arburu and his

cousin Juan de la Borda are to be quashed. Any part of their sentence still to be served is to be remitted, and they are to be informed that the proceedings have not excluded them from any honorable office.

10. The Tribunal is to publish an edict imposing silence regarding the whole question of witchcraft. Any person whose conscience may be troubling him in connection with these matters is to be enjoined not to discuss his problem with others but to go straight to one of the commissioners or to his own confessor, who can communicate the matter to the Tribunal. The same discretion is to be observed by persons who wish to accuse others of witchcraft.

11. Any persons who come of their own free will to confess anything about themselves or witness against others concerning these matters are to be freely admitted. Their statements are to be written down carefully with all the flaws and contradictions they may contain (as required by the ruling of the Inquisition); and if any testimony is made relating to accomplices, the witness is to be closely questioned so as to make plain what he in fact is able to witness.

12. No commissioner is to take evidence or make inquiries in these matters before he has informed the Tribunal and received express orders to proceed.

13. The commissioners are to be issued instructions on how to receive confessions of witchcraft. They are to be enjoined among other things to study the personal circumstances of those who come to confess and keep account of any details of background information that come to their notice. For these details will be of value when the Tribunal makes a decision regarding the confession. For their part, the inquisitors are to observe the greatest caution when appointing a commissioner to undertake further investigation of the case, and the inquisitors are to agree unanimously on the appointment.

14. Should fresh evidence be produced against any person previously under suspicion, his trial may be reopened, but the new evidence is to be entered as a continuation of his original case record, so that the question of his guilt may be resolved on the basis of both the old and the new testimonies. The vote may take place as soon as all three inquisitors are present, but before further action is taken the entire file with the inquisitors' vote and a copy of the new witchcraft instructions is to be remitted to *la Suprema*.

15. All voluntary *confitentes* who resort to the Tribunal are to have their cases dealt with mercifully, without delay. They are not to suffer imprisonment, confiscation of goods, or any other penalty. Those who make their confession to a commissioner are not to be summoned to the Tribunal. When their confessions have been examined by the inquisitors and their cases resolved, their reconciliation or absolution may be entrusted to the commissioner, and unless the case presents particular problems it may be expedited by the Tribunal summarily without the advice of the Council.

16. In order to secure an entirely impartial treatment of these cases, in future the Tribunal is to commit the investigations to a commissioner from a different archdeaconry, so that examination of witnesses and other inquiries are never undertaken by the commissioner from the accused person's home district.

17. The cases of witches who confess to having relapsed are to be dealt with in the same manner as those of first offenders described above. Whether they confess before the Tribunal or to an inquisitorial secretary, the inquisitors are, whenever possible, to absolve them *ad cautelam* without consulting *la Suprema,* and under no circumstances are these cases to be delayed.

18. It has been ascertained that the clause relating to witches (*brujos y brujas*) is not incorporated in the Edict of Faith published by other inquisitorial tribunals. For the sake of uniformity this clause should be deleted from the Edict of Faith of the Logroño Inquisition.

19. All letters, instructions, and ordinances concerning the witch question that have in the course of time been received from *la Suprema* by the Tribunal are to be bound in chronological order into a volume, preceded by a copy of the new instructions, so that all this information will always be at hand should fresh cases of this nature arise, or if *la Suprema* should request to examine the papers.

20. All employees of the Tribunal in *el secreto* are to be made acquainted with the new instructions, a copy of which is to be included among the *cartas acordadas.* Each year, when the Tribunal forwards its *relación de causas,* a report is to be made on the progress of this matter, what results have been achieved, and what steps have been taken in individual cases.[41]

The proposals for legislative reform that Salazar presented to *la Suprema* before his return to Logroño were extraordinarily radical. It was now up to the members of the Council to resolve whether they would adopt his proposals, and to what extent they would align themselves with the Council's new *fiscal*, Dr. Becerra.

5. THE NEW INSTRUCTIONS

By the end of August the Council had completed its deliberations and on the 29th the new instructions were signed and dispatched to Logroño.[42] They were prefaced by a letter to the Tribunal disclaiming in courteous but definite terms all responsibility for the errors that had been perpetrated in this matter:

> The papers concerning witchcraft sent in by your Inquisition with the various observations and comments made in your submissions have been studied with all the care and attention which such a serious matter demands. As for the cases dealt with, especially those from the auto de fe held in 1610, we now realize how essential it was for us to have been able to examine with due care all the old and new orders, directives, and instructions relating to similar cases which reposed in the archives of your Tribunal. We also should have been informed of the intimidation and physical violence which relatives, justices, and other persons have employed in various places against a number of the defendants accused of belonging to this sect, not to mention the other defects which have come to light in the trials. Therefore, we fully recognize the serious obstacles to establishing the truth in a matter which has been so complex and difficult to prove. To avoid a similar confusion in the future, and to remedy past and present errors, we have conferred with the inquisitor general, the Illustrious Lord Cardinal, and we are sending you the following articles and clauses. In future cases of this kind you are to proceed as follows:[43]

Thereupon followed the new instructions for cases of witchcraft. The thirty-two clauses are set out in table 14. The letter to the Tribunal concluded with the statement that the Council was herewith returning all the papers relating to this matter that had been forwarded by the Tribunal. Then followed the names of seven of the councillors — Tapia, Valdés, Zapata, Trejo, Pimentel, Ramírez, and Mendoza (in the customary order of seniority, see table 13) — and finally the signature of

Table 14. The Instructions of the Council, 29 August 1614, Compared
With Salazar's Draft and Other Prototypes

Summary of the thirty-two clauses	Occurrence in earlier texts
1. If the witches confess to murdering children or adults, the inquisitors are to ascertain (a) whether the victims died at the time referred to by the witches, (b) whether the deaths might have been from natural causes, and (c) whether there were any marks on the bodies or any other unusual circumstances concerning the deaths.	The Council to the Tribunal, 21 Feb. 1526.
2. The inquisitors are also to seek to discover (a) how the witches got into the house and by what means they left it, and (b) whether they were admitted by anyone, or simply entered by way of an open door or window.	Idem.
3. Concerning the meetings described by the witches in their confessions, the inquisitors are to find out (a) whether such meetings really took place, (b) by whom the witches were summoned to the gatherings, and (c) whether there were any outside witnesses to the witches' sabbaths who saw them practicing their evil arts.	Cf. Instructions of *la Suprema* dated 11 Mar. 1609 (chap. 4.4, above).
4. If the witches confess to killing cattle the owners are to be asked (a) whether the animals did in fact die, (b) how they died, and (c) whether marks were found on them.	
5. If the witches confess to destroying crops, inquiries are to be made as to (a) whether the damage really was inflicted, and (b) whether at the time in question the fields had been exposed to hail, fog, gales, or frost which in themselves were sufficient to cause the loss of the crops.	The Council to the Tribunal, 21 Feb. 1526.
6. If the witches confess to summoning up gales or hailstorms it must be determined whether these took place at a season when this kind of weather is a normal occurrence.	Idem.
7. The inquisitors are to instruct the commissioners and the priests to explain to the people that damage to crops is sometimes the way God punishes us for our sins, and sometimes is a natural consequence of bad weather. These things occur everywhere whether there are witches present in the district or not, and it is therefore most undesirable for people to believe that the witches are always to blame.	The Council to the Tribunal, 27 Nov. 1538 (quoted in Salazar's Fourth Report, clause 6).
8. In any concrete instance the inquisitors are to make efforts to verify whether the witches really did go to the *aquelarre* or in fact did not set foot outside the door on the nights when they maintain they had been to the gatherings. This can be ascertained by questioning those who live in the same house as the witch.	Instructions of *la Suprema* of 14 Dec. 1526 (quoted in Salazar's Fourth Report, clause 3).

Table 14, *continued*

Summary of the thirty-two clauses	Occurrence in earlier texts
9. Whenever a person comes to make a confession of witchcraft or to denounce others, his entire statement is to be written down in the same words and style that he himself uses and with all the contradictions he may make. Afterwards he is to be expressly questioned regarding his motives for making the confession and whether he has been exposed to violence or coercion in this connection. If he testifies against others, attempts must be made to substantiate what he says and to discover whether there is enmity between him and those he accuses of witchcraft.	Salazar's Seventh Report, clause 11. Idem.
10. No commissioner is to institute inquiries into these matters, either on his own initiative or as the result of a denunciation. He is to confine himself to receiving statements from the delinquent or witness and to send this information on to the Tribunal, which will instruct him further.	Idem, clause 12.
11. When judging the confessions the inquisitors are to give particular attention to estimating whether any part of the confession can be proved by outside witnesses, or whether any of the things that the witch confesses have occurred outside the gatherings.	
12. Whenever a witch or a witness comes to revoke his statement the revocation is to be accepted and entered as a continuation of the previous testimony. The inquisitors are to receive these people compassionately so that they may be free of the general and widespread fear of punishment after revocation. The Tribunal is to see that the commissioners receive these orders with express instructions to follow them.	The Council to the Tribunal, 28 June 1611 (quoted above p.252). Salazar's Seventh Report clause 3.
13. In the future, in the directives that the Tribunal may send to the commissioners for the examination of witnesses or for other investigations regarding witches, the rules and general practice of the Holy Office must be strictly adhered to. By issuing the directives in the manner they have done to date the witnesses' statements have been made valueless. For the commissioners — without putting the preliminary questions required by the standing instructions — have been reading the entire contents of the directives to the witnesses, thus giving them the opportunity to mention things of which they knew nothing.	Idem, clause 13.
14. Any person presenting himself in order to confess is to be received with compassion. When he has completed the confession of his errors he is to be asked	

Table 14, *continued*

Summary of the thirty-two clauses	Occurrence in earlier texts
whether he has held firm to Devil-worship even when outside the gatherings. He is to be questioned further on whether he anointed himself with the intention of going to the sabbath or when awake practiced other forms of apostasy. The cases are then to be decided according to the following general rules: *Adults* (women over twelve and men over fourteen) are to be reconciled only if they confess to having worshipped the Devil when awake. But because of the doubt prevailing in these cases this is to be enforced without confiscation of goods. The rest, who confess to having taken part in the *aquelarres*, but who have not persisted in apostasy when awake, are to be absolved *ad cautelam*. *Children* (girls under twelve and boys under fourteen) are without exception to be absolved *ad cautelam*.	Idem.
Reconciliation and absolution may be administered by the commissioners so that there will be no need for the witches to present themselves to the Tribunal.	Idem.
15. No person is to be imprisoned or sentenced solely on the basis of the witches' denunciations. If the witches in their confessions testify against others, the evidence is to be tested by means of investigations as stipulated in the present instructions, and only after these have provided confirmation may proceedings be initiated against the accomplices.	Instructions of *la Suprema* dated 14 Dec. 1526 (quoted in Salazar's Fourth Report, clause 3).
16. As soon as the secular or ecclesiastical courts discover that any case they have opened involves witchcraft, they are to assign it to the Holy Office. In such cases the inquisitors are to ascertain whether the accused persons or witnesses have been exposed to torture and if so what forms of torture were employed. They are further to establish on what grounds the case was opened and the evidence on which the charge was based. For if the evidence should not fulfill the legal requirements, the witches' confessions must be viewed with extreme care.	Instructions of *la Suprema* dated 14 Dec. 1526.
17. Those hitherto reconciled who may relapse are to be absolved *ad cautelam*. However, this is not applicable to persons who are reconciled from now on and later relapse. In such cases the Tribunal is to consult *la Suprema* and remit the trial record with the inquisitors' vote, at the same time drawing the attention of the Council to the present instructions.	Salazar's Seventh Report, clause 17. Instructions of *la Suprema*, 14 Dec. 1526.
18. Since witchcraft is a difficult matter in which the judges may be easily deceived it is essential for all three inquisitors to be present when the Tribunal determines	Instructions of *la Suprema* dated 14 Dec. 1526;

Table 14, *continued*

Summary of the thirty-two clauses	Occurrence in earlier texts
what investigations are to be made, and that all three inquisitors record their votes when this type of case is to be remitted to *la Suprema*.	see Salazar's Seventh Report, clause 14.
19. All the evidence resulting from the present cases is to be suspended so that — unless fresh evidence materializes — no legal proceedings can be instituted on the basis of the old evidence, and the suspects are not to be debarred from holding posts in the Holy Office.	Salazar's Seventh Report, clause 5.
20. Should fresh evidence emerge against any person previously under suspicion, thus requiring the case to be reopened, the fresh evidence is to be added to the original testimony. And when the inquisitors vote on these cases they are to take both the old and the new evidence into consideration. If the inquisitors resolve to suspend the case they need not inform *la Suprema*. However, if they decide to continue the trial, the entire case along with the inquisitors' verdicts and a copy of the present instructions is to be remitted to the Council. However, until a decision is reached, the accused or suspected person is not to be regarded meanwhile as debarred from honorable office.	Idem, clause 14.

Idem, clause 15. |
| 21. In order to make completely clear for future reference the degree of faith which can be placed in the testimonies and confessions hitherto received, the Tribunal is to examine the records and make additions regarding the precise circumstances of each individual case. Thus every detail relating to violence, coercion, or other conditions which diminish the reliability of the evidence is to be appended. | |
| 22. The cases of those persons who died during the trial are to be suspended and there will be no possibility for the *fiscal* of the Tribunal to reopen them (i.e. against the descendants of the accused). This is to be entered in the records, with a note to the effect that the descendants are not debarred from honorable office. | Idem, clause 8. |
| 23. The special nature of witchcraft cases and in particular the circumstances prevailing during the present trials make it necessary for us to make the following stipulations: The *sambenitos* of those who were burned or reconciled at the auto de fe of 1610 are not to be displayed in the churches, and the Tribunal is not to confiscate the property that was then sequestered. This is to be entered into the records with a note to the effect that the trial does not debar the children of the accused from | Idem, clause 6.

Idem, clause 7. |

Table 14, *continued*

Summary of the thirty-two clauses	*Occurrence in earlier texts*

holding posts in the Holy Office or from any other honorable office.

24. For the same reason neither are those who received lesser penalties, or were absolved, to be debarred from any kind of honorable office, and this is to be entered in their records.

Idem, clause 9.

25. The Tribunal is to make a detailed list of the goods sequestrated and the fines paid in connection with these cases. A detailed memorandum is also to be drawn up showing all the costs incurred by the Tribunal in this matter. On the basis of this information *la Suprema* will decide what is to be done with the property received from the accused persons.

26. The inquisitors are to issue a prohibition stating that no persons are to threaten or coerce others into making confessions of witchcraft or into exposing any person to unpleasantness on account of confessions they may already have made to the Holy Office.

Instructions of *la Suprema* dated 26 Mar. 1611, clause 9.

Also, the Tribunal is to summon the commissioners one at a time and instruct them to see that it is made known that the Inquisition — and in particular *la Suprema* — disassociates itself from the violence and abuses that have been inflicted, and deeply regrets that the local authorities (*los alcaldes de los lugares*) have, without any legal authority, exposed the suspects to such abuses in order to make them confess and witness against others.

Salazar's Seventh Report, clause 10. Idem, clause 1.

Finally, the commissioners are to be instructed to inform the people that for the moment the Holy Office will allow the High Court of Navarra to punish the guilty, but that any person who commits such abuses in the future will be severely punished by the Holy Office.

27. The High Court is not to be prevented from examining these cases and punishing guilty persons. The Tribunal is not to intervene, neither are the inquisitors, to attempt to influence the High Court by private intercession.

The Council to the Tribunal (mentioned above, p. 222).

28. Priests and confessors are to be supplied with the following instructions through the commissioners, if necessary in writing: If it comes to the knowledge of the priests, through the confessional or in any other way, that a person has employed the above methods of violence or coercion, they are to warn the person concerned that it is his duty to inform the Inquisition of the matter and that it is likewise his duty to report others he

Table 14, *continued*

Summary of the thirty-two clauses	Occurrence in earlier texts
knows to have used these methods. The priests are to assure those concerned that the Inquisition will assume they have acted out of Christian zeal and that therefore no punishment will be meted out for acts of this nature committed to date. The persons concerned are further to be warned that they are bound to make their declarations, both in order to relieve their consciences, and so that those who have been exposed to scandal may have their good name and reputation restored to them. Finally, the priests are to admonish the persons concerned with the warning that they will incur the punishment of the Inquisition if they commit any similar offenses in the future.	Salazar's Seventh Report, clause 1.
29. When the Tribunal delivers these instructions to the commissioners they are to be notified verbally to proceed with moderation when dealing with this type of case, and to observe these instructions to the last detail.	
30. The priests and confessors are to be instructed through the commissioners not to deny the sacraments to persons suspected of witchcraft unless expressly ordered to do so by the Inquisition.	Idem, clause 4.
31. Public discussion of the witch question has produced very undesirable consequences. It has divided the people into factions and caused private investigations to be carried out by self-appointed persons who sought to confirm their personal opinions. The Tribunal is therefore to issue an order imposing silence on these discussions. At the same time it must be announced that the matter may only be raised if anyone wishes to make a confession or statement to the Inquisition, and that the person concerned both before and after the hearing is under the usual obligation to preserve secrecy.	Idem, clause 10.
32. All the letters, instructions, and ordinances received to date from *la Suprema* concerning these matters are to be collected and bound together in chronological order. A copy of the present instructions is to be placed at the beginning of the volume. Thus all this material will always be at hand for the guidance of the inquisitors in future cases of this kind.	Idem, clause 19.

García de Molina, secretary to the Council. A postscript states that "Dr. Rodrigo de Castro y Bobadilla was also present during the deliberations but as he was absent on the day when the signatures were appended to the instructions, his signature does not appear. This is also the case with Fray Francisco de Sosa, bishop of Osma."[44] The former was a member of the Council, while the latter was not, so presumably he had been specially summoned by the inquisitor general to assist the Council in reaching a decision.

If we compare the instructions with Salazar's draft we see that the Council adopted almost all of his suggestions. They omitted only four clauses (nos. 2, 16, 18, and 20).[45] The rest of Salazar's draft was incorporated directly and some of his clauses were adopted almost word for word. *La Suprema* also drew on a variety of older instructions,[46] and it made a number of amendments which in some cases were quite as radical as Salazar's suggestions (see for instance clauses 9 and 20). However, all these alterations and amendments did not constitute such a large proportion of the material as to obscure the fact that Salazar had played the chief role in reshaping the instructions for witchcraft cases.

6. THE END OF THE PERSECUTION

The letter from the Council did not reach Logroño before 18 September, by which date Valle presumably already had left for France.[47] On 20 September Salazar and the new inquisitor, Antonio de Aranda y Alarcón,[48] acknowledged receipt of the fresh instructions. As senior inquisitor it was Salazar who dictated the Tribunal's letter and it therefore came to reflect his sense of elation:

> We are putting the instructions into operation immediately and observing them to the last detail. . . . With the Lord's aid we hope that this decision will be to the benefit of God's cause, to the relief of the whole of this troubled region, and to general confidence both throughout the district and within the walls of the Tribunal.[49]

One of the first tasks undertaken by the two inquisitors was doubtless to interview the commissioners — one by one, in order, as stipulated in the instructions, not to arouse too much notice.[50] It must have been a welcome duty to Salazar to instruct Lorenzo de Hualde from Vera, Felipe Díaz from Maestu, and Martín López from Larrea on how they were to act in the future. All the commissioners were given a copy of those parts of the instructions concerning them.[51]

The two inquisitors must also have lost no time in composing the edict the instructions required them to issue. "The Edict of Silence," as Salazar calls it in a report of 1617,[52] is now known only from a copy of the 1620s, but this is obviously a reprint of an earlier document issued shortly after the great witchcraft case had been decided. The edict begins with the usual formula (see figure 21): "We the apostolic inquisitors combating the heretical corruption throughout the whole kingdom of Navarra..." and continues thus:

> On the basis of the trial and the cases we have conducted in recent years against the witch sect in various parts of our district we have acquired great experience of the grave distortions of the truth which constantly impeded the investigations. Thus the *confitente* [witches] have been exposed to threats, terror, and abuses, as was also the case with those suspected of being witches. The public discussion [of the witch problem] and the secret coercion [used to make people confess] — not to mention the veritable wrangling that has taken place — have all contributed to confuse this affair. Therefore we now command that all concerned... shall cease the above-mentioned threats, coercion, and discussions, so that all may feel free to come to us — and only to us, or to one of the commissioners of the Holy Office — with the problems they may have in this connection. And this order stands regardless of whether one is a close relative of the witch, or considers that one has oneself been exposed to witchcraft.... Any person failing to comply with these orders will incur the severest penalties of the law for his disobedience, according to the degree of guilt and the details established in his particular case. Issued at the Holy Office of Logroño, the   162 [Date not filled in].[53]

In the report of 1617 Salazar also mentioned that a "special ruling" had been drawn up for the commissioners' examination of delinquents and witnesses in witchcraft cases.[54] This directive was presumably identical with a printed instruction of which two copies are extant. It is a four-page document bearing no indication of place, year, or printer (but to judge from the print it dates from the first half of the seventeenth century, see figure 22).[55] The directive is divided into fourteen clauses under the title "Instructions to be followed by the commissioners of the Holy Office when hearing confessions and statements in connection with crimes of witchcraft."[56] The greater part of the contents is derived from *la Suprema*'s instructions of 29 August 1614, and this is proof that the document cannot be of an earlier date.[57]

$\bar{J}^r$

1620

NOS LOS INQVISIDORES APOSTOLICOS contra la Heretica Prauedad y Apoſtaſia, en todo el Reyno de Naua-rra, Obiſpado de Calahorra, y la Calçada, Condado, y Señorio de Vizcaya, cō la Prouincia de Guipuzcoa, cō toda la tierra, y juriſdicion q̃ cae en el Arçobiſpado de Burgos de los montes de Oca a eſta parte, y ſu diſtriĉto &c. Por quanto de la proſecucion, y cauſſas q̃ ocurrieron de la ſeĉta de Brujos eſtos años paſſados en diuerſas partes de eſte diſtriĉto, ſacamos larga experiencia de los graues, y continuos inconuinientes que reciuia la verdad, y verificacion de ella que buſcamos, aſsi de las amenazas, temores, o violēcias hechas a los confi-tentes, o notados de tales culpas, como de las diſputas inducimentos, y otras platicas manuales, y deſordenadas de lo miſmo, ſegun que alpreſe nte tambien ſomos imformados: y recelamos q̃ ocurren en eſſa   y otras partes de ſu comarca, de tal manera que muchas perſonas ſocolor, y celo de amiſtad, o paren-teſco de los dichos notados, o de las perſonas, o criaturas pequeñas q̃ en ello tienten damnificados, an procurado, y diſpueſto que manifieſten en publico como effeĉtiuamente lo han hecho las ocaſsiones, y culpas de ſi, y de otros ter-ceros q̃ en eſtas ocaſiones vanamente ſe han eſparcido, y diuulgado. Para cuyo remedio, y que al ſanĉto Officio, y ſus miniſtros les quede toda libre, y de ſem-baraçada facultad de proceder a la aberiguacion, caſtigo, y remedio conuini-ente al ſeruicio de nueſtro Señor, y deſpacho de la Iuſticia. Por la preſéte exor-tamos, y mandamos a todas, y qualeſquier perſonas de qualquier eſtado, y con dicion que ſean que ſe abſtengan, y retraygan cada vno reſpetiuamente de ſu parte de las dichas a menazas, e inducimentos publicidad, o conferiencias re-feridas y q̃ con eſſo dexen libre facultad a cada vno de acudir a conſultar, o pe-dir el remedio conuiniente ſolo á nos, y a los Miniſtros, o Comiſſarios de eſte Sanĉto Officio en lo que fuere ſu conocimiento, ſin embargo de que por conjunto, o damnificado ſe pretenda tener, o téga por intereſſado para que aſsi tambien mejor ſeguarde, el ſecreto, y decoro en eſte caſſo que ſuele, y deue guardarſe en los de ma que ſon de la punicion, y caſtigo del Sanĉto Officio Lo qual aſsi hagan, y cumplan ſopena de que ſera caſtigada ſu inobediēcia, y tran-greſsiō por todo rigor de derecho conforme a la culpa y circūſtācias della que ſe verificare en cada vno. Dada en el Sāĉto Officio de la Inquiſiciō de Logroño a   dias de   de mil y ley ſcientos y veynte y

Figure 21.   The Edict of Silence, signed by Salazar and two other inquisitors.

INSTRVCCION QVEHAN
DE GVARDAR LOS COMISSARIOS DEL SANTO
Oficio enlas declaraciones, y teſtificaciones que recibieren
tocantes al crimen de Brugeria.

1   **L**O PRIMERO, Que las perſonas que vinieren de ſu volũtad a declarar, ô fueren llamados en los caſos neceſſarios, auiendo hecho el juramento acoſtũmbrado conforme a la Inſtrucciõ de Molde que ſe les dio con los titulos de Comiſſarios. Y declarando en voz ante el Notario del Santo Oficio, todo lo que tuuieren que dezir. Y hecho ſe muy capaz dello,ſe eſcriuira muy puntualmente,con el eſtilo,lenguage y contradiciones que lo dixeren ,preguntandoles que les ha mouido ha venir ha hazer la declaricion, y ſi para ello han ſido perſuadidas, atemori zadas, o forçadas las tales perſonas, y por quien : y eſcriuiendo puntualmente lo que reſpondieren.

2   Y auiendo dicho , que ayan ydo y halladoſe preſentes a las juntas , y aquelarres de las bruxas, declaren primero el principio que tuuieron para yr, quanto ha, y como fueron la primera vez, y deſpues. Y ſi para ello fueron hablados primero, por quien, y en que tiempo y ocaſion, y a que ora, antes,o deſpues de acoſtarſe, o auiendoſe ya començado a dormir, o eſtando deſpiertas. Y ſi ſe les pidio primero ſu conſentimiento en aquella,o otra ocaſion antes, y todo lo que en razon de ello paſsò. Y ſi para yr a las dichas juntas y aquelarres,ſe vntaron,como,con que,y donde, y con que intencion, ſi para yr corporalmente , o para dormirſe. Y ſi ay diferencia del vnto para yr,ò para hazer maleficios,y con ꝗ coſas, y ceſt†   mo:

Figure 22.   Front page of the special ruling for the commissioners in future witchcraft cases. Undated four-page print.

While there exists some uncertainty as to *when* the commissioners were summoned, *when* the Edict of Silence was issued, and *when* the directive for the examination of witnesses was printed, we know exactly when the Tribunal complied with *la Suprema*'s orders to present accounts of all the costs incurred in connection with the witchcraft case (see table 14, clause 25). This was done immediately on receipt of the Council's letter. By 27 September Salazar and Aranda had already dispatched the account with a long letter.[58] The statement showed that when the expenses of the prisoners' subsistence, the auto de fe, and the two journeys of visitation were totalled, the Tribunal had spent in all 39,460 *reales*. The two inquisitors explained in their letter that by selling the witches' confiscated goods (see beginning of chapter 11.B.4) they had acquired 9,837½ *reales*. The deficit of the Tribunal had thus been reduced to 29,623 *reales* and of this 19,276 *reales* were still owed by the prisoners who had not yet paid for their stay in prison.[59]

However, it was the opinion of the inquisitors that it would be wrong to attempt to recover this sum, considerable though it was:

> These poor mountain people of Navarra — who are still suffering from the persecution and chastisement they have been subjected to — would be alarmed and distressed if we now forced them to produce what they neither have nor are in a capacity to pay. It thus seems preferable to apply the mercy that Your Eminence may be inclined to show them.[60]

But here the inquisitor general did not comply with Salazar's suggestion; justice was one thing and bills quite another. On 6 October the Council wrote back to the Tribunal stressing that there could be no question of releasing the witches from their obligation to pay for their subsistence while in prison. Therefore by means of courteous application the Tribunal was to ensure that all those with means paid what they owed.[61]

Shortly after the Tribunal had received this letter Salazar was on his way to Madrid. The inquisitor general had selected him for a new mission; he was to inspect the Court of Confiscations at the Inquisition of Granada. After carrying out investigations lasting for almost two years, Salazar was finally able to reveal that the treasurer to the Tribunal had embezzled several hundred thousand *reales*.[62]

So it was that when Valle returned from his health cure in November 1614 he found himself alone with the new inquisitor and with the new instructions for witchcraft cases. Some remarks that he appended to a copy of the instructions witness to the disappointment he felt over the resolutions of *la Suprema.* For instance, he commented on Instruction 12, relating to *revocantes,* that witches who had made false revocations ought also to be permitted to reaffirm their first confessions. He further commented on Instruction 26, which treats of the abuses to which the suspects had been subjected, that the Inquisition should also regret the fact that persons who were witches and who wished to report themselves had been exposed to violence and coercion and prevented from making their confessions.[63]

But if Valle had been rendered powerless to continue his campaign, he was still able to act obstructively. He did not for instance hasten to put the new instructions into operation. It had been stipulated that those of the commissioners who were unable to get to Logroño were to be sent a copy of the instructions, but more than a year went by before such an important commissioner as the abbot of Urdax received his copy. Some time later, on 16 January 1616, Fray León de Araníbar wrote enthusiastically to Valle to acknowledge the receipt of the instructions and their effect. It was now seven years since Urdax and Zugarramurdi had been ravaged by the witch epidemic. Fray León wrote:

> I cannot describe to Your Eminence the momentous impact the instructions have had. They have quietened the consciences and souls of so many persons who, on account of violence, pressure, or coercion, had confessed to being witches and had incriminated many others. The instructions have also served to resolve the state of irresolution to which the priests and confessors had been reduced over this problem. For many of these witches went to them with tears and grief in order to revoke their confessions, but on account of the fear they have always lived in of being punished, it was quite impossible for the confessors to persuade these people to report themselves to the agents of the Holy Office and repeat their statements there.
>
> I am herewith forwarding Your Eminence twenty-six revocations and I am of the opinion that in the future so many will come forward to retract their confessions that we shall be obliged to question whether they are all telling the truth. For the present I will request Your Eminence to inform me whether we are also to receive revocations from all the

witches who are minors, or from what age upwards they should be accepted.[64]

Doubtless Valle was unable to share Fray León's enthusiasm. The Tribunal had already received over a hundred revocations.[65] On the other hand he could not ignore *la Suprema*'s new instructions. He therefore chose the third possibility, that of simply ignoring Fray León's letter.

Fray León's report covered the development of events in the Baztán Valley only, but the report that Salazar sent to *la Suprema* at the beginning of 1617 confirms that there was a similar situation in the rest of Navarra. In it he wrote that the eighteen hundred witches and four thousand suspects, as well as all their dependents and the local authorities, were now living "in such a state of peace and understanding . . . that it seems utterly incredible. No one," continued Salazar, "could have imagined that with the imposition of silence on the witch question it would have been possible to combat the craze to such an extent that today it is as if the problem had never existed."[66]

7. THE FATE OF THE INVOLVED

The sources do not reveal very much about the subsequent fate of María de Jureteguía and the other "witches" who survived the auto de fe. They were perhaps among the twenty-six *revocantes* who went to Fray León at Urdax;[67] perhaps they took their false confessions with them to the grave. We possess more detailed accounts only for the two witch ecclesiastics. On 4 November 1613 the priest Juan de la Borda was released from the monastery at San Millán where he had been confined since the auto de fe.[68] He then went immediately to Madrid to avail himself of the inquisitor general's dispensation, in order that he could resume his ministry.[69] The monk Fray Pedro de Arburu, who had been placed in custody at the Premonstratensian monastery at Miranda de Ebro, was not released until September 1614.[70] He straightway returned to the monastery at Urdax which some time later paid his debt of 537 *reales* to the Tribunal.[71] Five years later, when the Logroño Inquisition was undergoing inspection, the priest and the monk were both questioned regarding certain personal possessions that they had lost during their period of detention in the secret prison of the Tribunal. The questioning took place at Urdax and Elizondo, respectively, and sought to establish whether the jailer Juan Martínez had purloined the articles. It is not necessary to dwell upon the details of the priest's quilt valued at five ducats and the monk's "pillow with two pillow-slips, worth at least two ducats," to demonstrate that the two "priest witches" had reestablished their reputation. We now find mention of Juan de la Borda as priest at a conventual church in the neighborhood of the Velate Pass — the pass that Valle rode across in 1609 in order to get to Zugarramurdi. Pedro de Arburu on the other hand had remained a friar at the monastery at Urdax.[72]

We do not possess much information regarding what happened afterwards to the district commissioners, but there are a few details relating to three of those who played a considerable part in the witch persecution. It would seem that Fray León died shortly after writing his letter acknowledging the new instructions. Fray Josef de Elizondo, who was second-in-command at the monastery and who had taken part in the preaching crusade and accompanied Salazar on his journey of visitation, was promoted to abbot and became a member of the parliament of Navarra, and he took over Fray León's post of inquisitorial commissioner at Logroño.[73] Young Lorenzo de Hualde, the inquisitorial commissioner at Vera, soon afterwards lost his influential ally in the Pays de Labourd, for shortly after the witch persecution the lord of Urtubie was deprived of the patronage of the livings of Vera and Alzate.[74] But Hualde retained his post, and the villagers of Vera were obliged to resign themselves to his presence for over thirty years more, for he did not die until the middle of the century.[75]

The bishop of Pamplona — and later of Sigüenza — Antonio Venegas de Figueroa, died on 8 October 1614.[76] Thus he barely survived to experience the victory of "the witches' party" of which he had been the uncrowned leader. On the other hand another of the witches' defenders, the Jesuit Solarte, lived on for many years after the issuing of the new instructions,[77] but it is an open question as to whether he ever came to know the effects of his journey to Las Cinco Villas. As will be recalled, all that was revealed of the decision of *la Suprema* was what was published in "the Edict of Silence"; the rest was retained within the closed circle of the Inquisition.

The *fiscal* to the Tribunal, Doctor Isidoro de San Vicente, led a somewhat unsettled life following his stay at Logroño. After having been an inquisitor on Mallorca he went to Zaragoza and later to Galicia, where he stayed from 1620 to 1622.[78] At the end of the 1620s he returned to Logroño, where he soon became the senior inquisitor.[79] According to a contemporary source San Vicente was unpopular wherever he happened to be and apparently was even "sacked" from several inquisitions.[80] However, this did not prevent him from ending up as a member of *la Suprema*. As an old man San Vicente wrote a manual for inquisitors which, judging from the number of copies which are still extant, was widely employed.[81] One chapter in the manual deals with witchcraft trials, and here San Vicente admits the difficult nature of the subject, while at the same time firmly asserting the underlying reality behind the witches' confessions.[82]

The three inquisitors who had fought the battle of the witches did not have much contact with each other after 1614. Becerra continued in his post as *fiscal* to *la Suprema* and in 1617 was promoted to councillor of the Inquisition.[83] Before his death in 1619[84] he compiled a lengthy report on counterfeiters.[85] Valle remained at the Tribunal of Logroño with the new inquisitor Aranda. He continued to be troubled by gallstones and later by a kidney complaint. In the spring of 1615 *la Suprema* granted Valle a further leave period in order that he could again visit the health spa in France, and at the same time the visitation for that year was cancelled, thus allowing Aranda to remain at the Tribunal to deal with matters there.[86] The following summer Aranda went on visitation,[87] so when Salazar returned from Granada in July he found himself alone with Valle; but they had only a short time together for by August, Valle, at the age of sixty-three a sick and bitter man, was dead.[88]

Salazar found the new inquisitors at Logroño equally incompatible.[89] This was no doubt the reason for his transfer in 1618, much against his will, to the Inquisition at Murcia in southeast Spain.[90] At the official inspection at Logroño the following year the staff was questioned in the customary manner and asked whether the inquisitors had worked harmoniously together. All the witnesses answered with one voice that there had previously been numerous quarrels, but that after Salazar had left for Murcia the inquisitors and their subordinates had been in complete agreement.[91] On 16 March 1619 Salazar was sent to the tribunal at Valencia "on account of the unrest in this inquisition in connection with what is described as the events of 3 March," as Salazar wrote in his autobiography.[92] Thus it seems that *la Suprema* once again made use of his talents. In 1622 Salazar returned to the Tribunal at Logroño as senior inquisitor;[93] in 1628 he became *fiscal* to the Council of the Inquisition and in 1631 a member of *la Suprema*.[94] In this capacity he was present at the great general auto de fe which was held in the Plaza Mayor in Madrid in 1632.[95] Salazar's idealism did not grow dull with passing time. Even in the lofty surroundings of the Council he continued to express his opinions unreservedly. Thus in 1632 he sharply criticized the inquisitor general for promising individuals posts before they were vacated.[96] And the following year, when according to royal ordinance *la Suprema* was divided into two separate chambers, Salazar composed a report to Philip IV. In it he detailed, with his usual frankness, all the shortcomings exhibited during the first two months of existence of the new system.[97] The king seems to have taken heed of the criticism, for the two-chamber system proved to be only a brief episode in the long history of *la Suprema*.

Salazar died in 1635 at the age of seventy-one, a member of *la Suprema* and a canon of the Jaén cathedral. In the same year, Lope de Vega, the duke of Lerma, and other distinguished persons died.[98] Salazar's name was soon forgotten. Not until the archives of the Inquisition were made available for research in the nineteenth century and Lea discovered Salazar's papers did his efforts as "the witches' advocate" become generally known.[99] The few pages dedicated to him in Lea's great work on the Spanish Inquisition were enough to gain him world repute, and enough to inspire Charles Williams in 1941 to dedicate his book *Witchcraft* "to the immortal memory of Alonso de Salazar Frías."[100]

EPILOGUE

EA RIGHTLY DESCRIBES SALAZAR'S visitation of 1611 as "the turning point in the history of Spanish witchcraft." A leitmotiv in the debate on witch belief that was carried on in the Spanish Inquisition during the sixteenth century had been the question of whether to employ the chastisement of fire or the mercy of the Edict of Grace. Salazar saw how the witches materialized under the glaring spotlight of publicity, and vanished when no interest was shown in them. He realized that it was neither the Edict of Grace nor punishment that was required, but something entirely different: discretion.

During the years succeeding 1614 and up to the end of the 1620s we can follow Salazar and the new inquisitors at Logroño in their efforts to make the secular judges continue to respect the Inquisition's ancient jurisdiction over witchcraft cases — after it had become clear to everyone that the witches were no longer receiving the severe punishment which people thought they deserved. Peace still continued to reign in northern Navarra, but other regions soon became the scene of large-scale witch persecutions. Remarkably enough these took place in areas that had escaped the persecutions carried out from 1609 until 1611. Thus in the summer of 1616 a witch epidemic erupted in northern Vizcaya in the neighborhood of Bilbao. The Tribunal immediately dispatched "the Edict of Silence" for publication there, but the patience of the populace and the secular authorities was short-lived. Through the influence of the Council of Castilla they managed to have a royal commission issued to the High Court judge (*el corregidor*) of Vizcaya, which authorized him to institute proceedings against witches without the interposition of the Inquisition. In

two years he prepared no less than 289 witch cases for sentencing. However, thanks to the intervention of Salazar the
campaign in Vizcaya did not end in mass burnings. The king's
commission was withdrawn, the witches were absolved, and
the 289 trial records were transferred to the Tribunal, which
suspended all the cases. Similar epidemics ravaged Guipúzcoa
and the province of Burgos, where the authorities at Pancorvo
succeeded in burning eight witches in 1621.

This development caused *la Suprema* to consider the witch
problem once again. In 1623 Salazar compiled a copious report
covering all aspects of the witch problem since 1614. One of the
main points in the report was, to use Salazar's own words,
"the tragedy at Pancorvo." The trial records had been forwarded to the Tribunal for examination but as the Council had
instructed the inquisitors not to intervene they had returned
the records, and eleven days later the witches had been
burned. Together with Salazar's report a great deal of the
documentation from 1614 was forwarded to *la Suprema*, and
this time the jurisdiction of the Inquisition in witch cases seems
to have been definitively established.

The large-scale persecutions in the Basque provinces at the
beginning of the seventeenth century were paralleled in other
regions of northern Spain where witch belief was firmly en-
trenched and the authorities supported the populace and
strove energetically to continue burning witches. In the northwest, in Galicia, a witch-hunt was in process in 1611, and in
the 1620s a judge at Cangas condemned several witches to the
stake. In both cases the Inquisition intervened and ensured
that the witches escaped with light sentences. In the northeast,
in Cataluña, the secular authorities hanged more than three
hundred witches between 1616 and 1619, but here as well the
persecutions were halted by the Holy Office demanding the
restoration of its jurisdiction in these cases. Thus there are
clear indications that after pursuing a moderate "witch policy"
in the sixteenth century, with the Logroño auto de fe Spain
was at the point of joining forces with the rest of Europe. If *la
Suprema* had chosen to disregard Salazar and align itself with
Becerra and Valle, the consequences would have defied
imagination.

The instructions of 1614 are particularly admirable when
seen in the light of the fact that they were the expression of a
skepticism felt by only a minority of Spanish bureaucrats.

Thus until well into the seventeenth century many inquisitors considered that witches ought to be burned. It was largely owing to the centralized method of government of the Inquisition and the authority of *la Suprema* that it was possible to implement a decision that was to a great extent unpopular and thus to bring about the suspension of witch burning about a century before the remainder of Europe changed its policy.

But it was only in the suspension of the burnings that Spain took the lead. The new instructions did not abolish witch trials; rather the trials increased considerably throughout the Spanish Empire, and there were several instances of tribunals attempting to send a witch to the stake, but each time the sentence was mitigated by *la Suprema*. Spain was to continue holding witch trials long after this type of case had been abandoned by all other European courts. As late as 1791 the Inquisition in Barcelona conducted a case against a woman who confessed to having pledged herself to the Devil and taken part in witches' sabbaths. Some of the intellectual premises retained their hold into the nineteenth century, for in 1813 witch belief was expressed in the parliament of Cádiz by one of the deputies, the learned Fray Maestro Alvarado.

By concentrating upon the Logroño trial and the events that led to the instructions of 1614 it has been necessary to leave a number of questions out of consideration. Thus it would be interesting to subject the role of *la Suprema* to closer examination. The Council of the Inquisition dealt with witch cases from other tribunals than the one at Logroño, and the marked caution which characterized the Council's methods rested on the experiences they had accumulated throughout the sixteenth century. It would also be advantageous to study in closer detail the way in which belief in witchcraft was disseminated in Spain. There is much to indicate that there was never any persecution of witches in places lacking popular witch belief. The fact that southern Spain was free from witches provided *la Suprema* with a basis for comparison and must undoubtedly have contributed to a great extent to the formation of the skeptical attitude toward the persecutions in northern Spain. I believe this geographical factor to have been far more decisive than the assertion, so frequently advanced, that the Spanish Inquisition was so occupied in dealing with the Jews and the Moors that it could not afford to spend much time on the witches.

It would also have been interesting to examine the intellectual background of Salazar. In his consistent application of the inductive method, his strict insistence on empiricism, and his refusal to rely on older authorities, Salazar was far ahead of his time. His revolutionary documents, which ought to have been published three and a half centuries ago to the benefit of the whole western world, contain not only the key to an understanding of the European witch craze, but also give Salazar a place in the history of ideas as an early empiricist.

It is also to be hoped that some psychologist or psychiatrist will look more closely into the phenomenon of the dream epidemic which I have diagnosed as the main reason for the outbreak of the witch craze described in the present study. The *aquelarre*-dreams were a typical example of what is known to modern psychology as "stereotyped" dreams. These are inevitably the result of some form of indoctrination and are mostly characterized by the clear and distinct impressions recalled by individuals when awake. It is clear that the dream epidemic in the mountains of Navarra resulted from mass suggestion evoked by the rumors from France, the sermons of the preachers, and the spectacular auto de fe at Logroño, witnessed by thirty thousand people. We can follow the epidemic step by step and see how all develops according to the fundamental laws of communication science. I do not know whether dream epidemics have been studied elsewhere, but there is no doubt that the phenomenon is a psychological reality. We do not need to go outside the history of witchcraft to find parallels to the Basque pattern. Both in southern France and Germany and in northern Sweden we find mass trials with dreaming "child witches" as main accusers. Here indeed lies an unexplored field awaiting comparative or still better interdisciplinary study.

In spite of the research that remains to be done, I still hope with the present study to have made my modest contribution to the general study of European witchcraft. Some of the conclusions which Salazar, the bishop of Pamplona, and others reached through sober-minded investigations invite hypotheses which might prove to be applicable not only to Spain, but to large areas of the European continent:

Firstly, that the belief in witchcraft in its theological form — in witches as a sectarian organization practicing the complete inversion of Christianity, including pacts and fornication with the Devil — was so irrelevant to the functional popular belief in witches that it did not become a permanent tradition, but was forgotten (or became anecdotal history) in the intervals between the great witchcraft epidemics, and that people therefore had to be instructed through preachers or secular agitators before a new mass persecution could be initiated.

Secondly, that the accounts of a hallucinogenic witches' salve represent an old pseudo-scientific attempt to give the witch phenomenon a rational explanation, and that the many sixteenth- and seventeenth-century reports of experiments carried out on witches in order to obtain proofs of the dream-inducing effects of their "flying ointments" could not bear a critical re-examination.

Thirdly, that the persecution of witches was often instigated by people who gained economic or social advantage from them. They saw in zealous Christian officials, such as judges, inquisitors, and bishops, an excellent instrument with which to forward their decidedly wordly interests.

I believe that with the present study I have been able to demonstrate that witchcraft and witch craze are two different phenomena and that in the future we will have to distinguish between them in order to reach a better understanding of the dynamics of witch-hunting. The two are related to each other, but the general idea that one is just a reinforced form of the other is an unacceptable simplification. The witch craze is an explosive amplification caused by a temporary syncretism of the witch beliefs of the common people with those of the more specialized or educated classes. In Europe we could say that we have the traditional witchcraft of the villages and the demonological witchcraft theories of the intellectuals. The home of the learned tradition was in the studies of theologians and jurists; as long as it stayed there it was harmless. The danger appeared when the priest from the pulpit or the judge in court tried to apply learned theory to the concrete cases which occurred in daily life. It was in those situations that the potential for a new pattern of witchcraft arose — that dangerous creation which would take both high and low by surprise, the "witch craze." Because of its monstrous form it could only exist over a shorter period, as it would otherwise lead to the complete breakdown of society. Table 15 sums up the findings of our present study and gives an outline of how the two patterns can be distinguished. These could be developed

Table 15. Materials for a Dynamic Theory of Witchcraft

Aspect	*Witchcraft*	*Witch craze*
Means of transmission	Long-term oral tradition	Momentary propaganda, rumors
Social function	Part of cognitive system	Disfunctional
	Part of moral system Safety-valve for non-accepted social aggression	Disfunctional Same, but in explosive form which tears society into pieces
Mythological superstructure	Scanty and un-systematic	Abundant and elaborated
Harm to individuals by witchcraft (*maleficium*)	Important (a condition for initiat-ing a trial)	Unimportant
Connection or compact with the Devil	Unimportant	Important (the accusations concentrated on this point)
Tradition at local level	Uninterrupted (continuous)	Periodic (discontinuous)
Candidates for the witch role	Individuals who do not fit into the community: old people, widows, beggars	All sorts of people, especially children and young people
Percentage of the local population	One or two people in each village	Up to half of the population
Geographical areas	Europe (with some exceptions as e.g. southern Spain), Africa, Colonial America	Germany, eastern France, Savoy, the Pyrenees, the Low Countries, and northern Sweden
Parallels in modern society and twentieth-century history	Discrimination against deviants ("madmen," "homosexuals," "communists," revolutionists"), mobbing in the schools	The persecution of Jews in Nazi Germany, and . . .

further into what might be termed a dynamic theory of witch-craft.

To be sure, these considerations are all based on the assumption that Margaret Murray's theory of the existence of an organized witch cult has no basis in fact whatsoever. She still has a good many adherents — due perhaps to the fact that her theory is the most exciting one available. However, no stronger argument can be presented against the Murray school than the investigations of Salazar, which clearly show that his nearly two thousand witches were not members of any secret confederation, who, under cover of darkness, gathered in out-of-the-way places to perform heathen rituals.

Books about witches have a strange appeal for us, perhaps because there is still such an aura of mystery about the subject. I only hope that the present study of Salazar and the witches may not seem at all "exciting," but that it may promote the understanding that belief in witchcraft is an example of myth-making about socially marginal groups and the tragic consequences for their members. The peculiarity of the witch classification is that the group is fictitious, nobody belongs to it; but individuals who deviate from the norms of their society are the first to be supposed to be members of this secret confederation, where all virtues of the society are inverted. The European witch craze is now history, but in principle it continues to repeat itself. Indeed, a characteristic of this kind of myth-making is that it continually returns in a new and plausible disguise. We shall always need men with courage enough to tear away the mask, men of integrity — like Salazar.

WITCH LIST
Introduction: Witches Examined by the Inquisition of Logroño, 1609-1614

LMOST 2,000 WITCHES WERE EXAMINED IN the course of the proceedings; 31 were sentenced at the auto de fe (see table 5, above), 65 were reconciled in the Tribunal by virtue of the Edict of Grace, and 6 were reconciled or absolved after the expiration of the period of grace. To these 102 trials came the cases of all those who never passed through the court room of the Tribunal at Logroño, but who were dealt with on the journeys of visitation. Some 50 cases were the result of Inquisitor Valle's witch-hunt in the Pyrenees in 1609 (see chapter 7, above), and a further 1,802 cases were dispatched when his colleague Salazar visited the witches two years later with the Edict of Grace (see chapter 11, above). Except for a small part of Salazar's visitation book all the original records are missing. But thanks to a large body of secondary materials which have come down to us in the form of references, abstracts, and copies of entire files, the original documentation can be reconstructed to such a point of perfection that we can maintain that with the exception of Valle's visitation, where we do not know the exact outcome, the number of cases listed below is complete.[a] If new inquisitorial documentation should turn up, as happened a few years ago with the *Pamplona Manuscript,* this will only help us to fill in names and details which are still lacking.

Names of the accused appear in the original spelling except for a slight normalization according to modern Spanish orthography. Christian names have been modernized, as have been the names of villages. When a name, an age, or a village appears in italics it means that this information is found only in the *Pamplona Manuscript* (hereafter abbreviated PMS). After the name of each village follows the abbreviated name of its province: *Navarra*, *Guipúzcoa*, Pays de *Labourd*, *Logroño*, *Alava*, and *Burgos*.

Besides functioning as a survey of all the witchcraft cases, the list serves several other purposes: It can be used as a concordance to the many reports the inquisitors left behind them, in which the witches are listed under different numbers; parts 2 and 3, the reconstruction of Valle's and Salazar's visitation books, serve as tables of contents for these two manuscripts given so much discussion in the preceding chapters and notes; finally our list attempts to identify all the individuals who were tried on more than one occasion — for example first on the visitation of Valle and later in the Tribunal, or first in the Tribunal and later on the visitation of Salazar (see the cross references under "Miscellaneous" in the tables). As mentioned, the list is not an enumeration of persons, but of cases. However, if we subtract the 40[b] retrials from the total of 1,948[c], we can establish the total number of persons involved in this mass trial at 1,908.

1. THE 102 WITCHES TRIED IN THE TRIBUNAL AT LOGROÑO, 1609-1614

Sources for part 1: *First Report of the Auto de fe, Second Report of the Auto de fe,* and *Third Report of the Auto de fe* (here abbreviated *1st, 2nd,* and *3rd Report*); the *Pamplona Manuscript* (abbr. *PMS*), especially the register of 84 witches reconciled at Logroño (abbr. *PMS List A*), reproduced in IDOATE *Documento* pp. 177-180 (for convenience, reference is made here to the pages in Idoate's edition); the list of "Witches reconciled and absolved by the Edict of Grace" (*Rdo 15-76c*) contained in the *Relación de causas 1610/11*; and the *Relación de causas 1613/14* (abbr. *Rel. 1613/14*).

---

a. There are strictly speaking three more exceptions. First, the witches who died in the Tribunal's prison leaving their trials unfinished (see the discussion in chapter 11 n. 111, below). Secondly, those witches whose confessions Salazar brought with him when he set out from Logroño but whose files were returned to the Tribunal after his journey, because these people had failed to appear during the visitation. There was a total of 338 confessions (117 from males over age 14 and females over 12; the rest from child witches), but half of them did not present themselves to Salazar to be reconciled or absolved (see chapter 11 n. 13, below). Thirdly, the 81 *revocantes* listed below in the survey of *Volume "F"* do not include those persons who retracted their confessions after the expiration of the period of grace (see near end of chapter 13.6, above). Finally it should be noted that the list does not include all the secular witch trials conducted by more or less local authorities.

b. For the first 21 see below, case nos. 103-108, 452, 457, 462-465, 493-501; the remaining 19 retrials are found only once in the Witch List, see case nos. 502-520, below. They were, however, counted twice in the statistics of Salazar's journey of visitation (see the note to table 10 in chapter 11.C.7, above, and cf. the table of the 19 files in chapter 11 n. 49, below).

c. The total of 1,948 is made up of 102 plus 50 plus 1,802 *minus* 6, the last figure being the cases of the 6 *relapsos*. Salazar counted them twice in his statistics (see table 10, above), but in contrast to the other instances of retrials it appears that the *relapsos* never had more than one file each and that these remained in their original places in the visitation book (see e.g. case nos. 223 and 241) without being removed to form part of another series as was the case with the files of the *revocantes*. For the sake of clarity in my reconstruction of Salazar's visitation book (Witch List part 3, below) it seemed therefore convenient to subtract these six cases in advance from Salazar's statistics.

Cases 1-31. The 31 People Sentenced in the
Auto de Fe of 7 and 8 Nov. 1610

Case No.	Imprisoned[a]	Name, age, village, province	Number in:		
			1st&2nd Reports	3rd Report	PMS List A
1	[14]-2-09	Graciana de Barrenechea, 80, Zugarramurdi, Na	1	32	7
2	''	Miguel de Goiburu, 66, Zugarramurdi, Na	2	33	8
3	''	Estevanía de Yriarte, 36, Zugarramurdi, Na	3	34	5
4	''	María de Yriarte, 40, Zugarramurdi, Na	4	35	6
5	27-1-09	Estevanía de Navarcorena, 80, Zugarramurdi, Na	5	36	4
6	''	María Pérez de Barrenechea, 70 (46), Zugarramurdi, Na	6	37	3
7	3-3-10	Mari Juanto (de Aguirre), 60, Vera, Na	7	38	16
8	Sept. 09	Martín Vizcar, 80, Zugarramurdi, Na	8	39	11

a. For dates of imprisonment see above, chapters 4 and 8 passim.

Case No.	Imprisoned	Name, age, village, province	Number in: 1st&2nd Reports	3rd Report	PMS List A
9	27-1-09	María de Jureteguía, 22, Zugarramurdi, Na	9	25	1
10	''	Juana de Telechea, 38, Zugarramurdi, Na	10	26	2
11	[14]-2-09	Juanes de Goiburu, 37, Zugarramurdi, Na	11	27	10
12	''	Juanes de Sansín, 20, Zugarramurdi, Na	12	28	9
13	Sept. 09	María Presona, 70, Zugarramurdi, Na	13	29	13
14	''	María Chipía de Barrenechea, 52, Zugarramurdi (Urdax), Na	14	30	14
15	''	María de Echegui, 40, Zugarramurdi (Urdax), Na	12	31	12
16	3-3-10	Beltrana de la Fargua, 40, Vera, Na	16	40	17
17	Dec. 09	Juanes de Lambert, 27, Rentería, Gui	17	41	15
18	3-3-10	Juanes de Yribarren, 40, Echalar, Na	18	42	18
19	Dec. 09	María de Zozaya y Arramendi, 80, Rentería, Gui	19	43	19
20	Sept. 09	Juanes de Echegui, 68, Zugarramurdi, Na	20	40	
21	''	María de Echalecu, 40, Zugarramurdi, Na	21	45	
22	Nov. 09	Juanes de Odia y Berechea, 60, Zugarramurdi, Na	22	46	
23	Sept. 09	Estevanía de Petrisancena, 37, Urdax, Na	23	47	
24	''	María de Arburu, 70, Zugarramurdi, Na	24	48	
25	''	María Bastán de la Borda, 68, Zugarramurdi, Na	25	49	
26	''	María de Echachute, 54, Zugarramurdi, Na	26	50	
27	''	Graciana Xarra, 66, Urdax, Na	27	51	

Case No.	Imprisoned	Name, age, village, province	Number in:		
			1st&2nd Reports	3rd Report	PMS List A
28	Sept. 09	Petri de Juangorena, 36, Zugarramurdi, Na	28	52	
29	''	Domingo de Subildegui, 50, Zugarramurdi, Na	29	53	
30	''	Fray Pedro de Arburu, 43, Urdax, Na	30	54	
31	''	Don Juan de la Borda y Arburu, 34, Fuenterrabía, Gui	31	55	

Cases 32-96. The 65 Cases Reconciled in the Tribunal by the Edict of Grace (Nov. 1610 through Summer 1611)

Case No.	Impris- oned	Confes- sion	Recon- ciliation	Name, age, village, province. Miscellaneous	Rdo	No. in PMS List A
32		25-8-10[a]	6-2-11	María de Lecumberri, 20, Zugarramurdi, Na. See case no. 103	15	29
33		27-8-10[a]	6-2-11	Juana de Telechea (Garagarre), 20, Zugarramurdi, Na. See case no. 104	16	27
34		31-8-10[a]	''	María de Burga, 17, Zugarramurdi, Na. See case no. 105	17	28
35		5-9-10[a]	''	María de Lecumberri, 14, Zugarramurdi, Na. See case no. 106	18	31
36		9-9-10[a]	7-2-11	María Pérez de Burga, 12 (14), Zuga-rramurdi, Na See case no. 107	19	30
37		11-12-10	14-2-11	Juanes de Narvarte, 15, Santesteban, Na	20	24
38		4-2-11	8-2-11	Cristóbal de Alcoz, 14, Santesteban, Na	21	39

a. *Relación de causas 1610/11* has 1610 in both version A (f. 441[v]) and version B (f. 454[r]); we should, however, read 1609, see chapter 7 n. 11, below.

Case No.	Impris- oned	Confes- sion	Recon- ciliation	Name, age, village, province. Miscellaneous	Rdo	No. in PMS List A
39	[1611]	4-3-11	14-5-11	María de Zuraurre, 41, Santesteban, Na	22	22
40		14-5-11	14-5-11	María Miguel, 50, Santesteban, Na	23	21
41		6-3-11	31-3-11	Catalina de Arce, 25, Santesteban, Na	24	48
42		26-3-11	(Died)	María de Herminana (Arminana), 90, Santesteban, Na	25	72
43		24-3-11	24-3-11	Graciana de Arce, 15, Santesteban, Na	26	23
44		15-4-11	4-5-11	María de Dindart, 40, Santesteban, Na	27	32
45		19-4-11	7-5-11	María de Donesteve, 53, Santesteban, Na	28	33
46		20-4-11	4-5-11	Catalina de Porto, 60, Santesteban, Na	29	34
47		20-4-11	4-5-11	María de Saldies, 45, Santesteban, Na	30	35
48		29-3-11	31-3-11	Josef de Yrisarri, 14, Santesteban, Na	31	25
49		15-4-11	4-5-11	Tomasa de Yturen, 80, Santesteban, Na	32	38
50		23-4-11	14-5-11	Petri del Espinar, 70, Santesteban, Na	33	37
51		2-5-11	5-5-11	María Pérez de Labayen, 50, Santesteban, Na (see case no. 496); = ? María de Barbarena, 32, Elizondo, Na	34	58
52	[Feb.] 1611	28-2-11	6-3-11	Graciana de Olberro, 80, Santesteban, Na	35	36
53		29-1-11	9-4-11	Juanes de Nescacoa (Enezcaco), 18, Elizondo, Na	36	56
54		5-5-11	7-5-11	María de Ansorena, 70, Elizondo, Na	37	55
55		6-5-11	10-5-11	Catalina de Oyargun (Oyarzum), 20, Elizondo, Na	38	57
56		7-5-11	9-5-11	Mari Juan Anchorenea, 22, Elizondo, Na	39	51

Case No.	Impris- oned	Confes- sion	Recon- ciliation	Name, age, village, province. Miscellaneous	Rdo	No. in PMS List A
57		10-5-11	13-5-11	Mari Juan de Vergara, 26, Elizondo, Na	40	59
58	Spring 1611	21-4-11	4-5-11	Catalina de Araníbar, 30, Zubieta, Na. See case no. 494	41	78
59	''	22-4-11	4-5-11	Mari Juan de Larrayn, 40, Zubieta, Na	42	61
60	''	13-5-11	14-5-11	Pedro de Arrosa, 50, Zubieta, Na. See case no. 495	43	79
61		9-2-11	12-2-11	Miguel de Juangorena, 16, Legasa, Na	44	68
62		9-2-11	12-2-11	Tomás de Mariberti- cena, 18, Legasa, Na	45	69
63		30-5-11	4-6-11	Martín de la Aspidia, 76, Ituren, Na	46	62
64	3-3-10	8-7-11	21-7-11	María de Erausate, 48, Vera, Na	47	42
65	''	19-7-11	19-7-11	María de Aranaz, 28, Vera, Na	48	41
66	''	9-8-11	12-8-11	Juana Legasa Cucurro, 72, Vera, Na	49	46
67	''	22-7-11	30-7-11	Dominja de Casanova, 40, Lesaca, Na	50	43
68	''	30-7-11	8-8-11	Felipe de Vizcancho Casanova, 40, Lesaca, Na	51	44
69	''	4-8-11[b]	15-8-11[b]	Doña María de Endara (Berrizaun y Endarra alias Olandrea), 25, Echalar, Na	52	45
70		10-10-09	22-11-10	Diego de Marticorena, 14, Echalar, Na. See case no. 108	53	20
71	3-3-10	24-7-11	30-7-11	Magdalena de Agramonte, 36, Rentería, Gui	54	40
72		30-3-11	31-3-11	Agustín de Aguirre, 14, Rentería, Gui	55	26

b. We should probably read the date of confession as 4-7-11 and that of reconciliation as 15-7-11, see chapter 11 n. 117, below.

Case No.	Impris- oned	Confes- sion	Recon- ciliation	Name, age, village, province. *Miscellaneous*	Rdo	No. in PMS List A
73		1-6-11	9-6-11	Catalina de Echeva- rría, 50, Fuente- rrabía, Gui. See case no. 493	56	80
74	[Nov.] 1610	7-6-11	30-6-11	Graciana de Amézaga, 40, Oronoz, Na	57	65
75		18-3-11	31-3-11	Juana de Arráyoz, 24, Zuraurre, Na	58	49
76		28-3-11	31-3-11	María de Aldabe, 29, Sumbilla, Na	59	50
77		3-8-11	9-8-11	Catalina de Eguilcui, 12, Aránzazu, Gui	60	53
78		3-8-11	9-8-11	Juana de Zuloaga, 13, Aránzazu, Gui	61	54
79		3-8-11	9-8-11	María de Lorenceneco, 13, Aránzazu, Gui	62	52
80	[June]c 1611	18-?-11c	19-8-11c	Domingo de Orlaneche, 35, Logroño, Lo	63	64
81		[June]d 1611	Ab- solved *ad caute- lam*	Juanes de Sorraiz (*Solaez*), 9, Logroño, Lo	64	63
82		25-3-11	21-4-11	Juan Díaz de Alda, 80, Araya, Al	65	70
83e		8-7-11	15-7-11	María de Eguilaz (*Aguilar*), 70, Amézaga, Al	66	71
84		2-8-11	3-9-11	Don Diego de Basurto, 95, Ciordia, Na. See case no. 498	67	74
85		21-6-11	23-6-11	Francisca de Bertol, 32, *Arenaza*, Al	68	73

c. We should probably read June and not August in all these dates, see chapter 11 n. 125, below.

d. For date of confession see end of chapter 11.B.3, above.

e. In *PMS* f. 46ᵛ (IDOATE *Documento* p. 158) María de Eguilaz is stated to be *mujer principal*, i.e. a woman of noble family.

Case No.	Impris- oned	Confes- sion	Recon- ciliation	Name, age, village, province. *Miscellaneous*	Rdo	No. in PMS List A
86		21-7-11	21-7-11	Gracia González, 26, Cicujano, Al. See case no. 501	69	81
87		17-8-11	19-8-11	Inés de Corres, 66, Corres, Al	70	75
88		18-8-11	18-8-11	Ana de Corres, 56, Maestu, Al. See case no. 497	71	82
89[f]		[1611]	Ab- solved *ad caute- lam*	María de Eguino, 11, Eguino, Al. See case no. 499 = ? María Ybáñez,12, Cicujano, Al	72	84
90	[1611]	26-5-11	4-6-11	Catalina de Pajares, 50, Miranda de Ebro, Bu	73	66
91		28-6-11	30-6-11	María de Otazu, 16, Labastida, Al	74	67
92[g]		[Spring] 1611	[Spring] 1611	María de Zubieta, 18, Santesteban (*Zubieta*), Na	75	60
93[g]		''	''	Pedro de Zubieta, 18, Santesteban, Na	76	47
94[h]		[1611]	[1611]	*María González, 40, Corres, Al*	[76a]	76
95[h]		[1611]	[1611]	*María Pérez, 65, Atauri, Al*	[76b]	77
96[h]		[1611]	[July] 1611	*Magdalena de Area, 56, Cicujano, Al.* See case no. 500	[76c]	83

f. These two might even be identical with a third girl, twelve-year-old María de Corres from Corres, Al (*Rte* 59), see the discussion in chapter 11, n. 182, below.

g. In the *Relación de causas 1610/11* it is stated only that María and Pedro de Zubieta confessed and were reconciled [at the Tribunal] and that Salazar afterwards brought their files with him on the visitation. Consequently their reconciliation must have taken place before 22 May 1611, when Salazar set out on his journey (see beginning of chapter 11.A.3, above).

h. These three witches are not included in the *Relación de causas 1610/ 11*; they must have been reconciled after the report, on 15 Oct. 1611, was submitted to *la Suprema*; see the excursus in chapter 11 n. 160, below. For María González see further chapter 11 n. 194, below; for María Pérez, alias Mariquita de Atauri, see chapter 11.C.4, above.

Cases 97-102. The 6 Cases Reconciled in the Tribunal After the
Expiration of the Edict and Before the New Instructions for
Witchcraft Cases (1612 through 29 Aug. 1614)[a]

Case no.	Confession	Reconciled or absolved ad cautelam	Name, age, village, province	No. in Rel. 1613-14	Extracts in PMS (Idoate)
97	24-2-13, 5-11-13	3-12-13	Gracia Luxea, 16, Uztárroz, Na	16	p. 171
98	5-8-12, 6-11-13	9-11-13	Pascuala Miguel, 11, Uztárroz, Na	17	p. 171
99	7-11-13	9-11-13	Gracia Miguel, 7, Uztárroz, Na	18	p. 171
100	22-11-13	26-11-13	Cristóbal de Mayza (Mayz), 16, Lizárraga, Na	19	
101[b]	[1613]	[1613]	Isabel Folca [old, Villarreal, Al]	27	
102[c]	[1613]	[Summer] 1614	Juanes de Goizueta, 40, [Oyarzun, Gui]		pp. 99-100

a. There is no mention of these persons in the *PMS*'s register of the 84 witches reconciled at Logroño, but several of them are referred to in the text of the manuscript.

b. According to *Rel. 1613/14* f. 513ᵛ-514ᵛ Isabel Folca was an old beggar woman from Cataluña. She was on a pilgrimage to Santiago de Compostela when a 12-year-old witch finder in Alava accused her of being a witch. The inquisitorial commissioner of Villarreal sent her to the Tribunal. Her case is mentioned in *Fourth Report of Salazar* so it must have been concluded before 3 Oct. 1613.

c. For Juanes de Goizueta see above, chapters 12.3, 13.3; and below, chapter 13 n. 29. In the *PMS* he is referred to as no. 85 in the register of witches reconciled at Logroño (f. 24ʳ, IDOATE *Documento* p. 99); obviously Becerra and Valle anticipated events when they wrote their memorial in 1613, for Juanes de Goizueta was never reconciled and was not included in the list which ends with no. 84. Strangely enough he was not even included in the yearly reports of completed cases, neither in the *Rel. 1613/14* nor in *Relación de causas 1614/15*.

2. RECONSTRUCTION OF VALLE'S ONE-VOLUME VISITATION BOOK FROM HIS JOURNEY OF 1609

Sources for part 2: For the stipulated 50 witchcraft confessions see the calculation in chapter 7 n. 120, below. Our reconstruction of Valle's missing visitation book is based on references, abstracts, and copies of entire files contained in the following manuscripts: *Volume "F" of Salazar's Visitation Book* (here abbr.

VolF); *Examination of Valle's Visitation Book* (abbr. *EVV*); *Relación de causas 1610/11 (B)* (abbr. *RDC*); the *Pamplona Manuscript* (abbr. *PMS*, with reference to pages in IDOATE *Documento*). For Valle's Visitation Book see above, chapters 7.2 near end, and beginning of 7.3, with notes 22, 27, 29, and 31 and tables 2 and 3. A case number is assigned only when we definitely know that a person actually made a witchcraft confession; witnesses to witchcraft and persons who made depositions of other kinds are identified without any case number.

Cases 103-150. The some 50 witches' confessions
contained in the missing volume

Case no.	Folios	Date of confession	Name, age, village, province. Miscellaneous	Sources
	[1-92] Visitation at Zugarramurdi [23 Aug. through late Sept. 1609]			Chap. 7.2, above
	4-6		María de Ximildegui, 20, Zugarramurdi, Na	PMS pp. 59, 73-75
103		25-8-09	María de Lecumberri, 20, Zugarramurdi, Na. See case no. 32	RDC f. 454^r
104		27-8-09	Juana de Telechea, 17, Zugarramurdi, Na. See case no. 33	RDC f. 454^r
105		31-8-09	María de Burga, 15, Zugarramurdi, Na. See case no. 34	RDC f. 454^r
106		5-9-09	María de Lecumberri, 12, Zugarramurdi, Na. See case no. 35	RDC f. 454^r
107		9-9-09	María Pérez de Burga, 12, Zugarramurdi, Na. See case no. 36	RDC f. 454^r
	93-131 Visitation at Lesaca, 23 Sept. through 14 Oct. 1609			EVV f. 1524^v-1525^r
108		10-10-09	Diego de Marticorena, 14, Lesaca, Na. See case no. 70	RDC f. 456^v
	[132-268] Visitation at San Sebastián, late Sept. through 20 Nov. 1609			EVV ff. 1530^v-1531^r
109	147 ff.		Juanes de Bustiola, child witch	PMS p. 87
	170-179	4-11-09	Magdalena de Echasana and her daughter María de Esponda	EVV f. 1525^r

Case no.	Folios	Date of confession	Name, age, village, province. *Miscellaneous*	Sources
110	179-183	5-11-09	Juana de Esponda, child witch	*EVV* ff. 1525ʳ-1526ʳ
	183ᵛ-186ᵛ	6-11-09	Depositions of 4 persons	*EVV* f. 1526ʳ⁻ᵛ
	187ʳ-190ᵛ	7-11-09	Depositions of 3 persons	*EVV* ff. 1526ᵛ-1527ʳ
111 112	190ᵛ-197	8-11-09	Confessions of 2 persons concerning witchcraft	*EVV* ff. 1527ᵛ-1528ʳ
	197-202a	9-11-09	Depositions of 6 persons	*EVV* f. 1528ᵛ
	202a-202c	10-11-09	Depositions of 3 persons	*EVV* ff. 1528ᵛ-1529ʳ
	203-204	11-11-09	Depositions of 2 persons	*EVV* f. 1529ʳ⁻ᵛ
	205-212	12-11-09	Depositions of 4 persons	*EVV* ff. 1529ᵛ-1530ʳ
113	220 ff.	17-11-09	María Martín de Legarra, 31, Lesaca, Na. See case no. 457	*VolF* ff. 108ʳ-117ᵛ
	263-268ᵛ	19-11-09	Depositions of 6 persons	*EVV* f. 1530ʳ⁻ᵛ
	269-375 ff. *Visitation at Tolosa, 20 Nov. through mid-Dec. 1609*			*Chap. 7.3, above*
114	278 ff.		Juana de Goyenechea, 22	*PMS* pp. 84-85
	299ᵛ-303ᵛ	3-12-09	Depositions of 2 persons	*EVV* f. 1530ʳ⁻ᵛ
		&4-12-09	Depositions of 3 persons	*EVV* f. 1530ʳ⁻ᵛ
	309-323	7-12-09	Depositions of 2 persons	*EVV* f. 1531ʳ⁻ᵛ
		&8-12-09	Deposition of 1 person	
		&9-12-09	Deposition of 1 person	
	317 ff.ᵃ	[8-12-09]	Magdalena de Masalde, 22	*PMS* pp. 79-80, 163
115	332 ff.	11-12-09	María de Gardel, 72, Lesaca, Na. See case no. 452	*VolF* ff. 70ʳ-72ᵛ
116	337 ff.	12-12-09	María de Dindur, 40, Lesaca, Na. See case no. 462	*VolF* ff. 144ʳ-150ᵛ

---

a. Idoate *Documento* p. 79 has an error in the transcription: "Fol. 3, y de la Visita" should read "fol. 317 de la Visita."

Case no.	Folios	Date of confession	Name, age, village, province. Miscellaneous	Sources
117	372 ff.	13-12-09	Juanes de Picabea, 11, Lesaca, Na. See case no. 463	*VolF* ff.156^r-158^r
118	375 ff.	13-12-09	Gracia de Lizárraga, 17, Lesaca, Na. See case no. 464	*VolF* ff. 164^r-165^v
119		14-12-09	María de Yturría, 9, Echalar, Na. See case no. 465	*VolF* ff. 170^r-172^v

[120-150] The remaining 31 witches whose confessions cannot be identified

3. RECONSTRUCTION OF SALAZAR'S EIGHT-VOLUME VISITATION BOOK FROM HIS JOURNEY OF 1611

According to Salazar himself, the records of his visitation filled over 5,600 folios. These were bound into 8 volumes designated "A" through "H," of which only *Volume "F" of Salazar's Visitation Book*, and a single file from volume "E," the *Trial Record of María de Ulibarri*, have been preserved. However, thanks to Salazar's special method of reference, giving the letter of the volume followed by the first page of the file (see above, p. 319 f.), we are able to reconstruct the contents of the other seven volumes to a large extent.

Sources for part 3: The above-mentioned extant materials, *Second* and *Fifth Report of Salazar* (referred to collectively as *Salazar Reports*), and the *Pamplona Manuscript* (especially the second list of witches, abbr. *PMS List B*, containing those reconciled on the visitation of Salazar and reproduced in IDOATE *Documento* pp. 180-188, although with several errors in the transcription). This last source first came to light after my survey of the lost parts of the eight-volume visitation book had been constructed on the basis of the *Salazar Reports* alone; it confirmed the accuracy of the reconstruction, and at the same time contributed a wealth of new details.

Finally, a word about the makeup of the table: Dots between lines indicate that at this point in the manuscript there were presumably one or more files of which we have no knowledge. Here, as elsewhere in our list, italics are used to indicate that this information is known only through the *PMS*. In the column headed "References in" are given both the reference number that Salazar uses in his two reports and that (those) which his colleagues use in the *PMS*. These reference numbers appear in many different connections and for the sake of brevity I have refrained from adding the sources for each number except for a few instances where a critical note seemed necessary.

Where Salazar's reports and the *PMS* have conflicting reference numbers, criticism of the sources is based on the following two criteria: either the *criterion of space* or the *criterion of place*. The former presumes each file to have had a certain minimum length. A reconciliation case in volumes "B" through "E," for example, always filled at least four folios (one folio of title page, two pages of confession, and four pages taken up by the forms of reconciliation). If the person was under 25 years old, the reconciliation would invariably be preceded by the two-page form of the *curaduría* (see chapter 11 n. 18, below); that made five folios, and as the file often included previous confessions made before the visitation as well as a number of blank pages because of the use of double sheets, the average reconciliation file would seem to have been some ten folios. Thus if two consecutive reference numbers are quite close together, as for instance "B 601" and "B 603," we can deduce that one of them must be wrong, since a file of only two folios is unthinkable.

According to the other criterion, that of *place*, the cases of each of the categories (reconciled, absolved *de levi,* and child witches) may be assumed to have succeeded each other in the volume in the same sequence as the journey of visitation proceeded in the geographical sense of the word (see the discussion of serial numbers in chapter 11 n. 49, below). One exception to this is the category of *reconciliados,* who were divided into two series, one in volumes "B" through "D" and the other in volume "E" (see chapter 11 n. 184, below). For instance, when a certain María de Yráizoz from Lizaso appears under two different reference numbers, we can determine which reference is correct by seeing where the other files from the neighborhood of Lizaso appear in the visitation book (see case no. 193, below).

Cases 150a-150gg. Depositions Concerning Witchcraft
Contained in the Lost Volume "A"[a]

Case no.	Folios	Name, age, village, province. Miscellaneous	References in: Salazar Reports	PMS	No. in PMS List B
150a	13	María de Jornarena, 60, Ezcurra, Na	A 13	A 13	119
150b	46	Fray Domingo de Velasco, San Sebastián, Gui	A 46		
150c	63	María de Echeverría, Vera, Na	A 63		
150d	67	Isabel de Castro, 12, San Sebastián, Gui	A 67		
150e	75	Simona de Gaviria, "old," San Sebastián, Gui	A 75		
150f	84	Ana de Olite, "child-witch," Santesteban, Na	A 84		
150g	' '	Juana de Xubil, "child-witch," Santesteban, Na	A 84		
150h	' '	María de Arráyoz, "child-witch," Santesteban, Na	A 84		
150i	85	Magdalena de Oiz, "child-witch," Santesteban, Na	A 85		
150j	' '	Juanes de San Estevan, "child-witch," Santesteban, Na	A 85		
150k	86	Martín de Alcoz, "child-witch," Santesteban, Na	A 86		
150l	' '	Tomás de Jaunearaz, "child-witch," Santesteban, Na	A 86		
150m	87	Martín de Saldías, "child-witch," Santesteban, Na	A 87		
150n	88	Juanes de Bastán, "child-witch," Santesteban, Na	A 88		
150o	' '	Graciana de Zubieta, "child-witch," Santesteban, Na	A 88		
150p	89	Mari Sáenz, "child-witch," Santesteban, Na	A 89		
150q	' '	Mariana Ancochela, "child-witch," Santesteban, Na	A 89		
150r	' '	Catalina de Valencia, "child-witch," Santesteban, Na	A 89		

---

a. As a matter of fact this section should have had no case numbers, for all the persons in this volume were examined as witnesses whether they were witches or not. However, some of the witnesses made a witchcraft confession in some other part of the visitation book, so for convenience I have also given case numbers to the present section.

Case no.	Folios	Name, age, village, province. *Miscellaneous*	References in: Salazar Reports	PMS	No. in PMS List B
150s	185	Lucía de Ciriano, 14	A 185		
150t	200	Francisco Mortínez de Aranoz (*Aranz*), 43 (74), *Aranaz*	A 200	A 20	
150u	264 ff.	Doña Francisca de Alaba, a nun	A 264, A 267, A 271, A 274		
150v	291	María de Abechuco	A 291		
150w	297	Testimony by the two inquisitorial secretaries concerning a witches' heeting at Santesteban, Midsummer night 1611 (see chap. 11.C.6, above)	A 297		
150x	351 ff.	Investigations concerning deaths of the two infants of Leiza, Na (see chap. 11.C.6, above)	A 351, A 355, A 361		
150y	362 ff.	Juan de Garaicoechea (*Garaicoche*), 28, *Oronoz*	A 367	A 362	178
150z	376	*Catalina de Aremburu, 14, Aurtiz, Ituren, Na*		A 376	120
150aa	379	*Catalina de Berentena, 12, Aurtiz, Ituren, Na*		A 379	121
150bb	381	*María Martín de Sagarbía, 12, Aurtiz, Ituren, Na*		A 381	122
150cc	389	Mari Sáenz de Ormaechea, 60, San Sebastián, Gui	A 389		
150dd	410 ff.	Records from the experiments concerning the witches' ointments and powders (see chaps. 11.C.6 and 12.2, above)	A 410		
150ee	453- [475]	Records from the experiments concerning the witches' meeting places (see chaps. 11.C.6 and 12.2, above)	A 453		
	457	Examination of 3 witnesses in Iráizoz, Na	A 457		
	460	Examination of witnesses in Zubieta, Na	A 460		
	464	Examination of "the 3rd and 4th" witnesses in Sumbilla, Na	A 464		

Case no.	Folios	Name, age, village, province. *Miscellaneous*	References in: Salazar Reports	PMS	No. in PMS List B
	465	Examination of witnesses at Donamaría, Na	A 465		
	466	Examination of witnesses at Alzate, Vera, Na			
150ff	473	Examination of Catalina de Lizardi, 17, Vera, Na, concerning the witches' meeting places. See case no. 260	A 473		
150gg	475	Examination of cowitnesses to Catalina de Lizardi at Vera, concerning witch heeting	A 475		

Cases 151-197. The 47 Reconciled Witches Included in the Lost Volume "B"

Case no.	Folios	Name, age, village, province. *Miscellaneous*	References in: Salazar Reports	PMS	No. in PMS List B
151	1 ff.	Catalina de Labayen, *60, Santesteban, Na*	B 1	B 1	33
152	11 ff.	Juana de Garro	B 11		
153	23 ff.	Juana de Elizondo, *40, Santesteban, Na*	B 23	B 23	34
154	33 ff.	Catalina de Gaztelu, *14, Gaztelu, Na*	B 33	B 35	130
155	43 ff.	Juanes de Micho, *14, Gaztelu, Na*		B 43	35
156	63 ff.	Juana de Miguelena, *19, Donamaría, Na*	B 603[a]	B 63	36
157	87 ff.		B 87		
158	97 ff.	Female witch who gave birth to toad	B 97		
159	136 ff.	*María de Zocanibar, 24, Arce, Donamaría, Na*		B 136	37
160	148 ff.	*Pedro de Dindarte, 15, Elgorriaga, Na*	B 148	B 148 B 149	38, 129

a. According to the criterion of space, "B 603" is an error for "B 63," cf. case no. 191, below.

Case no.	Folios	Name, age, village, province. Miscellaneous	References in: Salazar Reports	PMS	No. in PMS List B
161	172 ff.	Graciana de Barazurren, 16, Elgorriaga, Na	B 172	B 172	39
162	194 ff.	María de Lesaca, 60, Elgorriaga, Na	B 194	B 194	40
163	218 ff.	María Miguel, 12, Elgorriaga, Na		B 218	1
164	239 ff.	Mari Juan de Laspiria, 16, Ituren, Na		B 239	41
165	251 ff.	Miguel de Olagüe, 15, Ituren, Na	B 251	B 253	129a
166	271 ff.		B 271		
167	281 ff.	Miguel de Hurroz (Ustárroz), 70, Ituren, Na	B 281	B 281	42
168	303 ff.	Pedro de Laspiria, 18, Ituren, Na	B 303	B 303	43
		[=] Martín de Laspidia, 18, Ituren, Na		B 305	2
169	315 ff.	María de Mariarena, 60	B 371[b]		
		[=?] Mariana Maxirena, 28, Zubieta, Na		B 315	44
		[=] María Maxirena, 28, Zubieta, Na		B 319	123
		[=?] María de Maxiarena, 60, Zubieta, Na		B 371[b]	175
170	327 ff.		B 327		
171	335 ff.		B 335		
172	347 ff.	Tomás de Gualde, 30, Zubieta, Na		B 347	45
173	363 ff.	Juanes de Zubieta, 30, Zubieta, Na		B 363	46
174	371 ff.	María de Larraspe, 14, Zubieta, Na	B 371[b]	B 371	46a
175	383 ff.	María de Mozotadie, 26, Oiz, Na	B 383	B 383	46b
176	403 ff.	Graciana de Azpilqueta, 60, Oiz, Na	B 403	B 403	47
		[=] Graciana de Azpilcueta, 60, "Haoiz" (i.e. Oiz), Na		B 409 B 412	132

b. In gloss 28 of *Second Report of Salazar* "B 371" is stated to be the file of María de Mariarena, but in gloss 86 the same file is said to contain the record of María de Larraspe. While we cannot decide whether the age of María de Mariarena was 28 or 60, it is probable that the great confusion in the witch list of the *PMS* is due to the fact that the colleagues used both the original files and Salazar's reports for their compilation.

Case no.	Folios	Name, age, village, province. Miscellaneous	References in: Salazar Reports	PMS	No. in PMS List B
177	419 ff.	Catalina de Zozaya, 20, Oiz, Na		B 419	48
178	429 ff.	Graciana de Yturri, 60, ... Almándoz, Na		B 429	49
179	458 ff.	Juana de Argarate, 60, Sumbilla, Na	B 458	B 458	50
180	468 ff.	Graciana de Aguirre, 15, ... Sumbilla, Na	B 468	B 468	51
181	487 ff.	María Juan de Azpeleta, 50, Sumbilla, Na		B 487	52
182	494 ff.	(?)	B 494c		
183	499 ff.	María de Jaureguía, 70	B 499		
184	509 ff.	Mari Juan de Pijarena ...... (Pixarerena), 14, Sumbilla, Na	B 509	B 512	53
185	529 ff.	Mari Miguel de Torrena, 30, Azcárraga, Na	B 529	B 529	54
186	541 ff.		B 541		
187	555 ff.	Sancho de Yráizoz, 60, Iráizoz, Na		B 555 B 556	55
188	567 ff.	Miguel de Yráizoz, 60, Iráizoz, Na	B 567	B 567 B 569	56 131
189	579 ff.	María de Ortiz Garaicoa, 60, Iráizoz, Na	B 579	B 579	57
190	591 ff.	María de Yriza (Oriza), 80, Beruete, Na	B 591	B 591 B 592	58
191	601 ff.	Lope de Elzaburo, 74, Beruete, Na	B 601	B 601 B 604	59
192	611 ff.		B 611		
193	625 ff.	María de Yráizoz, 94, Lizaso, Na	B 625	B 162d	60
194	635 ff.		B 635		
195	643 ff.	Magdalena de Arteche, 16, Arriba, Na		B 643	61
196	651 ff.	Martín de Ygunén, 60, Igunín, Donamaría, Na = Martie de Yguñén, 64, Igunín, Donamaría, Na	B 651	B 652 B 654	62
197	663 ff.	Juana de Lanz, 20, Lanz, Na	B 663	B 663	63

c. According to the criterion of space there is reason to doubt that this reference number is correct. It appears only once, in gloss 1 of *Second Report of Salazar,* and it might be an error for "B 194," see case no. 162, above.

d. According to our criterion of place "B 162" must be an error for "B 625."

Cases 198-247. The 50 Reconciled Witches
Included in the Lost Volume "C"

Case no.	Folios	Name, age, village, province. *Miscellaneous*	References in: Salazar Reports	PMS	No. in PMS List B
198	1 ff.	Juan de Saldías alias Juanes de Estevecorena *(alias Buru Urdina)*, 80, Elizondo, Na	C 1	C 2, C 4, C 6, C 7, C 9,	9
	......				
199	35 ff.		C 35		
200	45 ff.	María de Echeverría	C 45		
	......				
201	87 ff.	Pedro de Estebecorería	C 87		
202	97 ff.		C 97		
203	107 ff.		C 107		
	......				
204	124 ff.		C 124		
205	133 ff.	*Marito alias María Miguelena, 50, Elizondo, Na*	C 133	C 133	156
206	147 ff.	*Marichipi de Charrarena, 20, Elizondo, Na*	C 147	C 151	157
	......				
207	163 ff.		C 163, C 165		
208	173 ff.	María de Yriarte	C 173		
	......				
209	205 ff.		C 205		
210	209 ff.		I 209		
	......				
211	227 ff.		C 227		
212	235 ff.		C 235		
213	245 ff.	*María de Mendibe, 12, Elvetea, Na*	C 245	C 246	136a
214	255 ff.	Juanes de Sastrerena *(Santsetena), 16, Elvetea, Na*	C 255	C 257	137
215	265 ff.		C 265		
216	273 ff.	*María de Echevarría, 13, Elvetea, Na*	C 273	C 274	138
217	281 ff.		C 281		
218	285 ff.		C 285		
	......				
219	301 ff.	*María de Lesaca, 40, Oyeregui, Na*	C 301	C 301	122a
	......				
220	331 ff.		C 331		
221	336 ff.	*Gracia de Xaurigizar, 22, Narvarte, Na*		C 336, C 337	133
	......				
222	357 ff.	*María de Arechea, 32, Irurita, Na*		C 357, C 359	10

Case no.	Folios	Name, age, village, province. Miscellaneous	References in: Salazar Reports	PMS	No. in PMS List B
223	365 ff.	María de Tanborín Xarra, 16, Irurita, Na. Reconciled 23 June 1611, confessed to a relapse 23 July 1611 (see chap. 11.A.7, above)	C 365	C 365 C 377	3
224	381 ff.	Pierres de Arguialde, 60	C 381		
		= *Pierres de Alquiane, 60, Irurita, Na*		C 385	4
		= *Pierres de Alquinalde, 60, Irurita, Na*		C 381	124
225	393 ff.	*Juanes de Arrechea, 60, Irurita, Na*	C 393[a]	C 396[a]	5
226	403 ff.	*María Juan Nicotena, 40, Irurita, Na*	C 403	C 403	7
		= *Mari Juan Nicotena, 43, Irurita, Na*		C 403	159
227	413 ff.		C 413		
228	425 ff.	Miguel de Oteiza, 70, Irurita, Na	C 425	C 425	160 173
229	441 ff.		C 441		
230	457 ff.	Juanes de Dolagaray, 65, Irurita, Na	C 457	C 457	161
231	477 ff.	*Juana de Yturrimozta, 70, Arráyoz, Na*	C 477	C 477	8
		[=] *Juana de Yturre, 70, Arráyoz, Na*		C 481	134
232	489 ff.	*Sabadina de Celaieta, 16, Arráyoz, Na*	C 489	C 489	155
233	501 ff.	*Catalina de Yrigoién, 23, Ciga, Na*	C 501	C 504	136
234	531 ff.	*Catalina de Mendiburu, 20, Ciga, Na*	C 531	C 531	158
235	540 ff.	*Graciana de Mendiguro, 13, Ciga, Na*		C 540, C 541, C 545	11
236	561 ff.		C 561		
237	571 ff.	*María de Maiora, 17, Ciga, Na*		C 571, C 576	12
238	597		C 597		
239	615 ff.	*Juanes de Soraburu, 80, Ciga, Na*	C 615	C 615, C 618	6

a. "C 393" and "C 396" must refer to the same file; a reconciliation file of only 3 folios is inconceivable.

Case no.	Folios	Name, age, village, province. Miscellaneous	References in: Salazar Reports	PMS	No. in PMS List B
240	619 ff.		C 619[b]		162
241	643 ff.	Catalina de Echetoa, 14, Zugarramurdi, Na. Reconciled 28 July 1611, confessed to a relapse two months later on 3 Aug. (see chap. 11.A.7, above)	C 643	C 644	23
242	657 ff.	María de Aitajorena, 17, Urdax, Na	C 657	C 657	163
243	687 ff.	Juana de Echegui, 18, Zugarramurdi, Na	C 687	C 689	135
244	697 ff.	María de Odia, 60, Zugarramurdi, Na	C 697	C 697 C 669	24 164
245	709 ff.	Sabadina de Echetoa, 60	C 709		
246	719 ff.	Graciana de Maritorena, 33, Urdax, Na	C 719	C 721	139
247	729 ff.	Graciana de Barrenechea, 24, Urdax, Na	C 729	C 729 C 732	25

b. This reference number might be in error; it appears only once (*Second Report of Salazar* gloss 1). However, according to the space criterion a preceding file of only four folios is conceivable, although not very probable.

Cases 248-290. The 43 Reconciled Witches Included in the Lost Volume "D"

Case no.	Folios	Name, age, village, province. Miscellaneous	References in: Salazar Reports	PMS	No. in PMS List B
248	...... 13 ff.	María de Alzuara, 14, Lesaca, Na	D 13	D 13	169
249	29 ff.		D 29		
250	55 ff.	Juana de Antoco, 13, Lesaca, Na	D 55	D 55	142
251	65 ff.	Juanes de Alberro	D 65		
252	86 ff.		D 86		

Case no.	Folios	Name, age, village, province. Miscellaneous	References in: Salazar Reports	PMS	No. in PMS List B
253	102 ff.	Verónica Larrayn, 14, Aranaz, Na		D 102	26
254	122 ff.		D 122		
255	130 ff.	Graciana de Martilopicena, 25, Aranaz, Na		D 130	27
256	142 ff.		D 142		
257	152 ff.	Mari Martín de Aguirre, 22, Vera, Na	D 152	D 152, D 154	20
258	164 ff.	Sabadina de Aguirre, 70, Vera, Na	D 164	D 164, D 166, D 167	21 28
259	174 ff.	María de Peña, 14, Vera, Na =? case no. 453	D 174	D 174	144
260	184 ff.	Catalina de Lizardi, 17, Vera, Na	D 184	D 184 D 193	22 29
261	196 ff.	Catalina de Esponda, 14, Vera, Na	D 196	D 196	170
262	210 ff.	Graciana de Permosa, 19, Vera, Na	D 210	D 210	30
263	225 ff.	Graciana de Miranda, 16, Vera, Na	D 225	D 225	31
264	239 ff.	Martín de Jalinena [under 14], Vera, Na	D 239		
265	253 ff.	Pedro de Serasti, 11 (sic), Vera, Na	D 253		
266	273 ff.		D 273[a] D 275[a]		
267	305 ff.	Martín de Sarrate, 17, Vera, Na	D 305	D 305	13
268	317 ff.		D 317		
269	327 ff.	Gracia de Xauriguizar, 19, Vera, Na		D 327	32
270	337 ff.	Juanes de Gamio, 15, Lecaroz, Na	D 337	D 337	166
271	359 ff.	Juanes de Labaqui, 16	D 359[b]		166a
272		Graciana de Aldalor, 14, Lecaroz, Na		D 359[b]	
273	370 ff.	Catalina de Lecheberro, 15, Lecaroz, Na	D 370	D 370	167

a. According to the criterion of space "D 273" and "D 275" must refer to the same files; a reconciliation file consisting of only three folios is inconceivable.

b. One of these two references is obviously wrong, but it is impossible to decide which: The name of Juanes de Labaqui appears only in *Fifth Report of Salazar* clause 11, and Graciana de Aldalor is mentioned only in *List B* of the *Pamplona Manuscript*.

Case no.	Folios	Name, age, village, province. Miscellaneous	References in: Salazar Reports	PMS	No. in PMS List B
274	389 ff.	Graciana de Estilartea, 13, Lecaroz, Na	D 389	D 389	14 141
275	399 ff.	María San Juan de Echandía, 17, Fuenterrabía, Gui	D 399	D 399	165
276	411 ff.	Isabela García, 14, Fuenterrabía, Gui	D 411	D 412	140
277	420 ff.	Juana de Muría (Miura), 50, Fuenterrabía, Gui	D 420	D 420 D 423	15 168
278	440 ff.	Mari Martín de Yllarra, 70, Fuenterrabía, Gui	D 440	D 440 D 442	16
279	451 ff.		D 451		
280	473 ff.	Juanes de Bastida, 80		D 473 D 453^c	179
281	494 ff.	Magdalena de Orzaiz, 23, Lesaca, Na	D 494	D 494^d	143
282		Magdalena de Yanci, 13, Fuenterrabía, Gui		D 494^d	145
283	502 ff.	María de Yturregui, 26, Fuenterrabía, Gui	D 502	D 502 D 506	17 145
284	522 ff.	María Miguel (de Oyanburen), 44, Fuenterrabía, Gui	D 522	D 522 D 524	18
285	532 ff.	María López de Oiarzábal, 15, Fuenterrabía, Gui	D 532	D 532	171
286	549 ff.^{e}	Martín de Hualde, 15, Fuenterrabía, Gui		D 549	177
287	551 ff.		D 551		
288	557 ff.	Juanes de Lizardi, 14, Fuenterrabía, Gui		D 557	146
289	600 ff.		D 600		
290	685 ff.	Gracia de Arreche, 19, Ciboure, La		D 685 D 686	19

c. Cf. *PMS* f. 36^r; IDOATE *Documento* p. 130 has "D 493," but this is due to a misreading.

d. One of these two references is wrong. However, it is impossible to decide which, as the *Salazar Reports* give the reference number without name.

e. According to the criterion of space a file of only two folios is inconceivable, but it must be remembered that while Salazar invariably refers to the first page of the file his colleagues often make reference to some page inside the file.

Cases 291-355. The 65 Reconciled Witches
Included in the Lost Volume "E"

Case No.	Folios	Name, age, village, province. Miscellaneous	References in: Salazar Reports	PMS	No. in PMS List B
	· · · · · ·				
291	9 ff.	María de Echevarría alias Zunda, 80 (70), Oronoz, Na. The sixth in the list of witches who confessed to a relapse (see chap. 12 n. 47, below).	E 9	E 9	64 172
292	16 ff.	*María de Zunda, 80,*	E 16	E 18	65
293	21 ff.		E 21		
294	33 ff.	*Catalina de Zunda, 27, Oronoz, Na*	E 33	E 36,[a] E 35	66 147
295	43 ff.		E 43		
296	52 ff.	*Mari López de Aula, 19, Oronoz, Na*	E 52	E 53	67 176
297	61 ff.	*María de Arechea, 14, Errazu, Na*	E 61	E 61	174
298	71 ff.	*María Miguel, 52, Errazu, Na*		E 71	68
299	80 ff.	*María de Olaga, 15, Errazu, Na*		E 80	69
300	91 ff.	*Margarita de Holaga, 24, Errazu, Na*		E 91	70
301	100 ff.		E 100		
302	106 ff.	*Graciana de Esjumda [?], 15, Errazu, Na*		E 106, E 107	71
303	114 ff.	*Graciana de Garaycochea, 14, Errazu, Na*	E 114	E 115, E 116	72
304	127 ff.	*Margarita de Zubipunta, 20, Errazu, Na*		E 127	73
305	140 ff.[b]	*Lorenzo de Narvarte, 17, Goizueta, Na*		E 140	148
306	143 ff.		E 143		
307	148 ff.	*Miguel de Gortairi, 63, Arizcun, Na*		E 148	74
308	159 ff.		E 159		

a. Corrected from 33.

b. According to the criterion of space a file of only three folios is inconceivable, but as previously mentioned the *Pamplona Manuscript* often makes reference to some page inside the file. We might therefore conjecture that the case began at folio 139 or earlier.

Case no.	Folios	Name, age, village, province. Miscellaneous	References in: Salazar Reports	PMS	No. in PMS List B
309	163 ff.	María de Gortairi, 26, Arizcun, Na		E 163ᶜ	75
310	169 ff.	María de Ycacetea, 12, Arizcun, Na	E 169	E 170	76
311	177 ff.	Juanes de Perlichinecoa (Perlichecoa), 13	E 177		
312	185 ff.	Eñeco de Elorga, 14, Arizcun, Na	E 185	E 187	
313	190 ff.	Estevanía de Escobereta, 60	E 190		
314	195 ff.	Catalina de Bozate, 19, Arizcun, Na	E 195	E 196	78
315	199 ff.		E 199		
316	206 ff.	Pierres de Alfaro, 14, Arizcun, Na		E 206	79
317	223 ff.	Juana de Arizcun, 19, Arizcun, Na	E 223 E 227	E 224	80
318	236 ff.	Catalina de Labaqui, 60, Azpilcueta, Na		E 236	81
319	247 ff.	Juanot de Chabarri, 80, Azpilcueta, Na	E 247	E 248	82
320	256 ff.	María de Yrugingo, 12, Azpilcueta, Na	E 256	E 257	125 150
321	259 ff.		E 259ᵈ		
322	266 ff.		E 266		
323	270 ff.	María de Bizarrorena, 14, Azpilcueta, Na		E 270	83
324	285 ff.		E 285		
325	293 ff.	María de Larralde, 15	E 293		
326	303 ff.		E 303		
327	311 ff.	María de Errazuri, 14, Arizcun, Na	E 311	E 312	84
328	316 ff.		E 316		
329	324 ff.	Mari Juan de Sastrearena, 12, Arizcun, Na		E 324	85
330	342 ff.	Juanes de Yturalde, 15, Arizcun, Na		E 342	86
331	351 ff.	Gracianato de Oyeretena, 14	E 351		

c. "E 159" and "E 163" probably refer to the same file, although we cannot exclude the possibility that María de Gortairi's file was preceded by a different one of only four folios.

d. "E 259" which only appears once (*Second Report of Salazar* gloss 8) must be an error in copying, otherwise the preceding file would have been of only three folios and this is not conceivable according to the criterion of space.

Case no.	Folios	Name, age, village, province. Miscellaneous	References in: Salazar Reports	PMS	No. in PMS List B
332	361 ff.	Martín de Errazuri, 14, Arizcun, Na	E 361	E 365	87
333	371 ff.	Martín de Sastrearena, 15, Arizcun, Na	E 371	E 372	88
334	381 ff.	María de Machintorena, 14, Arizcun, Na	E 381	E 384	149
335	391 ff.	Catalina de Sastrearena, 17, Arizcun, Na. Her file would seem to have extensive (see chap. 11.A. 5, above, and *Second Report of Salazar* gloss 66, where the examination of a certain Mari Gorriti is stated to have been entered as well)	E 391	E 393	89
336	*413 ff.*		E 413		
337	*429 ff.*		E 429		
338	*439 ff.*		E 439		
339	*450 ff.*	Martín de Arasun, 18, Areso, Na		E 450	90
340	461 ff.	Catalina de Aresu, 52, Areso, Na. Reconciled at San Sebastián (*Second Report of Salazar* clause 4)	E 461	E 462	91
341	469 ff.		E 469		
342	473 ff.	Martín de Alcoz, 17, Areso, Na	E 473	E 474-475	92
343	512 ff.	Martín de Babazarte, 40, Inza, Na		E 512, E 517	93
344	537 ff.		E 537		
345	548 ff.	María de Gorriti, 70, "Ayabar" [=Aibar, Na]		E 548	94
346	566 ff.	Cristóbal de Echarrique, 15, "Ayabar" [= Aibar, Na]		E 566	95
347	583 ff.	María de Onsalona (Ansorena), 32, "Ychazun" [= Izascun, Gui]		E 583	96
348	596 ff.	Mari Martín de Aristizábal, 14, Urnieta, Gui		E 596	97
349	617 ff.	Bárbara de Yradi (Yrari), 40, San Sebastián, Gui. Reconciled at San Sebastián (*Second Report of Salazar* clause 68). Her	E 617	E 619	98

Case no.	Folios	Name, age, village, province. Miscellaneous	References in: Salazar Reports	PMS	No. in PMS List B
		trial was initiated by the secular authorities (see chap. 11.C.2, above) so the file was presumably extensive			
350	632 ff.	*Magdalena de Arreche, 13, Rentería, Gui*		E 632	99
351	642 ff.	*Magdalena de Yriarte, 14, Rentería, Gui*		E 642	100
352	651 ff.		E 651		
353	664 ff.	*Gracia de Olasorena, 14, Saldía[s], Na*		E 664	101
354	671ʳ- 683ᵛ	María de Ulibarri, 36, Corres, Al. Reconciled at Vitoria, 29 Nov. 1611ᵉ	E 671 E 661	E 673	102
355	687 ff.	*María de Ochoa, 18, Arroyabe, Al*		E 687	103

Cases 356-440. The Remaining 85 Reconciled Witches
Whose Files Were Also to be Found
in Volumes "B" to "E"ᶠ

e. This file has been preserved and is the previously cited *Trial Record of María de Ulibarri*. The original foliation 671-683 indicates that it was torn out of a volume (i.e. vol. "E"), and from the title page (f. 671ʳ) we learn that this was no. 289 of the total of 290 witches reconciled by Salazar; see below, chap. 11 n. 200, and above, chap. 12.2.

f. Judging from the missing files in our reconstruction — indicated by dots between lines — there would have been space for about 70 files; but this is already too many, for with the 19 *revocantes* whose cases were withdrawn from the series of *reconciliados* (see the table at chap. 11 n. 49), we are in fact missing information on only 66 files. Our reconstruction seems furthermore to prove that the volumes "B" to "E" were not given folio numbers until *after* the removal of the files of the 19 *revocantes*.

Cases 441-521. The 81 *Revocantes* Contained in the
Extant *Volume "F" of Salazar's Visitation Book*[a]

Case no.	Rte	Folios[b]	Name, age, state, village, province. (Previous conf.) Conf., Recon.; Rev. Additional examinations.[c]	Orig. Serial No.[d]	References in: Salazar Reports	PMS	PMS List A/B
441	1	1r-3v 4r-v	Graciana de Serorena, 40, m., Ciga, Na. (17 & 21-3-11 Elizondo) Rev. 23-7-11 Elizondo	"Rte 1"			
442	2	7r-9v 10r-v	María de Echenique, 26, m., Ciga, Na. (25-2-11 Elizondo) Rev. 23-7-11 Elizondo	"Rte 2"			
443	3	13r-15v 16r-v	María de Aynz, 15, unm., Ciga. Na. (21-2-11 Elizondo) Rev. 24-7-11 Elizondo	"Rte 3"			
444	4	19r-21r 22r-v	María de Goyeneche, 20, unm., Ciga. Na. (21-2-11 Elizondo) Rev. 24-7-11 Elizondo	"Rte 4"			
445	5	25r-27r 28r-29r	Juana de Aldeco, 16, unm., Ciga, Na. (21-2-11 Elizondo) Rev. 29-7-11 Elizondo	"Rte 5"			
446	6	31r-33v 34r-35r	María de Garagarre, 15, unm., Oronoz, Na. (6 & 10-1-11 Elizondo) Rev. 29-7-11 Elizondo	"Rte 6"			
447	7	37r-39r 40r-v	María Martín de Graxiarena, 20, unm., Arráyoz, Na. (30-12-10 Arráyoz) Rev. 29-7-11 Elizondo	"Rte 7"			
448	8	43r-45r 46r-47r	María de Arizcum (Aldecoa), 23, unm., Arráyoz, Na. (30-12-10 Arráyoz) Rev. 29-7-11 Elizondo	"Rte 8"			
449	9	49r-51r 52r-53r	María de Hualde, 40, m., Lecaroz, Na.	"Rte 9"			

a. The title is rather misleading since vol. "F," as has been stated, contains the files of only eighty *revocantes*. The eighty-first *revocante*, however, clearly belongs in the same context (see case no. 521, below).

b. In order that the reader may get an idea of the usual length of the visitation file, the page numbers have been given on two or three separate lines, as the case may be. The page numbers in the first line refer to what one might call the trial proper, the page numbers in the second line to the revocation, and where there is a third line, it refers to additional examinations. If we look at the first 61, who recanted their confessions immediately (that is to say before a reconciliation had taken place), we see that the trial proper requires three folios, one for the title page and two for the confessions. The records of the proceedings for the 19 who first were reconciled and then later appeared to revoke their confessions are considerably longer, from six to eight folios, depending on whether or not they include confessions made before the Edict of Grace was declared. It is precisely these norms of length we have arrived at in our reconstruction of the lost volumes "B" through "E," which contained the files of the reconciled. On this premise we may well speculate as to whether those who were recorded on eight folios in the lost volumes were witches who had confessed before the edict, while those whose records filled only six folios were witches who had first presented themselves during the visitation. However, the blank pages frequently left at the end of the files because of the use of double sheets makes these considerations uncertain.

c. Under the heading "state," married, unmarried, and widow(er) are respectively abbreviated to m., unm., and w. "Previous confessions" are both those made before the visitation began, and those made on the publication of the edict but before Salazar had come to the region in question. Following the parentheses are all the hearings undertaken on the actual journey of visitation: confession, *curaduría* (a declaration of guardianship for all those under 25 years of age), reconciliation, revocation, and additional examinations. Where no name is given, the hearings were undertaken by Salazar himself or by some member of his staff; however, in the case of the examination dates in parentheses the name of the inquisitorial commissioner has been excluded for the sake of brevity (compare case nos. 502-520 with table 7, above, where the names of the commissioners who received the previous confessions are stated).

d. "Rte" is the abbreviation of *Revocante*, and "Rdo" that of *Reconciliado*; for a discussion of these original serial numbers see chap. 11 n. 49, below; they should not be confused with our abbreviations *Rdo* and *Rte*, used elsewhere (see above, near end of Abbreviations and Conventions).

Case no.	Rte	Folios	Name, age, state, village, province. (Previous conf.) Conf., Recon.; Rev. Additional examinations.	Orig. Serial No.	References in: Salazar Reports	PMS	PMS List A/B
450	10	57r-59r 60r-v	Graciana de Larralde, 20, unm., Lecaroz, Na. (10-2-11, Lecaroz) Rev. 30-7-11 Elizondo	"Rte 10"			
451	11	63r-64v 65r-66r	María de Arotzarena, 36, unm., Oronoz, Na. (6-1-11 Elizondo) Rev. 30-7-11 Elizondo	"Rte 11"			
452	12	69r-72v 73r-v	María de Gardel, 74, w., Lesaca, Na. (11-12-09 Tolosa) Rev. 8-8-11 Lesaca. See case no. 115	"Rte 12"			
453	13	77r-79r 80r-v	María de Peña, 22, unm., Vera, Na. (28-3-10 Vera) Rev. 16-8-11 Vera =? case no. 259	"Rte 13"	F 77		
454	14	83r-87r 88r-89r 89r-v	Hipólita de Arbiza, 15, unm., Yanci, Na. (23-2-10 Lesaca) Rev. 8-8-11 Lesaca. Ratification of revocation and an additional hearing Vera 16-8-11	"Rte 14"	F 83		
455	15	91r-93v 94r-95r 95r-96r	Mariana de Apecechea, 12, unm., Yanci, Na. (20-2-10 Lesaca) Rev. 8-8-11 Lesaca. Ratification of the rev. and an additional hearing 16-8-61 Vera	"Rte 15"	F 91[e]		
456	16	99r-102v 103r-v 103v-104r	Juana Fernández de Arbiza, 13, unm., Yanci, Na. (3-2-10 Lesaca) Rev. 8-8-11 Lesaca. Additional hearing 17-8-11 Vera	"Rte 16"	F 99		
457	17	107r-117r 118r-119r	María Martín de Legarra, 33, unm., Lesaca, Na. (17-11-09 San Sebastián) Rev. 11-8-11 Lesaca. See case no. 113	"Rte 17"	F 107		

e. In *Second Report of Salazar* gloss 73, erroneously called Joana de Apecechea.

Case no.	Rte	Folios	Name, age, state, village, province. (Previous conf.) Conf., Recon.; Rev. Additional examinations.	Orig. Serial No.	References in: Salazar Reports	PMS	PMS List A/B
458	18	123r-124v 625r-v	Ana de Martilopicena, 20, unm., Aranaz, Na. (13-5-11 Lesaca) Rev. 11-8-11 Lesaca	"Rte 18"			
459	19	129r-131r 132r-133r	Catalina de Juangotenea, 37, w., Aranaz, Na. (13-3-11 Lesaca) Rev. 11-8-11 Lesaca	"Rte 19"			
460	20	135r 136r-137r	Margarita de Lizatea, 50, m., Aranaz, Na. Rev. 11-8-11 Lesacaf	"Rte 20"			
461	21	139r 140r-141r	Gracia de Galarza, 52, unm., Aranaz, Na. Rev. 11-8-11 Lesacaf	"Rte 21"	F 139g		
462	22	143r-150v 151r-152r 152r-v	María de Dindur (Chipito), 40, unm., Lesaca, Na. (12-12-09 Tolosa) Rev. 13-8-11 Lesaca. Additional hearing 13-8-11 Lesaca. See case no. 116	"Rte 22"			
463	23	155r-158r 159r-160r	Juanes de Picabea, 13, unm., Lesaca, Na. (13-12-09 Tolosa) Rev. 14-8-11 Lesaca. See case no. 117	"Rte 23"			
464	24	163r-165v 166r-v	Gracia de Lizárraga, 19, unm., Lesaca, Na. (13-12-09 Tolosa) Rev. 17-8-11 Lesaca to commissioner Domingo de San Paul. See case no. 118	"Rte 24"			
465	25	169r-172v 173r	María de Yturría, 10, unm., Echalar, Na. (14-12-09 Tolosa) Rev. 19-8-11 Vera. See case no. 119	"Rte 25"			
466	26	175r 176r-v	Martín de Gorosorroeta, 12, unm., Vera, Na. Rev. 19-8-11 Verah	"Rte 26"			
467	27	179r-181r 182r-v	Mari Martín de Garagarre, 12, unm., Oronoz, Na. (10-1-11 Oronoz) Rev. 29-7-11 Elizondo	"Rte 27"			
468	28	185r-189r 190r-v	Gracia de Berrotarán, 15, unm., Fuenterrabía, Gui. (16-6-11 Fuenterrabía) Curaduría and rev. 23-8-11	"Rte 28"			

469	29	193r-195v 196r-v 197r-v	María de Azaldegui, 17, unm., Fuenterrabía, Gui. (16-6-11 Fuenterrabía) *Curaduría* and rev. 23-8-11 Fuenterrabía. Additional hearing 20-9-11 San Sebastián	"Rte 29"	
470	30	199r-201v 202r-v	Catalina de Alonso, 14, unm., Oyarzun, Gui. (20-6-11 Fuenterrabía) *Curaduría* and rev. 24-8-11 Fuenterrabía	"Rte 30"	
471	31	205r-209r 210r-v 210v-211v	Sabadina de Echetoa, 17, unm., Fuenterrabía, Gui. (13-6-11 Fuenterrabía) *Curaduría* and rev. 25-8-11 Fuenterrabía. Additional hearing 16-9-11 San Sebastián	"Rte 31"	
472	32	213r-215r 216r-v	Juanes de Oyarzábal, 15, unm., Fuenterrabía, Gui. (19-6-11 Fuenterrabía) *Curaduría* and rev. 25-8-11 Fuenterrabía	"Rte 32"	
473	33	219r-221v 222r-v	Beltrán de Echegaray, 16, unm., Fuenterrabía, Gui. (20-6-11 Fuenterrabía) *Curaduría* and rev. 26-8-11 Fuenterrabía	"Rte 33"	
474	34	225r-227r 227r-v	Isabela de Gijón, 11, unm., Fuenterrabía, Gui. (7-6-11 Fuenterrabía) Rev. 25-8-11 Fuenterrabía	"Rte 34"	
475	35	229r-231r 232r-v 232v-235v	María de Yanci, 70, m., Fuenterrabía, Gui. (5-6-11 Fuenterrabía) Rev. 22-8-11 Fuenterrabía. Additional hearings 27 & 28-8-11 at Fuenterrabía and 23 & 24-9-11 at San Sebastián	"Rte 35"	F 229

f. These two files consist only of title page and revocation. In marginal notes (ff. 136r and 140r, respectively) it is stated that the files do not appear among "the visitation documents," although the commissioner of Lesaca certifies to having received the confessions during Holy Week 1611.

g. In *Second Report of Salazar* gloss 73, she is stated to be 80 years old, but this is clearly an error in copying.

h. The file consists of only title page and the revocation. According to a statement (f. 176r) the confession was made "more than a year ago" to the commissioner of Lesaca.

Case no.	Rte	Folios	Name, age, state, village, province. (Previous conf.) Conf., Recon.; Rev. Additional examinations.	Orig. Serial No.	References in: Salazar Reports	PMS	PMS List A/B
476	36	237ʳ-239ʳ 240ʳ⁻ᵛ	Gracia de Amorena, 20, unm., Elvetea, Na. (15-3-11 Elizondo) Rev. 24-8-11 Elizondo to commissioner Fray León de Araníbar	"Rte 37"			
477	37	243ʳ-245ʳ 246ʳ⁻ᵛ	Catalina de Unidearena, 60, m., Arráyoz, Na. (30-12-10 Arráyoz) Rev. 29-8-11 Elizondo to commissioner Fray León de Araníbar	"Rte 38"			
478	38	249ʳ-251ʳ 252ʳ⁻ᵛ	Marichipi de Barreneche, 19, unm., Arráyoz, Na. (30-12-10 Arráyoz) Rev. 29-8-11 Elizondo to commissioner Fray León de Araníbar	"Rte 39"			
479	39	255ʳ-258ᵛ 255ʳ⁻ᵛ	Juanes de Soraburu y Mayora, 22, unm., Ciga, Na. (28-3-11 Elizondo) Rev. 29-8-11 Elizondo to commissioner Fray León de Araníbar	"Rte 40"			
480	40	263ʳ-265ᵛ 266ʳ⁻ᵛ	María de Sansetena, 36, unm., Elveta, Na. (13-2-11 Elizondo) Rev. 24-8-11 Elizondo to commissioner Fray León de Araníbar	"Rte 41"			
481	41	269ʳ-273ʳ 274ʳ⁻ᵛ	María de Yturreguía, 40, m., Irurita, Na. (15-4-11 Elizondo; same day confession of her 10-year-old son, Martín de Yturregui, ff. 271ʳ-273ʳ) Rev. 26-8-11 Elizondo to commissioner Fray León de Araníbar	"Rte 42"			
482	42	277ʳ-279ᵛ 280ʳ	María Gómez, 16, unm., San Sebastián, Gui. Conf. 15-9-11 San Sebastián; Rev 24-9-11 San Sebastián	"Rte 45"	F 277		
483	43	281ʳ-283ᵛ 284ʳ	Marichipi de Garaycoeche, 20, unm., Lecaroz, Na. (28-2-11 Elizondo) Rev. 18-9-11 Elizondo to commissioner Fray León de Araníbar	"Rte 46"			

		Folios	Details	"Rte"	F	A
484	44	287r-290v, 291r-v	Mariana de Eraso, 13, unm., Asteasu, Gui. (28-8-10 Tolosa) Rev. 13-10-11 Tolosa	"Rte 47"		
485	45	295r-300v, 295r	García de Gortegui, 19, unm., Ciboure, La. (15-6-11 Fuenterrabia) Rev. 12-9-11 San Sebastián[i]	"Rte 49"		
486	46	303r-307v, 307v-308r	Catalina Fernández de Lecea (Otrollo), 80, unm., Araya, Al. (25-6-11 Amézaga) Rev. 26-11-11 Salvatierra	"Rte 51"	F 303	
487	47	313r-318r, 318v-319r	Ana Sáenz de Ylarduya, 70, w., Ilarduya, Al. (28-6 & 2-7-11 Amézaga) Rev. 27-11-11 Salvatierra	"Rte 52"	F 313	
488	48	321r-323r, 323r-324r, 324r-325r	Magdalena de Elorza, 50, w., Atauri, Al. (20-9-11 Maestu) Ratification and Rev. 29-11-11 Vitoria. Additional hearing 30-11-11 Vitoria	"Rte 53"	F 321	
489	49	327r-328v, 330r-v	Agueda de Muróa, 14, unm., Larrea, Al. (11-11-11 Larrea) Rev. 30-11-11 Vitoria	"Rte 55"	F 327	
490	50	333r-335r, 336r-v	Ana García (de Arriola), 10 (13), unm., Larrea, Al. (9-11-11 Larrea) Rev. 30-11-11 Vitoria	"Rte 54"	F 333	
491	51	339r-342v, 343r-v	Catalina de Echetoa, 16, unm., Almándoz, Na. (23-6-11 Elizondo) Rev. 22-11-11 Elizondo to commissioner Fray León de Aranibar	"Rte 55 [bis]"	F 339	
492	52	347r-349r, 350r-v	Juana de Echetoa, 50, w., Almándoz, Na. (26-3-11 Elizondo) Rev. 22-11-11 Elizondo to commissioner Fray León de Aranibar	"Rte 56"	F 347	
493	53	353r-355r, 356r-357v	Catalina de Echevarría, 60, w., Fuenterrabia, Gui. Rev. 29-8-11 Fuenterrabia. See case no. 73	"Rte 36"	F 253[j]	A:80

---

i. This is the case referred to below (chapter 11 n. 67) where the forms were left blank and bound with the file. Folio 298r-v is the form for the *curaduría* (see chapter 11 n. 18, below) and folios 299r-300v are the forms for reconciliation.

j. In *Second Report of Salazar* gloss 55, obviously an error for "F 353." The visitation file consists of title page, two certificates referring to her reconciliation at Logroño, and the revocation.

Case no.	Rte	Folios	Name, age, state, village, province. (Previous conf.) Conf., Recon.; Rev. Additional examinations.	Orig. Serial No.	Salazar Reports	PMS	PMS List A/B
494	54	359ʳ 360ʳ⁻ᵛ	Catalina de Aranibar, 26, unm., Zubieta, Na. Rev. 17-9-11 San Sebastián. See case no. 58	"Rte 43"			A:78
495	55	363ʳ 364ʳ⁻ᵛ	Pedro de Arrosarena, [50, m.], Zubieta, Na. Rev. 19-8-11 on his deathbed at Zubieta to the commissioner Miguel de Yrisarri. See case no. 60	"Rte 44"	F 363		A:79
496	56	367ʳ 368ʳ-369ᵛ	María Pérez Sarrayl, 60, w., Santesteban, Na. Rev. 12-10-11 Santesteban to commissioner Miguel de Yrisarri. The revocation is preceded by a letter from the commissioner to the Tribunal. See case no. 51	"Rte 48"			
497	57	373ʳ	Ana de Corres, 55, w., Maestu, Al. Rev. 22-12-11 Vitoria. See case no. 88	"Rte 57"	F 373		A:82
498	58	377ʳ 378ʳ-380ʳ	Don Diego de Basurto, 95, priest, Ciordia, Na. Rev. 18-11-11 Alsasua. With a letter from the commissioner of Salvatierra to the Tribunal, dated 8-12-11. See case no. 84	"Rte 50"	F 377		A:74
499	59	383ʳ 384ʳ⁻ᵛ	María de Corres, 12, unm., Corres, Al. Rev. 23-12-11 Vitoria. See case no. 89	"Rte 58"	F 383		A:83
500	60	387ʳ 388ʳ-389ʳ	Magdalena de Arza, 60, unm., Cicujano, Al. Rev. 27-12-11 Vitoria. See case no. 96	"Rte 59"	F 387ᵏ		A:83
501	61	391ʳ 392ʳ-393ʳ	Gracia González, 24, m., Cicujano, Al. Rev. 27-12-11 Vitoria. See case no. 86	"Rte 60"	F 391		A:81

			Rdo	F	F	B	
502	62	395r-403v, 404r-405v	"Rdo 24"				Juanes de Arroqui y Labayen (Aguirre), 40, m., Zubieta, Na. (16-4-11 Zubieta) Conf. 4-6-11 Santesteban, Recon. 28-6-11 Santesteban; Rev. 14-7-11 Ezcurra. (Cf. table 7, above)
503	63	409r-416v, 417r-418r	"Rdo 59"				Mari Pérez de Larralde, 18, unm., Ciga, Na. (6-2 & 25-2-11 Elizondo) Conf. 10-6-11 Santesteban, Recon. 26-6-11 Santesteban; Rev. 30-7-11 Elizondo. (Cf. table 7, above)
504	64	421r-428v, 429r-v	"Rdo 32"	F 421			María de Saldías, 19, unm., Zubieta, Na. (17-2-11 Elizondo) Conf. 6-6-11 Santesteban, Recon. 28-6-11 Santesteban; Rev. 17-9-11 San Sebastián. (Cf. table 7, above)
505	65	435r-452v[1], 453r-v	"Rdo 33"	F 435[m]			Gracia de Macuso y Marquesarena, 16, unm., Zubieta, Na. (25-2-11 Elizondo) Conf. 6-6-11 Santesteban, Recon. 28-6-11 Santesteban; Rev. 19-9-11 San Sebastián. (Cf. table 7, above)
506	66	455r-460v, 461r-v	"Rdo 26"				Hernautón de Arrosarena, 20, unm., Zubieta, Na. (11-2-11 Elizondo) Conf. 4-6-11 Santesteban, Recon. 28-6-11 Santesteban; Rev. 17-9-11 San Sebastián. (Cf. table 7, above)
507	67	465r-472v, 473r-v	"Rdo 8"	F 463[n]	F 468[n]	B:151	Juana de Labayen, 40, m., Zubieta, Na. (15-4-11 Zubieta) Conf. 2-6-11 Santesteban, Recon. 26-6-11 Santesteban; Rev. 17-9-11 San Sebastián. (Cf. table 7, above)

k. In *Second Report of Salazar* gloss 82, erroneously called Magdalena de Ara.

l. There is an error in the pagination resulting in a jump from f. 439 to f. 450.

m. In *Fifth Report of Salazar* § 20, corrupted to Garciana de Mascusio.

n. "F463," in *Second Report of Salazar* gloss 8, is an error for "F 465." By checking the reference of the *PMS*, "F 468," with the original manuscript we can observe that the colleagues have skipped the title page and previous hearing and jumped to the proper visitation record, which was initiated with the confession made on 2 June at the visitation at Santesteban. However, while Salazar invariably gave the title page, we are far from observing any fixed rule in the references of his colleagues.

Case no.	Rte	Folios	Name, age, state, village, province. (Previous conf.) Conf., Recon.; Rev. Additional examinations.	Orig. Serial No.	References in: Salazar Reports	PMS	PMS List A/B
508	68	477r-484v, 485r-v, 485v-487v	María de Mindeguía, 40, m., Zubieta, Na. (16-4-11 Zubieta) Conf. 6-6-11 Santesteban, Recon. 22-6-11 Santesteban; Rev. 17-9-11 San Sebastián. Additional hearings 16 & 17-10-11 at Ituren by the commissioner Juan de Monterola. (Cf. table 7, above)	"Rdo 30"	F 472°, F 437°, F 486	F 478	B:126
509	69	491r-496v, 497r-498r	Juana de Hualde, 27, unm., Zubieta, Na. (20-2-11 Zubieta) Conf. 3-6-11 Santesteban, Recon. 28-6-11 Santesteban; Rev. 17-10-11 at Ituren to commissioner Juan de Monterola. (Cf. table 7, above)	"Rdo 12"	F 491	F 491	B:152
510	70	503r-509v, 510r-v	Magdalena de Eraso, 15, unm., Fuenterrabía, Gui. (10-6-11 Fuenterrabía) Recon. 22-8-11 Fuenterrabía; Rev. 8-10-11 San Sebastián. (Cf. table in chapter 11 n. 49, below)	"Rdo 70"	F 503		
511	71	513r-520v, 521r-v	Mari Juan de Juanescongoa, 50, w., Zubieta, Na. (15-4-11 Zubieta) Conf. 2-6-11 Santesteban, Recon. 26-6-11 Santesteban; Rev. 17-10-11 at Ituren to the commissioner Juan de Monterola. (Cf. table 7, above)	"Rdo 9"	F 513		
512	72	527r-533v, 534r-535r	María de Garbisu, 16, unm., Fuenterrabía, Gui. (10-6-11 Fuenterrabía) Recon. 22-8-11 Fuenterrabía; Rev. 3-10-11 at Fuenterrabía to commissioner Martín de Berrotarán, and a second rev. 8-10-11 San Sebastián. (Cf. table in chapter 11 n. 49, below)	"Rdo 69"			

513	73	539r-544v 545r-546r	Juanes de Ugarte, 16, unm., Fuenterrabía, Gui. (11-6-11 Fuenterrabía) Recon. 22-8-11 Fuenterrabía; Rev. 1-10-11 San Sebastián. (Cf. table in chapter 11 n. 49, below)	"Rdo 68"	F 539
514	74	547r-554v 555r	Graciana de Plaza, 40, m., Lecaroz, Na. (10-2-11 Lecaroz) Conf. 29-7-11 Elizondo, Recon. 29-7-11 Elizondo; Rev. 24-10-11 on her deathbed at Lecaroz to commissioner Fray León de Araníbar. (Cf. table in chapter 11 n. 49, below)	"Rdo 153"	G 547[p]
515	75	559r-566v 567r-568v	Juana de Yrurita, 40, w., Zubieta, Na. (18-4-11 Zubieta) Conf. 4-6-11 Santesteban, Recon. 28-6-11 Santesteban; Rev. 24-10-11 at Goizueta to commissioner Juan de Monterola. (Cf. table 7, above)	"Rdo 19"	F 568
516	76	571r-575v 576r-v	Tomás de Saldías, 14, unm., Zubieta, Na. Conf. 4-7-11 Santesteban, Recon. 5-7-11 Santesteban; Rev. 24-8-11 at Goizueta to commissioner Juan de Monterola.[q] (Cf. table 7, above)	"Rdo 126"	
517	77	581r-587v 588r-589r	Catalina de Yrurita (Sanchocoa), 16, unm., Zubieta, Na. (11-2-11 Elizondo) Conf. 4-6-11 Santesteban, Recon. 24-6-11 Santesteban; Rev. 29-10-11 at Goizueta to commissioner Juan de Monterola. (Cf. table 7, above)	"Rdo 23"	

o. "F 472" in gloss 1 of *Second Report of Salazar* is an error in copying. "F 437" in gloss 10 of the same report might be an error for F 477. The gloss cites 20 persons who stated that they got wet if it rained when they journeyed to the sabbath. If we check the file of *Rte* 65 ("F 435") we find nothing of this kind, but *Rte* 68 ("F 477") on the other hand did make such a statement (f. 481r).

p. In *Second Report of Salazar* gloss 77, obviously an error for "F 547."

q. In the revocation reference is made to two previous confessions, one to the local authorities of Zubieta and another to the commissioner Fray León de Araníbar (see f. 576r-v).

Case no.	Rte	Folios	Name, age, state, village, province. (Previous conf.) Conf., Recon.; Rev. Additional examinations.	Orig. Serial No.	Salazar Reports	PMS	PMS List A/B
518	78	593r-599v 600r-v	Hernautón de Hualde, 60, m., Zubieta, Na. (19-2-11 Elizondo) Conf. 3-6-11 Santesteban. Recon. 28-6-11 Santesteban; Rev. 29-10-11 at Goizueta to commissioner Juan de Monterola. (Cf. table 7, above)	"Rdo 10"			
519	79	607r-612v 613r	Juanes de Bastanbide, 15, unm., Fuenterrabía, Gui. (12-6-11 Fuenterrabía) Recon. 23-8-11 Fuenterrabía; Rev. 23-11-11 at Fuenterrabía to commissioner Martín de Berrotarán. (Cf. table in chapter 11 n. 49, below)	"Rdo 247"			
520	80	617r-625v 626r-v	María de Dindart (Yndarte), 56, m., Lecaroz, Na. (14-3-11 Elizondo) Conf. 29-7-11 Elizondo, Recon. 29-7-11 Elizondo; Rev. 20-12-11 at Elizondo to commissioner Fray León de Aranibar. (Cf. table in chapter 11 n. 49, below)	"Rdo 152"			
521	81		Mari Martín, 40, Lecaroz, Nar				

r. This file does not form part of *Volume "F."* Presumably the recantation was received by some commissioner who forwarded the record to the Tribunal when the files of the 80 *revocantes* were already bound. But Salazar added a summary of this case to his survey of people who revoked their confession (see p. 318, above, and *Second Report of Salazar* gloss 79).

Cases 522-562. The 41 Witches Absolved *de Levi*
Contained in the Lost Volume "G"

Case no.	Folios	Name, age, village, province. Miscellaneous	References in: Salazar Reports	PMS	No. in PMS List B
522	1 ff.	María de Peloa, 11, Donamaría, Na	G 1	G 2	104, 127
523	11 ff.	Juanes de Yberíbar, 14, Ituren, Na	G 11	G 11	105
524	19 ff.	Miguel de Echachipía, 14, Zubieta, Na	G 19	G 20	106
525	27 ff.	Sancho de Aldaz, 14, Olagüe, Na	G 27	G 28	107
526	41 ff.	María de Serauren (Sorauren)	G 41		
527	55 ff.	Catalina de Aldátegi	G 55		
528	63 ff.	Catalina de Cortejeneco, 12, Zubieta, Na	G 63	G 64 G 66	108
529	67 ff.		G 67		
530	71 ff.	María Martín de Sagardía, 13, Aurtiz, Ituren, Na	G 71	G 72	109
531	79 ff.		G 79		
532	87 ff.	Pedro de Capearena, 15, Aurtiz, Ituren, Na	G 87	G 88 G 90	109a 154
533	97 ff.		G 97		
534	105 ff.	María de Zarandía	G 105		
535	. . . . . . 121 ff.	María de Datereberea (Datueberea or Atuberea) =María de Betebería, 12, Elizondo, Na	G 121	G 128	110
536	129 ff.	Juanesto de Bozate	G 129		
537	137 ff.		G 137		
538	145 ff.	María de Ordoqui [girl, Arizcun, Na?][a]	G 145		
539	153 ff.	María de Ormaechea (Ormacea), 30, Errazu, Na	G 153	G 154 G 155	111
540	166 ff.	Catalina de Soraburu	G 166		
541	. . . . . . 184 ff.	María de Garaicoche, 12, Urdax, Na	G 184	G 185	112
542	194 ff.	Juanes de Echegoiem, 14, Yanci, Na	G 194	G 195	113
543	202 ff.	María de Perugurría (Petrigurría)	G 202		

---

a. Cowitness to Catalina de Sastrearena (case no. 335) on the visitation at Elizondo (see chapter 11 n. 86, below).

Case no.	Folios	Name, age, village, province. Miscellaneous	References in: Salazar Reports	PMS	No. in PMS List B
544	218 ff.		G 218		
545	226 ff.	Catalina de Xaurigi, 15, Vera, Na		G 226 G 227	164
546	238 ff.	María de Permosa	G 238		
547	246 ff.	*Juan Pérez de Echevarría, 12, Lesaca, Na*	G 246	G 249	128
548	256 ff.	Catalina Pérez de Reina	G 256		
549	266 ff.	Felipe de Agesta, *14, Vera, Na*	G 266	F 271[b]	153
550	278 ff.	Catalina de Busti *(de Dibusti), 30, Vera, Na (Mendionde, La)*	G 278	G 279, G 281, G 282	115, 118, 128
551	294 ff.	Ana de Xamateleo	G 294		
552	302 ff.	María de Alsueta, *16, Sumbilla, Na*	G 302	G 303	116
553	336 ff.	María de Oteiza, 12	G 336 G 356[c]		
554	348 ff.		G 348		
555	360 ff.	*Juanes de Azparren, 13, Villanueva de Araquil, Na*	G 360	G 361	117
556	370 ff.	Francisca González, 47	G 370 F 370[d]		
557	382 ff.		G 382		
558	388 ff.		G 388		
559	394 ff.		G 394		

[560-562] The remaining three absolved witches whose files were also to be found in this volume.

b. "F 271" is an error for "G 271" (see case no. 481, above).

c. While the former reference appears thrice in *Second Report of Salazar* (gloss 1, 45b, and 71), "G 356" appears only in gloss 25 of the same report. It must therefore be an error in copying so that we should read "G 336."

d. "F 370" is an error in copying, see case no. 496, above.

Cases 563-1,948. The 1,384 Child Witches Contained in the Lost Volume "H"[a]

Case no.	Folios	Name, age, village, province. Miscellaneous	References in: Salazar Reports	PMS	No. in PMS List B
563	 52		H 52		

Case no.	Folios	Name, age, village, province. Miscellaneous	References in: Salazar Reports	PMS	No. in PMS List B
564	 91	Catalina de San Estevan	H 91		
565	 94	Catalina de Garaicochea	H 94		
566	 132	Juanes, 10, "son of the [black]smith"[b]	H 132		
567	133	Estevanía de Zalderi, 10	H 133		
568	134	Martín de Sastrearena, 80[c]	H 134		
569	 182	Marichipi de Huarte, 9	H 182		
570	 185	Catalina de Yturralde, 9	H 185		
571	 198	María de Zamarguillearena, 10	H 198		
572	 204	Juanes de Chirripa, 8	H 204		
573	 212	Juanes de Arreche, 9	H 212		
574	. . . . . . 248	Francisco de Echeverría, 11, Vera, Na	H 248		
575	290 ff.	Juanico de Aguirre, 12, Fuenterrabía[d]	H 290		
576	470	Gracianato de Legarrea, 10	H 470		
577	 526	Francisco de Echevarría, 8	H 526		
578	 529	María de Zabala, 8	H 529		

[579-1,948] The remaining 1,371 child witches whose files were also to be found in this volume. For the total of 1,948, see Introduction to Witch List, above.

a. If we sum up the folios of the preceding volumes we reach a total of 4,260 folios. As previously mentioned, the whole visitation book consisted of some 5,600 folios. According to these figures it would seem that the extent of volume "H" must have been over 1,300 folios, an average of one folio or two pages to each of the 1,384 files contained in this volume.

b. See *Second Report of Salazar* gloss 45.

c. See *Second Report of Salazar* gloss 45. It is, however, strange to find this old man among the child witches; 80 might be an error in copying for 8 years.

d. The file of this boy must have been of some length, for he managed, as Salazar puts it, to mention 147 persons in his list of accomplices (see *Second Report of Salazar* clause 64).

NOTES

NOTES TO CHAPTER 1

1. Margaret Alice MURRAY *The Witch-Cult in Western Europe* London & Oxford 1921; reprinted with foreword by Steven Runciman, Oxford 1962 (hereafter cited as MURRAY *Witch-Cult*). Parts of the contents were previously published in the periodical *Man* 18 (1918) 60-62, 81-84, 101-104, 148-153, 188-191; 19 (1919) 55-58, 137-140.

2. Wilhelm Gottlieb SOLDAN *Geschichte der Hexenprozesse aus den Quellen dargestellt* Stuttgart 1843; 2nd ed. revised by H. L. J. Heppe, Stuttgart 1880; 3rd ed. revised by M. Bauer, München 1912; 4th ed. revised by Will-Erich Peuckert, Darmstadt 1967.

3. Joseph HANSEN *Zauberwahn, Inquisition und Hexenprozess im Mittelalter und die Entstehung der grossen Hexenverfolgung* München & Leipzig 1900; *Quellen und Untersuchungen zur Geschichte des Hexenwahrs und der Hexenverfolgung* Bonn 1901, Hildesheim 1963.

4. Henry Charles LEA *A History of the Inquisition of the Middle Ages* New York 1888, 3 vols., reprinted New York 1955; *A History of the Inquisition of Spain* New York 1906-07, 4 vols., photographic reprint New York 1966 (hereafter cited as LEA *Inquisition of Spain*); "Notes for a History of Witchcraft" (1909) published by Arthur C. Howland with introduction by George Lincoln Burr (1938) under the title *Materials Toward a History of Witchcraft* Philadelphia 1939, 3 vols., also New York & London 1957. See also the Lea bibliography in Edward Sculley BRADLEY *Henry Charles Lea: A Biography* Philadelphia 1931, pp. 374-381.

5. MURRAY *Witch-Cult* p. 9.

6. Idem p. 9 ff.

7. Murray's book was reviewed by George L. Burr in *American Historical Review* 37 (1922) 78-83; and by W. R. Halliday in *Folklore* 33 (1922) 224-230. Her theories have since been vigorously disputed by Cecil E. EWEN *Some Witchcraft Criticism* London 1938; by Eliot E. ROSE *A Razor for a Goat* Toronto 1962; and most recently by Norman COHN *Europe's Inner Demons* London, Sussex University Press, 1975, Paladin ed., Frogmore 1976 pp. 107-120.

8. Montague SUMMERS *The History of Witchcraft and Demonology* London & New York 1926, reprinted London 1965. The book contains a valuable bibliography of English pamphlet literature 1566-1751. Reviewed by Lynn Thorndike in *The Nation* (New York) 12 January

1927, and elsewhere. For Summers's additional studies of witch belief see the bibliography in Joseph JEROME *Montague Summers. A Memoir* London 1965, pp. 91-92; the same author expresses doubts as to whether Summers ever was ordained as a Catholic priest, see op. cit. chap. 2, "Reverend in What Church?".
9. SUMMERS 1926 p. xiv.
10. Idem p. xii.
11. Augustin CALMET (Abbe de Simons) *Traité sur les apparitions des esprits* Paris 1751 (2nd ed.) vol. I p. 138 (cited by Summers in his note 66).
12. SUMMERS 1926 p. 133.
13. Gerhard ZACHARIAS *Satankult und Schwarze Messe. Ein Beitrag zur Phänomenologie der Religion* Wiesbaden 1964 (the author is somewhat uncritical but has assembled an interesting body of material and included long quotations from the sources in translation); pp. 320-321 of Julio CARO BAROJA *Las brujas y su mundo* Madrid 1961, treat of a "witches' sabbath" with parody of the Mass and sexual orgies held in 1952 on an isolated Basque farm in the Pyrenees in the neighborhood of the town of "V.," i.e. Valcarlos. In 1964 Caro Baroja and I visited the doctor who had been Caro Baroja's informant and who now lived in San Sebastián; he told us that the initiator of the "witches' sabbath" was a man who had spent many years in South America. The doctor was therefore unable to say with certainty whether it was an instance of an old Basque tradition, but the case is still awaiting closer investigation; Francis KING *Ritual Magic in England: 1887 to the Present Time* London 1970. From my studies in the Archivo Histórico Nacional (Madrid) I can adduce two instances of collective satanism: *Leg* 2022 No. 64 fol. 10^r-18^r, 31^r-32^v (proceedings taken in 1653 against a group of practitioners of black magic in Alicante who invoked the devil Cojuelo); and *Leg* 3730 Expediente 180 (statements of evidence against a priest at Cañedo, Gestoso parish, La Coruña, denounced for having held a black mass in a chapel at Cañedo in March 1803; 11 other persons were present and the ceremony took the form of invoking the assistance of the Devil in a treasure hunt). See also Henry T. F. RHODES *The Satanic Mass* London 1954.
14. Most of these books have been written with a keen eye on the popularity that fantastic theories seem to hold for the general public, and we can therefore ignore them. Among the more serious attempts to continue along the lines of Murray's research are the following: Arne RUNEBERG *Witches, Demons and Fertility Magic: Analysis of their Significance and Mutual Relationship in West-European Folk Religion* Helsingfors 1947; Carlo GINZBURG *I benandanti: Ricerche sulla stregoneria e sui culti agrari tra Cinquecento e Seicento* Turin 1966 (resumé and extracts in English in E. W. MONTER (ed.) *European Witchcraft* New York 1969 pp. 158-164); Tamás KÖRNER "Boszorkányszervezetek Magyarországon [The Hungarian witch organization]" *Ethnographia* 80 (1969) 196-211 (with German and Russian summary).
15. Geoffrey PARRINDER *Witchcraft: A critical study of the belief in witchcraft from the records of witch-hunting in Europe yesterday and Africa today* Harmondsworth, Pelican Books, 1958, passim. Two important studies of English witch belief diverge sharply from Margaret Murray:

see Alan D. J. MACFARLANE *Witchcraft in Tudor and Stuart England* London 1970, 2nd ed. New York 1970 (the ed. cited below) passim; and Keith THOMAS *Religion and the Decline of Magic* London 1971 pp. 514-515.

16. Lucy MAIR *Witchcraft* London 1969 (World University Library) p. 230.

17. Idem p. 229.

18. Gerald B. GARDNER *Witchcraft Today* London 1954 (with preface by Margaret Murray!), *The Meaning of Witchcraft* London 1959, and the novel *High Magic's Aid* London 1949. See also Stewart FARRER *What Witches Do* London 1971.

19. See KING 1970, chap. 21, "The contemporary Witch-Cult." While not a scholarly investigation of the type for which I have been looking, it nevertheless contains much valuable first-hand information. King denies any possibility of the modern witch societies having been engendered by Murray's book, but he has not succeeded in detecting any pre-Murray movement. The oldest coven he is aware of is one which was operating in the New Forest in the 1930s and 1940s. On the other hand he demonstrates in a convincing manner that Gerald B. Gardner's writings "were responsible for the mushroom-growth of the witch-cult in the fifties and sixties" (p. 179). King estimates the number of active witches in England at between one thousand and two thousand (p. 176).

20. See Lauritz GENTZ "Vad förorsakede de stora häxprocesserna [What caused the great trials for witchcraft]" *Arv* 10 (1954) 1-39 (with English summary); A. J. CLARK "Flying Ointments" in MURRAY *Witch-Cult* pp. 279-280 (Appendix V); Rossell Hope ROBBINS *The Encyclopedia of Witchcraft and Demonology* London 1959 pp. 364-367 (article on "Ointment, Flying"); Will-Erich PEUCKERT "Ergänzendes Kapitel über das deutsche Hexenwesen" in Julio CARO BAROJA *Die Hexen und ihre Welt* Stuttgart 1967 p. 313f. The subject of "witch unguents" has not yet been investigated in sufficient depth where Europe is concerned, but is dealt with in an interesting article by an American ethno-pharmacologist (see Michael J. Harner "The Role of Hallucinogenic Plants in European Witchcraft" in Michael J. HARNER (ed.) *Hallucinogens and Shamanism* New York, Oxford University Press, 1973 pp. 125-150).

21. Carlos CASTANEDA *The Teachings of Don Juan: A Yaqui Way of Knowledge* Berkeley & Los Angeles, University of California Press, 1968.

22. Idem p. 91.

23. Idem p. 92

24. Idem pp. 93-94.

25. Idem pp. 70-71. Doubts, however, as to Castaneda's veracity, or, indeed, as to the very existence of his *brujo* don Juan, have been expressed in certain quarters, see *Time,* 5 March 1973, pp. 30-35.

26. Traugott Konstantin OESTERREICH *Die Besessenheit* Langensalza 1921 (English translation by D. Ibberson *Possession: Demonical and Other* New York 1930, 1966); Etienne DELCAMBRE "La psychologie des inculpés lorrains de sorcellerie" *Revue historique de droit français et étranger* 32 (1954) 383-403, 508-526; George ROSEN "A study of the

Persecution of Witches in Europe as a Contribution to the Understanding of Mass Delusions and Psychic Epidemics" *Journal of Health
and Human Behaviour* I (1960) 200-211.

27. For instance, the possession of the nuns of Loudun in 1633, see
Aldous HUXLEY *The Devils of Loudun* London 1952, Harmondsworth,
Penguin Books, 1971.

28. For instance, the Salem trial of 1692, see Chadwick HANSEN
Witchcraft at Salem New York 1969.

29. Recommended further reading: ROBBINS 1959 (although a
popular interpretation based on somewhat outdated theories, it contains a wealth of detail and the hitherto most comprehensive bibliography of the early literature). MONTER 1969 (a selection of early and
later writings on witches translated into English); H. C. Erik MIDEL-
FORT "Recent Witch Hunting Research, or Where Do We Go from
Here?" *Papers of the Bibliographical Society of America* 62 (1969) 373-420
(information covering the various lines of research and a bibliography
of 509 works published after 1940); and COHN 1976 (an important
study of the origins of the European witchcraft mythology).

30. For the circular letter of the inquisitor general, dated 25 Feb.
1611, see below, chapter 11.A.1.

31. Pedro de Valencia in the introduction to his First Discourse, see
n. 32, below.

32. *Lib* 1231 ff. 608^r-629^r, Pedro de Valencia to inquisitor general,
Madrid, 20 Apr. 1611, *title:* "Acerca de los cuentos de las brujas,
discurso de Pedro de Valencia dirigido al Illustrísimo Señor Don
Bernardo de Sandoval y Rojas, Cardenal, Arzobispo de Toledo, In-
quisidor General de España" (*Beginning and ending:* "Habiendo leido
un papel impreso... Dios guarde la persona de Vuestra Señoría
Illustrísima. En Madrid, 20 de abril 1611 años"), hereafter cited as *First
Discourse of Pedro de Valencia.*

33. Idem f. 608^{r-v}.

34. Idem f. 608^v.

35. Cf. BN, MS 7579 Part I ff. [1-19], *title:* "Suma de las relaciones de
Logroño cerca de las brujas..." (*Beginning and ending:* "Prestóme un
caballero... correctione Sanctae Ecclesiae Romanae"), undated,
hereafter cited as *Second Discourse of Pedro de Valencia.* For the various
auto de fe accounts see chapter 9.5, below.

36. *First Discourse of Pedro de Valencia* ff. 608^v-609^r. See MURRAY
Witch-Cult pp. 179-180, which also discusses the probability of the
Devil using an artificial phallus.

37. *First Discourse of Pedro de Valencia* ff. 612^v, 613^v.

38. Idem ff. 614^r-615^v. Hereafter follows a passage in which Pedro
de Valencia first calls into question the opinion of one of the leading
authorities of the time, the Jesuit Martín del Río (the author of *Disquisitionem magicarum* Louvain 1599; 7th ed. Lyon 1608). The latter
asserted — according to Pedro de Valencia — that certainly God
would not permit the Devil to play such tricks at the expense of
innocent people. But to this Pedro de Valencia replies that he is not so
sure, for everything that is otherwise said to take place among the
witches in fact presupposes a quite extraordinary sanction on the part
of God; in fact there exists no method to determine whether it is the

person himself, or his spirit or apparition (*espíritu o fantasma*) which appears at these meetings, for even the witches themselves are not able to distinguish between them. On the other hand, he argues, it is well known that witches who anoint themselves in the presence of others, and then fall asleep, afterwards recount everything that they have dreamed as if they had experienced it in reality. Hence, unless the contrary can be proven, we must assume that the events recounted by the witches are nothing but their dreams, concluded the Spanish humanist (idem ff. 615^v-616^r). This account may serve as an example of the philosophical problems that confronted the scholars of witchcraft, who had to reckon with God, the Devil, and the spiritual bodies of human beings as accepted realities.

39. Idem ff. 628^r-629^r.

40. Pedro de Valencia's discourses were published by Manuel SERRANO Y SANZ: "Discurso de Pedro de Valencia acerca de los quentos de las brujas y cosas tocante a magia . . ." *Revista de Extremadura* 2 (1900) 289-303, 337-347; and "Segundo discurso de Pedro de Valencia acerca de los brujos y sus maleficios" *Revista de Archivos, Bibliotecas y Museos* 3d series, vol. II (1906) 445-454. Except for the discussion in LEA *Inquisition of Spain* vol. IV pp. 229-230 and CARO BAROJA 1961 pp. 259-262, I have not seen any mention of Pedro de Valencia in modern contributions to the history of witchcraft.

41. E. E. EVANS-PRITCHARD "Witchcraft" *Africa* 8 (1935) 417-418. The article prefaces the rest of the volume (pp. 423-560) which was entirely dedicated to witchcraft studies.

42. In the trials of village wizards and wise women there are so many examples of anti-witchcraft and current belief in witches that they provide a very valuable source of information regarding popular witch belief in the sixteenth and seventeenth centuries. The actual witch trials on the other hand generally offer a distorted view in this respect, since they reflect acute situations in which the popular remedies against enchantment had already been tried and had failed. A third group of trials, which it may also be profitable to include, are those of people tried for *maleficium* or harmful sorcery. The trials of sorcerers invariably elucidate what forms of black magic were actually practiced in a particular country and in a particular period, while the pure witch trials give only details of the various types of sorcery of which people *accused* each other. I can illustrate the latter with an example. In sixteenth- and seventeenth-century Denmark it was quite common to accuse witches of sorcery with wax dolls, which were baptized with the names of actual enemies and then punctured with pins in order to cause the death of the victim. However, I have not found a definite proof of this form of image-magic ever having been practiced in Denmark. In Spain, on the contrary, there is no doubt that this kind of sorcery took place. In 1614, for instance, the Inquisition of Toledo tried a woman for having killed her former lover in this way and the record contains a detailed account of her actions (*Leg* 2105 Exp. 3). This woman was accused of *maleficia* and an implicit pact with the Devil, but the proceedings, and this is noteworthy, contain no mention of her having ever met the Devil let alone taken part in a witches' sabbath.

43. MACFARLANE 1970 passim.
44. The above is intended as a synthesis of the observations that I made during my studies of the archives in Spain and Denmark. For the time being, for reference to Denmark see Gustav HENNINGSEN "Trolddom og hemmelige kunster [Sorcery and secret arts]" in Axel STEENSBERG (ed.) *Dagligliv i Danmark 1620-1720* Copenhagen 1969 pp. 161-196, 727-731; and "Hekseforfølgelser [Witch persecutions]" idem pp. 353-376, 736-738. See also MACFARLANE 1970 and THOMAS 1971, both of which offer exhaustive analyses of popular English witch belief in the sixteenth and seventeenth centuries. On the whole the observations of these two writers are in agreement with those I have myself made in Denmark and Spain, but with one important exception: the witches' sabbath. This phenomenon, which was so widespread on the European continent, was of only slight consequence in England (cf. George Lyman KITTREDGE *Witchcraft in Old and New England* Cambridge, Mass., 1929, and New York 1956, in particular chap. 16, "The Compact and the Witches' Sabbath").
45. E. E. EVANS-PRITCHARD *Witchcraft, Oracles and Magic among the Azande* Oxford 1937.
46. Of particular importance is Clyde KLUCKHOHN *Navaho Witchcraft* Cambridge, Mass., 1944; S. F. NADEL *Nupe Religion* London 1954 (especially chap. 6, "Witchcraft and Anti-witchcraft"); but see also John MIDDLETON & E. H. WINTER (eds.) *Witchcraft and Sorcery in East Africa* London 1963; Mary DOUGLAS (ed.) *Witchcraft: Confessions and Accusations* London 1970 (lectures delivered at a symposium on witch belief held 3-6 April 1968 in honour of Evans-Pritchard); Max MARWICK (ed.) *Witchcraft and Sorcery: Selected Readings* Harmondsworth, Penguin Books, 1970 (dedicated to Evans-Pritchard).
47. MAIR 1969 pp. 7-9.
48. This is also true of A. D. J. Macfarlane's impressive study of witchcraft in Essex in the sixteenth and seventeenth centuries (MACFARLANE 1970 part 4, "A comparative framework: Anthropological studies"). He demonstrates, on the other hand, the value of applying a social-anthropological outlook to the immense amount of material lying in the archives of local law-courts, instead of relying only upon printed sources.
49. This was the subject of my thesis "En strukturanalyse af heksetroen i et dansk kulturmiljø [A structural analysis of witch belief in a Danish cultural milieu]" presented at the University of Copenhagen in 1962. Unfortunately, many of the informants and even some of the "witches" being still alive, my thesis has remained unpublished.
50. See Gustav HENNINGSEN "Informe sobre tres años de investigaciones etnológicas en España" *Ethnica: Revista de Antropología* 1 (1971) 61-90.
51. M. FORTES "The Structure of Unilineal Descent Groups" *American Anthropologist* 55 (1953) 18.
52. See Gustav HENNINGSEN "Fatalism in its Systematic Aspect and Fatalism in its Functional Context" in Helmer RINGGREN (ed.) *Fatalistic Beliefs in Religion, Folklore and Literature: Papers read at the Symposium on Fatalistic Beliefs held at Åbo on the 7th-9th of September, 1964* Stockholm 1967 pp. 184-186.

53. RUNEBERG 1947 pp. 14-90 offers an attempt at this type of comparison.

54. HANSEN 1900 p. 55.

55. Cf. however the Edict of Rothar, King of Lombardy, of 643, in which it is expressly stated that Christians ought not to believe "ut mulier hominem vivum intrinsecus possit comedere [that a woman can devour a living person from within]"; cited in HANSEN 1900 p. 59 n. 4.

56. HANSEN 1900 p. 60. And see further the thorough exposition of the development of witch belief ca. 400-1230, idem chap. 2 pp. 36-121.

57. Cf. HANSEN 1900 pp. 78-87. *Canon Episcopi* text in HANSEN 1901 pp. 38-39 (English translation in ROBBINS 1959 pp. 75-77).

58. HANSEN 1900 chap. 4; HANSEN 1901 pp. 449-454; LEA 1957 pp. 230-232. The data of these authorities must be compared with COHN 1976 chap. 7 "Three forgeries and another wrong track" and Richard KIECKHEFER *European Witch Trials: Their Foundation in Popular and Learned Culture, 1300-1500* Berkeley & Los Angeles, University of California Press, 1976. Cohn and Kieckhefer have revolutionized the established history of Medieval witch-hunting by demonstrating that the sources on fourteenth-century mass trials are forgeries, and that the origin of the European witch craze is therefore to be found in the fifteenth century, and not as hitherto believed in the thirteenth or fourteenth centuries.

59. See ROBBINS 1959 pp. 143-147 "Early writers on witchcraft (to 1550)"; and Hugh R. TREVOR-ROPER "The European Witch-craze of the Sixteenth and Seventeenth Centuries" in H. R. Trevor-Roper: *Religion, the Reformation and Social Change* London 1967 (also as separate publication: *The European Witch-Craze* Harmondsworth, Penguin Books, 1969). It is worth noting that the chronological adjustment by Cohn and Kieckhefer (see preceding note) has reaffirmed some early writers on witchcraft who agreed in calling the witches a "new sect" dating from the first decade of the fifteenth century (cf. LEA 1888 III pp. 497-499).

60. On *Malleus Maleficarum* and its authors see HANSEN 1901 pp. 360-408. The year of publication is stated by Hansen to be 1487, while Robbins gives it as 1486 (see ROBBINS 1959 p. 337 and the bibliography, no. 958).

61. HANSEN 1900 pp. 473-475; TREVOR-ROPER 1967 pp. 101-102.

62. For the limited distribution of witch-hunting in this period see the chronological lists of sorcery and witchcraft trials in HANSEN 1901 pp. 445-613 (1240 to 1540) and KIECKHEFER 1976 pp. 108-147 (1300 to 1499). An exception to this pattern is the witch-hunt at Arras in northern France 1459-60 (see LEA 1888 III pp. 519-530 and COHN 1976 pp. 230-232).

63. However, in a recent article it has been demonstrated that the European witch-craze wave did not stop at the Carpathian Mountains as it is generally believed; see Zoltán KOVÁCS "Die Hexen in Russland" *Acta Ethnographica Academiae Hungaricae* 22 (1973) 51-87.

64. TREVOR-ROPER 1967 pp. 136-137.

65. Idem p. 90.

66. Idem pp. 188-189.

67. Copenhagen recess of 6 Dec. 1547, paragraphs 8 and 17, cited by J. C. JACOBSEN in *Danske Domme i Trolddomssager* [Danish judgments in sorcery cases] Copenhagen 1966 p. 141.

68. TREVOR-ROPER 1967 p. 143.

69. MAIR 1969 pp. 186-187, which cites A. D. Macfarlane's unpublished Ph.D. dissertation of 1967: "Witchcraft Prosecutions in Essex 1560-1680." See Alan MACFARLANE "Witchcraft in Tudor and Stuart Essex" in DOUGLAS 1970 pp. 91-99. For Macfarlane's book see n. 15 above.

70. In the case of Denmark see HENNINGSEN 1969b pp. 359, 363, 366, 376. In the case of Spain my assertion is based on an examination of all the *relaciones de causas* of the tribunals of the Inquisition in Navarra and Galicia. In this latter region the Inquisition dealt with about three hundred cases of witchcraft and sorcery between 1565 and 1816, but there was not one instance of a death sentence being pronounced.

71. HENNINGSEN 1969b p. 353.

72. Florencio IDOATE "Brujerías en la montaña de Navarra en el siglo XVI" *Hispania Sacra* IV (1951) pp. 7 (n. 16), 8.

73. See Gustav HENNINGSEN "Hekseforfølgelse efter 'hekseprocessernes tid': Et bidrag til dansk etnohistorie. ["Witch persecution after the era of the witch trials. A contribution to Danish ethnohistory]" *Folk og kultur* 1975, pp. 98-151 (with English summary); and e.g. ROBBINS 1959 p. 368 f. (England 1751); SOLDAN 1880 chaps. 26-27 passim (Europe and America in the eighteenth and nineteenth century).

74. *Le Nouvel Observateur* 15 March 1976, pp. 48-50.

75. ROBBINS 1967 p. 1.

76. Idem p. 3.

77. TREVOR-ROPER 1967 p. 161.

78. Cf. Balthasar BEKKER *De betoverde Weereld* Amsterdam 1691-1693.

79. Cf. Johan WEYER *De praestigiis daemonum et incantationibus ac veneficiis* Basel 1563.

80. Reginald SCOT *Discovery of Witchcraft* London 1584, republished Carbondale, Southern Illinois University Press, 1965, with introduction by Hugh Ross WILLIAMSON. See THOMAS 1971 p. 573 n. 1, where Trevor-Roper is criticized for misinterpretation. "Scot," says Thomas, "admitted the reality of imposters, poisoners, scolds, and deluded persons, but he made no concessions to the notion that they had any supernatural power."

81. See Friedrich von SPEE *Cautio criminalis* Rinteln 1631.

82. TREVOR-ROPER 1967 pp. 175-176.

83. A very similar criticism can be found in MACFARLANE 1970 p. 9, which concludes that "The real defect of the essay [of Trevor-Roper] is that its tone implies that we know a great deal about 'witchcraft' and all that is needed is synthesis. In fact we know far too little." See also Lawrence STONE "The Disenchantment of the World" *The New York Review of Books* XVIII:9 (2 Dec. 1971) 17-24.

84. TREVOR-ROPER 1967 p. 125.

85. See William SARGANT *Battle for the Mind: A Physiology of Conversion and Brain-Washing* London 1957, 7th edition, London, Pan Books, 1970, which treats of the same conception, see e.g. p. 177.

86. In some countries the mercy meted out to penitent and confessing witches was limited to beheading or strangulation, so that they escaped being burned alive (see ROBBINS 1959 p. 179).

87. ROBBINS 1959 pp. 289-293; a complete translation of the letter of Burgomaster Junius is to be found in G. L. BURR (ed.) *The Witch-Persecution* Philadelphia 1897.

88. Robert Jay LIFTON *Thought Reform and the Psychology of Totalism: A Study of "Brainwashing" in China* London 1962 p. 41.

89. See M. J. FIELD *Religion and Medicine of the Gã People* second edition London 1961 (first edition 1937) chap. 4 "Witchcraft."

90. See LIFTON 1962 chap. 5 "Psychological Steps," where the brainwashing process is divided up into the following stages: (1) the assault upon identity; (2) the establishment of guilt; (3) self-betrayal; (4) the breaking point: total conflict and basic fear; (5) leniency and opportunity; (6) compulsion to confess; (7) channelling of guilt; (8) re-education: logical dishonoring; (9) progress and harmony; (10) final confession: the summing up; (11) rebirth; (12) release: transition and limbo.

91. See LEA *Inquisition of Spain* IV p. 211; CARO BAROJA 1961 pp. 213-220; and chap. 8.5 of the present work. A thorough-going examination of Spanish witch persecutions of the sixteenth century is still lacking, but I would call attention to the following important sources: *Lib* 572 ff. 134^v-135^r (letter of 24 Jan. 1508, from *la Suprema* to the tribunal at Calahorra, concerning the goods confiscated from the witches of Guipúzcoa who had been burned by the Inquisition); *Lib* 832 ff. 262^r-263^v (*méritos* from the witch trial of 1508 at Vizcaya); *Lib* 316:I f. 120^r and II ff. 51^r-53^r (concerning the witch persecutions of 1517 in the district of the Barcelona tribunal); *Lib* 317 f. 215^v (the Edict of Grace to the witches at Jaca and Ribagorza, district of the Zaragoza tribunal, published 12 June 1521); *Lib* 397 f. 229^v (note to the effect that the Edict of Grace to the witches was also published in the district of the Calahorra tribunal on 16 July 1521).

92. *Lib* 833 ff. 86^r-89^r (*relación de causas* from the tribunal at Calahorra for the period 20 Nov. 1555 to 19 Jan. 1557, nos. 21-24 concerning four witches from western Guipúzcoa, who "were banished from their [respective] villages to other villages in various regions."

93. E.g. Alfonso Tostado (ca. 1440), quoted in LEA 1957 pp. 189-191; Alphonsus de Spina, whose *Fortalicium fidei* (written ca. 1458-60) was printed at Strassburg 1471 (or earlier), as the first book on witchcraft (see LEA 1957 pp. 285-295); Martín de ARLES Y ANDOSILLA, dean of Aibar (Navarra), canon of Pamplona, author of *Tractatus de superstitionibus* Lyon 1510 (2nd ed. Paris 1517), believed by Lea to have been inspired by the witch persecution in the Basque provinces in 1507 (LEA *Inquisition of Spain* IV p. 211). A reedition of this early treatise on Basque witchcraft with new information about its author can be found in the following article: José GOÑI GAZTAMBIDE "El tratado 'De supersticionibus' de Martín de Andosilla" *Cuadernos de etnología y etnografía de Navarra* III (1971) 249-322.

94. See *Lib* 573 ff. 128^r-128 *bis*^{r} (*title*: "Bruxas: Dubia quae in causa presenti videntur diffinienda"); other transcripts in *Lib* 1325 ff. 54^r-58^r and the Bodleian Library "Arch. Seld 130" (accessions no. according

to Lea). The witch polemic at Granada in 1526 is only briefly mentioned by Lea (*Inquisition of Spain* IV pp. 212-214) and a few other authors (among them S. TUBERVILLE *La Inquisición Española* Mexico 1948 p. 104).

95. See LEA *Inquisition of Spain* IV pp. 209-225; Augustín GONZÁLEZ DE AMEZÚA Y MAYO *"El casamiento engañoso"* y *"El coloquio de los perros": Novelas ejemplares de Miguel de Cervantes Saavedra. Edición crítica con introducción y notas* Madrid 1912 p. 188 and passim (a most scholarly contribution to the history of witch belief and magic in Spain).

96. Pierre DE LANCRE *Tableav de l'Inconstance des mavvais Anges et Demons. Ov il est amplement traicté de la Sorcelerie et Sorciers . . . Avec Vn Discours contenant la Procedure faicte par les Inquisiteurs d'Espagne et de Nauarre, à 53. Magiciens, Apostats, Iuifs, et Sorciers, en la ville de Logrogne en Castille le 9. Nouembre 1610 . . .* [Motto:] *Maleficos non patieris viuere. Exod.* 22 Paris, Nicolas Buon, 1612, another ed. Paris, Jean Berjou, 1612; revised ed. Paris, Nicolas Buon, 1613 (hereafter cited as DE LANCRE *Tableau*). At the Bibliothèque de la Ville de Bordeaux I have had the opportunity of comparing the two Buon editions (accession nos. S 1173 and MF 1373 respectively). The first edition has a somewhat smaller type page. It can be seen that the second edition has been revised and that de Lancre has made a few amendments (for instance on p. 357 an item from 1613); but the chief innovation is Ziarnko's large engraving (inserted between pp. 118 and 119), which is absent from the first edition. Concerning the population estimate of 30,000 in the Pays de Labourd, see DE LANCRE *Tableau* p. 38.

97. See Pierre DE LANCRE *L'incredvlité et Mescreance dv Sortilege plainement convaincve . . .* Paris, Nicolas Buon, 1622 p. 10, where de Lancre explains that his *Tableau* "contains all the trial records of the most notorious witches that we have either condemned to death, or banished, or sent back to the said Parlement" and "resembles the register or record of evidence, containing the examination and proceedings which formed the basis of their sentences" (idem p. 11).

98. Robert MANDROU *Magistrats et sorciers en France au XVIIe siècle: Une analyse de psychologie historique* Paris 1968 p. 19.

99. This must be the place for a short outline on the bibliography of Basque witch trials. Most of the literature may be ignored as it derives solely from printed sources. The remaining part may be divided into three groups according to which records are relied upon. The following studies are based on materials in the archives of southern France: Francisque HABASQUE *Episodes d' un procés en sorcellerie dans le Labourd au XVIIe siècle (1605-1607)* Biarritz 1912; V. LESPY "Les sorcières dans le Béarn (1393-1672)" *Bulletin de la société des sciences, lettres et arts de Pau* 2d series 4 (1874-75) 28-86. Based on materials in the archives of northern Spain are the following: Juan de A. ARZADÚN "Las brujas de Fuenterrabía. Proceso del siglo XVII, el 6 de Mayo de 1611" *Revista internacional de estudios vascos* 3 (1909) 172-181, 357-374; Dario de AREITIO "Las brujas de Ceberio" *Rev. intern. de estud. vascos* XVIII (1927) 654-664; Julio CARO BAROJA "Las brujas de Fuenterrabía (1611)" *Revista de dialectología y tradiciones populares* 3 (1947) 189-204; Florencio IDOATE *La brujería* Pamplona 1967, and op. cit. n. 72, above; José María IRIBARREN "Interesante documento sobre las brujas de Zugarr-

amurdi" *Príncipe de Viana* 4 (1944) 422-427. Finally there are the studies based on materials originating from the Spanish Inquisition. As mentioned in our Preface this documentation was briefly studied by Henry Charles Lea at the turn of the century (LEA *Inquisition of Spain* IV pp. 211-237). All subsequent studies derive solely from Lea, with the exception of Julio Caro Baroja, who published the Salazar manuscript of the Biblioteca Nacional and three other documents on Basque witchcraft in the same library (CARO BAROJA "Cuatro relaciones sobre la hechicería vasca" *Anuario de Eusco-Folklore* 13 [1933] 85-145). After my rediscovery (in Dec. 1967) of the documentation used by Lea and a wealth of hitherto completely unknown materials concerning the famous trial at Logroño in 1610, I published a preliminary analysis in the Autumn of 1969 announcing a forthcoming study which is the present book, see Gustav HENNINGSEN "The Papers of Alonso de Salazar Frias. A Spanish Witchcraft Polemic 1610-14" *Temenos* 5 (1969) 85-106, hereafter cited as HENNINGSEN *Papers of Salazar*. Part of the documentation, that contained in the important *Leg* 1679, was presented by Julio Caro Baroja in a long exposition which appeared in Spring 1970 although the annual says 1969 (see Julio CARO BAROJA "De nuevo sobre la historia de la brujería (1609-1619)" *Príncipe de Viana* 30 (1969) 265-328 hereafter cited as CARO BAROJA *De Nuevo*. To this may be added Florencio Idoate who published an Inquisition manuscript which turned up in AGN (Florencio IDOATE *Un documento de la Inquisición sobre la brujería en Navarra* Pamplona 1972, hereafter cited as IDOATE *Documento*), and J. Simón Días who in 1946-48 wrote two articles on the history of the Inquisition of Logroño in the sixteenth century (cited in chap. 3 n. 30, below). If he had proceeded into the seventeenth century he would doubtless have discovered the Salazar documents. For a recent survey of Basque witchcraft with more bibliography, see also the article by Idoia ESTORNES ZUBIZARRETA on "Brujería" in *Diccionario Enciclopédico Vasco* Vol. V, San Sebastián 1974 pp. 531-559.

100. DE LANCRE *Tableau* pp. 391-406 (Livre V, Discours III).

101. See MURRAY *Witch-Cult,* in the index "Basses-Pyrénées" refers without exception to de Lancre's *Tableau;* the Logroño auto de fe is cited on pp. 29, 63, 71-72, 88, 111, 122, 148, 164, 165, 176, 179, 181, 190, and 198; and SUMMERS 1926 passim, but the latter also cites Mongastón's pamphlet of 1611, e.g. pp. 112-113 and 159-160 (for the pamphlet see chap. 4 n. 14, below). Another historian familiar with de Lancre and Mongastón's pamphlet is Jules Michelet. However, his interpretation of the Basque witch persecution is just as erroneous as Summers's and Murray's (Jules MICHELET *La Sorcière* Paris 1862 chap. 16).

102. The complaint is no longer extant, but it is referred to in the Royal Decree of 17 Jan. 1609, Archive départementale de la Gironde, Fond I B (Registre du Parlement de Bordeaux) vol. 19 ff. 123^v-124^v, published in A. COMMUNAY *Le conseiller Pierre de Lancre* Agen 1890 pp. 52-53 (Appendix VII); cf. MANDROU 1968 p. 134.

103. DE LANCRE *Tableau* pp. 65, 142. Jean (de Paule) d'Amou was *bailli* of Labourd 1590-1620 (see Jean-Auguste BRUTAILS *Inventaire*

sommaire des archives départementales antérieures á 1790 Bordeaux 1925 pp. 60, 90).

104. See DE LANCRE *Tableau* p. 142; COMMUNAY 1890 p. 54 n. 4.

105. The decree of 10 Dec. 1608 is now known only through the Royal Decree of 17 Jan. 1609 (see n. 102). By a resolution dated 4 Feb. 1609 the Bordeaux parliament sought to limit the authority of the commission judges to exclude them from pronouncing death sentences and from examining prisoners under torture. But a new Royal Decree of 18 Feb. 1609 (Archive départementale de la Gironde Fond I B vol. 19 ff. 124ᵛ-125ᵛ, reprinted in COMMUNAY 1890 pp. 54-55) forced the parliament to yield and also authorized the validity of the commission for six months from the date of registration. The registration took place on 5 June 1609 (COMMUNAY 1890 p. 55) and the commission thus ran until 5 Dec. the same year. The complicated prelude to the witch-hunt of de Lancre and d'Espaignet has been erroneously described by various writers. This is also the case with my own short account in the article in *Temenos* (HENNINGSEN *Papers of Salazar* p. 88), which was based on ROBBINS 1959 p. 299. For the life of de Lancre see COMMUNAY 1890; for d'Espaignet see J. MAXWELL *Un magistrat hermetiste: Jean d'Espaignet, president au parlement de Bordeaux* Bordeaux 1896.

106. See COMMUNAY 1890 pp. 56-57 (Appendix V), letter of 22 June 1609 from the parliament at Bordeaux to the authorities at Bayonne, which gives notice of the departure of de Lancre and d'Espaignet. A further letter dated 28 June calls upon the town to provide hospitality for the two judges (COMMUNAY 1890 p. 56 n. 3), so presumably at this stage they were still residing at Bordeaux.

107. See n. 105, above.

108. See DE LANCRE *Tableau* p. 456. D'Espaignet was simultaneously charged to visit the coastal islands in order to settle a frontier question, but it is hardly likely, as some writers maintain, that he left de Lancre to deal with the witch trials on his own. It is clear that the two judges worked as a team most of the time, and as late as 11 Sept. we find them together at Bayonne, where the town entertained them ceremoniously with wine (COMMUNAY 1890 p. 57). This may possibly have coincided with the great witch-burning at Bayonne, described in de Lancre's *Tableau* pp. 110-111.

109. See e.g. SOLDAN 1880 II p. 162; ROBBINS 1959 p. 298; MANDROU 1968 p. 505. I was recently confirmed in my suspicion by being able to check Mandrou's reference to *Factums et arrest du Parlement de Paris contre des bergers sorciers exécutez depuis peu dans la province de Brie* Paris 1695 pp. 63-64, where it is said about d'Espaignet and de Lancre "qu'ils firent bruler plus de six cens personnes" and where reference is given to "l'ouvrage de Pierre de Lancre," obviously his *Tableau*. I am grateful to Dr. Alfred Soman, Paris, who located two copies of this rare pamphlet, one in Bibliotheque de l'Arsenal (8º-J.-5542) and another in the Newberry Library. In the preface of the *Tableau* de Lancre mentions 80 + 500 witches which makes nearly 600, but all these were definitely not burned (see the following note).

110. The basis for this calculation is a systematic transcript of the Labourd witches mentioned in de Lancre's *Tableau*. De Lancre himself

distinguished between these two groups, see the unpaginated preface (at signature mark oiij) where de Lancre relates that he saw the Devil's mark on eighty *"insignes sorciers"* and five hundred *"tesmoins."* Where fuller details are lacking or where minors are concerned I have listed people in the category of witch witnesses. The witches were geographically assigned to the following towns (figures for the numbers of priest witches, actual witches, and witch witnesses, respectively, follow in parentheses): Ascain (1, 2, 2); Bayonne (0, 2, 0); Biarritz (0, 1, 1); Bordegain (1, 0, 0); Ciboure (3, 3, 2); Hendaye (1, 2, 1); Jatxou (1, 4, 0); Saint-Jean-de-Luz (1, 1, 2); Saint Pée (1, 6, 4); Sare (0, 1, 3); Urrugne (1, 5, 4); Ustaritz (0, 2, 3); Villefranque (0, 0, 1); the Pays de Labourd without detailed specification (2, 5, 12). For the sake of space I refrain from appending page references.

111. One of the three priests was from Ascain and the two others from Ciboure (DE LANCRE *Tableau* pp. 452, 429). As regards the other eight priests, two were from Ascain (pp. 92, 96), one from Saint-Jean-de-Luz (p. 111); one from Urrugne (p. 224); two (or more) from Ustaritz (p. 112); and the origin of two was not stated (pp. 129, 363).

112. DE LANCRE 1622 p. 816.

113. See *Leg* 1679 Exp. 2.1 No. 21[a] f. 16^r (ff. 1^r-17^r, Salazar to inquisitor general, Logroño, 24 March 1612; received at Madrid 31 March. Submitted together with paper containing the notes or *Glosses* (*Leg* 1679 Exp. 2.1 No. 6 ff. 1^r-6^r, *title:* "Brujas: La glosa del papel y relación precedente [Witches: The glosses of the preceding report]"). Both papers published elsewhere as SD Text 12, hereafter cited as *Second Report of Salazar*. See analysis in chapter 12.2, below.

114. See DE LANCRE *Tableau* passim; and *Leg* 1679 Exp. 2.1 No. 31[e] ff. 1^r-2^r (ff. 1^r-9^r, *title:* "Relación hecha a Don Antonio Venegas de Figueroa, Obispo de Pamplona, del Consejo de Su Magestad, por las personas que Su Señoría ha ocupado — ansi religiosos como otras — en los lugares donde se ha dicho que hay esta mala secta de brujos y brujas, comenzando desde el mes de junio del año de 1610 [though in fact it begins in 1609] hasta el mes de diciembre del mismo año [though it continues into 1611]." Published elsewhere as SD Text 8, hereafter cited as *The Bishop's Report*).

NOTES TO CHAPTER 2

1. *Lib* 832 f. 170^r (ff. 170^r-171^v, "Méritos del proceso de Juanes de Goyburu . . ." [ca. 7 Jan. 1613], hereafter cited as *Méritos of Juanes de Goiburu*); cf. *Lib* 832 f. 172^{r-v} (ff. 172^r-174^r, "Méritos del proceso de Juanes de Sansín . . ." [ca. 7 Jan. 1613], hereafter cited as *Méritos of Juanes de Sansín*).

2. The basis of my calculation is a census (*apeo*) of 1646, in which the population of Zugarramurdi was stated to be 38 *vecinos* and 1 *habitante*, i.e. 39 families. If we allow 5 persons to each family this corresponds to 196 inhabitants (see AGN, Sección de Estadística, Legajo 2, Carpeta 19 f. 51^{r-v}, *apeo* at Zugarramurdi undertaken 17 Sept. 1646 by Fray Bernardo de Aguirre on orders from the abbot of Urdax). No figures are extant for Urdax. In a letter to the official in charge of the census, dated Elizondo, 18 Sept. 1646, Fray Bernardo explained

that he had not compiled a list for Urdax, as the place consisted only of the monastery and 8 families of farm laborers (*granjeros*) who worked on the monastery farm (see loc. cit. f. 50[r-v]). The 8 families included 40 individuals. Adding those from Zugarramurdi we thus arrive at a total of 236 inhabitants. If we also take the 13 monks at the monastery we get 249 inhabitants. But to this we must also add the servants of the monastery, and when we further consider that 20 people lost their lives during the witch trial in 1609-12, it seems reasonable to estimate the total number of inhabitants of Urdax and Zugarramurdi in about 1608 at roughly 300. For the Urdax monastery see also Norbert BACKMUND *Monasticon Praemonstratense* Straubing 1949 passim.

3. See n. 2, above and AGN, Secc. de Estadística, Legajo 2, Carpeta 19 f. 49[r] (the Abbot Fray Lorenzo de Virrit to the official in charge of the census, Urdax, 18 Sept. 1646). In the letter Fray Lorenzo explains that the two villages are under his jurisdiction, and that on this as on previous occasions no census has been taken of the residents of Urdax, since they are neither *vecinos* nor *habitantes* but merely *bordeantes* [*sic*], who are the concern of the monastery and have no property of their own. The sources do not indicate whether the residents of Zugarramurdi were freeholders or copyholders, but it is clear that in any case they had a *jurado* and some *diputados* (see Fray Bernardo's letter, loc. cit. f. 49[r]).

4. See table 4, below, auto de fe nos. 5, 6, 10, 9, 1, 4, 3, 2, 11, 12, 13, 24, 25, 27, 26, 14, 15, 21, 23, 8, 20, 29, 30, 28, and 22.

5. *Lib* 835 ff. 394[r], 395[r] (ff. 386[r]-400[r] "Sentencia de Graciana de Barrenechea, Estevanía y María de Yriarte sus hijas y Miguel de Goiburu; brujos del aquelarre de Cigarramurdi [*sic*]," hereafter cited as *Joint Sentence*. This sentence is in fact part of a larger document (see chap. 8.6) which includes a title page (f. 385[r]), the *Joint Sentence* (ff. 386[r]-400[r]), the sentence of María de Zozaya (ff. 401[r]-420[r]), and finally a list of the persons to be brought forth at the auto de fe, *title:* "Relación de las personas que saldrán al auto y breve sumario de los delitos que han cometido" (ff. 421[r]-424[r]). The last of these sections will hereafter be cited as *First Report of the Auto de fe*).

6. *Joint Sentence* f. 394[r].
7. EVANS-PRITCHARD 1937 chap. 4.
8. *Joint Sentence* f. 395[r].
9. Idem f. 393[r].
10. Idem f. 393[r].
11. Idem 393[v].
12. Idem f. 394[v].
13. Idem f. 395[r-v].
14. Idem 395[v].
15. Idem ff. 393[r]-395[v].
16. See María Pilar de TORRES *La Navarra húmeda del Noroeste* Madrid 1971.
17. *Joint Sentence* f. 391[v].
18. Idem ff. 391[v]-392[r].
19. To borrow Fortes's term; see chap. 1 n. 51.
20. *Lib* 835 f. 340[r-v] (ff. 340[r-v], 345[r]-351[v] "Relación de las personas que

saldrán al auto de la fe . . ." [before 31 Oct. 1610], hereafter cited as *Second Report of the Auto de fe,* SD Text 2).

21. AGN, MS without signature, f. 13ᵛ (iii + 60 folios, *title:* "Inquisición de Navarra. Cuaderno de actos comprobados de brujos," hereafter cited as *Pamplona Manuscript.* It was recently published, pp. 42-193 in: IDOATE *Documento;* see chap. 12.5, below.

22. *Second Report of the Auto de fe* f. 340ᵛ (SD Text 2); cf. *Pamplona Manuscript* ff. 13ᵛ-14ʳ (IDOATE *Documento* pp. 73, 75).

23. See HABASQUE 1912 passim.

24. DE LANCRE *Tableau* pp. 363-364, where de Lancre relates of 16-year-old Jeannette d'Abadie of Ciboure that she had "watched for many nights in the church in the above-mentioned place *according to the custom there* in order to prevent the witches taking them to the sabbath" (italics added). De Lancre relates of the same girl (op. cit. p. 130) that as early as nine months before 16 Sept. 1609 (i.e. in Jan. 1609) she had begun to keep watch at night in the Ciboure church. This is the basis of my assumption that the witch epidemic in this village had erupted at the beginning of Dec. 1608, or perhaps even earlier.

25. *Second Report of the Auto de fe* f. 340ᵛ (SD Text 2); for María de Jureteguía's age see f. 349ᵛ. There is some uncertainty as to whether the statements of age relate to 1609, when the witches were arrested, or to 1610, when the sentences were pronounced. I have decided to assign them, here and below, to the date of the arrests, since there is nothing to indicate that the inquisitors took the trouble to amend the ages even when a trial lasted longer than a year.

26. *Second Report of the Auto de fe* ff. 340ᵛ, 349ᵛ no. 14 (SD Text 2). Regarding the fit suffered by María de Jureteguía, see SARGANT 1970 chap. 5 "Techniques of religious conversion" passim. According to Sargant, fear is a means of increasing suggestibility. Thus there would seem to be a direct psychological connection between the young woman's excited protest and her later total acceptance of the role of witch.

27. *Second Report of the Auto de fe* ff. 344ᵛ-345ʳ (SD Text 2); Fray Felipe de Zabaleta is mentioned in *Méritos of Juanes de Goiburu* f. 170ʳ.

28. *Joint Sentence* f. 395ᵛ.

29. Idem ff. 395ᵛ-396ʳ. On witches seen by people, see below in chap. 7.2.

30. Idem f. 396ʳ. As regards style and content this episode in the witches' confession might very well be based on a popular witch tradition. "The witches," it is stated in the joint sentence, "seized hold of the mill, which rested on four supports. They lifted up the whole mill and carried it over to a hilltop . . . and this was attended by great hilarity . . . for 80-year-old Graciana de Barrenechea and some of her contemporaries, who had to exert themselves considerably to carry the heavy object, kept saying 'Out here, lasses, and in there, beldames! [*Aquí mozas, y en casa viejas*].' After having amused themselves with the mill for a while the witches returned it to its site." Another variant of the rhyme of the witches, "En Casa biejo y aqui moço . . ." is found in a record of a trial in Bilbao, see Pablo FERNÁNDEZ

ALBALADEJO *La crisis del antiguo régimen en Guipúzcoa, 1766-1833* Madrid 1975 p. 135.

31. *Méritos of Juanes de Goiburu* f. 170ʳ⁻ᵛ; *Méritos of Juanes de Sansín* f. 172ʳ⁻ᵛ. On toads as imps or familiar spirits see chap. 5.5, below.

32. See chap. 4 sections 2 and 3, below. The information contained in the first two columns of the table are based on the three different accounts of the auto de fe that were composed by the inquisitors at Logroño: (1) *First Report of the Auto de fe* (see n. 5, above); (2) *Second Report of the Auto de fe* (SD Text 2); and (3) *Lib* 835 ff. 356ʳ-369ᵛ, *title:* "Relación de las personas que salieron al auto de la fe que se celebró en la Inquisición de Logroño, domingo 7 días del mes de noviembre y, el lunes siguiente deste año y de otras causas despachadas en la sala," forwarded to the Council, 29 Nov. 1610 (see chapter 9.5 along with n. 53), hereafter cited as *Third Report of the Auto de fe.* The figures in the third column refer to the numbers allotted the delinquents in the *Second Report of the Auto de fe* ff. 349ʳ-350ᵛ (SD Text 2); see case nos. 1-31 of our Witch List.

33. *Pamplona Manuscript* f. 35ʳ (IDOATE *Documento* p. 128).

34. Her age is given as 70 in all three reports of the auto de fe. On the other hand in the *Pamplona Manuscript* her age is given as 46 (IDOATE *Documento* p. 100); and two of her children are mentioned, Juanes de Burua and María de Borda (f. 24ᵛ). If María can be proved to be identical with the 15-year-old María de Burga or the 12-year-old María Pérez de Burga (see table 2, below), we should give preference to the age given by the *Pamplona Manuscript,* since a 70-year-old could not possibly be the mother of such young children. In *Third Report of the Auto de fe* f. 366ᵛ it is stated that María Pérez de Barrenechea made three of her children witches, but the ages of the children are not stated.

35. The sources (see e.g. *Joint Sentence* f. 396ᵛ) mention Juanes de Sansín as being the nephew (*sobrino*) of Miguel de Goiburu. Since their surnames are not identical I conclude that the relationship was on the maternal side.

36. The relationship between the Zugarramurdi witches — never before thoroughly investigated — shows that Julio Caro Baroja is incorrect in assuming that Graciana de Barrenechea was married to Miguel de Goiburu (CARO BAROJA 1961 p. 251). It is quite possible that he was influenced by Pío Baroja's short story, "La Dama de Uturbide" (1916), which portrays them as man and wife.

37. *Joint Sentence* f. 389ʳ; the initiation took place when Graciana was 15 years old (see chap. 5.4, below).

38. For two daughters initiated by Graciana de Barrenechea, see chap. 5.4, below.

39. See *Lib* 796 f. 396ʳ, Joan de Hiriarte's application to the Tribunal, dated Logroño 3 Aug. 1616, in which he states that he is the son of Joanes de Marigorri and María de Hiriarte (not to be confused with her sister of the same name). He was seeking dispensation from the Inquisition in order that he might be enabled to enter the priesthood, irrespective of the fact that his maternal aunts and his grandmother had been convicted of witchcraft.

40. *Joint Sentence* f. 396ᵛ and *Third Report of the Auto de fe* f. 366ᵛ. However, see near beginning of chap. 12.3, below, where Juanes de Goiburu is stated to have five children.

41. *Joint Sentence* f. 389ᵛ.

42. For son and nephew initiated by Miguel de Goiburu, see chap. 5.4, below.

43. *Joint Sentence* f. 395ᵛ. It is not very clear from the sources, whether Miguel de Goiburu and his son Juanes de Goiburu lived together or in different households, but the latter is most probable; see e.g. *Pamplona Manuscript* f. 31ᵛ (IDOATE *Documento* p. 118).

44. Cf. below, chap. 10 n. 5-7 where there is mention of yet another witch from the Zugarramurdi district with the surname Barrenechea.

45. *Joint Sentence* f. 392ʳ.

46. It would be interesting to discover whether there was a Basque tradition for reconciliation with witches in this manner. To date, however, I have discovered only one case of a somewhat similar nature. This took place in 1611 in the Baztán Valley, where an old woman made a public confession of witchcraft in church and begged the congregation for forgiveness (AGN Proceso 5257 f. 28ʳ).

NOTES TO CHAPTER 3

1. *Note on further reading:* For Reformation and Counter-Reformation Europe see: A. G. DICKENS *Reformation and Society in Sixteenth Century Europe* New York 1966, and *The Counter-Reformation* New York 1969; J. H. ELLIOT *Europe Divided 1559-98* London 1968; Henry KAMEN *The Iron Century: Social Change in Europe 1550-1660* London 1971. Except in the case of Spain, relatively little research has been undertaken into the history of the Inquisition in more recent time. There is no survey comparable to Lea's *Inquisition of the Middle Ages.* Reference to particular studies may be found in E. van der VEKENÉ *Bibliographie der Inquisition* Hildesheim 1963. There is an exceptionally rich body of literature concerning the Spanish Inquisition, but the chief works are nevertheless still LEA *Inquisition of Spain* (particularly vols. II and III, the chapters on organization and practice), and Ernst SCHÄFER *Beiträge zur Geschichte des spanischen Protestantismus und der Inquisition im sechzehnten Jahrhundert. Nach den Originalakten in Madrid und Simancas bearbeitet* Gütersloh 1902, 3 vols. (particularly the introduction). I would maintain, while according due respect to later historians, that none can match these two in their general mastery of the archives of the Inquisition. The brilliant tradition of scholarship of Simancas was disrupted in many respects when in 1908-16 the archives of the Council of the Inquisition were transferred to Madrid and incorporated in the Archivo Histórico Nacional with new accession numbers. This meant that the references in Lea and Schäfer were rendered obsolete, and as no printed catalogue was issued, many scholars abandoned the attempt to trace their way back to the original sources and simply contented themselves with the information offered by these two experts (see HENNINGSEN *Papers of Salazar* pp. 85-87, and note that Lea's *Inquisition of Spain* was reprinted

in 1966 without any attempt at all to bring the references up to date). A third major work is Juan Antonio LLORENTE *Histoire critique de l'Inquisition d' Espagne, depuis l'epoque de son établissement par Ferdinand V jusq'au règne de Ferdinand VII. Tirée des pieces originales des archives du Conseil de la Suprême et de celles des Tribuneaux subalternes du Saint Office... Traduite de l'espagnol sur le manuscrit et sous les yeux de l'Auteur par Alexis Pellier* Paris 1817-1818, 4 vols. The original manuscript of Llorente appeared later in the extremely rare ten-volume edition *Historia crítica de la Inquisición de España* Madrid [or Paris?] 1822. The author of this pioneer work was in the privileged position of having been a secretary to the Council of the Inquisition. In addition to this he had access to a great deal of source material no longer extant. Recommended as a brief guide — chiefly based on Lea, but having regard to more recent research — is Henry KAMEN *The Spanish Inquisition* London 1965. See also Gustav HENNINGSEN "Los archivos y la historiografía de la Inquisición Española," paper read at the *Simposium interdisciplinario de la Inquisición Medieval y Moderna, Copenhagen 5-9 Sept. 1978*, scheduled for publication 1980.

A number of writers have drawn parallels between the types of secret police found in the twentieth century and during the Inquisition, see e.g. SARGANT 1970 pp. 130, 169-170, 186-194, and LIFTON 1961 pp. 454-461. However, the question of how far these parallels can be extended has yet to be investigated. A considerable amount of material for comparison is to be found in Simon WOLIN and Robert M. SLUSSER (eds.) *The Soviet Secret Police* London 1957, particularly in the following two contributions: A. GRIGORIEV "Investigative Methods of the Secret Police" p. 180 ff.; E. A. ANDEREVICH "Structure and Functions of the Soviet Secret Police" p. 96 ff. I must admit, however, that I am not in a position to verify the statements made by the authors of the above works.

2. This, for instance, was the practice of the Logroño Inquisition, see *Lib* 791 f. 417^{r-v} (Tribunal to Council, 20 Sept. 1596).

3. Distribution of the Bible in the vernacular was prohibited in Spain from 1551 to 1782, see LEA *Inquisition of Spain* III pp. 528-530; H. C. LEA *Chapters from the Religious History of Spain* Philadelphia 1890 pp. 44-56.

4. The immunity of agents of the Inquisition from prosecution did not, however, cover a number of more serious crimes, such as treachery to the state, rape, and highway robbery; see LEA *Inquisition of Spain* I chap. 4 (especially p. 436).

5. When Philip II wished to consult a distinguished surgeon, who had been arrested by the Inquisition, he tendered several applications to the inquisitor general. When the latter finally deigned to reply he did so in a statement declaring that *if* the person was in the prisons of the Inquisition, he could not be taken out, nor could it even be revealed whether he was or was not a prisoner (LEA *Inquisition of Spain* II pp. 472-473). Lea's source is the important manuscript in the Royal Library of Copenhagen, Ny. Kgl. Samling 213 2° f. 335^r.

6. To use Lifton's term, cf. chap. 1 n. 90, above.

7. *Instrvciones del Santo Oficio de la Inquisicion... Puestas por Abecedario por Gaspar Isidro de Argüello, Oficial del Consejo* Madrid 1630

(hereafter cited as ARGÜELLO *Instrucciones*) f. 12ᵛ (instruction iv). This manual recapitulates the Instructions of Sevilla 1484, Valladolid 1488, Sevilla 1485, Avila 1498, Sevilla 1500, Medina 1504, Madrid 1516, and Toledo 1561. These last-named Instructions, issued by the inquisitor general Fernando Valdés occupy one third of the volume and are to be found on ff. 27ʳ-38ᵛ §§ 1-81. The instructions of the Holy Office were printed several times. The first edition was *Copilacion de las Instrvciones del Officio de la sancta Inquisicion . . . por mandado del . . . Señor don Alonso Manrique* Granada 1536; a revised edition was issued Madrid 1576 (reprinted Madrid 1612, Madrid 1627) and this is the one which Argüello reedited and supplied with an index (see VEKENÉ 1963 nos. 14, 77, 133, 150, and 152).

8. *Orden qve comvnmente se gvarda en el Santo Oficio de la Inquisicion, acerca del processar en las causas que en el se tratan, conforme à lo que està proueydo por las instruciones antiguas y nuevas. Recopilado por Pablo Garcia, secretario del Consejo de la Santa General Inquisicion. Van en esta segunda impression añadidas algunas cosas y puestas otras en mejor orden* Madrid 1607 (hereafter cited as GARCÍA *Orden de procesar*) f. 10ᵛ. The first edition (Madrid 1568) was issued to all provincial tribunals together with *Carta Acordada* No. 46 (*Lib* 497 f. 106ʳ⁻ᵛ). For other editions see VEKENÉ 1963 nos. 103 (Madrid 1591), 104 (Madrid 1592) and 151 (Madrid 1628).

9. GARCÍA *Orden de procesar* ff. 10ᵛ-11ʳ. See LIFTON 1962 p. 21, where the French Dr. Vincent's "first interrogation" in the Chinese prison seems to have been conducted according to these principles. The examining judge: "The government never arrests an innocent man . . . The government knows all about your crimes . . . It is now up to you to confess everything to us, and in this way your case can be quickly solved and you will soon be released."

10. An instance of interruption of the preliminary hearings is mentioned at the end of chap. 4.3, below.

11. ARGÜELLO *Instrucciones* f. 30ʳ § 21.

12. "Es obligado (como Christiano) a amonestarle, que confiesse verdad, y si es culpado en esto, pida penitencia." (ARGÜELLO *Instrucciones* f. 30ʳ § 23).

13. Lea gives an example of the ratification remaining in force for three years, but this was a rare exception (LEA *Inquisition of Spain* II p. 548).

14. ARGÜELLO *Instrucciones* f. 30ᵛ § 28.

15. GARCÍA *Orden de procesar* f. 22ᵛ.

16. ARGÜELLO *Instrucciones* f. 32ʳ § 38.

17. Idem f. 32ᵛ § 39; see GARCÍA *Orden de procesar* f. 26ʳ, where the formula varies somewhat.

18. ARGÜELLO *Instrucciones* f. 32ᵛ § 40. But see GARCÍA *Orden de procesar* f. 27ʳ, which states that in the case of a death sentence the inquisitors are always to forward the trial record to *la Suprema* for examination, and that the Council must authorize the sentence before the execution can take place. This regulation was instituted by means of *Carta Acordada* No. 45, of 19 June 1568 (*Lib* 497 f. 106ʳ), repeated in *Carta Acordada* No. 95, 14 Oct. 1574 (*Lib* 497 f. 158ᵛ-159ʳ), where the

authority of the regulation was extended to cover sentences of interrogation under torture.

19. ARGÜELLO *Instrucciones* f. 6^r § 15 (the Instructions of Sevilla 1484).

20. Renunciation of heresy was made by means of formulae which varied according to how great a degree of suspicion the accused was under. The formulae are to be found in GARCÍA *Orden de procesar* ff. 38^r-39^r ("Abjuracion de vehementi") and 39^r-40^r ("Abjuracion de leui"). Renunciation of heresy was employed both in cases where the charge was considered insufficiently proved and in those where the accused had made a confession, but to offenses which were of a minor nature.

21. ARGÜELLO *Instrucciones* f. 33^v § 45.

22. Idem ff. 33^v-34^r §§ 48-50.

23. *Lib* 1244 f. 231^v (ff. 228^r-232^r; printed Edict of Faith from Logroño, lacking place and year). For description of the Edict of Faith see chap. 6, below.

24. A section in the Edict of Faith charged people to report *reconciliados* together with children and grandchildren of *condenados* (burned heretics) who had broken the regulations for *infamia* enforced on them. However, such persons were on the whole subjected only to lighter punishment by the Inquisition; but the frequency of the cases throughout the sixteenth and seventeenth centuries demonstrates how the Inquisition kept them under observation. Perhaps above all they underscore the difficulty of enforcing such regulations in a society like that of Spain where the system of social values was (and is) so completely centered on the concept of *honor* and its opposite *vergüenza* (shame).

25. During Senator Joseph McCarthy's "witch-hunt" for Communists in the USA from 1950 to 1954 there were many instances of a reversion to the practice of the Inquisition, when people were charged with the demand that they prove their innocence. The method was very pertinently defined by Senator Hubert Humphrey as "Anglo-Saxon jurisprudence upside down," see A. Rebecca CARDOSO "A Modern American Witch-Craze" in MARWICK 1970 pp. 369-377.

26. See the examples in LEA *Inquisition of Spain* III p. 108, to which can be added another from the account of an auto de fe from the Toledo Inquisition in the eighteenth century, see Gustav HENNINGSEN "La colección de Moldenhawer en Copenhague: Una aportación a la archivología de la Inquisición española" *Revista de Archivos, Bibliotecas y Museos* LXXX (1977) 209-270, the auto de fe manuscript (Ny Kgl. Samling 218^d 2° No. 41) at p. 268 f.

27. The capacity varied somewhat from tribunal to tribunal, and from about 1600 on there was also a considerable decrease in the number of cases. This will be seen more clearly from the forthcoming index of the relaciones de causas of the Spanish Inquisition which I am preparing in collaboration with the Spanish historian, Jaime Contreras, see Gustav HENNINGSEN "El 'banco de datos' del Santo Oficio: Las relaciones de causas de la Inquisición española" *Boletín de la Real Academia de la Historia* CLXXIV (1977) 547-570. An excellent survey of the activity of a single tribunal during the entire period of the Spanish

Inquisition is Jean Pierre DEDIEU "Les causes de foi de l'Inquisition de Tolède (1483-1820): Essai statistique" *Mélanges de la Casa de Velázquez* XIV (1978) 143-171.

28. This was the case with the bishop of Pamplona, Antonio Venegas de Figueroa, who had formerly been an inquisitor at Granada (see his biography, chapter 7 n. 66, below).

29. Bernardo de Sandoval y Rojas (d. 1618), the protector and benefactor of Cervantes, was a member of the highest aristocracy in Castilla (see beginning of chap. 8.6, below). He had been bishop of Pamplona from 1588 to 1595, and from there moved to Jaén in southern Spain, where he was bishop (and thus the superior of Salazar, see chap. 3.3) until he was appointed archbishop of Toledo, see Fray Prudencio de SANDOVAL *Catálogo de los obispos que ha tenido la Santa Iglesia de Pamplona* Pamplona 1614 ff. 135ᵛ-136ʳ; Basilio Sebastián CASTELLANO DE LOSADA (ed.) *Bibliografía eclesiastica* (30 volumes, Madrid 1848-68) XXV (1865) pp. 963-964.

30. For the history of the Tribunal during the second half of the sixteenth century see J. SIMÓN DÍAZ "La Inquisición en Logroño (1570-1580)" *Berceo* I (1946) 89-119; "La Inquisición en Logroño (1580-1600)" *Berceo* III (1948) 83-96.

31. *Lib* 1338 f. 41ʳ (Juan de Ramírez, *juramento*, or oath of allegiance sworn on accession to the post of *fiscal* to *la Suprema*, Madrid, 18 Mar. 1608).

32. *Lib* 794 f. 346ʳ, Becerra to the Council, 29 Aug. 1608. Becerra reports in his letter that his colleague, *licenciado* Pedro Guerra y Dosal, died on 27 Aug. 1608.

33. *Leg* 1372 Exp. 2, "Información de la genealogía y limpieza del doctor Alonso Becerra . . . ," anno 1600; see *Lib* 835 f. 27, the end of a report of a small auto de fe held on 19 Aug. 1601, in which it is stated that Becerra took office as an inquisitor at Logroño on 26 Mar. 1601.

34. The inquisitors' seniority was calculated from the date of their appointment. If, for example, Valle had become an inquisitor in 1599, he would automatically have taken precedence as senior inquisitor at Logroño, regardless of the fact that Becerra had been serving this tribunal for more than seven years. See *Lib* 497 ff. 65ʳ-66ʳ, *Carta Acordada* No. 15, 1 Sept. 1534.

35. *Leg* 1259 Exp. 22, "Información de la genealogia y limpieza . . ." of Valle, anno 1603.

36. *Lib* 577 ff. 471ᵛ-472ʳ, appointment of Valle as *secretario de cámara* for the inquisitor general, Valladolid, 10 Apr. 1603.

37. Juan Antonio Llorente is in error when he states (*Histoire critique* 1818 IV p. 262) the date of Acevedo's death as being 8 July 1607, since in fact he did not die until 9 Aug. 1608 (information kindly supplied by Professor Quintín Aldea, Madrid).

38. On account of a lacuna in the registers of the Council, I have been unable to trace Valle's appointment as inquisitor. We find his signature as *secretario de cámara* to Inquisitor General Acevedo as late as 6 July 1608 (*Lib* 367 II f. 241ᵛ). The first evidence of his inquisitorship at Logroño is his signature on a letter to the Council dated 23 Dec. 1608 (*Lib* 794 f. 274ʳ). The appointment must have been made between these two dates. If we are to believe Salazar's statement that he was

the first inquisitor to be appointed by Sandoval y Rojas (23 Mar. 1609, see end of chap. 3.3), this means that Valle's appointment must have taken place under Acevedo, and therefore before the latter's death on 9 Aug. 1608.

39. Laso de Vega had been appointed inquisitor at Murcia. See Becerra's letter of 29 Aug. 1608 to the Council (*Lib* 794 f. 346^r), which contains a request for Laso to remain long enough to make the new *fiscal* conversant with the work.

40. San Vicente's age is calculated according to his own statement of 1619, when he gives his age as 40. On this occasion he also states that he served as *fiscal* at Logroño from Sept. 1608 until Sept. 1612 (see *Leg* 1683 Exp. 1 ff. 731^r-738^r, Examination of San Vicente, Zaragoza, 30 Aug. 1619). San Vicente's title as *fiscal* to the Inquisition at Logroño is dated Madrid, 7 July 1608 (*Lib* 367 II f. 239^{r-v}).

41. Huerta y Rojas's age is calculated according to his own statement of 1619, when he states it as 40 (see *Leg* 1683 Exp. 1 ff. 823^r-833^r); he took up his post on 29 Aug. 1608 (*Lib* 794 f. 346).

42. *Lib* 794 f. 422^r, Tribunal to Council, 20 June 1609. Salazar's age is calculated according to his own statement of 1619, when he gives it as 54, see *Leg* 1683 Exp. 1 f. 786^r (ff. 749^r-789^r, *Examination of Salazar at Valencia* 28, 29, 30, 31 Aug. and 1 Sept. 1619 in connection with *la Suprema's* inspection of the Logroño Tribunal).

43. For Salazar's family history see Alfonso QUINTANO RIPOLLÉS *Un linaje burgalés: La casa de Quintano y sus enlazados* Madrid 1967 pp. 518-523. For a biography of Salazar see the forthcoming study by Luis CORONAS TEJADA "Unos años en la vida y reflejos de la personalidad del Inquisidor de las brujas (1564-1609)" *Boletín del Instituto de Estudios Giennenses* C (1980), in preparation.

44. Bernardo de Sandoval y Rojas, as bishop of Jaén, was Salazar's superior during the period 1595-98. This fact goes far to explain the trust that this influential man placed in Salazar. It cannot have been by mere coincidence that Salazar's career as an ecclesiastical diplomat commenced in the very same year that Sandoval was appointed cardinal. To an even greater degree than emerges from his *Autobiography* (see n. 45, below), Salazar seems to have been the future inquisitor general's right-hand man. This is worth bearing in mind later on, when we examine Salazar's attitude toward the other two inquisitors at Logroño.

45. The above is based on Salazar's curriculum vitae, *Leg* 2220 No. 21 ff. 2^r-5^v, hereafter cited as *Autobiography* (ff. 2^r-13^r, "Relación de los Inquisidores que hay en esta Inquisición del reino de Navarra que reside en esta ciudad de Logroño, de sus salarios y ayuda de costa, edad, órdenes, prebendas y grados de letras," dated 4 June 1622; the part comprehending Salazar's curriculum vitae is published in Gustav HENNINGSEN "Alonso de Salazar Frías, ese famoso inquisidor desconocido" in *Homenaje a Julio Caro Baroja* Madrid 1978 pp. 581-586). As in Valle's case, I have been unable to discover Salazar's appointment in the registers. According to his own statement (*Autobiography* f. 4^r) it took place on 23 Mar. 1609 and this would conform with the fact that shortly afterwards the king authorized the payment of in-

quisitor's salary to Salazar in a *cédula real de salario,* issued in Madrid, on 6 Apr. 1609 (*Lib* 251 Part I f. 161ʳ).

46. See extract near the beginning of chap. 6, below.

47. For the inquisitorial agents' duty of keeping their Tribunal informed regarding everything that occurred in their region, see LEA *Inquisition of Spain* II p. 270 with n. 3 (Lea's reference to "Lib. 939" is outdated (cf. n. 1, above) and should now read *Lib* 1231).

48. *Lib* 794 f. 434ʳ⁻ᵛ, application by Fray León de Araníbar for the post of *calificador,* registered by Inquisitor Valle when on visitation at Urdax, 8 Sept. 1608.

49. *Lib* 794 f. 405ʳ (ff. 404ʳ-405ʳ, Tribunal to Council, 15 Sept. 1609). See José GOÑI GAZTAMBIDE *Los Navarros en el Concilio de Trento y la Tridentina en la Diócesis de Pamplona* Pamplona 1947 p. 89 and fig. 6 with map of the diocese of Pamplona showing the four deaneries of Fuenterrabía, Las Cinco Villas, Santesteban, and Baztán, which in 1567 were transferred from the see of Bayonne to that of Pamplona. It is of interest to us to consider that this circumstance produced the situation wherein all the more senior priests holding livings in the area in 1608 had been appointed by the bishop of Bayonne.

50. The information derives from a hearing held by Narvarte, 6 June 1612, in which he also states that he is 63 years old (AGN, Proceso 5257 f. 50ʳ). I do not possess any knowledge about when he became a *familiar.* However, there is a fairly complete list of the persons who became agents of the Tribunal during the period 1608-12 (*Leg* 1683 Exp. 1 ff. 66ʳ-76ᵛ, "Relación de las informaciones de . . . limpieza . . . ," 6 Mar. 1612, composed by the *fiscal* San Vicente; see beginning of chap. 12.1), and as his name does not appear among these I assume that his appointment must be of an earlier date. His name occurs in the papers of the Inquisition for the first time on 30 Dec. 1610 where he is assisting Fray León de Araníbar as notary at the examination of a witch at Arráyoz (*Leg*1679 Exp. 2.2 ff. 38ʳ-39ʳ), but he seems to have been examining witches from the beginning of 1609 (see chaps. 4.1 and 7.3, below).

51. See beginning of chap. 7.2, below, and *Leg* 1679 Exp. 2.1 No. 29[a] f. 5ᵛ, where Salazar, in 1613, states that Domingo de San Paul is over 80 years old (ff. 1ʳ-10ʳ, Salazar to inquisitor general, Logroño, 3 Oct. 1613, hereafter cited as *Fourth Report of Salazar,* published elsewhere as SD Text 14, analyzed in chap. 12.7, below).

NOTES TO CHAPTER 4

1. *Leg* 1679 Exp. 2.1 No. 18, Tribunal to Council, 13 Feb. 1609; received in Madrid 2 March, hereafter cited as *Tribunal's Letter of 13 Feb. 1609; Third Report of the Auto de fe* f. 360ᵛ passim; also see chap. 8 n. 10, below.

2. See *Tribunal's Letter of 13 Feb. 1609* which mentions "the hearings that were undertaken by the commissioner [*las informaciones recibidas por el comisario*]"; regarding the notary, see above, pp. 50 and 119.

3. However, the emergence of the *Pamplona Manuscript* has enabled us to identify one of the witnesses as María de Jureteguía's father-

in-law (see chap. 12.6, below). Another of the witnesses was possibly the miller, Martín de Amayur (see chaps. 4.7 and 7.2, below).

4. *Tribunal's Letter of 13 Feb. 1609.*

5. See *Fourth Report of Salazar* ff. 2ᵛ-3ʳ (SD Text 14).

6. *Tribunal's Letter of 13 Feb. 1609.* A copy of the Granada Instructions of 14 Dec. 1526 is to be found in *Lib* 319 ff. 348ʳ-350ᵛ (see chap. 1.6, above). Regarding the instructions of 12 Sept. and 2 Oct. 1555 see *Fourth Report of Salazar* f. 2ʳ⁻ᵛ (SD Text 14 §§ 7 and 8). In the letter of 13 Feb. 1609 the inquisitors also mentioned that they had seen a large number of trial records of witches who had been reconciled on two different occasions, and, moreover, that they had seen the instructions that the inquisitor general "sent last." But since the letter did not furnish more precise details it is difficult to see what the inquisitors were referring to there.

7. *Tribunal's Letter of 13 Feb. 1609.*

8. This information emerges first in a letter from the Tribunal to the Council, 10 Sept. 1611 (*Lib* 795 f. 192ʳ).

9. *Tribunal's Letter of 13 Feb. 1609.*

10. The *Tribunal's Letter of 13 Feb. 1609* mentions that four witches had been imprisoned but does not give their names. However, these appear in *la Suprema*'s reply dated 11 Mar. of the same year (see n. 34 below and tables 1 and 4). When Julio Caro Baroja asserts that the first group contained six witches, his calculation is based on a misinterpretation of the letter from the Tribunal in question, which causes considerable confusion in his next explanation (CARO BAROJA *De nuevo* pp. 269-270, 272). When listing the manuscripts he opts to correct the inquisitors: "Letter from the same, containing the trial records of 4 (*sic*, but there were more than that)" (idem p. 324 n. 33).

11. The date is stated both in *Méritos of Juanes de Goiburu* (f. 170ʳ) and in *Méritos of Juanes de Sansín* (f. 172ʳ).

12. *Third Report of the Auto de fe* f. 360ᵛ.

13. Idem ff. 360ᵛ-361ʳ.

14. Ff. 6ᵛ and 7ᵛ of *Relacion de las personas qve salieron al avto de la Fee, qve los señores Doctor Alonso Bezerra Holguin, del Abito de Alcantara; Licenciado Iuan de Valle Aluarado; Licenciado Alonso de Salazar Frias, Inquisidores Apostolicos del Reyno de Nauarra, y su distrito, celebraron en la Ciudad de Logroño, en siete, y en ocho dias del mes de Nouiembre, de 1610. Años. Y de las cosas y delitos por que fueron castigados.* Printed by Juan de Mongastón, Logroño 1611, hereafter cited as MONGASTÓN *Relación.*

15. *Third Report of the Auto de fe* f. 360ᵛ, see *Fourth Report of Salazar* f. 3ᵛ (SD Text 14) and *Lib* 794 f. 433ʳ (ff. 433ʳ⁻ᵛ and 440ʳ, Tribunal to Council, 26 Sept. 1609, received in Madrid 6 Oct.). In the *Pamplona Manuscript* f. 52ᵛ there is one more fragment of Jureteguía's confessions (IDOATE *Documento* p. 174).

16. *Third Report of the Auto de fe* ff. 365ᵛ-366ʳ. However, in the *Pamplona Manuscript* (ff. 19ᵛ, 33ᵛ, 52ᵛ-53ʳ) there are several extracts from Telechea's confessions (IDOATE *Documento* pp. 88, 124, 128-129, 174). The last of these fragments is also found in the pamphlet, MONGASTÓN *Relación* f. 8ʳ.

17. *Third Report of the Auto de fe* f. 366ᵛ. In addition there are a number of long extracts from María Pérez's confessions in the *Pam-*

plona Manuscript ff. 1ᵛ, 4ᵛ, 19ᵛ, 29ᵛ, 33ᵛ, 53ʳ (IDOATE *Documento* pp. 47, 53, 88, 113, 124, 175).

18. *Third Report of the Auto de fe* f. 366ᵛ.

19. MONGASTÓN *Relación* f. 13ᵛ. A number of additional fragments of Estevanía's confessions appear in the *Pamplona Manuscript* ff. 1ᵛ, 4ᵛ, 11ᵛ, 29ᵛ, 31ᵛ, 35ʳ⁻ᵛ, 43ʳ, 48ᵛ (IDOATE *Documento* pp. 48, 53-54, 67, 113, 118-119, 127-128, 148, 163).

20. *Tribunal's Letter of 13 Feb. 1609.* Regarding the dating of the fragments of the four confessions cited above it must be admitted that they were not necessarily all made during the preliminary hearings, since throughout the entire period of the trial supplementary hearings were held. But we can assign the confessions of the two eldest witches to 1609 without any doubt, since they both died in that year (see chap. 8.2, below).

21. *Fourth Report of Salazar* f. 3ᵛ (SD Text 14).

22. *Joint Sentence* (of Graciana de Barrenechea, María and Estevanía de Yriarte, and Miguel de Goiburu) f. 396ʳ; *Méritos of Juanes de Goiburu* f. 170ʳ; *Méritos of Juanes de Sansín* f. 172ʳ.

23. The *Tribunal's Letter of 13 Feb. 1609* mentions only Graciana de Barrenechea (the inquisitors call her Graciana de Yriarte, after her husband), but thanks to the detailed trial records (see n. 22, above) it is possible to identify all six without difficulty.

24. *Tribunal's Letter of 13 Feb. 1609.*

25. It may possibly be the *fiscal's clamosa* which is reproduced in the first part of the *Joint Sentence* (ff. 386ʳ-387ᵛ).

26. *Tribunal's Letter of 13 Feb. 1609.*

27. The reasons for placing the date at 14 Feb. are as follows: (1) the *Tribunal's Letter of 13 Feb. 1609* indicates that even then the six witches were still at liberty, although it had already been decided that they were to be imprisoned; (2) the statements in Juanes de Goiburu's and Juanes de Sansín's *méritos* relate that the six witches reached Logroño about *ten* days after the first four witches had been confined in the Inquisition prison (i.e. about 6 Feb.); (3) the information in Juanes de Goiburu's *méritos* that the six witches had waited for a reply from the inquisitors for *eight* days. If we count eight days from 6 Feb. (see point 2) we reach 14 Feb.

28. We know from the regulations of the Inquisition that men and women were separated while in prison, but we possess no information regarding whether the three men and three women were placed in solitary confinement or whether any of them shared cells. However, there are many indirect indications in the sources that the former was the case (see chap. 4.6, below).

29. *Joint Sentence* f. 387ᵛ; GARCÍA *Orden de Procesar* ff. 8ᵛ-10ᵛ.

30. *Joint Sentence* ff. 387ᵛ-388ʳ; see GARCÍA *Orden de Procesar* ff. 10ᵛ-11ʳ.

31. It is nowhere directly mentioned that the inquisitors decided to discontinue the preliminary hearings, but it is suggested indirectly in the sources. Thus, the summaries of the trials of all six witches mention the first and second, but not the third (preliminary) hearing (see *Joint Sentence* ff. 388ʳ, 389ʳ, 389ᵛ; *Méritos of Juanes de Goiburu* f. 170ᵛ; and *Méritos of Juanes de Sansín* f. 173ʳ). As we mentioned previously (in

chap. 3.2, above), the three preliminary hearings were normally completed during the first ten days after imprisonment, but in this case they lasted for more than six months (see chaps. 4.5 and 4.6, below). The reason for the inquisitors' decision appears in a letter to the Council, dated 10 July 1610, which states that the six witches had "conspired to make denial before the Holy Office [*se habían conjurado para negar en este Santo Oficio*]." This letter provides the clue by which the whole problem of the Logroño trial can be solved, and is discussed in chap. 4.6, below.

32. The date is found in the *Tribunal's Letter of 13 Feb. 1609*.

33. *Lib* 332 f. 230^r, Council to Tribunal, 7 Mar. 1609.

34. *Leg* 1679 Exp. 2.1 No. 7, Council to Tribunal, 11 Mar. 1609. This is the letter which contains the names of the four witches (see above, n. 10), although in a distorted form (here reproduced with the original's spelling): "Maria Perez de Barranchea, Juan Fechelle, Maria de Guaritaguia, Stefania de Nauarcorena." Julio Caro Baroja reproduces these names with quite different spellings (CARO BAROJA *De nuevo* p. 270 n. 20), which is strange, since the handwriting in this document is clearly legible.

35. Much of this questionnaire has already been published in English translation, see HENNINGSEN *Papers of Salazar* p. 89, and the full text is now available in CARO BAROJA *De nuevo* pp. 270-271.

36. See the instructions to the inquisitors in Navarra of 14 Dec. 1526 (*Lib* 319 f. 349^r § 9) and 11 July 1537 (*Lib* 322 ff. 145^v-146^r). However, the main source of *la Suprema*'s fourteen questions seems to have been the Instructions to the Barcelona Tribunal of 3 Dec. 1548 (*Lib* 322 II ff. 56^v-57^r).

37. *Lib* 322 ff. 231^v-232^r, Council to Tribunal, 11 Mar. 1609. This is *la Suprema*'s copy, entered in the so-called Libro 17 of letters from the Council to the inquisitions of Aragón and Navarra. It differs from the Tribunal's copy consulted above (see n. 34) in that it omits the fourteen questions. But on the other hand the present version contains the whole of the second half of the letter which is missing in the Tribunal's copy. In this part of the letter the Council reports the finding of an old letter written by a certain Avellaneda, who was an inquisitor in Navarra, to the archbishop of Sevilla, the inquisitor general (Alfonso Manrique). The old letter bears no date, the Council states, but it is assumed to be from 1526. The original of the letter was enclosed in order that the Tribunal could identify it more closely. Julio Caro Baroja has written at some length on Avellaneda (CARO BAROJA 1961 pp. 214-217, 220). However, I have my suspicions that this inquisitor may never have existed owing to the fact that apart from this letter his name does not appear in the registers of *la Suprema*.

38. Becerra's visitation is mentioned in the correspondence to *la Suprema* (*Lib* 794 ff. 99^{r-v}, 106^r). With regard to the inquisitors' duty of going on visitation by turns, see beginning of chap. 6, below.

39. *Leg* 1679 Exp. 2.1 No. 12, Tribunal to Council, 22 May 1609. In his analysis of this letter Julio Caro Baroja arrives at a total number of twelve witches, of which six were *negativos* and four were *confitentes* (*sic*), thus adding up to ten! (CARO BAROJA *De nuevo* p. 272, see p. 323, where the letter is erroneously dated 12 May 1609). But in this case

Caro Baroja is merely reaping the consequences of his misinterpretation of the letter of 13 Feb. 1609 (see above, n. 10).

40. See above, chap. 3 n. 42.

41. This was *la Suprema*'s argument in another letter, which urged Valle to set out on visitation without further delay (*Lib* 332 f. 244ʳ, Council to Tribunal, 16 June 1609).

42. The letter of 11 July is no longer extant. However, it is mentioned in the Council's letter to the Tribunal of 21 July 1609 (*Lib* 332 f. 251ᵛ) and 24 July 1609 (Idem ff. 252ᵛ-253ʳ). The dating of the Tribunal's letter as 11 June in a later communication from *la Suprema* must undoubtedly be due to error (*Lib* 334 f. 273ʳ, Council to Tribunal, 11 Oct. 1614). This letter from *la Suprema* states that the Council is returning the file that the Tribunal sent down on "11 June 1609." However, the Tribunal is directed to make a copy of it and then return it. Thus it is very probable that the file containing the old instructions regarding witches is still extant in the archives of *la Suprema* in the Inquisition section of the Archivo Histórico Nacional, although I have not been able to find it.

43. *Lib* 332 ff. 252ᵛ-253ʳ, Council to Tribunal, 24 July 1609. The instructions are referred to as "the manner for proceeding in these cases [*el modo de proceder en esas causas*]." It is possible that some of the clauses were assimilated at the beginning of the new instructions of 29 Aug. 1614 (for which see table 14, below).

44. *Leg* 1679 Exp. 2.1 No. 40, Tribunal to Council, 4 Sept. 1609; for the rules regarding the publication of the indictment, see chap. 3.2, above.

45. See further William Sargant's excellent exposition of how false confessions are elicited, SARGANT 1970 pp. 165-196.

46. According to Lifton there are eight psychological themes which are predominant in a brainwashing milieu: (1) control of human communication; (2) "mystical manipulation," i.e., behavior motivation with reference to a "higher purpose"; (3) a demand for purity, that creates a "guilty milieu" and a "shaming milieu"; (4) a cult of confession; (5) a "Sacred Science"; (6) a loading of the language by thought-terminating clichés; (7) a subordination of human experience to the claims of doctrine; and (8) a "dispensing of existence" according to the concept that those who set themselves apart from society have no right to existence (see LIFTON 1962 chap. 22 "Ideological Totalism"). If for our purpose we substitute for Lifton's "Sacred Science" the Holy Catholic Faith, we find that all these conditions were present in the secret prisons of the Inquisition.

47. This unconscious pulling of the wool over each other's eyes is not at all unique to the Inquisition. Thus Sargant writes: "Even the most conscientious police examiner is liable to make the same mistakes as the equally conscientious Freud, and in the Russian purges, where emotional tension must have risen far higher than it usually does in the atmosphere of an English police station, or on a psychotherapeutic couch, the examiner and the prisoner must often have built up between them complete delusional systems. For the prisoner may be completely innocent, but the police examiner is required to continue the examination until he has dragged the truth

out of him, which means that he must himself come to believe what has been confessed" (SARGANT 1970 p. 176).

48. ARGÜELLO *Instrucciones* f. 37ʳ § 72, or "la instrucción 72 de las nuevas," as the inquisitors call it in their letter of 10 July 1610 (see n. 49, below).

49. *Lib* 795 ff. 41ᵛ-42ʳ (ff. 41ʳ-42ʳ, Tribunal to Council, 10 July 1610, received at Madrid 30 July).

50. *Joint Sentence* f. 389ʳ.

51. Dating according to A. CAPPELLI *Cronologia, cronografia e calendario perpetuo* 2nd enlarged ed., Milano 1930.

52. *Joint Sentence* f. 389ʳ.

53. Idem f. 388ʳ.

54. Idem ff. 388ʳ-389ʳ.

55. Idem ff. 394ᵛ-395ʳ.

56. For Salazar's criticism of the manner in which the witches' confessions were recorded, see chap. 12.7, below.

57. *Joint Sentence* f. 389ʳ; for the letter of 22 May, see beginning of chap. 4.5, above.

58. *Méritos of Juanes de Sansín* f. 173ʳ.

59. The *Joint Sentence* merely states that Miguel de Goiburu denied being a witch at the first and second hearing, and subsequently "after many days" himself requested a hearing, when he made confession (f. 389ᵛ).

60. *Méritos of Juanes de Goiburu* ff. 170ᵛ-171ʳ.

61. Idem f. 171ʳ.

62. Idem f. 171ʳ⁻ᵛ.

63. The example is taken from LEA *Inquisition of Spain* III p. 232. The Inquisition's production of evidence and the concept of *acto positivo* demand investigation by a legal expert.

64. S. F. NADEL "Witchcraft and Anti-Witchcraft in Nupe Society" *Africa* 8 (1935) 423-447, the quotation at p. 426.

65. *Joint Sentence* f. 399ʳ. On the late appearance of the counterfeit phenomenon in the trial, see chap. 7.2, below.

66. Idem f. 399ʳ, cf. the *Pamplona Manuscript* f. 48ʳ (IDOATE *Documento* p. 162), where the same explanation is reported with fewer details.

67. *Joint Sentence* f. 397ʳ.

68. Idem 397ʳ.

69. The *Pamplona Manuscript* informs us further that the six witches answered two more of the questions on the list. Four of the six replied affirmatively to Question 10, on whether they spoke together and discussed what happened at the sabbaths (IDOATE *Documento* pp. 67-69). Estevanía de Yriarte replied to Question 12, on whether the witch unguent made them fall asleep, that she was awake and dressed when she took part in the sabbaths, and the three men (Miguel de Goiburu, Juanes de Goiburu, and Juanes de Sansín) added that they anointed themselves before leaving (IDOATE *Documento* p. 54, but in line 28 for *juntaban* read *untaban*).

NOTES TO CHAPTER 5

1. In addition to the *Joint Sentence* we can add large portions of the *Pamplona Manuscript* owing to the fact that the present chapter was written before this new source was discovered by Florencio Idoate. The most important details, however, have been inserted in the notes. See also the analysis in table 12 which shows how much of each of the first 18 *confitente* witches' confessions is cited in the *Pamplona Manuscript*. For a comparison between the material in the *Joint Sentence* and the *Second Report of the Auto de fe*, see below, chap. 8.6.

2. See below, chap. 8.2.

3. In order to facilitate a comparison with the material presented by Murray, I have as far as possible arranged the contents of this chapter in the same order as used in MURRAY *Witch-Cult* (see the chapters entitled "The God," "Admission Ceremonies," etc.). Thus I have sought to avoid making references in the notes to every parallel, except in a few important instances; but in consideration of those who may hold different opinions, in presenting the Spanish material I have endeavored to include everything that the Murrayists might wish to cite in support of their theories.

4. *Joint Sentence* f. 389ʳ.

5. See chap. 4.6, above; "Joan Gaicoa," more correctly *Jaun Goicoa*, is the Basque word for God. It means literally "Lord of High." In comparison it is interesting to note that the Basque word for devil is *dabria*.

6. *Joint Sentence* ff. 389ᵛ-390ʳ; see MURRAY *Witch-Cult* pp. 62-63, where the faint voice is explained as being due to the fact that the "Devil" wore a mask. Incidentally, most of Murray's examples here, as in other instances, are taken from DE LANCRE *Tableau* (see above, chap. 1 n. 101).

7. MONGASTÓN *Relación* f. 7ᵛ: "Graciana de Barrenechea (Reyna del Aquelarre) dize que es de vn grauissimo, y malissimo olor."

8. *Joint Sentence* f. 388ᵛ.

9. Idem f. 389ʳ.

10. See *Méritos of Juanes de Goiburu* f. 170ᵛ, *Méritos of Juanes de Sansín* f. 173ʳ; for María de Yriarte see *Joint Sentence* f. 388ᵛ.

11. Martín ALONSO *Enciclopedia del idioma* Madrid 1968 I p. 444.

12. *Joint Sentence* f. 390ᵛ, in the manuscript written "veroscoberro."

13. Idem ff. 389ʳ, 398ᵛ.

14. Idem f. 390ᵛ.

15. Idem f. 398ʳ.

16. Idem f. 390ᵛ.

17. Idem f. 388ᵛ.

18. Idem f. 390ᵛ.

19. As stated by some children to the author and his wife, when we were on a visit to the Zugarramurdi grotto on 23 June (the day of Midsummer Night) 1970.

20. *Joint Sentence* f. 390ᵛ.

21. Idem f. 391ʳ. See MONGASTÓN *Relación* f. 9ʳ⁻ᵛ and IDOATE *Documento* pp. 85-86, where a number of episodes connected with

taboo-breaking are recorded. The originator of all these accounts was Miguel de Goiburu. The other five witches do not seem to have recounted this type of story.

22. This was somewhat younger than what was considered by the Inquisition to be the age of discretion (12 for girls and 14 for boys). According to the rules of the Inquisition a person could not be required to renounce heresy if he had not reached the age of discretion (ARGÜELLO *Instrucciones* f. 11ʳ § 12). As the crux of the witches' initiation ceremony was the abjuration of Christianity, according to the logic of the inquisitors the Devil would be obliged to utilize a similar practice.

23. Miguel de Goiburu in *Joint Sentence* f. 389ᵛ; *Méritos of Juanes de Sansín* f. 173ʳ.

24. *Joint Sentence* f. 396ᵛ.

25. María de Yriarte in *Joint Sentence* f. 388ʳ⁻ᵛ, Estevanía de Yriarte idem f. 389ʳ, Graciana de Barrenechea idem f. 389ʳ⁻ᵛ; see *Méritos of Juanes de Goiburu* ff. 170ᵛ-171ʳ.

26. *Joint Sentence* f. 389ʳ.

27. Idem f. 389ʳ⁻ᵛ.

28. Idem ff. 388ʳ⁻ᵛ, 398ᵛ.

29. Idem ff. 389ᵛ-390ʳ; see MONGASTÓN *Relación* f. 7ʳ, where the Devil's blessing is described almost identically, and for which also Goiburu's confession is the sole source.

30. *Méritos of Juanes de Goiburu* f. 171ʳ.

31. *Méritos of Juanes de Sansín* f. 173ʳ.

32. This information *did*, however, come to light in the *Pamplona Manuscript*. Miguel de Goiburu declared that his toad was dressed in "different shades of yellow [*differentes colores que correspondían a amarillo*]" (IDOATE *Documento* p. 103); and Juanes de Goiburu related that his toad was dressed in black and green (idem p. 105). Strangely enough, however, this source fails to record Sansín's description of the colors worn by his uncle's and cousin's toads (idem p. 104). It is possible that the authors of the *Pamplona Manuscript* (the inquisitors Becerra and Valle) did not want to preserve these small discrepancies in the witnesses' statements and therefore deleted the details of the colors from the passage relating to the dressed toads which was transcribed from Juanes de Sansín's trial record.

33. *Joint Sentence* f. 396ᵛ.

34. On María's age, see sixth paragraph of present section.

35. *Joint Sentence* f. 389ʳ: "more than 14 years ago," i.e. ca. 1595, when Estevanía was about 22 years old.

36. Idem f. 396ᵛ.

37. *Méritos of Juanes de Goiburu* f. 170ᵛ.

38. *Méritos of Juanes de Sansín* f. 173ʳ.

39. The validity of this view has been greatly strengthened by the body of additional material that has come to light in the *Pamplona Manuscript*.

40. Here and below I shall refer to the four witches' confessions collectively, since the *Joint Sentence* ceases to distinguish between the individual confessions. Thanks to the recently discovered *Pamplona Manuscript*, where the extracts from the trial record always identify

the speakers, this problem is no longer insoluble. Since, on the other hand, the *Joint Sentence* contains many details that are not cited in the *Pamplona Manuscript,* the project would only be partially viable.

41. *Joint Sentence* ff. 391ᵛ, 397ʳ.

42. Idem f. 398ʳ; *Méritos of Juanes de Goiburu* f. 171ʳ; *Méritos of Juanes de Sansín* f. 173ᵛ.

43. *Joint Sentence* f. 390ᵛ; *Méritos of Juanes de Sansín* f. 173ʳ.

44. See MURRAY *Witch-Cult* chap. 5 secs. 3 and 4.

45. *Joint Sentence* ff. 390ᵛ-391ʳ.

46. Idem f. 391ᵛ.

47. *Pamplona Manuscript* f. 25ʳ (IDOATE *Documento* p. 102); see above, chap. 4.2.

48. *Joint Sentence* f. 398ᵛ; see *Méritos of Juanes de Goiburu* f. 171ᵛ and *Méritos of Juanes de Sansín* f. 173ᵛ.

49. See MURRAY *Witch-Cult* chap. 6 sec. 3. Murray's assertion that "among the witches there appears to have been a definite rule that no girl under puberty had sexual intercourse with the Devil" (p. 175) is also for that matter valid among the Zugarramurdi witches, who did not have sexual intercourse with the Devil before they reached the age of 14 (*Joint Sentence* f. 398ᵛ).

50. Idem f. 398ᵛ. See *Méritos of Juanes de Goiburu* f. 171ᵛ and *Méritos of Juanes de Sansín* f. 173ᵛ, where these two male witches admit to having had homosexual intercourse with each other both at the witches' sabbaths and in the fields in broad daylight.

51. *Joint Sentence* f. 396ᵛ; regarding the week's delay see above, chap. 4 n. 27.

52. *Joint Sentence* f. 398ʳ⁻ᵛ; see *Méritos of Juanes de Goiburu* f. 171ᵛ and *Méritos of Juanes de Sansín* f. 173ᵛ. See also MURRAY *Witch-Cult* chap. 5 sec. 7, "The Sacrament," particularly pp. 148-149, where a considerable part of de Lancre's chapter on the auto de fe at Logroño is cited. Presumably de Lancre's source was Mongastón's pamphlet or the handwritten report sent by the inquisitors to French witch-judge M. de Gourgues (see below, chap. 9.5).

53. *Joint Sentence* f. 399ʳ. For the late appearance of the motif of the Midsummer Night ritual, see chap. 7.2, below. It seems likely that the whole of the Black Mass episode was appended to the witches' confessions late in the summer of 1609. This probability is indicated by the statements in the inquisitors' letter dated 15 Sept. 1609 (see chapter 7 n. 17, below) and Salazar's vote of 8 June 1610 (see below, chap. 8.7).

54. *Joint Sentence* f. 399ʳ⁻ᵛ; see *Méritos of Juanes de Goiburu* f. 171ᵛ, and *Méritos of Juanes de Sansín* f. 173ᵛ. The witches also exhumed the bodies of the children they had killed with their evil arts (see María de Yriarte's statement in *Joint Sentence* f. 395ʳ). It is characteristic of Murray's selective treatment of the sources that these hideous feasts receive no mention in her section on the banquet at the witches' sabbath (MURRAY *Witch-Cult* chap. 5 sec. 5, "The Feast") or in the section on child sacrifice (idem pp. 156-159).

55. *Joint Sentence* f. 399ʳ; see *Méritos of Juanes de Goiburu* f. 171ᵛ and *Méritos of Juanes de Sansín* f. 173ᵛ. Juanes de Goiburu confessed that now and again the witches gathered at his house for a feast, and that

on one of these occasions they had dug up the body of his son and eaten it (*Third Report of the Auto de fe* f. 366ʳ). The eldest witches dined in a third manner, on the bones of long-dead Zugarramurdi residents, which they dug up in the churchyard and brought as sacrifice to the Devil. This normally occurred once or twice a month, and the Devil showed his gratitude by strengthening their old gums to enable them to chew the bones (*Joint Sentence* f. 399ᵛ).

56. Idem f. 399ʳ.

57. Idem f. 399ʳ.

58. Idem f. 399ᵛ, see *Second Report of the Auto de fe* f. 348ᵛ (SD Text 2), where the plant is called *belarrona*, i.e. belladonna or deadly nightshade.

59. *Joint Sentence* f. 392ᵛ.

60. Idem f. 393ʳ; see *Second Report of the Auto de fe* ff. 348ᵛ-349ʳ (SD Text 2).

61. *Joint Sentence* ff. 391ᵛ, 392ʳ.

62. Idem f. 392ʳ⁻ᵛ; see *Méritos of Juanes de Sansín* f. 173ᵛ.

63. *Joint Sentence* ff. 391ᵛ, 392ᵛ; see *Méritos of Juanes de Goiburu* f. 171ᵛ.

64. *Joint Sentence* ff. 392ᵛ-393ʳ.

65. Idem ff. 392ᵛ, 393ʳ.

66. Idem f. 391ᵛ.

67. Miguel de Goiburu confessed to having given some witch powder to the stonemason Petri de Juangorena's pig, so that it sickened and died, and said this was in revenge for the pig having constantly ruined Goiburu's fields (*Joint Sentence* f. 394ᵛ).

68. Miguel de Goiburu and Graciana de Barrenechea confessed that the Zugarramurdi Devil and his witches once flew to the coast at Saint-Jean-de-Luz and out over the sea for a league. Here they produced a storm which caused some ships to collide. But when one of the sailors held up a cross toward the witches they and the Devil fled away (idem f. 391ʳ). The same episode is recounted in Mongastón's pamphlet which states that there were six ships (MONGASTÓN *Relación* f. 9ᵛ). One seventeenth-century writer connects the witches' confessions at the auto de fe at Logroño in 1610 with the loss of General (*sic*) Don Antonio de Oquendo's fleet off the Isthmus of Bidart in 1607, when more than 800 men were drowned. This manuscript was later published, see Lope MARTÍNEZ DE ISASTI *Compendio historial de la . . . provincia de Guipúzcoa* San Sebastián 1850 p. 240.

69. See table 4 in chap. 8.1, below.

70. MURRAY *Witch-Cult* Appendix III A, pp. 249-254.

71. Julio Caro Baroja's classification of seven grades of witches, which is based solely on his interpretation of Mongastón's pamphlet (see CARO BAROJA 1961 pp. 249-251), is unconvincing. The new source material clearly illustrates that in the view of the inquisitors — which to my mind is the decisive criterion — there were only three witch grades. This division into three groups is most clearly apparent in the *Second Report of the Auto de fe* ff. 345ᵛ-346ʳ (SD Text 2).

72. For the Devil's marking of children and their duty to guard toads, see chaps. 5.4 and 5.6, above.

73. See *Joint Sentence* ff. 387ᵛ, 389ᵛ, 390ᵛ, 396ᵛ; *Méritos of Juanes de Goiburu* f. 173ʳ.

74. *Joint Sentence* f. 397ʳ. This presumably reflects a Basque antiwitchcraft tradition.

75. Idem f. 396ᵛ; *Méritos of Juanes de Sansín* f. 173ʳ.

76. Idem f. 173ᵛ; see chap. 4.2, above, where 22-year-old María de Jureteguía tells that she was received into the sect, but never became a senior witch.

77. See the prologue to the *Joint Sentence*, where it is stated that all four witches are "authorized to manufacture poison [*tienen... autoridad de hacer ponzoñas*]," and where the rights and duties attached to the senior grade are described in some detail (*Joint Sentence* f. 387ᵛ).

78. Idem f. 387ʳ.

79. Idem ff. 391ᵛ, 398ʳ.

80. See chap. 4.2, above.

81. See chap. 4.2, above.

82. *Joint Sentence* f. 387ʳ⁻ᵛ.

83. Idem ff. 387ʳ, 387ᵛ.

84. *Méritos of Juanes de Goiburu* f. 171ᵛ.

85. *Méritos of Juanes de Sansín* f. 173ᵛ.

86. *Joint Sentence* f. 397ʳ. The child witches were also flogged for not guarding the toads properly, and the adult witches for breaking the sabbath taboo and speaking the name of Jesus.

87. Idem ff. 391ʳ, 391ᵛ.

88. Idem f. 391ʳ.

89. Idem f. 397ᵛ. This instance puts the number of ships at eight, but the *Joint Sentence* does not indicate whether it refers to the episode discussed above (see n. 68).

90. *Joint Sentence* f. 397ʳ⁻ᵛ.

91. See near beginning of chap. 4.5, above.

92. See above, nn. 21 and 29. Reading the quotations from Miguel de Goiburu's trial record in the *Pamplona Manuscript* has confirmed my opinion of him as a good raconteur (see IDOATE *Documento* pp. 54, 63, 65-66, 67, 85-86, 95-96, 98, 113-114, 122, 124-125, 139, 141, 149-151, 164).

93. *Joint Sentence* f. 397ᵛ. The witches' general assembly is mentioned neither in the *Pamplona Manuscript* nor in any of the other auto de fe reports, but the subject appears again (1610) in the confessions of some child witches of Echalar (see below, chap. 10.4).

94. Although in principle this is an assertion I continue to maintain, I have to admit that judging from the citations in the *Pamplona Manuscript* the individual witches' confessions were fuller in detail than I had originally believed (see table 11 in chap. 12.5, below). But on this point we must take into consideration the fact that the *Pamplona Manuscript* reflects only one particular aspect of the witches' confessions, that which in some way or other could be used as evidence of *actos positivos* or to prove the existence of witchcraft (see below, chap. 12.5).

95. After studying the copy that I had sent him of the description in

the *Joint Sentence* of the dressed toads (see above, chap. 5.5 with n. 43), Dr. Harner wrote to me: "This is the first time I have encountered such a specific reference to the use of toad extract in a flying ointment and I consider it most important. . . . I am firmly convinced that flying ointments contained hallucinogens capable of inducing the effects described" (Harner to Henningsen, 28 Dec. 1970).

NOTES TO CHAPTER 6

1. *Note on further reading:* It is remarkable that there is so little research on the inquisitorial journeys of visitation that were so integral a part of the activity of the Inquisition. In fact, apart from the passages in LEA (*Inquisition of Spain* II pp. 91-101, 238-241) I have been unable to find any supporting literature. It was therefore necessary for me to examine a great deal of unpublished material before I was able to write this chapter (see, however, the recent article published by a young French historian and collaborator of mine, Jean Pierre DEDIEU "Les inquisiteurs de Tolède et la visite du district" *Mélanges de la Casa de Velázquez* XIII [1978] 235-256). It is to be hoped that the subject will be investigated thoroughly in the future. Special attention must be called to three important manuscripts. The *first* is an undated *Modo de proceder* which, judging from its contents, dates from the beginning of the seventeenth century. It contains a long chapter entitled "Lo que se ha de hacer en visita" (*Lib* 1259 ff. 130ᵛ-134ᵛ, hereafter cited as *"What is to be undertaken on Visitation."*) The first part of this text is identical with the thirteen paragraphs of instructions for inquisitorial visitations found in *Carta Acordada* No. 51, 26 Nov. 1569 (*Lib* 497 ff. 121ʳ-123ᵛ), see below, notes 31, 33, 36. The remainder of the text contains a number of supplementary details regarding the usual procedures for visitations. The *second* manuscript is the *Modo de proceder* in the Biblioteca Nacional (Madrid) so often cited by Lea in his *Inquisition of Spain,* but which I only recently succeeded in locating on account of Lea's obsolete reference "MSS D122." The accessions number is now MS 798. Judging from the contents the date of the manuscript is approximately 1640 (this year is mentioned on f. 5ᵛ). On ff. 50ᵛ-61ʳ there is a long series of instructions and forms of procedure as used on journeys of visitation by the Inquisition of Llerena. The *third* manuscript bears the title "Orden que se ha de guardar en la visita [Rules to be observed on the visitation]," *Lib* 1229 ff. 168ʳ-169ʳ. This was merely a copy of *Carta Acordada* No. 51, which was sent to the Llerena tribunal in 1596. This manuscript volume is of interest because it contains some printed texts which all have a bearing on inquisitorial visitations: (1) "Iuramento que a de hazer el pveblo antes que se lea el Edicto de la Fe" (f. 171ʳ); (2) the Llerena tribunal's Edict of Faith and Anathema (ff. 172ʳ-177ʳ); and (3) "El orden que se a de tener qvando se lea la carta de Anathema" (f. 178ʳ). These texts are familiar from other examples, discussed below in notes 10 ("Juramento"), 7 (Edict of Faith "Type B"), and 22 ("El Orden . . . quando se lea la carta de Anathema"). The texts are all undated, but as all the contents of this manuscript volume seem to relate to the end of the sixteenth century we may assume that these are the oldest examples.

2. ARGÜELLO *Instrucciones* f. 13ᵛ.

3. *Lib* 497 ff. 270ʳ-272ʳ, *Carta Acordada* No. 225, 25 Jan. 1607 (§ 3).

4. Idem f. 191ʳ⁻ᵛ, *Carta Acordada* No. 119, 21 June 1578; see LEA *Inquisition of Spain* II p. 240.

5. *Carta Acordada* No. 225 § 1 (n. 3, above); see LEA *Inquisition of Spain* II p. 240.

6. Manuel RODRÍGUEZ LUSITANO *Svmma de casos de consciencia, con aduertencias muy prouechosas para Confessores* Salamanca 1598 3 vols. I should like to take this opportunity of thanking Antonio Odriozola (Pontevedra), the bibliographer, who in 1968 presented me with his copy of this extraordinarily interesting old book. It is a manual for confessors, and here we may read of buying and selling, millers and bakers, dancing and card-playing, forgers and prostitutes, baptism, marriage, and burial — about all the details of everyday life in sixteenth-century Spain, in fact, though naturally regarded from the moral point of view. Here too are articles on the *precepto pascual* (I pp. 162-163); heresy as one of the "reserved sins" (I pp. 347-349); and the seal of confession (II pp. 200-203). It is stated of the latter that the priest is bound to silence "to such a degree that he must not reveal even crimes of heresy, of which he is informed in the confessional" (p. 201); there are, however, two exceptional instances when the priest may break the "seal of the confessional": "One is if the person confessing is himself in agreement.... The other [is] if the confessor knows about it [the same] from another quarter...." (p. 202).

7. Here and below I refer to the Edict of Faith of the Logroño Inquisition, an undated printed copy which is found in *Lib* 1325 ff. 228ʳ-232ʳ, hereafter cited as *The Logroño Edict*. The same volume contains printed examples from the majority of the other tribunals. It is clear that all these edicts were sent to *la Suprema* in anticipation of a revision in 1632. The Logroño Edict — and this also applies to most of the edicts from other tribunals in this volume — agrees almost to the letter with a printed Edict of Faith from the Córdoba Inquisition, which according to a superscription was published at Baeza on 3 June 1607 (*Lib* 1325 ff. 239ʳ-243ᵛ). This provides a firm basis for the date of one version of the Edict of Faith, which we may term "Type B." This eight-page version probably dates back as far as 1581, for we know that in this year *la Suprema* sent a revised edition of the Edict of Faith to all tribunals (*Lib* 497 f. 202ʳ⁻ᵛ, *Carta Acordada* No. 129, 15 Feb. 1581). An Edict of Faith from Valencia, which is reprinted by Llorente (*Historia crítica* 1822 X pp. 230-250) may also be classified as "Type B." An older and considerably shorter version, "Type A," is the Edict of Faith from Mexico, 1571, published by Lea, and which, it should be noted, is handwritten (LEA *Inquisition of Spain* II pp. 587-590). No other examples of this version are known. However, the tradition of edicts of faith can be traced back to the very beginning of the sixteenth century thanks to the copy of a printed Edict of Faith issued in Valencia in 1512 which is preserved in the Cambridge University Library, see John Langdon DAVIES (ed.) *The Spanish Inquisition: A Collection of Contemporary Documents* London 1966 (Jackdaw Publications No. 5) exhibit no. 6a (where the edict is reproduced) and 6b (where it is translated into English). A third and later version, "Type C," is found in edicts of

faith extant from after 1632 up to the end of the seventeenth century. This type may be recognized from the reference to a papal brief relating to *solicitantes* (i.e. unchaste confessors), dated 30 Aug. 1622 (folio 2^r), and to the passage on astrology, which takes up almost two pages, to which "Type B" only devotes twelve lines. A printed example of "Type C," from the Toledo Inquisition, is endorsed 18 Mar. 1696 and is in the Biblioteca Nacional (Madrid) MS 718 ff. 74^r-81^r. It consists of eleven pages of Edict of Faith followed by four pages of Anathema.

8. *What is to be undertaken on Visitation* f. 131^r. Not until 1575 was the ruling introduced for the Edict of Faith to be read in monasteries as well (see *Lib* 497 ff. 177^r-178^r, *Carta Acordada* No. 103, 14 Oct. 1575).

9. BN, Manuscript 2440 f. 427^r, "Instrvccion. El orden que se a de tener en publicar el Edicto de Fè, y Anathema. . . ."

10. *Lib* 1244 f. 127^v, "Juramento." Printed oath prefacing an Edict of Faith of "Type B" from before 1632 (see n. 7, above). The same oath recurs in *What is to be undertaken on Visitation* f. 134^r and in GARCÍA *Orden de Procesar* f. 72^v-73^r, in both instances with slight variations. The latter work was published in 1608.

11. *The Logroño Edict* f. 228^r.

12. Idem f. 228^{r-v}.

13. Idem ff. 228^v-230^v.

14. Idem ff. 230^v-231^r.

15. Idem f. 231^{r-v}.

16. Idem ff. 231^v-232^r.

17. BN, MS 2440 f. 427^r (n. 9, above).

18. Idem.

19. Here and below I have used a printed anathema from the Inquisition at Valladolid, BN MS 2440 ff. 422^r-423^r, hereafter cited as *Anathema of Valladolid*. It is undated but may be assumed to date from the beginning of the seventeenth century, since it is found together with a printed Edict of Faith of "Type B" from the same Tribunal.

20. *Anathema of Valladolid* f. 422^r.

21. Idem f. 422^v.

22. Idem ff. 422^v-423^r; *Lib* 1325 f. 249^r, "El orden que se a de tener qvando se lea la carta de Anathema", undated printed instruction, judging from the typography from the first half of the seventeenth century. The instruction contains the texts of both antiphon and response. It is stated that the psalm "Deus Laudam meam" is to be found in "los Maitines del Sabado."

23. *Anathema of Valladolid* f. 423^r.

24. Idem f. 423^r; *Lib* 1325 f. 249^r (n. 22, above); *What is to be undertaken on Visitation* ff. 132^v-133^v.

25. The details of these variations obviously need thorough research. However, it is my impression that the variation is far greater in the texts of the tribunals' anathemas than in the edicts of faith. The Anathema cited by Lea (*Inquisition of Spain* II pp. 95-96) is the one mentioned in n. 7 above from Toledo 1696 (Lea's reference, op. cit. p. 96 n. 1, "MS D 118," is now obsolete and should read MS 718).

26. *Lib* 1244 ff. 243^r-244^v.

27. *Leg* 2042 Exp. 8 f. 14ʳ (*Relación de visita* of the Inquisition of Galicia carried out in 1581, no. 94, against Nuño Vázquez, *vecino* of the parish of Racamonde, testified to by two witnesses).

28. *Lib* 795 f. 359ʳ § 9 (ff. 357ʳ-368ʳ, Salazar to inquisitor general, Logroño, 24 Mar. 1612 (a); received at Madrid 31 Mar., hereafter cited as *First Report of Salazar*. The first eight paragraphs are reproduced as SD Text 11, and the whole manuscript is described below in chap. 12.2).

29. Idem ff. 359ᵛ-360ʳ § 13. The name of the priest was Juan de Ribera Yrigoyen.

30. *What is to be undertaken on Visitation* f. 132ʳ⁻ᵛ.

31. *Carta Acordada* No. 51, 26 Nov. 1569, § 3 (n. 1, above).

32. *First Report of Salazar* f. 367ʳ §§ 51-52.

33. *Carta Acordada* No. 51, 26 Nov. 1569, §§ 2 and 10 (n. 1, above).

34. See LEA *Inquisition of Spain* II p. 239. For Lea's reference "MS D 122" read now BN MS 798. A journal of this type is extant from the inquisitor Juan de Espina Velasco's journey of visitation in Sardinia, 23 Feb. through 24 May 1640 (*Lib* 783 ff. 227ʳ-279ᵛ). The author provides details regarding receptions and etiquette as well as additional interesting information; for instance, wherever he went the inquisitor bought bread to distribute among the poor. It is quite surprising to discover that the same inquisitor was ill for most of the journey and spent a great deal of his time in bed. Finally the journal describes how on arrival home he sank into a chair in utter exhaustion.

35. For inquisitors' canopy see below, chap. 11.A.3 and 11.C.3; for the traveling altar see *Second Report of Salazar* f. 4ᵛ (SD Text 12).

36. *Carta Acordada* No. 51, 26 Nov. 1569, §§ 8-12 (n. 1, above).

37. *What is to be undertaken on Visitation* f. 133ᵛ. It is further stated that the report is to be sent in after being voted on by the Tribunal, and is to be in duplicate, one copy to be sent to the Council and the other to the inquisitor general.

38. In the oath of secrecy the witness swore not to reveal anything to others of what he had heard or said, or had been questioned about in connection with the case at hand. See the formula in GARCÍA *Orden de Procesar* ff. 1ᵛ-2ʳ.

39. For instance *Leg* 2889, Inquisition of Galicia, *Relación de causas* 1619/20, nos. 1 and 11.

40. See LEA *Inquisition of Spain* II p. 240.

41. *Lib* 497 f. 270ʳ, *Carta Acordada* No. 225, 25 Jan. 1607.

42. *Lib* 497 f. 191ʳ⁻ᵛ, *Carta Acordada* No. 119, 21 June 1578.

43. In 1607 the visitation was made by the inquisitor Becerra (see chap. 4 n. 38, above); in 1609 by Valle (see chap. 7, below); in 1611 by Salazar (see chap. 11, below); in 1616 by the inquisitor Aranda (see chap. 13.7, below); and in 1617 again by Salazar (see chap. 13.7, below). A somewhat different list of journeys of visitation is given by Salazar in 1619, see *Examination of Salazar at Valencia* ff. 781ᵛ-782ʳ.

NOTES TO CHAPTER 7

1. *Lib* 332 f. 251ᵛ, Council to Tribunal, 21 July 1609.

2. *Lib* 332 ff. 252ᵛ-253ʳ, Council to Tribunal, 24 July 1609. In translating the end of the letter I have attempted to give an interpretation. In the original the quotation runs: "pues el principal juicio de esta materia consiste en la prueba y verificación que se hiciere de estos actos y cosas visibles y permanentes."

3. These instructions to Valle must not be confused with the *modo de proceder*, or guide to procedure in witch cases, which was also forwarded to the Tribunal on this occasion but which unfortunately was not preserved (see p. 60).

4. *Lib* 794 f. 462ᵛ (ff. 462ʳ-463ʳ, Tribunal to Council, 22 Aug. 1609; received in Madrid 4 Sept.).

5. See *Leg* 1683 Exp. 1 f. 1525ᵛ (ff. 1524ᵛ-1531ᵛ, Examination of Valle's visitation book and other papers of the Tribunal during *la Suprema*'s inspection in 1619-20, hereafter cited as *Examination of Valle's Visitation Book*).

6. See above, chap. 4.5. Valle's journey took him via Pamplona, where he made a stop and presumably stayed Tuesday night (see below, near end of chap. 7.3).

7. *Lib* 794 f. 459ʳ⁻ᵛ, Valle to Tribunal, Urdax 20 [Aug.] 1609; received in Logroño 24 Aug. For Monterola see above, chap. 4.2.

8. *Lib* 794 ff. 461ʳ⁻ᵛ, 464ʳ, Tribunal to Council, 25 Aug. 1609; received in Madrid 4 Sept. The inquisitors wrote that they had received Valle's letter of 20 Aug., and they continued by telling *la Suprema* that they were sure that the Edict of Faith was read "last Sunday" (i.e. 23 Aug.). If Valle followed the usual practice of the Inquisition, the Anathema must have been published the following Sunday (see above, chap. 6).

9. The most important sources are (1) *Lib* 835 ff. 449ʳ-458ᵛ, hereafter cited as *Relación de causas 1610/11 (B)* (another copy, *(A)*, is found idem, ff. 438ʳ-443ᵛ), where these five witches are numbered 15-19, the first ones on the list of "Witches reconciled and absolved by the Edict of Grace" (see case nos. 32-36 of Witch List); (2) *Salazar's Vote of 8 June 1610* (see below, chap. 8.7); and (3) a letter from the abbot of Urdax, discussed below in chap. 10.1.

10. The age of the first witch is stated in the inquisitors' letter (assuming that she is identical with María Chipía, see below, chap. 7.2). The ages of the other four are calculated on the basis of the facts given two years later in *Relación de causas 1610/11 (B)* f. 454ʳ, which originate from the beginning of 1611, and where the five witches are said to be respectively 20, 20, 17, 14, and 12 years old.

11. The dates of the hearing are also given in *Relación de causas 1610/11 (B)* f. 454ʳ. Placing the year as 1610 is obviously erroneous and it should be 1609.

12. The *Pamplona Manuscript* f. 53ʳ (IDOATE *Documento* p. 174). This provides an additional example of the belief that the evil arts could be inherited by members of certain families. Note that María de Lecumberri's grandmother, Estevanía de Navarcorena, was also a witch (table 1, above).

13. For María Pérez de Barrenechea and her daughters (see table 1, above, chap. 2 n. 34, and chap. 10 n. 7, below).

14. See preceding note.

15. See chap. 2, above. The *Pamplona Manuscript* reproduces two lengthy passages from the depositions of María de Ximildegui to Valle at Urdax (IDOATE *Documento* pp. 59, 73-75). The first of the quotations is stated to have been copied from folios 4, 5, and 6 in the visitation book. From this we can deduce that the French girl must have been one of the first to be questioned by Valle. It must presumably be due to a misunderstanding when Salazar mentions her as one of the five who presented themselves and made witchcraft confessions to Valle (see below, chap. 8.7). María de Ximildegui seems to have appeared only as a witness. Possibly Salazar confused her with María de Lecumberri (senior) see table 2, above.

16. The emergence of the *Pamplona Manuscript* has improved the position since it gives a number of quotations from the confessions made by the same witches two years later, when they presented themselves at Logroño to be reconciled through the Edict of Grace, see IDOATE *Documento* pp. 52, 58, 165, 168-169 (Joana de Telechea, case no. 33); *52, 56, 64,* 133, *165, 170* (María de Burga, case no. 34); 58, *64, 67, 88, 141,* 169 (María de Lecumberri, senior, case no. 32). The italicized page numbers signify that there is no quotation, but only a reference to the trial record is made. María de Lecumberri (junior) and María Pérez de Burga are not named, but they are listed as nos. 30 and 31 respectively in the register of the *Pamplona Manuscript* (f. 54ᵛ, IDOATE *Documento* p. 178), case nos. 35 and 36.

17. *Lib* 794 ff. 404ʳ-405ʳ, Tribunal to Council, 15 Sept. 1609; received in Madrid 6 Oct. The inquisitors state that the letters from Valle were received by the Tribunal on 11 Sept.

18. *Lib* 794 f. 440ʳ (ff. 433ʳ⁻ᵛ, 440ʳ, Tribunal to Council, 26 Sept. 1609, received in Madrid 6 Oct.).

19. The *Pamplona Manuscript* states that all the witches' confessions agreed on this point (IDOATE *Documento* p. 158); but if we study table 11, Acto no. 28 "Demon as substitute," we notice the remarkable fact that not a single reference is made to any one of the first ten witches' trial records. Since nevertheless the subject is mentioned in the *Joint Sentence* (see chap. 4.7, above), presumably some of the four witches must have mentioned the counterfeit phenomenon at a later hearing. These could only have been Miguel de Goiburu and María de Yriarte, since the two others, Graciana de Barrenechea and Estevanía de Yriarte, had already died in Sept. 1609 (see below, chap. 8.2).

20. See chap. 5.8, above. The quotations in the *Pamplona Manuscript* (IDOATE *Documento* pp. 163-165) show that the first four witches to be imprisoned in January, and Graciana de Barrenechea, who died in September, made no mention of this topic in their confessions (see table 11, below).

21. The latter has been confirmed to a great extent by the *Pamplona Manuscript* (IDOATE *Documento* passim).

22. *Examination of Valle's Visitation Book* f. 1524ᵛ.

23. *Leg* 1679 Exp. 2.1 No. 40 f.1ʳ⁻ᵛ, Tribunal to Council, 4 Sept. 1609; received in Madrid 15 Sept.

24. *Lib* 794 f. 433ᵛ (T./C. 26-9-1609; n. 18, above). Probably it is this imprisonment that is referred to in an account, *Lib* 832 ff. 159ʳ-162ʳ,

title: "Memoria y relación de lo que ha gastado la Inquisición de Logroño en el negocio de brujos desde el año de 1609, así en dos visitas y el auto de fe y otras partidas como en alimentar los presos," undated but datable to 27 Sept. 1614, hereafter cited as *Accounts of 27 Sept. 1614* or *Food Accounts* (for the dating see below, chap. 13.6 with n. 58). On f. 161ᵛ of this account there is an entry of 180 *reales* "for a monk [Fray Felipe de Zabaleta] who carries out the services of priest at Zugarramurdi and who helped Juan de Yerro, the porter, with the imprisonment."

25. *Examination of Valle's Visitation Book* f. 1525ʳ.

26. Cf. *Lib* 794 f. 443ʳ, where Becerra and Salazar at the end of a letter to the Council concerning other matters (24 Oct. 1609) stated that Valle had now moved on to hold a visitation at San Sebastián, and that in the near future they would write to the Council regarding the letters they had recently received from their colleague. Unfortunately none of these letters (neither those from Valle nor the promised one from the Tribunal) have been preserved.

27. *Examination of Valle's Visitation Book* f. 1530ᵛ. It is stated here that Valle left San Sebastián on 19 Nov. 1609 and reached Tolosa the same day with his companions, Francisco Pardo, the secretary, and Juan de Yerro, the porter. "19 November" is possibly an error in transcription, as an original letter in Valle's hand is dated San Sebastián 20 Nov. 1609 (see below, n. 34). I have adhered to Valle's dating, though in fact it is impossible to decide which of the two dates is the correct one.

28. On 14 Dec. 1609 Valle interrogated nine-year-old María de Yturría of Echalar on the visitation at Tolosa (see below, chap. 7.5).

29. See *Examination of Valle's Visitation Book* ff. 1524ᵛ-1525ʳ, where it is stated: "And likewise I [i.e. *la Suprema*'s visitor] testify and confirm that what appears in the visitation book from the journey in 1609, which was undertaken by the inquisitor . . . Valle Alvarado with Francisco Pardo, *notario del secreto*, is attested to by the above-mentioned Francisco Pardo, on folios 93 and 131 respectively, that they arrived at Lesaca on 23 September of the year in question and stayed in that town until 14 October of that year."

30. Idem f. 1530ʳ⁻ᵛ.

31. Note that a transcript of a witch confession made at Tolosa on 13 Dec. 1609 (see below, table 3, *Rte* 24) is stated to have been copied from Valle's visitation book "Folio 375 [ff.]," *Leg* 1679 Exp. 2.1 f. 165ᵛ (ii + 626 folios, a parchment volume with the back title: "F. Pamplona Calahorra. Revocantes de sus confesiones hechas en la secta de brujas 1611. El licenciado Alonso de Salazar Frías." At f. iʳ the heading: "Las personas revocantes que ha habido en la secta de brujos desde 29 de mayo de 1611, que se publicó el edicto de gracia, contenidos en este volumen letra F.," hereafter cited as *Volume "F" of Salazar's Visitation Book*). The majority of the hearings must have been witchcraft cases, but Valle also recorded other types of heresy cases; see the reconstruction of his visitation book in Part 3 of the Witch List.

32. See below, table 3 and chap. 7.6.

33. *Lib* 794 ff. 448ʳ-449ᵛ, 445ʳ, Valle to Tribunal, San Sebastián, 13 Nov. 1609, received at Logroño 16 Nov. In his introduction Valle

wrote that he received his colleagues' letter dated 26 Oct. on 3 Nov. (that letter was not preserved, but on this occasion the Tribunal forwarded a copy of a 1595 witch trial to Valle, see below, chap. 7.3). He had not replied before because the postal services were very poor and communication slow. Now, however, he had met a certain Joan Fernández, who was going to Logroño, and he was availing himself of this opportunity.

34. *Lib* 794 f. 447^{r-v}, Valle to Tribunal, San Sebastián, 20 Nov. 1609 (see n. 27, above), received in Logroño 27 Nov.

35. *Lib* 794 f. 445^r (Valle/T. 13-11-1609; n. 33, above).

36. Idem ff. 449^v, 445^r.

37. *Lib* 794 f. 447^{r-v} (Valle/T. 20-11-1609; n. 34, above).

38. Idem f. 447^v.

39. See below, chap. 8.4.

40. BN MS 2031 f. 133^r (ff. 133^r-136^v, "Relación que hizo el Doctor Lope de Isasti, presbitero y beneficiado de Lezo, que es en Guipúzcoa, acerca de las maléficas de Cantabria, por mandado del Señor Inquisidor Campofrío en Madrid" dated 1618; published in Julio CARO BAROJA "Cuatro relaciones sobre la hechicería vasca" *Anuario de Eusco-Folklore* 13 [1933] 85-145).

41. See *Lib* 795 f. 6^{r-v}, Tribunal to Council, 2 Jan. 1610; received in Madrid 22 Jan. The letter states that the two witches were transferred from the prison at Rentería a few days after Valle had returned from visitation (i.e. shortly after 17 Dec. 1609). The remainder of the letter concerns these two witches, and it appears that Lambert was reported on Valle's visitation and imprisoned by the secular authorities at Rentería at about the same time as María de Zozaya.

42. *Lib* 794 ff. 448^v-449^r (Valle/T. 13-11-1609; n. 33, above).

43. Idem f. 449^{r-v}.

44. *Lib* 794 f. 446^r, Ximenes de Oco to Valle on the visitation Pamplona, 1 Nov. 1609; received at San Sebastián 6 Nov.

45. *Lib* 794 f. 449^v (Valle/T. 13-11-1609; n. 33, above): "Y lo bueno es que tengo descubierto un aquelarre en aquellos lugares que están junto a la villa de Santesteban, con dos testigos, uno de 19 y otro de 15 años; y están testificadas las personas que acusan."

46. It would be interesting to discover whether there is any connection between this case and an action for slander from Goizueta in 1609 (AGN Proseso No. 9177). This action was brought by Catalina de Alduncín and her son, relatives of the parish priest of Goizueta. They charged Joanes de Zubillaga and Magdalena de Leiza with having circulated false rumors to the effect that Catalina de Alduncín was a witch. At the end of the trial the High Court of Navarra sentenced the two slanderers to two years' banishment. See Florencio IDOATE *La brujería* Pamplona 1967 (*Navarra. Temas de cultura popular* 4) pp. 26-27. Unfortunately the trial record was not in its place when I visited the archive in 1970.

47. *Lib* 794 f. 448^r (Valle/T. 13-11-1609; n. 33, above). For the witches in the Araiz Valley see Florencio IDOATE *El Señorío de Sarria* Pamplona 1959, section "El señor de Andueza y los brujos" (pp. 285-289 with Appendix No. 38 "Confession of witchcraft made 1 Feb. 1595 at

Andueza Castle by María Miguel de Oreza, Inza"). For the intervention of the Inquisition in this trial see *Fourth Report of Salazar* ff. 2ᵛ-3ʳ (SD Text 14 § 11).

48. See above, near beginning of chap. 6.

49. *Lib* 795 f. 6ʳ⁻ᵛ (T./C. 2-1-1610; n. 41, above).

50. *Lib* 794 f. 451ʳ, Juan de Bidazabal to Tribunal, Motrico, 19 July 1609; received in Logroño 27 July.

51. *Lib* 794 f. 458ʳ⁻ᵛ, *Licenciado* Juan Pérez de Mutio to Tribunal, San Sebastián, 24 July 1609; received in Logroño 13 Aug.

52. Idem f. 458ᵛ.

53. *Lib* 794 ff. 462ʳ-463ʳ (T./C. 22-8-1609; n. 4, above). The ruling that the Inquisition should not take proceedings against foreigners for heresy committed outside Spanish territory had been established in earlier letters from *la Suprema* (6 May 1597; 22 Dec. 1604; 8 Oct. 1605). The inquisitors referred to these communications in their next letter to the Council, dated 25 Aug. 1609.

54. *Lib* 794 f. 460ʳ⁻ᵛ, Francisco de Espilla to Tribunal, Oñate, 19 Aug. 1609; received in Logroño 24 Aug.

55. *Lib* 794 ff. 461ʳ⁻ᵛ, 464ʳ (T./C. 25-8-1609; n. 8, above).

56. DE LANCRE *Tableau* p. 38.

57. *Lib* 794 f. 433ᵛ (T./C. 26-9-1609; n. 18, above). In this letter d'Espaignet is mentioned only as "el presidente"; in a sense this might well allude to de Lancre. The passage concerning the seven small trial records is obscure in the original: "siete procesillos de actos comprobados de las cosas que han confesado estos brujos." My translation should be seen as a suggested interpretation.

58. *Lib* 333 f. 8ʳ⁻ᵛ, Council to Tribunal, 10 Oct. 1609. The letter refers to "los siete procesos de actos comprobados en la materia de brujos" (see the quotation from the inquisitors' letter, preceding note).

59. See *Lib* 333 f. 22ᵛ, Council to Tribunal, 10 Dec. 1609, which contains a brief message to Valle to remain where he is and await further orders. The message to Valle is repeated in a further letter (*Lib* 333 ff. 27ᵛ-28ʳ, Council to Tribunal, 23 Dec. 1609) when the Edict of Grace to the witches was also forwarded. This edict is not extant, but its contents are recorded in the Council's letter to the Tribunal of 23 Dec. and in another letter, a *consulta*, from the Council to the inquisitor general, who at that time was at Toledo (*Lib* 333 ff. 24ʳ-25ʳ, Council to Inquisitor General, 11 Dec. 1609).

60. *Lib* 795 f. 6ʳ (T./C. 2-1-1610; n. 41, above).

61. See our mention of Valle's letter of 13 Nov. 1609, chap. 7.3, above.

62. This letter has not been preserved but its contents are known from two later letters, see *Leg* 1679 Exp. 2.1 No. 35 f. 1ʳ, Tribunal to Council, 8 Feb. 1611 and idem No. 22 f. 1ʳ, Tribunal to Council, 9 Mar. 1611.

63. *Lib* 333 ff. 33ᵛ-34ᵛ, Council to Tribunal, 25 Jan. 1610, received in Logroño 5 Feb.

64. *Lib* 795 f. 9ʳ (ff. 8ʳ-9ᵛ, Tribunal to Council, 13 Feb. 1610, received in Madrid 2 Mar.).

65. Las Cinco Villas was under the civil jurisdiction of the *merindad* of Pamplona, which was itself subject to the High Court of Navarra.

Navarra was divided into five *merindades* (Pamplona, Estella, Tudela, Sangüeza, and Olite). A census from 1637 calculated the total population of Navarra as 27,942 *vecinos* (or 139,710 inhabitants). According to the same count the *merindad* of Pamplona numbered 7,944 *vecinos* (or 39,720 inhabitants). These figures are taken from José YANGUAS Y MIRANDA *Diccionario de antigüedades del Reino de Navarra* (3 vols. 2nd ed. Pamplona 1964) II pp. 428-430 (article "Población"). For ecclesiastical jurisdiction Las Cinco Villas formed a deanery under Pamplona. It was one of four deaneries which until 1567 were under the jurisdiction of the bishop of Bayonne in France (see above, chap. 3 n. 49). According to a census of 1645/46 (AGN, Seccion de Estadística, Legajo 1-2) Las Cinco Villas (Vera, Echalar, Lesaca, Yanci, and Aranaz) contained a total population of 2,730 inhabitants.

66. Antonio Venegas de Figueroa was born about 1550; he was the son of Don Luis de Venegas y Figueroa, ambassador to Philip II in Vienna, and Doña Guiomar de Saá, lady-in-waiting to the Infanta Doña María. He studied theology at Salamanca, where he took his licentiate. He must have become a canon at Toledo shortly afterwards, since this was his position in 1592, when he entered the service of the Inquisition (see *Leg* 1371 No. 4, Examination of Venegas's *limpieza de sangre* 1592). From 1596 to 1599 we find him serving as third inquisitor in Granada (*Leg* 2607, letters from the Granada tribunal to the Council, 1594-1599). He was a member of the Council from 1600 to 1606 (*Lib* 1338 f. 27^r contains his *juramento* or oath of allegiance on his accession to the position of *conciliario* on 23 Dec. 1600; and in *Lib* 367 II f. 147^r we find him on *la Suprema*'s payroll for the last time, on 25 Feb. 1606. Here he is mentioned as already being bishop of Pamplona and therefore receiving only two-thirds of the annual salary of 500,000 *maravedis*). Thus Venegas must have been acquainted with Valle at the time when the latter was secretary to inquisitor general Acevedo (see chap. 3.3, above). In 1612 Venegas was translated from Pamplona to the wealthy and sought-after bishopric of Sigüenza. He died on 8 Oct. 1614, just as he had been appointed president of the Council of Castilla (*Consejo de Castilla*). It is to be hoped that a biography of this interesting character will be produced one day; for the time being we must be content with the mention in Toribio MINGUELLA Y ARNEDO *Historia de la Diócesis de Sigüenza y de sus Obispos* (Madrid 1910-13, 3 vols.) III pp. 10-14.

67. *Leg* 1679 Exp. 2.1 No. 26[b] ff. 1^r-2^v, No. 31[a] f. 1^r, Venegas to inquisitor general, 4 Mar. 1611; received in Madrid 14 Mar., hereafter cited as *First Letter of the Bishop* (SD Text 5).

68. *Leg* 1679 Exp. 2.1 28[b] ff. 1^r-5^v, Tribunal to Council, 14 Feb. 1611, received in Madrid 28 Feb. The diocese of Pamplona included Navarra and all the eastern part of Guipúzcoa as far as the port of Motrico (see the map in José Goñi's book, reference chap. 3 n. 49, above).

69. See the biography in n. 66, above.

70. See below, n. 72.

71. The source is the parish register at Errazu, Baztán Valley, which I visited in 1968. The parish priest there showed me a list of episcopal visitations which I understood to be based on a "Libro de cuentas de

fábrica." Visitation No. 22 listed Venegas's journey of 1610, when the parish priests from the Baztán Valley were summoned to Elizondo on 10 Mar. 1610. The same source mentions episcopal visitations held on 22 May 1601 (Visitation No. 19); 4 Aug. 1607 (Visitation No. 20); 23 July 1608 (Visitation No. 21); 5 Sept. 1611 (Visitation No. 23); and 12 Apr. 1613 (Visitation No. 24).

72. Unfortunately the letter is not extant, but it is mentioned by Venegas in his second letter to the inquisitor general, *Leg* 1679 Exp. 2.1 No. 31[d] ff. 9^r-10^r, Venegas to Inquisitor General, 1 Apr. 1611, received in Madrid 21 Apr., hereafter cited as *Second Letter of the Bishop* (SD Text 7). It is presumably the same letter which is referred to by the inquisitors in their letter to the Council of 14 Feb. 1611 (n. 68, above), when they state that the bishop wrote to the Tribunal requesting that the distinguished María de Endara of Echalar should be taken to Logroño secretly and not together with the other witches who were being arrested by the Inquisition. María de Endara was imprisoned on 3 Mar. 1610. The Tribunal complied with the bishop's request and she was taken to Logroño by the priest Miguel de Oragaray (Inquisitors' letter of 14 Feb. 1611, f. 1^{r-v}).

73. *First Letter of the Bishop* f. 2^v (SD Text 5).

74. *The Bishop's Report* f. 2^r (SD Text 8).

75. *Lib* 795 ff. 101^r-102^r, Tribunal to Council, 16 Jan. 1610, received in Madrid 30 Jan.

76. The case is now known only through *Relación de causas 1610/11 (B)* f. 456^v in which Diego de Marticorena is listed as No. 53. It states here that he "confessed at the visitation on 10 Oct. 1609," and that later he went to Logroño and was reconciled on 22 Nov. 1610. The *Pamplona Manuscript* cites some fragments of his confession (IDOATE *Documento* passim).

77. Among these eleven are "María de Berrizaun y Endara alias Olandrea" and "Catalina de Topalda, serora" (*Volume "F" of Salazar's Visitation Book* f. 172^{r-v}).

78. See above, chap. 7.3, where it appears from Valle's two letters that eight children and two adult women from Lesaca had confessed and testified to the witch coven in their town. There seems every probability that we can identify one of the adult women as María Martín de Legarra (see above, table 3, *Rte* 17). To these we may add three adult witches from Lesaca who confessed at Tolosa (see table 3, *Rte* 12, 22, and 24). The total number of adult *confitente* witches would therefore be five. One of the eight child witches, Diego de Marticorena, had already confessed at the visitation at Lesaca. Eleven-year-old Juanes de Picabea made a confession at Tolosa (table 3, *Rte* 23). This brought the number of child witches to nine. However, besides these fourteen witches from Lesaca, we must also take into account an unknown number of witches from this town who made their confessions to Valle at Tolosa (see also below, n. 120).

79. This is a conclusion based on a close analysis of the six extant confessions of witchcraft (see table 3). In 1645/46 the population of Lesaca was ca. 1,190 (see below, table 6).

80. See *Volume "F" of Salazar's Visitation Book* f. 101^{r-v} (*Rte* 16, Juana de Arbiza's confession to the inquisitorial commissioner Domingo de

San Paul, Lesaca, 20 Feb. 1610), where it is stated of no. 22 in the list of witch accomplices, eight-year-old Mari Juri de Aranaz, that she is the one who "made a voluntary confession to Your Eminence [i.e. Valle] in the City of Tolosa," and the record goes on to say that the witches actually fetch her from San Sebastián and take her to the witches' sabbaths at the before-mentioned town [Yanci]". This presumably indicates that the girl lived at San Sebastián.

81. *Volume "F" of Salazar's Visitation Book* f. 109ᵛ (*Rte* 17).

82. *The Bishop's Report* f. 2ʳ⁻ᵛ (SD Text 8).

83. Idem f. 1ʳ⁻ᵛ; for an unabbreviated version of this quote, see HENNINGSEN *Papers of Salazar* p. 93.

84. DE LANCRE *Tableau* is possibly referring to Hualde on pp. 407-408: "A secular priest who was conversant with the Basque tongue presented himself to us in order to serve as interpreter, and to explain the statements of the witnesses and the hearings of the witches." See idem pp. 414-415, where de Lancre again mentions this priest.

85. See below, p. 133 and n. 94.

86. There is of course only indirect evidence of this, see the letters from Hualde and the Tribunal quoted below, p. 136 f.

87. *Examination of Valle's Visitation Book* f. 1525ʳ, which records 12 witnesses at Lesaca, questioned 25-27 Sept. 1609, who testified to Juan Martínez de San Paul's *limpieza de sangre*.

88. *Leg* 1679 Exp. 2.1 No. 8[a] f. 2ʳ (ff. 1ʳ-2ᵛ, Hernando de Solarte to the Provincial of the Jesuits, Bilbao, 17 Jan. 1611, hereafter cited as *First Letter of Solarte*, SD Text 3. In almost all the sources this priest is named as "*el licenciado* Yrisarri," but he signs himself with a Christian name on a death certificate of 1611 (see below, chap. 11 n. 118).

89. See *The Bishop's Report* f. 4ʳ (SD Text 8).

90. *Volume "F" of Salazar's Visitation Book* f. 118ʳ⁻ᵛ.

91. Idem f. 118ᵛ.

92. Idem ff. 108ʳ-117ᵛ. This too is an extract from my analysis of the six extant witchcraft confessions (cf. n. 79, above, and case no. 457).

93. See *The Bishop's Report* f. 5ʳ⁻ᵛ (SD Text 8). The same event is mentioned in MONGASTÓN *Relacíon* f. 8ᵛ and in the *Pamplona Manuscript* (IDOATE *Documento* pp. 170-171).

94. *Lib* 795 f. 99ʳ (ff. 99ʳ-100ʳ, Hualde to Tribunal, Vera, 11 and 12 Jan. 1610; received in Logroño 16 Jan.).

95. Idem f. 99ʳ. It is stated of Beltrana de la Fargua in the *Third Report of the Auto de fe* f. 367ʳ, that "nine witnesses, the three adults and priests, made statements testifying that she had admitted out of court [*extrajudicialmente*] that she was a witch." And further that she and "the five accomplices, one of whom was an adult woman" confessed immediately after the publication of the Edict of Faith (*luego que se leyeron los edictos de la fe*). I must admit that I cannot see how this can agree with the facts given by the other sources, which make it clear that the witches at Vera failed to report themselves during Valle's visitation at Lesaca.

96. *Lib* 795 f. 99ᵛ (Hualde/T. 11 Jan. 1610; n. 94, above). The source of the Latin invocation is the Gospel of St. John 19.19 and 1.14. The blessing seems to be of liturgical origin. Information kindly supplied by the Danish Jesuit Father Bjørn Højbo.

97. Idem f. 99ᵛ.
98. Idem f. 99ᵛ.
99. Idem f. 99ᵛ.
100. Idem f. 100ʳ.
101. *Lib* 795 f. 98ʳ⁻ᵛ, Vera Town Council to Tribunal, Vera, 12 Jan. 1610; received in Logroño 16 Jan. The town seal of Vera is affixed to the letter which is signed by Juanes de Zaldua and Pedro de Alzate.
102. *Lib* 795 f. 101ʳ (T./C. 16-1-1610; n. 75, above).
103. Idem ff. 101ʳ, 102ʳ. See *Lib* 795 f. 99ʳ (Hualde/T. 11-1-1610; n. 94, above), in which one of the child witches is mentioned as "the boy who was at Tolosa." Valle's letter from San Sebastián makes no mention of an *aquelarre* at Vera, so the other child witch from Vera must likewise have gone to Tolosa to report to him.
104. For Diego de Marticorena, see n. 76, above.
105. *Volume "F" of Salazar's Visitation Book* ff. 170ʳ, 170ᵛ (*Rte* 25).
106. Idem ff. 170ʳ-172ʳ.
107. Idem f. 173ʳ.
108. Here and below this mass psychosis or "dream epidemic" is described in purely phenomenological terms. I shall attempt a psychological interpretation below, in the Epilogue.
109. According to the Tribunal's statistics, by 9 Mar. 1611 a total of 796 witches had been found in Las Cinco Villas (see table 6, figures for Vera, Echalar, Lesaca, Yanci, and Aranaz with Sumbilla). After this date the Inquisition received confessions from at least 3 other witches in Las Cinco Villas (*Rte* 13, 18, and 19), and these denounced 50, 6, and 5 accomplices respectively (see *Volume "F" of Salazar's Visitation Book* ff. 78ʳ-79ʳ, 124ʳ⁻ᵛ, 130ʳ⁻ᵛ). However, in addition to this there were all the witchcraft confessions from Las Cinco Villas which had been made in the spring of 1611, about which only brief reference is made in the *Pamplona Manuscript*'s list of witches reconciled during Salazar's visitation, which included many witches from Las Cinco Villas (see IDOATE *Documento* pp. 180-188). It is impossible to determine whether these confessions had been made before or after the witch statistics of the Tribunal had been compiled on 9 Mar. 1611. But it can hardly be an exaggeration to assume that the number of suspects mounted to a thousand. This means that out of a total population of almost three thousand (see n. 65, above), every third inhabitant was suspected of being a witch. With regard to the revocations we know quite definitely that 15 witches from Las Cinco Villas revoked their confessions in the course of the summer of 1611. *Volume "F" of Salazar's Visitation Book* contains all their trial records. Five of them were from Lesaca (*Rte* 12, 17, 22, 23, 24); 4 from Aranaz (*Rte* 18, 19, 20, and 21); 3 from Yanci (*Rte* 14, 15, and 16); 2 from Vera (*Rte* 13 and 26); and 1 was from Echalar (*Rte* 25). Cf. case nos. 452-466.
110. *Leg* 1679 Exp. 2.1 ff. 2ᵛ, 3ᵛ (T./C. 14-2-1611; n. 68, above).
111. Idem f. 2ʳ. This is the source for the names of the three priests in Echalar (Labayen, Oragaray, and Urrutía) mentioned above in chap. 7.6.
112. María de Endara (case no. 69) was as we have seen above in this section denounced by María Martín de Legarra (case no. 457), and by

nine-year-old María de Yturría (case no. 465). The latter testified also against María de Topalda, who was in fact the above-mentioned *serora* or sacristan (see above, n. 76). For the imprisonment of María de Endara and María de Topalda see n. 72, above, and table 8.

113. *Lib* 795 f. 3^{r-v}, Tribunal to Council, 30 Aug. 1610; received in Madrid 14 Sept. This letter was written immediately after María de Endara had informed the inquisitors, during a hearing she had herself requested, that she was pregnant, and that the father of the child was the priest Labayen (which was the reason for her requesting permission to write and inform him). The inquisitors went on to tell *la Suprema* that they were convinced that María de Endara was telling the truth, for Labayen had twice put in an appearance in Logroño. The first time he came on the pretext of being on a pilgrimage to Santiago de Compostela, and the second time he declared that he was on the way home from the pilgrimage. But it was obvious that the purpose of his visits to Logroño had been to obtain information about the two women, María de Endara and Catalina de Topalda, at the secret prison of the Inquisition. The Tribunal's letter of 14 Feb. 1611 (n. 68, above) reveals fresh facets of this romance. The inquisitors relate among other things how during one of his visits to Logroño Labayen was received in audience by Becerra, when he was impudent enough to try to convince the inquisitor that the two imprisoned women were not witches. Becerra had grown angry and threatened him with imprisonment for opposing the Inquisition. The audience ended with Labayen bursting into tears and imploring forgiveness for his lack of self-control. Additional material is also to be found in *Leg* 1683 Exp. 1 ff. 1067^{r}-1071^{v}. Regarding María de Endara see also below, chaps. 11.B.1 and 11.B.4.

114. See below, table 6, figures for Yanci.

115. The confessions of the three witches from Yanci are to be found in *Volume "F" of Salazar's Visitation Book*: *Rte* 14 (Hipólita de Arbiza, 15 years old) ff. 83^{r}-89^{v}; *Rte* 15 (Mariana de Apecechea, 12 years old) ff. 91^{r}-96^{r}; and *Rte* 16 (Juana Fernández de Arbiza, 13 years old) ff. 99^{r}-104^{r}.

116. Idem. f. 105^{r}.

117. *Lib* 795 ff. 8^{r}-9^{v} (T./C. 13-2-1610; n. 63, above).

118. Idem f. 8^{v}, see table 8.

119. See below, table 8, which is an attempt to reconstruct the list of 16 witches.

120. *Lib* 795 f. 41^{r} (T./C. 10-7-1610; chap. 4 n. 49, above). Although the details are somewhat obscure it may nevertheless be worthwhile to attempt to make an approximate calculation of the total number of witchcraft confessions obtained on this visitation. It will be recalled that in his letter of 13 Nov. from San Sebastián Valle stated that to date he had received 15 confessions from child witches and at this point he does not seem to have obtained any confessions from adult witches, apart from that of María Chipía at Zugarramurdi (see table 2, above). On 20 Nov. 3 more confessions had come from Lesaca and 15 from Fuenterrabía (see above, pp. 117 and 118). In Tolosa at least 5 more witchcraft confessions were made (see table 3) and besides these we

have various references to a dozen or so witnesses in Tolosa, the majority of whom must presumably have been considered witches. We thus come to a total of about 50 witches, and there can hardly have been many more than this, cf. case nos. 103-150.

121. See *Lib* 333 f. 37ʳ, Council to Tribunal, 3 Feb. 1610, in which *la Suprema* grants permission for Hualde to be appointed inquisitorial commissioner, providing that his *limpieza de sangre* is in order.

NOTES TO CHAPTER 8

1. See *Lib* 794 f. 43ᵛ (T./C. 26-9-1609; chap. 7 n. 18, above): " . . . When our colleague sent us the enclosed letters he also sent 9 women and 3 men, one of whom was the priest. The following day we received the monk and two of the men, who, as he relates in his letter, had fled. Thus we now have 15 in all." According to the priest's own statement, made in 1614, he was first taken from Fuenterrabía to Urdax by a brother of the Inquisition (*Lib* 832 ff. 163ʳ-164ʳ, petition from Don Juan de la Borda presented to the Tribunal 23 Sept. 1614).

2. Cf. *Lib* 794 f. 448ᵛ (Valle/T. 13-11-1609; chap. 7 n. 33, above). Here Valle writes that he that very morning received the Tribunal's letter of 6 Nov. with the warrant for the arrest of Juanes de Odia Barrenechea. He goes on to say that he has already taken him into custody and has him in safe keeping in the prison at San Sebastián. In his second letter from San Sebastián (*Lib* 794 f. 447ʳ, Valle/T. 20-11-1609; chap. 7 n. 34, above) Valle writes that he is now sending some *familiares* to Logroño with "Juanes de Berechea [*sic*] alias de Odia." The brothers of the Inquisition took Valle's letter with them which means that Juanes de Odia must have arrived in Logroño on 27 Nov. when the Tribunal received the letter. It is possibly Juanes de Odia who is referred to in the *Accounts of 27 Sept. 1614* f. 161ᵛ where a sum of 52 *reales* is put down to "expenses in connection with a runaway witch."

3. See above, chap. 7.3 and n. 41.

4. During the inspection of the Tribunal in 1619-20 the visiting inquisitor surveyed the prisons as well, and inquired of each prisoner whether he was treated well or had any complaints. It appears from this *visita de cárceles* (*Leg* 1683 Exp. I ff. 197ʳ-201ᵛ) that the secret prison consisted of 20 cells, "9 on the first floor and 11 on the ground floor [*las nueve de ellas altas y las once bajas*]." Assuming that the Tribunal practiced the usual method of confining two prisoners only in each cell, the secret prison would therefore have accommodated at most 40 persons. For the placing of prisoners in the penitentiary, see below, chap. 8.2.

5. See above, near end of chap. 7.6

6. See *Lib* 795 ff. 8ᵛ-9ʳ (T./C. 13-2-1610; chap. 7 n. 64, above), where the inquisitors write: "Since the secret prison is cramped and there is insufficient space for those already confined there, we have decided to adapt some rooms in the *casa de penitencia,* where 12 of the above-mentioned persons who are women can be held, and the remaining 4 who are men can be detained in the Dominican monastery of Valcuerno."

7. See below, table 8, in which I have attempted to reconstruct the list of 16 witches.

8. See below, chap. 9.1, and nos. 32-52 in *Second Report of the Auto de fe* ff. 350^v-351^v (SD Text 2).

9. See beginning of chap. 8.5, below.

10. In the *Third Report of the Auto de fe* it is stated of María de Jureteguía that she "was imprisoned together with three other persons [see above, chap. 4.2] on the basis of the testimony of eight witnesses that they had made extrajudicial confessions of being witches and declared many things of this sect and accused many persons of being their accomplices" (Idem f. 360^v). Regarding all the other witches from Zugarramurdi it is merely stated that they were imprisoned "on the basis of the same testimony [*por la misma testificacion*]" (Idem ff. 366^r-367^r, 368^r-369^r).

11. According to Mongastón's pamphlet María de Echalecu confessed to having been taken to the *aquelarre* by Graciana de Barrenechea (see below, chap. 8.3); note that Graciana de Barrenechea besides initiating her two daughters had instructed "a relative [*su conjunta*] whom she named" in the arts of witchcraft (*Joint Sentence* f. 396^v).

12. See n. 2 above, where it is stated that Juanes de Odia was also called by the surname Barrenechea; unless we read *Barechea* as in *First Report of the Auto de fe* f. 423^v, *Second Report of the Auto de fe* f. 350^r (SD Text 2), and *Third Report of the Auto de fe* f. 368^v. The first spelling is supported by *Lib* 1158 f. 72^r (*la Suprema*'s register of verdicts).

13. *Third Report of the Auto de fe* f. 369^{r-v}.

14. Idem f. 369^r.

15. Idem f. 368^{r-v}.

16. Idem f. 366^r; cf. f. 368^r, where it is stated of Juanes de Echegui that one of the witnesses against him was his own daughter, who was reconciled.

17. Idem 366^r.

18. Idem 366^v; the surname Aguirre (or Aguerra) appears in a letter from Hualde at Vera to the Tribunal (see above, chap. 7.6 with n. 94).

19. *Third Report of the Auto de fe* f. 366^r. Presumably their mother had instructed them. According to the fresh information supplied by the *Pamplona Manuscript* she too was a witch and all three lived together at Zugarramurdi (IDOATE *Documento* pp. 54-55, 57-58, 67-68).

20. See below, chap. 8.3 passim.

21. In order that the evidence could be used against others, the witnesses were required to confirm their statements at a later interrogation. Normally this "ratification" was not undertaken before proceedings had been opened against the person concerned (see chap. 3.2, above), but the regulations of the Inquisition allowed ratification to be undertaken in advance, *ad perpetuam* (i.e. permanently), if, for instance, there was a danger of the witness dying.

22. *Lib* 794 f. 462^v (T./C. 22-8-1609; chap. 7 n. 4, above).

23. *Lib* 794 f. 433^{r-v} (T./C. 26-9-1609; chap. 7 n. 18, above).

24. *Lib* 794 f. 444^v (f. 444^{r-v}, Tribunal to Council, 28 Nov. 1609).

25. Idem f. 444^v; see *Third Report of the Auto de fe* f. 368^v, where it is

stated that none of the monks, doctors, or any of the others who tended Juanes de Echegui during his illness could persuade him to go to confession.

26. As a *negativo* he was in a state of excommunication and it was not possible to release him from this as long as he did not confess — or his innocence was not established.

27. The letter of 21 Aug. 1610 is now known only through a mention in the Tribunal's letter of 30 Aug. 1610, see n. 28, below.

28. *Lib* 795 f. 2ʳ (f. 2ʳ⁻ᵛ, Tribunal to Council, 30 Aug. 1610; received in Madrid 15 Sept. 1610). The letter names only María de Zozaya, María de "Chalegua" and Mari Juanto. Of the other three it is merely stated that they belong to different *aquelarres* and are among those "we are holding in order to proceed with their trials [*que tenemos presos para que se vayan haciendo sus procesos*]." This would most probably seem to refer to the March group of prisoners, whose trials had been postponed until after the auto de fe. After three had been sent to the auto de fe, thirteen remained of this group and of these five died before their cases came up (see below, chap. 11.B.1). As far as Estevanía de Petrisancena, Martín Vizcar, and Juanes de Odia are concerned, however, the conclusion is certain that they died during this epidemic — if not in August, then very shortly afterwards. The information in the auto de fe reports and the *Food account* (see table 4, above) indicate this indirectly. Another source states of Juanes de Odia that he died after he had been in the Tribunal's prison for 11 months (i.e. from 27 Nov. 1609 to ca. 27 Aug. 1610), *Second Report of Salazar* f. 7ᵛ (SD Text 12 § 35).

29. See above, table 4. As mentioned earlier the food allowance was 1 *real* per day. In the *Food account* María de Yriarte is put down for 526 *reales*. This corresponds to the period from 27 Feb. 1609 to 9 Aug. 1610 (526 days).

30. *Joint Sentence* f. 400ʳ. This also supplies a proof of the effectiveness of the inquisitors' "brain-washing."

31. *Lib* 795 f. 2ʳ⁻ᵛ (T./C. 30-8-1610; n. 28, above). It is interesting to note that Salazar's description of Juanes de Odia's death reveals a view that differs from that of his colleagues: "He sickened," writes Salazar in his second report, "with an illness declared to be a fever and from this he died without any suspicion of foul play, as can be inferred from the declarations of the doctors who visited him at that time." *Second Report of Salazar* f. 7ᵛ (SD Text 12 § 35). Possibly the witches were attacked by typhus (*tabardilla*). The prison guard at the penitentiary, Martín de Ygarzabal, was certainly infected with typhus after attending the sick witches (see *Lib* 795 f. 504ʳ⁻ᵛ, application for an increase in wages from Martín de Ygarzabal presented to the Tribunal 25 Jan. 1613).

32. *Third Report of the Auto de fe* ff. 366ᵛ-367ʳ, 368ʳ⁻ᵛ.

33. The emergence of the *Pamplona Manuscript* has considerably increased our knowledge of these witches' confessions. I have only referred to the new material to a limited extent in the notes to this chapter, and I should here, as before, call attention to table 11, below.

34. *Third Report of the Auto de fe* f. 366ʳ.

35. Idem f. 367ʳ.

36. MONGASTÓN *Relación* f. 11ʳ; see IDOATE *Documento* p. 141.

37. *Third Report of the Auto de fe* ff. 366^r, 366^v.

38. *Leg* 1679 Exp. 2.1 No. 27 f. 1^r (1^r-2^r, Hualde to Tribunal, 10 Jan, 1611; received in Logroño 22 Jan.). See MONGASTÓN *Relación* f. 8^r. However, in all the inquisitors' reports these two sisters are stated to be *vecinos* of Zugarramurdi. Possibly they had not moved to Vera until Valle was on visitation at Urdax and Zugarramurdi. Perhaps these are the women who are indicated in the Tribunal's letter to *la Suprema* dated 26 Sept. 1609, which refers to "two [witches] who left as soon as our colleague arrived in order to hold the visitation session" (*Lib* 794 f. 433^v; chap. 7 n. 18, above). See also the *Pamplona Manuscript* f. 44^v, where María Presona herself relates that she moved to Vera and lived with her sister (IDOATE *Documento* p. 152).

39. See MONGASTÓN *Relación* f. 8^{r-v}.

40. *Third Report of the Auto de fe* ff. 366^r, 366^v. Cf. *Pamplona Manuscript* which cites the two sisters' confessions in greater detail (IDOATE *Documento* p. 127).

41. MONGASTÓN *Relación* f. 11^v; see below, n. 68.

42. *Third Report of the Auto de fe* f. 367^r; MONGASTÓN *Relación* f. 7^r. See IDOATE *Documento* p. 108; *Lib* 1252 f. 400^r (ff. 391^r-400^r, "Relación que un ministro del Santo Oficio... envió a Valladolid...." For this MS see also below, chap. 9 n. 23.

43. *Third Report of the Auto de fe* ff. 367^v-368^r. One of the four boys must undoubtedly have been 14-year-old Diego de Marticorena, who confessed on the visitation (see above, chap. 7 n. 76).

44. Idem f. 367^v.

45. MONGASTÓN *Relación* f. 8^r; see *Third Report of the Auto de fe* f. 367^v.

46. MONGASTÓN *Relación* f. 4^v; see IDOATE *Documento* p. 99.

47. MONGASTÓN *Relación* f. 11^v.

48. Idem ff. 9^v-10^r; he is here named Juanes de Echalar. See *Pamplona Manuscript* ff. 18^r-19^r, where the event is stated to have occurred when Juanes de Yribarren was ten years old (IDOATE *Documento* p. 86).

49. *Third Report of the Auto de fe* f. 367^v.

50. MONGASTÓN *Relación* f. 10^r. Estevanía de Telechea is presumably identical with Estevanía de Navarcorena, note that her husband's surname was Telechea (see table 4, above).

51. *Lib* 832 f. 156^{r-v}, "Relación de los méritos del proceso de Don Juan de la Borda Arburu, clérigo presbítero, capellán de Fuenterrabía y natural de Zugarramurdi en el Valle de Baztán," undated but appears to have been written between Nov. 1613 and Mar. 1614, hereafter cited as *Méritos de Juan de la Borda*.

52. *Third Report of the Auto de fe* f. 368^v.

53. *Lib* 795 f. 6^v (T./C. 2-1-1610; chap. 7 n. 41, above).

54. *Lib* 835 ff. 401^r-420^r, "Sentencia de María de Zozaya y Arramendi, bruja del *aquelarre* de Rentería," hereafter cited as *Sentence of María de Zozaya*. Other fragments of her confessions are given in MONGASTÓN *Relación* ff. 7^r, 11^v, 14^r; in the *Pamplona Manuscript* (see IDOATE *Documento* pp. 49, 55, 68, 108, 115, 122-123, 130-131, 134, 138, 143, 148-149, 152, 159-160); and in *Third Report of the Auto de fe* f. 368^r.

55. *Sentence of María de Zozaya* ff. 403^r, 405^r, 417^v.

56. Idem ff. 412^v-414^v.

57. Idem f. 415^r. See MONGASTÓN *Relación* f. 14^r.

58. *Sentence of María de Zozaya* ff. 415ᵛ-417ʳ. In support of my assumption that María de Zozaya was not questioned until some time after her arrival in Logroño is a statement that she "was lying sick in the prison of the Inquisition before she began to make the present confession" (Idem f. 418ʳ). On the other hand the same source later states that "she was arrested a month ago" (Idem f. 418ᵛ). If we assume that María de Zozaya was imprisoned about 20 Nov., this would agree with her being transferred to Logroño at the end of December. It is possible that the inquisitors commenced the hearings immediately after María de Zozaya's arrival, and later discontinued them on account of her illness.

59. Idem f. 403ʳ⁻ᵛ.

60. Idem ff. 403ᵛ-404ʳ.

61. See idem ff. 404ʳ-412ᵛ.

62. Idem ff. 403ᵛ, 405ʳ.

63. Idem f. 403ᵛ; see e.g. *Volume "F" of Salazar's Visitation Book* ff. 71ᵛ (*Rte* 12), 111ʳ (*Rte* 17), 148ᵛ (*Rte* 22), 156ʳ (*Rte* 23), and 164ᵛ (*Rte* 24).

64. *Sentence of María de Zozaya* f. 404ᵛ; see e.g. *Volume "F" of Salazar's Visitation Book* ff. 92ʳ (*Rte* 15), 102ʳ (*Rte* 16), 156ʳ (*Rte* 23), and 164ʳ (*Rte* 24).

65. *Sentence of María de Zozaya* f. 409ʳ.

66. *Leg* 1683 Exp. 1 f. 22ʳ (ff. 19ʳ-23ᵛ, Salazar to Inquisitor General, Logroño, 2 Mar. 1611; hereafter cited as *Memorial of 2 Mar. 1611*).

67. *Sentence of María de Zozaya* ff. 414ᵛ-415ᵛ.

68. The situation has been altered by the appearance of the *Pamplona Manuscript* although it quotes only small fragments of Mari Juanto's confessions (IDOATE *Documento* pp. 54-55, 58, 67-68, 127, and 159). The last quotation (on p. 159) deals specifically with Mari Juanto's substitute-demon but only discusses this in general terms without any reference to the episode with the eggs related above in chap. 8.3 from Mongastón's pamphlet. It would therefore seem that Mongastón assigned the egg episode to Mari Juanto in error, when in fact María de Zozaya was the sole author of this story.

69. If the record of the civil proceedings which were instituted by the authorities of Rentería against María de Zozaya in 1609 could be discovered, many of these problems would undoubtedly be solved. In addition, we should gain a fascinating insight into the development of witch persecution in this small town.

70. *Sentence of María de Zozaya* f. 415ᵛ.

71. Idem ff. 408ᵛ-409ʳ.

72. Idem f. 414ʳ⁻ᵛ.

73. Idem f. 414ʳ. It is also stated here that the sleep-inducing powder is obtained from a "blue, or rather, dark purple" flower, which grows among the stones on the mountain slopes. The plant grows to a height of half a yard (*como un codo de alto*) and is "the thickness of two or three fingers." The witches collect this plant in the summer and after having dried it (and ground the stalks to powder?) they mix it with human bones, toads' legs, and some of the liquid they extract from the dressed toads. The powder is so potent that the witches need only sprinkle some of it on the window sill to lull the people of the house to sleep.

74. Idem f. 415^r.

75. Idem f. 414^v.

76. Idem f. 406^{r-v}.

77. Idem f. 418^{r-v}.

78. Idem f. 417^v.

79. *Lib* 794 f. 433^v (T./C. 26-9-1609; chap. 7 n. 18, above).

80. *Lib* 795 ff. 8^v-9^v (T./C. 13-2-1610; chap. 7 n. 64, above). The letter does not reveal who had made the four confessions, but the possibilities are limited to six (see table 4, above, where all from groups one, two, and six can be excluded together with the *negativos* of groups three through five). The two *confitente* witches whose trials had not yet been completed were probably María de Zozaya and Juanes de Lambert. It will be recalled that they were transferred from Rentería at the end of December, having already made a temporary confession there. It is more difficult to determine the identities of the other two witches, but there are only four possibilities: Martín Vizcar, María Presona, María Chipía de Barrenechea, and María de Echegui. The assumption that it was the first two of these is supported by a statement in a later letter in which the inquisitors described how they made Martín Vizcar and María Presona go to confession (see below, chap. 8.5).

81. See *Lib* 795 f. 41^v (T./C. 10-7-1610; chap. 7 n. 49, above).

82. *Lib* 835 ff. 352^r-355^r, the *fiscal* San Vicente to [Inquisitor General], Logroño [10 July] 1610; [received in Madrid 30 July]; hereafter cited as *Memorial of San Vicente 1610*.

83. Idem ff. 352^r-355^r.

84. Compare the above with *Fourth Report of Salazar* ff. 1^r-3^r (SD Text 14 § 1).

85. *Memorial of San Vicente 1610* f. 355^{r-v}; see HENNINGSEN *Papers of Salazar* p. 90.

86. *Lib.* 795 f. 41^v (T./C. 10-7-1610; chap. 4 n. 49, above).

87. Idem ff. 41^v-42^r.

88. With the *first letter* (*Lib* 333 f. 98^{r-v}, Council to Tribunal, 9 Sept. 1610 (a)) *la Suprema* returned the trial records of 13 witches, whose cases the Tribunal, as the Council's letter states, "have voted unanimously." The names of the 13 witches are in the margin (table 4, auto de fe nos. 10, 9, 4, 11, 12, 13, 14, 15, 8, 17, 7, 16, 18; i.e. all the *confitente* witches still alive in July 1610 who had been granted reconciliation by the Tribunal). With the *second letter* (*Lib* 333 f. 99^{r-v}, Council to Tribunal, 9 Sept. 1610 (b)) *la Suprema* returned the trial records of five deceased *confitente* witches, who were to be reconciled in effigy: auto de fe nos. 5, 6, 1 (erroneously named Juanes de Yriarte, after her husband), 3, and 2 (see table 4). With the *third letter* (*Lib* 333 f. 99^r, Council to Tribunal, 9 Sept. 1610 (c)) *la Suprema* returned the trial records of nine *negativos* still alive in July 1610: auto de fe nos. 24, 25, 27, 26, 21, 23, 29, 28, and 22, who were to be burned. Also returned with this letter was the trial record of María de Zozaya, who was to be burned together with the *negativos* because she had been a proselytizer (see chap. 8.5, above). This accounts for 28 of the 31 trial records. The two ecclesiastics' records (see below, n. 90) were returned with a *fourth letter*, dated 9 Sept. 1610 (d). The 31st witch was

Juanes de Echegui. He had long since died a *negativo* in prison (see above, chap. 8.2) and was to be burned in effigy. *La Suprema* had already returned his record to the Tribunal with an earlier letter (*Lib* 333 ff. 95ᵛ-96ʳ, Council to Tribunal, 28 Aug. 1610). The remaining 30 records were not dispatched until 13 Sept. 1610. They were taken to Logroño by the inquisitorial secretary Agüero (see *Lib* 333 f. 100, Council to Tribunal, 13 Sept. 1610). Agüero arrived at Logroño with the records on 23 September.

While working on the notes I discovered that some of the above-mentioned records are also recorded in *Lib* 1158 ("Libro primero de votos . . . en causas de fe [de las inquisiciones de Aragón]"). The ten *negativos*, who were condemned to the stake, are registered on ff. 71ᵛ-74ᵛ under the date 9 Sept. 1610 (see *third letter* above). Under the same date are recorded the five who were to be reconciled in effigy (cf. *second letter*, above), idem ff. 74ᵛ-76ᵛ. Finally under the same date is recorded *la Suprema*'s verdict on the two witch ecclesiastics (see below, n. 90). It ordains that they are both to be examined under torture regarding the charges that witnesses had brought against them (*que . . . sea puesto a cuestión de tormento sobre lo testificado*), idem ff. 76ᵛ-77ᵛ. Apart from various alterations in names, the register of sentences contains nothing new. The judgments of the other witches are not recorded in this source.

89. *Lib* 333 f. 98ʳ⁻ᵛ (C./T. 9-9-1610 (a) n. 88, above).

90. *Lib* 333 f. 99ᵛ, Council to Tribunal, 9 Sept. 1610 (d). The letter makes no mention of *la Suprema*'s decision but merely refers to the instructions inserted by the Council in the original trial records.

91. See *Third Report of the Auto de fe* f. 369ʳ⁻ᵛ; *Méritos of Juan de la Borda* f. 156ʳ⁻ᵛ.

92. *Lib* 795 f. 1ʳ (Tribunal to Council, 12 Oct. 1610 (a); received in Madrid 19 Oct.).

93. LEA *Inquisition of Spain* III p. 2.

94. *Lib* 795 f. 1ʳ⁻ᵛ (T./C. 12-10-1610 (a); n. 92, above).

95. *Lib* 795 f. 74ʳ (f. 74ʳ⁻ᵛ, Tribunal to Council, 12 Oct. 1610 (b); received in Madrid 19 Oct.).

96. *Lib* 333 f. 108ʳ⁻ᵛ (Council to Tribunal, 20 Oct. 1610; received in Logroño 24 Oct.).

97. *Lib* 795 f. 10ʳ (Tribunal to Council, 24 Oct. 1610, no date of receipt).

98. Francisco (Gómez) de Sandoval y Rojas, prime minister to Philip III, had been elevated to the rank of duke, of Lerma, in 1599. His paternal grandfather (the first count of Lerma, Bernardo de Sandoval y Rojas, d. 1536) was also the inquisitor general's grandfather. The two men were thus first cousins (see D. A. de Burgos: *Blasón de España* I parte, Tomo 3. Madrid 1858 pp. 270-274). Further reference to be made to the monograph on the duke of Lerma, in preparation by Don José Antonio Martínez Bara, assistant director of the Archivo Histórico Nacional (Madrid).

99. *Lib* 795 f. 24ᵛ, Tribunal to Council, 1 Nov. 1610; received in Madrid 5 Nov.

100. *Lib* 835 f. 385ʳ, the title page of the documents mentioned chap. 2 n. 5, above.

101. *Lib* 795 f. 10ʳ (T./C. 24-10-1610; n. 97, above).

102. *Second Report of the Auto de fe* (SD Text 2). An application from Luis de Huerta, in his own hand, dated 29 Nov. 1610 (*Lib* 795 f. 5ʳ), enables us to identify the handwriting. In the same volume are holograph letters from the secretary, Juan de Agüero, attesting Huerta's application.

103. *Lib* 835 f. 343ʳ, Tribunal to King, 31 Oct. 1610 (to be published as SD Text 1).

104. See *Lib* 835 f. 341ʳ, Tribunal to Duke of Lerma, 1 Nov. 1610.

105. Salazar's *Memorial of 2 Mar. 1611* f. 20ʳ⁻ᵛ.

106. *Lib* 795 f. 24ᵛ (T./C. 1-11-1610; n. 99, above).

107. *Lib* 333 f. 113ᵛ (ff. 113ᵛ-114ᵛ, Council to Tribunal, 6 Nov. 1610).

108. *Leg* 1679 Exp. 2.1 No. 30 [c] f. 1ʳ⁻ᵛ, "Para la causa de María de Arburu y las demas personas que salieron al auto," hereafter cited as *Salazar's Vote of 8 June 1610*. The whole transcript is written in Salazar's hand and marked with the signature "CC." It was forwarded to *la Suprema* on 3 Oct. 1613 as a supplement to *Fourth Report of Salazar*, see f. 3ʳ of this report (SD Text 14 § 13).

109. *Salazar's Vote of 8 June 1610* f. 1ʳ. The names are reproduced here in the order in which they appear in the MS. It is possible that Lazaro de Badarán should be placed second. For it is stated in a *carta acordada* that when the bishop wishes to participate in the Tribunal's *consultas de fe* he is to be seated next in eminence to the senior inquisitor (*Lib* 497 f. 247ʳ⁻ᵛ, *Carta Acordada* No. 192, 27 Jan. 1601). However, this ruling would seem to have applied only to the bishop in person, and not to his substitute, *el ordinario*. No. 5 is mentioned only as "el licenciado Amasa, Juez de bienes confiscados de este Santo Oficio." His full name appears on a document dated 31 July 1607 (*Lib* 835 f. 265ʳ). In a letter to *la Suprema* on the subject of the lack of advisers to the Tribunal it is stated of Amasa that besides being a judge of confiscations he also served as *consultor* (*Lib* 795 f. 107ʳ⁻ᵛ, Tribunal to Council, 28 Mar. 1610; received in Madrid 20 Apr.). For *las consultas de fe* see also above, chap. 3.2.

110. See ARGÜELLO *Instrucciones* f. 32ᵛ § 40.

111. See above, chap. 8.5; and below, table 12 § 11.

112. *Fourth Report of Salazar* f. 3ʳ (SD Text 14 § 13).

113. *Salazar's Vote of 8 June 1610* f. 1ʳ. María de Ximildegui is probably an error for María de Lecumberri (senior), see above, chap. 7 n. 15.

114. Idem f. 1ʳ. This is in agreement with the inquisitors' letter of 15 Sept. 1609, in which the Black Mass is mentioned as one of the new elements in the witches' confessions which had not emerged until the visitation at Zugarramurdi and Urdax (see above, chap. 7.2). On the other hand, Salazar's statement that Estevanía de Yriarte did not mention the Black Mass in her confession at all appears to be incorrect, see below, table 11; and IDOATE *Documento* pp. 163-164.

115. *Salazar's Vote of 8 June 1610* f. 1ʳ⁻ᵛ.

116. Salazar's style is marked by its abstruseness. It might almost be said that he wrote as he thought, without paying much regard to fluency or clarity of expression. Nevertheless he seems to have been a man who commanded attention. The bishop of Calahorra, Don Pedro de Castillo, who spent many years in Madrid with Salazar, relates that

the latter was much respected in government circles and was renowned for his scholarship and lucid opinions in debates (*Leg* 1683 Exp. 2 ff. 454^r-457^r, testimony of the bishop of Calahorra regarding Salazar, given 8 July 1620 in connection with the inspection of the Tribunal in Logroño). The vote of 8 June 1610 is presumably a résumé, composed by the secretary, of Salazar's verbal exposition; the result is therefore a further condensation of Salazar's already extremely ponderous style.

117. *Salazar's Vote of 8 June 1610* f. 1^v.

118. Idem f. 1^v. I find some difficulty in interpreting the meaning of the last words of Salazar's vote and therefore I quote the text of the original: "y así es de parecer que sea puesta a cuestión de tormento para que manifieste la intención de las cosas que contra ella resultan, y también los demás complices que se hallaron con ella."

119. Salazar's *Memorial of 2 Mar. 1611* f. 20^v.

NOTES TO CHAPTER 9

1. See *Third Report of the Auto de fe* ff. 346^r-360^v, nos. 1-24. In the *Second Report of the Auto de fe* the reports of the cases are in a different order. The witches are placed first (nos. 1-31) and are followed by the other delinquents (nos. 32-52), see SD Text 2. No. 8 (Juan de Pancorbo), no. 9 (Juan Pérez de Heineta), and no. 10 (Magdalena López) in the *Third Report of the Auto de fe* are not present in the *First* or *Second Report of the Auto de fe*. Presumably these three cases were made ready for the auto de fe at the last moment.

2. *Third Report of the Auto de fe* nos. 17-22; *Second Report of the Auto de fe* nos. 34-39 (SD Text 2).

3. *Third Report of the Auto de fe* nos. 24, 23, 16; *Second Report of the Auto de fe* nos. 32, 33, 42 (SD Text 2).

4. *Third Report of the Auto de fe* nos. 3-15; *Second Report of the Auto de fe* nos. 40-41, 43-50 (SD Text 2).

5. *Third Report of the Auto de fe* nos. 1-2; *Second Report of the Auto de fe* nos. 51-52 (SD Text 2).

6. See Salazar's *Autobiography* f. 4^v.

7. See LEA *Inquisition of Spain* III pp. 209-229 (chapter on "The Auto de fe"). My attention was recently drawn to a very detailed and hitherto unknown description of the ceremonial at an auto de fe in Córdoba held on 21 Jan. 1590 (*Lib* 1259 ff. 121^r-129^r). This is followed by a memorandum of all that is to be prepared in readiness for an auto de fe (Idem ff. 129^r-130^v).

8. See the *relaciones* of the autos de fe of 24 Sept. 1600 (*Lib* 835 ff. 17^r-27^r), 19 Aug. 1601 (Idem ff. 28^r-35^v), 1 Sept. 1602 (Idem ff. 64^r-89^v), and 20 July 1603 (Idem 96^r-111^r), with 37, 30, 41, and 35 delinquents respectively.

9. See *Lib* 834 ff. 802^r-815^r, *Relación* of the auto de fe of 14 Nov. 1599, with 51 delinquents, 13 of whom were burned (eight of these in effigy).

10. This is a general impression obtained from my studies of the *relaciones de causas*. I shall substantiate the argument in my yet unpub-

lished index to the *relaciones de causas* of the Spanish Inquisition, see HENNINGSEN 1977b and chap. 3 n. 26, above.

11. See MONGASTÓN *Relación* ff. 2^r, 2^v.

12. MONGASTÓN *Relación* f. 2^v; *Lib* 795 f. 17^v (ff. 17^v-16^v [sic], Tribunal to Council, 13 Nov. 1610; received in Madrid 22 Nov.).

13. See *Lib* 795 f. 17^v (T./C., 13-11-1610; n. 12, above); MONGASTÓN *Relación* f. 2^v.

14. See fig. 12, where the stage is raised above ground level, but which in contrast to the one described here is closed at the rear by two boxes with an altar between them.

15. MONGASTÓN *Relación* f. 2^v. One pulpit only is shown in fig. 12, but there are two pulpits in, for instance, Francisco Rizi's painting of the great auto de fe in Madrid in 1680 on the Plaza Mayor, where the rest of the stage bears much resemblance to that described by Mongastón. Rizi's painting is in the *Museo del Prado,* and a portion of it is reproduced in KAMEN 1965, facing p. 215.

16. MONGASTÓN *Relación* f. 2^v, see *Accounts of 27 Sept. 1614* f. 160^v, where a sum of 80 *reales* is registered for "some benches which were broken."

17. See idem f. 161^r, where a sum of 42 *reales* records "hire of windows."

18. Idem f. 160^v.

19. In 1607 the porter Juan de Yerro's *ayuda de costa* amounted to 10,000 *maravedis* (*Lib* 367 II f. 273^r). The *ayuda de costa* formed a sixth part of the wage. The porter's annual wage must therefore have been 60,000 *maravedis,* or ca. 1,765 *reales* (in 1608 1 *real* was equal to ca. 34 *maravedis*).

20. *Accounts of 27 Sept. 1614* ff. 160^v-161^r.

21. Idem f. 161^r.

22. Idem ff. 160^v-161^r; items in the account add up to 2,541 *reales,* or about 86,400 *maravedis.* In comparison we may note that around 1600 the Seville Inquisition spent some 112,500 *maravedis* on each auto de fe and in 1624 spent 396,374 on a single auto de fe (KAMEN 1965 p. 194).

23. *Lib* 1252 ("Libro 44 ... para la recopilación") ff. 391^r-400^r, *title*: "Relación que un ministro del Santo Oficio de la Inquisición de Logroño envió a Valladolid [sic] al tesorero Gamez, comisario del Santo Oficio, de lo sucedido en el auto de fe que se celebró en Logroño a 7 de noviembre 1610." (*Beginning and ending*: Hasta la vispera del auto ... de Logroño y Noviembre 14 1610"). Besides this manuscript, hereafter cited as *Report of an Official (A),* another copy *(B)* is in *Lib* 1259 ff. 147^v-159^r. While the author of this hitherto unknown auto de fe report is not known, the recipient can be identified as the inquisitorial commissioner Diego de Gamiz, who was treasurer of the cathedral chapter (*iglesia colegial*) in Vitoria (and not in Valladolid, as stated in the title of the two above-mentioned manuscripts), see *First Report of Salazar* f. 485^r § 43.

24. *Report of an Official (A)* f. 391^r.

25. *Lib* 795 f. 17^v (T./C. 13-11-1610; n. 12, above).

26. MONGASTÓN *Relación* f. 2^r; see *Lib* 795 f. 17^v (T./C. 13-11-1610; n. 12, above).

27. See chap. 8.5, above. For the monks see n. 29, below.

28. See chap. 3.2, above.

29. In the *Account of 27 Sept. 1614* (f. 161ʳ) there is an item of 147 *reales* "for cakes for breakfast for the prisoners, brothers of the inquisition, and the monks who kept vigil [with the condemned prisoners]."

30. The chief sources for my reconstruction of the first day of the auto de fe are: *Lib* 795 f. 17ᵛ (T./C. 13-11-1610; n. 12, above); MONGAS-TÓN *Relación* f. 2ʳ⁻ᵛ; *Third Report of the Auto de fe* ff. 356ʳ-360ᵛ, 365ᵛ-369ʳ. In MONGASTÓN *Relación* f. 2ʳ it is stated that six people had scourges around their necks, but in the *Third Report of the Auto de fe* only five people were listed as condemned to whipping (nos. 2, 13, 15, 16, and 26). Another point over which there is uncertainty is the question of whether the auto de fe commenced with an open-air Mass. The fact that a sermon was preached might indicate this, but since I have been unable to trace any definite evidence I prefer to assume that the sermon was given outside the context of a Mass. Not until the great auto de fe in Madrid in 1680 is there a definite report of the Mass forming an integral part of the auto de fe (see KAMEN 1965 p. 192).

31. MONGASTÓN *Relación* f. 2ᵛ; *Lib* 795 f. 17ᵛ (T./C. 13-11-1610; n. 12, above).

32. MONGASTÓN *Relación* ff. 2ᵛ-3ʳ.

33. *Third Report of the Auto de fe* f. 356ʳ, no. 1.

34. Idem f. 356ʳ⁻ᵛ, no. 2.

35. Idem ff. 357ᵛ-358ʳ, no. 14.

36. Idem f. 359ʳ⁻ᵛ, no. 21. In the *Second Report of the Auto de fe* (SD Text 2) these four cases (see notes 33-36, above) are numbered 52, 51, 41, and 39. For Dionisio de Lerma see also *Lib* 795 ff. 554ʳ-553ʳ [*sic*], Tribunal to Council, 24 Sept. 1613; received at Madrid 5 Oct.

37. *Joint Sentence* ff. 386ʳ-400ᵛ. To read out a page of manuscript takes about 5 minutes; therefore 30 pages must have taken about 150 minutes or 2½ hours. María de Zozaya's sentence is written in fairly large script (see *Sentence of María de Zozaya* ff. 401ʳ-420ʳ). To read out a page of this manuscript takes 3 minutes; therefore 39 pages must have taken about 117 minutes or two hours (see above, chap. 9.3).

38. MONGASTÓN *Relación* f. 3ʳ. Cf. *Lib* 795 f. 17ᵛ⁻ʳ [*sic*] (T./C. 13-11-1610; n. 12, above): "It was necessary to cut short some of the final sentences in order to complete them that day."

39. MONGASTÓN *Relación* f. 3ʳ; *Lib* 795 f. 17ʳ (T./C. 13-11-1610; n. 12, above). The three other heretics were to be reconciled from the sects of Mahomet, Luther, and the Law of Moses, see *Second Report of the Auto de fe* f. 350ᵛ (SD Text 2).

40. MONGASTÓN *Relación* f. 3ʳ; see the form of reconciliation in GARCÍA *Orden de procesar* ff. 32ᵛ-34ᵛ.

41. *Lib* 795 f. 17ʳ (T./C. 13-11-1610; n. 12, above).

42. MONGASTÓN *Relación* f. 3ʳ.

43. Idem f. 3ʳ⁻ᵛ.

44. Idem f. 14ᵛ.

45. *Report of an Official (B)* ff. 147ᵛ-148ʳ.

46. Idem f. 159ʳ.

47. *Lib* 795 f. 17ᵛ (T. / C. 13-11-1610; n. 12, above).

48. Idem 16ᵛ.

49. See above, near end of chap. 8.5. The trial records of the monk and the priest were returned to the Tribunal by *la Suprema* on 30 Oct. 1610 (*Lib* 333 f. 112^{r-v}). The Council's decision is entered in *la Suprema*'s "Libro primero de votos de Aragón" (*Lib* 1158 ff. 78^{r-v}), under the date mentioned above. The final judgments are in the *Third Report of the Auto de fe* f. 369^{r-v}, nos. 54-55.

50. See above, chap. 8.6.

51. *Lib* 795 ff. 17^r-16^v [*sic*] (T./C. 13-11-1610; n. 12, above). Monsieur de Gourgues — or in the inquisitors' orthography, "Mus de gorgos" — can be identified with the help of BRUTAILS 1925 pp. 84 and 107. From this it appears that the distinguished French guest must have been Armand de Gourgues, who was a parliamentary councillor at Bordeaux from 8 Jan. 1610 to 24 April 1630.

52. *Lib* 333 f. 122^r, Council to Tribunal, 25 Nov. 1610. It is quite probable that the report in question could have come into de Lancre's possession at a later date. For although the chief source for his chapter on the auto de fe in Logroño (see above, chap. 1.7 and n. 100) would seem to have been one of the printed reports (either Mongastón's or Varesio's) de Lancre seems to have resorted to other sources as well. Presumably the abbot of Urdax, Fray León, is referring to the activities of Armand de Gourgues when he writes three months later in a letter to the Tribunal: "The judges from the Parliament at Bordeaux who have been appointed to deal with witchcraft cases this year have gone to the other extreme from the judges of the previous year. If no facts or external evidence [*actos positivos y exteriores*] are available, they will neither institute proceedings nor receive evidence. They have gone so far as to release many of those who had been imprisoned. This will greatly damage the Pays de Labourd." (*Leg* 1679 Exp. 2.1 No. 11 f. 3^r; see chap. 10 n. 34, below). If Monsieur de Gourgues had not felt any skepticism at the outset he must certainly have acquired some at the auto de fe in Logroño.

53. See the covering letter *Lib* 835 f. 433^r, Tribunal to Council, 29 Nov. 1610.

54. See my edition of *Second Report of the Auto de fe* (SD Text 2) where in two cases I have made use of alternative readings from the *Third Report of the Auto de fe*.

55. Francisco Romero de Castilla and Henry Charles Lea are presumably the only scholars to have been aware of the existence of the unprinted reports of the auto de fe. See Francisco ROMERO DE CASTILLA "Extracto del inventario de los papeles de Inquisición, que procedentes del antiguo Consejo Supremo de la misma, se trasladaron al Archivo General de Simancas en el año de 1850" *Revista de Archivos, Bibliotecas y Museos* 1st Series, vol. III (1873) 118-121, 136-140, 149-155, 168-170, 182-187, where on p. 152 it is stated that "lib. DLXIV" (now *Lib* 835) contains "important notes pertaining to the witch sect [*apuntes notables sobre la secta de los brujos*]"; and see LEA *Inquisition of Spain* IV p. 227 n. 1, which refers to the letter to the king dated 1 Nov.; we have previously noticed that this is bound in with the *Second Report of the Auto de fe*, see the folio numbers referred to in chap. 2 n. 20 and chap. 8 n. 103, above. It should be possible to make inquiries at the Lea Library in Philadelphia to ascertain whether the

auto de fe reports were among the transcripts which Lea had sent over from the archives in Simancas in the 1890s. See also HENNINGSEN *Papers of Salazar* pp. 85-88. The unprinted auto de fe reports referred to by Agustín González de Amezúa in the erudite introduction to his "El coloquio de los perros" (see GONZÁLEZ DE AMEZÚA 1912 pp. 155-157 n. 5) are all transcripts of Mongastón's pamphlet.

56. Presumably this is the pamphlet which is referred to in a *Relación de causas* 1616/17 (*Lib* 835 f. 578^{r-v}, No. 3), which mentions "the ballads which were made about the auto de fe of the witches [*las coplas que se hicieron del auto de las brujas*]." The broadsheet ballad was soon prohibited; in fact, *la Suprema* ordered the Tribunal to confiscate all existing copies, see *Lib* 333 f. 147^r § 15 (ff. 144^r-147^r, Council to Tribunal, 26 Mar. 1611; received at Logroño 31 Mar., hereafter cited as *Instructions of 26 Mar. 1611* (SD Text 6).

57. GONZÁLEZ DE AMEZÚA 1912 pp. 156-157 n. 5, where the signature on the Biblioteca Nacional's copy is stated to be "V.-73-12"; and see CARO BAROJA 1961 p. 257 n. 4, where the ballad with the same signature is stated to have been lost. My attempt to order the ballad from the Biblioteca Nacional failed to produce anything. It is to be hoped that the ballad will come to light when the collections in the library are revised.

58. GONZÁLEZ DE AMEZÚA 1912 pp. 155-156 n. 5. On the basis of the fragments cited by Amezúa I feel we can maintain it is definite that the Burgos account is not identical with any of the extant reports (manuscript or printed). On the other hand, it is possible that the Burgos account was the source of *Second Discourse of Pedro de Valencia* on the witches. In any case, Pedro de Valencia certainly did not use Mongastón's pamphlet. The various accounts of the auto de fe which have emerged are so numerous that a special study of them with reference to textual criticism is required. For I would emphasize that I myself have had time to undertake only enough research to form a basis for the above comments, which are basically no more than a provisional impression.

59. See *Third Report of the Auto de fe* f. 360^v no. 25.

60. Idem ff. 365^v-366^r no. 26.

61. Idem ff. 367^v-368^r no. 42.

62. Idem f. 367^{r-v} no. 40.

63. Idem f. 367^v no. 41.

64. See LEA *Inquisition of Spain* III p. 160.

65. See above, chap. 9.5 and n. 49.

66. As time went on cracks began to appear in the edifice constructed by the inquisitors. María Presona, who died in the summer of 1611, recanted all her confessions on her deathbed. See *Fourth Report of Salazar* f. 3^v (SD Text 14 § 15) where Salazar states that a certain person who had been reconciled at the auto de fe, and had served her sentence in the penitentiary, made an extrajudicial revocation before she died. This unnamed prisoner, who must have been one of the ten survivors of the auto de fe (see table 5, nos. 9-18, above) may almost certainly be identified as María Presona. María de Echegui, who was released in the autumn of 1611, went to the commissioner at Urdax

and recanted what she had confessed at Logroño. When María de Jureteguía and her maternal aunt María Chipía came back to their neighbors at Zugarramurdi they were strongly advised to recant their confessions, but held back for fear of the consequences (see p. 325, below). Becerra and Valle had completely ignored their nocturnal conversation in the prison, which had been reported by the jailer (see chap. 4.2, near end). But in 1613 Salazar sent a report to *la Suprema* declaring that these two women had confided to one another that they were not witches (see p. 348, above). After the first two recantations the ratio of *confitentes* to *negativos* was 17 to 14 (ten plus the two priests and the two who recanted), and if the two unofficial recantations are added the balance tilted in favor of the *negativos*.

67. *Examination of Salazar at Valencia* f. 779ʳ.

68. *Lib* 795 f. 159ʳ (ff. 158ʳ-161ᵛ, Tribunal to Council, 15 June 1611, with a postscript, ff. 157ʳ⁻ᵛ, 165Eʳ, dated 17 June 1611; received at Madrid 26 June). The inquisitors relate here that Venegas had twice been invited to the auto de fe, and that twice shortly before the auto de fe he passed through Logroño without paying a visit to the Tribunal, where they would have been more than willing to show the bishop the witches' confessions in order to, as the inquisitors' letter states, "if possible open his eyes."

NOTES TO CHAPTER 10

1. N.B.: In the preceding chapters we have been able, as it were, to examine all the extant documentation. However, in the present chapter the source material is so extensive that it will be necessary to confine ourselves to defining the chief elements and analyzing some of the most important documents. In particular, it has been necessary to omit much of interest concerning the persecutors of the witches. Where the defenders of the witches are concerned, I have deliberately subjected the sources to a brief examination only, since practically everything they wrote is recorded in SD, the text volume to this work. Therefore, in the present chapter I have felt it to be of primary importance to illuminate the background to these contributions to the witch-belief polemic.

2. See chap. 7.6, above, "The Witch-hunt in Las Cinco Villas."

3. Besides the actual accusations of witchcraft which are witnessed to by the slander trials in Goizueta and the unknown town in the neighborhood of Santesteban (see above, chap. 7.3 and n. 45-46), I have found two interesting examples of how Valle's visitation had a certain effect on witch belief far beyond the bounds of Zugarramurdi and Las Cinco Villas. 20-year-old María de Garaycoechea (*Rte* 43) from Lecaroz in the Baztán Valley declared that previously the witches held their sabbath once a week, but after Valle had been on visitation and published "his edicts" they gathered every single night (confession to Fray León de Araníbar, 28 Feb. 1611, in *Volume "F" of Salazar's Visitation Book* f. 282ʳ). A 70-year-old man, Miguel de Ustárroz, from Ituren in the Ezcurra Valley (case no. 167) described something similar to Salazar in 1611, see *Leg* 1679 Exp. 2.1 No. 29[c] 12ᵛ § 11 (ff. 11ʳ-15ʳ,

Salazar to Inquisitor General, Jaén, 7 Jan. 1614, hereafter cited as *Fifth Report of Salazar*, to be published as SD Text 15). However, the most important evidence of the limited spread of the witch craze in 1609 and the first half of 1610 is to be found in two slander trials from 1611 and 1612, from Elgorriaga (AGN Proceso 506, see below, p. 220 f.) and Arráyoz (AGN Proceso 5257, see Bibliography, below). In both cases a great many witnesses were questioned as to when the witch persecutions had commenced, and they had all answered that they had not flared up until the end of 1610.

4. *Rte* 13, María de Peña, 21, Vera, confessed to the commissioner at Echalar on 28 Mar. 1610 (*Volume "F" of Salazar's Visitation Book* ff. 77^r-79^r); *Rte* 44, Mariana de Eraso, 12, Asteasu (Guipúzcoa), confessed to the commissioner at Tolosa on 28 Aug. 1610 (idem, ff. 287^r-290^v). However, the inquisitors' statement in the letter dated 10 July 1610 that the Tribunal continued to receive new witchcraft confessions from the commissioners in the infested area (see above, end of chap. 7), indicates that some of the witchcraft confessions that were lost may have stemmed from this period.

5. *Lib* 795 f. 75^{r-v} (ff. 75^r-76^r, Fray León to Tribunal, Urdax, 4 Oct. 1610; received at Logroño 11 Oct.).

6. See idem f. 75^v.

7. Fray León states that María de Burga (case no. 36) also bears the surname Barrenechea. She may therefore have belonged to the large witch family of that name at Zugarramurdi (see end of chap. 2, above).

8. *Lib* 795 f. 75^v (Fray León/T. 4 Oct. 1610; n. 5, above).

9. Idem f. 75^v. See AGN, Proceso 506 f. 33^v, where it is stated that the village council of Elgorriaga themselves sent for Fray León. The witch epidemic did not break out in this village until November 1610 (see idem f. 26^r). For this interesting trial instituted by the High Court of Navarra against two town councillors and other witch persecutors at Elgorriaga, see below, chap. 10.4.

10. *Lib* 795 ff. 75^v-76^r (Fray León/T. 4 Oct. 1610; n. 5, above).

11. I have not succeeded in identifying Fray Josef's niece at Elizondo. Strangely enough, she is not on the list of reconciled witches in *Relación de causas 1610/11*. But this in itself might indicate that the Tribunal did give Fray Josef the required permission and entirely refrained from taking proceedings against the girl.

12. *Lib* 795 f. 41^r (T./C. 10-7-1610; chap. 4 n. 49, above).

13. *Lib* 835 f. 341^r (T./Duke 1-11-1610, chap. 8 n. 104, above).

14. *Lib* 795 f. 7^{r-v}, Tribunal to Council, 14 Dec. 1610; received in Madrid 22 Dec. Elgorriaga is not named directly, but is mentioned as "another town situated a quarter of a league [about a mile]" from Santesteban.

15. Idem f. 7^r. For the outbreak at Santesteban see AGN, Sala A, Legajo 1975, trial of Gracián de Yrisarri and accomplices instituted by the High Court of Navarra in Pamplona on 18 Dec. 1610. The accuser was the citizen Pedro de Garro from Santesteban, and the case was one of slander, first and foremost consisting of accusations of witchcraft directed against the accuser and his wife by the above-mentioned Gracián and his family. The two parties were neighbors

and the witnesses' evidence provides us with a vivid picture of a quarrel carried on from house to house between the two neighbors on 13 Dec. 1610, during which the accusations of witchcraft were made. It is significant, however, that the "witches," Pedro de Garro and his wife, won the case.

16. *Relación de causas 1610/11 (B)* f. 454^r, no. 20; *Lib* 795 f. 7^{r-v} (T./C. 14-12-1610; n. 14, above).

17. *Lib* 795 f. 42^{r-v} (T./C. 10-7-1610; chap. 4 n. 49, above). See *Lib* 246 ff. 77^{r-v}, which contains three letters dated 20 Dec. 1527, which were sent to the bishop of Calahorra, the Dominican provincial, and the Franciscan provincial. These were all instructed to send preachers into the mountains to preach against the witches.

18. *Lib* 333 ff. 85^v-87^v, Council to King, 3 Aug. 1610.

19. Biblioteca de la Real Academia de la Historia, MS 9-29-5-5944, Varios Documentos, Tomo 4 f. 174^{r-v}, King to Archbishop of Burgos, 5 Sept. 1610. A postscript states that similar letters were sent to the bishops of Pamplona, Calahorra, and Tarazona, to the Franciscan provincials at Burgos and Guipúzcoa (*Cantabria*), to the provincials of the Dominicans, Trinitarians, Mercedians, Carmelites, and Jesuits at Castilla, and finally to the head of "los ministros" in Aragón (*y a él de los ministros de Aragón*).

20. *Leg* 1679 Exp. 2.1 No. 28 [b] f. 2^v (T./C. 14-2-1611, chap. 7 n. 68, above).

21. Idem ff. 2^v-3^r; see *First Letter of the Bishop* f. 1^v (SD Text 5), where the bishop mentions the persons he has sent up to the area.

22. See *First Letter of Solarte* f. 1^r, where Solarte relates that he reached Lesaca a week before Advent. In 1610 the first Sunday in Advent fell on 28 Nov. (see CAPPELLI 1930), thus "a week before" must have been ca. 21 Nov. 1610.

23. *Leg* 1679 Exp. 2.1 No. 28 [b] f. 2^v (T./C. 14-2-1611; chap. 7 n. 68, above). Hernando de Solarte — not Golarte, as Julio Caro Baroja reads the name (CARO BAROJA *De nuevo* p. 280 *et passim*), nor Solartes, as I myself have rendered the name (HENNINGSEN *Papers of Salazar* p. 91 *et passim*) — came from a Jesuit college in Bilbao (see *First Letter of Solarte* f. 2^v). The other Jesuits were presumably from the same college, but there is also the possibility that they were from Pamplona. For in the above-mentioned letter from the Tribunal to the Council the inquisitors state that they have been informed that the provincial of the Jesuits was in Pamplona. The name of the head of the Jesuits was Gaspar de Vegas, see *Leg* 1679 Exp. 2.1 No. 28 [a] f. 2^v, the reverse of the letter, ff. 1^r-2^v, of Hernando de Solarte to Gaspar de Vegas at Valladolid, "Provincial of the Society of Jesus in the province of Castilla etc.," Bilbao, 26 and 27 Jan. 1611 (with copies of two letters to Solarte from the *licenciado* Martín de Yrisarri, dated Yanci, 13 and 21 Jan. 1611), hereafter cited as *Second Letter of Solarte* (SD Text 4). The purpose of Gaspar de Vegas's visit to Pamplona must almost certainly have been consultation with the bishop, Venegas de Figueroa. Whether the other Jesuits came from Pamplona or Bilbao it seems certain that they accompanied Solarte. For according to the information revealed by the Tribunal, only one group from this order was active in the area. We know nothing of Solarte other than that he was

a young man; in the letter of 14 Feb. the inquisitors call him *hombre mozo* (loc. cit. f. 5ᵛ).

24. For the homeward journey via Santesteban see *Leg* 1679 Exp. 2.1 No. 31[b] f. 5ʳ, Hernando de Solarte to the Bishop of Pamplona, Oyarzun, 25 Mar. 1611, hereafter cited as *Solarte's Letter to the Bishop* (SD Text 9). A wealth of details from the Jesuit's journey is given in *First Letter of Solarte, Second Letter of Solarte,* and in *Leg* 1679 Exp. 2.1 No. 31[c] ff. 6ʳ-7ʳ, *title:* "Memoria de las personas que por engaño y violencia dijeron a ministros de la Inquisición contra sí y contra otros en Las Cinco Villas de Navarra," [25 Mar. 1611], hereafter cited as *Solarte's Report to the Bishop* (SD Text 10). The Spanish original is published in CARO BAROJA *De nuevo* pp. 285-286, n. 55.

25. *Lib* 795 f. 152ᵛ (ff. 152ʳ-153ᵛ, Tribunal to Council, 9 Apr. 1611; received in Madrid 19 Apr.).

26. See chap. 10.4 and n. 63, below, from which it appears that the Franciscans had met the bishop in Pamplona before they reached Logroño and delivered the written report to the Tribunal, which is mentioned in the letter of 9 Apr. 1611, but which unfortunately is not extant. For the date of the meeting in Pamplona see also below, n. 60.

27. Fray Domingo de Sardo is mentioned in the inquisitors' letter of 9 Apr. 1611 (*Lib* 795 f. 153ʳ). Another of the Franciscans was Father Cigarroa (see *Volume "F" of Salazar's Visitation Book* f. 549ᵛ). For Domingo de Sardo's participation in Salazar's journey of visitation see below, chap. 11.A.3.

28. See the heading to *The Bishop's Report* (SD Text 8). The Spanish title is rendered above, chap. 1 n. 114.

29. For actuation of Franciscan fathers during the witch-hunt, see e.g. below, chaps. 10.4 and 11.C.6.

30. *Leg* 1679 Exp. 2.1 No. 27 f. 1ʳ (Hualde/T. 10-1-1611; chap. 8 n. 38, above).

31. *The Bishop's Report* ff. 6ᵛ-8ᵛ (SD Text 8); AGN, Proceso 506 passim; AGN Proceso 5257 passim.

32. AGN Proceso 506 f. 28ᵛ (ff. 28ʳ-30ʳ, hearing of 48-year-old Miguel de Yzeretea, Elgorriaga, as a witness in the case against the two *jurados*).

33. *The Bishop's Report* ff. 5ᵛ-6ʳ (SD Text 8). I have not succeeded in identifying the herdsman Yricia (but see below, chap. 11 n. 111). Juana de Argarate does not appear to have been imprisoned by the Inquisition. On the contrary, her name is on the *Pamplona Manuscript's* list of witches who were reconciled during Salazar's visitation (IDOATE *Documento* p. 182 no. 50). Presumably this means that she was imprisoned by the secular authorities in Aranaz. She is also mentioned in *Volume "F" of Salazar's Visitation Book* ff. 84ʳ and 130ʳ, as mistress of *Rte* 14 and *Rte* 19 respectively.

34. *Leg* 1679 Exp. 2.1 No. 11 ff. 1ʳ-3ᵛ, Fray León to Tribunal, Elizondo 29 Jan. 1611; received in Logroño 4 Feb. Only very few of the witchcraft confessions enclosed by Fray León with this letter are preserved in *Volume "F" of Salazar's Visitation Book* (see below, n. 47).

35. *Leg* 1679 Exp. 2.1 No. 11 f. 2ʳ (Fray León/T. 29-1-1611; preceding n.).

36. Idem f. 2ᵛ.

37. Idem f. 1ʳ. In the letter of 14 Dec. 1610 (n. 14, above) the Tribunal had requested permission to imprison two witches at Santesteban. *La Suprema* granted this in a letter of 24 Dec. 1610 (*Lib* 333 f. 126ʳ). The two witches are also mentioned in a letter from the dean of Santesteban to the Tribunal (*Leg* 1679 Exp. 2.1 No. 13[a] f. 1ʳ⁻ᵛ, Miguel de Yrisarri to Tribunal, Santesteban, 31 Jan. 1611; received in Logroño 4 Feb.). One of the two prisoners was 50-year-old María Baxco de Dindart (identical with 40-year-old María de Dindart, case no. 44); the other was Graciana de Moquerra, presumably identical with 80-year-old Graciana de Olberro (case no. 52). The dean's letter was accompanied by the confessions of these two women and those of two other witches, all written down by Miguel de Yrisarri personally (loc. cit. ff. 2ʳ⁻3ʳ). The dean's letter with the four confessions was received by the Tribunal simultaneously with Fray León's papers, so they were obviously taken to Logroño by Fray León's messenger.

38. *Leg* 1679 Exp. 2.1 No. 11 f. 1ʳ (Fray León/T. 29-1-1611; n. 34, above).

39. Idem f. 2ʳ.

40. *Leg* 1679 Exp. 2.1 No. 20 f. 1ᵛ (ff. 1ʳ⁻4ᵛ, Tribunal to Council, 9 Mar. 1611(a); received in Madrid 14 Mar.).

41. *Leg* 1679 Exp. 2.1 No. 23[b] f. 1ʳ⁻ᵛ, "Report of the places where *aquelarres* have been exposed, of the *confitente* delinquents who have made confession, and of the number of suspected persons in each place" [9 Mar. 1611], hereafter cited as *Statistics of 9 March 1611*.

42. There was a particular explanation for the persecution that took place outside this area. Thus, there is an obvious connection between the confessions from Tafalla (table 6 no. 17) in southern Navarra, and from the four towns in Alava (nos. 23-26), and the auto de fe, as all these towns are situated relatively close to Logroño. Most of the confessions from the towns of Arriba and Lezaeta in the Araiz Valley in Navarra (nos. 15-16) were presumably made during Valle's visitation in 1609. This was the case at Rentería for at least 17 of the 27 confessions recorded (see above, p. 117 f.).

43. One can also detect an emerging saturation point where those under suspicion are concerned; and this becomes clearer when we compare the lists of accomplices in some of the extant confessions preserved in *Volume "F" of Salazar's Visitation Book*. From these it can be seen that the witches did not denounce their neighbors at random but referred on the whole to the same persons.

44. See *Lib* 795 f. 204ᵛ (ff. 204ʳ⁻207ʳ, Tribunal to Council, 5 Oct. 1611; received in Madrid 15 Oct.).

45. See below, chap. 11.C.5.

46. *Lib* 795 f. 153ᵛ (T./C. 9-4-1611; n. 25, above).

47. See *Volume "F" of Salazar's Visitation Book Rte* 1-11, 27, 36-41, 43, 51-52, 63-66, 69, 74, 77-78, 80.

48. *Volume "F" of Salazar's Visitation Book Rte* 1, 9, 10, 36, 39, 40, 43, 51, 52, and 80. Four of these confessions (*Rte* 1, 39, 51, 52; made 17, 28, 26, and 26 Mar. 1611 respectively) related to previously denounced witches' sabbaths. The remaining seven were from new *aquelarres: Rte*

41 (15-4-1611) exposed an *aquelarre* in Irurita; *Rte* 9, 10, 43, and 80 (confessions made 14 Mar., 10 Feb., 28 Feb., and 14 Mar. respectively) exposed a witch coven at Lecaroz; *Rte* 36 and 40 (confessions made 15 Mar. and 13 Feb. respectively) exposed a witch gathering at Elvetea. Some of the confession dates are earlier than 9 Mar. 1609, but as Fray León did not forward them until later they were not included in the Tribunal's statistics.

49. No witchcraft confessions are extant from Elizondo and Errazu, but from the above-mentioned letter of 29 Jan. 1611 (*Leg* 1679 Exp. 2.1 No. 11 ff. 2^r and 2^v) it appears that Fray León exposed witch confederacies in them as well.

50. *Solarte's Report to the Bishop* f. 6^{r-v} (SD Text 10); *First Letter of Solarte* f. 2^r (SD Text 3).

51. See idem f. 2^r.

52. See idem f. 2^r. I would point out here that I have allowed myself a moderately free interpretation bearing in mind that the source is reproduced as SD Text 3 where the reader may follow up my reference and ascertain whether he agrees with me.

53. *First Letter of Solarte* f. 1^{r-v} (SD Text 3). Hualde's 16-year-old nephew may almost certainly be identified as Joanes de Hualde, son of Domenja de Peruchena. In *Rte* 13, confession of 21-year-old María de Peña (of Vera) these two are named as nos. 29 and 30 in the list of accomplices (*Volume "F" of Salazar's Visitation Book* f. 79^r). Domenja de Peruchena is also mentioned by Hualde in the letter of 10 Jan. 1611 as one of the dangerous witches at Vera, and it is here that we learn that she is Hualde's sister-in-law (*mi cuñada*) *Leg* 1679 Exp. 2.1 No. 27 f. 1^v (Hualde/T. 10-1-1611; chap. 8 n. 38).

54. *First Letter of Solarte* f. 2^r (SD Text 3). We have no further information regarding Father Juan López. He was possibly one of the Jesuits who accompanied Solarte.

55. See *Lib* 795 f. 153^r (T./C. 9-4-1611; n. 25, above), where the Tribunal states, giving Domingo de Sardo as the source, that Yrisarri had even received a reply from Rome.

56. *Leg* 1679 Exp. 2.1 No. 27 f. 1^r (Hualde/T., 10-1-1611; chap. 8 n. 38, above).

57. Idem No. 1[a], f. 1^{r-v}, Hualde to Tribunal, Vera, 12 Jan. 1611; received in Logroño 24 Jan.

58. See idem f. 1^r.

59. Idem f. 1^v. The Jesuits are here called *"los padres teatinos."* Twenty-one-year-old María de Peña's confession (see above, n. 53) was made on 28 Mar. 1610 to the inquisitorial commissioner at Lesaca. In addition to Hualde's sister-in-law and 16-year-old nephew she had denounced 48 other residents of Vera as witches (see *Volume "F" of Salazar's Visitation Book*, ff. 77^r-80^v).

60. On 4 Mar. 1611 the bishop wrote to the inquisitor general that he had called his emissaries to a meeting in order to discuss the witch question, see *First Letter of the Bishop* f. 1^v (SD Text 5). On 1 Apr. 1611 the bishop forwarded his report together with the letter and the report he had received from Solarte after having concluded his own report, see *Second Letter of the Bishop* f. 10^r (SD Text 7). The meeting in Pamplona must have taken place between these two dates. Regarding

the participation of the Franciscans, see above, n. 26. The Jesuits do not seem to have been present, in any case Solarte was not, as his letter is dated Oyarzun (Guipúzcoa) 25 Mar. 1611, *Solarte's Letter to the Bishop* f. 5ʳ (SD Text 9).

61. See *Lib* 795 f. 152ᵛ (T./C. 9-4-1611; n. 25, above).

62. See Solarte's statement in the letter of 25 Mar. 1611 (loc. cit. n. 60, above).

63. *Lib* 795 ff. 158ᵛ-159ʳ (T./C. 15-6-1611; chap. 9 n. 68, above). The witch unguents and the dressed toads are also mentioned in a later letter, *Lib* 795 f. 152ᵛ (T./C. 9-4-1611; n. 25, above).

64. See *Lib* 795 ff. 157ᵛ, 158ᵛ-159ᵛ (T./C. 15 & 17-6-1611; chap. 9 n. 68, above). The name of the postmaster (*el correo mayor*) was Joan de Arbelaiz (idem).

65. AGN, Proceso 506, 198 folios (see n. 9, above). The sentence of the two *jurados*, Joanes de Legasa (20 years old) and Martín de Yzurrena, and their three accomplices, is at the end of the trial record (f. 196ᵛ).

66. *Lib* 795 f. 159ᵛ (T./C. 15-6-1611; chap. 9 n. 68, above).

67. See *Leg* 1679 Exp. 2.1 No. 30 f. 1ʳ-ᵛ, Tribunal to Viceroy, 17 May 1611. This is a copy written by Salazar himself and marked with the signature "EE." The copy was forwarded to *la Suprema* in Oct. 1613 as a supplement to *Fourth Report of Salazar*, see f. 4ᵛ (SD Text 14). The other letters to the viceroy (the Duke of Ciudad Real) are known only through a mention in the Tribunal's letter to *la Suprema* of 15 June 1611 (n. 66, above).

68. The viceroy's reply is discussed in detail in the Tribunal's letter of 15 June 1611 (*Lib* 795 f. 160ʳ; chap. 9 n. 68, above). Unfortunately the interesting memorial has not come to light in the Archivo Historico Nacional, and thus it may possibly be in the viceroy's archive, which, according to information kindly supplied by Professor Ismael Sánchez Bella, appears to have been preserved in Pamplona.

69. *Lib* 795 f. 157ʳ-ᵛ (T./C. 17-6-1611; chap. 9 n. 68, above).

70. *Lib* 333 ff. 170ᵛ-171ʳ, Council to Tribunal, 28 June 1611.

71. Salazar's *Memorial of 2 Mar. 1611* ff. 19ʳ-ᵛ, 22ʳ-ᵛ. After this was written I discovered a report on Salazar's behavior written two weeks previously by Becerra (*Leg* 1683 Exp. 1 f. 40ʳ-ᵛ, Becerra to Inquisitor General). This shows us the other side of the coin. Becerra stated that he could no longer put off informing the inquisitor general of the problems created by Salazar at the Tribunal. Ever since his arrival in June 1610 Salazar had shown the utmost arrogance. Becerra had tried to make him see reason in vain, and Salazar had not improved. It was impossible to work with him, as he wanted to argue about every detail, and he could spend an entire sitting discussing trivialities. Becerra concluded his letter by saying that in spite of the great favor, according to Salazar's own declarations to his colleagues, afforded him by the inquisitor general, he, Becerra, felt obliged to report these matters since the Tribunal could not continue in this manner.

72. *Leg* 1679 Exp. 2.1 No. 32 ff. 1ʳ-2ʳ, vote of the three inquisitors, in the Tribunal courtroom on 3 Mar. 1611 in the morning; see CARO BAROJA *De nuevo* p. 290, where the names of the four witches are cited. The four witches were all reconciled by the Tribunal, see case nos.

58-60 and, for the fourth, María de Echevarría Mateorena, see *Accounts of 27 Sept. 1614* f. 160ʳ and *Second Report of Salazar* f. 16ᵛ (SD Text 12 § 74). Three of them later recanted their confessions, see case nos. 494-495 and *Second Report of Salazar*, loc. cit.

73. *Leg* 1679 Exp. 2.1 No. 28 ff. 1ʳ-2ʳ, 5ʳ (T./C. 14-2-1611; chap. 7 n. 68, above). This letter, which I have quoted from so frequently, contains a detailed commentary on Solarte's first and second letters.

74. Marginal note by inquisitors on f. 1ʳ of *Second Letter of Solarte* (SD Text 4).

75. See *Lib* 795 f. 153ʳ⁻ᵛ (T./C. 9-4-1611; chap. 10 n. 25, above).

76. Idem f. 153ʳ; see *Second Letter of the Bishop* f. 9ᵛ (SD Text 7) where the bishop forwards Martín de Yrisarri's suggestion to the inquisitor general.

77. *Lib* 795 f. 153ᵛ (T./C. 9-4-1611; n. 25, above).

78. *Memorial of 2 Mar. 1611* f. 19ᵛ.

79. *Lib* 333 f. 170ᵛ (C./T. 28-6-1611; n. 70, above).

NOTES TO CHAPTER 11

1. *Instructions of 26 Mar. 1611* (SD Text 6).

2. The inquisitor general's letter of 25 Feb. 1611 is no longer extant, but the contents are quoted at the commencement of the inquisitors' letter, *Leg* 1679 Exp. 2.1 No. 20 f. 1ʳ (T./C. 9-3-1611(a); chap. 10 n. 40, above).

3. Idem ff. 1ᵛ-4ᵛ.

4. See below, n. 5, 6, and 7.

5. *Leg* 1679 Exp. 2.1 No. 14 f. 1ʳ, the bishop of Calahorra to the inquisitor general, Santo Domingo de la Calzada, 6 Mar. 1611; received in Madrid 14 Mar. The letter written by the inquisitor general to the bishop of Calahorra is not extant, but it can be seen from the reply that it was dated 25 Feb. 1611.

6. *First Letter of the Bishop* (SD Text 5) f. 1ʳ. The bishop of Pamplona refers to a letter from the inquisitor general which has been lost, but which, like those mentioned above, was dated 25 Feb. 1611.

7. Neither is the letter from the inquisitor general to Pedro de Valencia extant, but it is mentioned by the latter in his reply of 20 Apr. 1611, with, however, no mention of the date (see above, chap. 1.2). Since the inquisitor general's letters to the Tribunal, to the bishop of Calahorra, and to the bishop of Pamplona were all dated 25 Feb., I am inclined to assume that they were in the nature of a circular. I therefore imagine that a copy would have been sent to Pedro de Valencia on the same day that it was sent off to the others.

8. *The Bishop's Letter* with the report and enclosures were received in Madrid on 21 Apr. 1611, see marginal note to *Second Letter of the Bishop* f. 9ʳ (SD Text 7).

9. *Instructions of 26 Mar. 1611* (SD Text 6).

10. Julio Caro Baroja cannot understand why it was Salazar's lot to administer the Edict of Grace, "since he was the most junior inquisitor." He considers that a number of reasons combined to make the choice fall on Salazar, and assumes that it was implemented by orders from the highest quarters (see CARO BAROJA *De nuevo* pp.

273-291). However, no such orders from *la Suprema* are to be found, and in my opinion Caro Baroja's speculations are unnecessary. The explanation is perfectly simple: following the practice already mentioned, the inquisitors (according to *Carta Acordada* No. 119) were to go on visitation by turns (see above, chap. 6) and on this occasion it was Salazar's turn (see beginning of chap. 4.5).

11. See *Fourth Report of Salazar* f. 4ᵛ (SD Text 14 § 21).

12. *Lib* 795 f. 152ʳ⁻ᵛ (T./C. 9-4-1611; chap. 10 n. 25, above).

13. Salazar was entrusted with a total of 338 *confitente* witches' records, but only 117 were old enough for reconciliation, the rest — girls under 12 and boys under 14 — were to be absolved *ad cautelam*, see *Fifth Report of Salazar* f. 13ᵛ (SD Text 15 § 16). A number of these trial records are preserved, either in the original or as transcripts, in *Volume "F" of Salazar's Visitation Book*.

14. Note that the prosecutor San Vicente had actually compiled a list of suspects in May (see chap. 10.3, above), and that it was the usual practice to present such lists to the inquisitors to take with them on visitation (see near end of chap. 6, above).

15. See *Volume "F" of Salazar's Visitation Book* passim. In the *Fourth Report of Salazar* f. 7ᵛ (SD Text 14 § 34), he himself says that he used both "the ordinary set of questions," which, judging from the reference, means the fourteen questions from *la Suprema* (see chap. 4.4, above), and a shorter list of eight questions (reproduced below, chap. 11.C.6).

16. *Leg* 1679 Exp. 2.1 No. 31 [f] f. 1ᵛ (ff. 1ʳ-3ʳ, Salazar to Inquisitor General, Fuenterrabía, 4 Sept. 1611; received in Madrid 12 Sept., hereafter cited as *Letter from Fuenterrabía*).

17. *Instructions of 26 Mar. 1611* f. 145ᵛ (SD Text 6 § 6).

18. Examples of these printed formulae may be seen in *Volume "F" of Salazar's Visitation Book*. There are two types. In proceedings against adults (*Rte* 62, 67, 68, 69, 71, 74, 75, 78, 80) one printed formula only is used, a renouncement of heresy (see e.g. f. 402ʳ⁻ᵛ). In proceedings against those who were under 25 (*Rte* 63, 64, 65, 66, 70, 72, 73, 76, 77, 79) both the abjuration of heresy and another printed formula containing a declaration of guardianship (*curaduría*) have been used (see e.g. f. 414ʳ). These persons, being minors, were to be supported during the reconciliation proceedings by a guardian (*curador*). Regarding the reconciliation see further below, near end of chap. 11.A.5.

19. *Instructions of 26 Mar. 1611* merely states that the Edict of Grace is to be published "in its original form and in authentic copies" (SD Text 6 § 1). My assumption that the edict was printed rests merely on the fact that a large number of copies would have been needed, since it was to be published in many places.

20. See *Instructions of 26 Mar. 1611* ff. 145ᵛ-146ʳ (SD Text 6 § 9), in which the Tribunal is directed to proclaim this kind of instruction, and note that a similar printed edict is extant of a slightly later date (see chap. 13.6, below).

21. *Lib* 795 f. 154ʳ (f. 154ʳ⁻ᵛ, Tribunal to Council, 7 May 1611).

22. *Lib* 251 ff. 163ᵛ-164ᵛ, copy of royal decree dated Aranjuez, 25 Apr. 1611.

23. *Lib* 333 ff. 154ᵛ-155ʳ, Council to Tribunal, 29 April 1611.

24. The details of the conditions regarding this amnesty for the witches appear in the instructions of 26 Mar. for Salazar's visitation. Therefore there remains only the question of whether the Edict of Grace was so formulated that it could serve the witches as a guide in what they were to confess. This was the case with other edicts of grace from the Inquisition — for instance, that to the mystics, the *alumbrados*, in which all the errors of the sect were described in minute detail (see e.g. *Lib* 1231 ff. 643ʳ-653ᵛ, Edict of Grace to the *alumbrados* of Sevilla, dated Madrid, 9 May 1623). We cannot entirely exclude the possibility that the Edict of Grace to the witches in the district of Logroño may have been formulated in this manner, but there is nothing in the sources that provides any indication of this. On the contrary, Salazar tells of several persons who reported themselves in order to take advantage of the edict to the witches, but who during the interrogation were unable to tell him anything at all regarding witchcraft, see *Second Report of Salazar* ff. 14ʳ, 15ᵛ (SD Text 12 §§ 62, 68).

25. *Lib* 795 f. 154ᵛ (T./C. 7-5-1611; n. 21, above).

26. *Letter from Fuenterrabía* f. 1ʳ; cf. *First Report of Salazar* f. 357ʳ (SD Text 11).

27. See *Second Report of Salazar* f. 7ᵛ (SD Text 12 § 33).

28. *First Report of Salazar* f. 357ʳ (SD Text 11). On Fray Domingo de Sardo see above, chap. 10.4, and on Fray Josef de Elizondo see above, chap. 10.1

29. See *Accounts of 27 Sept. 1614* f. 161ᵛ, in which it is shown that these two together with a third monk between them were paid a total of 1,620 *reales* as salary for their preaching during Salazar's visitation.

30. *Leg* 1679 Exp. 2.1 No. 30, Tribunal to bishop of Pamplona, Logroño 21 May 1611. The letter was later forwarded by Salazar to *la Suprema* as an enclosure with his *Fourth Report* f. 8ᵛ (SD Text 14 § 39). Julio Caro Baroja reproduces it in his dissertation, but the conclusion is erroneously transcribed: instead of the meaningless "mros (?) y a V. S." it should read "n[uest]ro s[eñ]or g[uard]e a V. S." (CARO BAROJA *De nuevo* p. 291).

31. See reference in preceding note, and cf. *Fourth Report of Salazar* f. 9ʳ (SD Text 14 § 39).

32. *Lib* 795 f. 487ʳ (ff. 485ʳ-487ʳ, Tribunal to Council, 23 Mar. 1613); for the bishop's canopy, see chap. 11.C.3, below.

33. *Second Report of Salazar* f. 17ʳ (SD Text 12 § 77).

34. See *Lib* 795 f. 157ʳ (T./C. 17-6-1611; chap. 9 n. 68, above), where Becerra and Valle cite a letter from Salazar (since lost).

35. *Letter from Fuenterrabía* f. 1ʳ. Cf. *First Report of Salazar* f. 357ʳ (SD Text 11), where the towns are named in a slightly different order and two more towns, Amaya and Arizcun, are added to the list (inserted between Elizondo and Urdax). Amaya and Arizcun are situated in the Baztán Valley and were possibly visited by Salazar in the days from 25 to 27 July, when it appears that he was not at Elizondo (see n. 38, below). If this was the case it would prove that Salazar in fact traveled in the circular manner decided by the Tribunal in its plan of operation formulated earlier in the spring (see above, chap. 11.A.1 § 11).

36. *Volume "F" of Salazar's Visitation Book* f. 573ʳ, reconciliation of

Tomás de Saldías (*Rte* 76) at Santesteban on 5 July 1611 (see below, table 7, Serial No. "126").

37. The revocation of *Rte* 62, *Volume "F" of Salazar's Visitation Book* f. 417ʳ; see chap. 11.A.6, below.

38. The dates of interrogations in *Volume "F" of Salazar's Visitation Book* ff. 4ʳ (*Rte* 1), 10ʳ (*Rte* 2), 16ʳ (*Rte* 3), 22ʳ (*Rte* 4), 28ʳ (*Rte* 5), 34ʳ (*Rte* 6), 40ʳ (*Rte* 7), 46ʳ (*Rte* 8), 52ʳ (*Rte* 9), 60ʳ (*Rte* 10), 65ʳ (*Rte* 11), 182ʳ (*Rte* 27), 551ʳ (*Rte* 74), 622ʳ (*Rte* 80), see under hearings at Elizondo in case nos. 441-451, 467, 514, and 520.

39. On 3 Aug. Salazar seems to have been staying at Zugarramurdi, see his mention of Catalina de Echetoa, chap. 11.A.7, below, and compare this with *Second Report of Salazar* f. 8ᵛ (SD Text 12 § 42), where Salazar describes the investigations he undertook himself at the witches' meeting place, Berroscoberro Meadow, outside Zuga-rramurdi. Regarding Valderro (i.e. Erro, five miles from Aescoa) and conjecture as to when Salazar may have been there, see idem f. 16ʳ (SD Text 12 § 71) and see below, chap. 11.A.7 and n. 106.

40. See *Volume "F" of Salazar's Visitation Book* ff. 73ᵛ (*Rte* 12), 118ʳ (*Rte* 17), 132ʳ (*Rte* 19), 136ʳ (*Rte* 20), 140ʳ (*Rte* 21), 151ʳ (*Rte* 22), 159ʳ (*Rte* 23); see under hearings at Lesaca in case nos. 452, 457, 459-463.

41. Interrogation dates in *Volume "F" of Salazar's Visitation Book* ff. 80ʳ (*Rte* 13), 89ʳ (*Rte* 14), 95ʳ (*Rte* 15), 103ᵛ (*Rte* 16), 173ʳ (*Rte* 25), 176ʳ (*Rte* 26); see under hearings at Vera in case nos. 453-456, 465, and 466.

42. The dates given for the interrogations at Fuenterrabía are 22, 23, and 25-29 August, see *Volume "F" of Salazar's Visitation Book* ff. 190ʳ (*Rte* 28), 196ʳ (*Rte* 29), 210ʳ (*Rte* 31), 216ʳ (*Rte* 32), 222ʳ (*Rte* 33), 227ʳ (*Rte* 34), 232ʳ, 232ᵛ, and 234ʳ (further interrogations of *Rte* 35), 356ʳ (*Rte* 53), 507ʳ (*Rte* 70), 531ʳ (*Rte* 72), 542ʳ (*Rte* 73), 610ʳ (*Rte* 79); see case nos. 468, 469, 471-475, 493, 510, 512, 513, and 519.

43. The date for the publication of the Edict of Grace at Fuenterrabía appears in *Volume "F" of Salazar's Visitation Book* ff. 226ʳ and 230ʳ. Almost all the Fuenterrabía witches mentioned in n. 42, above, had previously made confession to the local inquisitorial commissioner, immediately after the publication of the edict in June.

44. See *First Report of Salazar* f. 357ʳ (SD Text 11) where it is stated that on the whole of this visitation the Edict of Faith was only pub-lished in four towns: Fuenterrabía, San Sebastián, Azpeitia, and Vitoria.

45. Idem f. 357ᵛ.

46. *Lib* 795 f. 155ʳ, Tribunal to Council, 28 May 1611. In the letter, which is concerned with other matters, it is stated that Salazar "to-morrow Sunday is to publish the Edict of Grace" at Santesteban and that on the same day the Tribunal (i.e. Becerra and Valle) will order its proclamation at Logroño "and other places."

47. Miguel de Yrisarri — not to be confused with Martín de Yrisarri, the priest at Yanci (chap. 10.4, above) — had, as has been previously mentioned, taken an active part in the great witch-hunt of the winter (see chap. 10.1, near end). As early as January he had requested that he be appointed inquisitorial commissioner, and in this connection Fray León de Araníbar carried out investigations into his *limpieza de*

sangre (*Leg* 1679 Exp. 2.1 No. 11 f. 3ᵛ, Fray León de Aranibar/T. 29-1-1611; chap. 10 n. 34, above). From a letter written in April it appears that the appointment had been made by this date (see *Lib* 333 ff. 154ᵛ-155ʳ, T/C 29-4-1611; n. 23, above).

48. See *First Report of Salazar* f. 358ʳ (SD Text 11 § 4), which mentions the crowds at the first sessions at Santesteban and Elizondo.

49. The 13 original visitation cases from the session at Santesteban are to be found in *Volume "F" of Salazar's Visitation Book*. These are all placed at the end of the volume with 6 other records. While the first 61 trial records in *Volume "F"* are clearly enough provided with the serial numbers of *revocantes* (Nos. "1"-"55," "55 bis"-"60"), the last 19 records are not numbered consecutively. This puzzled me considerably until I began to suspect that these might be fragments of a serial numbering of *reconciliados*. For the 19 records differ from the others on one point. The witches did not revoke their confessions until *after* a reconciliation had taken place. Besides this, we know from a direct statement in *Salazar's Fourth Report* f. 8ʳ (SD Text 14 § 35), that it was not until a later date that these records were withdrawn from their position among the reconciled and placed together with the other *revocantes*. No regard was paid to either of the two numberings when the volume was bound, and thus the numbers must have been inserted when the records were still unbound and in loose sheets. It is important to produce the numbering of the 19 reports in greater detail for, as was shown in table 7, they provide the key to a quantitative demonstration of the way in which the number of witchcraft confessions increased almost day by day during Salazar's visitation. If we start with the original numbers and align them with the time and place of the various interrogations of the witches, we get the accompanying illuminating table (Confession 1 shows confessions made *before* the period of grace came into force. Confession 2 shows confessions made *after* the period of grace came into force). If we compare the dates in the first and second columns of confessions, we can see clearly that the 19 records must have acquired their numbers while still lying in the sheaf with those of the other reconciled witches. (Regarding the other records in this group, totalling 290, which were bound, except for one single record, in the lost volumes "B"-"E" of Salazar's visitation book, see near end of chap. 12.2, below.) The remaining part of the table reflects the principle by which this serial numbering was undertaken, and it is of the greatest importance to assist us in reconstructing Salazar's visitation. The witches were not — as might have been expected — allotted numbers after being reconciled; rather they were allotted them as soon as they were ready for reconciliation (i.e. immediately after they had confessed or had confirmed a previous confession made before the publication of the Edict of Grace). The four records from Fuenterrabía (Nos. "68"-"70" and "247") seem to contradict this interpretation, but here there were special circumstances. We have already mentioned the publication of the edict at this town (chap. 11.A.3) and we have information from quite another quarter that a notary from Fuenterrabía was at Santesteban on 13 June 1611 and that he gave Salazar some witch records (Caro Baroja 1947 p. 190 f.). He could thus on this occasion very well

have obtained the three confessions made from 10 and 11 June. As far as the fourth one is concerned the fact that it was not made until 12 June may well explain why the notary did not take it with him to Santesteban. Presumably it would have been kept at Fuenterrabía until Salazar arrived there, and it thereby received the higher serial number "247" (note that when Salazar completed this part of the visitation at Fuenterrabía he had reconciled a total of 271 witches, see quote near beginning of chap. 11.A.7, below).

50. *Instructions of 26 Mar. 1611* ff. 144^v-145^v (SD Text 6 §§ 3, 6).

Chapter 11, note 49

Orig. serial number	Rte	Confession 1, place		Confession 2, place		Reconciliation, place	
'8"	67	15 Apr.,	Zubieta	2 June,	Santesteban	26 June,	Santesteban
'9"	71	"	"	"	"	"	"
'10"	78	19 Feb.,	Elizondo	3 June,	"	28 June,	"
'12"	69	20 Feb.,	Zubieta	"	"	"	"
'19"	75	18 Apr.,	"	4 June,	"	"	"
'23"	77	11 Feb.,	Elizondo	"	"	24 June,	"
'24"	62	16 Apr.,	Zubieta	"	"	28 June,	"
'26"	66	11 Feb.,	Elizondo	"	"	"	"
'30"	68	16 Apr.,	Zubieta	6 June,	"	22 June,	"
'32"	64	17 Feb.,	Elizondo	"	"	28 June,	"
'33"	65	25 Feb.,	"	"	"	"	"
'59"	63	6 Feb.,	"	10 June,	"	26 June,	"
'68"	73			11 June,	Fuenterrabía	22 Aug.,	Fuenterrabía
'69"	72			10 June,	"	"	"
'70"	70			"	"	"	"
'126"	76	?	Santesteban	4 July,	Santesteban	5 July,	Santesteban
'152"	80	14 Mar.,	Elizondo	29 July,	Elizondo	29 July,	Elizondo
'153"	74	10 Feb.,	Lecaroz	"	"	"	"
'247"	79			12 June,	Fuenterrabía	23 Aug.,	Fuenterrabía

51. *Leg* 1683 Exp. 2, loose letter placed inside the end of the volume, f. 2^r (ff. 1^r-3^v, Salazar to Inquisitor General, [Valencia, posterior to 27 Aug. 1619], hereafter cited as *Salazar's Letter from Valencia*).

52. *Volume "F" of Salazar's Visitation Book* f. 493^r (*Rte* 69).

53. ARGÜELLO *Instrucciones* f. 13^v § 15.

54. See table 7, Serial Nos. "8," "9," "10."

55. See n. 49, above.

56. For these groups see below, chap. 12.2, subsection "Salazar's Visitation Book."

57. *Volume "F" of Salazar's Visitation Book* f. 438^r (*Rte* 65).

58. Cf. n. 49, above.

59. *Volume "F" of Salazar's Visitation Book* f. 469^r (*Rte* 67).

60. Idem f. 595^{r-v} (*Rte* 78).

61. Idem f. 584^r (*Rte* 77).

62. Idem f. 582^{r-v} (*Rte* 77).

63. Cf. LEA *Inquisition of Spain* II pp. 582-585.

64. *Volume "F" of Salazar's Visitation Book* f. 572^v (*Rte* 76).

65. See *Volume "F" of Salazar's Visitation Book* ff. 401^r-403^v (*Rte* 62), 426^r-428^v (*Rte* 64), 450^r-452^v (*Rte* 65), 458^r-460^v (*Rte* 66), 494^r-496^v (*Rte* 69), 564^r-566^v (*Rte* 75), 585^r-587^v (*Rte* 77), 597^r-599^v (*Rte* 78). See Table 7, nos. "10," "12," "19," "23," "24," "26," "32," "33."

66. It was in connection with this ratification that minors (persons under 25 years of age) were allotted a guardian (*curador*), see n. 18, above.

67. In the trial record of García de Gortegui (*Rte* 45) we even have an instance in which all the forms have been preserved in incompleted condition. This 19-year-old witch had confessed on 15 June 1611 to the commissioner at Fuenterrabía. By the time that Salazar reached the town, García de Gortegui had moved to France. So a messenger was dispatched to fetch him in order that he could be reconciled. But García de Gortegui told the messenger to return with the message that he was not a witch and had no need of reconciliation (see the entry on the title page of his record, *Volume "F" of Salazar's Visitation Book* f. 295^r). Thus the manuscript and printed forms for his reconciliation were not used, but they were nevertheless bound up with his record, and this gives us clear proof of how much in fact was prepared and written in advance (Idem ff. 298^r-300^v).

68. *Leg* 1683 Exp. 2 f. 431^r (ff. 430^v-434^v, examination of Francisco Ladrón de Peralta, Logroño 9 April 1620, in connection with the previously mentioned inspection of the Tribunal).

69. See below, chap. 11.A.7, and also *Volume "F" of Salazar's Visitation Book* where three witches from Yanci (*Rte* 14, 15, 16) recanted their confessions in the presence of Fray Domingo de Sardo at Lesaca on 8 Aug. 1611, and repeated the revocations a week later to Salazar at Vera.

70. Catalina de Sastrearena's record was on folios 391-411 in the now lost volume "E" of Salazar's visitation book (case no. 335). One might have expected to find long extracts of her confessions in the *Pamplona Manuscript* but strangely enough this is not the case. Becerra and Valle list her as no. 89 in their second list of witches (f. 58^r), and

here we learn for the first time that she came from the village of Arizcun in the neighborhood of Elizondo. But otherwise there is no mention of her. The only reason for her inclusion on the list is that her trial record is referred to four times, "no. 89," see ff. 6ʳ, 7ᵛ, 10ʳ, and 11ʳ (IDOATE *Documento* pp. 57, 60, 64, 67, and 183).

71. *Second Report of Salazar* f. 7ʳ and *Glosses* f. 4ʳ (SD Text 12 § 30 and gloss 50).

72. Idem f. 3ʳ and *Glosses* f. 2ʳ (§ 8 with gloss 18).

73. Idem f. 7ʳ (§ 29).

74. Idem f. 2ᵛ and *Glosses* f. 2ʳ (§ 7 with gloss 14).

75. *Second Report of Salazar* f. 2ᵛ and *Glosses* ff. 1ᵛ-2ʳ (SD Text 12 § 7 with gloss 13).

76. Idem f. 3ʳ and *Glosses* f. 2ʳ (§ 8 with gloss 17).

77. Idem f. 2ʳ and *Glosses* f. 1ʳ⁻ᵛ (§ 2 with gloss 6). Another singular case was 18-year-old Joana de Echegui who differentiated herself from the others in that she declared that she flew to the sabbath in the form of a fly, idem f. 2ʳ and *Glosses* f. 1ʳ (§ 2 with gloss 5).

78. See *Fifth Report of Salazar* f. 13ᵛ (SD Text 15 § 17), where Catalina's trial is cited verbatim.

79. It should be noted that this was written before the discovery of the *Pamplona Manuscript* in the spring of 1971, which confirmed my hypothesis that Catalina came from Arizcun (see n. 70, above, and see also on the finding of the MS, below, chap. 12.5, beginning).

80. The distance between Arizcun and Santesteban is practically double. However, nothing is known as to where the Arizcun witches held their meetings. If Salazar's statement is correct it must have been somewhere midway between the two towns.

81. *Second Report of Salazar* f. 4ʳ⁻ᵛ (SD Text 12 § 16).

82. Idem f. 4ᵛ and *Glosses* f. 3ʳ (§ 16 with gloss 33); as for the four witches see case nos. 311, 314, 331, and 538.

83. *Second Report of Salazar* f. 4ᵛ (SD Text 12 § 16).

84. See DE LANCRE *Tableau* pp. 143-144.

85. *Second Report of Salazar* f. 4ᵛ (SD Text 12 § 16).

86. Idem f. 4ᵛ and *Glosses* f. 3ʳ (§ 16 with gloss 37). Two of the three witches, Joanes de Perlichinecoa ("E 177") and Graciana de Oyeretena ("E 351") had also been present when, as described above, the Devil and some witches burst into the chamber and set fire to Salazar after having bound him to his chair (compare gloss 35 and gloss 33 of *Second Report of Salazar*). We are thus faced with the conclusion that the authors of these confessions, i.e. the witches cited in glosses 33, 35, and 37 (case nos. 311, 314, 327, 331, 335, 538), must have been previously acquainted with each other's stories. On the other hand, this does not prove that they all came from Arizcun. It is perfectly possible that some of them may have met for the first time at Elizondo, and as they might well have waited there for several days before being interrogated, they would have had plenty of time in which to meet and tell each other witch stories.

87. *First Report of Salazar* f. 362ʳ.

88. See *Fourth Report of Salazar* ff. 3ᵛ-4ʳ (SD Text 14 § 16).

89. Idem f. 4ʳ (§ 16) where Salazar quotes from the lost letter from his colleagues at some length.

90. *Lib* 795 f. 159ᵛ (T./C. 15-6-1611; chap. 9 n. 68, above).

91. *Lib* 333 ff. 170ᵛ-171ʳ (C./T. 28-6-1611; chap. 10 n. 70, above).

92. For this recantation, from the peasant Joanes de Arroqui at Zubieta, see below, chap. 11.C.6.

93. There were in fact 81 *revocantes,* but the 81st *revocante*'s trial record was not preserved. It concerned a certain Mari Martín, who is mentioned in the *Second Report of Salazar,* the *Glosses* f. 6ʳ (SD Text 12 gloss 79). A complete list of the 80 extant records is given in the original table of contents to *Volume "F" of Salazar's Visitation Book,* which is reproduced in Caro Baroja's dissertation (CARO BAROJA *De nuevo* pp. 326-328). See also the list of the 81 *revocantes,* case nos. 441-521.

94. *Second Report of Salazar* f. 13ʳ (SD Text 12 § 60). It is not without reason that Salazar attributes so much importance to his own attitude at Santesteban. For although permission to undertake revocations was granted only in the form of an internal communication to the commissioners, it was never officially published. All the same, news of it was of course rumored abroad, though some time passed before it became public knowledge. The trial records in *Volume "F" of Salazar's Visitation Book* clearly illustrate this situation. From the total of 67 *revocantes* from northern Navarra and Fuenterrabía, only 37 recanted while the visitation was taking place in their district, the rest — 31 in all — did not come forward until after Salazar had left. Some sought him out at later sessions. Thus, during the visitation at San Sebastián he was visited by six witches from Zubieta in Navarra. Salazar had himself reconciled five of them at Santesteban (see table 7, nos. "8," "26," "30," "32," and "33"), the sixth (*Rte* 54 = *Rdo* 41) had been reconciled at Logroño. They now came this great distance in order to recant their confessions. Other witches from the mountains of Navarra went to Urdax, Santesteban, and Arano, where the commissioners continued to receive recantations until Christmas.

95. *Letter from Fuenterrabía* f. 1ʳ.

96. Idem f. 1ʳ⁻ᵛ.

97. For the case of Olagüe see *Second Report of Salazar* f. 16ʳ (SD Text 12 § 71).

98. *Letter from Fuenterrabía* f. 2ʳ.

99. Idem f. 2ʳ.

100. As *relapsos* these were normally liable to be condemned to the stake, cf. beginning of chap. 11.A.6, above.

101. *Letter from Fuenterrabía* f. 1ᵛ. Cf. *Second Report of Salazar* ff. 8ʳ, 9ʳ (SD Text 12 §§ 37 and 42), where respectively María de Tanborín's and Catalina Echetoa's confessions after recantation are cited in detail; see also case nos. 223 and 241.

102. *Letter from Fuenterrabía* ff. 1ᵛ-2ʳ.

103. See *Fourth Report of Salazar* f. 5ʳ (SD Text 14 § 24).

104. This information appears in a letter from Becerra and Valle to *la Suprema,* 24 Mar. 1612, see below, chap. 12 n. 2.

105. *Letter from Fuenterrabía* f. 2ʳ⁻ᵛ.

106. Idem ff. 2ᵛ-3ʳ. There is otherwise nothing to indicate that Salazar visited Valcarlos. It is possibly a lapsus for Valderro (see map 4

and chap. 11.A.3, above). Of course, the possibility cannot be excluded that for instance during his stay at Fuenterrabía Salazar made a detour through the Pays de Labourd to Valcarlos, which is easily accessible from that direction. In support of this theory it can be mentioned that after the visitation at Vera Salazar sent the priest and commissioner in that town, Lorenzo de Hualde, to Roncesvalles, which is in the neighborhood of Valcarlos, and later went there himself (regarding this, see below, chap. 11.C.5).

107. *Letter from Fuenterrabía*, f. 2^v.

108. *Lib* 333 ff. 201^v-202^r, Council to Salazar, 12 Sept. 1611.

109. These marginal notes, written by a staff member of *la Suprema*, are in fact the draft of the above-mentioned letter to Salazar. The hand is difficult to identify although it is not likely that of the inquisitor general.

110. *Lib* 333 f. 201^v, Council to Tribunal, 12 Sept. 1611.

111. We have definite information regarding only 11 of the 16 witches in the group of Mar. 1610. Nos. 1, 5, and 6 in table 8 are mentioned in the auto de fe reports; nos. 2 and 7-12 in *Relación de causas 1610/11*; and finally there is mention of no. 3 in a letter from Hualde to the Tribunal of 10 Jan. 1611. In his letter the commissioner of Vera reported that the death of the witch Juanes de Aguirre Luberriseme in the secret prison of the Tribunal was rumored throughout the whole countryside (see HENNINGSEN *Papers of Salazar* p. 91). But we have no direct information regarding the last five witches, although there is a considerable amount of indirect information which enables us to ascertain with a fair amount of certainty who they may have been. Firstly, it is clear from the Tribunal's letter of 13 Feb. 1610 that the prisoners came from Vera, Lesaca, Yanci, Echalar, and Rentería, and not from other towns (see near end of chap. 7.6, above). Secondly, this same letter states that the group consisted of 12 women and 4 men — in other words we are missing information about one man and four women (see near beginning of chap. 8, above). Thirdly, the *Accounts of 27 Sept. 1614* contain a complete list of all the witches who received food rations in the prison of the Tribunal during the period from 1609 through 1613, where board, as mentioned earlier, was charged at a rate of one *real* a day. Now, if we first take all men prisoners with total food rations of over 100 *reales* and exclude all names previously known to us, we obtain the following possibilities (the figures in parentheses represent food costs in *reales*): *Food Accounts* nos. 7, Juan Pérez de Ibarburu (362); 41, Pedro de Samatelu (188); 53, Pedro de Andrade (976); and 87, Pedro Ortiz de Manco (124). Regarding the unknown fourth man who died in prison we know from another quarter that he was still alive after 5 Oct. 1611 (see p. 275, above). This corresponds to over 19 months' imprisonment, which would mean at least 570 *reales* in food charges. Out of those mentioned above Pedro de Andrade is the one who fulfills the conditions most satisfactorily. We can use the same method in order to identify the four unknown women. If we take all women prisoners with food charges of over 100 *reales*, excluding all previously known names, the following nine possibilities emerge: *Food Accounts* nos. 37, Catalina de

Antoco (294); 39, María de Guyarte (111); 40, Magdalena de Yparra-
guerri (189); 44, Margarita de Casanova (193); 45, Catalina de Ydiarzabal, and 46, Magdalena de Arander (777 together); 55, Magdalena
de Argareta (395); 62, María de Arayoz (280); and 65, María Semper
(136). None of these appear in *Relación de causas 1610/11*, which means
that they died in prison without having made a confession. By combining this result with other source material we are enabled to isolate
five possibilities with a reasonable degree of certainty. Thus Magdalena de Arander is only at first sight unknown to us, for by means of
a letter dated 9 Feb. 1611 from Rentería to the Tribunal (*Leg* 1679 Exp.
2.1 No. 1[b]) she may be identified as Magdalena de Agramonte (see
table 8 no. 12), who according to *Relación de causas 1610/11* was one of
the group of Mar. 1610. Since her food charges are assessed together
with those of her mother, Catalina de Ydiarzabal, the latter was
presumably imprisoned at the same time. Catalina de Topalda was a
prominent witch at Echalar who had already been reported during
Valle's visitation in 1609 (see chap. 7.6, above). According to a statement in the Tribunal's letter of 14 Feb. 1611 (chap. 7 n. 68, above) she
was imprisoned at the same time as María Endara (table 8 no. 11).
Margarita de Casanova and Catalina de Antoco were dangerous
witches in Lesaca who were thus reported during Valle's visitation,
see *Volume "F" of Salazar's Visitation Book* ff. 114ʳ, 116ᵛ (*Rte* 17), 149ᵛ (*Rte*
22), 157ᵛ (*Rte* 23), 165ᵛ (*Rte* 24). Magdalena de Argareta (or Argarate)
was the most notorious witch in Yanci at the beginning of 1610, see
Volume "F" of Salazar's Visitation Book ff. 84ʳ (*Rte* 14), 94ʳ (*Rte* 15) and
100ʳ (*Rte* 16). The account does not work out accurately — it contains
one too many (table 8 nos. 16 or 16a) — but without further source
material I think we are obliged to leave the matter here.

112. Her arrest, which took place some time in Nov. 1610, came
about owing to the numerous witnesses and complaints made
against her in Oronoz. The preliminary hearings were held at the end
of Nov. and beginning of Dec. 1610 (*Relación de causas 1610/11* f. 456ᵛ,
Rdo 52).

113. See idem ff. 455ᵛ-456ᵛ. The same source reveals that some of
the witches had already been interrogated as early as the spring of
1610, but that most of their cases were not taken up until the autumn,
after the auto de fe was over. However, they all continued to deny the
charges right up to the spring of 1611, when they were informed of the
Edict of Grace.

114. *Lib* 795 f. 161ʳ (f. 161ʳ⁻ᵛ, Tribunal to Council, 9 July 1611(a);
received in Madrid 21 July). On the same occasion (f. 161ᵛ) the inquisitors wrote that they were still holding seven (corrected from
eight in the manuscript) witches, who had not yet confessed. Compare this with point 3 of the memorandum of the *fiscal*, below, chap.
11.B.4 and n. 127.

115. *Relación de causas 1610/11* f. 456ᵛ-457ʳ (*Rdo* 57).

116. See *Lib* 795 f. 164ᵛ (ff. 164ʳ-165ʳ, Memorandum of the *fiscal* San
Vicente, 9 July 1611; received in Madrid 21 July, hereafter cited as *San
Vicente's Memorandum of 9 July 1611*) where María de Endara is referred
to as "the rich widow from Echalar with the ten thousand gold
ducats."

117. *Relación de causas 1610/11* f. 456ᵛ (*Rdo* 52); the copy of María de Endara's confession of 4 July 1611 in the *Pamplona Manuscript* ff. 61ʳ-65ʳ (IDOATE *Documento* pp. 188-193). It is true that the first of these two sources states that the confession took place on 4 Aug. and the reconciliation on "15 [Aug.]." But as it is obvious that 4 Aug. is a lapsus for 4 July, it must surely be correct to read the date of the reconciliation as 15 July.

118. An original death certificate in the hand of Martín de Yrisarri is enclosed with the papers relating to the inspection of the Tribunal in 1619-20 (*Leg* 1683 Exp. 1 f. 1072ʳ).

119. *Lib* 795 f. 208ʳ (ff. 208ʳ-209ᵛ, Memorandum of the *fiscal* San Vicente, 3 Oct. 1611; received in Madrid 15 Oct., hereafter cited as *San Vicente's Memorandum of 3 Oct. 1611*).

120. *Leg* 1683 Exp. 1 f. 806ʳ (ff. 806ʳ-808ᵛ, Valle to [Commissioner of Salvatierra] 24 July [1614]). This courageous man was *el licenciado* Domingo Ruiz de Luzuriaga, who was renowned for his learning and who had previously been attached to the University of Alcalá (*persona grave y docto que fue colegial mayor en Alcalá*), *First Report of Salazar* f. 365ʳ § 41.

121. *San Vicente's Memorandum of 3 Oct. 1611* f. 208ʳ.

122. *Leg* 1679 Exp. 2.1 No. 17 f. 1ʳ (ff. 1ʳ⁻ᵛ, Tribunal to Council, 9 July 1611(d); received in Madrid 21 July).

123. Idem f. 1ʳ⁻ᵛ. See *Pamplona Manuscript* f. 15ʳ⁻ᵛ (IDOATE *Documento* pp. 78-79), which gives extracts from the statements of the seven persons and other testimony regarding witch sabbaths in Logroño. A long extract from the Tribunal's letter is in CARO BAROJA *De nuevo* pp. 295-296.

124. *Lib* 333 f. 179ʳ, Council to Tribunal, 23 July 1611(c).

125. See *Relación de causas 1610/11* f. 457ʳ (*Rdo* 63), where the statement that he confessed on "18 [August]," must be a lapsus for 18 June. The date of reconciliation should therefore be read as 19 June and not 19 August. I consider it extremely unlikely that the Tribunal would have kept him in prison for two months after he had made confession.

126. Idem f. 457ʳ (*Rdo* 64).

127. It should be noted, however, that San Vicente miscalculated in the case of the three who appeared at the auto de fe, of whom only one had died (see table 8 nos. 1, 5, 6).

128. *San Vicente's Memorandum of 9 July 1611* ff. 164ʳ-165ʳ.

129. *Lib* 795 f. 163ʳ, Tribunal to Council, 9 July 1611 (c); received in Madrid 21 July.

130. *San Vicente's Memorandum of 9 July 1611* ff. 164ᵛ-165ʳ. As the end of the quotation is translated somewhat freely, I append the text of the original, *Fol. 165ʳ*: "aunque no se pueden negar muchos embelecos y engaños del Demonio que puede haber en materia de complices."

131. We may safely assume that *la Suprema's* letter had reached Logroño by this time. If this had not been the case the Tribunal would not have been able to inform Salazar on his visitation of the permission to receive revocations. It will be recalled that Salazar made use of this permission as early as 14 July (see above, chap. 11.A.6).

132. See *Lib* 333 f. 178ʳ⁻ᵛ, Council to Tribunal, 23 July 1611(b). This

letter considers points 1, 2, and 4 of the *fiscal*'s memorandum. For the sake of accuracy the Council also complied with point 4, but the idea of ratifying the confessions of the oldest witches never seems to have been acted upon.

133. *Lib* 333 f. 179ᵛ, Council to Tribunal, 23 July 1611(a).

134. *Relación de causas 1610/11* f. 457ʳ (*Rdo* 65); *Leg* 1675 Exp. 2.1 No. 19 f. 1ʳ (ff. 1ʳ-2ʳ, Tribunal to Council, 12 Aug. 1611; received in Madrid 23 Aug.). The letter is given further consideration by Julio Caro Baroja with, however, uncertainty as to the date, which he gives in one place as 12 Aug. and in another as 17 Aug. (CARO BAROJA *De nuevo*, pp. 296, 324).

135. See *Lib* 795 f. 205ᵛ (T./C. 5-10-1611; chap. 10 n. 44, above).

136. We do not know how many journeys Pedro Ruiz made. One of them would seem to have covered the period from June until the beginning of July (see the dates of the hearings in n. 156, below). On 14 July he seems to have been back in Logroño with an old witch from Amézaga, who on this date repeated a confession she had made to Pedro Ruiz a week before in her home town, see *Relación de causas 1610/11* f. 457ʳ (*Rdo* 66).

137. *Relación de causas 1610/11* f. 457ᵛ (*Rdo* 67).

138. *Leg* 1679 Exp. 2.1 No. 19 ff. 1ʳ-2ʳ (T./C. 12-8-1611; n. 134, above). The names of the two priests in the Borunda Valley are not stated, but they were probably a 76-year-old priest and commissioner in Bacaicoa, Juan Martínez de Larraiza (see below, chap. 11.C.5), and the priest at Alsasua, Miguel de Arramendía, an old friend Salazar had taken with him on his journey of visitation to serve as inquisitorial notary, see table 7 and *Fourth Report of Salazar* f. 8ᵛ (SD Text 14 § 38).

139. *Leg* 1679 Exp. 2.1 No. 19 f. 2ʳ (T./C. 12-8-1611; n. 134, above).

140. *Lib* 333 ff. 189ᵛ-190ʳ, Council to Tribunal, 23 Aug. 1611.

141. We possess previous knowledge of this priest through an application in 1608 for the vacant post of inquisitorial notary at Santa Cruz de Campezo (*Lib* 794 f. 32ʳ⁻ᵛ). The appointment does not seem to have been confirmed before some time in the course of 1609 (see *Leg* 1683 Exp. 1 f. 1456ᵛ).

142. *Volume "F" of Salazar's Visitation Book* ff. 322ʳ-323ʳ (*Rte* 48).

143. Both at Zugarramurdi, where the seeds of the persecution had been sown locally, and in the mountains of Navarra and in Guipúzcoa, where the campaign had to a great extent been the work of the Tribunal, the witch-hunt had been enthusiastically supported by the populace. In Alava the sole motive for the witch-hunt seems to have been the immediate need of the Tribunal for fresh evidence to support its position in Madrid and towards Salazar. The persecution was carried out by the special emissaries of the Tribunal assisted by some of the local commissioners. Although hitherto unknown methods were applied the results were negligible. In the process the agents of the Inquisition made themselves exceedingly unpopular with the people. For the total score of the witch-hunt in Alava see the table in n. 156, below.

144. *Leg* 1683 Exp. 1 f. 76ʳ. The information is stated to have been taken from the Tribunal's *Libro de ausencia* (i.e. "register of absence").

145. The dates of the publication of the two edicts are unknown, but we can calculate them reasonably accurately. In Salazar's letter to the Tribunal of 28 Sept. 1611 (see n. 146, below) he states that the Anathema was published during the week after San Vicente's departure. Since the publication had to be made on a holiday, the date would presumably have been Sunday 25 Sept. The Edict of Faith was normally read on the preceding Sunday: in this case 18 Sept. This agrees satisfactorily with the publication of the Edict of Grace, which judging from another source took place on 11 Sept. (see n. 173, below), that is to say, the Sunday before the Edict of Faith. Regarding the Dominican monk who preached at the publication of the Edict of Faith, see *Second Report of Salazar* f. 15ʳ (SD Text 12 § 67).

146. *Lib* 795 f. 203ʳ⁻ᵛ, Salazar to Tribunal, San Sebastián, 28 Sept. 1611; received at Logroño 6 Oct.

147. Cf. pp. 251, above, and 277, below.

148. See the quotation in chap. 12.1, below, where in a letter dated 3 Feb. 1612 Becerra says that he has been in bed "for seven months." This takes us back to July. We cannot exclude the possibility that the cause of Becerra's illness was the sharply reprimanding letter from *La Suprema* which had arrived just at this time.

149. *San Vicente's Memorandum of 3 Oct. 1611* ff. 208ʳ-209ʳ.

150. Idem f. 209ʳ⁻ᵛ.

151. Endorsement idem f. 209ᵛ.

152. *Lib* 795 ff. 204ʳ-207ʳ w)t.-c. 5-10-1611; chap. 10 n. 44, above).

153. Idem ff. 204ᵛ-205ʳ.

154. Idem f. 205ʳ.

155. Idem f. 205ʳ. It seems reasonable to identify the shepherd as Pedro de Andrade (table 8 no. 4). We cannot in fact discover how long he spent in the secret prison of the Inquisition. There is little possibility of identifying the woman *negativa* (see table 8 and n. 111, above).

156. Idem f. 205ʳ. The other information available proves on comparison to reveal a similar total of witches. However, what is particularly interesting in the inquisitors' letter of 5 Oct. 1611 is that it gives the exact figures for the result of the summer's witch-hunt. This in turn leads us to the conclusion that the 17 witches mentioned in the inquisitors' letter must on balance be identical with those mentioned in *Relación de causas 1610/11 (Rdo)*, *Volume "F" of Salazar's Visitation Book (Rte)*, and other sources. However, nos. 1-12 in the table cannot be definitely identified with the 12 who were reconciled at Logroño. Thus it is doubtful whether the Tribunal included no. 1 (who had been reconciled even before the publication of the edict) and no. 8 (who had been arrested by a judge at Miranda de Ebro). As for those five who had confessed but who had not yet reached Logroño, four can be identified with certainty because their trial records are extant (see nos. 13-16 in the table). As for no. 17, it is doubtful whether she was included in the inquisitors' reckoning (see n. 182, below).

157. In the *fiscal's* memorandum it is stated that 20 priests were under suspicion, but that only one (i.e. Diego de Basurto) had confessed. We can identify the two *aquelarres* with certainty as those discovered by the inquisitorial commissioners at Eguino and Maestu

respectively (see map 7 and table 9). The 300 suspects mentioned in clause 1 of San Vicente's document (near beginning of chap. 11.B.7, above) must almost certainly refer to these two *aquelarres* in eastern Alava. If we look at the table in n. 156, the figures almost tally. Nine of the witches are from the Maestu district (nos. 4-7, 10-12, 15, 16). Six are from the surrounding district of Eguino (nos. 1-3, 13-14, and 17). The Tribunal's statement listed seven confessions from Eguino, so our list is incomplete on this point. Only two of the witches on the list came from elsewhere (nos. 8 and 9).

158. *Lib* 795 ff. 205ᵛ-206ʳ (T./C. 5-10-1611; chap. 10 n. 44, above).
159. Idem ff. 206ʳ-207ʳ.

Chapter 11, note 156

No.	Name, age, domicile	Confession	Inquisitorial commissioner	Reconciled at Logroño	References
1.	Juan Díaz de Alda, 80, Arraya	25 March	Pedro Ruiz, Eguino	21 April	*Rdo* 65
2.	María de Eguilaz, 71, Amézaga	8 July	ʺ	15 July	*Rdo* 66
3.	Diego de Basurto, 95, Ciordia	28 June	ʺ	3 Sept.	*Rdo* 67, *Rte* 58
4.	Francisca de Bertol, 32, Arenaza	21 June	[Felipe Díaz, Maestu]	23 June	*Rdo* 68
5.	Gracia Gonzáles, 26, Cicujano		[ʺ]	21 July	*Rdo* 69, *Rte* 61
6.	Inés de Corres, 66, Corres		[ʺ]	19 Aug.	*Rdo* 70
7.	Ana de Corres, 56, Maestu		[ʺ]	18 Aug.	*Rdo* 71, *Rte* 57
8.	Catalina de Pajares, 50, Miranda de Ebro (Burgos province)	26 May		4 June	*Rdo* 73

160. Idem f. 207ʳ. This was, however, not completely correct (see chap. 11.A.6, above, near beginning).

Excursus. Shortly afterwards Valle submitted the Tribunal's annual report of completed cases, the *Relación de causas 1610/11* we have so frequently cited. It consisted of a total of 76 cases, the great majority of which were witch cases. Nos. 15-76 comprised the list of the 62 "Witches reconciled and absolved by the Edict of Grace" (see case nos. 32-96). The first witch had been reconciled on 22 Nov. 1610 (*Rdo* 53, Diego de Marticorena, see chap. 7.6, above); the last on 19 Aug. 1611 (*Rdo* 70, Inés de Corres; n. 156, no. 6 in the table). Thus the statement in Valle's accompanying letter that the period covered from

				30 June	
9.	María de Otazu, 16, La Bastida (southern Alava)	28 June			*Rdo* 74
10.	María González, 40, Corres		[Felipe Díaz, Maestu]		*Rdo* 76a
11.	María Pérez (alias Mariquita de Atauri), 65, Atauri		Felipe Díaz, Maestu		*Rdo* 76b
12.	Magdalena de Arza, 56, Cicujano		['']		*Rdo* 76c, *Rte* 60
13.	Catalina Fernández, 80, Arraya	25 June	Pedro Ruiz, Eguino		*Rte* 46
14.	Ana Sáenz, 70, Ilarduya	28 June	''		*Rte* 47
15.	Magdalena de Elorza, 50, Atauri	20 Sept.	Felipe Díaz, Maestu		*Rte* 48
16.	María de Ulíbarri, 36, Corres	9 Sept.	Martín Pérez, Campezo		See chap. 11.C.4
17.	María de Eguino, 11, Eguino		[Pedro Ruiz, Eguino]		*Rdo* 72

20 July 1610 to 20 July 1611 (*Lib* 795 f. 202ʳ, Tribunal to Council, 15 Oct. 1611; received in Madrid 28 Oct.), was not quite accurate. Twenty-six of the witches had been reconciled during the period following the publication of the Edict of Grace on 29 May 1611, but eight of these had remained in the Tribunal prison for a further period (see table 8, above). After the *Relación de causas 1610/11* had been submitted, three more witches were reconciled by the Tribunal at Logroño. I have supplied them with *Rdo* numbers as with the other witches for the sake of convenience, but their names are found only in the *Pamplona Manuscript* list of witches reconciled by the Tribunal (see IDOATE *Documento* p. 180 nos. 76, 77, 83, numbered respectively by me *Rdo* 76a, 76b, and 76c, see table in n. 156, above).

161. *Lib* 333 f. 213ᵛ, Council to Tribunal, 25 Oct. 1611.

162. *Leg* 1679 Exp. 2.1 No. 16 f. 1ʳ-2ʳ, Tribunal to Council, 15 Nov. 1611. In a way it is strange that the Tribunal made no mention of Juanes de Goiburu and Juanes de Sansín. It is true that they were not detained in the penitentiary, but their cases completely paralleled those of the two women and it would therefore have seemed natural for them to have benefited from the Edict of Grace. But in fact the two men, as well as the priest and the monk, were to serve the sentence imposed on them at the auto de fe for another two years, before they were at length released (see chaps. 12.3 and 13.7, below),

163. *Lib* 333 f. 241ʳ⁻ᵛ, Council to Tribunal, 29 Nov. 1611.

164. *First Report of Salazar* f. 357ʳ (SD Text 11).

165. *Volume "F" of Salazar's Visitation Book* ff. 295ʳ (12 Sept.), 210ᵛ (16 Sept.), 197ʳ (20 Sept.), 234ᵛ (23 Sept.), 235ʳ (24 Sept.), 545ʳ (1 Oct.), 534ᵛ (8 Oct.); see respectively case nos. 485, 471, 469, 475, 513, and 512.

166. Idem f. 291ʳ (*Rte* 44); see case no. 484.

167. Idem f. 378ʳ (*Rte* 58); see case no. 498.

168. Idem ff. 307ᵛ (*Rte* 46), 318ᵛ (*Rte* 47); see case nos. 486, 487.

169. Idem ff. 323ʳ (*Rte* 48), 330ʳ (*Rte* 49), 347ʳ (*Rte* 57), 384ʳ (*Rte* 59), 388ʳ (*Rte* 60); see case nos. 488, 489, 497, 499, and 500.

170. *Second Report of Salazar* ff. 4ᵛ, 9ʳ (SD Text 12 §§ 16, 43).

171. Note that we have an interrogation date of 12 Sept. (see n. 165, above) and compare this with the calculations in n. 145, above.

172. We know that while he was at Azpeitia Salazar received two letters; one was from Fray León de Araníbar, dated Elizondo 30 Oct. 1611 (*Leg* 1679 Exp. 2.1 No. 30, with the old signature "FF"); the other was from the bishop of Bayonne in France, dated Bayonne 5 Nov. 1611 (*Leg* 1679 Exp. 2.1 No. 5).

173. See *Volume "F" of Salazar's Visitation Book* f. 279ᵛ (*Rte* 42), where 16-year-old María Gómez of San Sebastián refers to the Edict of Grace in her confession of 15 Sept. This proves that the Edict of Grace must already have been in force in San Sebastián on this day, which was a Thursday. Therefore the publication cannot have taken place on any other day but Sunday 11 Sept. 1611.

174. *Lib* 795 f. 203ʳ (Salazar/T. 28-9-1611; n. 146, above).

175. Idem f. 203ʳ.

176. Idem f. 203ʳ⁻ᵛ. The witch that Salazar reconciled was 40-year-old Bárbara de Yradi (see IDOATE *Documento* p. 184 no. 98). One of the

other imprisoned witches from San Sebastián was called María Lucea, see *Volume "F" of Salazar's Visitation Book* f. 278ʳ.

177. *Volume "F" of Salazar's Visitation Book* ff. 193ʳ-197ᵛ and 205ʳ-211ᵛ (*Rte* 29, María de Azaldegui, and *Rte* 31, Sabadina de Echetoa, respectively, both aged 17 and both from Fuenterrabía).

178. Idem ff. 197ʳ⁻ᵛ, 211ʳ⁻ᵛ.

179. Idem ff. 197ᵛ, 211ᵛ.

180. These two girls had been examined previously by Salazar at Fuenterrabía where he had summoned them for reconciliation, on 23 and 25 Aug. respectively. But during the ratification of their witch confessions they had broken down and admitted that it was all lies (idem ff. 196ᵛ and 210ʳ⁻ᵛ, respectively) and they were consequently not reconciled. It will be recalled, however, that the hearings took place in secret, so if the story of the four women on the mountainside is true, this means that the girls must have been double-dealing, and outwardly giving the impression that they had been reconciled on an equal footing with the other *confitente* witches at Fuenterrabía.

181. *Volume "F" of Salazar's Visitation Book* ff. 287ʳ-291ᵛ (*Rte* 44).

182. *Volume "F" of Salazar's Visitation Book* ff. 304ʳ-308ʳ (*Rte* 46, Catalina Fernández de Lecea), 314ʳ-319ʳ (*Rte* 47, Ana Sáenz de Ylarduya), 321ʳ-325ʳ (*Rte* 48, Magdalena de Elorza), 327ʳ-330ᵛ (*Rte* 49, Agueda de Murúa), 333ʳ-336ᵛ (*Rte* 50, Ana de Arriola), 373ʳ-375ʳ (*Rte* 57, Ana de Corres), 377ʳ-380ʳ (*Rte* 58, Diego de Basurto), 383ʳ-384ᵛ (*Rte* 59, María de Corres), 387ʳ-389ʳ (*Rte* 60, Magdalena de Arza), 391ʳ-393ʳ (*Rte* 61, Gracia González). All these names recur in the table relating to the witch-hunt at Alava (n. 156, above), except for *Rte* 49 and *Rte* 50, who confessed after 5 Oct. 1611 (see case nos. 489, 490), and *Rte* 59, 12-year-old María de Corres from the village of Corres. This young girl told Salazar that she had been in Logroño with her mother, María González (*Rdo* 76a), but strangely enough she is not to be found on the list of reconciled witches. She may possibly be identical with *Rdo* 72, María de Eguino (no. 17 in table in n. 156), or with 12-year-old María Ibáñez from Cicujano, who is mentioned both in the *Pamplona Manuscript* (IDOATE *Documento* p. 180 no. 84) and in an alphabetical list of the 84 witch trials, which was completed at the Logroño Tribunal (*Leg* 1679 Exp. 2.1 No. 21 [b], an undated leaf without pagination (inserted in *Second Report of Salazar*), hereafter cited as *Abecedario*).

183. See chap. 11.C.4, below.

184. See Part 3 of our Witch List, simultaneously being a reconstruction of the lost volumes of Salazar's visitation book. Volumes "B"-"D" of the visitation book seem to have contained only the records of persons who had made a confession of witchcraft *before* the publication of the Edict of Grace. On the contrary Volume "E" seems to have contained a new series of *reconciliados,* consisting of witches who had not confessed until after the publication of the edict. If we then study the last records in our reconstruction of this volume we find that all the witches are from towns in eastern Guipúzcoa (Urnieta, San Sebastián, and Rentería), or western Navarra, which Salazar visited on the last lap of the journey (Saldías), or finally Alava (Corres, Arroyabe). The *Pamplona Manuscript* agrees with these facts

on f. 58^r, which refers to a large number of records in Volume "E" (IDOATE *Documento* p. 184 nos. 97-103).

185. See *First Report of Salazar* f. 357^v (SD Text 11 § 2) and cf. his comments on the commissioners, chap. 11.C.5, below.

186. *Volume "F" of Salazar's Visitation Book* ff. 378^r-379^r, the revocation of Diego de Basurto (*Rte* 58) at Alsasua, 18 Nov. 1611. After Salazar had arrived at Vitoria he received a letter from the inquisitorial commissioner at Salvatierra stating that Basurto had presented himself at Salvatierra and had there again repeated his previous confession. But Salazar sent a prompt reply to the commissioner telling him to proceed no further with this case for the time being (Idem f. 380^r, Domingo Ruiz de Luzuriaga to Salazar, Salvatierra, 6 Dec. 1611; received at Vitoria 6 Dec.).

187. Idem ff. 307^v-308^r (revocation of *Rte* 46).

188. Idem ff. 318^v-319^r (revocation of *Rte* 47).

189. Idem ff. 305^r-307^r, 315^r-318^r (confessions of *Rte* 46 and *Rte* 47, respectively).

190. See immediately below in this section, which shows that Salazar was still staying at Salvatierra on 27 Nov.

191. *Volume "F" of Salazar's Visitation Book* ff. 330^{r-v} (revocation of Agueda de Murúa (*Rte* 49), 14 years old), ff. 336^{r-v} (revocation of Ana de Arriola (*Rte* 50), 13 years old).

192. Idem ff. 322^r-323^r (Confession of *Rte* 48, 20 Sept. 1611 at Maestu), 323^r-325^r (recantations and new confessions of *Rte* 48, 29 and 30 Nov. at Vitoria). During the hearings at Vitoria, Magdalena de Elorza constantly vacillated between denial and confession. She admitted to being a witch four times, but finally stated that she definitely was not one.

193. Fray Pedro Ladrón's signature is appended to the hearings of several witches, see *Volume "F" of Salazar's Visitation Book* ff. 323^r (*Rte* 48), 328^v (*Rte* 49), 335^r (*Rte* 50), and he is mentioned in several other places, once as Fray Juan Ladrón (f. 330^r), obviously in error.

194. The five witches were *Rte* 57, Ana de Corres, 55, Maestu; *Rte* 59, María de Corres, 12, Corres; *Rte* 60, Magdalena de Arza, 60, Cicujano; *Rte* 61, Gracia González, 24, Cicujano (all in *Volume "F" of Salazar's Visitation Book*); and *Rdo* 76a, María González, 40, Corres (n. 156 above, no. 10 in the table). The latter was the mother of 12-year-old María de Corres (*Rte* 59) and is mentioned in a marginal note to the latter's trial record. This states that the mother was summoned, but that in contrast to her daughter and the other women she stood fast by the confession she had made at Logroño (*Volume "F" of Salazar's Visitation Book* f. 384^r).

195. Idem ff. 392^{r-v} (revocation of *Rte* 61).

196. Idem ff. 374^r-375^r (revocation of *Rte* 57).

197. *Lib* 333 ff. 241^v-242^r, Council to Salazar, 10 Dec. 1611, *but read*: 13 Dec. 1611 (a). In this, reference is made to a letter from Salazar, since lost, dated Vitoria 4 Dec. 1611. The letter from *la Suprema* states further that Salazar had appointed "Sunday the fourth day of this month" for the publication of the Edict of Faith, but this must be a lapsus for Sunday the third, because in 1611 the fourth of December

was a Monday. Regarding the dating of *la Suprema*'s letter as 13 Dec. 1611, see below, n. 198.

198. In *la Suprema*'s letter-book, n. 197, above, the letter is dated "10 Dec. 1611," but the correct date is more likely to have been 13 Dec. 1611. Firstly, Salazar refers to *la Suprema*'s letter under this date in his reply of 28 Dec. (see n. 199, below). Secondly, on 13 Dec. *la Suprema* wrote regarding the case to the Logroño Tribunal, and this would presumably have been on the same day, *Lib* 333 f. 245^r, Council to Tribunal, 13 Dec. 1611 (b). In this last-mentioned letter the Tribunal at Logroño was instructed to discover whether there was a precedent for the inquisitors in this district to preside under a canopy on their journeys of visitation. These investigations were carried out as slowly and meticulously as usual and two years later the Tribunal replied that a certain tradition did in fact exist for the inquisitors to use a canopy on their visitations (*Lib* 795 f. 487^r, Tribunal to Council, 23 Mar. 1613).

199. Cf. *Lib* 795 f. 224^r, Salazar to Council, Vitoria 28 Dec. 1611.

200. *Leg* 1679 Exp. 2.1 No. 41 ff. 671^r-683^v, *title page*: "Corres. 1611 [/] no. 289 Bruxa-gracia [/] Maria de Vlibarri. R[econcilia]da de hedad de 36 años. [Bottom of page]: 63," hereafter *Trial record of María de Ulibarri*. Both the foliation and various other sources combine to show that this record is in fact a fragment of the since lost Volume "E" of Salazar's Visitation Book. On this, see case nos. 291-355, particularly no. 354.

201. *Second Report of Salazar* f. 13^v (SD Text 12 § 61).

202. *Trial record of María de Ulibarri* ff. 672-676^r. Judging from the trial record, this commissioner seems to have been much more honest than the other inquisitorial agents in this area, for he reports the hearing in full; and, as it seems, in contrast to all other agents of the district of Logroño itself, he followed the instructions of the Inquisition to the letter and was careful to see that his notary took down all the questions together with the answers. In practically all the other hearings the questions put to the witches were omitted in the records. It is presumably also owing to the honesty of this commissioner that María de Ulibarri's list of accomplices, in contrast to all the other witchcraft confessions from the Alava district, includes no priests.

203. Idem f. 676^r.

204. Idem ff. 680^v-681^r. In her confession to Salazar, María went on to state that her mother had confided to her that she had witnessed against her in Logroño as well, but the truth was that she had never seen her at the witches' gatherings. Neither had María herself noticed her mother at the meetings at any time during the three years she had been a witch (Idem f. 681^r).

205. Idem ff. 678^v-680^r.

206. *First Report of Salazar* f. 362^r § 23.

207. Idem f. 363^r § 26.

208. Idem f. 362^{r-v} § 24.

209. Idem f. 362^v-363^r § 25. Note that *The Bishop's Report* ff. 1^r-2^r (SD Text 8 §§ 1-2) gives identical information regarding Hualde and the Lord of Urtubie (cited in chap. 7.6, above), and this might indicate

that Salazar's source was the bishop of Pamplona. For the Lord of Urtubie see also above, chap. 1.7.

210. *First Report of Salazar* ff. 363^{r-v} §§ 27-28.

211. Idem f. 363^v (§ 29). The names of the two familiars appear in *Volume "F" of Salazar's Visitation Book*, where they are shown to have participated in several witch-hearings at Fuenterrabía, and where their signatures appear. One of them, Pedro de Zuloaga, titles himself notary (see f. 189^r *et passim*).

212. See *First Report of Salazar* ff. 363^v-365^r §§ 30-40, consisting of a description of a succession of commissioners from Irún, Rentería, San Sebastián, Azpeitia, Orio, Guetaria, Deva, Motrico, Aibar ("Eybar"), Vergara, and Oñate.

213. See idem ff. 365^r, 365^v-366^r, where §§ 41 and 43 mention the commissioners in Salvatierra and Vitoria respectively.

214. Idem f. 361^v (§ 21).

215. Idem f. 365^{r-v} (§ 42).

216. Idem f. 366^r (§ 44).

217. See *Second Report of Salazar* f. 2^r (SD Text 12 § 4). Regarding the list of the fourteen questions, see above, chap. 4.4.

218. *Leg* 1679 Exp. 2.1 No. 30[i] f. 1^r. Salazar furnished this list of eight questions with the signature "HH" and with a note stating that these and other questions had been used in each occasion in the visitation book where the word *"Actos"* was found (see e.g. quotation in chap. 11.A.4, above). See also the text of *Instructions of 25 Mar. 1611* f. 146^{r-v} (SD Text 6 § 13).

219. *Leg* 1679 Exp. 2.1 No. 29[e] f. 17^r (ff. 17^r-20^v, *title*: "Relación y epílogo de lo que ha resultado de la visita que hizo el Santo Oficio en las montañas del Reyno de Navarra y otras partes con el Edicto de Gracia concedido a los que hubiesen incurrido en la secta de brujos, conforme a las relaciones y papeles que de todo ello se han remitido al Consejo," hereafter cited as *Sixth Report of Salazar* (to be published as SD Text 16). This report has been previously published by Julio Caro Baroja from another manuscript which is lodged in the Biblioteca Nacional (Madrid), MS 2031 ff. 129^r-132^v, see the Preface and chap. 1 n. 99, above. The two copies are identical except for the last section which is missing in the Biblioteca Nacional manuscript, see HEN-NINGSEN *Papers of Salazar* p. 102 n. 2). See also *Second Report of Salazar* ff. 9^v-10^r (SD Text 12 § 49).

220. This would seem to be indicated from the references to the investigation of the *aquelarres* in volume "A" of Salazar's lost visitation book, see *Second Report of Salazar*, the *Glosses* ff. 3^v, 4^v glosses "+", 60, and 69 (SD Text 12); and compare case nos. 150dd-150ff.

221. *Second Report of Salazar* ff. 9^v-10^r (SD Text 12 § 49); see *Sixth Report of Salazar* f. 17^r (SD Text 16).

222. *Second Report of Salazar*, the *Glosses* f. 4^v (SD Text 12 gloss 62).

223. *Volume "F" of Salazar's Visitation Book* ff. 404^r-405^v (*Rte* 62).

224. *Second Report of Salazar* ff. 10^{r-v} (SD Text 12 § 50), see *Sixth Report of Salazar* f. 17^r (SD Text 16).

225. *The Letter from Fuenterrabía* f. 2^v. See *Volume "F" of Salazar's Visitation Book* ff. 34^r-35^r (*Rte* 6) and 182^{r-v} (*Rte* 27), where two sisters

from Oronoz in the Baztán Valley admitted to Salazar that the witch salves they had handed over to the authorities in their district were faked.

226. *Volume "F" of Salazar's Visitation Book* ff. 485ᵛ-486ʳ (*Rte* 68) and 487ʳ⁻ᵛ (*Rte* 69).

227. Idem f. 521ᵛ (*Rte* 71).

228. Idem ff. 568ʳ⁻ᵛ (*Rte* 75) and 588ᵛ-589ʳ (*Rte* 77), mother's and daughter's statements respectively.

229. Idem ff. 388ᵛ (*Rte* 60) and 392ᵛ-393ʳ (*Rte* 61).

230. See *Second Report of Salazar* chap. III "Of the *actos positivos* or external proofs which we have endeavored to substantiate," where each of the 27 clauses of the chapter is devoted to one of these instances (SD Text 12 §§ 25-51).

231. Idem f. 7ᵛ (§ 33).

232. Idem f. 7ᵛ (§ 32).

233. Idem f. 9ᵛ (§ 48).

234. Idem f. 1ʳ (Introduction).

235. *First Report of Salazar* f. 357ᵛ (SD Text 11 § 2).

236. Idem f. 358ᵛ (§ 7). A Spanish translation of the papal bull against white witches and astrologists was printed in Francisco TOR-REBLANCA VILLAPANDO *Epitome delictorum sive de magia in qva aperta vel occvlta invocatio daemonis intervenit* (Sevilla 1618) 2 ed. Lyon 1678 pp. 536-541. Henry Charles Lea is of the opinion that the Spanish Inquisition withheld the bull until 1612, when a vernacular version was published (LEA *Inquisition of Spain*, IV pp. 189-190). However, Salazar's mention indicates that the papal bull must have been published earlier, or he would not have referred to it as being well-known in 1611.

237. *First Report of Salazar* ff. 358ᵛ-359ʳ (SD Text 11 § 7). A few years later the Tribunal instituted proceedings against two of these white witches, namely the priest Pedro Abad de Guebara at Vitoria and the innkeeper Diego López de Gamarra at Villarreal (which is also in Alava), see *Leg* 1679 Exp. 2.1 No. 4 f. 5ᵛ (ff. 3ʳ-8ᵛ, Tribunal to Council, 28 Jan. 1617; received in Madrid 9 Feb., hereafter cited as *Eighth Report of Salazar*).

238. Salazar's Report of the General Visitation Cases, of 8 Feb. 1612, is discussed below, chap. 12.1.

239. *Second Report of Salazar* f. 9ʳ (SD Text 12 § 44). See MARTÍNEZ DE ISASTI 1850 pp. 243-244, where a similar event is reported to have taken place in 1616 "somewhere in Guipúzcoa," only with the variation that the witch had appeared there in the form of a rabbit.

240. In the Roncal Valley the witch epidemic does not seem to have erupted until the summer of 1611, lasting until the end of 1613. Lorenzo de Hualde, the commissioner from Vera, must undoubtedly have been responsible for this. It will be recalled that Salazar had sent this fanatical witch persecutor on a special mission to the Roncal Valley. Regarding the witches from the Roncal Valley see also below, chap. 12 nn. 85, 110.

241. *Second Report of Salazar* f. 15ᵛ (SD Text 12 § 69). This is the famous quotation from Salazar that was published by Henry Charles

Lea in 1906 (LEA *Inquisition of Spain,* IV pp. 233-234) and that has since been cited by so many writers who have taken Lea as their source (see HENNINGSEN *Papers of Salazar* p. 85 n. 2).

NOTES TO CHAPTER 12

1. *Second Report of Salazar* f. 1[r] (SD Text 12); *Lib* 795 f. 230[r], Valle to Council, 14 Jan. 1612.

2. *Leg* 1679 Exp. 2.1 No. 26[a] ff. 1[r]-2[r], Becerra and Valle to Council, 24 Mar. 1612; received at Madrid 31 Mar., hereafter cited as *The Colleagues' Letter of 24 Mar.*

3. See *Second Report of Salazar* ff. 16[v]-17[r] (SD Text 12 § 76).

4. *Salazar's Letter from Valencia* f. 2[v]: "mas de cinco mil seiscientos foxas." Regarding Valle's visitation book see beginning of chap. 7.3, above.

5. *Lib* 795 f. 237[r-v], Becerra to [Juan Ramírez, the *fiscal* of the] Council, 17 Jan. 1612; received at Madrid 27 Jan.

6. *Leg* 1683 Exp. 1 f. 46[r-v], Becerra to Council [the secretary García de Molina?], 3 Feb. 1612; see idem f. 45[r-v], Becerra to Council [the *fiscal* Juan Ramírez?], 3 Mar. 1612.

7. The *fiscal* to the Tribunal, Isidoro de San Vicente, had reported the matter of the secretaries to the Council without the knowledge of the inquisitors, see *Leg* 1683 Exp. 1 ff. 31[r]-32[v], San Vicente to inquisitor general, 19 Jan. 1612; received at Madrid 12 Feb. Later the *fiscal* produced the larger report mentioned above (chap. 3 n. 50).

8. *Leg* 1683 Exp. 1 f. 46[v] (Becerra/Council 3-2-1612; n. 6, above).

9. An examination of the Tribunal's letters to *la Suprema* from the beginning of 1612 shows that Valle signed alone for the whole of the first half of Jan. After 24 Jan. Salazar's signature also appeared, but not until 13 Mar. was Becerra's signature adjoined. (It was a firm rule that the official letters of the Tribunal were to be signed by all inquisitors present.) See *Lib* 795 ("Libro 11º de cartas de la Inquisición de Logroño") *passim.*

10. *The Colleagues' Letter of 24 Mar.* f. 1[r].

11. There is mention of the lost report several times in the correspondence. For instance, in a letter to *la Suprema* Salazar stated that the report contained the 110 cases that had resulted from the visitation, in addition to the 1,802 witchcraft cases dealt with in connection with the Edict of Grace (*Lib* 795 f. 299[r-v], Tribunal to Council, 22 Sept. 1612, with a postscript by Salazar; received in Madrid 1 Sept.). In the *First Report of Salazar* (f. 359[v] § 12) there is a mention of three persons in Vitoria who had had revelations, and their cases are stated to have been numbered 102, 103, and 104 in the report covering the general visitation cases. In the *Fourth Report of Salazar* f. 5[r] (SD Text 14 § 23) it is mentioned that the report contained 17 witchcraft cases. Two of these receive further mention in §§ 44-45 of *Second Report of Salazar* f. 9[r-v] (see end of chap. 11.C.7, above).

12. *The Colleagues' Letter of 24 Mar.* f. 1[r].

13. Cf. *Second Report of Salazar* f. 17[r] (SD Text 12 § 77).

14. *Leg* 1683 Exp. 1 ff. 47[r]-48[r], Becerra to Council [the secretary Miguel García de Molina], 17 Mar. 1612.

15. Cf. *The Colleagues' Letter of 24 Mar.* f. 1ʳ.

16. Compare *The Colleagues' Letter of 24 Mar.* f. 1ʳ⁻ᵛ with the *Second Report of Salazar* ff. 14ᵛ, 16ᵛ (SD Text 12 §§ 66, 74) and with the *Fifth Report of Salazar* f. 14ᵛ (SD Text 15 § 21). The attempt at drawing up a list had been typical of Salazar in that it had consisted in a count of innocent persons, but this had in itself given an indication of how many were involved in the whole affair. In Volume "F" alone of the visitation book — the volume with the 81 *revocantes* — Salazar had listed accusations against 1,672 persons, but all these testimonies had been annulled by the "witches" having recanted their confessions. In the other volumes several thousands were reported as having participated in witches' sabbaths. It was impossible, however, to arrive at an exact figure: for one thing, the Tribunal had been informed of revocations *after* the records of the 81 *revocantes* had been put in order and separately bound; and for another, fresh revocations were likely to come in as long as the Edict of Grace was in force (after the last extension, the edict was valid until 29 Mar. 1612). On these grounds, which are set forth in the second report to the inquisitor general, Salazar had deliberately abstained from compiling the list of suspected people.

17. *The Colleagues' Letter of 24 Mar.* f. 1ᵛ.

18. See *Lib* 333 f. 281ʳ, Council to Tribunal, 31 Mar. 1612, where the receipt is confirmed.

19. See *la Suprema*'s endorsements at *First* and *Second Report of Salazar* (SD Texts 11 and 12) which indicate that the reports were received in Madrid on 31 Mar. 1612. In all probability the seven additional reports, which were in fact all addenda to Salazar's second report, were sent at the same time, see below, chap. 12.2 "The lost reports," and beginning of chap. 12.3.

20. *The Colleagues' Letter of 24 Mar.* ff. 1ᵛ-2ʳ.

21. *Lib* 333 f. 281ʳ (C./T. 31-3-1612; n. 18, above).

22. *Examination of Salazar at Valencia* f. 786ᵛ.

23. One receives this general impression when scanning the correspondence from this period, see *Lib* 795 ("Libro 11º de cartas de la Inquisición de Logroño" passim).

24. See chap. 3 n. 40, above. A Royal Decree of Salary (*Cedula real de salario*) shows that San Vicente became an inquisitor on Mallorca (*Lib* 366 f. 88ʳ⁻ᵛ).

25. *Leg* 1683 Exp. 1 f. 29ᵛ (ff. 29ʳ-30ʳ, Memorial of San Vicente, 13 July 1612, read at the Tribunal on 20 July, forwarded on 21 July and received in Madrid 23 July).

26. *Leg* 1683 Exp. 2 f. 425ᵛ (ff. 425ʳ-426ᵛ, Examination of San Vicente, Zaragoza 22 April 1620; see n. 27, below).

27. Idem f. 425ʳ⁻ᵛ. Together with 23 other people San Vicente was questioned regarding Salazar's behavior during the time when he was an inquisitor at Logroño, and also as to his character in general. These inquiries (22 Apr.-8 July 1620) were held at Salazar's own request in order that he might be cleared of a number of accusations that had been made against him during the inspection of the Tribunal at Logroño. There is a wealth of information here for anyone desirous

of making a closer study of Salazar's personality; see *Leg* 1683 Exp. 2 ff. 417^r-458^r, hereafter cited as *Witnesses in Favor of Salazar*.

28. *Leg* 1683 Exp. 1 f. 731^v (Interrogation of San Vicente at Zaragoza, 30 Aug. 1619; chap. 3 n. 40, above).

29. *Leg* 1683 Exp. 2 ff. 438^v-439^r (ff. 437^v-439^r, interrogation of Gregorio de Leguizamo at Logroño, 12 Apr. 1620; one of the witnesses in Salazar's favor, see n. 27, above).

30. *Title:* "Carta de todo lo que ha resultado generalmente de la visita y edicto de gracia. Carta primera." The first eight paragraphs are to be reproduced as SD Text 11.

31. *Instructions of 26 Mar. 1611* f. 146^r (SD Text 6 § 12).

32. *First Report of Salazar* f. 358^r (SD Text 11 § 5).

33. *Instructions of 26 Mar. 1611* f. 147^r (SD Text 6 § 14).

34. *First Report of Salazar* f. 358^r (SD Text 11 § 6).

35. "Lo que ha resultado de toda la visita y publicación del edicto en el negocio de la secta de brujos. Carta Segunda." (SD Text 12).

36. Idem f. 1^v (Introduction).

37. Idem ff. 1^r-2^r (§ 1).

38. Idem f. 2^{r-v} (§§ 2-4).

39. Idem ff. 2^v-3^r (§§ 5-8).

40. Idem f. 3^{r-v} (§ 9). The grammatical complexity of the passage cited reflects to some extent the convolutions of Salazar's style. I want to express my gratitude to Carmelo Lisón Tolosana and his wife Julia Donnald for valuable help with the interpretation and the translation.

41. Idem ff. 3^v-6^r (§§ 10-24).

42. Idem ff. 6^r-10^v (§§ 25-51).

43. Idem ff. 9^v-10^v (§§ 49-50).

44. Idem ff. 10^v-16^r (§§ 52-70) passim.

45. Idem ff. 15^v-16^r (§§ 69-72).

46. Idem f. 1 (Introduction).

47. In *Salazar's Second Report* he refers to "the separate survey of the 81 *revocantes* (f. 12^r, SD Text 12 § 58) and in another place to a visitation file, "E 9," which is "recorded as no. 6 in [the survey of] relapsos" (idem f. 6^r § 25). The experiment with the witches' meeting-places is stated to be "summarized in a separate survey" (Idem f. 10^r § 49), and this is also stated of the investigations which were made into the nature of the witches' ointments and powders (Idem f. 10^v § 50).

48. Manuel SERRANO Y SANZ *Autobiografías y memorias* Madrid 1905 p. cvi (Nueva Biblioteca de Autores Españoles II); see CARO BAROJA *De nuevo* p. 267 n. 6. After the Napoleonic Wars the Inquisition was reestablished; it functioned until 1820. In the letters from the Logroño Tribunal to *la Suprema* during this period there are many references to the way in which this inquisition had been totally destroyed. "The beautiful building," as one letter described it, had been burned and leveled with the ground, and the archives of the Tribunal had been scattered to the four winds (*Leg* 2248, letters from the Tribunal to the Council 1814-1820, passim). See also F. J. GÓMEZ *Logroño Histórico* Logroño 1893 p. 629.

49. See table 3 chap. 7.6, above; for the nineteen who recanted their confessions, see the table in chap. 11 n. 49, above.

50. *Trial Record of María de Ulibarri*, see case no. 354.

51. See HENNINGSEN *Papers of Salazar* p. 97.

52. *Second Report of Salazar* f. 1ʳ⁻ᵛ (SD Text 12 Introduction).

53. Idem f. 2ᵛ and *Glosses* f. 1ᵛ (§ 6 with gloss 12).

54. *Trial Record of María de Ulibarri* f. 681ᵛ.

55. For instance, Simona de Gabiria's testimony regarding the witch in the shape of a dog (see end of chap. 11.C.7, above), which, according to the note to the *Second Report of Salazar*, was to be found in Volume "A" of Salazar's visitation book, f. 75 (*Glosses* f. 4ᵛ, gloss 64). Considerable extracts from Volume "A" also appear in the *Pamplona Manuscript* (see IDOATE *Documento* pp. 75-77 passim). In certain cases, when Salazar was not in possession of the earlier confession, the witches' revocations were recorded in Volume "A," and later a copy was made which was bound into Volume "F" together with the other *revocantes*, see e.g. *Volume "F" of Salazar's Visitation Book* f. 360ʳ⁻ᵛ (*Rte* 43 Catalina de Araníbar).

56. See *Second Report of Salazar, Glosses* ff. 3ᵛ, 4ᵛ, 5ʳ (SD Text 12) where glosses "+," 60, and 69 refer to Volume "A" of Salazar's visitation book and state where the experiments took place: A 453 (Santesteban), A 457 (Iráizoz), A 460 (Zubieta), A 463 (Sumbilla), A 464 ("2nd and 4th witnesses at Sumbilla"), A 465 (Donamaría), A 466 (Alzate), 473 (Vera). In other words we can take it that the record of the interrogation of each individual filled less than a page.

57. *Second Report of Salazar, Glosses* f. 5ʳ (SD Text 12 gloss 70).

58. Wherever Salazar mentions witches reconciled on the visitation he makes reference to Volumes "B," "C," "D," or "E," and not to other volumes. On close examination, these prove to be the witches whose records appear in these four volumes who were all old enough to be reconciled. None of the women were under 12 and none of the men were under 14 years of age. See the reconstruction of Volumes "B"-"E" in Witch List, case nos. 151-440, above.

59. Regarding the 19 records see the survey in chap. 11 n. 49, above.

60. Regarding the 81st *revocante*, see chap. 11 n. 93, above; see also the survey of Volume "F," case nos. 450-521.

61. According to the *Second Report of Salazar*, the *Glosses* f. 5ʳ (SD Text 12 gloss 72), trial records of the witches who abjured *de levi* were in Volume "G"; see also the survey in Witch List, case nos. 522-562.

62. Idem f. 3ᵛ (gloss 45). It is stated that the testimony of an 80-year-old witch is placed with the confessions of the child witches in Volume "H." See also the reconstruction of Volume "H" in Witch List, case nos. 563-1,948.

63. It is to be noted that this is the case only with María de Tanborín Xarra ("C 365"), Catalina de Echetoa ("C 643"), and María de Echevarría ("E 9"), for the records of the two child witches mentioned by Salazar in the letter from Fuenterrabía (see chap. 11.A.7) were presumably included in Volume "H" together with those of the other children.

64. The *Glosses* of the *Second Report of Salazar* (SD Text 12) passim.

65. *Sixth Report of Salazar* f. 17ʳ⁻ᵛ (SD Text 16).

66. *Leg* 1683 Exp. 1 f. 26ʳ, Salazar to Inquisitor General, 20 May 1612; received in Madrid 29 May. Presumably, although it is not mentioned in the letter, the Tribunal was instituting a case against some of the

hechiceros or against the 17 *brujos* about whom Salazar had received complaints; for otherwise it is not easy to see what connection these cases had with Salazar's first and second reports.

67. *Lib* 795 f. 346ʳ (f. 346ʳ⁻ᵛ, Becerra and Valle to Council, 28 May 1612).

68. *MS:* "y también porque la gran multitud de cosas que se van recopilando y hay que sacar de actos infalibles que se van comprobando."

69. Idem f. 346ʳ⁻ᵛ.

70. *Lib* 795 f. 299ᵛ (T./C. 22-9-1612; n. 11, above). The application of the secretary Huerta y Rojas, dated 10 July 1612, is to be found idem f. 266ʳ.

71. *Lib* 333 ff. 332ᵛ-333ᵛ, Council to Tribunal, 2 Oct. 1612.

72. *Lib* 333 f. 339ʳ, Council to Tribunal, [13] Oct. 1612; see *Lib* 795 f. 309ʳ, Tribunal to Council, 6 Nov. 1612, in which the receipt of *la Suprema*'s letter is confirmed.

73. *Lib* 333 ff. 351ᵛ-353ʳ, Council to Tribunal, 24 Dec. 1612. Among other things, a directive aimed at Becerra (see chap. 10.4, above) runs that if one of the inquisitors opposes a decision none of the others may carry it through, and this applies equally to the most senior inquisitor. Likewise no inquisitor is to be acrimonious toward a colleague who opposes his opinion when cases are being voted upon. This was a reprimand for Valle (for Valle, see end of chap. 7, above; and for Becerra, see about Salazar's *Memorial of 2 Mar.* 1611 in chap. 10.4 along with n. 71).

74. There are two almost identical applications from Juanes de Sansín, apparently written by himself. They were presented to the Tribunal on 9 and 16 Feb. 1612 respectively (*Lib* 795 ff. 241ʳ and 243ʳ respectively). Juanes de Goiburu's application (which seems not to have been written by himself) was presented to the Tribunal on 16 Feb. 1612 (Idem f. 242ʳ⁻ᵛ). Both applications were sent on to the Council on 28 Feb. 1612, and the Council replied with a request to be sent the *méritos* of their trials (*Lib* 333 ff. 268ᵛ-269ᵛ, Council to Tribunal, 2 Mar. 1612). However, these *méritos* or summaries of the trial records (see the references in chap. 2 n. 1, above) took the Tribunal a whole year to complete, and not until 5 Mar. 1613 were they dispatched together with a vote from the inquisitors concerning two petitions of Juanes de Sansín and Juanes de Goiburu (see immediately below in this section).

75. *Lib.* 832 f. 169ʳ (ff. 169ʳ-169 Aʳ, Tribunal to Council, undated [5 Mr. 1613(a)] (see n. 78, below); received in Madrid 13 Mar.). The gist of Salazar's argument was that any objection to such permission was invalid on the basis of the investigations carried out, the reports of which now reposed in the archive of the Tribunal, and which had also been referred to *la Suprema.* Besides, in the last few days the Tribunal had received another proof of the validity of the results reached by Salazar on his journey of visitation, namely in the examination of Catalina de Echevarría, who had been sent for from Fuenterrabía at the request of *la Suprema;* see *Leg* 1683 Exp. 1 f. 17ʳ (ff. 17ʳ-18ʳ, Memoran-

dum of Salazar, read at the Tribunal on 15 June 1613; received in Madrid 1 July, hereafter cited as *Salazar's Memorandum of 15 June*).

76. *Lib* 832 ff. 169ᵛ-169Aʳ (T./C. 5-3-1613(a); n. 75, above).

77. *Lib* 795 f. 446ʳ, Tribunal to Council, 5 Mar. 1613 (b). The commissioner in the Oyarzun Valley was the priest Sebastian de Zuaznabar. He had been appointed by Valle on the latter's journey of visitation in 1609 (*Leg* 1683 Exp. 1 f. 1461ʳ). See also *Lib* 835 ff. 518ʳ-519ᵛ (ff. 517ʳ-532ᵛ, hereafter cited as *Relación de causas 1614/15*) case 2, summary of two trials against Pedro de los Reyes. The first trial was instituted with imprisonment on 10 May 1613 and ended shortly before Christmas with a sentence of exile for life from the district of the Logroño Inquisition. The second trial was instituted after the Tribunal had received information that the young witch-finder and *saludador* had again been active in Guipúzcoa. The peasants from the village of Ydiarzabal had come riding right down to Villafranca to persuade him to go home with them in order to cure (*saludar*) their cows and children, who were bewitched. It had not been necessary for him to expose the witches, for the peasants had given him the information straightaway. Following preliminary investigations Pedro de los Reyes was imprisoned for the second time on 31 Jan. 1614. The case ended with a fresh banishment and a fine of 22,000 *maravedis*. The case is interesting for the information on Basque antiwitchcraft traditions that it provides, although there is no space to deal with the subject here. Regarding Juanes de Goizueta (see below, chap. 13.3).

78. *Lib* 334 ff. 26ᵛ-27ʳ, Council to Tribunal, 14 Mar. 1613 (a). To begin with the receipt of five letters from the Tribunal, dated 5 March, is acknowledged, among these the letter concerning Juanes de Sansín and Juanes de Goiburu, which thus may be dated (see n. 75, above). The conclusion of these two Zugarramurdi trials appear from a marginal note to the *Méritos of Juanes de Goiburu* f. 170ʳ: "Exempt them from wearing *sambenitos* and release them. The lords Valdés, Zapata, Castro, Trejo..." This is clearly the draft of a letter to the Tribunal concerning the Council's decision.

79. *Lib* 334 f. 30ʳ⁻ᵛ, Council to Tribunal, 14 Mar. 1613 (b). The same day, *la Suprema* returned the cases against Pedro de los Reyes and Juanes de Goizueta with detailed instructions to the Tribunal for dealing with them (*Lib* 334 ff. 29ʳ-30ʳ, Council to Tribunal, 14 Mar. 1613 (c)).

80. *Lib* 334 f. 45ᵛ (f. 45ʳ⁻ᵛ, Council to Tribunal, 24 Apr. 1613; received at Logroño 5 May).

81. *Leg* 1679 Exp. 2.1 No. 30 (with the original signature "+ + +") f. 1ʳ⁻ᵛ, copy of Salazar's vote written in his own hand. In a (presumably later) heading Salazar states that the vote was taken as a consequence of the Council's letter of 23 Apr. 1612 (*sic*), but this must be a lapsus for 23 Apr. 1613. Salazar's heading is reproduced by Julio Caro Baroja, with, however, a misreading: "sentencia" for "conferencia" (CARO BAROJA *De nuevo* p. 325 No. 64).

82. *Lib* 795 f. 509ʳ⁻ᵛ, Becerra to Council, 31 May 1613; received 12 June.

83. *Lib* 334 f. 71ʳ, Council to Tribunal, 12 June 1613. For the *Carta Acordada* see chap. 6, above, with n. 41.

84. *Salazar's Memorandum of 15 June* ff. 17ʳ-18ʳ.

85. *The first item* was the case of Catalina de Echevarría (see n. 75, above), concerning which Salazar had composed a written verdict as long ago as 9 Jan., but his colleagues had not yet committed themselves. *The second item* concerned the annual journey of visitation. Salazar had long since given a written opinion on this as well, but his colleagues had not yet decided to commit their opinion to paper (presumably Salazar knew nothing about Becerra's letter to the inquisitor general of 31 May). *The third, fourth, and fifth items* concerned three applications for posts of inquisitorial agents. *The sixth item* concerned his colleagues' opinion on the affair of the witches which they had promised, at the end of March the previous year, to send "in the near future," but which was still not forthcoming and was therefore delaying a solution to the witch problem as a whole. The *seventh, eight, and ninth items* concerned some witch-plagued valleys in northeastern Navarra: Valderro, Aescoa, and Val de Roncal. These had all sent deputations to the Tribunal requesting a speedy solution to their problem. The Tribunal, however, had done nothing. *The tenth and eleventh items* concerned two parish priests who a long time ago had applied to become inquisitorial commissioners. One was Martín de Lesaca of Gainza in Guipúzcoa, the other was Miguel de Arramendía of Alsasua in the Borunda Valley (see chap. 11.B.5, above, along with n. 138). Their "purity of blood" (*limpieza de sangre*) had long since been verified, but Becerra and Valle had been opposed to making a decision regarding their applications. (They had both been denounced as witches by persons who had since retracted their confessions, but as Salazar reveals in another connection his colleagues expected fresh evidence to be produced against them.) *The twelfth item* concerned an application from the inquisitorial secretary Juan de Agüero, and the *thirteenth and final item* concerned a certain Diego Benito of Fuenterrabía who had caused a scandal by spreading stories about how he had made the daughter of the Tribunal's jailer at Logroño pregnant. See *Lib* 334 f. 80ʳ⁻ᵛ, Council to Tribunal, 2 July 1613, where Salazar's memorandum is returned with a message to the Tribunal to send the Council more detailed information regarding these matters, particularly in regard to the jailer's daughter.

86. *Lib* 334 ff. 75ᵛ-76ʳ, Council to Tribunal, 20 June 1613; received 3 July. "It is now more than a year ago," *la Suprema* wrote, "that we sent you the report regarding the witches proved guilty on the visitation . . . made by your colleague the previous year, in order that you should vote on the cases in the usual manner." This letter shows complete ignorance of the contents of Salazar's reports, which are mentioned as if they were an entirely routine visitation report (with the one exception that it dealt only with witches). The letter is thus an indirect proof that *la Suprema* had kept their promise to Becerra and Valle not to read Salazar's reports.

87. *Lib* 795 f. 526ʳ, Tribunal to Council, 6 July 1613, received in Madrid 18 July.

88. See below in present section and *Fourth Report of Salazar* f. 1^r (SD Text 14 § 1).

89. On *la Suprema*'s payroll for 1606 (see chap. 7 n. 67, above) Fernando de Acevedo is classed as *fiscal* to the Council (*Lib* 367 f. 147^v). On 5 July 1610 he became bishop of Osma, and on 2 June 1613 he was appointed archbishop of Burgos (see *Boletín Eclesiástico del Arzobispado de Burgos* 16-17 (1873-1874) pp. 188-189; Patritium GAUCHAT *Hierachia Catholice* München 1935 IV p. 123).

90. *Leg* 1683 Exp. 1 ff. 803^r-804^r (ff. 803^r-805^r, Valle to [the archbishop of Burgos, Fernando de] Acevedo, July 1613). Only the draft of Valle's letter is extant. It later came into Salazar's possession, and when he was questioned at Valencia in connection with the inspection of the Tribunal at Logroño in 1619, he handed it over to *la Suprema* (see Idem f. 786^v-787^r). Valle's letter must have been written after 3 July 1613, since it mentions *la Suprema*'s direction to the inquisitors to employ the whole of the month of July in completing their deliberations on the affair of the witches (see immediately above). July is spoken of in the letter as "this month" and promise is made that the completed reports will be "sent off in a week's time." As the reports were not sent in until the beginning of August, Valle's letter to the archbishop can be dated at approximately the end of July 1613.

91. Idem ff. 804^r-805^r.

92. *Lib* 795 f. 525^{r-v}, Tribunal to Council, 3 Aug. 1613 (although manuscript has "3 July"); received in Madrid 21 Aug. According to an endorsement by *la Suprema* on the back of the letter, it must have been written on 16 July. There is, however, a statement by Salazar that the letter was written on 23 July. Finally, we have Valle's own statement that the letter with his own and Becerra's memorials was forwarded "at the beginning of August." I am therefore most inclined to put the date of the letter at 3 Aug. 1613 (see my exposition to Florencio Idoate cited in IDOATE *Documento* p. 33).

93. *Lib* 795 f. 532^r, Valle and Salazar to inquisitor general, 17 Aug. 1613; received in Madrid 29 Aug.

94. According to *Lib* 1338 (f. 54^r) Becerra swore the oath of allegiance to *la Suprema* and acceded to the post of *fiscal* on 19 Oct. 1613 (cf. table 13, chap. 13.1, below). On the other hand, according to my calculations, he was in Logroño as late as 17 Oct.

95. *Leg* 1679 Exp. 2 No. 30[a] (original signature "AAA"), Memorandum of Salazar dated 1 Oct. (corrected from Sept.) 1613, hereafter cited as *Salazar's Memorandum of 1 Sept.* The extant manuscript is a copy written in Salazar's hand. The correction to 1 Oct. was most probably made many years later by Salazar in error. The correct date must have been 1 Sept., since on 17 Sept. two of the cases Salazar had complained about were dealt with. This occurred when the cases against Juanes de Goizueta and Pedro de los Reyes were voted on, and forwarded to *la Suprema* on this date (cf. *Lib* 795 f. 535^{r-v}, Tribunal to Council, 17 Sept. 1613; received in Madrid 25 Sept.). In the memorandum mentioned above Pedro de los Reyes is called by the name Cristóbal de Mayza, but here Salazar is guilty of another lapsus (see near end of present section, along with n. 111).

96. *Leg* 1683 Exp. 1 f. 28^{r-v}, Salazar to Inquisitor General, 24 Sept. 1613; received in Madrid 8 Oct.

97. Cf. idem f. 28^{r}: "because of the inconveniences, which I describe in the enclosed document (*por los inconvenientes que envio apuntados*)."

98. *Leg* 1679 Exp. 2.1 No. 29[g] ff. 25^{r}-26^{r}, Memorandum of Salazar, undated [24 Sept. 1613 (?)] *Heading:* "Para que el Consejo apresurase sin dilación alguna la resolución de este negocio," to be published as SD Text 13, hereafter cited as *Third Report of Salazar*. The manuscript is among some of Salazar's papers from 1614 (see the description of the contents of this archive file in CARO BAROJA *De nuevo* p. 324 Nos. 49-54). I have, therefore, previously been of the opinion that this memorandum must date from 1614 as well (see HENNINGSEN *Papers of Salazar* p. 102, where it is dealt with as Salazar's Sixth Report). The redating has been made partly on the grounds of the support given by the quoted allusion in the letter of 24 Sept. 1613, and partly on an analysis of the entire contents; for in fact the introductory remarks and much of what Salazar says in this memorandum only make sense if we presuppose a situation which necessitated his colleagues in the Tribunal being persuaded to allow *la Suprema* to decide the matter. The use of Your Grace (*Vuestra Merced*) also indicates the Tribunal. If Salazar had been writing during his sojourn at the Council of the Inquisition in 1614 he would presumably have addressed himself to the inquisitor general, who would have been addressed as Your Eminence (*Vuestra Alteza*).

99. *Third Report of Salazar* ff. 25^{r}, 26^{r} (SD Text 13 Introduction and § 7).

100. See *Fourth Report of Salazar* f. 8^{v} (SD Text 14 § 37), in the passage: "the incomprehension shown by them toward my effort to bring these matters to a general decision." This is another vital clue to my dating the *Third Report of Salazar* at Sept. 1613 (see n. 98, above). Regarding Becerra and Valle's report of 3 Oct. 1613 see also below, chap. 12.7.

101. See the introduction to the *Fourth Report of Salazar* f. 1^{r} (SD Text 14 § 1).

102. *Leg* 1683 Exp. 1 ff. 801^{r-v} (ff. 801^{r}-802^{v}, Valle to [the Council], undated [late Oct. 1613]). The letter is extant only in the form of Valle's draft, which, as with the letter to the archbishop of Burgos, fell into the hands of Salazar and was later delivered to *la Suprema* in 1619 (see n. 90, above). Valle may have written his letter *after* Becerra's departure for Madrid to take up his new post (19 Oct. 1613, see n. 94, above). On the other hand it may have been written before the receipt of *la Suprema*'s letter confirming that Becerra and Valle's memorials had been received (see n. 105, below).

103. Idem f. 802^{r}.

104. Idem f. 802^{r-v}.

105. *Leg* 1679 Exp. 2.1 No. 29, Council to Salazar, 24 Oct. 1613. This copy in Salazar's own hand has previously been made use of by Julio Caro Baroja and me (CARO BAROJA *De nuevo* p. 324 No. 49; HENNINGSEN *Papers of Salazar* p. 95). In the meantime two further copies have emerged, one the entry in *la Suprema*'s letter book (*Lib* 334 f. 120^{v}), and the other the original, which is among some of Salazar's

papers from the inspection of the Granada Tribunal 1614-16 (*Leg* 1958 Exp. 1 f. 11ʳ⁻ᵛ). Regarding the visitation at Granada, see chap. 13.6, below.

106. *Leg* 1679 Exp. 2.1 No. 4[o] ff. 1ʳ-4ʳ, Memorandum of Salazar, read in the Tribunal 13 Nov. 1613. *Title:* "Los apuntamientos que yo el Inquisidor, *licenciado* Alonso de Salazar Frías he significado en el Tribunal cerca del discurso que en él se leyó a tres de octubre pasado sobre el negocio de brujas por respuesta que daban los señores Inquisidores Alonso Becerra y *licenciado* Juan de Valle Alvarado mis colegas a otro mío, que en carta de veinte y cuatro de marzo de mil seiscientos y doce había yo remitido al Consejo, es como se sigue:," hereafter cited as *Salazar's Memorandum of 13 Nov.* The somewhat obscure title holds the clue to the date of the colleagues' "Memorial C," which is discussed below. The translation is as follows: "The following are the considerations which I . . . Salazar Frías delivered in the Tribunal in connection with . . . Becerra and Valle Alvarado's opinion on the witch-affair, which was read there on 3 Oct. 1613, and in which my colleagues argued against another consideration which I had forwarded to the Council with my letter of 24 Mar. 1612" (i.e. *Second Report of Salazar*).

107. *Lib* 795 f. 580ʳ, Salazar to inquisitor general, undated; received in Madrid 9 Nov. 1613.

108. *Lib* 334 f. 130ʳ⁻ᵛ, Council to Tribunal, 9 Nov. 1613.

109. *Lib* 795 f. 577ʳ, Valle and Salazar to Council, 19 Nov. 1613; received in Madrid 5 Dec.

110. Summaries of the trial records of the three witches from the Roncal Valley are to be found in *Lib* 835 ff. 507ᵛ-509ʳ cases 16-18 (ff. 500ʳ-514ʳ, hereafter cited as *Relación de causas 1613/14*). Gracia Luxea was age 16 and the two child witches, the sisters Pascuala and Gracia Miguel, were 11 and 7, respectively. They had all made confession to the local inquisitorial commissioner. Pascuala and Gracia Miguel on 5 Aug. and 7 Nov. 1612, respectively; Gracia Luxea on 24 Feb. 1613. The late dates of these confessions may indicate that the witch craze in the Roncal Valley erupted as a more or less direct result of the visit of Hualde, the priest from Vera, to this district (see above, chap. 11.C.5). As well as in the above-mentioned summaries the confessions of these three girls are mentioned in the *Pamplona Manuscript* (IDOATE *Documento* p. 171).

111. *Relación de causas 1613/14* f. 509ʳ⁻ᵛ case 19. According to this source Cristóbal de Mayza did not report to the Tribunal until 22 Nov. 1613. This confirms our suspicion that the mention of his name in *Salazar's Memorandum of 1 September* is due to Salazar's having confused him with Pedro de los Reyes (see n. 95, above).

112. Strictly speaking the disagreement concerned only the two 16-year-old witches. (The cases of the two child witches were voted on 9 Nov. and here the inquisitors agreed that they should be absolved *ad cautelam, Relación de causas 1613/14* ff. 508ᵛ-509ʳ cases 17, 18.) Gracia Luxea's case was voted on 9 Nov. and was sent in to *la Suprema* on the same day. In their letter to *la Suprema* the inquisitors asked permission to continue to reconcile those witches who might appear at the Tribunal, despite the fact that the Edict of Grace had expired (*Lib*

795 f. 578^r, Tribunal to Council, 9 Nov. 1613(b); received in Madrid 19 Nov.). The case against Christóbal de Amayza (his name is spelt thus in the letter) was voted on 26 Nov., and was forwarded to *la Suprema* on the same day (*Lib* 795 f. 576^r, Tribunal to Council, 26 Nov. 1613). The decision of the Council appears in the Tribunal's report of cases completed 1613/14. The Tribunal received instructions to release both witches, though the 16-year-old Cristóbal was to be whipped in the Tribunal prison first, *Relación de causas 1613/14* ff. 508^v, 509^v.

113. In the letters from the Tribunal to the Council, Salazar's signature appears for the last time on 29 Nov. 1613 (*Lib* 795 passim).

114. *Fifth Report of Salazar* (SD Text 15), see the analysis, last part of chap. 12.7, below).

115. In the original this key passage runs (author's italics): "Remitimos con esto lo que está acabado que son dos cuadernos, *el uno* de actos positivos y cosas que resultaron de las confesiones de éstos brujos, y *el otro* de los actos comprobados." (*Lib* 795 f. 525^v, T./C. 3-8-1613; n. 92, above).

116. Idem f. 525^v.

117. See IDOATE *Documento* p. 7 and p. 33, where Idoate quotes information supplied by me for the dating of this important manuscript. Thanks to the photostat copy I have been able to make use of the *Pamplona Manuscript* ever since June 1971 (after the first 11 chapters of this book were completed). Florencio Idoate's published edition was not available until the spring of 1972.

118. See IDOATE *Documento* p. 33.

119. It is also possible that the manuscript was sent to the successor to Antonio Venegas in the bishopric of Pamplona, Prudencio de Sandoval, who was interested in witchcraft. In the spring of 1970 I visited the archives at Burgos, Pamplona, and other places in northern Spain with the intention of unearthing copies of the then quite unknown "Memorial A." No positive results emerged from my journeying, so that the discovery of the manuscript in the Archivo General de Navarra was all the more welcome. Likewise, scrutiny of the archives of *la Suprema* (now housed in the Archivo Histórico Nacional, Madrid) has not revealed any of Becerra and Valle's memorials. The only discovery I have made is a list of 22 *actos positivos* which agrees in the main with the list of contents of Memorial "A" (see IDOATE *Documento* pp. 42-46). It bears the heading: "Various subjects. Witches exposed in Navarra and the mountains at the beginning of the year 1609 [*Materias varias. Brujas que se descubrieron en Navarra y montañas por principios del ano de 1609*]" (written 1600 in error), and is in *Lib* 1280 ff. 645^r-646^r.

120. Juan de Agüero Albear was senior secretary and had been on the staff of the Tribunal since 1602 (see *Leg* 2220 f. 10^v). Examples of his handwriting are to be found e.g. in *Lib* 795 ff. 5^r and 209^v.

121. *Pamplona Manuscript* f. 53^v (IDOATE *Documento* p. 175 and the facsimile on p. 176).

122. Since Florencio Idoate has not subjected the disposition of the manuscript to a detailed analysis, the description which follows will not be superfluous. In order to clarify the survey I have numbered the sections. The parentheses contain, firstly, reference to the *Pamplona*

Manuscript, followed by the page number in Florencio Idoate's edition:

1. Title page with the title: "Witches. Inquisition of Navarra. Volume containing acts which were proved on the basis of what the witches themselves declared [*Brujas. Inquisición de Navarra. Cuaderno de actos comprobados de brujos*]." At the top of the right-hand margin is a note in Valle's handwriting, but this is discussed below in section 6 on the lost memorials (f. i^r, p. 33).

2. List of contents with short description of 32 acts of witchcraft. This list bears the heading: "Résumé of the *actos positivos* in this volume and references to the pages on which each is discussed [*Sumario de lo que contienen los actos positivos de este cuaderno y a cúantas fojas está cada uno*]" (ff. ii^r-iii^r, pp. 42-46).

3. A collection of material with reports and extracts from the witches' trial records grouped under 32 chapters, each treating one *acto positivo*. This section bears the heading: "Evidence of the acts committed by the witches while awake, by night and by day, outside the gatherings; together with another body of evidence relating to what they do at the *aquelarre*. The confessions of the witches prove that everything actually does take place and cannot be dismissed as dreams or illusions, and this is apparent from the evidence which — while omitting much — is reported in what follows [*Actos positivos de las cosas que los brujos hacen como tales brujos estando despiertos de día y de noche fuera de sus juntas y aquelarres, y otras que proceden de las que se hacen en ellos, las cuales pasan real y verdaderamente sin que se pueda pretender que intervenga sueño ni ilusión, como consta por sus confesiones, y entre otros muchos se refieren aquí los siguientes*]" (ff. 1^r-53^v, pp. 46-175).

4. Register of 84 witches who were reconciled at Logroño after having made their confessions. The first 19 on the list are the *confitente* witches from the auto de fe, while the rest are witches reconciled by the Tribunal after the Edict of Grace had taken effect (ff. 54^r-55^v, pp. 177-180).

5. Register of 179 witches reconciled by Salazar on the journey of visitation (ff. 56^r-60^r, pp.180-188).

6. Copy of María de Endara's confession at the Tribunal made on 4 July 1611. Folio 3^v states that this section is copied from "the volume with proved acts [*el cuaderno de actos comprobados*]," i.e. Memorial "B" (ff. 61^r-65^r, pp. 188-193).

123. See the *Pamplona Manuscript* (IDOATE *Documento* p. 52), where it is stated that the beginning of María de Endara's confession is to be found in "the volume with the facts that have been proven [i.e. Memorial "B"], fol. 27," but this is immediately corrected to: "I mean at the end of this volume" (*que va en el cuaderno de actos comprobados, fol. 27. Digo que va al fin de este cuaderno*).

124. However, in the original version, the list of contents (our sections 4 and 5) of Memorial "A" seems to have been placed first.

125. *Pamplona Manuscript* ff. 6^v-7^v (IDOATE *Documento* pp. 57-60).

126. Loc. cit. n. 125, above.

127. IDOATE *Documento* pp. 46-53.

128. Idem pp. 53-57.

129. Idem pp. 170-175.

130. Idem p. 161.

131. Idem pp. 70-84. Unfortunately, this source was not vouchsafed to Margaret Murray. But it will be intriguing to see what her followers will make of the *Pamplona Manuscript*'s endless lists of "proofs" of the existence of the West European witch cult.

132. Idem pp. 77-78. It is interesting to note that this is the same Catalina de Echetoa who some time after her reconciliation came to Salazar to tell him she had suffered a relapse (see chap. 11.A.7, above).

133. See IDOATE *Documento* pp. 66-67, where reference is made to the volume with "the facts that have been proved." Regarding the miller, see also end of chap. 4.7, above.

134. See IDOATE *Documento* p. 81. Regarding the witches' attempt to carry off María de Jureteguía, see chap. 2, above.

135. See IDOATE *Documento* p. 81.

136. See idem pp. 101-108, where strangely enough the description of "the dressed toads" does not make any reference to the evidence in "Memorial B."

137. See the references to *"el cuaderno de los actos comprobados,"* idem pp. 66-67, 70-84, 132-133, 170-171.

138. MS: "El libro encuadernado en pergamino es también de actos comprobados, pero en aquel se compreuban los actos singulares y individuales que confesaron las brujas con otros testigos, y en éste se compreuban con actos singulares las cosas comunes que uniformemente confiesan los brujos" (IDOATE *Documento* p. 33).

139. See above, near end of chap. 12.3, where Valle states in his letter at the end of Oct. 1613 that all that remains to be done is the fair-copying of "the remaining sections" of his and Becerra's vote (i.e. "Memorical C"). The greater part of this document, however, must already have been complete by 3 Oct., when it was read in the Tribunal in the presence of Salazar (see the heading to *Salazar's Memorandum of 13 Nov. 1613*, n. 106, above, and see *Fourth Report of Salazar* f. 1ʳ (SD Text 14 § 1).

140. See below, in particular table 12 and end of chap. 12.7.

141. See *Fifth Report of Salazar* ff. 12ʳ-15ʳ (SD Text 15 §§ 8-24).

142. See *Fourth Report of Salazar* f. 6ʳ⁻ᵛ (SD Text 14 § 28).

143. Idem ff. 7ᵛ-9ᵛ (SD Text 14 §§ 33-45).

144. See e.g. idem f. 8ᵛ and f. 9ʳ, where Salazar has interchanged two clauses (§ 37 and § 41).

145. Idem ff. 1ʳ, 9ᵛ.

146. Idem f. 1ʳ (§ 1).

147. The nine mass witch trials, or *complicidades,* to which Salazar refers, were: 1526; 1531 (a), witches in northern Navarra; 1531 (b), witches in northwestern Guipúzcoa; 1538; 1555; 1576 (a), witches in the province of Santander; 1576 (b), witches in the Baztán Valley; 1595; and 1596 (see *Fourth Report of Salazar* ff. 1ᵛ-3ʳ (SD Text 14 §3-12).

148. Idem f. 2ʳ (§ 6).

149. Idem f. 3ʳ⁻ᵛ (§ 14); Juan de Espinas appears to be an error for Petri del Espinar (case no. 50).

150. Idem f. 4ᵛ (§ 19).

151. Idem f. 3ᵛ (§ 16).

152. Idem f. 4ᵛ (§ 21).

153. Idem f. 5ʳ (§ 22).

154. Idem f. 5ᵛ (§ 25).

155. *Leg* 1679 Exp. 2.1 No. 30 (with the original signature "GGG"), Domingo de San Paul to Tribunal, 2 June 1613; received at Logroño 8 July. The letter bears an endorsement by Salazar. A marginal note to the *Fourth Report of Salazar* f. 5ᵛ (SD Text 14 § 25) shows that the Lesaca commissioner's letter was sent down to the Council as an appendix to this report.

156. *Fourth Report of Salazar* ff. 5ᵛ-6ʳ (SD Text 14 § 27).

157. Idem f. 6ʳ⁻ᵛ (§§ 28-29).

158. Idem f. 8ᵛ (§ 39). Regarding the translation of Venegas, see chap. 7 n. 66, above.

159. *Fourth Report of Salazar* f. 9ʳ (SD Text 14 § 42).

160. Idem f. 9ᵛ (§ 43).

161. Idem ff. 9ᵛ-10ʳ (Epilogue).

162. *Fifth Report of Salazar* (SD Text 15). As mentioned above, end of chap. 12.3, this report is merely a new version of *Salazar's Memorandum of 13 Nov.* An introduction and six new clauses have been added to the report, while on the other hand Salazar has excised the conclusion of his memorandum, but otherwise the two versions are identical apart from a few alterations in style. The following survey shows in detail the relationship between the two versions (figures outside the parentheses refer to the clauses in the *Fifth Report,* while figures in parentheses refer to the clauses in the *Memorandum*): Introduction; 1 (1); 2 (2); 3; 4; 5 (3); 6 (4); 7; 8 (5); 9 (6); 10 (7); 11 (8); 12 (9); 13 (10); 14 (11); 15 (12); 16 (13); 17 (14); 18 (15); 19 (16); 20 (17); 21 (18); 22; 23; 24; (18 bis).

163. *Fifth Report of Salazar* f. 11ʳ⁻ᵛ (SD Text 15 § 3).

164. Idem f. 11ᵛ (§ 3).

165. Idem ff. 11ᵛ-12ʳ (§§ 5-7).

166. Idem f. 14ᵛ (§ 23).

167. Idem f. 15ʳ (§ 24).

NOTES TO CHAPTER 13

1. *Leg* 1958 Exp. 1 f. 12ʳ, Council to Salazar, 4 Feb. 1614.

2. Salazar appears to have been highly esteemed in Madrid and to have had many friends in the Council of the Inquisition; see the eulogies on Salazar made in 1619 by his contemporary Pedro del Castillo, the bishop of Calahorra, who had known him since 1594 (*Witnesses in Favour of Salazar* ff. 454ʳ-457ʳ).

3. *Leg* 1958 Exp. 1 f. 13ʳ⁻ᵛ, Juan Zapata Osorio to Salazar, Madrid, 7 Mar. 1614.

4. Idem f. 15ʳ, Council to Salazar, 11 Mar. 1614 (a). A copy of this letter (*Leg* 1679 Exp. 2.1 No. 29 f. 16ʳ) is erroneously dated 2 Mar. 1614 (see CARO BAROJA *De nuevo* p. 307 and HENNINGSEN *Papers of Salazar* p. 95).

5. *Leg* 1958 Exp. 1 f. 14ʳ, Juan Zapata Osorio to Salazar, Madrid, 11 Mar. 1614 (b).

6. On account of a lacuna in the registers of *la Suprema* no payrolls for the Council members are extant for the years around 1614. I have therefore been obliged to reconstruct the list with the aid of other sources, the most important of which are (1) *Lib* 334, letters from *la Suprema* to the tribunals in Aragón and Navarra from 8 Jan. 1613 to 5 May 1615, signed by members of the Council according to seniority; (2) *Lib* 367 II, "Registro de titulos y provisiones... del Inquisidor General Acebedo 1603-1608"; (3) *Lib* 366 "Registro Primero de Cámara del Inquisidor General Cardenal Sandoval 1610-1618"; and (4) *Lib* 1338 "Libro de los juramentos..." 7 Aug. 1574 to 22 Dec. 1635. All these registers are arranged chronologically, so for the sake of brevity I shall not give a reference for each individual council member's appointment and oath of allegiance (dates in parentheses). I should like to express my gratitude to Dr. Patric Williams for checking my dates of the councillors and for lending me his unpublished article: "The Council of Inquisition under Philip III (1598-1621)." The most senior councillor, Juan Tapia, in addition to being councillor for Castilla was also a member of the small council of Spanish sheep-farmers, el Consejo de la Mesta. There is a colored sketch of a meeting of this council which depicts him with two other councillors. The sketch is in the D. G. Moldenhawer collection at the Royal Library of Copenhagen, *Collectio libellorum ad historiam inquisitionis hispanicae* (Sign. 4-252ᶜ-2º). For other members of *la Suprema*, see below, n. 44.

7. *Lib* 334 f. 188ʳ⁻ᵛ, Council to Tribunal, 15 Mar. 1614.

8. Idem ff. 188ᵛ-189ʳ, Council to Inquisitor General at Toledo, Madrid, 15 Mar. 1614.

9. *Lib* 796 f. 15ʳ, Council to Inquisitor General at Toledo (the original letter with the inquisitor general's marginal note).

10. Oral statement from Professor Ismael Sánchez Bella, University of Pamplona.

11. Royal Library of Copenhagen, NKS 128ᶜ 4º, pp. 80-81 (4+ 96 pp., D. G. Moldenhawer's copy from 1784 of the Spanish manuscript "Origen y fundación de las Inquisiciones de Espana" in Biblioteca de la Real Academia de la Historia (Madrid); hereafter cited as *Origen y fundación*). The manuscript gives a brief outline of the history of the Spanish Inquisition, but it is first and foremost a description of the customary practice employed by the Council of the Inquisition in the mid-seventeenth century. The author is anonymous, but as his historical presentation is based on sources held in the archives of *la Suprema*, and his description of the life of the Council is pictured as from within its walls, he was presumably a member of the Council of the Inquisition himself. As far as time is concerned, the description must stem from between 1643 (the date of Diego de Arce Reinoso's appointment to the post of inquisitor general) and 1654 (on p. 92 of the manuscript the date of 16 Aug. 1654 is given). Naturally a source originating from such a late date must be utilized with some reservation, but since *la Suprema* was a markedly conservative institution, conditions in 1650 were unlikely to have altered radically from the period with which we are occupied. The author of the manuscript appears to have been José de Ribera, *secretario* of *la Suprema* at the time of Philip IV, see HENNINGSEN 1977 p. 214.

12. Idem p. 81. There are only two secretaries and one reporter on the payroll of *la Suprema* for 1606 (*Lib* 367 f. 147ʳ⁻ᵛ), but two secretaries and two reporters seem to have been the normal complement.

13. *Origen y fundación* pp. 67-68.

14. See *Lib* 367 II f. 148ʳ⁻ᵛ (payroll of 1606).

15. *Origen y fundación* p. 66.

16. Idem pp. 50-51, 61-62.

17. Idem pp. 66-67.

18. Idem p. 80.

19. Idem p. 62; see idem p. 49, where it is stated that the Council consists of six clerical members and two non-clerical assessors from the Council of Castilla.

20. Idem pp. 67-68. Regarding the king's secretary, see p. 80. Information regarding the ceremonial of the Council is also available in an inventory taken in connection with the removal from Valladolid to Madrid in 1606 (*Lib* 490 ff. 40ᵛ-41ᵛ).

21. *Origen y fundación* p. 75.

22. Idem p. 72, see idem pp. 69-70.

23. *Lib* 796 f. 41ʳ, Tribunal to Council, 9 Apr. 1614; received in Madrid 15 Apr. See idem f. 40ʳ, Tribunal to Council, 5 Apr. 1614; received in Madrid 17 Apr., which is almost a repetition but which states in addition that Juanes de Goizueta had been ill for some time. See also idem f. 42ʳ, Tribunal to [Miguel García Molina], 9 Apr. 1614; and *Accounts of 14 Sept. 1614* f. 160ʳ, where the subsistence allowance for Juanes de Usueta (*sic*) while in the Tribunal prison is put at 522 *reales*.

24. *Lib* 334 f. 198ʳ, Council to Tribunal, 17 Apr. 1614.

25. Idem ff. 198ᵛ-199ʳ, Council to Tribunal, 19 Apr. 1614. Also at this time *la Suprema* seems to have written to all the other inquisitorial tribunals requesting them to send in any information in their possession concerning old ordinances and instructions for dealing with witches (see *Lib* 335 ff. 134ʳ-135ʳ, Council to Tribunal, 17 Dec. 1616), but unfortunately none of this material seems to have been preserved.

26. *Lib* 796 f. 35ʳ, Tribunal to Council, 23 Apr. 1614; received in Madrid 2 May. However, the last papers *la Suprema* sent for did not arrive until 10 May; see idem f. 49ʳ, Tribunal to Council, 2 May 1614; received in Madrid 10 May.

27. *Lib* 796 f. 36ʳ, Fray León de Araníbar to Tribunal, Elizondo, 14 Apr. 1614; forwarded to *la Suprema* with the Tribunal's letter of 23 Apr. (see n. 26, above).

28. Idem f. 50ʳ, Valle to Council, 7 May 1614; received in Madrid 13 May.

29. See *Lib* 334 f. 224ʳ, Council to Tribunal, 11 July 1614. The trial record is no longer extant and there is no summary of the case in the Tribunal's *relaciones de causas*. From other sources, however, it can be seen that Juanes de Goizueta was released *ad cautelam*, see *Eighth Report of Salazar* f. 5ᵛ and *Pamplona Manuscript* f. 24ʳ⁻ᵛ (IDOATE *Documento* p. 99 n. 73).

30. *Leg* 1683 Exp. 1 ff. 807ᵛ-808ʳ (Valle/Commissioner of Salvatierra 24-7-1614; chap. 11 n. 120, above).

31. *Relación de causas 1613/14*, ff. 500ʳ-514ᵛ. It appears from an en-

dorsement on Valle's accompanying letter of 14 Aug. 1614 that the report was received in Madrid on 23 Aug. (*Lib* 796 f. 156ʳ).

32. *Sixth Report of Salazar*, the Spanish title is given in chap. 11 n. 219, above.

33. This last section is not found in the copy in the Biblioteca Nacional (see chap. 11 n. 219, above).

34. *Leg* 1679 Exp. 2.1 No. 29 ff. 21ʳ-24ʳ, *title:* "Copia de una carta que el Ilustrísimo Señor Cardenal, Inquisidor General quiso escribir a ciertos prelados de estos reinos sobre el negocio de la complicidad de brujas para que ayudasen con su consejo a la resolución que se había de tomar en él [Consejo] de la Inquisición, donde primero habían sido consejeros — Aunque después no se escribió a nadie." (See CARO BAROJA *De nuevo* pp. 307, 324 No. 52; HENNINGSEN *Papers of Salazar* p. 102).

35. *Lib* 334 f. 234ʳ, Council to Tribunal, 11 Aug. 1614.

36. See *Lib* 796 f. 151ʳ et passim.

37. *Lib* 796 f. 213ʳ, Valle to inquisitor general, 2 Sept. 1614; received in Madrid 6 Sept.

38. See *Lib* 796 f. 166ʳ et passim. Valle's signature does not appear again on the letters of the Tribunal before 8 Nov. (f. 205ʳ et passim), but by then Salazar was already on his way to Granada, see a letter from Salazar dated Madrid, 7 Nov. 1614 (idem f. 216ʳ).

39. *Leg* 1679 Exp. 2.1 No. 29[g] ff. 27ʳ-28ᵛ, Memorandum of Salazar 1614, *title:* "Lo que convenía proveer en el remedio de este negocio de secta de brujas," hereafter *Seventh Report of Salazar* (SD Text 17). The other copy is to be found idem No. 24[a] ff. 1ʳ-2ᵛ. The two manuscripts are present in Julio Caro Baroja's list of contents of capsule 1679 (CARO BAROJA *De nuevo* p. 324 Nos. 54 and 40 respectively); see also HENNINGSEN *Papers of Salazar* p. 102.

40. *Seventh Report of Salazar* f. 27ʳ (SD Text 17 Introduction).

41. Idem ff. 27ʳ-28ᵛ (SD Text 17).

42. *Lib* 334 ff. 244ᵛ-253ʳ, Council to Tribunal, 29 Aug. 1614, *title:* "Instrucción en la materia de brujos, sobre la resolución que se tomó a primero de septiembre 1614 en vista de los papeles, que de la visita que hizo el licenciado Salazar Frías, resultaron," hereafter cited as *Instructions of 29 August 1614* (SD Text 18). Besides the copy in *la Suprema*'s letter book that has been utilized here, a considerable number of copies are in existence (see HENNINGSEN *Papers of Salazar* p. 103 n. 10; and below, n. 63).

43. *Instructions of 29 August 1614* ff. 244ᵛ-245ʳ (SD Text 18).

44. Idem f. 253ʳ. Rodrigo de Castro y Bobadilla was the fourth councillor, see table 13, above. Fray Francisco de Sosa was a former member of *la Suprema* (sworn in 24 Mar. 1609), but was now, since 23 Sept. 1613, serving as bishop of Osma in northern Spain. The day before the signing of the instructions an important person was sworn in as a member of *la Suprema*, but he is not known to have taken part in the decision; his name was Fray Luis de Aliaga y Martínez, and he was to succeed Sandoval y Rojas as inquisitor general (for references see n. 6, above).

45. *The first* omitted clause, clause 2 in the draft, moved that the commissioners at Vera, Maestu, and Larrea should be punished. In

this instance *la Suprema* wisely chose not to call anyone to account, but merely to warn against repetitions in the future (Instruction 28). *The second,* clause 16 in the draft, moved that in the future it should always be a commissioner from a different archdeaconry who heard the evidence in cases of witchcraft. No doubt *la Suprema* felt this would be too impractical. *The third,* clause 18 in the draft, moved that the sentence regarding witches should be omitted from the Edict of Faith of the Logroño Inquisition. This was no doubt omitted because the passage, in direct contradiction of what Salazar had stated (see above, chap. 13.4, clause 18 of Salazar's draft), appeared in the Edict of Faith of most other tribunals (see chap. 6 along with n. 7 and 14, above). *The fourth,* clause 20 in the draft, moved that every year the Tribunal was to forward a report on the witch situation. The Council may have considered such a project to be far too complicated to put into practice.

46. Among other things, several clauses from the instructions of Granada, dated 14 Dec. 1526 (see chap. 1.6, above) were included. Salazar had drawn the inquisitor general's attention to these old instructions in his *Fourth Report* (see SD Text 14 § 3). *La Suprema* had likewise resorted to the instructions of 26 Mar. 1611 (SD Text 6) and to the epoch-making letter of 28 June of the same year (see near end of chap. 10.4, above). I have been unable to trace an original source for clauses 1-6 of the new instructions. However, apart from the wording, most of the contents are in fact to be found in a letter containing instructions for witch trials sent by *la Suprema* to the Tribunal on 21 Feb. 1526 (*Lib* 319 ff. 270ʳ-271ᵛ).

47. For Valle see end of chap. 13.3, above. The date of receipt of the new instructions is mentioned in the Tribunal's letter of 20 Sept. 1614, see n. 49, below.

48. Antonio de Aranda Alarcón, previously *fiscal* to the Inquisition at Córdoba, had been appointed inquisitor at Logroño as of 5 July 1614 (*Lib* 366 f. 167ᵛ-168ᵛ). His signature appears for the first time on the Tribunal's letters on 6 Sept. 1614 (see *Lib* 796 f. 160 et passim).

49. *Lib* 796 f. 168ʳ, Tribunal to Council, 20 Sept. 1614; received in Madrid 20 Oct.

50. See above, table 14, clauses 26, 28-30.

51. *Eighth Report of Salazar* f. 45ʳ.

52. Idem f. 45ᵛ; see *Leg* 1679 Exp. 2.1 No. 4 f. 32ᵛ (ff. 32ʳ-35ᵛ, Tribunal to Council, 11 Oct. 1623; received in Madrid 25 Oct., hereafter cited as *Ninth Report of Salazar*). Julio Caro Baroja misread the date as 11 Oct. 1613 and interpreted the second inquisitor's signature as that of Pedro Hurtado de Gabiria, when it is in fact Pedro Bohorquez Quintanilla. Salazar's ninth report was therefore not given the detailed treatment it deserved in Caro Baroja's article (see CARO BAROJA *De nuevo* pp. 304, 323, no. 17 of the Index).

53. *Lib* 271 f. 1ʳ. This copy of the printed edict bears Salazar's signature followed by those of two other inquisitors (strangely enough the date is not inserted, but it must be between 1622 and 1628, when Salazar was senior inquisitor at Logroño, cf. chap. 13.7, below). In a letter from the Council to the Tribunal dated 17 Oct. 1629, reference is made to a similar edict, which is stated to be found in "the

great volume of verdicts [*el libro grande de votos*], fol. 149" (*Lib* 822 f. 335ʳ). Unfortunately, my attempts to locate this manuscript volume have been unsuccessful. Possibly the reference is not to the archives of *la Suprema* but of the Tribunal, which were not preserved.

54. *Eighth Report of Salazar* f. 45ʳ⁻ᵛ.

55. One of the copies is to be found in the collected material for a history of the Spanish Inquisition which was brought home by the Danish theologian D. G. Moldenhawer (1753-1823) from a visit to Spain in the 1780s and is now in the Royal Library at Copenhagen (N. kgl. S. 213 2° ff. 379ʳ-380ᵛ). This copy has long been considered unique (see LEA *Inquisition of Spain* IV p. 237 n. 1; HENNINGSEN *Papers of Salazar* p. 103 n. 10). However, a second copy was recently discovered by the author in the Archivo Histórico Nacional (*Lib* 1237 ff. 342ʳ-343ᵛ). For another set of printed instructions, see n. 57, below.

56. For the original title see HENNINGSEN 1977 p. 260.

57. Comparison shows that the ruling was based on instructions 2, 4-5, 8-10, and 12-14. On the other hand, some of the contents are to a considerable extent in keeping with the original attitude of the Tribunal. For instance, in clause 7 the commissioner is instructed to inquire whether any person has been able to deal one of the witches a blow during their nocturnal attack, and thus been enabled to recognize the witch the next day by the injury. Perhaps it was Valle who insisted on that type of question being included. Thus the directive was a compromise between the old and the new. However, the new received sufficient emphasis to ensure against future errors. My friend Dr. Angel Gari Lacruz has recently found a different set of printed instructions, much closer to the original version of *la Suprema*, whose *Instructions of 29 Aug. 1614*, clauses 1-12 and 26-31, are reproduced almost literally. A copy is found inserted in a manuscript volume of the Biblioteca Universitaria de Zaragoza (MS 104) with documents pertaining to the Inquisition of Logroño: *Instrvcion para los comissarios del Santo Officio, en las aueriguaciones tocantes al crimen de Brugeria,* 3 pages, no place or date, but the year "1669" added. The clauses are number 1 through 17, and the last, with the standing order to return the document to the Holy Office in case of the commissioner's death, appears to be copied from clause 14 of the printed instructions mentioned above, n. 55.

58. *Lib* 832 ff. 158ʳ⁻ᵛ, 165ʳ⁻ᵛ, Tribunal to Council, 27 Sept. 1614; received in Madrid Oct. 1614.

59. Idem f. 158ᵛ; see *Accounts of 27 Sept. 1614* ff. 160ᵛ-162ʳ.

60. *Lib* 832 f. 165ʳ (T./C. 27-9-1614; n. 58, above).

61. *Lib* 334 ff. 270ᵛ-271ʳ, Council to Tribunal, 6 Oct. 1614.

62. *Leg* 1958 Exp. 1-2 passim, Salazar's papers from the inspection of the Court of Confiscations at the Granada tribunal 1614-1616.

63. *Leg* 1679 Exp. 2.1 No. 29 f. 33ʳ⁻ᵛ. Valle's remarks are a direct extension of a copy of the instructions of 29 Aug. 1614 written in Salazar's hand (idem ff. 29ʳ-32ʳ).

64. Fray León de Araníbar's letter of 16 Jan. 1616 is not extant, but a long extract from it is quoted in the *Eighth Report of Salazar* f. 46ʳ⁻ᵛ.

65. *Eighth Report of Salazar* f. 46ᵛ.

66. Idem ff. 45ᵛ-46ʳ.

67. Cf. pp. 325 and 382 f., above.

68. *Méritos of Juan de la Borda* f. 156ᵛ.

69. See *Lib* 832 f. 157ʳ, Application from Juan de la Borda to the Inquisitor General, Madrid, 2 May 1614. According to a marginal note to the *Méritos of Juan de la Borda* f. 156, dispensation was granted on 26 Aug. 1614.

70. While Juan de la Borda's sentence had been for only three years, that of Pedro de Arburu had been for ten years' confinement in a monastery, see *Third Report of the Auto de fe* f. 369ᵛ. Thus with the new instructions six years of Fray Pedro de Arburu's sentence were remitted. A letter of 9 Aug. 1616 from the Tribunal to the Council mentions an application from Fray Pedro at Urdax asking for a certificate from *la Suprema* similar to that granted to his cousin, Juan de la Borda (*Lib* 796 f. 367ʳ). The Council complied with the application immediately (see *Lib* 335 f. 110ʳ, Council to Tribunal, 17 Aug. 1616).

71. *Accounts of 27 Sept. 1614* f. 159ʳ; see *Leg* 1683 Exp. 1 f. 1290ʳ (ff. 1289ʳ-1290ᵛ, Examination of Pedro de Arburu, Urdax, 29 Dec. 1619).

72. *Leg* 1683 Exp. 1 ff. 1288ʳ-1289ʳ, Examination of Juan de la Borda, Elizondo, 27 Dec. 1619; idem ff. 1289ʳ-1290ᵛ, Examination of Pedro de Arburu (n. 71, above).

73. The hearings of Juan de la Borda and Pedro de Arburu (nn. 71 and 72, above) were held by Josef de Elizondo, who here designates himself as "abad del monasterio de Urdax, diputado del Reino de Navarra y comisario de la Santa Inquisición" (*Leg* 1683 Exp. 1 ff. 1288ʳ, 1289ʳ).

74. See CARO BAROJA *De nuevo* p. 287 f.

75. I have seen a volume containing baptisms and marriages in the parish archive of Vera, which unfortunately, on account of several fires, is somewhat incomplete. It begins in 1616 and continues up to about 1650, but Hualde's signature appears for the last time on 29 Mar. 1644.

76. See chap. 7 n. 66, above.

77. In the Archivo Histórico Nacional, Sección de Jesuitas, I have found letters from Solarte to the provincial of the Jesuits from ca. 1620.

78. Bernardo BARREIRO DE VÁZQUEZ VARELA "Archivos secretos. Adiciones y notas a una lista de Inquisidores de Galicia desde el establecimiento... hasta... 1700" *Galicia Diplomática* III (1888) 153-155, 164-166, 178-181, 187-189, 194-197, and 201-203. San Vicente is mentioned on p. 179. Regarding San Vicente's life in Mallorca and in Zaragoza, see above, chap. 12.1 with n. 24. After leaving Galicia San Vicente was for a considerable time an inquisitor in Toledo.

79. In 1629 he signed as second inquisitor to the Logroño Tribunal and in 1630 as first inquisitor (*Lib* 802-803, letters from the Tribunal to the Council 1628-1631): cf. *Lib* 1244 ff. 195ʳ-196ʳ, Payroll of the Tribunal of Logroño for [1632].

80. Bernardo Barreiro (loc. cit. n. 78, above) quotes statements from the Galicia tribunal's letters to *la Suprema* (see *Leg* 2889 passim).

81. BN, MS 18.715 No. 11 ff. 1ʳ-53ᵛ, title: "Papel del Señor Don Isidoro de San Vicente que habiendo sido inquisidor en diversas inquisiciones fue después del Consejo Supremo de Inquisición" hereafter cited as *San Vicente's Manual*. This manual was edited from

another copy in the Biblioteca Nacional, MS 831, in Elias AMÉZAGA *Guia del perfecto Inquisidor* Bilbao 1968 pp. 284-309. A third copy, Biblioteca Nacional MS 8660 (olim V 377) was used by Lea, who did not, however, realize who the author was (cf. LEA *Inquisition of Spain* IV p. 240). In the archive of *la Suprema* in the Archivo Histórico Nacional there are yet more copies in the above-mentioned series of *libros para la recopilación* (n. 55, above).

82. *San Vicente's Manual* chap. 13, pp. 296-297 in Amézaga's edition (see preceding note). Here San Vicente gives several extracts from the *Instructions of 29 Aug. 1614* which, he writes, "are to be found in the Tribunal at Logroño." This, however, does not prevent him from referring to Bernardo de Como and asserting him to be one of the leading authorities on the subject. Bernardo de Como was an inquisitor at Lucerne and was responsible for one of the largest witch persecutions of the 16th century (HANSEN 1901 pp. 34, 510). In about 1510 he wrote a document entitled *De strigiis*, which was later published (Milan 1566, Rome 1584; see ROBBINS 1959 p. 562 no. 79 and RUSSEL 1972 p. 365).

83. Becerra's oath of allegiance made on his accession to the post of councillor is dated 28 Aug. 1617 (*Lib* 1338 f. 66^r; n. 6, above).

84. I have found no documentation regarding the death of Becerra, but his signature ceases to appear in the Council's letters in 1619.

85. *Lib* 1251 ff. 11^r-67^r, *title:* "Tratado de D. Alonso Becerra sobre tocar al Santo Oficio el delito de moneda falsa cometida por familiares." Undated.

86. *Lib* 796 f. 244^r, Valle to inquisitor general, 5 May 1615; received in Madrid 16 May; see *Lib* 334 f. 330^r, Council to Tribunal, 16 May 1615, in which the visitation is cancelled and Valle is granted three months' leave.

87. See *Lib* 796 f. 365^r, Tribunal to Council, 1 July 1616, in which Valle informs *la Suprema* that on 27 June Aranda left on visitation to the southwestern region of the Tribunal.

88. On 30 July Salazar's signature again appears on the letters of the Tribunal. He and Valle are both signatories until 9 Aug., but as early as 7 Sept. Salazar speaks of Valle as his deceased colleague (*Lib* 796 ff. 328, 331, 350 et passim). It was while ordering Valle's papers that Salazar came into possession of the letters mentioned above (see chap. 11 n. 120, chap. 12 nn. 90 and 102, and *Examination of Salazar at Valencia* ff. 786^v-787^r).

89. At first Salazar and Aranda were alone together. In 1617 Juan de Vallejo arrived, and as he had greatest seniority he took the post of senior inquisitor. This meant that Salazar was again relegated to the position of third inquisitor as in the time of Becerra and Valle (see *Lib* 797 passim). Salazar's relationships with his colleagues in the Tribunal during this period are revealed with some clarity in his remarks during the inspection of the Tribunal in 1619 (*Examination of Salazar at Valencia* ff. 770^r-778^v et passim). Salazar relates that things grew to such a pitch that he was blamed when the weather was bad in Logroño (Idem f. 778^{r-v}).

90. See *Autobiography* f. 4^r, where Salazar states that the appointment as inquisitor at Murcia took place on 3 Aug. 1618. He himself

regarded it as a banishment (*Salazar's letter from Valencia* f. 3^{r-v}). The "banishment" occurred when Salazar's old patron Sandoval y Rojas was still inquisitor general (he did not die until 7 Dec. that year, see LLORENTE 1817-18 IV p. 262).

91. See Question 3 in the list of questions from the inspection of the Tribunal in 1619 (*Leg* 1683 Exp. 1 f. 742^r) and the replies from e.g. the *fiscal* Gregorio de Leguizamo, the secretaries Juan Zorrilla, Francisco de Peralta, Francisco Pardo, Lázaro de Badarán, and the porter Pedro de Gamarra (ff. 293^v, 383^r-385^r, 409^v, 597^v-599^r, 614^v, 632^{r-v}).

92. *Autobiography* f. 4^r. At this date Fray Luis de Aliaga had just become inquisitor general (LLORENTE 1817-18 IV p. 262).

93. See *Autobiography* f. 4^r, where the appointment is dated 16 Feb. 1622. It occurred shortly after Andrés Pacheco had succeeded to the office of inquisitor general (12 Feb. 1622, LLORENTE 1817-18 IV p. 263).

94. Salazar's oath of allegiance on his accession to the post of *fiscal* to *la Suprema* is dated 27 July 1628 (*Lib* 1338 f. 150^v). On account of a lacuna in the *"Libro de juramentos"* from 1629 to 1635, I have been unable to find any reference to his appointment as councillor, but his signature appears on the letters of *la Suprema* from 12 July 1631 onwards (see *Lib* 822 f. 394^r et passim).

95. See Emilio MENESES GARCÍA "Construcción del tablado para el auto de fe de 1632" *Revista de Archivos, Bibliotecas y Museos* 3d Series Vol. 72 (1965) 363-392, especially p. 375.

96. Salazar's censure took the form of a memorandum dated 29 May 1632 (*Lib* 1267 f. 150^{r-v}). The inquisitor general was Antonio de Zapata y Mendoza, who on the orders of Felipe IV retired in the same year (LLORENTE 1817-18 IV p. 263).

97. *Lib* 1267 ff. 148^r-149^v, Salazar to Philip IV, Madrid (no date) 1633. Salazar's memorandum comprises eight clauses and follows immediately (f. 147^{r-v}). This occurred while Fray Antonio de Sotomayor was inquisitor general. Like his predecessor, he was obliged to retire on orders from the king in 1643 (LLORENTE 1817-18 IV p. 264).

98. The statement is to be found in the pamphlet *Muertes de personas insignes y señores* (Madrid), copy in the Biblioteca Nacional (Madrid), sign. 6-2/3639. See CARO BAROJA 1961 p. 268 with n. 35.

99. See CARO BAROJA *De nuevo* pp. 265-267, 316-317, and HENNINGSEN *Papers of Salazar* pp. 85-86, 102, and n. 9.

100. Charles WILLIAMS *Witchcraft*, London 1941.

GLOSSARY

Abad. Abbot; in Navarra, Galicia, and other parts of Spain, also a parish priest.

Abjuración. Renunciation of heresy in general and especially of the heresy of which the accused is suspected. Abjuration *de levi* entailed no special penalty in case of reincidence, but abjuration *de vehementi* involved burning after reincidence.

Acto positivo. Positive indication, tangible proof.

Ad cautelam. Absolved. Absolved by the benefit of doubt.

Alcalde. Mayor.

Alguacil. Constable or executive officer of the Inquisition, in charge of imprisonments.

Aquelarre. Witches' sabbath, literally "field of the goat" (*aquelarre* is the Castilian spelling of the Basque word *akellarre*, from *akerr* 'he-goat' and *larre* 'meadow').

Autillo. Small auto de fe, usually held in a church.

Auto de fe. Literally "act of faith." A ceremony where sentences were pronounced and those delinquents who had been condemned were handed over to the civil authorities who carried out the burnings. An auto de fe was usually held in a public square.

Ayuda de costa. An annual payment to the officials of the Inquisition forming one-sixth of the ordinary salary.

Bachiller. "Bachelor," the lowest university degree, ranking under those of *licenciado* and *doctor*.

Brother of the Inquisition. See *Familiar*.

Brujería. Witchcraft, the secret rites supposed to be carried out by the societies of male and female "witches" (*brujos y brujas*).

Calificador. Theological unsalaried official of the Inquisition who acted as censor and determined whether charges of the accused involved heresy.

Cárceles secretas, las. The secret prison, literally "the secret prison-cells." The place where the accused was isolated during the trial.

Carta acordada. A circular letter, usually issued to all the tribunals of the Inquisition by *la Suprema*. The *cartas acordadas*, or subsequent regulations promulgated by the Council of the Inquisition, were supplemental to the printed instructions of the Spanish Inquisition.

Casa de penitencia. Literally "house of penance," the punitive prison or house of correction where the persons sentenced to do penance by the Inquisition were secluded.

Comisario. Local commissioner of the Inquisition, usually being a parish priest.

Confitente. Adj., "having made confession"; subst., a delinquent who has confessed his crimes.

Consiliario. Councillor, member of *la Suprema*.

Consulta de fe. Conference where judgment is passed in cases of heresy, cf. *consultor.*

Consultor. Unsalaried official who assisted the inquisitors as legal or theological adviser in the *consultas de fe.*

Council of Inquisition. See *Suprema, la.*

Curador. Guardian whose assistance was required when the accused was under 25 years old.

Curaduría. The *curador*'s oath of guardianship.

De levi, De vehementi. See *Abjuración.*

Doctor. "Doctor," the highest university degree, ranking over those of *bachiller* and *licenciado.*

Dogmatizante. Agitator and proselytizer for a heretical movement.

Doli capaz. Capacity to act with evil intention. Children under six or seven years were according to Roman law *doli incapaces.*

Ducado. Spanish gold coin until the end of the sixteenth century, and later a unit of account equalling 375 *maravedís.*

Edad de discreción. Age of discretion, by Torquemada fixed at twelve for girls and fourteen for boys.

Edicto de fe. Edict of Faith, a comprehensive list or catalogue of all forms of heresy, designed for reading out in the churches.

Edicto de gracia. Edict of Grace, a formula denouncing a specific kind of heresy and granting a period for voluntary confessions.

Ensalmador. Literally a "charmer," folk healer.

Escribano real. Notary or scribe of the royal justice.

Expediente. Dossier.

Familiar. Unsalaried lay agent of the Inquisition, usually a member or Brother of its fraternity, the *Hermandad de San Pedro Martir.*

Fiscal. Prosecutor of the Inquisition.

Fray. Title used by friars. Abbreviated Fr.

Habitante. Inhabitant.

Hechicería. Sorcery, the magical techniques of village wizards and sorceresses (*hechiceros* and *hechiceras*) and of folk healers or "wise" men and women (*curanderos* and *curanderas*).

Hermandad de San Pedro Martir. The fraternity of the Inquisition.

Infamia. Infamy.

Inquisidor general. Grand inquisitor, the president of *la Suprema* and the head of the Spanish Inquisition.

Jubileo. Letter of indulgence.

Jurado. Village elder.

Legajo. File.

Legua. Spanish league, equivalent to 5.572 kilometers or 3.5 miles.

Libro de testificados. Literally "Book of denounced persons," i.e. the "secret files" of people suspected of heresy, kept by each tribunal of the Inquisition.

Libro de visita. Literally "visitation book." A volume wherein were recorded all the hearings and transactions carried out on a *visita de distrito*.

Libro de votos. Minute book of verdicts of the Inquisition.

Licenciado. Holder of a university degree, intermediate between that of *bachiller* and *doctor*.

Limpieza de sangre. Literally "purity of blood," i.e. having no heretics as ancestors. Applicants for posts in the Holy Office were, at their own expense, obliged to provide documentary proof of family purity.

Maravedí. Smallest unit of account, cf. *real* and *ducado*.

Merindad. The district of a royal judge, *merino*.

Méritos. Literally "merits." Summary of a trial record.

Modo de proceder. Manual of procedure.

Negativo. Adj., "denying"; subst., "denier," one who pleads not guilty.

Nomina. Charm, literally "list," e.g., of holy names or magical words.

Ordinario, el. The bishop in his capacity as judge, here used of the bishop's delegate in the jury of the Inquisition.

Precepto Pascual. The obligation of all Catholics of going to communion between Lent and Whitsun.

Real. Aragonesian unit of account equal to 34 maravedís (in 1608 the annual wage of a porter of the Inquisition was 1,500 *reales* plus 300 *reales* of *ayuda de costa*, and a prisoner's food was calculated at one *real* per day).

Ratificación. Ratification, the act of confirmation of a declaration to the Inquisition required before the evidence could be used against others. Normally this "ratification" was not undertaken before proceedings had been opened against the person concerned, but the regulations of the Inquisition allowed ratification to be undertaken in advance (*ad perpetuam*), if, for instance, there was a danger of the witness's dying.

Reconciliado. Reconciled, released from the state of excommunication.

Relación de causas. Report submitted by a tribunal of the Inquisition to *la Suprema* containing summaries of the cases completed in a certain period.

Relación de visita. Report submitted by a tribunal of the Inquisition to *la Suprema* containing the cases resulting from a *visita de distrito*.

Relajado. Literally "handed over" (to the secular authorities), i.e. sent to the stake.

Relapso. A former delinquent who has relapsed.

Relator. Literally "reporter," an official of *la Suprema* in charge of filing the incoming correspondence and making summaries of the appeal cases.

Renunciation of heresy. See *Abjuración*.

Revocante. An accused who recants his confession.

Sabbath, witches'. See *Aquelarre*.

Saludador. Literally "healer," a folk healer with a special gift, also used of a witchfinder.

Sambenito. A corruption of *saco bendito*, "blessed sack," the penitential garment prescribed by the Inquisition.

Secretario de cámara. Private or confidential secretary of the inquisitor general.

Secretario del Secreto. Secretary to the inquisitors of a tribunal with admittance to *el Secreto*.

Secreto, el. Literally "the Secret," i.e. the office and archives of a tribunal of the Holy Office to which only the inquisitors and their confidential staff had admittance.

Sorcery. See *Hechicería*.

Suprema, la. Abbreviation of *el Consejo de la Suprema y General Inquisición*, the Council of Inquisition, with fixed residence in Madrid as of 1608.

Vecino. A citizen or inhabitant of a special area; here used as head of family; one *vecino* is reckoned to every five inhabitants.

Visita de cárceles. Inspection of the inquisitorial prisons.

Visita de distrito. Provincial inspection carried out by the Inquisition.

Visita de tribunal. La Suprema's inspection of a tribunal of Inquisition.

Witchcraft. See *Brujería.*

Witches' sabbath. See *Aquelarre.*

Wizard. See under *Hechicería.*

BIBLIOGRAPHY

1. ALPHABETIC LIST OF THE SIXTY KEY DOCUMENTS.[a]

Abecedario, undated (chap. 11 n. 182) *Leg* 1679 Exp. 2.1 No. 21[b] 1 folio.

Accounts of 27 Sept. 1614 (chap. 7 n. 24) *Lib* 832 ff. 159^r-162^r.

Anathema of Valladolid, undated (chap. 6 n. 19), printed copy in BN MS 2440 ff. 422^r-423^r.

Autobiography, Salazar's, [4 June 1622] (chap. 3 n. 45) *Leg* 2220 No. 21 ff. 2^r-5^v. Published in HENNINGSEN 1978 pp. 583-586.

Auto de fe, First Report of the, [Oct. 1610] (chap. 2 n. 5) *Lib* 835 ff. 421^r-424^r.

Auto de fe, Second Report of the, [31 Oct. 1610] (chap. 2 n. 20) *Lib* 835 ff. 340^{r-v}, 345^r-351^v, to be published as Text 2 in *The Salazar Documents.*

Auto de fe, Third Report of the, [29 Nov. 1610] (chap. 2 n. 32) *Lib* 835 ff. 356^r-369^v.

Bishop, First Letter of the, 4 Mar. 1611 (chap. 7 n. 67) *Leg* 1679 Exp. 2.1 No. 26[b] ff. 1^r-2^v, No. 31[a] f. 1^r, to be published as Text 5 in *The Salazar Documents.*

Bishop, Second Letter of the, 1 Apr. 1611 (chap. 7 n. 72) *Leg* 1679 Exp. 2.1 31[d] ff. 9^r-10^r, to be published as Text 7 in *The Salazar Documents.*

Bishop's Report, The, [1 Apr. 1611] (chap. 1 n. 114) *Leg* 1679 Exp. 2.1 No. 31[e] ff. 1^r-9^r, to be published as Text 8 in *The Salazar Documents.*

Borda, Méritos de Juan de la [between Nov. 1613 and Mar. 1614] (chap. 8 n. 51) *Lib* 832 f. 156^{r-v}.

Colleagues' Letter of 24 Mar. [1612], *The* (chap. 12 n. 2) *Leg* 1679 Exp. 2.1 No. 26 [a] ff. 1^r-2^r.

---

a. The chapter and note numbers in parentheses indicate where in the present work each of the sixty key manuscripts is mentioned for the first time and fully described.

Food Accounts. See *Accounts of 27 Sept. 1614.*

Goiburu, Méritos of Juanes de, [ca. 7 Jan. 1613] (chap. 2 n. 1) *Lib* 832 ff. 170ʳ-171ᵛ.

Instructions of 26 Mar. 1611 (chap. 9 n. 56) *Lib* 333 ff. 144ʳ-147ʳ, to be published as Text 6 in *The Salazar Documents.*

Instructions of 29 Aug. 1614 (chap. 13 n. 42) *Lib* 334 ff. 244ᵛ-253ʳ, to be published as Text 18 in *The Salazar Documents.*

Joint Sentence, [Oct. 1610] (chap. 2 n. 5) *Lib* 835 ff. 386ʳ-400ʳ.

Letter from Fuenterrabía, Salazar's, 4 Sept. 1611 (chap. 11 n. 16) *Leg* 1679 Exp. 2.1 No. 31[f] ff. 1ʳ-3ʳ.

Logroño Edict, The, undated (chap. 6 n. 7), a printed copy in *Lib* 1244 ff. 228ʳ-232ʳ.

Memorial of 2 Mar. 1611, Salazar's (chap. 8 n. 66) *Leg* 1683 Exp. 1 ff. 19ʳ-23ᵛ.

Origen y fundación, [José de Ribera's, posterior to 1654] (chap. 13n. 11) Royal Library of Copenhagen, Ny kgl. Saml. 128ᶜ 4⁰ 4 + 96 pp.

Pamplona Manuscript, Becerra and Valle's, [Autumn 1613] (chap. 2 n. 21, see also chap. 12 n. 122) AGN, manuscript without signature, published 1972 by Florencio Idoate (IDOATE *Documento*).

Relación de causas 1610/11 (chap. 7 n. 9), one copy *(A)* in *Lib* 835 ff. 438ʳ-443ᵛ, another *(B)* in *Lib* 835 ff. 449ʳ-458ᵛ.

Relación de causas 1613/14 (chap. 12 n. 110) *Lib* 835 ff. 500ʳ-514ʳ.

Relación de causas 1614/15 (chap. 12 n. 77) *Lib* 835 ff. 517ʳ-532ᵛ.

Report of the General Visitation Cases (chap. 11 n. 238); for information on this lost document see above, p. 309 and chap. 12 n. 11.

Report of an Official, 14 Nov. 1610 (chap. 9 n. 23), one copy (A) in *Lib* 1252 ff. 391ʳ-400ʳ, another (B) in *Lib* 1259 ff. 147ᵛ-159ʳ.

Salazar, First Report of, 24 Mar. 1612 (chap. 6 n. 28, see also chap. 12 n. 30) *Lib* 795 ff. 357ʳ-368ʳ; the first eight paragraphs to be published as Text 11 in *The Salazar Documents.*

Salazar, Second Report of, 24 Mar. 1612 (chap. 1 n. 113, see also chap. 12 n. 35) *Leg* 1679 Exp. 2.1 No. 21[a] ff. 1ʳ-17ʳ, including the *Glosses* idem No. 6 ff. 1ʳ-6ᵛ; to be published as Text 12 in *The Salazar Documents.*

Salazar, Third Report of, [24 Sept. 1613(?)] (chap. 12 n. 98) *Leg* 1679 Exp. 2.1 No. 29[g] ff. 25ʳ-26ʳ; to be published as Text 13 in *The Salazar Documents.*

Salazar, Fourth Report of, 3 Oct. 1613 (chap. 3 n. 51) *Leg* 1679 Exp. 2.1 No. 29[a] ff. 1ʳ-10ʳ; to be published as Text 14 of *The Salazar Documents.*

Salazar, Fifth Report of, 7 Jan. 1614 (chap. 10 n. 3) *Leg* 1679 Exp. 2.1 No. 29[c] ff. 11ʳ-15ʳ; to be published as Text 15 in *The Salazar Documents.*

Salazar, Sixth Report of, [Summer 1614] (chap. 11 n. 219; see also chap. 13.3) *Leg* 1679 Exp. 2.1 No. 29[e] ff. 17ʳ-20ᵛ; to be published as Text 16 in *The Salazar Documents.* Another copy is found in the BN MS 2031 ff. 129ʳ-132ᵛ and was published by Julio Caro Baroja in 1933 (CARO BAROJA 1933 pp. 131-145).

Salazar, Seventh Report of, [Summer 1614] (chap. 13 n. 39; see also chap. 13.4) *Leg* 1679 Exp. 2.1 No. 29[g] ff. 27ʳ-28ᵛ; to be published as Text 17 in *The Salazar Documents;* another copy idem No. 24[a] ff. 1ʳ-2ᵛ.

Salazar, Eighth Report of, 28 Jan. 1617 (chap. 11 n. 237) *Leg* 1679 Exp. 2.1 No. 4 ff. 3ʳ-8ᵛ.

Salazar, Ninth Report of, 11 Oct. 1623 (chap. 13 n. 52) *Leg* 1679 Exp. 2.1 No. 4 ff. 32ʳ-35ᵛ.

Salazar at Valencia, Examination of, 28 Aug.-1 Sept. 1619 (chap. 3 n. 42) *Leg* 1683 Exp. 1 ff. 749ʳ-789ʳ.

Salazar, Witnesses in Favor of, [1620] (chap. 12 n. 27) *Leg* 1683 Exp. 2 ff. 417ʳ-458ʳ.

Salazar's Letter from Valencia [posterior to 27 Aug. 1619] (chap. 11 n. 51) *Leg* 1683 Exp. 2, loose letter inside the volume.

Salazar's Memorandum of 15 June 1613 (chap. 12 n. 75) *Leg* 1683 Exp. 1 ff. 17ʳ-18ʳ.

Salazar's Memorandum of 1 Sept. 1613 (chap. 12 n. 95) *Leg* 1679 Exp. 2.1 No. 30[a] f. 1ʳ.

Salazar's Memorandum of 13 Nov. 1613 (chap. 12 n. 106) *Leg* 1679 Exp. 2.1 No. 4[o] ff. 1ʳ-4ʳ.

Salazar's Visitation Book, Volume "F" of, 1611 (chap. 7 n. 31) *Leg* 1679 Exp. 2.2 2 + 626 folios, see the survey of this manuscript in Witch List, above (case nos. 441-520). The three first pages with the original index are published in CARO BAROJA *De nuevo* pp. 326-328.

Salazar's Vote of 8 June 1610 (chap. 8 n. 108) *Leg* 1679 Exp. 2.1 No. 30[c] f. 1ʳ⁻ᵛ.

Sansín, Méritos of Juanes de, [ca. 7 Jan. 1613] (chap. 2 n. 1) *Lib* 832 ff. 172ʳ-174ʳ.

San Vicente 1610, Memorial of, [10 July] (chap. 8 n. 82) *Lib* 835 ff. 352ʳ-355ʳ.

San Vicente's Memorandum of 9 July 1611 (chap. 11 n. 116) *Lib* 795 ff. 164ʳ-165ʳ.

San Vicente's Memorandum of 3 Oct. 1611 (chap. 11 n. 119) *Lib* 795 ff. 208ʳ-209ᵛ.

San Vicente's Manual, [posterior to 1639] (chap. 13 n. 81) BN MS 18.715 No. 11 ff. 1ʳ-53ᵛ; another copy, BN MS 831, was published in AMÉZAGA 1961 pp. 284-309.

Solarte, First Letter of, 17 Jan. 1611 (chap. 7 n. 88) *Leg* 1679 Exp. 2.1 No. 8[a] ff. 1^r-2^v; to be published as Text 3 in *The Salazar Documents.*

Solarte, Second Letter of, 26 and 27 Jan. 1611 (chap. 10 n. 23) *Leg* 1679 Exp. 2.1 No. 28[a] ff. 1^r-2^r; to be published as Text 4 in *The Salazar Documents.*

Solarte's Letter to the Bishop, 25 Mar. 1611 (chap. 10 n. 24) *Leg* 1679 Exp. 2.1 No. 31[b] f. 5^r; to be published as Text 9 of *The Salazar Documents.*

Solarte's Report to the Bishop, [25 Mar. 1611] (chap. 10 n. 24) *Leg* 1679 Exp. 2.1 No. 31[c] ff. 6^r-7^r, reproduced in CARO BAROJA *De nuevo* pp. 285-286 n. 55; to be published as Text 10 in *The Salazar Documents.*

Statistics of 9 Mar. 1611 (chap. 10 n. 41) *Leg* 1679 Exp. 2.1 No. 23[b] f. 1^{r-v}, reproduced in CARO BAROJA *De nuevo* pp. 283-284 (printed with catastrophic errors, cf. the revised edition in CARO BAROJA 1970 p. 305 f.).

Tribunal's Letter of 13 Feb. 1609 (chap. 4 n. 1) *Leg* 1679 Exp. 2.1 No. 18 f. 1^{r-v}.

Ulibarri, Trial Record of María de, 9 Sept. - 29 Nov. 1611 (chap. 11 n. 200) *Leg* 1679 Exp. 2.1 No. 41 ff. 671^r-683^v; see also case no. 354.

Valencia, First Discourse of Pedro de, 20 Apr. 1611 (chap. 1 n. 32) *Lib* 1231 ff. 608^r-629^r; another copy, BN MS 7579 Part II, was published by M. SERRANO Y SANZ in *Revista de Extremadura* 2 (1900) 289-303, 337-347.

Valencia, Second Discourse of Pedro de, undated (chap. 1 n. 35) BN MS 7579 Part I ff. [1-19], published by M. SERRANO Y SANZ in *Revista de Archivos, Bibliotecas y Museos* 3rd series vol. II (1906) 445-454.

Valle's Visitation Book, Examination of, [1620] (chap. 7 n. 5) *Leg* 1683 Exp. 1 ff. 1524^v-1531^v.

Visitation, What is to be undertaken under, [early 17th century] (chap. 6 n. 1) *Lib* 1259 ff. 130^v-134^v.

Zozaya, Sentence of María de, [Oct. 1610] (chap. 8 n. 54) *Lib* 835 ff. 401^r-420^r.

2. *LIBROS* AND *LEGAJOS* CONSULTED IN THE *SECCION DE INQUISICIÓN* OF THE ARCHIVO HISTORICO NACIONAL (MADRID).[b]

Lib 246 (olim Lib. 5). Ff. 1-192 contain the original "Libro 4° Tomo 2°"

b. The references given in parentheses, e.g. (olim Lib. 5), are those of the Archive of Simancas. Because of the great scholarship of Lea and Schäfer they are still of importance. For the transfer of the archives of the Inquisition from Simancas to Madrid in 1908-1916, see chap. 3 n. 1, above.

of royal decrees in favor of the Inquisition; ff. 193-233, the rest of the volume, are a copy book of letters and provisions of the inquisitors general 1517-1534.

Lib 251 (olim Lib. 10). Ff. 1-291 are the original "Libro 8º Tomo 2º" of royal decrees in favor of the Inquisition; ff. 292-381 containing provisions of the inquisitors general from the first decades of the 17th century originally constituted a separate volume.

Lib 271 (olim Lib. 30). "Libro 4º de decretos reales y consultas originales" 1620-1629.

Lib 316 (olim Lib. 72). *Part I* contains the original "Libro 1º" of letters from *la Suprema* to the inquisitions of Aragón and Navarra (1514-1517); *Part II* is "Libro 2º" of the same series (1517-1519).

Lib 317 (olim Lib. 73). "Libro 3º" of the same series (1519-1523).

Lib 319 (olim Lib. 75). "Libro 4º Tomo 2º" of the same series (1523-1529).

Lib 322 (olim Lib. 78). *Part I* contains "Libro 7º" of the same series (1536-1546); *Part II* another volume of the same series (1547-1548).

Lib 332 (olim Lib. 88). "Libro 17º" of the same series (1606-1609).

Lib 333 (olim Lib. 89). "Libro 18º" of the same series (1609-1613).

Lib 334 (olim Lib. 90). "Libro 19º" of the same series (1613-1615).

Lib 335 (olim Lib. 91). "Libro 20º" of the same series (1615-1618).

Lib 366 (olim Lib. 117). A copy book of provisions of the confidential secretariat (*secretaria de cámara*) of Inquisitor General Bernardo de Sandoval y Rojas (1610-1618).

Lib 367 (olim Lib. 118). *Part I* contains the papers concerning an inspection of the tribunal of Llerena; *Part II* is a copy book of provisions of the confidential secretariat of Inquisitor General Acevedo (1603-1608).

Lib 490 (olim 233). "Libro 2º" of provisions of the inquisitor general, payrolls etc. (1599-1633).

Lib 497 (olim Lib. 240). "Libro 1º" of the unprinted instructions of the Inquisition, containing the *cartas acordadas* no. 1-450 (1513-1631).

Lib 572 (olim Lib. 311). "Libro 1º" of letters from *la Suprema* to the inquisitions of Castilla (1499-1525).

Lib 573 (olim Lib. 312). "Libro 2º" of the same series (1525-1540).

Lib 577 (olim Lib. 316). "Libro 6º" of the same series (1569-1610).

Lib 783 (olim Lib. 513). "Libro [2º]" of *relaciones de causas* of the Inquisition at Sardinia (1592-1688).

Lib 791 (olim Lib. 521). "Libro 7º" of letters from the Inquisition at Logroño to *la Suprema* (1593-1596).

Lib 794 (olim Lib. 524). "Libro 10º" of the same series (1607-1609).

Lib 795 (olim Lib. 525). "Libro 11º" of the same series (1610-1613).

Lib 796 (olim Lib. 526). "Libro 12°" of the same series (1614-1616).

Lib 797 (olim Lib. 527). "Libro 13°" of the same series (1617-1619).

Lib 802 (olim Lib. 532). "Libro 18°" of the same series (1628-1629).

Lib 803 (olim Lib. 533). "Libro 19°" of the same series (1630-1631).

Lib 822 (olim Lib. 552). "Libro 1°" of letters from *la Suprema* to the Inquisition at Logroño (1619-1633).

Lib 832 (olim Lib. 561). "Libro 2°" of *relaciones de causas* of the Inquisition at Logroño, containing *méritos* of trials (1594-1678).

Lib 833 (olim Lib. 562). "Libro 3°" of the same series, containing *relaciones de causas* (1538-1580).

Lib 834 (olim Lib. 563). "Libro 4°" of the same series, containing *relaciones de causas* (1581-1599).

Lib 835 (olim Lib. 564). "Libro 5°" of the same series, containing *relaciones de causas* (1600-1617).

Lib 836 (olim Lib. 565). "Libro 6°" of the same series, containing *relaciones de causas* (1618-1636).

Lib 1158 (olim Lib. 866). "Libro 1° de votos de Aragón," i.e. of verdicts in cases of faith in the inquisitions of Aragón and Navarra (1571-1616).

Lib 1229 (olim Lib. 937). "Libro 17°" of a series of miscellanies "para la recopilación."

Lib 1231 (olim Lib. 939). "Libro 19°" of the same series.

Lib 1237 (olim Lib. 945). "Libro 26°" of the same series.

Lib 1244 (olim Lib. 952). "Libro 33°" of the same series.

Lib 1251 (olim Lib. 960). "Libro 43°" of the same series.

Lib 1252 (olim Lib. 961). "Libro 44°" of the same series.

Lib 1259 (olim Lib. 968). "Libro 51°" of the same series.

Lib 1267 (olim Lib. 976). "Libro 59°" of the same series.

Lib 1280 (olim Lib. 989). "Apparently a volume pertaining to the same series of miscellanies "para la recopilación."

Lib 1325 (olim Lib. 1034). A volume pertaining to another series of miscellanies.

Lib 1338 (olim Lib. 1055). "Libro 1°" of oaths of allegiance sworn by officials on accession to posts at *la Suprema* (1574-1635).

Leg 1259 (olim Leg. 75 de la Sala 44). "Legajo 5" of letter "J" of examinations of *limpieza de sangre* of applicants for posts in the inquisitions of Aragón and Navarra.

Leg 1371 (olim Leg. 187 de la Sala 44). "Legajo 3" of letter "A" of examinations of *limpieza de sangre* of applicants for posts in the inquisitions of Castilla.

Leg 1372 (olim Leg. 188 de la Sala 44). "Legajo 4" of letter "A" of the same series.

Leg 1679 (olim Leg. 100 de la Sala 51). "Inquisición de Logroño. Procesos de fe, Legajo 1." A capsule of documents pertaining to the extinguished archives of the Inquisition at Logroño. These records were borrowed by *la Suprema* and never returned, and thus saved from destruction. They are divided in two parts, of which the latter, *Expediente 2*, is of extreme importance for our study. It contains nearly all the reports of Salazar and a wealth of other letters and documents related to the great witch trial (1609-1614) and to the Tribunal's handling of the witch problem throughout the following ten years (*Exp. 2.1*), and it contains also a huge parchment volume with another of our main sources: *Volume "F" of Salazar's Visitation Book (Exp. 2.2)*. According to *Ninth Report of Salazar*, which is in fact a letter from the Tribunal to the Council, dated 11 Oct. 1623, the precious documentation was forwarded to *la Suprema* on this occasion (see *Ninth Report of Salazar* passim).[c]

---

c. Julio Caro Baroja, whose study is based exclusively on this capsule, has given a thorough survey of its contents (see CARO BAROJA *De nuevo* pp. 323-328, "Indice de los papeles del legajo 1679, 2"). He uses letters to subdivide an archive signature, when it refers to more than one document. This is the same principle that I have followed (see e.g. the reference "No. 21[a]" in first item of Key Documents, above). But we do not always coincide in our numbering. However, the reader who wants to compare my references with Caro Baroja's list may easily identify the documents, except for a few cases where Caro Baroja has misread or left out the date. *Additions and corrections to Caro Baroja's list:* (No. 5) Undated memorial of Salazar; the date should be 13 Nov. 1613, i.e. *Salazar's Memorandum of 13 Nov. 1613*. (No. 16) Letter dated 21 July 1613; read 21 July 1623, not cited in our study. (No. 17) Memorial to the Council signed by Salazar and Hurtado de Gabiria, 11 Oct. 1613; read 11 Oct. 1623, i.e. *Ninth Report of Salazar*. (No. 19) The document characterized as "Report of witnesses and glosses to the preceding papers" is in fact the notes to the paper listed by Caro Baroja as No. 36, i.e. *Second Report of Salazar* with the *Glosses*. It appears that Caro Baroja was not aware of the connection between these two parts of the same manuscript. (No. 27) Letter dated 12 May 1609; read 22 May 1609, see chap. 4 n. 39, above. (No. 48) Memorial of Salazar dated 3 Oct. 1612; read 3 Oct. 1613, i.e. *Fourth Report of Salazar*. (No. 57) Memorial of Salazar dated 1 Oct. 1613. The date in the manuscript is, however, corrected from 1 Sept. 1613, which I consider to be the right one, see chap. 12 n. 95, above. (No. 61) Copy dated 27 May 1611; read 17 May 1611, see chap. 10 n. 67. (No. 62) Undated letter of Fray León de Araníbar; the date is 30 Oct. 1611, see chap. 11 n. 172, above.

Leg 1683 (olim Leg. 104 de la Sala 51). "Inquisición de Logroño, expedientes de visitas, legajo 2°." This capsule contains two huge volumes, *Exp. 1* and *Exp. 2.*, with more than 2,500 folios of records from *la Suprema*'s inspection of the Inquisition at Logroño 1619-1620.

Leg 1958 (olim Leg. 377 de la Sala 51). "Inquisición de Granada, Expedientes de visitas, Legajo 2°." The capsule contains two volumes of records from *la Suprema*'s inspection of the Inquisition at Granada undertaken by the inquisitor Alonso de Salazar Frías (1614-1616).

Leg 2022 (olim Leg. 441 de la Sala 51). "Inquisición de Murcia, Relaciones de causas, Legajo 2°." *Relaciones de causas* 1562-1682.

Leg 2042 (olim Leg. 460 de la Sala 51). "Inquisición de Santiago o Galicia, Relaciones de causas, Legajo 1°." *Relaciones de causas* 1565-1680.

Leg 2105 (olim Leg. 522 de la Sala 51). "Inquisición de Toledo, Expedientes varios, Legajo 1."

Leg 2220 (olim Leg. 66 de la Sala 39^d). "Legajo 1" of letters from the Inquisition at Logroño to *la Suprema* (1564-1699).

Leg 2248 (olim Leg. 94 de la Sala 39). "Legajo 29°" of the same series (1814-1820).

Leg 2607 (olim Leg. 450 de la Sala 39). "Legajo 6" of letters from the Inquisition at Granada to *la Suprema* (1594-1599).

Leg 2889 (olim Leg. 733 de la Sala 39). "Legajo 7" of letters from the Inquisition of Galicia to *la Suprema* (1620).

Leg 3730 (olim Leg. 1616 de la Sala 39). A capsule of a series containing bills of indictments (*alegaciones fiscales*) from various inquisitions.

3. MANUSCRIPT IN ARCHIVES OTHER THAN THE ARCHIVO HISTÓRICO NACIONAL.

ARCHIVO GENERAL DE NAVARRA, PAMPLONA.

AGN, without signature. "Brujas. Inquisición de Navarra. Cuaderno de actos comprobados de brujos." i.e. the *Pamplona Manuscript*.

AGN, *Sección de Procesos*, Proceso 506. The record of a trial instituted in 1611 by the High Court of Navarra against two village elders of

----

d. The series of *legajos* formerly placed in room 39 of the *Archivo de Simancas* consisted of capsules in quarto, while those formerly placed in room 51 of the same archive were a series of capsules in folio. This division still existed until the late 1960s when the Archivo Histórico Nacional decided to unfold the papers in the quarto series.

Elgorriaga for defamation (i.e. witchcraft accusations) and maltreatment of two residents of their village.

AGN, *Sección de Procesos*, Proceso 5257. The record of a trial instituted in 1612 by the High Court of Navarra against a village elder and other local authorities of Arráyoz for defamation (i.e. witchcraft accusations) and maltreatment of eight women of their village.

AGN, *Sección de Procesos*, Proceso 9177. The record of a trial before the High Court of Navarra of two villagers of Goizueta in 1609. Both were sentenced to two years' banishment for having circulated rumors to the effect that Catalina de Alducín, a relative of the parish priest, was a witch.

AGN, *Sección de Procesos*, Sala A, Legajo 1975. Record of trial instituted by the High Court of Navarra on 18 Dec. 1610 against a citizen of Santesteban for slander (i.e. witchcraft accusations) against another citizen of the same town.

AGN, *Sección de Estadística*, Legajo 1-2. Records of a census (*apeo de casas, vecinos y moradores*) undertaken in the towns and villages of northern Navarra in 1644, 1645, and 1646.

BIBLIOTECA NACIONAL, MADRID.

BN, MS 718 (olim D 118). A volume of letters, reports, and printed materials originating from the Council of Inquisition (16th-17th centuries).

BN, MS 798 (olim D 122). A collection of forms and instructions of the Spanish Inquisition originally pertaining to a certain Don Jacinto Fernández de la Peña.

BN, MS 831 (olim D 119). A volume entitled "Las cosas que se han de observar y practicar en las inquisiciones . . ." (i.e. a copy of *San Vicente's Manual*).

BN, MS 2031 (olim G 115). A volume of miscellaneous Inquisition papers, inter alia the copy of *Sixth Report of Salazar* published by Julio Caro Baroja in 1933, and the report on witchcraft in Guipúzcoa written by Doctor Lope Martínez de Isasti in 1618 and published by Caro Baroja in 1933 (see chap. 7 n. 40, above).

BN, MS 2440 (olim F 333). A volume of miscellaneous Inquisition papers (16th and 17th centuries).

BN, MS 7579 (no anterior signature). A volume containing copies of (1) *Second Discourse of Pedro de Valencia*, and (2) *First Discourse of Pedro de Valencia*. 76 folios.

BN, MS 8660 (olim V 377). A file containing a copy of *San Vicente's Manual*. 53 folios (consulted by Henry Charles Lea, see LEA *Inquisition of Spain* IV p. 240).

BN, MS 18.715[11]. A file containing another copy of *San Vicente's Manual*.

BIBLIOTECA DE LA REAL ACADEMIA DE LA HISTORIA, MADRID (abbr. BRAH).

BRAH 9-29-5-5944 (olim Est. 27, Gr. 5ª E. No. 129). Collección de Documentos y Privilegios, Tomo 4.

ROYAL LIBRARY OF COPENHAGEN.

Udenlandsk afdeling, 4-252ᶜ-folio. "Collectio libellorum ad historiam Inquisitionis hispanicae."

Ny kgl. Samling 128ᶜ 4º. D. G. Moldenhawer's copy of [Jóse de Ribera's] manuscript entitled "Origen y fundación de las Inquisiciones de España" (i.e. *Origen y fundacion*) 2 folios + 97 pages.

Ny kgl. Samling 213 2º. The "Codex Moldenhawerianus," a dictionary of the instructions and *cartas acordadas* of the Spanish Inquisition from its foundation to the second half of the 18th century. For this important manuscript, which was one of the main sources for Lea's *Inquisition of Spain*, see HENNINGSEN 1977 pp. 234-237, 259-261.

Ny kgl. Samling 218ᵈ 2º. A folder containing 41 original documents concerning the Spanish Inquisition and D. G. Moldenhawer's notes for a history of the same institution (see description of the collection in HENNINGSEN 1977 pp. 264-269).

4. BOOKS AND ARTICLES CONSULTED.

Quintín ALDEA VAQUERO et al. (eds.) *Diccionario de Historia Eclesiástica de España* 4 vols. Madrid 1972-75.

Elias AMÉZAGA *Guía del perfecto Inquisidor* Bilbao 1968.

Bengt ANKARLOO *Trolldomsprocessarna i Sverige* [The witchcraft trials in Sweden] Stockholm 1971 (English summary).

Telésforo de ARANZADI "Aproposito de brujerías" *Revista internacional de estudios vascos* 19 (1928) 142-144.

Darío de AREITIO "Las brujas de Ceberio" *Revista internacional de estudios vascos* 18 (1927) 654-664.

Gaspar Isidro de ARGÜELLO (ed.) *Instrvciones del Santo Oficio de la Inquisicion, sumariamente, antiguas, y nueuas. Pvestas por Abecedario por Gaspar Isidro de Arguello Oficial del Consejo* Madrid, Imprenta Real, 1630 (for other editions, see chap. 3 n. 7, above).

Martín de ARLES Y ANDOSILLA *Tractatus de superstitionibus* Lyon 1510; 2nd ed. Paris 1517; for a 3rd ed., see below GOÑI GAZTAMBIDE 1971.

Juan A. de ARZADÚN "Las brujas de Fuenterrabía. Proceso del siglo XVII, el 6 de mayo de 1611" *Revista internacional de estudios vascos* 3 (1909) 172-181, 357-374.

Kurt W. BACK and Alan C. KERCKHOFF *The June Bug: A Study of Hysterical Contagion.* New York 1968.

Norbert BACKMUND *Monasticon Praemonstratense. Id est, Historia circariarum atque canoniarum candidi et canonici Ordinis Praemonstratensis* Straubing 1949.

Bernardo BARREIRO DE VÁZQUEZ VARELA "Archivos secretos. Adiciones y notas a una lista de Inquisidores de Galicia desde el establecimiento... hasta... 1700" *Galicia Diplomática* III (1888) 153-155, 164-166, 178-181, 187-189, 194-197, 201-203.

Kurt BASCHWITZ *De strijd met den duivel. De heksenprocessen in het licht der massapsychologie* Amsterdam 1948; German version *Hexen und Hexenprozesse; die Geschichte eines Massenwahns und seiner Bekämpfung* München 1963; Spanish version *Brujas y persecuciones de brujas* Barcelona 1968.

Balthasar BEKKER *De betoverde Weereld* Amsterdam 1691-1693; English version *The World Bewitched* London 1695.

Bartolomé BENNASSAR et al. *L'Inquisition Espagnole XVe-XIXe siècle* Paris 1979.

José BERRUEZO "La brujería en el país vasco" in: 1er *Congreso de Etnología y Folklore en Braga 1956* Lisboa 1963 vol. I pp. 263-281.

Francesco BOLZONI *Le Streghe in Italia* Rome, Universale Cappelli, 1963.

Guiseppe BONOMO *Caccia alle streghe. La credenza nelle streghe dal secolo XIII al XIX con particolare riferimento all'Italia* Palermo 1959.

Agostino BORROMEO "Contributo allo studio dell'inquisizione e dei suoi rapporti con il potere episcopale nell'Italia spagnola del Cinquecento" *Annuario dell'Istituto Storico Italiano per l'età moderna e contemporanea* XXIX-XXX (1977-78) 219-276.

Edward Sculley BRADLEY *Henry Charles Lea. A Biography* Philadelphia 1931.

Jean-Auguste BRUTAILS *Inventaire sommaire des archives départementales antérieures a 1790* Bordeaux 1925.

George Lincoln BURR (ed.) *The Witch-Persecution* Philadelphia 1897 (same as *Translations and Reprints from the Original Source of European History* vol. 3 no. 4).

Augustin CALMET *Dissertation sur les apparitions des anges, des démons, et des esprits, et sur les revenans et vampires de Hongrie, de Bohême, de Moravie, et de Silésie* Paris 1746; (2nd. ed.) *Traité...* Paris 1751.

A. CAPPELLI *Cronologia, cronografia e calendario perpetuo* Milano 1930.

Julio CARO BAROJA "Cuatro relaciones sobre la hechicería vasca" *Anuario de Eusco-Folklore* XIII (1933) 85-145.

———. "Las brujas de Fuenterrabía (1611)" *Revista de dialectología y tradiciones populares* 3 (1947) 189-204.

———. *Los vascos* San Sebastián 1949, 2nd. ed. Madrid 1958.

———. *Las brujas y su mundo* Madrid 1961; English version *The World of the Witches* Chicago 1964; German version *Die Hexen und ihre Welt* Stuttgart 1967 (with a supplementary chapter by Will-Erich PEUCKERT); French version *Les sorcières et leur monde* Paris 1972.

———. *Vidas mágicas e Inquisición* 2 vols. Madrid 1967.

———. *El Señor Inquisidor y otras vidas por oficio* Madrid 1968.

———. "De nuevo sobre la historia de la brujería (1609-1619)" *Príncipe de Viana* 30 (1969) 265-328; reprinted in: Julio CARO BAROJA *Inquisición, brujería y criptojudaísmo* Barcelona 1970 pp. 183-315.

———. *Etnografía histórica de Navarra* 3 vols. Pamplona 1971-72.

———. "Problemas psicológicos, sociológicos y jurídicos en torno a la brujería en el País Vasco" en *Primera Semana Internacional de Antropología Vasca* Bilbao 1971 pp. 63-86.

———. *Estudios vascos, V. Brujería vasca* San Sebastián 1975.

———. "El ballet del inquisidor y la bruja" *Historia 16,* Special Issue: *La Inquisición* (Dec. 1976) 87-97.

Carlos CASTANEDA *The Teachings of Don Juan. A Yaqui Way of Knowledge* Berkeley & Los Angeles, University of California Press, 1968.

Basilio Sebastián CASTELLANO DE LOSADA (ed.) *Biografía Eclesiástica* 30 vols. Madrid 1848-68.

Norman COHN *Europe's inner Demons. An Enquiry Inspired by the Great Witch-Hunt* London, Sussex University Press, 1975; Paladin ed., Frogmore 1976.

A. COMMUNAY *Le conseiller Pierre de Lancre* Agen 1890.

John Langdon DAVIES (ed.) *The Spanish Inquisition. A Collection of Contemporary Documents* London 1966 (Jackdaw Publications No. 5).

F. Trevor DAVIES "Magic and Witchcraft in Post-Medieval Spain" *The Rationalist Annual* (1948) 57-66.

Jean Pierre DEDIEU "Les inquisiteurs de Tolède et la visite du district. La sedentarisation d'un tribunal (1550-1630)" *Mélanges de la Casa de Velázquez* XIII (1977) 235-256.

———. "Les causes de foi de l'Inquisition de Tolède (1483-1820): Essai statistique" *Mélanges de la Casa de Velázquez* XIV (1978) 143-171.

Pierre DE LANCRE *Tableav de l'Inconstance des mavvais Anges et Demons. Ov il est amplement traicté de la Sorcelerie et Sorciers. Livre tres-cvrievx et tres-vtile, non seulement aux Iuges, mais à tous ceux qui viuent soubs les loix Chrestiennes. Avec Vn Discours contenant la Procedure faicte par les Inquisiteurs d'Espagne et de Nauarre, à 53. Magiciens, Apostats, Iuifs, et Sorciers, en la ville de Logrogne en Castille le 9. Nouembre 1610. En laquelle on voit, combien l'exercice de la Iustice en France, est plus iuridiquement traicté, et auec de plus belles formes qu'en tous autres Empires, Royaumes, Republiques et Estats* Paris, Nicolas Buon, 1612; another ed. Paris, Berjou, 1612; revised ed. Paris, Nicolas Buon, 1613.

———. *L'Incredvlité et Mescreance dv Sortilege plainement convaincve. Ov il est amplement et cvrievsement traicté, de le verité ou Illusion du Sortilege, de la Fascination, de l'Attouchement, du Scopelisme, de la Diuination, de la Ligature ou Liaison Magique, des Apparitions: Et d'vne infinité d'autres rares et nouueaux Subjects* Paris, Nicolas Buon, 1622.

Étienne DELCAMBRE *Le concept de la sorcellerie dans le duché de Lorraine aux XVIᵉ et XVIIᵉ siècles* 3 vols. Nancy 1948-51.

———. "Les procès de sorcellerie en Lorraine. Psychologie des juges" *Tijdschrift voor Rechtsgeschiedenis* 21 (1954) 389-419.

———. "La psychologie des inculpés lorrains de sorcellerie" *Revue historique de droit français et étranger* 32 (1954) 383-403, 508-526.

A. G. DICKENS *Reformation and Society in Sixteenth-Century Europe* London 1966.

———. *The Counter-Reformation* New York 1969.

Mary DOUGLAS (ed.) *Witchcraft: Confessions and Accusations* London 1970.

J. H. ELLIOT *Europe Divided 1559-98* London 1968.

Idoia ESTORNES ZUBIZARRETA "Brujería" in: *Diccionario Enciclopédico Vasco* Vol. V, San Sebastián 1974 pp. 531-559 (*Enciclopedia general ilustrado del País Vasco*).

Evans E. EVANS-PRITCHARD "Witchcraft" *Africa* 8 (1935) 417-422.

———. *Witchcraft, Oracles and Magic among the Azande* Oxford 1937.

Cecil L'Estrange EWEN *Some Witchcraft Criticism* London 1938.

Stewart FARRER *What Witches Do: The Modern Coven Revealed* London 1971.

Pablo FERNÁNDEZ ALBALADEJO *La crisis del antiguo régimen en Guipúzcoa, 1766-1833* Madrid 1975.

M. J. FIELD *Religion and Medicine of the Gã People* London 1961 (First edition 1937).

Meyer FORTES "The Structure of Unilineal Descent Groups" *American Anthropologist* 55 (1953) 17-41.

Pablo GARCÍA *Orden qve comvnmente se gvarda en el Santo Oficio de la Inquisicion, acerca del processar en las causas que en el se tratan, conforme à lo que està proueydo por las instruciones antiguas y nuevas. Recopilado por Pablo Garcia, secretario del Consejo de la Santa General Inquisicion. Van en esta segunda impression añadidas algunas cosas y puestas otras en mejor orden* Madrid, Luis Sánchez, 1607; 1st. ed. Madrid 1568 (see chap. 3 n. 8, above).

Gerald B. GARDNER *High Magic's Aid* London 1949.

———. *Witchcraft Today* London 1951; 2nd. ed. with introduction by Margaret MURRAY London 1954.

———. *The Meaning of Witchcraft* London 1959.

Lauritz GENTZ "Vad förorsakede de stora häxprocesserna [What caused the great trials for witchcraft]?" *Arv* 10 (1954) 1-39 (English summary).

Carlo GINZBURG *I benandanti. Ricerche sulla stregoneria e sui culti agrari tra Cinquecento e Seicento* Torino 1966; 2nd. ed. Torino, Piccola Biblioteca Einaudi, 1972.

F. J. GOMEZ *Logroño Histórico* Logroño 1893.

José GOÑI GAZTAMBIDE *Los Navarros en el Concilio de Trento y la Tridentina en la Diócesis de Pamplona* Pamplona 1947.

———. "El tratado 'De superstitionibus' de Martín de Andosilla" *Cuadernos de etnología y etnografía Navarra* III (1971) 249-322.

Agustín GONZÁLEZ DE AMEZÚA Y MAYO "El casamiento engañoso" y "El coloquio de los perros": *Novelas ejemplares de Miguel de Cervantes Saavedra. Edición crítica con introducción y notas* Madrid 1912.

Francisque HABASQUE *Episodes d'un proces en sorcellerie dans le Labourd au XVIIᵉ siecle (1605-1607)* Biarritz 1912.

Chadwick HANSEN *Witchcraft at Salem* New York 1969.

Joseph HANSEN *Zauberwahn, Inquisition und Hexenprozess im Mittelalter und die Entstehung der grossen Hexenverfolgung* München & Leipzig 1900.

———. *Quellen und Untersuchungen zur Geschichte des Hexenwahns und der Hexenverfolgung* Bonn 1901; Hildesheim 1963.

Michael J. HARNER (ed.) *Hallucinogens and Shamanism* New York, Oxford University Press, 1973.

Gustav HENNINGSEN "Fatalism in its Systematic Aspect and Fatalism in its Functional Context" in: Helmer RINGGREN (ed.) *Fatalistic Beliefs in Religion, Folklore and Literature. Papers read at the Symposium on Fatalistic Beliefs held at Åbo on the 7th-9th September, 1964* Stockholm 1967 pp. 184-186.

———. "Trolddom og hemmelige kunster [Sorcery and secret arts]" in: Axel STEENSBERG (ed.) *Dagligliv i Danmark 1620-1720* Copenhagen 1969 pp. 161-196, 727-731.

———. "Hekseforfølgelser [Witch persecutions]" in: Axel

STEENSBERG (ed.) *Dagligliv i Danmark 1620-1720* Copenhagen 1969 pp. 353-376, 736-738.

— — —. "Informe sobre tres años de investigaciones etnológicas en España" *Ethnica*. *Revista de Antropología* 1 (Barcelona 1971) 61-90; Danish version in *Nord Nytt* 1969 No. 3/4 20-31.

— — —. "The Papers of Alonso de Salazar Frias. A Spanish Witchcraft Polemic 1610-14" *Temenos*. *Studies in Comparative Religion Presented by Scholars in Denmark, Finland, Norway and Sweden* 5 (1969) 85-106.

— — —. "Witch-Belief in Daily Life" in: *VIIme Congrès international des sciences anthropologiques*. *Moscou 3 aout-10 aout 1964* vol. VIII Moscow 1970 pp. 38-41.

— — —. *The European Witch-Persecution* Copenhagen 1973 (DFS-Translations No. 1); Danish version in *Jordens folk* 7:3 (1971) 112-131.

— — —. "Hekseforfølgelse efter "hekseprocessernes tid." Et bidrag til dansk etnohistorie [Witch-persecution after the "era of the witch trials." A contribution to Danish ethnohistory]" *Folk og Kultur* 1975 98-151, with English summary.

— — —. "La colección de Moldenhawer en Copenhague. Una aportación a la archivología de la Inquisición española" *Revista de Archivos, Bibliotecas y Museos* LXXX (1977) 209-270; Danish version in *Fund og Forskning* XXII (1975-76) 121-176.

— — —. "El 'banco de datos' del Santo Oficio: Las relaciones de causas de la Inquisición española" *Boletín de la Real Academia de la Historia* CLXXIV (1977) 547-570, also as *Dansk Folkemindesamling. Studier* No. 12, Copenhagen 1978, with English summary.

— — —. "Alonso de Salazar Frías. Ese famoso inquisidor desconocide" in *Homenaje a Julio Caro Baroja* Madrid 1978 pp. 581-586.

— — —. "Las víctimas de Zugarramurdi: El origen de un gran proceso de brujería" *Saioak. Revista de Estudios Vascos* 2 (1978) 182-195.

— — —. "Inkvisition og etnografi [Inquisition and ethnography]" *Jordens Folk* 9:2 (1973) 66-83, also as *Dansk Folkemindesamling. Studier* No. 9 Copenhagen 1973, with English summary.

— — —. "Kloge folk og 'Kloge Søren' [Folk healers and Søren the Healer]" in: Gustav HENNINGSEN & George NELLEMAN *Det farlige liv* Copenhagen, Nationalmuseet, 1978.

— — —. "Hver by sin heks [No town without its witch]" *Skalk* 1979:3 pp. 21-30.

— — — & Marisa REY-HENNINGSEN *Hekse og hellige kvinder* [Witches and holy women] Copenhagen 1977 (DFSNYT 77/1).

— — —. "The Inquisition and Society. Report from the Interdisciplinary Symposium on the Medieval and Modern Inquisition, Copenhagen, 5-9 Sept. 1978" *NIF Newsletter* 6:4 (1978) 2-4; Spanish version in: *Arbor* CIII (1979) 213-216.

————. Jens Chr. V. JOHANSEN & Ditlev TAMM "16.000 jyske domme. En sagtypologisk analyse af Hofman-Bangs regest til Viborg Landstings dombøger 1569-1805 [16,000 Jutland judgments. A case-typology analysis of Hofman-Bang's register of the court rolls of the High Court at Viborg for the period 1569-1805]" *Fortid og nutid* XXVIII (1979) 240-270, with English summary.

Aldous HUXLEY *The Devils of Loudon* London 1952; Harmondsworth, Penguin Books, 1971.

Florencio IDOATE "Brujerías en la montaña de Navarra en el siglo XVI" *Hispania Sacra* IV (1951) 193-218.

————. *El Señorío de Sarria* Pamplona 1959.

————. *La brujería* Pamplona 1967 (*Navarra. Temas de cultura popular* 4).

———— (ed.) *Un documento de la Inquisición sobre la brujería en Navarra* Pamplona 1972.

José María IRIBARREN "Interesante documento sobre las brujas de Zugarramurdi" *Príncipe de Viana* 4 (1944) 422-427.

J.C. JACOBSEN *Danske Domme i Trolddomssager* [Danish judgments in sorcery cases] Copenhagen 1966.

Joseph JEROME *Montague Summers. A Memoir* London 1965.

Henry KAMEN *The Spanish Inquisition* London 1965; Spanish version *La Inquisición Española* Barcelona & Mexico 1967.

————. *The Iron Century. Social Change in Europe 1550-1660* London 1971.

Richard KIECKHEFER *European Witch Trials: Their Foundations in Popular and Learned Culture, 1300-1500* Berkeley and Los Angeles, Univ. of California Press, 1976.

Francis KING *Ritual Magic in England: 1887 to the Present Time* London 1970.

George Lyman KITTREDGE *Witchcraft in Old and New England* Cambridge, Mass. 1929; New York 1956.

Clyde KLUCKHOHN *Navaho Witchcraft* Cambridge, Mass. 1944.

Alan KORS and Edward PETERS (eds.) *Witchcraft in Europe: A Documentary History* Philadelphia, University of Pennsylvania Press, 1972.

Zoltán KOVÁCS "Die Hexen in Russland" *Acta Ethnographica Academiae Scientiarum Hungaricae* 22 (1973) 51-87.

Támás KÖRNER "Boszorkányszervezetek Magyarországon [The Hungarian Witch Organisation]" *Ethnographia* 80 (1969) 196-211, with German and Russian summary.

Henry Charles LEA *Chapters from the Religious History of Spain* Philadelphia 1890; New York 1967.

————. *A History of the Inquisition of the Middle Ages* 3 vols. New York

1888; New York 1955.

— — —. *A History of the Inquisition of Spain* 4 vols. New York 1906-07; New York 1966.

— — —. *Materials Toward a History of Witchcraft* 3 vols. Philadephia 1939 published by Arthur C. HOWLAND with an introduction by George Lincoln BURR; New York & London 1957.

V. LESPY "Les sorciers dans le Béarn (1393-1672)" *Bulletin de la société des sciences, lettres et arts de Pau* 2nd series vol. IV (1874-75) 28-86.

Robert Jay LIFTON *Thought Reform and the Psychology of Totalism. A Study of "Brainwashing" in China* London 1962.

Carmelo LISÓN TOLOSANA *Brujería, estructura social y simbolismo en Galicia* Madrid, Akal Editor, 1979.

— — —. *Ensayos de Antropología Social* Madrid 1973.

Lista alphabetica de las ciudades, villas, y lugares, tocantes à los distritos de las Inquisiciones de España residentes en las Ciudades de Córdoba, Lleréna; Sevilla, Granàda, Mùrcia, Valéncia, Barcelòna, Zaragóza, Logròño, Santiàgo de Galicia, Valladolíd, Cuénca y Tolèdo No date or place [Madrid 18th century].

Juan Antonio LLORENTE *Histoire critique de l'Inquisition d'Espagne, depuis l'epoque de son établissement par Ferdinand V jusq'au règne de Ferdinand VII, Tirée des pieces originales des archives du Conseil de la Suprême et de celles des Tribuneaux subalternes du Saint Office . . . Traduite de l'espagnol sur le manuscrit et sous les yeux de l'Auteur par Alexis Pellier* 4 vols. Paris 1817-18; Spanish version *Historia crítica de la Inquisición de España* 10 vols. Madrid [or Paris?] 1822.

Alan D. J. MACFARLANE *Witchcraft in Tudor and Stuart England* London 1970; New York, Harper Torchbooks, 1970.

Lucy MAIR *Witchcraft* London, World University Library, 1969; Spanish version *La brujería en los pueblos primitivos actuales* Madrid 1969.

Robert MANDROU *Magistrats et sorciers en France au XVIIᵉ siècle. Une analyse de psychologie historique* Paris 1968.

Lope MARTÍNEZ DE ISASTI *Compendio historial de la provincia de Guipúzcoa* [Manuscript from 1625] San Sebastián 1850; reprinted Bilbao, *La Gran Enciclopedia Vasca*, 1972.

Max MARWICK (ed.) *Witchcraft and Sorcery. Selected Readings* Harmondsworth, Penguin Books, 1970.

J. MAXWELL *Un magistrat hermetiste. Jean d'Espagnet, president au parlement de Bordeaux* Bordeaux 1896.

P. MAYER *Witches. Inaugural lecture delivered at Rhodes University* Grahamstown, Rhodes University Press, 1954.

Emilio MENESES GARCÍA "Construcción del tablado para el auto de fe de 1632" *Revista de Archivos, Bibliotecas y Museos* 3rd series vol. 75 (1965) 363-392.

Jules MICHELET *La Sorcière* Paris 1862; English version *Satanism and Witchcraft* New York 1939; Spanish version *La bruja* Barcelona 1970 (with preface by Robert Mandrou).

John MIDDLETON & E. H. WINTER (eds.) *Witchcraft and Sorcery in East Africa* London 1963.

H. C. ERIK MIDELFORT "Recent Witch Hunting Research, or Where Do We Go from Here?" *Papers of the Bibliographical Society of America* 62 (1968) 373-420.

―――. "Witchcraft and Religion in Sixteenth-Century Germany: The Formation and Consequences of an Orthodoxy" *Archiv für Reformationsgeschichte* 72 (1971) 266-278.

―――. *Witch Hunting in Southwestern Germany 1562-1684: The Social and Intellectual Foundations* Stanford University Press, 1972.

Toribio MINGUELLA Y ARNEDO *Historia de la Diócesis de Sigüenza y de sus Obispos* 3 vols. Madrid 1910-1913.

Juan de MONGASTÓN (ed.) *Relacion de las personas qve salieron al Avto de la Fee, qve los señores Doctor Alonso Bezerra Holguin, del Abito de Alcantara; Licenciado Iuan de Valle Aluarado; Licenciado Alonso de Salazar Frias. Inquisidores Apostolicos, del Reyno de Nauarra, y su distrito, celebraron en la Ciudad de Logroño, en siete, y en ocho dias del mes de Nouiembre, de 1610. Años. Y de las cosas y delitos por que fueron castigados* Logroño, Juan de Mongastón, 1611.

E. W. MONTER (ed.) *European Witchcraft* New York 1969.

―――. "Patterns of Witchcraft in the Jura" *Journal of Social History* 5 (1971) 1-25.

―――. "Witchcraft in Geneva, 1537-1662" *Journal of Modern History* 43 (1971) 179-204.

―――. "The Historiography of European Witchcraft: Progress and Prospects" *The Journal of Interdisciplinary History* 2 (1972) 435-451.

―――. *Witchcraft in France and Switzerland: the Borderlands During the Reformation* Ithaca, Cornell University Press, 1976.

Margaret Alice MURRAY *The Witch-Cult in Western Europe* London & Oxford 1921; Oxford 1962 (with foreword by Steven RUNCIMAN).

S. F. NADEL "Witchcraft and Anti-Witchcraft in Nupe Society" *Africa* 8 (1935) 423-447.

―――. "Witchcraft in four African Societies" *American Anthropologist* 54 (1952) 18-29.

―――. *Nupe Religion* London 1954.

N. NARBARTE IRAOLA *Diccionario etimológico de apellidos vascos* 2nd ed. Pamplona 1968.

Traugott Konstantin OESTERREICH *Die Besessenheit* Langensalza 1921; French version *Les possédes. La possession démoniaque chez les primitifs, dans l'antiquité, au moyen age et dans la civilisation moderne*

Paris 1927; English version *Possession, Demonical and Other* New York 1930, 1966.

Alfonso OTAZU "Brujería y régimen señorial en la Montaña atlántica de Navarra (1600-1620)" in: *Homenaje a Julio Caro Baroja* Madrid 1978, pp. 827-842.

Geoffrey PARRINDER *Witchcraft. A critical study of the belief in witchcraft from the records of witch-hunting in Europe yesterday and Africa today* Harmondsworth, Pelican Books, 1958, Spanish version *La brujería* Buenos Aires 1958.

Mario N. PAVIA *Drama of the Siglo de Oro: A study of Magic, Witchcraft and other Occult Beliefs* New York 1959.

J. PROBST "Les survivances dans le Pyrénées Occidentales (magie, sorcellerie et croyances populaires)" in: *5ᵐᵉ Congrès de l'U.H.A.S.O.* Tarbes 1914 pp. 173-188.

Alfonso QUINTANO RIPOLLÉS *Un linaje burgalés: La casa de Quintano y sus enlazados* Madrid 1967.

Henry T. F. RHODES *The Satanic Mass. A Sociological and Criminological Study* London 1954.

Martín del RÍO *Disquisitionem magicarum* Louvain 1599; 7th ed. Lyon 1608.

Rossell Hope ROBBINS *The Encyclopedia of Witchcraft and Demonology* London 1959.

Manuel RODRÍGUEZ LUSITANO *Svmma de casos de consciencia, con aduertencias muy prouechosas para Confessores* 3 vols. Salamanca 1598.

Francisco ROMERO DE CASTILLA "Extracto del inventario de los papeles de Inquisición, que procedentes del Antiguo Consejo Supremo de la misma, se trasladaron al Archivo General de Simancas en el año de 1850" *Revista de Archivos, Bibliotecas y Museos* 1st. series vol. III (1873) 118-121, 136-140, 149-155, 168-170, 182-187.

Eliot E. ROSE *A Razor for a Goat* Toronto 1962.

George ROSEN "A Study of the Persecution of Witches in Europe as a Contribution to the Understanding of Mass Delusions and Psychic Epidemics" *Journal of Health and Human Behavior* 1 (1960) 200-211.

Arne RUNEBERG *Witches, Demons and Fertility Magic. Analysis of their Significance and Mutual Relationship in West-European Folk Religion* Helsingfors 1947.

Jeffrey Burton RUSSEL *Witchcraft in the Middle Ages* Ithaca & London, Cornell University Press, 1972.

Fray Prudencio de SANDOVAL *Catálogo de los obispos que ha tenido la Santa Iglesia de Pamplona* Pamplona 1614.

William SARGANT *Battle for the Mind. A Physiology of Conversion and Brain-Washing* London 1957; 7th ed. London, Pan Books, 1970.

Ernst SCHÄFER Beiträge zur Geschichte des spanischen Protestantismus und der Inquisition im sechzehnten Jahrhundert. Nach den Originalakten in Madrid und Simancas bearbeitet 3 vols. Gütersloh 1902; Aalen 1969.

Ulrich Friedrich SCHNEIDER Das Werk 'De Praestigiis Daemonum' von Weyer und seine Auswirkungen auf die Bekämpfung des Hexenwahns. Duplicated Dr. jur. dissertation, Bonn University 1951.

Reginald SCOT Discoverie of Witchcraft London 1584; republished by Hugh Ross WILLIAMSON (ed.) Carbondale, Southern Ill. University Press, 1965.

Manuel SERRANO Y SANZ (ed.) "Discurso de Pedro de Valencia acerca de los quentos de las brujas y cosas tocantes a magia..." Revista de Extremadura 2 (1900) 289-303, 337-347.

———. Autobiografías y memorias Madrid 1905 (Nueva Biblioteca de Autores Españoles II).

———. "Segundo discurso de Pedro de Valencia acerca de los brujos y sus maleficios" Revista de Archivos, Bibliotecas y Museos 3rd series, vol. II (1906) 445-454.

José SIMON DÍAZ "La Inquisición en Logroño (1570-1580)" Berceo I (1946) 89-119.

———. "La Inquisición en Logroño (1580-1600)" Berceo III (1948) 83-96.

Wilhelm Gottlieb SOLDAN Geschichte der Hexenprozesse aus den Quellen dargestellt Stuttgart 1843; Stuttgart 1880 (rev. by H. L. J. HEPPE); München 1912 (rev. by Max BAUER); Darmstadt 1967 (rev. by Will-Erich PEUCKERT).

Alfred SOMAN "Les proces de sorcellerie au Parlement de Paris (1565-1640)" Annales: Economies. Sociétés. Civilisations XXII (1977) 790-814.

———. "The Parlement of Paris and the Great Witch Hunt (1565-1640)" Sixteenth Century Journal IX:2 (1978) 31-44.

Friedrich von SPEE Cautio criminalis Rinteln 1631; German version ed. and trans. by Joachim-Friedrich RITTER Cautio Criminalis oder rechtliches Bedenken wegen der Hexenprozesse Weimar 1939.

Alphonsus de SPINA Fortalicium fidei Strasbourg [1471 or earlier].

Jacob SPRENGER & Heinrich INSTITORIS Malleus maleficarum Cologne [1487]; English version by Montague SUMMERS London 1928, paperback edition New York, Dover Publications, 1971.

Lawrence STONE "The Disenchantment of the World" The New York Review of Books XVIII:9 (2 Dec. 1971) 17-24.

Montague SUMMERS The History of Witchcraft and Demonology London & New York 1926; London 1965.

John TEDESCHI "Preliminary Observation on Writing a History of the Roman Inquisition" in: F. F. CHURCH & T. GEORGE *Continuity and Discontinuity in Church History* Leiden 1979.

Keith THOMAS *Religion and the Decline of Magic. Studies in popular beliefs in sixteenth and seventeenth century England* London 1971.

Francisco TORREBLANCA VILLALPANDO *Epitome delictorum sive de magia in qua aperta vel occulta invocatio daemonis intervenit* Sevilla 1618; Lyon 1678.

María Pilar de TORRES *La Navarra húmeda del Noroeste* Madrid 1971.

Hugh R. TREVOR-ROPER "The European Witch-craze of the Sixteenth and Seventeenth Centuries" in: *Religion, the Reformation and Social Change* London 1967; also as separate publication *The European Witch-Craze* Harmondsworth, Penguin Books, 1969.

A. S. TUBERVILLE *The Spanish Inquisition* London 1932; Spanish version *La Inquisición Española* Mexico 1948.

E. van der VEKENÉ *Bibliographie der Inquisition* Hildesheim 1963.

Johan WEYER *De praestigiis daemonum et incantationibus ac veneficiis* Basel 1563.

Charles WILLIAMS *Witchcraft* London 1941.

Simon WOLIN & Robert M. SLUSSER (eds.) *The Soviet Secret Police* London 1957.

José YANGUAS Y MIRANDA *Diccionario de antigüedades del Reino de Navarra* 3 vols. San Sebastián 1840-43; 2nd. ed. Pamplona 1964.

Gerhard ZACHARIAS *Satanskult und Schwarze Messe. Ein Beitrag zur Phänomenologie der Religion* Wiesbaden 1964.

Russell ZGUTA "Witchcraft Trials in Seventeenth-Century Russia" *American Historical Review* 5 (1977) 1187-1207.

INDEX

Abad, Fausto, 288 (Table 9)
Abad, Francisco, 288 (Table 9)
Abad, Sancho, 288 (Table 9)
Abad de Audizana, Martín, 288 (Table 9)
Abad de Lecea, Juan, 288 (Table 9)
Abad de Suso, Martín, 289 (Table 9)
Abad Ochoa, Juan, 289 (Table 9)
Abiria, Francisco Ochoa de, 270, 289 (Table 9)
Accomplices. See Confederates
Acevedo, Fernando de, 329-331, 337, 535 n. 90, 536, n. 102
Acevedo, Juan Bautista de, 46, 48, 49, 459 n. 37, 459-460 n. 38, 481 n. 66
Actos positivos: Becerra-Valle letter, 311; Becerra-Valle verdict, 336, 337-341, 342, 343-345; discussed, 65-67; new instructions, 373; *Pamplona Manuscript,* 471 n. 94; Salazar reports, 314-317, 346, 349-350, 353 (Table 12); *la Suprema,* 295-296; Valle letter, 330; mentioned, 466 n. 63. See also Experiments
Adultery, 102, 534
Africa, 9, 12-13, 22, 303-304, 392 (Table 15)
Agents, 49, 95
Age of discretion, 468 n. 22
Age of Enlightenment, 1
Agramonte, Magdalena de (case no. 71), 261 (Table 8)
Agüero, Juan de, 313, 337, 364, 492 n. 88, 493 n. 102

Aguirre, Bernardo de, 451-452 n. 2
Aguirre, Mari Juan de. *See* Juanto, Mari
Aguirre, Martín de, 262
Aguirre Luberriseme, Juanes de, 260 (Table 8), 515 n. 111
Ajamil, 214 (Table 6)
Alarcón, Antonio de Aranda y, 377, 381, 385, 545 n. 48
Alava: Edict of Grace, 262, 264; Logroño Tribunal, 49; Salazar report, 302-303; Salazar visitation, 236, 252, 279, 282, 285, 291, 294, 301, 304; statistics, 214 (Table 6); visitation, 229; witch-hunt, 269-270, 275, 287, 294; mentioned, 364
Albéniz, 288 (Table 9)
Alcántara, 46, 359 (Table 13)
Alda, Juan de, 289 (Table 9)
Alda, Juan Díaz de, 269
Aldea, Quintín, 459 n. 37
Aldoín, Pedro López de, 288 (Table 9)
Alduncín, Catalina de, 479 n. 46
Alegría, Juan Martínez de, 288 (Table 9)
Alegría, 214 (Table 6), 269, 285, 288 (Table 9)
Alençon, 18
Aliaga y Martínez, Luis de, 544 n. 44
Almándoz, 216, 252
Alps, 14, 15, 16
Alsasua, 279, 282, 289 (Table 9), 294
Alsatte, Tristan de Gamoba d'. *See* Urtubie, Lord of